S0-ARY-874

KATHERINE MANSFIELD'S
LETTERS
TO
JOHN MIDDLETON MURRY
1913-1922

ALSO BY
KATHERINE MANSFIELD

POEMS (1924)
Her collected verse.

JOURNAL OF KATHERINE MANSFIELD (1927)
An account of herself in relation to her work.

THE LETTERS OF KATHERINE MANSFIELD (1929)
Her intimate and revealing letters to a wide variety of people.

NOVELS AND NOVELISTS (1930)
A collection of literary essays.

THE SHORT STORIES OF KATHERINE MANSFIELD
(1937)
*All the stories ever written by one of the modern masters of the art, with
an introduction by J. Middleton Murry.*

THE SCRAPBOOK OF KATHERINE MANSFIELD (1940)
*Unpublished stories, poems, journal entries, sketches and critical
comments selected by J. Middleton Murry from a trunkful of manuscript
left by Katherine Mansfield.*

THESE ARE BORZOI BOOKS
PUBLISHED BY ALFRED A. KNOPF, INC.

Katherine Mansfield 1911

PR
9639.3
.M258
Z556
1951

6025
A 5.7
Z 5 56
1951

1951

S6561

KATHERINE MANSFIELD'S LETTERS

TO

JOHN MIDDLETON MURRY

1913—1922

Edited by

John Middleton Murry

WITHDRAWN

ALFRED A. KNOPF: NEW YORK

1951

L. C. catalog card number: 51-12071

THIS IS A BORZOI BOOK,
PUBLISHED BY ALFRED A. KNOPF, INC.

Copyright 1929, 1951 by Alfred A. Knopf, Inc. All rights reserved. No part of this book may be reproduced in any form without permission in writing from the publisher, except by a reviewer who may quote brief passages and reproduce not more than three illustrations in a review to be printed in a magazine or newspaper. Manufactured in the United States of America.

FIRST AMERICAN EDITION

PUBLISHER'S NOTE

AN extensive collection of Katherine Mansfield's letters was published in two volumes in 1929. This publication contained approximately 200,000 words, and included letters to various friends as well as to Mr. Murry.

The present volume is virtually a new book. It is one-third as long again as its predecessor, although containing only the letters written by K. M. to her lover and husband. He (Mr. Murry) has restored all the passages omitted from the letters on their first appearance.

ILLUSTRATIONS

KATHERINE MANSFIELD 1911   *frontispiece*

J. MIDDLETON MURRY 1912   *facing page* 40

KATHERINE MANSFIELD 1913   60

KATHERINE MANSFIELD 1915   120

KATHERINE MANSFIELD 1916   240

KATHERINE MANSFIELD 1918   360

KATHERINE MANSFIELD 1920   520

KATHERINE MANSFIELD'S
LETTERS
TO
JOHN MIDDLETON MURRY
1913-1922

LETTERS OF KATHERINE MANSFIELD

I first heard of Katherine Mansfield in the autumn of 1911. *W. L. George sent me a 'fairy story' of hers for 'Rhythm', with an enthusiastic note about her. The story intrigued and puzzled me, and I returned it saying that I did not understand it, and asking if she would send something else. After a little delay, she sent 'The Woman at the Store', which impressed me mightily. I accepted it on the spot in a letter which said, very truly, that it was by far the best story that had been offered to 'Rhythm'. At about the same time I bought for two shillings in Dan Rider's shop a reviewer's copy, conspicuous by its bright orange wrapper, of her 'In a German Pension' which was published in December* 1911. *I was still more, and more intimately, impressed by this collection of stories which seemed to express, with a power I envied, a revulsion from the brutality of life akin to my own.*

I conceived a strong desire to meet Katherine Mansfield, and W. L. George kindly arranged it. I have given an account of the meeting and the subsequent ripening of my acquaintance with Katherine Mansfield in my autobiography 'Between Two Worlds,' which serves as a background to these letters up to the moment when that narrative ends, in the winter of 1918. *In April* 1912, *when I left Oxford to try my fortunes as a journalist in London, Katherine generously invited me to take a room in her flat at* 69 *Clovelly Mansions, Grays Inn Road. After a few weeks we recognized our love for one another. We became lovers, and expected to be married soon. But, for some reason, Katherine's husband, whom she had left shortly after their marriage three years before, delayed divorcing her for six years. We were not actually married until May* 3, 1918.

*We set our hearts on retiring into the country. The way seemed open when Katherine Mansfield's publisher, who traded as Stephen Swift, offered to take over the responsibility of 'Rhythm' and to give us a joint salary of £*10 *a month as editors. Katherine had an allowance from her father of £*100 *a year; I was making about £*5 *a week from the 'Westminster Gazette'. It seemed that we could well afford to say good-bye to London (and its indecent curiosity about us) and hide ourselves in the country. We found a beautiful little house at Runcton, near Chichester, furnished it by hire purchase, and proceeded to be happy in August* 1912. *Our happiness was short-lived. Within two or three months Stephen Swift was declared bankrupt. The editorial salary on which we counted to pay for our furniture vanished. Still worse, it appeared that he* *had not, as he promised, taken over the responsibility for 'Rhythm'; he had merely taken the proceeds and left the printing order in my name. I suddenly discovered that I was in debt to the printers for some £400. Very generously, but unwisely, in order to save me from bankruptcy, Katherine undertook to pay the whole of her allowance to the printers month by month. The furniture was taken away from the house in Runcton by the firm which had supplied it, and we returned, sadder but not much wiser, to London.*

Our unwisdom was apparent in our determination to keep 'Rhythm' in being. We took a three-roomed flat at 57 Chancery Lane, had the name of the magazine painted on the ground-glass door, and called it an office. Katherine undertook the grim job of canvassing for advertisements, while I toiled away at my journalism. But it was a grievous burden. Katherine became unwell. In the early summer of 1913 Gilbert and Mary Cannan found us a small cottage at Cholesbury which we persuaded Gordon Campbell to share with us. Katherine stayed there during the week, in order to get on with her own writing, while Gordon Campbell and I went down for the week-ends.

That was the first time, since we began to live together, that Katherine and I had been separated. Here her letters to me begin. The name Tig by which she signed, and by which I called her, grew out of a joint signature which we used for some articles on the theatre in 'Rhythm'. We signed them 'The Two Tigers'. Subsequently, the name was frequently softened to Wig.

Cholesbury,

Dear Jack, (Summer, 1913)

This is just 'good morning' to you.

It has been a warm bright day here—very quiet. Immediately you had gone the house fell fast asleep, and it refuses to wake up or so much as smile in a dream until next Friday. I feel that I have been here a long time—and that it's New Zealand. I'm very happy, darling. But when you come into my thoughts I refuse you, quickly, quickly. It would take me a long time away from you before I could bear to think of you. You see, when I am not with you, every little bit of you puts out a flaming sword.

Jack dear, (Summer, 1913)

Yes, Friday *will* be fun. I am beginning to 'pretend' that you are a sailor—trading with all sorts of savages from Monday until Friday and that *The Blue Review*[1] is your schooner and Secker the Fish-Eyed Pilot.

[1] For its last three numbers *Rhythm* became *The Blue Review*.

Could you not write a long—complicated—extremely insulting—symbolical serial round that idea with minute, obscene descriptions of the savage tribes . . .?

Thank you for Pa's letter. He was cheerful and poetic, a trifle puffed up, but very loving. I feel towards my Pa man like a little girl. I want to jump and stamp on his chest and cry 'You've *got* to love me'. When he says he does, I feel quite confident that God is on my side.

It is raining again today, and last night the wind howled and I gloomed and shivered, and heard locks being filed and ladders balanced against windows and footsteps padding upstairs . . . all the old properties jigged in the old way. I'm a lion all day, darling, but with the last point of daylight I begin to turn into a lamb and by midnight—mon Dieu!—by midnight the whole world has turned into a butcher!

Yes, I like Boulestin very much. There's something very sympathetic about him.

Goodbye for today, darling.

Tig

Jack dearest,   (Summer, 1913)

The postman knocked into my dream with your letter and the back door key. I had locked myself in three times three with Mrs Gomm's key, but I am glad you sent me ours.

I have begun the story and mean to finish it this evening: it feels pretty good, to me.

Walpole's letter was a little too strenuous. (What is a beautiful picture?) But I prefer that to Gilbert's[1] one remark: 'Davies steeped in Bunyan'. Oh dear! I'm afraid Walpole is having his birthday cake far too soon—like all our young men (except Jack and Tig). What a surprise for them when we sit down at the heads of their tables—all among their cake crumbs and groaning little tummies—you, with a laurel wreath on your darling head, and me trailing a perfectly becoming cloud of glory.

Pride is a charming, sheltering tree: but don't think I'm resting in it, I'm only standing underneath with my eyes turned up, for a moment's grace.

Last night Mrs Gomm and I had a glass of dandelion wine, and over it I heard how Mrs Brown's petticoat had dropped off in the hurdle race 'King Edward's Coronation time'. Such goings on!

[1] Gilbert Cannan.

3

Goodbye for today. I love you. 'Not tomorrow, not the next day, but the next.' Tell me what train you are coming by. I cannot quite believe that you are coming back here. I feel—quite alone and as if I were writing to someone in the air—so strange.

Three reviews tomorrow.   Monday (Summer, 1913)

Am I such a tyrant, Jack dear—or do you say it mainly to tease me? I suppose I am a bad manager, and the house seems to take up so much time if it isn't looked after with some sort of method. I mean . . . when I have to clear up twice over or wash up extra unnecessary things I get frightfully impatient and want to be working. So often this week, I've heard you and Gordon talking while I washed dishes. Well, someone's got to wash dishes and get food. Otherwise—'There's nothing in the house but eggs to eat'. Yes, I hate hate *hate* doing these things that you accept just as all men accept of their women. I can only play the servant with a very bad grace indeed. It's all very well for females who have nothing else to do . . . and then you say I am a tyrant, and wonder because I get tired at night! The trouble with women like me is—they can't keep their nerves out of the job in hand. And [on] Monday, after you and Gordon and Lesley[1] have gone I walk about with a mind full of ghosts of saucepans and primus stoves and 'Will there be enough to go round?' . . . and you calling (whatever I am doing) '*Tig,* isn't there going to be tea? It's five o'clock', as though I were a dilatory house-maid.

I loathe myself today. I detest this woman who 'superintends' you and rushes about, slamming doors and slopping water—all untidy with her blouse out and her nails grimed. I am disgusted and repelled by the creature who shouts at you, 'You might at least empty the pail and wash out the tea-leaves!' Yes, no wonder you 'come over silent.'

Oh, Jack, I wish a miracle would happen—that you would take me in your arms and kiss my hands and my face and every bit of me and say 'It's all right, you darling thing. I quite understand'.

All the fault of money, I suppose.

But I love you, and I feel humiliated and proud at the same time: that you *don't* see—that you *don't* understand and yet love me puzzles me . . . .

Will you meet me on Wednesday evening at the Café Royal at about

[1] Lesley Moore (L.M.) was the professional name of Ida Baker, Katherine's devoted friend.

4

10.30? If you can't be there, let me know by Wednesday morning . . .
I'll come back and sleep at '57' if I may, even though I *don't* live there.
Jack—Jack—Jack.

Your wife

Tig

Jack dearest, (Summer, 1913)

I sent your glasses yesterday, packed—I hope—carefully enough.
Thank you for the money: I'm going to start again keeping a strict
account of every penny I spend and then we can see where the screw is
loose or the shoe pinches—or whatever it is.

Last night as I got into bed the bed refused to have me and down I
flew with my feet up in the air. I was terrified but I couldn't help
laughing—and once started I kept on. It seemed no end of a joke to be
all alone in what R.C.[1] would call 'the profound stillness of the June
night' and to be served that age old trick.

'Mrs Walter' is here today and we're having clean pinnies from head
to foot. Such relief that I've written my reviews again and started my
Epilogue.[2]

I went in to see Baby Gomm this morning. He was sucking. Such a
pretty sight as a rule. But Mrs Gomm's sharp worn face above him
somehow filled me with horror.

You poor darling! Having to write to me at such 'impossible hours'.
Well, assert yourself and 'be hanged if you will'. I'd rather wait for the
afternoon post or until you feel 'I want to talk to Tig'. So treat me like
that in future.

I'll phone you when I get to London tomorrow, but I know
Wednesday is your busy day and I don't want on any account to
disturb you.

Things have straightened out in my mind and I'm rather ashamed
that I told you . . . what I did yesterday. It sings in my ears rather like
the wail of the little girl left behind on the fence . . . more anger than
anything else.

I kiss your eyes and your soft furry ears and your darling frightening
mouth.

I am your

Tig

Café Royal at 10.30 if I don't hear from you tomorrow.

[1] Richard Curle.
[2] Katherine was contributing sketches under this title to *The Blue Review*.

Dear Jack,   (Summer, 1913)

I've nursed the *Epilogue* to no purpose. Every time I pick it up and hear 'You'll keep it to six,' I *can't* cut it. To my knowledge there aren't any superfluous words: I mean every line of it. I don't 'just ramble on' you know, but this thing happened to just fit 6½ pages. You can't cut it without making an ugly mess somewhere. I'm a powerful stickler for form in this style of work. I hate the sort of licence that English people give themselves . . . to spread over and flop and roll about. I feel as fastidious as though I wrote with acid. All of which will seem, I suppose, unconvincing and exaggeration. I can only express my sincerest distress (which I do truly feel) and send you the *Epilogue* back. If you and Wilfrid[1] feel more qualified for the job . . . oh, do by all means—but I'd rather it wasn't there at all than sitting in *The Blue Review* with a broken nose and one ear as though it had jumped into an editorial dog-fight.

It's a queer day, with flickers of sun. The *Epilogue* has worried me no end—and I can still hear, tossing about, the aftermath of that thunder 'It's not fair. Swinnerton can do it . . . You've got to cut it' . . . etc., etc. Can't you cut a slice off the D. Browne?[2] I really am more interesting than he is—modest though I be . . . .

                                                        Tig

Don't think of this letter. I'm frightfully depressed today. I love you, darling. Do not let us forget that we love each other. Your sad beyond words

        Tig

My dearest,   (Tuesday, Summer, 1913)

I am sorry for my anxiety of yesterday. It was not to be silenced at all except by your wire. Don't know what came over me—but I don't feel very well, and I suppose that was the reason. Nothing much—headache. Your letter—thank you, and the news was good. Johnny[3] is a darling. F——[4] a rather dangerous fraud. Albert[5] 'very sweet'. I'm glad you saw Abercrombie. Gilbert called here yesterday, and I gave him his proof. He brought back your baccy pouch and some French books. Mrs. Gomm is here today, and my room is very clean and bright with a fire. It's dull—grey—inclined to rain. I am sending you some reviews.

[1] W. W. Gibson helped us editorially.   [2] Denis Browne contributed on music.
[3] J. D. Fergusson.   [4] A Polish 'friend'.   [5] Albert Rothenstein.

6

Take care of yourself. I'm better today—except that I'm all burning up inside with a raging fire ... but, my God, it's good to be here.

On Thursday we'll see each other. Take my love.

Tig

P.S. I don't know whether you will roar at me, darling, for doing these books in this way. But they lent themselves to it, and I thought if you read the review you would see that it's almost silly to notice them singly and that they gain like this. If wrong, return the thing, and I'll do you two little ones.

Dear Jack,   (Summer, 1913)

F——is taking this for me. Will you phone Ida to come to Chancery Lane and see about this box, because some things of his are in the top of my box and he had better have them all? The story is really rather what I'd thought. He has had false promises and believed them. It's no use discussing it. He promises to pay you back in little sums of £1 and £2.

About B. and Gaudier—I can't write. Gilbert will deal with B. as she deserves. I am worried and anxious about you all the time. Gilbert will silence B. Mary says he's seldom angry and when he is he's dreadful—that's true. He'll believe nothing but truth of you. He is devoted to you. He said, 'I wish Jack would always come to me' . . . Mary said 'Oh, I'd like to put my arms round him and hug him'.[1]

Do not answer the door after office hours. During office hours don't answer yourself. Come tomorrow. My letter from G.[2] says divorce papers will be served in a day or two. No damages and no costs for us to pay.

I've seen the farm, and we all agree it's perfect.

All these things to comfort you a little. But come here, and I will tell you all. I wait for you until tomorrow.

Phone Ida to come at 7 and F—— will then come for his box. If impossible for her then make some arrangement. I am going to telegraph you now.

Your
Tig

Wednesday

Dear Jack,   (Summer, 1913)

No letter from you today. I am sending you the B. drawings this

---

[1] The episode to which this refers is described in *Between Two Worlds* pp. 246-7.
[2] Katherine's husband.

7

evening. Enough string came with my parcel from Ida to make it possible. If you want any meat (and if—oh, well, no—not necessarily) bring down some with you, please, dear. *Meat* and *tea*. That is all we want. It is a very grey day again, here, half raining—and a loud roaring noise in the trees. This morning a robin flew into my room. I caught it. It did not seem at all frightened but lay still and very warm. I carried it to the window and I cannot tell you what a strange joyful feeling—when the little bird flew out of my hands. I am very sorry you did not write to me. I count on your letters in the morning and always wake up early and listen for the postman. Without them the day is very silent.

Do you want to drive tomorrow? Let me know in time.

Goodbye for today, my darling.

Tig

The '*Blue Review*' came to an end in the summer of 1913, in July if I remember rightly. We gave up the flat and 'office' in Chancery Lane, and lived for a little while at Chaucer Mansions, Baron's Court. Finding it too burdensome to pay Katherine's allowance of £8 6s. 8d. a month regularly over to the printer, we gave him notice that at the end of the first year we would cease to do so. The remainder of the debt did not really belong to us but to Stephen Swift. The printer threatened me with proceedings in bankruptcy. We told him to do what he liked.

We breathed more freely for the decision, and promptly decided to go abroad. D. H. Lawrence and Frieda, his wife, who had become our friends during the last months of 'Rhythm' and 'The Blue Review', pressed us to go and live with them at Lerici. It was very tempting; but it involved my living on Katherine's small allowance: for I could see no way at all of earning any money in Italy, and it was a matter of honour with me not to live on Katherine's money. (I now think it was a mistaken conception of honour, and that Lawrence had a truer conception of the obligations of love than I.) But I thought I might manage to earn enough to keep myself in Paris by reviewing French books for the 'Times Literary Supplement'. Accordingly, in December 1913, Katherine and I went to live at 31 rue de Tournon, Paris. Unfortunately, I did not succeed in making the necessary £2 a week. In February 1914 I was called to London for my public examination in the bankruptcy court. During this visit, J. A. Spender came to my rescue by offering me the art-criticism of 'The Westminster Gazette'. The following letters were written to me while I was in London, where I stayed with Gordon and Beatrice Campbell.

31 rue de Tournon, Paris,
Sunday morning.
(February, 1914)

Your letter this morning was a lovely surprise. I had not hoped to hear from you until tomorrow at earliest. Thank you, darling.

Everything is quite all right, here. Your room feels cold and it smells faintly of orange-flower water or furniture polish—a little of both. I spent a great part of the day reading Theocritus and, late last night, happening upon our only Sainte-Beuve, I found the first essay was all about him. What I admire so much in your criticism—your *courteous* manner: Sainte-Beuve has it to perfection.

Do not worry about me. I am not in the least frightened, but if Campbell abuses me too heartily, tell him 'I am not one of a malignant nature, but have a quiet temper'.[1]

It's a spring day. The femme de ménage is cleaning the windows and I've had a bath.

Take every care of yourself.

Tig

Dear Jack,   (February, 1914)

If you are staying so long, I had better send you this to answer. Do not worry about anything here. We are all right. I am afraid I am rather childish about people coming and going—and just now, at this moment when the little boy has brought me your telegram, the disappointment is hard to bear.

Your room is ready for you. It looks lovely. Do whatever is best, dear, but remember that all the people are very little and that really and truly we are awfully strong.

Very well, dear.

Tig

Wednesday,
Well, Jack dear,   (February, 1914)

I expect I did not understand your wire quite fully. Telegrams are always frightening. Now that I've read your letter, I am able to write to you more sensibly. You are right to stay until the matter of the bankruptcy is fixed up. I quite understand that, dear, and I am thankful

---

[1] This is a translation of a fragment of Sappho. 'In fr. 72 she says of herself, "I am not one of a malignant nature, but have a quiet temper".' *Sappho: A Memoir and Translation*, by H. T. Wharton, London, 1887.

they are more or less nice. Don't rush and don't consider me. If you find it more convenient to stay longer, just wire me.

Now about the other and 'more important' affair. This is difficult to discuss by letter. I do not think it is any good your staying anywhere if you are worried about money. A constant strain like that wears you out quicker than anything. If we cannot live over here on £10 a month (and we can't) there's an end of this place for the present. I *think* you had better do what you think—I mean take the *Westminster* job for at least a year and feel the security of a regular £5 a week for that time. Your work needs freedom from these grinding fears. About exchanging flats, I expect it would not be difficult. But it would take time, I am sure.

What is at the back of your darling mind? Is it your idea to stay at Campbell's and me to stay here until the exchange is effected? Tell me quite plainly, won't you? Did you take a return ticket? Would you rather stay on now and save the money and manage things by letter? You know, Jack darling, quite seriously speaking, I can be happy in any place where we are together, but without you all places alike are deserted for me. No more now.

Tig

Don't send any more postcards—like you did today, please dear. Excuse writing. Tired.

Cheque enclosed   Thursday,

My dear one,   (February, 1914)

You are good to me! Two letters this morning and a telegram yesterday afternoon. I wished that I might have sent you one in return but I thought you would not expect it so I . . . guarded the money. It would be a great relief to talk over everything, but by the time you get this letter it will be Friday morning and unless your plans have changed you will have no time to reply to me except 'in person'. I talked over 'the business' with you yesterday as much as I could by letter and without you. Depend upon us—we're quite strong enough now to find a way out of our difficulties and we *will* and be happy, too, and do our work. (By being happy I mean happy together in the 'odd times', you know). And if I can get a room in London that hasn't another opening out of it and isn't the logical end of a passage I can work there as well as anywhere—supposing we arrange to leave here at once.

I read the letter that you wrote me with Lesley and my breast ached, my dearest.

Tig

Can you let me know the *exact time* of your arrival? If you feel you'd rather keep the money, don't worry to, but I have been very careful of my money here, and everything is paid up to date—the two weeks' laundry *and* the femme de ménage—and I have 60 francs left.

Monday morning,
(February, 1914)

Dear Jack,

I am glad that Campbell is looking after you—glad, too that you went to see W.L.G.[1] That was a good idea. Lesley writes me—the weather is beastly—and here it is so warm and sunny that I have sat with my window open yesterday and today. (Yes, dear, mentioned 'with intent'.) I wish you would buy a pair of shoes as well as the pepper and salt trousers. Try to. You want them so badly and I've no faith in these cheap boulevard beauties.

Everything here 'is just the same'. The femme de chambre is singing in the kitchen—a most improbable song. It runs along—very blithe and nice—for about five notes and then it *drops*—any distance you like, but a little deeper each time. If the 'aspects' were not good that song would frighten me no end . . . *provided* that I was in a little house on the edge of the steppes with a mushroom-shaped cloud over it and no smoke coming out of the chimney etc., etc. But things being what they are, my romantic mind imagines a kind of 15th century French Provincial Ride-a-Cock-Horse—you know the business . . . dashing off on some one's knee to get a pound of butter and being suddenly 'tumbled into the gutter'. Which, after all, is a very pleasant place to fall. I wonder if Queens played this Disturbing Game with their youngest pages.

My door has been mended. I am told that a workman came at nine, wrenched out the remains of the old panel, tapped the wood with an iron hammer, slapped in a new panel, clattered over the hall—but I did not hear a sound. I slept until a quarter to ten.

You will tell me the exact time of your arrival, won't you? If it is early morning I'll not meet you, but at any other time I'd like to go to the station. You have all my love.

Tig

No letters have come. I sent a 'bleu' on Saturday for you.

[1] W. L. George, at whose house I first met Katherine.

We decided that I should accept the art-criticism of 'The Westminster', and that we must return to London. We arrived practically penniless. Gordon Campbell put us up and gave us some money till I could find my feet again. We lived in various rooms in Chelsea until the outbreak of the war. The Lawrences, who had now returned to England and become bosom friends, went to live in a cottage at Cholesbury. We wanted to be near them, but the nearest cottage we could find was a mile and a half away from them at The Lee.

Rose Tree Cottage was cold and damp. The totally unexpected happening of the war bewildered and depressed me; and it drove the more conscious and sensitive Lawrence to despair. When Lawrence and I desponded together, as we frequently did, Katherine found it very oppressive. She suffered severely from fibrositis. To add to the difficulties my work as art-critic on 'The Westminster' came practically to an end. I remember staring gloomily at a cheque for 16s. which was my earnings for a week.

At this time, at the Lawrences' cottage, we met S. S. Koteliansky who had come to visit them. He became, almost immediately, Katherine's staunch and life-long friend.

In January the Lawrences left Cholesbury for Greatham in Sussex, where Viola Meynell had lent them a magnificent modern cottage. Shortly after, Katherine met her brother, Leslie Heron Beauchamp, who had arrived from New Zealand to serve in the British army. I think the meeting planted in Katherine's imagination the first germ of the 'novel' about New Zealand which was eventually to be realized as 'Prelude' and 'At the Bay'. He also gave her the money to go to France.

During the early part of 1915 Katherine made three separate stays in France. The motive of her first journey was partly to escape from the unhappiness and depression of Rose Tree Cottage, but mainly to meet Francis Carco, the French novelist, whom we had known when we were in Paris in the winter of 1913–14, and with whom Katherine now imagined she was in love. He was stationed near Gray, in the military zone, which she had difficulty in entering. However, the meeting took place on February 19. But the excitement of the adventure which had sustained her was short-lived, and there was a severe reaction.

There is no doubt that, so far as her conscious intentions went, Katherine at this time had decided to leave me for good. She thought she could look back, with a tenderness in which there was a tinge of condescension, to 'the three years' idyll', as she called it. But, strangely enough, I knew her better than she knew herself; and though her departure made me sad, I did not take it tragically. I was certain that she would return. In the meantime, I went to stay with the

Lawrences at Greatham. After about a week I had a telegram to say that she was returning. She was obviously disillusioned, and fell ill.

When she recovered, she decided, in a different spirit and with a different purpose, to return to Paris to write. Carco had placed his little flat at 13 Quai aux Fleurs at her disposal, and she thought that she would be able to live there on about a pound a week. But before going she went to stay with the Lawrences at Greatham. The following letter was written during her visit to them.

Greatham,
Saturday afternoon.

My darling Bogey, (March 13, 1915)

I came here by a fly with a man with a black patch on his eye. It was a most complicated journey. I kept thinking of my 'wandering boy' and the journey in the dark that you told me of, and when we took the tenth turning my hand flew out to you. This is a very nice cottage and I feel like you that ours is sordid in comparison. This bathroom! This thick white distemper! And a fire in one's bedroom all dancy in the dark!

I gave Lawrence your love, and he sends his and so does Frieda. They love you, both of them. I have talked a good deal of your book. Lawrence wants to review it for some paper. It's a good idea, I think.

Brother sent me a letter today, asking me to spend a week-end with him in London—so I had to wire him. I have seen Mrs. Saleeby. She called me 'Katherine'. I don't know why that touched me. I like her, but she seems to me unhappy: she appeals to me. Mary keeps your letter, but you said you were coming here soon, and Mrs. Saleeby says if the promise is not kept 'there will be no holding Mary'.

The country is lovely—sand and pine hills, daffodils in flower, violets and primroses in plenty, and on the marshes this morning there were almost as many seagulls as we saw in Rye.

I am sitting writing to you, and Frieda and Koteliansky are talking. My brain is wispy a little, my precious dear. I hope you and Goodyear[1] are all right in the cottage.

I shall be in London tomorrow and I will take that 6.25 train from Marylebone. Send Collins for me, will you please?

My work is snapping at my heels, but I have to Down Rover it, so far.

---

[1] Frederick Goodyear, see *Journal* p. 58.

Bogey, *did* you see a book here called *Irene Iddesleigh*? It is such a treat. I shall have to give you a copy: it is the ideal book to read in bed.

My Boge, I am very near you and I feel very free in my love. I do love you, you know, dearly—dearly. I want to talk to you.

The downs so free are lovely—but I cannot walk quite there. I am *much* better—the air is so good, and the hot baths with sea salt—very sumptuous!

If I were quite alone and writing to you I should say something different. I want to tell you something about myself—but I hardly know what it is—against the others talking. I expect you know better than I do. I have a notion that your intuition is almost angelic.

I hope C. was decent. I feel that I dislike him utterly—that he is a fool and no end of a beggar. However . . .

That's all, Bogey. Two little quick kisses.

Your

Tig

Katherine's second stay in Paris lasted from March 18 to the end of the month—a bare fortnight. The third was equally short: from May 5 to 19. Her purpose in these two journeys was twofold. She wanted to 'break through', as she used to say, in her writing: that is, to make a solid beginning with the 'novel' she had in mind. Equally, she wanted to reach a resolution of the turmoil of her emotional life. In this matter, her letters to me, which have now been arranged in the correct order and precisely dated, tell their own story.

During her second stay in France I was engaged in preparing two top-floor rooms at 95 Elgin Crescent for her return. She stayed there some five weeks during which the novel, after a number of false starts, took a more definite shape. Its name was settled: it was to be 'The Aloe', for I have lately discovered a letter of mine to her of May 11 which refers to it under that name, as a matter of familiar knowledge between us. Hitherto I had been under the impression that 'The Aloe' was not conceived until after the death of her brother in October 1915. Whether she actually wrote any considerable portion of it in Paris between May 5 and May 19 is doubtful, but I think that there can be no doubt that it is to 'The Aloe' she refers when she says: 'Ça marche, ça va, ça se dessine.' (May 8, 1915).

But the emotional turmoil did not subside easily; and so long as it existed Katherine was unable to realize 'The Aloe'. For that she depended upon inward peace—on 'being in some perfectly blissful way at peace' (letter of

14

February 3, 1918). She used that phrase to describe her condition while she was actually writing 'The Aloe' in the early spring of 1916 at the Villa Pauline, Bandol. Nor was it till that time that her emotional turmoil was fully resolved.

'Prelude'—which was the final form of 'The Aloe'—is now an accepted classic. Its revolutionary novelty, thirty years ago, is easily forgotten. Therefore it has seemed to be worth emphasizing that it was the final outcome of a prolonged period of gestation which probably lasted a full year.

1st Morning   13 Quai aux Fleurs, Paris,
My dearest darling,   (Friday, March 19, 1915)

I have just had déjeuner—a large bowl of hot milk and a small rather inferior orange—but still not dressed or washed or at all a nice girl, I want to write to you. The sun is very warm today and lazy—the kind of sun that loves to make patterns out of shadows and puts freckles on sleeping babies—a pleasant creature.

Bogey, I had a vile and loathsome journey. We trailed out of London in a fog that thickened all the way. A hideous little Frenchwoman in a mackintosh with a little girl in a dirty face and a sailor suit filled and overflowed my carriage. The child combed its hair with a lump of brown bread, spat apple in our faces—made the Ultimate impossible noises—ugh! how vile! Only one thing rather struck me. It pointed out of the window and peeped its eternal 'Qu'est-ce?' 'C'est de la *terre, ma petite*,' said the mother, indifferent as a cabbage.

Folkestone looked like a picture painted on a coffin lid and Boulogne like one painted on a sardine tin. Between them rocked an oily sea. I stayed on deck and felt nothing when the destroyer signalled our ship. We were 2 hours late arriving and then the train to Paris did not even trot once—sauntered—meandered. Happily an old Scotchman, one time captain of the *California*, that big ship that went down in the fog off Tory Island, sat opposite to me and we 'got chatting'. He was a Scotchman with a pretty, soft accent; when he laughed he put his hand over his eyes and his face never changed—only his belly shook. But he was 'extremely nice'—quite as good as 1s. Worth of Conrad. At Amiens he found a tea-wagon and bought ham and fresh rolls and oranges and wine and would not be paid, so I ate hearty. Paris looked exactly like anywhere else—it smelled faintly of lavatories. The trees appeared to have shed their buds. So I took a room (the same room) and piled up coats and shawls on my bed to 'sleep and forget'. It was all merely dull beyond words and stupid and meaningless.

But today the sun is out: I must dress and follow him. Bless you my dearest dear. I love you *utterly—utterly*—beyond words—and I will not be sad. I will not take our staying in our own rooms for a little as anything serious. How are you? What are you doing?

Address my letters to the post until I give you another address.

This is a silly old letter—like eating ashes with a fish-fork—but it is not meant to be. I rather wanted to tell you the truth. I read last night in the *Figaro* that the 16th Section (Carco's) are to be sent to TURKEY Alas, the day!

Jaggle, Bogey, love—tell me about you, your book, your rooms—everything.

Your

Tig

Paris,

Darling,   (March 19, 1915)

I went to Chartier to lunch and had a maquereau grillé and épinards à la crême. It was very strange to be there alone. I felt that I was a tiny little girl and standing on a chair looking into an aquarium. It was not a sad feeling, only strange, and a bit 'femme seule-ish'. As I came out it began to snow. A wind like a carving knife cut through the streets—and everybody began to run. So did I—into a café, and there I sat and drank a cup of hot black coffee. Then for the first time I felt in Paris.

It was a little café and hideous—with a black marble top to the counter *garni* with lozenges of white and orange. Chauffeurs and their wives and fat men with immense photographic apparatus sat in it—and a white fox-terrier bitch, thin and eager, ran among the tables. Against the window beat a dirty French flag, fraying out in the wind and then flapping on the glass. Does black coffee make you drunk—do you think? I felt quite *enivrée*, (Oh, Jack, I *won't* do this. It's like George Moore. Don't be cross.) and could have sat there years, smoking and sipping and thinking and watching the flakes of snow. And then you know the strange silence that falls upon your breast—the same silence that comes just one minute before the curtain rises. I felt that and knew that I should write here. I wish that you would write a poem about that silence sometime, my Bogey. It is so *peculiar*—even one's whole physical being seems arrested. It is a kind of dying, before the new breath is blown into you . . . As I write I can almost see the poem you will make —I see the Lord alighting on the breast of the man and He is very fierce. (Are you laughing at me?)

So after this intense emotion I dashed out of the café, bought some oranges and a packet of rusks and went back to the hotel. *Me voici!* The garçon has just polished the handles of the door. They are winking, and smelling somethink horrible. The sky is still full of snow—but everything is clear to see—the trees against the tall houses—so rich and so fine—and on the grey streets the shiny black hats of the cabmen are like blobs of Lawrence's paint.[1] It's very quiet. A bird chirrups—a man in wooden shoes goes by. Now I shall start working. Goodbye, my dear one.

The same night. Very strange is my love for you tonight. Don't have it psycho-analysed. I saw you suddenly lying in a hot bath, blinking up at me—your charming beautiful body half under the water. I sat on the edge of the bath in my vest waiting to come in. Everything in the room was wet with steam and it was night-time and you were rather languid. 'Tig, chuck over that sponge.' No, I'll *not* think of you like that. I'll shut my teeth and not listen to my heart. It begins to cry as if it were a child in an empty room and to beat on the door and say 'Jack—Jack—Jack and Tig.' I'll be better when I've had a letter.

Ah, my God, how can I love him like this! Do I love you so much more than you love me or do you too . . . feel like this?

Tig

Saturday morning. Just off to see if there are any letters. I'm all right, dearest.

Paris,

(Saturday, March 20th, 1915)

I don't know what you think of yourself but I think you're a little pig of a sneak. Not a letter—not a sign—not a copy of the *Saturday Westminster*—plainly nothing. Why are you so horrid? Or is it the post? I'll put it down to the post and forgive you, darling. A baby in arms could play with me today. The weather is so warm I'm sitting with the windows wide open and nothing but a thin blouse on (in a way of speaking). All the trees are popping and the air smells of mignonette. Big open barges full of stones are being towed by black and red beetles up the river. The steering men lean idly, legs crossed—

[1] At this time Lawrence was very busy painting little wooden boxes.

17

you know their way—and the water froths against the bows. The carts passing make a merry jingle and the concierge has put a pink hyacinth in her window. Bogey, (I'm a fool when I'm alone. I turn into a little child again) there is a woman on the opposite side of the river. She sits with her back against a tree, her legs stretched out in front of her, combing her long brown hair. To this side and to that she bends and then, with that charming weary gesture, she throws her head back and draws the comb all the length of it. If I were near enough I am sure I would hear her singing.

The idle time of the year is coming, Jaggle, when you can sit outside with a piece of bread and butter on your knee and watch it fristle— frisle. (How do you spell that?) I felt very flat when I bought *La Patrie* at midday and found that no Zeppelins had arrived after all. Unfortunately, I had already posted your letter, so you can laugh at me. This afternoon I am going to write about last night. I'll send it to you. Do what you like with it. Send it somewhere—will you, please? I don't want *anything* about Paris to go to the *New Age*. I must not make daisy-chains in Biggy B's meadows.

I dreamed last night about G.[1] I was at an opera with you sitting on a converted railway carriage seat and I heard G. talking of his wife to an American lady. Then he saw me and I went up and spoke to him. Just as I was saying I never had and never would love him etc. Mrs. Saleeby appeared and seeing us together she came up to me and kissed my hands and said, 'Oh, Katherine, I always felt such love for you—and now I know why' and she pressed me to her and said 'Caleb is at home, digging in the garden.' This so touched me that I nearly sacrificed myself on the spot, but I knew you were waiting for me in a little house in South Kensington. The opera had disappeared and I was sitting on the stump of a cut tree and G. leant against it toying with a top hat. So I pressed his hand awfully kindly, picked up a very large rabbit that was watching us, with twitching ears, and walked away, saying to G. over my shoulder 'There is always a beginning and an ending, George.' But he burst into tears and called 'Ah, my dear, *don't—don't* be so wonderful!' 'If that is the case,' thought I, 'I'm wasting myself. I shall take some inexpensive but good, dancing lessons.' Then I woke up.

Next day. After all I never wrote a thing. Yesterday I began reading and read on until past midnight. There are so many books of 'the young men' here and I glanced through a number to get an impression.

[1] Katherine's husband.

18

Heavens! what a set of lollipops! Really, I did not come across *one* that counted. Upon the same stage, with the same scenery, the same properties, to the same feeble little tune, one after one pipes his little piece, and the audience, being composed of a number of young men and females exactly like himself, with precisely the same burning desire to feel the limelight on their faces, applaud and flatter and cherish. You can't believe they were not all littered at a breath. Funny, if it weren't so damned ugly—and the trouble is that nobody will ever kick their little derrières for them because they haven't got 'em to kick—seulement, 'deux globes d'ivoire'! Afterwards I began to read Stendhal's *Le Rouge et le Noir*. You can imagine how severe and noble it seemed and does still by morning seem to me. But what I feel most deeply is—how *tragic* a great work of art appears. All these young 'nez-au-venticistes' have their place and their meaning in this world, but I seemed to see Stendhal with his ugly face and pot belly and little pig's legs confined within a solitary tower, writing his book and gazing through the window chink at a few lovely stars. (Don't whistle!)

I must go off to the post. I could write to you all day. It is raining fast and my lung hates the weather. I press your hand very hard, Jaggle. I believe in you and I love you profoundly today.

Goodbye for now, my darling.

Tig

Sunday early afternoon,
(March 21, 1915)

My darling one,

Still no letter—perhaps I can be certain of one tomorrow. I walked to the post this morning and then finding neither light nor murmur there, I went to the Luxembourg gardens. About 3 of the biggest chestnut trees are really in leaf today—you never saw anything lovelier, with pigeons and babies adoring. I walked and walked until at last I came to a green plot with the back view of the head and shoulders of a pa-man rising out of an enormous stone urn—d'une forme d'une carotte. Laughing with my muff as is my solitary habit, I sped to see his face and found that it was a statue of Verlaine. What extraordinary irony! The head seemed to me to be very lovely in its way—bashed in but dignified, as I always imagine Verlaine. I stayed a long time looking at that and then sunned myself off on a prowl. Every soul carried a newspaper. *L'Information* came out on orange sails. *La Patrie* lifted up its voice at the Métro stations. Nothing was talked of but the raid last night. (I'm trying to tell you about this raid but I'm sure I shan't be able to).

Oh, Jaggle, I was really rather fine. I came home late—I had been dining with B. at the Lilas. It was a lovely night. I came in, made some tea,—put out the lamp and opened the shutters for a while to watch the river. Then I worked until about one. I had just got into bed and was reading Kipling's *Simples Contes des Collines,* Bogey, when there was a sharp quick sound of running and then the trumpets from all sides blaring *Garde à vous!* This went on, accompanied by the heavy groaning noise of the shutters opening and then a chirrup of voices. I jumped up and did likewise. In a minute every light went out except one point on the bridges. The night was bright with stars. If you had seen the house stretching up and the people leaning out! And then there came a loud noise like *doo-da-doo-da* repeated hundreds of times. I never thought of Zeppelins until I saw the rush of heads and bodies turning upwards, as the *Ultimate Fish* (see *The Critic in Judgment*) passed by, flying high, with fins of silky grey. It is absurd to say that romance is dead when things like this happen. And the noise it made—almost soothing, you know, steady and clear *doo-da-doo-da*—like a horn. I longed to go out and follow it, but instead I waited, and still the trumpets blared—and finally when it was over I made some more tea and felt that a great danger was past and longed to throw my arms round someone. It gave me a feeling of boundless physical relief like the aftermath of an earthquake.

B.'s flat is really very jolly. She only takes it by the quarter at 900 francs a year—four rooms and a kitchen, a big hall, a cabinet and a conservatory. Two rooms open on to the garden. A big china stove in the salle à manger heats the place. All her furniture is second-hand and rather nice. The faithful M. conducts her shopping. Her own room, with a grey self-colour carpet, lamps in bowls with Chinese shades, a piano, 2 divans, 2 armchairs, books, flowers, a bright fire, was very unlike Paris, really very charming. But the house I think detestable. One *creeps* up and down the stairs. She has dismissed D. and transferred her virgin heart to P., who lives close by. Strange and really beautiful though she is, still with the fairy air about her and her pretty little head still so fine, she is ruined. There is no doubt of it. I love her, but I take an intense, cold interest in noting the signs. She says 'It's no good me having a crowd of people. If there are more than four I go to the cupboard and nip cognacs till it's all over for me, my dear' or 'Last Sunday I had a fearful crise. I got drunk on rhum by myself at the

Rotonde and ran up and down this street crying and ringing the bells and saying "Save me from this man!" There wasn't anybody there at all.' And then she says with a faint show of importance, 'Of course the people here simply love me for it. There hasn't been a real woman of feeling here since the war. But now I am going to be careful.'

Myself, I am dead off drink. I mean the idea of being drunk revolts me horribly. Last time I was drunk was with B. here and the memory stays and shames me even now. We were drunk with the wrong people. Not that I committed any sottise, but I hate to think of their faces and —ugh! no—I shall not drink again, like that, never—never.

As I write to you the concierge is doing the flat and she will persist in talking. Do I like flowers? Cold or heat? Birds or beasts? She is one of those women who can't lift or replace a thing without giving it its *ticket*. But she's a good soul and looks after me and fills the lamp without being told. Of course, everybody she ever knew has died a grisly death in this war—and the fact that Carco is going to Turkey seems to delight her beyond measure. 'Il ne reviendra jamais!'

Today everywhere they are crying 'Voici les jolies violettes de Parme!' and the day is like that. Under the bridges floats a purple shadow. I must start working. (I believe now she is dusting simply to spite me and to keep me off my work. What a bore these women are!)

How are you managing, dearest? Does the housekeeper come up? Oh, Jack, write often. I am *lost, lost* without letters from you. Things haven't got their real flavour. Keep me very close to your heart in my own place. Dearest of all, I love you utterly.

I am your
Tig

Monday afternoon,
(March 22, 1915)

D. Bogey,

I have just had your first letter. But won't you have a little more money this week from *The Westminster*? And if you simply haven't enough to buy the necessities can't you go to Lawrence until a cheque comes—or is that impossible? I am frightfully sorry about all this and the curtains—what misery! Has Beatrice[1] got a pair she could *lend* you for the time being? I suppose all my suggestions sound silly and beside the mark, darling. Of course, the thing to do would be to have a band of the green lining material put down the outside of each curtain

[1] Beatrice Campbell.

Make Beatrice find you a little machinist. She would do it for almost nothing. The green stuff is ordinary casement cloth from Waring's. About the gas stove—they always take 8 to 10 days. I suppose you can buy *fish* and cook it on the Primus all right—can't you? Don't *live* on sardines!

My precious, how hideous it all sounds! I read your letter, and a very sweet big dropping rain fell on the pages all the while. I wonder if things are better. I wish I knew how much the furniture had cost to come to Elgin Crescent. Perhaps it would be a good thing to get Rose to send by Collins another chair or two and the round table as an *odd table*. I do not know exactly what else to suggest. Keep me posted with whatever news you can.

Your letter has dried me up. Nothing has happened here that will fit in with it at all: it all sounds 'silly'—my news—and of no earthly importance.

I've read a book by Rachilde, *L'Heure Sexuelle*. She is a fascinating creature, far more interesting than Colette—the *writer*. She started me off with a leap this morning.

Now I am on my way to tea with B.—a *pain d'épices* (only half one at 40) under my arm. But oh! what a horrible state of things in London with you. No, I'll recover from it, and I would a million times rather that you told me than that you remained silent.

Did you get a letter from me posted at Victoria? Perhaps the gas-man took it.

No, I stop writing. All my nerves are up in arms. Damn this bloody money! I won't even say that I kiss you, You don't want me to.

Tig

Monday night,

Dear Bogey, (March 22, 1915)

When I wrote to you this afternoon, I was not a nice girl—I know. Now, sitting writing to you by the light of a candle, with the whole house so quiet and closed and all the people in the cellars, I am sorry. The trumpets sounded about an hour ago. All the lights are out, except one on the bridge, very far, and one by the police station at the corner. I have been standing at the open window. Searchlights sweep the sky; they are very lovely, lighting up one by one the white clouds. Now and then someone passes, or a cart all dark gallops by. When the alarm sounded, the sirens and fire whistles and motors all answered. I was in the street and in a moment or two it was almost pitch dark— just here and there a flicker as someone lighted a cigarette. When I arrived at the Quai aux Fleurs and saw all the people grouped in the doorways, and when people called out, 'N'allez pas comme ça dans la rue!' I was really rather thrilled. The concierge, all the house, and an obscure little old man who is always on the scene on every occasion, asked me if I would 'descendre' but I hate the idea and I came up—of course all the gas was turned off—and hung out of the window. It was extremely terrifying suddenly; in fact (prosaic!) I was nearly sick! But after that the wonderful things happening and especially a conversation between a man at the fifth floor window and a thin man on the Quai got me over my mal d'estomac. These two were talking—their voices in the dark and the things they said—are unforgettable. Also a fool who came along the Quai whistling, his hands in his pockets, and as big drops of rain fell shouted with a laugh 'Mais ils seraient mouillés—ces canailles d'oiseaux!' The rain—the dark—the silence—the voices of the two men—the beauty of the river and the houses that seemed to be floating on the water . . . . Ah, Jack!

As I wrote that more bugles sounded. Again I ran into the bedroom with the lamp, again opened the window. A big motor passed, a man in front blowing a trumpet. You heard from far and near the voices raised, 'C'est fini?' 'Fini, alors?' The few people in the street ran blindly after the motor and then stopped.

I went on the landing with my big rusty key to put on the gas again, because it's cold and I wanted a fire. The little man came up the stairs, and of course, I couldn't find the letter or the number, and of course, he knew all about it. 'Attendez! Attendez! Voulez-vous aller voir si le gaz prend?' He was a far greater fool than I. But I mercied him bien and managed it myself.

These raids after all are *not* funny. They are extremely terrifying and one feels such a horror of the whole idea of the thing. It seems so cruel and senseless. And then to glide over the sky like that and hurl a bomb— *n'importe où*—is diabolic and doesn't bear thinking about. (There gc the trumpets again and the sirens and the whistles. Another scare!) All over, again.

At B's this afternoon there arrived 'du monde', including a very lovely young woman, married and *curious*—blonde—passionate. We danced together. I was still so angry about the horrid state of things.

23

(Oh God! It's all off again!) I opened the shutters; the motors flew by sounding the alarm. I can't talk about the tea-party tonight. At any rate it isn't worth it really. It ended in a great row. I enjoyed it in a way, but B. was very impossible—she must have drunk nearly a bottle of brandy and then at 9 o'clock I left and refused either to stay any longer or to spend the night there. She flared up in a *fury* and we parted for life again. It seemed such utter rubbish in the face of all this—now. A very decent and pleasant man saw me home, happily—otherwise I think I might have been sitting in a Y.M.C.A. until this moment—it was so very dark. But a lovely evening—very soft, with rain falling. B. makes me sad tonight. I never touched anything but soda-water and so I really realized how the other people played on her drunkenness, and she was so . . . half charming and such an *utter fool*.

It is raining fast now, on the shutters—a sound I love to hear. England feels so far away at this moment, oh, very far—and I am quite suddenly sad for you. I want you as I write—and my love rises, my darling, and fills my breast. Perhaps tomorrow in your letter you may sound happier. Oh, my little lover, my dear dearest, I shall write no more now—I must go to bed and drink some hot milk *pour me faire dormir tout de suite*,

Goodnight, my heart's treasure.

Tig

(March 23, 1915)

If you lean over the Pont St. Louis you look down on to a little court which is called Port de l'Hôtel de Ville. It is a pleasant cobbled square with poplars and lime trees growing against the wall. Where it slopes down to the river there are 2 upturned boats. An old man in a straw hat sat by one of them today tapping it over with a hammer and over the other two little boys wriggled, dabbling their hands in the water. There were some mattresses propped against the wall in the sun and a wooden frame set up covered with a square of red linen. An old woman in a lilac print dress with a white band over her head and under her chin was tossing grey flock and feathers on the linen square. An immense heap of them beside her was lifted and shaken and gathered up for her by a younger woman in black, wearing a cotton bonnet. It was very warm in the sun and the flock and feathers were so dusty that the two women coughed and sneezed as they worked, but they seemed very happy. I watched until the mattress was filled and folded over like a pie-crust. Then the young woman took a little camp-stool and sat down with a needle and thread stitching, and the old one replaced the 'buttons' in the cover with a long long needle like a skewer. Now and again the two little boys ran up to have their noses blown, or the old woman sang out something and they sang back . . . .

Whose fault is it that we are so isolated—that we have no real life—that everything apart from writing and reading is 'felt' to be a waste of time?

I walked on today and came to a garden behind Notre Dame. The pink and white flowering trees were so lovely that I sat down on a bench. In the middle of the garden there was a grass plot and a marble basin. Sparrows taking their baths turned the basin into a fountain and pigeons walked through the velvety grass, pluming their feathers. Every bench and every chair was occupied by a mother or a nurse or a grandfather, and little staggering babies with spades and buckets made mud pies or filled their baskets with fallen chestnut flowers or threw their grandfathers' caps on to the forbidden grass plot. And then there came a Chinese nurse trailing 2 babies. Oh, she was a funny little thing in her green trousers and black tunic, a small turban clamped to her head. She sat down with her darning and kept up a long birdlike chatter all the time, blinking at the children and running the darning needle through her turban. But after I had watched a long time I realized I was in the middle of a dream. Why haven't I got a real 'home'—a real life—why haven't I got a Chinese nurse with green trousers and two babies who rush at me and clasp my knees? I'm not a girl—I'm a woman. I *want* things. Shall I ever have them? To write all the morning and then to get lunch over quickly and to write again in the afternoon and have supper and *one* cigarette together and then to be alone again until bed-time—and all this love and joy that fights for outlet—and all this life drying up, like milk in an old breast. Oh I want life. I want friends and people and a house. I want to give and to spend (the P.O. savings bank apart, darling).

Tig

Thursday morning,
My own Bogey,   (March 25, 1915)

Yesterday I had your letters at last. But first, I *never* got a cross post-card about the sofa: you never mentioned it until this letter. Here are

25

the directions. Take a bus to Blandford Street which is off Baker Street. Walk down it, and turn into South Street. King has got a filthy little shop with a sewing machine in the window and some fly-blown cards which say 'Loose Covers'. More than that I can't tell you myself. Have you written to him and enclosed a stamped envelope? If not, I would do that *at once*.

You seem to have done perfect wonders with the rooms. The carpentering job I saw and heard as plain as if I'd been there—to the very sand-papering. All the things are floating in my brain on a sea of blue Ripolin. I feel those rooms will be lovely. If Frieda is there ask her about the curtains. She can sew, even though I don't think she'd have ideas. I saw such jolly low stools yesterday—very firm with rush seats, 1.75. I wish I could send you two or three. They are nice.

I had a great day yesterday. The Muses descended in a ring, like the angels on the Botticelli Nativity roof—or so it seemed to 'humble' little Tig, and I fell into the open arms of my first novel. I have finished a huge chunk, but I shall have to copy it on thin paper for you. I expect you will think I am a dotty when you read it, but, tell me what you think, won't you? It's queer stuff. It's the spring makes me write like this. Yesterday I had a fair wallow in it, and then I shut up shop and went for a long walk along the Quai—very far. It was dusk when I started, but dark when I got home. The lights came out as I walked, and the boats danced by. Leaning over the bridge I suddenly discovered that one of those boats was exactly what I want my novel to be. Not big, almost 'grotesque' in shape—I mean perhaps *heavy*—with people rather dark and seen strangely as they move in the sharp light and shadow; and I want bright shivering lights in it, and the sound of water. (This, my lad, by way of uplift.) But I *think* the novel will be alright. Of course, it's not what you could call serious—but then I can't be, just at this time of year, and I've always felt a spring novel would be lovely to write.[1]

Today I must go to Cook's with my last goldin sovereign in my hand to be changed. I am getting on all right as regards money and being very careful. Cooked vegetables for supper at 20 c. the demi-livre are a great find and I drink trois sous de lait a day. This place is perfect for working.

I read your letter yesterday in the Luxembourg Gardens. An old gentleman, seeing my tender smiles, offered me half his umbrella, and

[1] This was, almost certainly, not *The Aloe* but an abandoned novel called *Brave Love*.

26

I found that it was raining; but as he had on a pair of tangerine coloured eyeglasses, I declined. I thought he was a Conrad spy.

My own dear darling, what are you doing about a bed? Surely not that vile sofa all these nights?

I have adopted Stendhal. Every night I read him now, and first thing in the morning.

This is a vague letter, but it carries love and love and kisses from your
Tig

Friday evening,
Dearest darling,   (March 26, 1915)

I am in such a state of worry and suspense that I can't write to you tonight or send you anything. When I came back from the fruitless search for letters the concierge began a long story about an Alsatian in the house who had received yesterday a four page letter for the name of Bowden.[1] 'Another came today,' said she; 'I gave it back to the postman'. I literally screamed. I have *written* this name for her and she'd utterly forgotten it, thinking of me only as Mansfield. Since then I've simply rushed from post-office to post-office. The Alsatian is out. I'm waiting for her and the postman now. My heart dies in my breast with terror at the thought of a letter of yours being lost. I simply don't exist. I suppose I exaggerate—but I'd plunge into the Seine—or lie on a railway line—rather than lose a letter. You know, Bogey, my heart is simply crying all the time and I am frightened, desolate, useless for anything.

Oh, my precious—my beloved little Jag, forgive Tig such a silly scrawl.

But life ought not to do such things to you and me. I could *kill* the concierge—yes, with pleasure. 'Une lettre d'Angleterre dans un couvert bleu.'

Courage! But at this moment I am simply running as fast as I can and crying my loudest into your arms.

I will write you properly tomorrow. This is just to say that I love you and that you are the breath of life to me.

Tig

[1] Katherine's married name.

My Bogey, my little King.   (March 27, 1915)

I'm doing the unpardonable thing—writing in pencil, but I'm in bed still and having breakfast, so please forgive. I kep my eye upon the hole of the door until 12 o'clock last night when the Alsatian deigned to ascend. As she did *not* know this flat was occupied she had a pretty fright at sight of me in the inky darkness—but after a long disappearance when I decided to hit her if she had not got it she appeared. V'là! At the same time, carrying her little lamp and all wrapped up in a shawl and wonderfully beautiful, I thought, she put her hand on my arm— 'Att*a*ndez!' she said, and disappeared and brought me back a pink hyacinth growing in a pot. 'Ça s*a*nt de la vraie fleur!' said she. Then I came in and read your Monday night letter. I read it and then I read it again. Then I dropped it into my heart, and it made ever bigger circles of love, flowing over and over until I was quite healed of that torment of waiting. I love you, you know. I love you with every inch of me. You are wonderful. You are my perfect lover. There is nobody but you. Hold me, Bogey, when I write those words, for I am in your arms, your darling head in my hands and I am kissing—kissing.

The rooms sound lovely. I hope by now the sofa is there. I hope another cheque has come. The moment Kay[1] sends my money I will send some to you.

I think O. wants kicking—just that. Of course, what is peculiarly detestable is his habit of lying *so* charmingly—his 'I should be delighted, Katherina' rings in my ears. B. I have not seen since her famous party. It's an ugly memory. I am glad it happened so soon. I think next morning she must have felt horribly ashamed of herself, for she was drunk and jealous and everybody knew it. I am thankful that I stood firm. I feel so utterly superior to her now.

To tell you the truth, both of them are bitter because they have nearly known love, and broken, and we know love and are happy— Bogey, really and truly how happy we are! Now I am giving you all sorts of little hugs and kisses, and now big ones and long long kisses—

No, I really must get up. What a farce it is to be alone in bed in the spring when you are alive!

Tig

[1] The London Manager of the Bank of New Zealand.

                                            Saturday,
Dearest one,   (March 27, 1915)
   I am really worried about money for you. Will you have got another
cheque by now? I do hope to Heaven that you have. I always feel you
become wicked and don't spend enough on food if you're hard up and
you are really rather dependent on good meals—if you only knew it.
I shall be eating chestnut buds if Kay doesn't send me my money some
time next week. I don't know how money goes. I keep a strict account
(one of those amazing fourfold affairs in which we are so expert) and
every penny is reckoned, and yet, Bogey, it seems to fly. A franc in
Paris is really 8d in England just now. But don't think I am complaining, because I am not—merely stating my case—and I know my money
will come next week. I have asked Kay to send it through Cook's. It
is the simplest way and really the post-offices are merely a collection
of stools and stamp-paper. Yesterday, after I had nearly cried through a
grating about my lost letter, the man suggested brightly, cleaning his
nails on an old nib, 'Perhaps the postman *threw it away!* . . .'
   I wanted to tell you about a nice time I had on Thursday night. At
about seven I left the house buttoned up in my black and white coat
and went for a walk behind the Hôtel de Ville. I found most curious
places—and I found at last a little market where every third body was
either frying or eating Polish pancakes. The air smelled of them and of
'petits gris'—tiny snails which you bought by the shovelful. It began to
rain. Under an old stone arch 3 hags wrapped in black shawls were
standing—their hands crossed over their bellies. At their feet there lay
three little baskets of herbs—dry twigs, withered bundles and tiny
packets. Their heads were raised, watching the drizzle, and the green
light from a lantern fell on their faces. All of them were talking,
whether to each other or to themselves you could not tell, for their
voices did not pause. It sounded like a song. It was one of the most
ancient things I have ever seen or heard.
   Having a besoin to faire mon service, I went into one of those little
10 c. places. In the passage stood an immense fat and rosy old market
woman, her skirts breast high, tucking her chemise into her flannel
drawers, and talking to an equally fat old ouvrier, who began to help
her to arrange her affairs, saying as he tugged and buttoned, 'Mais tu
sais, *ma petite*, tu ne peux pas sortir comme ça'.
   I went on much further—then down an alley on to a quai. There was

                                29

a bird shop there. The window was flying with canaries and Java sparrows and green love-birds and white doves and parrots. Outside the shop two little girls were standing, their arms round each other's necks. One had rings in her ears and the other wore a bangle. They were watching the birds and eating an orange between them, quarter by quarter. The bird-seller was a dark young man with long black moustaches and narrow eyes . . . I don't know why, but I had a curious sensation that I was in a dream and that I had seen all this years and ages ago.

Finally, it poured so with rain that I hunted and I hollered and found a café—very poor—the people eating, chauffeurs and rag bags of people. But a woman came in, skinny, enceinte, but very alive, and a curious rough boy followed her. They were so wet that the woman said 'faut danser'. And they danced. As far as I could make out this is what they sang as they turned round and round. The people who ate banged with the bread on the table and the plates clattered.

> S'il en reste un bout, ce sera pour la servante.
> S'il en reste pas d' tout, elle se tapera sur l'ventre.
> Et zon zon zon Lisette, ma Lisette.
> Et zon zon zon Lisette, ma Lison.

All the while my hat dripped over the table. I kept taking it off and shaking it on the floor, but when the boy was greeted by a very smart young friend who came to my table and said 'Je veux manger une belle fricassée avec vous, ma fleur,' I paid and ran away.

The concierge has brought me another letter, written on Wednesday night. My darling, if you write me letters like that I'll not be able to bear my love. I simply adore you. But that old *beast* upstairs must be poisoned. Jaggle, don't give him another crumb, I *implore* you.[1] I think you were very brave, all the same. I am glad about the curtains and glad Kot came. Floryan is rather a hateful idea. No, you won't find anything of mine in the *New Age*, because I won't send them a line. I think Orage is too ugly.[2] No, *don't send me any money*—I haven't the need of it.

Here's a confession. I cannot write if all is not well with us—not a line. I do write in my own way through you. After all it is love of you

---

[1] This refers to a troublesome scrounging lodger on the floor above at Elgin Crescent.
[2] Katherine was completely reconciled to A. R. Orage in the year before her death.

now that makes me write and absolutely deep down when I write well it is love of you that makes me see and feel.

You darling—you darling. Je te veux.

Tig

(March 28, 1915)

Jack, I shan't hide what I feel today. I woke up with you in my breast and on my lips. Jack, I love you terribly today. The whole world is gone. There is only you. I walk about, dress, eat, write—but all the while I am *breathing* you. Time and again I have been on the point of telegraphing you that I am coming home as soon as Kay sends my money. It is still possible that I shall.

> Jack, Jack, I want to come back,
> And to hear the little ducks go
> Quack! Quack! Quack!

Life is too short for our love even though we stayed together every moment of all the years. I cannot think of you—our life—our darling life—you, my treasure—everything about you.

No, no, no. Take me quickly into your arms. Tig is a tired girl and she is crying. I want you, I want you. Without you life is nothing.

Your woman

Tig .

After spending five weeks at 95 Elgin Crescent, Katherine went to Paris for the third time on May 5, 1913.

Jeudi.

(May 6, 1915)

I cannot tell you how beautiful this place is by daylight. The trees on the island are in full leaf . . . I had quite forgotten the life that goes on *within* a tree—how it flutters and almost plumes itself, and how the topmost branches tremble and the lowest branches all swing lazy.

It is very warm today. All the windows are wide open. From early morning people have passed along the Quai carrying lilac . . . little stout men, the bunch upside down, looped to a finger by a knotted string—young girls carrying it along the arm—little children with their faces quite buried—and old fat women clasping the branches, just a frill of flower showing above their bosoms.

31

I ran out at seven to buy some oranges. Already the shops were open. Already the sausages were looped round a lilac jar—the tailoress, bent over the machine, had a piece in her bodice. (I don't tell you any more because you won't believe me. It's everywhere.) I'll tell you where I saw it first yesterday.

Jag. Oh, Tig, don't *harp* so.

Tig. Just this, and then I won't. But we drew up alongside a hospital train. From my window I could see into the saloon. There were pallet beds round the walls. The men, covered to the chin, never moved an inch. They were just white faces with a streak of hair on top. A doctor, stout and ruddy, with a fine blond beard, stood at the window drying his hands and whistling. All round the walls of the car kind female hands had placed big bunches of purple and white lilac. 'What lovely lilac!' said the people in the train with me. 'Look! how fine it is!' The wounded men did not matter a rap.

(Then came a cry from the étage above. 'Fermez vos persiennes s'il vous plaît!' But I wasn't in time. Whether the lady sheared a sheep outside her window or merely shook her bedroom mat, I do not know. A little of both. Damn her!)

And now there comes a little handcart with 3 babies in it and a quantity of newspapers. It is dragged by two other infants—men of about 8 or nine. They stopped outside here, let down a kind of false leg which steadied the cart and strolled over to the lavatory—talking—unbuttoning their breeches and shouting to the babies to keep tranquille. But alas! no sooner had they disappeared than the infants with screams of rage began throwing the papers into the wet gutter. Back rushed their lords and now they are picking up the muddy papers and the culprits hang their heads over the side of the wagon like people about to be guillotined ... terribly chastened.

(May 7, 1915)

Next morning. I went out to lunch yesterday at a very good little brasserie, overlooking Place du Châtelet—*and* cheap—quite as cheap as Chartier and frequented only by old men and a priest or two. Afterwards, like a fool, I took the Métro to the Palais Royal and went to look for Smith's to see if they had *The Golden Bowl*. Oh, that walk! It stretched for miles, and each moment I thought it was going to end. My leg finally trailed after me like a tired child. And they had not got *The Golden Bowl*. So I came home and worked and did not go out

32

again. We had the thunder last night and today it is silvery and now and then some rain falls.

I had a horrible dream about Lesley Moore last night, and then I dreamed that you came up here to see me dressed in khaki—very handsome and happy.

Tomorrow I will send you some work, darling.

I don't want to complain, Bogey, but I do think my leg is a bit off, don't you? It hurts like billy-o today. Goodbye for now, my dearest dear.

    Tig

Saturday afternoon,

Boge darling,
(May 8, 1915)

I shall write you my letter today in this café Biard whither I've come for shelter out of a terrific storm—rain and thunder. I'm soaked and my bones are in dismay already. It is the most absurd *rot* to have to think like an old pusson every time the rain falls. This is rheumatiz for a dead spit for me. But I'm not sad, dearest of all, I am only surprised at God.

I am writing my book. *Ça marche, ça va, ça se dessine*—it's good.[1]

Your letter this morning. Thank you, my Bogey. Letters really arrive very quickly. I hope you had one from me today. I was glad to hear of the good cheque. How much does that mean for the Bank? Seven quid, I make it. Get your Sickerts framed when you can to show yourself what a good and rich boy you are. Besides, I'd love to turn up my eyes at them when I come home.[2]

The conscription scare is only a false alarm, isn't it? Of course the *Daily Mail* shrieks it each day—but I don't like the idea of even a tentative *Times* leader. Tell me all you know—the idea is hideous. I wish to God I hadn't dreamed of you in khaki—but perhaps you were thinking and your thoughts reached me. But they would never make you go, would they? I'll say no more, Betsy, until I hear.

Last night I woke to hear torrential rain. I got up with a candle and made the shutters firm—and that awful line of Geo. Meredith's sang in my head. 'And Welcome Water Spouts that Bring Fresh Rain.' Then I dreamed that I went to stay with the sisters Brontë who kept a boarding-house called the Brontë Institut—*pain*fully far from the railway station, and all the way there through heather. It was a sober place with

---

[1] This refers to the first conception of *The Aloe*.

[2] Walter Sickert had given me several of his etchings.

linoleum on the stairs. Charlotte met me at the door and said, 'Emily is lying down'. Kot, I found, was also there, taking supper. He broke an orange into a bowl of bread and milk. 'Russian fashion,' said he. 'Try it. It's very good.' But I refrained.

Then the bell tinkled and the concierge gave me your letter .... How can all these people afford cabs? Even girls in pinafores without hats are jumping into fiacres. I cannot afford even the principle.

I found a photograph of Willy today. He looked like Edward VII in spirits of wine—an awful fathead. Of course, he has got *something*, but he's terribly small beer, I'm afraid. *And* a snob *and* heartless. So I feel. Frank Harris is writing pro-Germanics in *The Continental Times*. He is roaring down England and roaring up Germany. I feel very disgusted. 'And you?' (as they are always singing in Wagner's opera for a kick-off).

There goes Eve Balfour. Yes, it is. No, it isn't. Yes, it is. No, it isn't. Alas, another case of mistaken identity, like the darkey who was asked why he stole the old lady's parrot and said, 'A-aw Boss, Ah took it for a lark'.

Jag. 'Tig, what a *fool* you are today.'

Tig. 'But it won't stop raining, and I'm stuck, dearest, and wondering if the waiter will flick me away next time he comes.'

Tell me about your dinner-party. I shall have to face this music and 'plunge' after all. It is extremely hot and muggy and airless.

Goodbye for now, my darling.

I am always your
Tig

Saturday,
(May 8, 1915)

Dear Bogey,

The lamplighter is just going his rounds, but I am sitting in the dusk still. I have just come in from a small walk. I returned to the garden of Notre Dame. It was dusky already, and the smell of the flowery trees a wonder to enjoy. I sat again on a bench. Hardly anybody was there; an old man on the other end of my bench kept up a buzzing in his beard, and a few extremely wicked babies without any hope of bed played ball, just their heads and knees and flying hands to be seen. How black the tree stems were and how fine the leaves! They were like a tune given out in the bass with a wonderful running treble,—and above the trees uprose Notre Dame in all its venerable beauty. Little birds flew among the towers—you know the little birds that always fly about ruins. Looking at them I wanted to write a sonnet, using as an image of old age and the thoughts of old age flying out and returning, the tower and the birds. I shall write it one day.

I have been writing my book all the afternoon. How good the fatigue is that follows after!

Lovers are idling along the Quai. They lean over the parapet and look at the dancing water and then they turn and kiss each other, and walk a few steps further arm in arm and then stop again and again kiss. It *is* rather the night for it, I must say.

The rain stopped after I had posted your letter today, but it is still *un temps très lourd*. I bought a litre of white wine today for 45 c. (very good) and it is lying in a basin of water in the kitchen zinc. The butter and the milk sit on a brick outside the kitchen window. '*Some* summer,' as a fool at the music hall would say.

Write to me as often as you can, my dear love. Of course, no human being could compete with my effugions and well I knows it, but alone in furrin parts is not the same as being even as alone as I realize you are in England.

Sunday morning. I have just had your summer letter *and* the *D.N.* London does sound good, and the idea of drinking cider and then sitting in my special little garden was very alluring. I know that garden[1] better than any other in the world. I see it now as I write. But for some strange reason, I have always gone there to cry. I well remember one dreadful New Year's Eve when I went there and sat on one of the benches crying into a little black velvet muff with blue ribbons (Lesley had it after) and an awful old woman with a jet bonnet watched, a long time and then she sighed and said 'Well, that's 'ow it is, my dear'.

No, dearest darling, the Lawrences of course do not understand. I hope you posted the letter to them I gave you. What became of your dinner-party? I mean with Muirhead Bone. F.C. as you know simply doesn't exist for me.

I found last night in the letter-rack a copy of that song 'Dodo!' It is called *Idylle Rouge*. I send you a verse and the refrain. I had got it all wrong.

My work I'll send when it's copied out. A high strange wind blows today, but the sun shines. I dream—oh, I dream so strangely here. There is half past 9 o'clock. I am still in my sprigged nighty. I must get up.

---

[1] The little garden in Leicester Square.

(Yes, I want you, too. I want to lean against you and laugh and forget Time and his jangling bell. Yes, I want to be your lover. Darling!)

Tig

This goes on for verses of *Horrid Tragedy*. I'll sing it for you one day. It is really very 'pa' when sung.

> Quand on l'voyait
> On n'aurait pas dit
> A son air peu bra-va-che
> Que c'était un dangéreux bandit
> Un vrai chef d' a-pa-ches.
> C'est pour sa maîtresse
> Qu'il cambriolait
> Pour n' pas qu'ell'fass' la no-ce.
> Elle tremblait pour lui
> Car ell' l'adorait
> Et disait en l'berçant comme un gos-se

Refrain: Dodo, mon homm'
> Fais vit' dodo
> Tout près d' ta maît-res-se.
> Blotti dans mes bras
> T'oubliras bientôt
> Tes pensées mauvais's
> Bercé par ma ten-dres-se
> Serr' toi bien près de moi, j'ai peur
> Qu'un jour tes car-ess-es
> Ne vienn'nt à me manquer
> J' s'rais folle de douleur
> Car je t'aime 'ε tout mon cœur!

Sunday evening,
(May 9, 1915)

Instead of having dinner today I ate some bread and drank some wine at home and went to a cinema. It was almost too good. A detective drama, so well acted and so sharp and cruel, with a horrible décor—the environs of Calais. Wickedness triumphed to everyone's great relief, for the hero, an apache called 'L'Fantôme,' was an admirable actor. And there was a girl there, mistress of 'Bébé' and 'le faux curé', two other apaches. I wish you could have seen that girl act. She was very still, and then her gestures *sprang* from her. Pale, you know. A little round head and a black dress. All the while the orchestra played a tango that we have heard before, a very 'troubling' tune.

Before going in I walked up to the Luxembourg Gardens. But the Sunday crowd,—you know, the women mincing in their high boots like fowls in the wet, and the shop-walker men, and the 'Ah, c'est beau!' 'Dis! c'est joli,' 'C'est *très, très* joli,' 'Tout à fait beau.' I felt exactly as if I were dead.

It is very beautiful outside the window this afternoon. The wind shakes the trees so.

There was a great excitement a few minutes ago. I saw the policeman before the station below suddenly stiffen and then at the bottom of the steps that lead on to the quai—you know where I mean, below here?—there came a grey little frog squirming in the grip of two gendarmes. They were evidently hurting him, but my policeman flew to their aid. He got behind the man and suddenly thrust his hand between the man's legs. You should have heard the yell he gave and you should have seen the jerk that sent him forward. Life is a funny business.

Now there are birds wheeling and flying in the air and the sky is pink. It is evening. I have not spoken to anyone since Wednesday except to say 'Combien ça fait?' or to say 'Oui, c'est bien terrible,' to the concierge. It is curious for one who has been much alone—this *sinking back* into silence.

Monday. Oh, Bogey, I haven't got a letter. The *Daily News* came, and I even looked for a little message on the inside of the wrapper. It is ten o'clock. I shall start work and drown my disappointment. That means no news of you until tomorrow. And I love you. I love you.

Tig

I went out on the landing just now to get some water. The concierge was sweeping the stairs and the woman below me came out to talk to her. 'The little lady upstairs came in very late last night,' said she. 'Who?' 'La maîtresse de Francis Carco,' bawled the voice. 'No, she was not out at all. Ce n'est pas son habitude de sortir le soir,' said the concierge. I am still trembling with fury. I wanted to pack up and go that moment. I suppose people do not matter—but they certainly *can* hurt. And I've no letter from you all day, dear darling.

A letter from you.   Tuesday morning,
My dearest of all,   (May 11, 1915)

I have just got your Saturday letter, and you can imagine what I feel about the supper party and about ——. I could *murder* her. Everything you told me made me boil and made my heart fly out for my Bogey.

Poor Richard! The beginning of the day sounded very like a little you. But I envied him being on the Serpentine with you.[1] Lesley and I used to go in the old days, but I've never been since. It's a lovely thing to do.

Yesterday was simply hellish for me. My work went very well, but all the same, I suffered abominably. I felt so alien and so far away, and everybody cheated me, everybody was ugly and beyond words cruel. I finally got to such a state that I could go nowhere to eat because of the people and I could hardly speak. At half past ten I shut up shop and went to bed, but not to sleep. The three apaches of the cinema, L'Fantôme, Bébé and le faux Curé, tried the key of the door all night and tip-toed on the landing. Finally through the shutters there came two chinks of day. Do I sound foolish and cowardly? Oh, but yesterday was simply Hell. In the evening (I'd gone out to get a lamp glass. The concierge, with relish, had smashed mine) I sat in a little garden by a laburnum tree, I felt the dark dropping over me and the shadows enfolding me, and I died and came to life 'time and time again' as Mrs C. used to say. I went to buy bread at a funny shop. The woman hadn't got a nose and her mouth had been sewn up and then opened again at the side of her face. She had a wall eye. When she came into the lamplight with the bread I nearly screamed; but she clapped her poor hand to her head and smiled at me. I cannot forget it.

This morning things are better. It is such a fine day. But I could not stand a month of yesterdays. I'd come home in a coffin, Jaggle.

My darling, my dearest, your letter written so beautifully is on the table. It expresses you so. I love you with every bit of me. I am your own woman, your
                              Tig
Shut your eyes a minute. Hold me very hard. Now I am giving you little kisses, and now a big big kiss.

P.S. I have opened your letter again to say that your Sunday one is just come—so I am rich today with 2 letters. Don't cast your clouts

[1] My brother, then a small boy, had missed me at a rendezvous in London.

before May is out—in other words, keep your pants on, Boge. (How absurd it sounds!) I should have liked to see the sewing—but I shall, shan't I?

Found another BUG in the kitchen today. (Did I tell you about the first, which nearly bit off my hand?) And also a large black louse with white spots on it.

I am being so careful—careful of my money. You'd be surprised. Every sou is counted out and put down in my book. I detest money. Isn't it a long time since I've heard from Lesley?

I am sorry the sylph is cold to you, my dear love, and I hope the Lawrences were nicer.

The concierge has just refused to get me some milk. It's ½ past 11 and I've had no breakfast. She *is* a swine.

Tig

Café Biard. Rue de Rivoli,
Midi.

Dearest Boge darling,   (May 12, 1915)

Here's the history of my lunch. I decided I would never go to the brasserie again because there was a black cat that frightened me there, so today I sought pastures new. All were *impudently* full so I fell back on Chartier. I wanted something cheap so I ordered pied de veau. My strike! I got the exact contents of Magginalli's stomach as described by Dr. Spilsbury—hairs, feathers and all, and a hoof thrown in as 'make-weight', I suppose.[1] I had that removed, but still hungry, I ordered risotto milanais and got a lump of rice originally covered with tomato sauce, but the sauce had run on to somebody's crème d'Isigny in transit. Then I ordered compôte de rhubarbe. 'C'est fini.' And looking down at that moment I saw on my thumb an immense BUG dining in all possible comfort and half full already. That was the limit. I fled here—and this coffee is just like squeezed wet flannel.

I wonder if it is the war that has made the people here so hideous or if I am out of joint. They appear to me a nation of concierges. And the women look such drabs in their ugly mourning. I wish I had some new shoes and a straw hat. My head and my feet are always hot—but these are minor things. It is a brilliant fine day—everything shines.

The *fool* of a concierge has written to F.C. and said I am here. Consequence was a despairing letter at mid-day. If I will not write, will I at

---

[1] Maggie Nally was the victim of a recent London murder.

least see his friend Réné Bizet, 'très charmant avec beaucoup de talent', so that he can tell F.C. how I am. How absurd! Of course I won't.

How terrible it is that waiters must have flat feet! These are shuffling about—sweating—ugly. If they were turned out of their cafés whatever would they do?

Plainly nothing.

My book marche bien. I feel I could write it anywhere—it goes so easily and I know it so well. It will be a funny book.

Now I've finished my coffee, I am going. Goodbye, my precious.

Wig

Dear Boge,   (May 13 1915)

This is about the 4th letter I have written and torn up. (The others I mean. This I will send.) My rheumatism is simply dreadful. I am very tired with it—*dead* tired and sick of it, but my work goes 'all right'.

Fancy giving yourself up to loving someone for a fortnight—as you say you will do for Lawrence in the summer. My strike! I think you are quite right, but it does surprise me as an idea.

You *are* seeing a lot of people, Bogey. You always do when I am away. I wish I knew where Harris was in Paris. I've a perfect mania to see him and to hear his bitter laugh.

Quelle vie!

I send back this letter. I don't know what to say. *Why* do the fowls come in? I am ill and alone. Voilà tout!

Tig

                                 Friday afternoon,

My dearest darling,   (May 14, 1915)

I am determined to come home on Wednesday. I'll arrive at Victoria at 9 o'clock. My work is finished, my freedom gained. If I stay, they will (1) cut the gas off (2) arrest me as a spy (3) F.C. is coming to Paris at the end of next week. *Voilà des beaux raisons!* Besides which I have only to polish my work now; it's all really accompli. I am simply bursting to come.

If this throws you into a fury do not attend me à la gare—or come and don't recognize me, or something.

Ah, Bogey, be glad! Such a *good* Wig is coming back, with money in her pocket, too—for I have lived *most carefully*.

J. Middleton Murry 1912

But what with Bugs and no gas and a heart full of love and fun, I cannot cannot cannot stay alone. So there you are. Do my letters arrive all safely? I write every every day. I am very silly ce soir—drunk on a black coffee, dearest, I believe. But Life is fun—and I'll take up my leg and walk.

What perhaps is the source of my amusement is that I was marched off to the police station today—as I was here without *papiers de séjour*, I thought it was all up. *And* the cheek of those police. Where was my husband? How many children have you? 'None'. 'Pourquoi pas?' said the Inspector. I was a frozen Union Jackess.

There is a darling baby in this café with me. She is drowning her brioche in a cup of weak coffee—drowning it *deliberately* —holding it down with a spoon!

Dearest darling, I am hanging up the curtains in the little house today.[1] Ah, I do simply love you, you funny boy! Anoint your derrière, love, with zinc ointment. Buy steak for Wednesday. They are selling huge asparagus here—so big that it looks like the first sentence of a Willy novel.

I love love love you. Will this letter arrive on Monday? Then start the week with my arms tight round you a moment, for I adore you, Bogey, and I am only yours.

Wednesday then, dearest heart, I shall see your old grey hat at Victoria. But come on the platform this time—and I will lean out of the kerridge and wave.

Always your

Wig

Saturday afternoon,

(May 15, 1915)

I got very sane after I had written to you yesterday. I wish something in you didn't make me feel a 'silly' when I want to write at full tilt. It's because you never do; you're such a guarded and careful little Bogey—and so frightened I shall 'make a scene'. I won't, dear. I promise you. I'm not at *all* sure this afternoon whether I'll come on Wednesday or whether I'll wait a week. Perhaps I'd better wait a week. If I *do* come I *won't* wire, if I *don't* come I will wire. It's a fair toss-up. Yesterday evening I sat in a little parc and played with the idea with a *sou*. The

---

[1] We were preparing to take a house at 5 Acacia Road, St John's Wood.

sou said every time 'Yes, go,' but that was yesterday. Now this morning again your calm letter as though we were 'seule pour la vie' shook up against the apple-cart.

You sent me a letter from Lesley which was simply marvellous. She wrote, as she can, you know, of all sorts of things—brass and birds and little animals and herself and our friendship with that kind of careless, very intimate joy. There is something quite absolute in Leslie. She said at the end of a page 'Katie, dearie—what is *Eternity?*' She's about the nearest thing to 'eternal' that I could ever imagine. I wish she were not so far away. Things are so changed now. You and I still love each other, but you haven't the need of me you had then, and somehow I do always have to be 'needed' to be happy. I've expressed that abominably —and it's not even quite true, for what I call your need of me was more or less an illusion on my part. You're an amazing person in the way you can accept just so much and no more . . . No, I am beating about the bush and not really saying what I want to—*and* it really doesn't matter. But I do wish my tall pale friend were here to walk with and to sit with. You're not the slightest use, for it doesn't come natural to you to desire to do such things with me. It's I who plead like 'une petite pensionnaire' to be taken out on a Saturday afternoon or to a music hall.

A lovely woman sits in here with me. She's got a fool of a man with her that she hates beyond words. So would I. She wears a big rose under her chin. Her eyes are lovely, but very shadowed with a purple ring. She is not *only* bored, she is trying not to cry. Three fat jossers at a table near by are vastly amused. Two dirty little froggies, smoking pipes *à l'Anglaise* and ragging each other, are next to me. They occasionally sing at me or snap their fingers. They are the most hideous little touts. Blast them! Now—I might have known it—my lovely woman is playing a game of cards with her cavalier. Mon dieu! She does look lovely with her fan of cards in her hand—the other hand hovering over and her lips just pouting. I must go.

This is a fool of a letter. What makes you disgruntled? Is your book worrying you? No, I can't send any of mine because I'm too dependent on it as a whole under my hand. The BUGS are still flourishing in the kitchen. One violated me last night.

Pretty business this German-chasing! And a pity they have to photograph such decent, honest-looking wretches as the *belles proies*. It's a filthy trick. There's no difference between England and Germany when

42

the mob gets a hand in things. No difference between any nations on earth. They are all equally loathsome.

Goodbye for now, my dear. Hanged if I know whether I'll see you on Wednesday or not. If I do wire that I'm not coming, you might send me that £1—just to reassure me, will you?

Oh, Bogey—dearest.

Tig

In June or July 1915 we moved from Elgin Crescent to a pretty stucco house in St John's Wood, No. 5 Acacia Road, into which we gathered our belongings from Rose Tree Cottage. The house had a long garden with a tall pear-tree, where we played Badminton. The Lawrences had left Greatham and taken a little ground-floor flat in the Vale of Health, Hampstead, which backed on to the pond. We met often and planned 'The Signature' together, Koteliansky acting as a kind of business manager. The first number was issued in October 1915.

Katherine's brother came several times to see us there, and spent his last leave with us before going to the front. In November came the news that he had been killed by the explosion of a Mills bomb. The shock to Katherine was great, and she felt that she could live in the house no longer, but must leave it and England as soon as she could.

Meanwhile, the evident failure of 'The Signature', on which Lawrence had set great hopes, and a more grievous disaster—the suppression of his novel 'The Rainbow'—had convinced Lawrence that England had no use for him and turned his mind to the idea of emigrating to America; but he was not allowed to leave the country. I possessed a certificate of rejection for military service and had no difficulty in leaving with Katherine for the South of France. We arrived at Marseilles in mid-November.

Katherine was absorbed by her grief for her brother, and that set a barrier between us. At Marseilles she fell ill, though not very seriously, with what she called 'Marseilles fever'. We scouted along the coast for a place to settle. After a miserable fortnight at Cassis, where the weather mocked all our expectations, we hit upon Bandol. By that time, I had resolved to return to England. I felt—no doubt foolishly—that her dead brother had taken the place in her heart that belonged to me. After spending two or three days at Bandol, while Katherine settled in, I returned to England on December 7, 1915.

Hôtel Beau Rivage,
Bandol (Var),
France.

Wednesday morning,
(December 8, 1915)

My darling Bogey,

The 'comfortable party' brought me your letter this morning on my breakfast-tray. I read it and kissed it. It was wicked of you to send me the 5 francs, and awfully sweet of you. Doesn't the Havre-Southampton route mean a longer sea-journey? I am thankful you got a corner seat from Marseilles to Paris. I keep thinking about you, my Bogey. You were quite right to go back.

Yesterday after you had gone I bought some biscuits and oranges and after putting them in my room and entering the cost of them in my Account Book(!) I went for a walk. It was hot and sunny with big reine-claude waves breaking on the rocks. When I came back I picked my geraniums—toujours in a state of lively terror. I wanted to tell (1) the proprietor (2) the gardener (3) the girls hanging out the washing (4) anyone in and out of sight that I had permission. I even suspected that the white dog had been taught to hurle when the pensionnaires touched the flowers. But there they are in the lovely jug you gave me— *un joli petit bouquet*.

The crépuscule descended just as it did the day before. At six I took Jules Laforgue's rather cynical arm and descended to the salon and read until dinner time. A New Lady appeared in tight purple velvet, low neck and short sleeves, tiny waist, large pear-shaped derrière, big fat shoulders, marabout scarf, little round head with curls like escargots on the forehead. I was *quite overwhelmed*. After a chaste repast (your serviette, my precious, was still there—I got awfully sentimental over it) the man that we said was English, made me a leg and offered me two copies of the *Times*. I took about two hours reading them—picked them absolutely clean and decided that the English newspapers were the finest, etc., and that no other nation, etc., could possibly, etc. But they were packed with meat. . . . An attack on Lunn's father as a pro-German—attempted suicide of Miss Annesley Kenealy—Sir John Simon's attack on the *Times*—the King's first excursion in a Bath chair (Note the capital B. Heavens! What a dignity it gave!). After I had returned them the Englishman's lady opened a rapid fire. But I kept under cover and she changed her tactics and told me a lot of interesting

44

things. For instance: November is the very bad month of the year for the South of France. 'Parisians' never come then. December is early spring. The flowers begin—the jonquils and the oranges. The villas open and the Parisians arrive. The mistral *never* blows here—*never*. This place abounds in charming walks and one can buy a map of the forest paths for 50 centimes. (But shall I 'enter those enchanted woods,' do you think, Boge, even with a map of the paths? Courage! I must!) They are expecting 25 people at this hotel for Christmas. This was told to encourage me, I think—and so on until bed-time.

I woke early and for a long time forgot you were not with me but felt you beside me and only when I wanted to tell you my Extraordinary Dream, I remembered.

It is a lovely day again—very bright and warm. They are still digging up the garden and prizing up little rock borders with disused railway lines and telegraph poles. The boats with red sails are sailing on the sea and your ship is quite close in. Yesterday they lowered a boat and the exhausted crew 'tumbled' (see the *Lancet*)[1] into it and were rowed to shore.

That is all just now, my darling heart. Here's your toothpick that you left, and you also forgot to take your face-rag. But that I won't send. You can buy one (a wash-glove) for $4\frac{3}{4}$d anywhere.

You know I love you. I love you simply tremendously. I put my arms round you and kiss you.

Tig

Thursday morning: A little before ten,

My Bogey, (December 9, 1915)

I expect you are in London. I have just washed and dressed and put on my white broderie anglaise jacket (I really *do* look rather a pretty girl) and now I'm sitting in the sun by the open window smoking the first cigarette. The air is like silk today and there is a sheen upon the world like the sheen on a bird's wing. It's very quiet except for the gardener and his spade and warm as fine wool. Yesterday I walked to Sanary—which is the next bay to this, on the road that follows past the palm avenue. Really it was very hot. You walked along with your eyes and nose screwed up and breathed Hail Maries that you wouldn't freckle or be violated by a black soldier. But I wish you could have

---

[1] I do not understand the reference to *The Lancet*.

been there and seen that bay. There is a long beach there too and on the other side of the road fields of jonquils in flower. Two women one in grey and one in yellow with black straw hats were picking them. As I passed they stood up and held the big nodding bunches before their eyes to see who was passing. There is a tiny villa there, too—with a glass verandah and a small garden. It could not have more than 2 rooms. It looks right over the bay to the open sea. Behind it rears up an old rock covered with that pink heath and rosemary. A board on the gate said 'à louer.' I confess to hanging over the fence for a long time and dreaming . . . Coming home in the evening with driftwood to burn—the lamp on the round table—the jar of wild flowers on the mantelpiece . . . Sitting on the verandah in canvas chairs after supper and smoking and listening to the idle sea. But don't be frightened, dear one, you were not there. It was my Brother who sat on the verandah step stroking a kitten that curled on his knee.

Bogey, I think the Oxford Book of English verse is *very* poor. I read it for hours this morning in bed. I turned over pages and pages and pages. But except for Shakespeare and Marvell and just a handful of others it seems to me a mass of falsity. Musically speaking, hardly anyone seems to *even understand* what the middle of the note is—what that sound is like. It's not perhaps that they are even 'sharp' or 'flat'—it's something very much more subtle—they are not playing on the *very note itself*. But when, in despair, I took up the French Book I nearly sautéd from the fenêtre with rage. It's like an endless gallery of French salon furniture sicklied o'er with bed canopies, candelabra, and porcelain cupids, all bow and bottom. Of course, there *are* exceptions. Victor Hugo, by the way, reminded me very much of our white bull taking a railway ticket—to Parnassus. And I wasn't a bit 'surprised'.

Am I being a bit of a bore? I'll stop, my darling. You can think how I am longing to hear from you. You know what your letters mean,

My dear darling, I am always your little mate,

Tig

Friday,
Jag-Bog,   (December 10, 1915)

I don't know whether you expect me to write to you every day but I shall do so (D.V.) and you will too, won't you? Once a day really isn't too often and it's my only dear signal that you are well. Today came your Paris letter with the swindle from ——'s (which made me furious!) and the lady with the Dates. 'Net gain 4d.' *re* baggage was very *pa* of you. I heard you saying that. Darling, what a frightful adventure with O-Hara-San![1] What a Minx to take off her head like that! But you ought to have known, Bogey. You are always accusing me of the same thing . . . I hope you do see de la Mare. Thank you for sending me his note.

Yesterday I went for a long walk round by the sea towards St. Cyr (which is very beautiful and wild and like my N.Z.) and then I struck inland and came home by little lanes and crooked ways bordered with olive trees—past the flower farms. I thought I should never get home again. I got quite lost and though I kept hearing voices the walls were always in the way and when I peered through the gates there was never a soul to be seen except jonquils and daffodils and big blue violets and white roses. The sun went down. I passed a little villa called 'Allons-y' and coo-eed but a Fearful White Dog happily attached to a pump answered me so effectually that I decided to strike into a wood and have done with it. But at that moment a far too agile malignant-looking goat appeared—vaulted over a wall just ahead of me—I rushed in the opposite direction and got found at last.

My work is shaping for the first time today—I feel nearer it—I can see the people walking on the shore and the flowery clusters hanging on the trees . . . if you know what I mean. It has only been a dim coast and a glint of foam before.[2] The days go by quickly.

My precious one, I long for your first London letter. I expect it will arrive on Sunday or Monday—so I *must* be patient. Take care of yourself, my darling boy. Buy something for your hair and use it. Do keep warm. Buy yourself another pair of those pants. Do keep happy. Eat good food. Don't call this 'swank' on my part. It is not. Perhaps it *is* partly that I love to frown at you and give your tie a perfectly unnecessary little tug, even though you do say, 'For God's sake, woman, let me alone'.

I kiss you on your eyes and your lips and the top curl of your hair.

Tig

---

[1] A Japanese doll of Katherine's which she had lent me as a mascot. Her head came off on the journey. She never recovered. She was succeeded by another, eventually called Ribni, or Rib, after Captain Ribnikov, the Japanese spy in Kuprin's story of that name.

[2] This refers to a second attempt at *The Aloe*.

My dear one,

No letters today. I cannot hope to hear from you before Monday, I think. So I am not disappointed.

The weather has changed. Last night a wind sprang up—one of the lesser winds—a forlorn, piping creature that I don't remember having heard on land before—a wind I always connect with the open sea and night in the cabin—and a hollow dread that the land has gone for ever. I dreamed that I had a baby (Virtue always rewards me with this elfin child) and Grandmother was alive. I had been to sleep after it was born and when I woke it was night and I saw all the people in the house lying on their backs asleep too. And I was sure my baby was dead. For a long time I was too frightened to call anyone—but finally called to Grandmother and she came in and said, 'Nonsense, child, he's getting on beautifully' (as though 'he' were a cake in the oven). She brought him in to reassure me—a charming little creature in a flannel gown with a tuft of hair. So I got up and kissed Grandmother who handed me the baby and I went downstairs and met you in the street. The moon was shining—you looked lovely; it shone particularly on your grey felt hat which you wore à l'espagnole. But we were very poor; we lived in a tenement and you had put a banana box across two chairs for the baby. 'The only brick is,' you said—'how the hell can we go to a music hall?' Then I woke up, switched on the light and began to read Venus and Adonis. It's pretty stuff—rather like the Death of Procris.[1]

Yesterday I had de la veine and wrote in the afternoon and then went for a short walk along that bar that encloses the harbour. It was sunset. It's a good place to walk—the sea on either side rushed up and the town —just showing a glimmer of light here and there—looked marvellous. I sat on a stone and began thinking 'I believe it is perfectly necessary to one's spiritual balance to be somewhere where you can see the sun both rise and set etc., etc.,' and such like nonsense—trés sèrieuse—when I remarked a gazelle-like military form approaching, in blue with a braided cap. This ensemble, thought I, is exactly like the cover of a 95 centimes novel. Myself on a rock—a red sunset behind—this graceful form approaching . . . It came near—and then a blithe, cheerful, dead-sure voice positively hailed me. 'Vous vous promenez seule, Madame?' I had a good look at the upstart. Olive skin, silky eyebrows and silky

---

[1] i.e. the picture of that name in The National Gallery.

moustache. *Vain*—there is no word for it. I said 'Oui, Monsieur, seule.'
'Vous demeurez à l'Hôtel Beau Rivage, n'est-ce pas?' Silence. 'Je vous
ai déjà remarqué plusieurs fois.' (His French was right. Mine isn't).
Then I looked up at him like Frank Harris would look at Dan Rider
quoting Shakespeare—and he drew himself, saluted, said, 'Ah, pardon.
Je suis très indiscret.' I said *exactly* like Harris—'*Très* indiscret, Monsieur'
and walked home.[1] Scarcely had I gained the road when a gentleman
in a cape approached. 'Vous vous promenez seule, Madame?' But that
was a bit too steep. I said 'Non, Monsieur—avec une canne!' What a
race! They are like German commercial travellers! Send me a bulldog
in your next letter, sweetheart.

The sea is very choppy today. Far as you can see the waves break—
like a school of fishes. I love you. I am your own girl.

Wig

A windy Sunday,

Dearest and only one,   (December 12, 1915)

I really do think I may expect your first London letter tomorrow
and I ought to hear from Kay, too. I've not had a sign so far.

For some unaccountable reason, chéri, I've got our Marseilles fever
again with all its symptoms—loss of appetite—shivering fits—dysentery.
What on earth can it be? I really think it is a noisome fever from some
black man in a café near to the Vieux Port. At any rate it's horrid and I
am a ragged creature today. If I hadn't got William Shakespeare I
should be in the ultimate cart, but he reads well to a touch of fever.
However, I expect I shall be a better girl by the time you get this, so
don't go and worry, darling of my heart. I bought a most superior
exercise book yesterday for 4 sous *but* at about five o'clock the eternal
silence was broken by a rap at my door and a pretty creature with gold
rings in her ears, Spanish boots like Bogey's, and flashing eyes and teeth,
brought in a basket—My laundry. I only sent a *morsel*—the veriest
fragmint, and Lord! there was a bill for 3.15. *How* the rings, the teeth,
eyes and boots vanished—counting the precious money into her hand.
I paid for them, every one. I shall have to cut myself a little pair of
football shorts out of *Le Radical,* I can see that.

How are you? Where are you? What are you doing now? . . .

The salon, my dear, has become impossible ground while the wife

[1] For this incident see *Journal* page 39.

of that Englishman remains in this hotel. Did you remark her? She is a Belgian—I never met her like. She out-Belgians anything imaginable. However, I'll be even with her and put her to paper and have done with her. I shall creep to the post and back but that's my limit today. Otherwise I'll keep my room and try and write and read. Send me a book, precious, when you can. Take care of yourself. I kiss you, Bogey, I am

Tig

Sunday night before dinner,

My darling one, (December 12, 1915)

I have just put on my spencer, an extra *pair* of *stockings* and another shawlet and I'm still frozen. I rang for Mary Anne to make me a fire but she is evidently gone a junketing for I can't find her. The only minion I did find said they could not monte any bois until demain. Which seemed to me absurd. Suppose I were in convulsions and had to be wrapped in blankets and laid on an hearth (would that I were!)? Also I am as empty as the little French boy's tirelire and there's nothing to eat here.

And the salon is full of travellers a sitting round the fire and toasting of their unworthy toes. Oh, what a wretched little swinging-on-a-bare-twig of a goblin you have got tonight—and her maladies have been sich that she has been forcéd to guarder her chambre all day except for to post my letter. At about five I nearly swallowed the tea-spoon and had done with it. For I have added a sore throat to my fever and I am trying to gargle every 2 hours with 3 sous worth of borax and it tasted awful. Just when I wrote in my diary Adieu chère terre! a nice little boy who belongs to the hotel brought me a letter from you. It was a gift from heaven. Darling love, never was a letter more welcome. It was indeed one of my great-aunt Charlotte's 'direct answers' to prayers. I read it once and then twice and then I absorbed it, you know. If you are not careful and less sweet I shall say TOUJOURS, too, and then you'll be finally caught out. I do hope they give you a bed among the pottery, dear love.[1] Can you choose your own jug and basin from the stock? *I saw that shop the day Munro flouted me and nearly entered in.* (Forgive me; I am all sticky with eating so much and such continuous, continent Shakespeare.) You told me very little of Kot. *Didn't* he fall

---

[1] I found a room above The Peasant Shop in Devonshire St. Theobald's Road. Harold Munro's Poetry Bookshop was nearby.

down dead when he saw I wasn't there? And where did you sleep that first night, sirrah?

Ah, but I wanted you today. Today I have longed for you. Have you known that? Can I long for you so and you not know? It's a terrible thing to wonder over. But I am so bound up in you that 'us' is become a kind of separate and loving being that I can scarcely bear to part with and cannot understand why it should ever really leave me. Only pretend and then come back laughing into my arms. Dearest—dearest.

After lunch today a kind gentleman lent me an Historical Roman. (Je vous remercie, Maman! Bon soir, cher Père.) But I also saw the last 2 numbers of *La Vie Parisienne* left in the salon by a bald-headed old party who brought his own oysters to luncheon—

Monday morning—Then the bell rang for dinner and I went down and afterwards sat in the salon and talked with the lender of the Roman. What a night I spent, Bogey! My left leg rushed up to reinforce my other ills, and it has won the battle. In fact I'm a complete prisoner to it today and shall have to give this letter to foreign hands to post for I cannot walk at all. However, it's just my old rheumatism—you know what it's like. Dressing took me nearly 2 hours and I nearly gave it up, wore only one stocking, one leg of my 'pantalons' etc. today, but the old trick of looking at myself in the glass and saying 'Courage, Katherine' won after all—and here I am complete even to Flowering Gorse.[1]

I got 2 papers from Kot today. They will be a great feast and as always happens I am now so tied and bound, so *caged*, that I know I'll *sing*. I'm just on the point of writing something awfully good, if you know that feeling. So there is compensation.

The sun shines today but the wind is still high and 'foam flies white over rocks of black,' opposite.

I feel cut off from all human kind—but I am not sad today, sweetheart. I am *hoping* for a letter from you by the courier this afternoon. Give Kot my love.

Just a minute. I am in your arms,—and now,

Goodbye my treasure

Tig

I have opened my letter again to say there is a review of *Mother Goose* under the title 'Nursery Rhymes' in the *Lit. Sup.* for December

[1] Gênet Fleuri. Katherine's favourite perfume.

9th which is one of the most delightful reviews I ever read. If Delamare wrote it and you see him please say how enchanting I thought it was.

A week today you went away.   Tuesday,
My dear Heart,   (December 14, 1915)
    After giving your letter to my 'bonne' yesterday I gave up the fight and retired in good order to bed, where I am still. The day seemed very long yesterday, but I must say my 'bonne' was very good to me. She gave me an extra pillow, kept me supplied with boiling bottles, brought me Vichy, and my meals on a little round table, actually produced a bottle of alcool camphré and frictioned me and gave me some lime flower tea before I went to sleep. Not counting the number of times she put her fat face round the door and said nodding and *smiling* as only a Frenchwoman can—with an air of delighted gaiety(!) 'Vous souffrez toujours?' You see little Wig giving her smile for smile and nod for nod and saying 'Ah, oui, un peu!' She's the only creature I've seen. I am rather surprised that neither of the kind ladies who were so ready to welcome us to their haven should not at least have inquired. But no—And I must confess that notice that the repasts served in the rooms se paient en supplément rather rings in my ears. But Kay's money has come and as I am spending nothing else it will be *perfectly all right*. It is such a beautiful day today. Oh, so lovely. There seems to be a ring of light round everything. It is still and sunny—so still you could hear a spider spin. I dreamed last night that I sat by a fire with Grandmother and my brother and when I woke I still held my brother's hand. That is true. For my hands were not together. They were holding another hand. I felt the weight and the warmth of it—for quite a long time.
    I am hoping for a letter by this afternoon's post. Goodbye, my lovely one. Do not forget me and WRITE often to your
                               Tig
                      I am quite happy.

                              Tuesday,
Dearest of all,   (December 14, 1915)
    Don't you worry about me. My femme de chambre, when she goes off duty, leaves me in her 'friend's' charge and her 'friend' is a little spry creature with a pale blue nose who is very gentille indeed to me. 'Il ne

faut pas vous gêner,' she keeps saying to me. 'Je veux faire tout ce que je peux pour vous.' In fact, the servants here seem to think I'm a *dear* little thing! *And* after midday that Englishman, terribly shy, knocked at my door. It appears he has a most marvellous cure for just my kind of rheumatism. Would I try it? All this was explained in the most preposterous rigmarole, in an attempt to appear off-hand and at his poor unfortunate ease. I never saw a man so shy! Finally he says that if the pharmacien can't make it up here he will take the first train to Toulon this afternoon and get it for me. It is a rubbing mixture which he got off a German doctor one year when he was at Switzerland for winter sports and had an attack of sciatic rheumatism. It sounds to me—very hopeful—but I'd catch any straw! So I thanked him and bowing and humming and hawing he went off. I can't think what frightened him so. I shall have to put on a hat and a pair of gloves when he brings me back the unguent.

Oh, that postman is a tortoise, a detestable tortoise—half a tortoise. (Bogey, I am an awful little cod. My bed is going to my brain. Now I'll wait for your letter before I go on.)

Later. I did wait with a vengeance. At half past 3 I rang the bell. 'Le courier, a-t-il déjà passé?' 'Ah, oui, Madame—une *bonne* demi-heure!' 'Merci bien.' But when she had gone I confess I turned to the wall and cried bitterly . . . . I think mostly from rage. Then I began to think how my Father always always had time to write every single day to my Mother, etc., etc., etc. Then in despair I climbed out of bed, found a piece of ribbon and sat up and made myself a hat. Once before, I remember, when I was ill at Rottingdean and alone and waiting for a letter that didn't come I made myself a hat out of pins and fury and it was the hat of my life. So is this. But I am desperately disappointed, I must confess and I think it is awfully awfully cruel. Once I get better I'll forgive you if you don't write, but Oh—to lie in this silent room and know the postman has *been.* You wouldn't like it, Bogey.

Now I've had dinner, an omelette, some cauliflower and a stewed apple. I am getting thin. There are 2 hollows in my cheeks but no little love kisses them. My Englishman has arrived with his pot of ointment and refuses to take even a pin or a bead in payment. How kind he is— It's easy to see *he* hasn't lived with me 3 years.

I am very angry—but not really with you. You couldn't help your letter missing the post, I suppose. Or perhaps you were handing cups and saucers for that quiet lady with the cast eye.

I should like to be at a large circus tonight: in a box—very luxurious, you know, very warm, very gay with a smell of sawdust and elephants. A superb clown called Pistachio—white poneys, little blue monkeys drinking out of Chinese cups. I should like to be dressed beautifully, beautifully, down to the last fragment of my chemise—and I should like Colette Willy to be dressed just exactly like me and to be in the same box. And during the entr'actes while the orchestra blared Pot Pourri from *The Toreador* we would eat tiny little jujubes out of a much too big bag and tell each other all about our childhood.

A demain, then. *Are* you a darling? Oh, I forgive you. I love you. I hug your blessed little head against my breast and kiss you. I love you, you bad wicked precious adorable and enchanting Boge. I am,

Wig Tig

Dear Jack,

Wednesday,
(December 15, 1915)

I have opened my letter to say that now another day has come and again I have no news. I am sending the maid with a wire this morning, for I cannot but believe there is something terribly wrong. I do not deny that today I am *dreadfully anxious*.

Oh, Jack, I appeal even to your imagination as a novelist—do not leave me like this without news. It is so cruel—cruel. I weep bitterly as I write, but if you do not answer my wire I shall weep no more but face the fact that—no, I can't write it. Ever since Sunday my hope has been for letters, and I've not had one. Your silence makes me ashamed to so let you see my heart—and its need of you. I am still in bed.

Dear Jack,

Wednesday Night,
(December 15, 1915)

The maid came back with the wire. She couldn't send it. I had to appear in person with my papers—so it lies here. However, this afternoon I got your Sunday letter, so I know my fears were quite groundless. The room does not sound very comfortable. Thank you for sending me Belle's and Mother's letters. Belle's letter was awfully sweet and friendly, and my Mother's too I understood very deeply. I am sorry you should have waited for my letters before writing to me. That is what made the situation.

To tell you the truth, I feel exhausted now as though the sea which

54

has been tossing me so rudely has thrown me on a flat rock. Of course, I do not want you to write if you do not 'feel' like it, but you are a strange being, Jack, and you have hurt me terribly. You were so *sure* I would be lonely in this quiet room—but once away I suppose you 'forgot'. However, *I don't mind now*. It's all over. It is getting dark again—after a long bright day. The moon shines in my room. Goodnight, dearest.

Tig

Thursday night,
Dearest Boge, (December 16, 1915)

I am better but still in bed, for there is a bitter east wind blowing today and I feel it is not safe for me to start my normal life in it. I think my Englishman's stuff is going to do me a great deal of good and he has made me so perfectly hopeful—and has been in so many ways such a *comfort* to me. Should this stuff not quite cure me he has given me the address of a place in Normandy where one goes for a cure once a year. The cure only takes 3 weeks; it is a small inexpensive place and he says it's simply miraculous. Well, I am sure I can get my Father to give me a little extra a year for this purpose. 'You'll be skipping like a 2 year old after a week there' says my nice funny man. I am being rubbed twice a day and dieting carefully and only drinking Vichy. This man isn't really a doctor—He's the Head of Guy's Dental Hospital —but he is a queer delightful good-natured person and he has certainly been a comfort to me.[1]

I feel very sober today. I am afraid you will think my last letters very silly. They won't happen again. I understand you far better now, somehow,—and I'll not ask for the moon, either.

A knock at my door. A letter in pencil from you and funnily enough almost the second sentence is about crying for the moon. Thank you, darling, for your letter; it's an awfully sweet one. I do hope you get your studio at Haverstock Hill. It sounds really delightful—*et pas trop cher*. Your present room must be horrid. I am sorry, too—you do not know how sorry that we have not talked more about the things we have read and seen and felt. Still, it was fate, and can't be altered.

Kiss those fingers for me, dear one. Kiss the chewed up one and the grimy one and particularly the drunken old villain of a first finger.

Tell you all that I am doing? Why, Bogey, I'm lying down or sitting

[1] This was F. Newland Pedley, F.R.C.S. For an account of him see my *Katherine Mansfield, and other Literary Portraits*.

up in bed. All I'm feeling? Ah, I can't. I've lost the key just for the minute—you know how things get lost in bed.

Since I have been alone here the loss of my little brother has become quite real to me. I have entered into my loss, if you know what I mean. Always before that I shrank from the final moment—but now it is past.

As I write it is raining fast with a loud noise on the windows. I have the bed covered with copies of the *Times* marked at certain places with large blue crosses and a copy of *Le Temps* with arrows in the margin and 'This will interest you' written underneath. All from the same kind and only donor.

Again, my dear one, your last letter is very precious—such a Jag-like letter. I see every bit of you in the way you write your name.

Good-night, sweetheart, and bless you.

Always,
Wig

Vendredi,

My dear love, (December 17, 1915)

I am afraid the courier is past and my letters are drowned for it is as wild a day as ever I have seen—a sky like lead, a boiling sea, the coast hidden by thick mist, a loud noise of wind and such rain dashing on the windows. It is very cold, too; and (3.30) dark already. My maid, however, lit me a splendid fire this morning and after lunch when the room was warm I got up and am sitting by it now in the armchair. I don't feel *very grand* and though the fire isn't like that wretched affair at Cassis and burns merrily and warm, it seems to light the shadows and to prick an ear to the quiet—How quiet it is! except for the storm outside! Much quieter than Day's Bay![1]

No, the courier has just come and there *is* a letter after all, with no address, 'Somewhere in Hampstead.' I am glad you have moved there if you are more comfortable, darling. I am sure you were wretched doing your own chores in the other places. And I do hope you will soon be able to get your own studio and be free of your wretched worries in that respect. It always seems such a waste of time looking for a bed, especially for people like you and me who are so particular. I hope you have a big fire and a *good* breakfast, darling Bogey, and that you will now refresh yourself with one of your Turkish Bath tickets (which are in your 'gentleman's companion').

[1] Day's Bay near Wellington, N.Z. which is the scene of *At the Bay*.

I am sorry I made you sad about that little villa. I heard of another last night from my Englishman—four rooms—good stoves—electric light, heating, a verandah, a garden all furnished, and so sheltered that you can dine out every day—88 francs a month. The man who has just taken it says he buys fish at the market for practically nothing and rosebuds at 1d a dozen, so I should live off fish and rosebuds.—But no, I'll not speak of these things, for it's useless and foolish.

I'll remember that England and the Printing Press won the day and left me on the field. Don't think I don't understand. I do understand absolutely, my love. Ah, Bogey, as I write to you my heart is full of love for you and I long to press your head to my breast. Do not forget me. We have had the loveliest times together—you know. Shut your eyes, and so many sweet things press on your eyelids.

I am
Tig

Saturday,
(December 18, 1915)

I must write a little more for 'le temps' is so exciting. I had a very vivid dream last night that I and my brother were in Berlin without passports. We were having lunch in the waiting room of a railway station at a long table, with several German soldiers just back from the front with their equipment, etc. I see now the proud wives carrying the men's coats for them, etc. Suddenly in a dreadful pause I began to speak English. I said one woman reminded me of a Miss Lindsay, bootmaker's assistant on Lambton Quay.[1] In a flash I knew we were done for. Brother said, 'Make for the telephone box!' And as we got in a soldier smashed his helmet through the glass door. Crash! I woke to a violent peal of thunder. It was raining, hailing, the shutters flashed pale yellow with the lightning. I heard the bells ringing in the hotel— the servants in felt slippers running along the corridors. Bang! went the thunder, rolling and tossing among the hills. The air was so electric that one's hands and feet sang. Finally, I got up, put on my mackintosh and opened the shutters. I felt sure that I'd be struck, especially as my room, being at the corner, got the full force of the storm. It was a wonderful night. I shall never forget the dignity of the sea. It drew back from the land a long way. There were no waves, only a fold or two where it touched the shore—and it looked as cold as stone. Above

---

[1] Wellington, N.Z.

the coast the sky was bright silver and above that a bright fantastic green. As I opened the window I smelled the sharp smell of the wet blue-gum trees. Oh, it was exciting—it was lovely, and all the while the hail springing against the window pane and the loud thunder and the fluttering light. I rang for my breakfast and that became a kind of thrilling feast, too. I put the milk jug under the édredon when I had poured out my first cup of coffee and it stayed there warm as a pigeon and I had a second boiling cup. That seemed a miracle of ingenuity and forethought! Then the spry maid tripped in and lit the fire. I heard the little twigs crackling. She sat back on her heels and told me which rooms the water had flooded—when such a thing had happened before etc. I felt that I was going to jump out of bed, wash and dress as quickly as possible, pack a small bundle and catch the Ark at about half past ten. But it is half past ten now and the wind has dropped, 2 roosters are crowing somewhere and the sky is silver.

This letter will arrive dreadfully near Xmas and I have no present for you and I shall not be able to send you one—only my love, dearest, and my loyalty. I shall make them both into a little something that you can hang round your neck as a charm—like the Russians do. (Wouldn't you hate to). No, I shan't. But forgive me for not having a gift for you.

I am very much better—in fact to all intents and purposes *cured* I believe by that unguent. Here is a geranium—I quite forgot they were there. Here is your Xmas box, Bogey.

Wig

Sunday morning,

Dear Jag, (December 19, 1915)

From sheer laziness I am sitting up in bed. The 'l'eau chaude' is warming its enamel bosom before a fresh-lighted fire, and I ought to be up—but it's so pleasant here and the smell of burning wood is so delicious and the sky and the sea outside are all pearly. After I had written to you yesterday down came the rain again, and this time the courier really was drowned, so I got a letter of yours about the landlady etc., just this moment. You sound to be peculiarly snug in a way—a clean bed, a fire and a landlady who has a sense of the horrific—*très Anglaise!* But you mustn't send me money yet, not until you have more, darling. I'll keep this as an iron ration and buy myself a little tiny Noël —but guard your money. I hate to think you may want it, *et tout va bien chez moi, tu sais.*

My rheumatism this morning—*n'existe pas*. I've not been so free for a year. I can positively jump. I'm to go on using the unguent and my Englishman is going to give me the prescription today for he leaves here on Monday. He is also going to conduct me to the post and see I'm not cheated with my mandat from Kay—so that is all to the good. I dined down stairs last night. A good many people have arrived—and the hotel is rather changed. More flowers, more fire still and an 'atmosphere.' I met the 'Madame' on the stairs. Elle me demandait si je souffre toujours. I said no—said she 'Heureusement le climat est très sec!' What a *fool*, with rain teeming on everything! I paid a bill here too which was a relief off my mind.

Dear, *do* send me summat to read when you can. I am still confined to Shakespeare and the *Times*. I don't know what to ask for. I'd like a 1/- Dickens that I haven't read—or one I don't remember—but which is it? Oh, I'd like to read *Oliver Twist* again, for one. And I'll send you something for *The Signature*, but don't flatter me—I'm only the jam in the golden pill—and I know my place, Betsy.

You suddenly mentioned Belgians in connection with your studio— But what Belgians? I hope they don't wrest it from you. It sounded such a good place, and Haverstock Hill is près de Hampstead, isn't it? I must get up—this paper is being supported on the édredon and it's dreadfully heaving.

I have a presentiment that I shall never see Albion's shores again (but then I always feel like that when I'm away). Still, Bogey, in case I should be taken sudden, preserve these words and show them to the landlady.

It's such a Sunday morning—so quiet and so tending towards *la messe*—The lovely air must be the result of the storm, I suppose, for breathing is a delight. It's what you might call very *choice*, this morning, too.

I should like to embrace my Father this morning. He would smell of fine cloth, with a suspicion of cigar added, eau de Cologne, just an atom of camphorated chalk, something of fresh linen, and his own particular smell—his 'blood smell' as p'raps Lorenzo[1] would say.

Addio, dear love. Je suis à toi,

Tig

[1] D. H. Lawrence.

Sunday before Xmas,
My dearest love,   (December 19, 1915)

I have just got the letter that you wrote me on Thursday night, with the money in it. Papers have come, too, which I have not opened yet, and other letters are waiting—but I want to speak to you très sérieusement. Your letter made you 'real' to me in the deepest sense of the word, I believe, almost for the first time. You say just those things which I have felt. I am *of* you as you write just as you are *of* me.

Now I will say Toujours because now at last I know you. We are in a world apart, and we always shall be in a world apart—in our own kingdom which *is* finer and rarer. Shut the gates of it for a minute and let us stand there. Let us kiss each other, we three. Yes, Bogey, I shall love you *for always*.

                    Tig

Later

I've just read the *Times Lit. Sup.*, *The New Statesman*, *The Daily News*, and letters from Beatrice Campbell, Kay and Marie. For the papers many thanks, darling; they were a great feast. The *New Statesman* is a dead horse—but still—horse it is and there you are. Beatrice (très entre nous) wrote me a nice letter. She's a queer mixture for she is really loving and affectionate, and yet she is malicious. She was about you and Lawrence *re* me, you understand. How you were so happy on your own and a lot of rubbish, and how Lawrence had spoken against me at Clive Bell's. It is unpleasant hearing that kind of thing, and smells faintly of their drawing-room, which is a most distasteful memory to me. By the way, I wrote to Lawrence the other day—a wild kind of letter, if I think of it, and not fair to 'us'. You understand? It was just after I had been in bed and without letters, and I had a fit of positive despair, when life seemed to me to be absolutely over—and I wrote rather in that strain. I only tell you because when I have read your despairing letters to your friends I have always felt that you betrayed us and our love a little, and I feel if you should see mine (don't —for it's nothing and the mention is making it a mountain) you might feel a little the same. I am sorry I wrote it. To tell you the truth, I am come to the conclusion that our happiness rests with us and with nobody else at all, and that we ought to build for ourselves and by ourselves. We are very rich people, for we are real true lovers—and we are young and born in each other. Therefore, I think we ought to develop

60

Katherine Mansfield 1913

together—keep very close together (spiritually, mon chéri) and make ourselves, on our island, a palace and gardens and arbours, and boats for you and flowery bushes for me—and we ought not to court other people at all yet awhile. Later it will be different. Do you know what I mean and do you agree with me? Writing to you, I love you simply boundlessly. My love for you is always being new born; the heavenly dews descend upon it, and I'll not believe it is the same flower as yesterday—you see—how I believe in you! I have a store of belief in you that couldn't be exhausted! How I admire you! How I love you! We are two little boys walking with our arms (which won't quite reach) round each other's shoulders and telling each other secrets and stopping to look at things . . . . We must not fail our love.

At the end of your letter you ask me how long I am going to stay. I do not know at all, my precious. You'd better tell me what you think. Now I'll add a word tomorrow.

Lundi le matin,

(December 20, 1915)

A lovely 'gold dust' day. From early morning the fishermen have been passing and the little boats with red sails put out at dawn. I am dressed to go to the Post Office with my 2 mandats.

When I woke this morning and opened the shutters and saw the dimpling sea I knew I was beginning to love this place—this South of France. Yesterday I went for a walk. The palm trees after the rain were magnificent, so firm and so green and standing up like stiff bouquets before the Lord. The shop people, too, are very kind. You are a regular customer after a day or two—and my Englishman says they are very honest.

Last night in the salon I had a long talk with a woman who is here for her health—a woman about 50. She has been nursing since the beginning of the war somewhere near Arles. She is of the Midi and has a very pronounced accent which is *extremely* fascinating, and she knows and adores 'mon pays'. She told me all about the coast—about all sorts of places 'de toute beauté' and as she talked I began to see this place—not romantically, but truly. I like it and more than like it. This woman was reading the letters of Taine . . . . She told me such good stories of the black soldiers—I must not forget them. I hope I shall speak a great deal with her because she is very good for my French too. She has a good vocabulary and a way of *spacing* her words giving them a very nice, just quantity. Oh. Bogey, it is the most heavenly day. Every little tree feels it and waves faintly from delight. The femme de chambre called to the gardener just now as she beat the next door mattress out of the window—'Fait bon?' and he said, 'Ah, délicieux!' which seemed to me very funny for a gardener, especially this little chap. Now I must button my boots with a tiger's tail and go out.

Goodbye, dearest love

Tig

Tuesday,

(December 21, 1915)

My darling,

This will be just a note today, for I wrote you at such length yesterday. Last night at about 6.45 your telegram came. It was very worrying because now I am better and you are still getting letters to say that I am ill. That is the horrible part of distance. If ever I'm ill again, I'll [not] breathe a word of it. Oh, my precious darling, I am sorry you should have been so worried, and I hope my wires arrive early. The reason for the 2 wires was this. The courier who brought me the telegram said it was *défendu* to send wires in English from France from here, so I believed him and sent you the first cold acknowledgement, but then when he had gone I thought it was absurd and I hated to think of you getting that chill reply, so I ran to the post office. The postmaster said of course I could 'dire ce que vous voulez', and thankfully I sent the other. It was bright moonlight when I went to send your wire. I felt I could have spent pounds upon a long long telegram but you will understand that I used our secret word with intent in the English telegram. Is all well now, my dear love, and do you understand?

Last night I dreamed I was back in England looking everywhere for rooms behind the South Kensington Museum. It was pouring with rain and nearly dark—and the agent said 'How about a small house with a studio attached?' We were *seriously considering* this when I woke up and praised the Lord.

I am writing something for *The Signature,* but it will not be finished before Friday. That means you will get it on Tuesday. Is that time? It is called 'Et in Arcadia ego'. I hope you will like it.[1]

This is a scrappy and insufficient letter today, but you know that it is sent with all my love. How distracting it is that I cannot say how much

---

[1] Printed in *Journal* p. 130 but wrongly dated there.

I love you—however I may long to—but you know. You have written me such wonderful letters. It is strange. I feel that I only really know you since you went back to England. I feel as though a miracle had happened to you and you are rich and bathed in light. While I sit here writing to you time is not. I am one with our love for ever.

The fishing boats are putting out to sea. There is a breeze today and white wings in the sky—they mean happiness.

Again again I love you

Tig

Mercredi,

Bogey, my dearest love,   (December 22, 1915)

I wish you could see the winds playing on the dark blue sea today, and two big sailing vessels have come in and are rocking like our white boat rocked when you were here. The sea is what *I* call very high this morning and the clouds are like swans. It's a lovely morning; the air tastes like fruit!

Yesterday I went for a long scrambling walk in the woods, on the other side of the railway. There are no roads there—just little tracks and old mule paths. Parts are quite wild and overgrown, then in all sorts of unexpected faery places you find a little clearing—the ground cultivated in tiny red terraces and sheltered by olive trees (full of tiny black fruit). There grow the jonquils, daffodils, new green peas and big abundant rose bushes. A tiny (this word is yours really: it's haunting me today) villa is close by with a painted front and a well or a petite source at the bottom of the garden. They are dream places. Every now and then I would hear a rustle in the bushes and an old, old woman, her head tied up in a black kerchief would come creeping through the thick tangle with a bunch of that pink heath across her shoulders. 'B'jour ma petite dame' she would munch and nod—and with a skinny finger point me my way. Once I found myself right at the very top of a hill and below there lay an immense valley—surrounded by mountains—very high ones— and it was so clear you could see every pointed pine, every little zig-zag track—the black stems of the olives showing sooty and soft among the silvery green. One could see for miles and miles. There was, far in the distance, a tiny town planted on a little knoll, just like a faraway city in a Dürer etching, and now and again you would see two cypresses and then if you looked carefully you found a little house, for two cypresses side by side *portent bonheur*. On the other side of me there was

63

the sea and Bandol and the next bay, Sanary. Oh, Bogey, how I longed for my playfellow! Why weren't you with me? Why didn't you lean over the fence and ask the old, old man and hear him say it was the *immortelle* and it flowers for eight years and then dies and its yellow flowers come out in June. The sun went down as I found the Saint-Cyr road back to Bandol. The people were coming home and the children were running from school. As I came into Bandol I heard a loud chanting and down the Avenue des Palmiers came four little boys in white carrying a cross and incense braziers—an old priest with white hair chanting—four men following, each carrying a corner of a black and silver cloth—then a coffin carried on a table by six men and the whole village following—the last man of all being an old chap with a wooden leg. It was extremely fantastic and beautiful in the bright strange light.

No post came yesterday. I expect it was delayed. I am longing for a letter today, my precious. Do you feel in this letter my love for you today? It is as warm as a bird's nest, Bogey. But don't mind when i say that in all these walks and in all my growing love for this country and people I cannot but wish infinitely that you were here to share it and complete my happiness.

My own—my darling love. Take me in your arms and kiss me—and I will kiss you too and hold you, Bogey, and tell you all I can't write.

I am your woman,

Tig

As I write a *third* ship is coming in and you are walking on the deck in your corduroy trousers and Spanish boots—an Awful Knife in your sash. Can you see me if I wave?

Wednesday,

Bogey darling,   (December 22, 1915)

I received this yesterday and I don't know what to do with it.[1] How can I get the £2? Must I sign something or—*enfin* what must I do? If I have to sign it and return it to you mark the place for my signature with a pencil, will you, and instruct me how to proceed? It's an excellent advent for it will pay for all my unavoidable recent extras. It could not be more welcome. Don't send me *another farthing*, for I'll send it back. I am perfectly well, you know, not a touch of rheumatism, and I

---

[1] A Sola for £2.

64

am taking care of myself like Billy-O. Observe the spelling of Marie's name—Mrs Perkins.[1] But if we were together we'd have a TERRIFIC time with the £2—wouldn't we?

I have just had lunch—vin blanc and grilled sardines and carottes à la crême and saucisses pommes parmentier and oranges. One must *never* drink vin rouge in the Midi, on m'a dit. It's true the vin blanc is wonderful. I wish you had tasted it. Then I make these people give me toast at all my meals instead of the Van Gogh,[2] and that makes 'le repas deux fois plus discret'. I'm just off for a long promenade. If you were here, we could walk to Sanary—watch the fishermen pull in their nets, have coffee at the café on the quay, and come back by train, carrying a big bunch of yellow roses. Sanary is simply a bower of roses—pour *rien*, Monsieur.

Whether it is because I feel so well and my bête noire of rheumatism is gone, or whether it is the vin blanc *or* the climate or all three I don't know, but I feel so terribly happy this afternoon, I have such a désir vif d'embrasser quelqu'un *bien—bien*.

Mon plus que chéri—voici ma seconde lettre aujourd'hui—il faut que ça finisse—et tout de suite.

Can you send me Marie's £2 by a mandat international? I mean, isn't there a way to send money so that the postman comes and gives it you while you are in bed—pays you out of a bag. That used to happen to me. How is it done?

A bientôt, mon amour.

Tig

Dec. 23rd I think

Dearest,   (Thursday, December 23, 1915)

I had 2 short notes from you this morning written on Saturday and one on Sunday. They are arrived so late that I can only think the post is out of order with the Xmas mails—and we'll have to expect delays for a day or two. I (*unlike* you, false wretch) have never missed one day in writing to you. I expect by this time the letters are come. The *Daily Sketch* arrived yesterday. It's a fat rag and thank you for it, Jag dear, but don't be offended if I say I don't like it—will you? I am longing for my Colette books and I am also *absolutely certain* that letters from

[1] Katherine's sister.
[2] An ordinary French long *pain*, so christened because of a Van Gogh still-life containing one.

Lesley Moore have fallen into Farbman's hands.[1] Is Kot my enemy now? I feel he is. You know I have not heard from Lesley for a long time and I know she writes to me every week. My heart burns with rage when I think that her poor letters come and I do not see them. Chastise Kot for me—will you, Bogey?

I am glad you are going to Lady Ottoline's, darling, for Xmas. You are bound to have what Marie calls 'a very merry time'; I lay in bed this morning wondering how many wenches you'd taken under the misletoe and swear you'd been amorous of these three years. Tell me all about it, darling of my heart, and don't forget among your fairies to think of me on New Year's Eve.

The sailors in the sailing ships have been washing. They are all pegged out along the masts and spars. It's a very still, primrose and cowslip day. I am going to drive in a kerridge to that little Dürer town I told you of. The Englishman did not go away on Monday. He stayed till the end of the week to show me the different walks he has discovered here, and it is he who is taking me there this afternoon. How we get there heaven only knows, but he says there *is* a road. This man has certainly been awfully kind to me. You he cannot understand at all, and for all I say I am afraid you will remain a villain. I can't persuade him that I am more than six years old and quite able to take my own ticket and manage my own affairs. 'But why should you?' says he. 'What did he marry you for if it wasn't because he wanted to look after you?' He is 62 and old-fashioned at that. But I feel in a very false position sometimes and I can't escape from it. However, it's no matter.

I am glad Lawrence is nice to you and I think your lunch sounded quite *too horrid*. Please tell me how money is with you, Bogey. I don't like your sausage-and-mashed dinners—and your free meals. Thank goodness the Lady Ottoline will feed you well, and you'll have good baths and beds.

Ten new people are coming here today. There is a kind of flurry in the corridors.

You know I really am a little tempted to take a minute villa later on here. Would it be more expensive than living here, do you think? It's not that I don't like this hotel—I *do,* and (this is like my brother) I am awfully popular with all the people here—you would laugh. I know all their separate histories and married lives, etc. I sit and listen—they

[1] Michael Farbman had taken over 5 Acacia Road from us. Koteliansky also lived there. They were, of course, quite innocent of Katherine's not serious charge.

talk. I feel sometimes very much like Fergusson.[1] But a little villa with a handkerchief of garden is a very attractive idea. Talk to me about it. I am so sorry, love, that the Belgians have got your studio. Have you any other place in your eye?

Your two letters today for some reason have made me rather stiff— rather dumb. I feel it as I write—I don't know why. I feel I am talking over a fence, and my voice is tiny like a grasshopper's. Write to me again at length and know that this little stuffiness or dumbness *n'est rien* and that really and truly there isn't a fence and we are sitting hand in hand under a rhubarb leaf and I am showing you what I have got in my pocket and you are showing me what you have got in yours.

My dear love!

Tig

The Morning of Christmas Eve,
(Friday, December 24, 1915.)

My Very Dearest,

Yesterday I had *four* letters from you and a copy of the *Daily News*. I have never had such richness upon a single day—but my love, my darling, in all the letters you were worried about me and I simply curse myself for having told you about my rheumatism at all. Fool that I was! I will never, never do such a thing again. I am only praying that my telegram was not very delayed with the Xmas posts and that you go away for your festivities with a light heart. Oh Bogey, I do reproach myself, but it's over now, isn't it? and we are in harbour, aren't we? and you will be able to work in peace when you get back to London. I wish I had known how long you were staying, for I wanted to send you a small panier de fleurs for the New Year. They are in such profusion here and they can be safely sent to London.

Thank you for Lesley's two letters and for dear Marie's. She sent me as you know, a pair of mittens to write in, but apologised that they had no 'thum' as she has no one to teach her how to make one. If they are large enough for you, do wear them, my precious, and keep your knobbly hands warm. Oh, I wish I could *cherish* you as I long to. I wish I could care for you and hold you in my arms and say 'Yes, Boge, I know.'

Although you are as near me as my own blood, in one way, in another, here is the physical fact that you are not here—that when I go

[1] J. D. Fergusson, the painter.

for my walks and scramble on the rocks there is no Bogey somewhere with a little worn Homer in his hand—that when I fly round a particularly lovely corner, I do not see—coming to meet me—No, that idea, that you should come and meet me, happily—not as we have met at Tube Stations and street-corners—but you careless, whistling frightfully out of tune, is too sweet and too painful to imagine even in play. I can never be completely happy without you, and the nearer I feel to life and to being myself, the greater is my longing to have you with me—that is quite absolute and final.

Yesterday after I had posted your letter I went to the Market. You know where it is—in front of that square, curious little Church. Yesterday the Market was full of branches of roses—branches of mandarines and flowers of all kinds. There was also a little old man selling blue spectacles and rings 'contre la rhumatisme' and a funny, fat old woman waddling about and pointing to everything she wanted with a fat fowl that she held by the legs. The fowl was furious.

Then I went up to that untidy funny villa with the oranges growing against the walls, close to the cemetery—you know the one I mean? It has a long 'sticky' garden in front and a large blue board advertising apartements. White roosters peck among the gravel and all the paths are spanned over with brown sprigs of vine. The villa is stone and carved with doves, cauliflowers, lions, monkey trees and setting suns. Very gay.

In the garden, mounted on a very nervous chair, a huge old man in a blue apron and horn specs was snipping twigs, and below him a tiny little boy in pink and white socks was receiving them in his pinny. I asked if Mademoiselle Marthe lived there. Certainly, said the man, while the chair wobbled fearfully and then he stood up, raised his snippers, and hailed, 'Marthe, Marthe!' Open flew a window, out popped a little round head. 'On demande,' said the old man. Then a glass door opened and a little creature in a white cotton jacket, with red wool shoes on, stood smiling by me. I asked her if she would lift the shoulders of my brown jacket for me—and she said she would—but after the days of fête—n'est-ce pas? And then, her head a little on one side, with a charming timid smile and one hand with a silver ring on it keeping the sun from her eyes, she came to open the gate for me, because, she said, it was a very difficult gate. I went away longing to write a little play with this setting—I could even hear the music to it. I especially saw the garden by moonlight and the shadows of the oranges and Marthe with a shawl over her head—and her telling *him* it was a difficult gate.

Two of the big sailing ships have come right into the port this morning and are anchored close to the quai. I think they are unloading something; I must go and ask the paper woman all about it. She is a fund of cheerful gossip and she's a nice soul. When the air is 'frais' she produces a tiny charcoal bucket with a pierced lid, and says 'Warm your hands one good little moment'.

My dear! Ten *children* with their parents and 2 nurses arrived here last night. They are all 'une belle famille', as my maid says. I have not even seen them yet—but my brain reels at the idea of their weekly bills.

Bogey, Bogey, Bogey.

I am not going to write any more now for I am so longing to see you today and to talk to you that it's useless. Dear love, I am your

Tig

Do you want *any money*? Tell me your exact finances, will you? I am quite in the dark about so many things that concern you.

It is Xmas morning,

My Little King,   (Saturday, December 25, 1915)

The rain is pouring down and the sea is roaring out the Psalms. Even in the harbour the boats are rocking—but I am so happy and there are so many candles and angels burning on the tree that you have planted in my heart that I can hardly write to you. I want to come flying into your arms and I want us to stay close—close, kissing each other because we are in love. There is a large pine-cone on the fire. I put it on just before I began this letter—to be a kind of celebration. And do you remember that black-headed pin you stuck in my curtain to make it 'hang'. It's still there—it has got to look very like you. I am going to write a fearfully long letter this morning for if I do not I shan't be able to keep my heart from going off like a Xmas cracker.

Dear love—my own beloved—precious, marvellous and adorable little Boge. If I live to be the age of those first and original Pa men in the Bible, I shall never be able to love you enough. I quite understand God making Eternity. Catch hold of me, Bogey—stop me—oh, dearest, hold me close. My body trembles for love of you today. I can feel you in every minutest part of me.

Before I write any more, I must tell you something. I hope you don't kiss anybody at Lady Ottoline's. After all I have said, it does sound absurd! But I minded you kissing even Anne 'seriously'. I minded you *really* kissing. For this reason. If I wished to, I could not. There is no question of will or reason—but I have to be physically faithful because my body wouldn't admit any one else—even to kiss *really*, you know. That was why I wrote so stiffly about your going there for Xmas. Is this jealousy? I suppose it is. But you're mine—you're mine, and when we have not been lovers for so long, I feel I could not bear anyone else even to touch the threshold of your lips. But tell me *all* that happens at Lady Ottoline's and if you have kissed anybody (I'm laughing a little, precious, as I write that, because it is a little absurd) tell me and I'll bear it and understand and not take it to heart. Only *tell me* always. Now you'll say 'Good God! my goblin is changing into a dragon'. I'm not.

Two letters came from you today. In one you had been to see Lawrence (but I explained that away, didn't I?) and in the other, thank God, you had got my telegram at last. Ah, dear heart, really our stormy passage is over. Then, just as I had brushed my hair 100 times, I had your telegram. You couldn't have sent me a lovelier present. I keep on reading it and it looks so awfully funny and sweet because it's so written wrong—by the man here—and scratched over. 'Tenderest *lion*' (I read that *love*) 'Wonderful litters received perfectly harpy' and your name is *Mercy*!! It is even nicer like this. I feel as though fate did it on purpose to show that she really does love us and we really are her funny little children. . . .

Although it is damp and raining I have not even a touch of rheumatism. That cure is wonderful.

When I went out to put your letter in the Palais d'Azur yesterday, I found out why the boats had come in—for there was a procession of dark young sailors, bare legged, their bright blue trousers rolled to the thigh, in big full blouses and with their hair cropped 'en pudding', carrying on their shoulders little red kegs and filling them at the fountain. A great dispute went on because it was midday and the women had come to draw water, too, and the sailors would not take the kegs away and only laughed. They had a tiny boat rocking at the steps of the quai. On deck three sailors hung over the rail plucking three ducks. The feathers floated on the water. The boat is called the *Felicina* and she comes from Verragia. The other boat hasn't got a name. Today they are dressed and flying five or six snippets of flags.

Yesterday afternoon I went off by myself into the woods and spent all the afternoon exploring little tracks and 'chemins de chamois'. I picked such lovely daisies too, with pink tips. It got very faery after the sun went down—and when I got to the road to come home, still deep in the woods, there came a tinkle and round the corner came an old man with a herd of brindled goats. As I came into the town all the babies were flocking in the streets looking at Xmas toys. Heaven knows they are a sorry little show, but you should have heard the screams of joy—'Ah ah, le beau chemin de fer—Dis, dis! Qu'il est mignon le p'tit chien! Ah, la grande—la belle!' I began to look too and I nearly bought an elephant or a dog with one ear standing up—or a *lovely* tea-set with roses painted on it and a sugar basin with a tiny strawberry for the handle on the lid.

Then the Captain of the *Felicina* landed and came marching up the street—very grand—all gold braid—little clipped beard, stiff linen. He was followed by 2 sailors and he disappeared behind the bead curtain of the butcher's shop. Then another ship came sailing in—which makes *five*. Can you feel how thrilling they are in this tiny place? And how one longs to go on board and walk up and down little ladders?

There is a crêche in the Church. It has been all made by the children. It is simply beautiful. A landscape with painted cardboard houses—even shutters to the windows. A windmill—little bridges of twigs, fountains made of falling silver paper cut in strips—the roads all of fresh sand, the hills and the valleys all of moss that they gathered in the woods. Trees are planted in the moss and hung with silver stars (far too big for them). There are sheep under the trees, shepherds, holy men, the three Kings, one with a black face and awful whites to his eyes. Fat little angels perch in all sorts of places and in a neat cardboard grotto is Mary, St Joseph (a very old dotty) and a naked 'p'tit Chesau' as they say, who can open and shut his eyes. The priest was showing this Marvel to a baby when I was there but she could say nothing except in a very hushed voice. 'Il est tout nu.' The dove is also perched on a tree—a drunken fowl bigger than the ox or the ass—and out of the house there is the head of the innkeeper in a nightcap with a tassel on it telling Mary he hasn't got a room . . . .

My love, I have only time to run to the post with this. I love you, *love* you.

       I am always your own

Tig

Plus tard.

I have opened my letter (I am always doing that—it's like popping just one's head in again) to say that when I ran to the Post it was shut for all today and I am afraid this letter will not go until tomorrow, love. But I am glad I opened it for I want to ask you something.

Do you want me to come back? Do you think you will work better at your Dosty book[1] alone? Shall I stay here until it is finished, or until the Spring, or when? I am willing to come back today if you want me—you know that, my heart. But speak to me frankly about this, will you? And when you *do* want me back write me a note saying Hara is ill and that you would be very relieved if I would come to England immediately etc., just so that I will have a definite something to show the consuls and the passe-portiers. (We are still quite babies enough to play with dolls and I'd much rather pretend about Hara than about a real person. I would so see her, with her little hands in her kimono sleeves, very pale, and wanting her hair brushed.)

I have just had a Xmas dinner—very dreadful and indecent to be partaken of alone. The 'belle famille' had an *enormous* feed. I left the little tiny ones leaning back in their chairs with their legs stretched out, utterly helpless—and slightly the worse for wine. For even the baby who is not yet three drank until her glass rested on her nose, where she left it and blew into it and stared at me through the top. Now I am going for a walk with the Englishman who leaves definitely the day after tomorrow.

Later. It was a long walk through the woods and then we left the paths and he taught me *how* to climb as taught by the guides in Norway. It was boring beyond words but absolutely successful. We scaled dreadful precipices and got wonderful views. Then I had to learn *how* to descend and how to balance if the stones roll when you put your foot on them—what a pa man! All this of course he takes deadly seriously—and I find myself doing so too and I don't get one bit tired. I wish you could see my room. Even the blue glass vases we put away have had to come out for the big bouquets of yellow and pink roses. Tonight I have promised to dine with this pa man. I don't doubt I shall get a lecture on touring in Spain. I already know more about how to travel in Italy than any living being, I should think.

I am going to try to send you a nut-shell in this letter for a little hat.

[1] I was preparing to write a book on Dostoevsky.

It's dark now and the waves are beating right up the road among the palms.

Do you feel my love?

Always and toujours,

Tig

Colette has come. Thank you, love.

My own!   (Sunday, December 26, 1915)

Just a little note so as not to let the day pass. It is a lovely day, and even yesterday became fair after all. If you could but see my roses! I heard today from Kay whose card I send you (!), and from Father and Mother. Their letters I have just answered, Bogey. They made me very sad. Indeed I understand that as 'the silence' descends on them, their loss becomes ever greater. Now, for instance, that letters about him are infrequent and few—and the English mail arrives, as Father says, and seems each week to make the dreadful gap more real. Dearest, in my letter I wrote a great deal *about* you and Chummie. I wanted to make them feel that you had been real to each other and played together. I wish you would write a note to them. Please *do* if you can, but send it to *me* to post, for I have not told them that you have gone back to England. I thought it wiser not to; it was so difficult to explain from this distance, and not necessary.

I heard from Lawrence today. Shall I send you his letter? It left me cold. He wants us to join him, but you know we are not made to do that kind of thing, ever. We are two, rich and happy apart. If you do not want me back yet, Bogey (you understand) I would like to stay here a little longer.

I send you all my love.

Tig

Monday,

Dearest,   (December 27, 1915)

Just a line which may not reach you. It is 7-30 a.m. and I am just off to send the telegrams. I have been awake all night, hugging my joy. If you come, Bogey, in all probability I shall fly into two bits as the train comes in. I hate the journey over again for you. That is why I am putting 'Don't feel bound to,' but once you arrive you will be *happy*. I keep making out little lists and having conversations with imaginary charbonniers! Bogey, my heart, my treasure, I have been sent £10 10. 0.

for a Xmas present, which will come in handy. No more now. I will write again at length when your wire comes, if it says 'No', but until then I can't write. We can easily live here on £3 a week. A woman to 'do' for us only costs 15 to 20 francs a month. We shall become very brown indeed with little bits of orange peel in our hair. I am praying— to really the old God. I feel He can do it and will.

A Happy New Year, my little big husband,

Your infinitesimal wife,
Wig

The white bear is waving at you.[1]

Monday morning,
(December 27, 1915)

Even if you never came I cannot but love you more for the evening and the night and the morning I have spent thinking that you *are* coming. It was Sunday, so I could not send you a telegram until today. I somehow—Oh, how did I?—got through last evening by sitting in the salon among unreal fantastic people and sewing and talking. For I knew I would not sleep. I knew I would not sleep. What drowsy bliss slept in my breast! Oh Jack, I hardly dared to breathe.

A woman here told me how to buy our stores and what to pay and how to make soup with 2 sous worth of bones, and what day the woman with the good apples was at the market and how to manage une femme de ménage. I heard. I dared not look at her. I felt my smiles chasing in my eyes. I saw the villa—perhaps a cactus near the gate—you writing at a little table, me arranging some flowers and then sitting down to write too. Both of us gathering pine cones and driftwood and bruyère for our fire. I thought of what I would have ready for you, soup and perhaps fish, coffee, toast, because charbon de bois, which is *much* cheaper than coal, makes lovely toast, I hear—a pot of confitures, a vase of roses. And then I thought de notre bon lit et de nous deux tout seuls, seuls, cachés dans la nuit—The fire perhaps just tinkling, the sea murmuring outside, et vous et moi, mon chéri . . . with happiness fast asleep on the roof with its head under its wing, like a dove. And then I saw us waking in the morning and putting on the big kettle and letting in the femme de ménage. She hangs her shawl behind the kitchen door. 'Vous savez, il fait beau.'

[1] I do not remember 'the white bear', but it was probably one of Katherine's dolls.

74

Finally I could bear it no longer. I came up to my room and took a hot bath and then curled up in bed and smoked and tried to read a new Dickens. No use. The sea was very loud. I looked at the watch and saw it said 25 to 12 and then I went to sleep. When I looked again it was nearly four. So I turned on the light and waited, waited for day. How the light changed, I never shall forget. I put on my big purple coat and opened the shutters and sat on the window sill. It was all primrosy with black mountains. A sailing ship put out to sea. I saw all the little men on board, and how the sail was put up and how when it caught the breath of wind the ship went fast. Two more of our big ships, with a rattle of chains, hoisted anchor and put out to sea. I saw the bending, straining bodies of the men. And then came the fishers bringing in their pots. Then the first bird. At seven I heard my little maid lighting the stove, so I ran out and asked for my déjeuner—washed in cold water— kissed my roses—put on my goblin hat and flew into the garden. The market was there, with 2 funny Spaniards beating drums. Such flowers Such violets! But I kept my pennies for you and me. I thought I should have to have a small fête, so when I went to the post office I put *new Relief nibs* in all the awful old crusty pens. The sea and sky this morning are LITERALLY a DARK NAVY (see Aunt Li[1]). I sent your telegrams, ran home to find the maids beating the carpets and the white dog overslept and pretending he had been awake for hours on the Terrace. Now I am going with a gent in corduroys to look at a furnished villa of his.

This letter may never reach you for I shall not send it until your answer comes. Oh, my love, I cannot walk fast enough. My breast is eaten by love like the Spartan boy's inside. Love eats and eats at my heart and I feel everybody must know. I keep thinking 'We shall go to Sanary—to that little village in the mountains—I will show him all the walks,' and then I think of the long journey and perhaps you will not come. If you do, then it is the miracle.

There are faeries, faeries everywhere. I would not be surprised if I were to find them putting fir boughs in the hall and wreaths upon the door handles and swags and garlands over the windows.

Love presses on my forehead like a crown—my head is heavy— heavy—I must not think of you . . . . But I keep talking to myself in my Tig voice as though you could hear . . . . The other coming to France I can hardly remember. It was all so curious, so uncertain and so joyless. Was it? Or is it my fancy? I feel we are coming together for the first

[1] Aunt Li was a relative of Katherine's in New Zealand.

time. In your letter you say: 'We shall go from sunshine to sunshine.' Yes, that is just what I feel. Today, too, my brother smiles.

Two more ships have put out to sea. One had 11 sails and one had 12. And now a little destroyer has come rushing in. My only thought is. Are you on the destroyer? A little low grey boat snipping through the water like a pair of scissors.

Tuesday,

Boge, (December 28, 1915)

I ran about yesterday and surveyed the land, but it was only prospecting, and nothing definite. Then when I came in I found your happy letters and realized that the Xmas telegram had meant to explain that the villa, too, was not necessary any more. Then I had a most terrible feeling that you did not want to leave England and that it were better for you *not* to come again. You see, I love you so and I shan't be bitterly disappointed if you don't come. I want you to do what you please, my love, and I shall really understand and love you more because then I know you are free in our love as I am. So I rushed off in the dark and sent the third wire. Cost of wires that day, 9 francs. Happily, Lesley sent me 10/- for Xmas, so I spent that and did not feel so guilty. I'm sending it to you a little later with the *Sola* too.

My own, my little Bogè, I shall be glad when this is all settled. It's frightfully unsettling. This morning I am in terror lest you should come.

If you don't, I shall go on living here for a while, and then I will return later. I had such lovely letters from you, but I am a little bit distracted, my precious, and wish the crisis was over. Also, I have appointments with various people all day in case you should come . . . .

But my love will always endure and it will never be faint or be less. You must believe that—for it is true for ever. Neither shall I be unhappy nor think the miracle is anything but postponed.

Wig

Feel how I love you.

The White Bear sends O Hara San his respects.

Wednesday early,

Dearest only, only one. (December 29, 1915)

Of course I really *don't* expect you and yet . . . . I am waiting for the answer to the telegram and I can't stop my heart leaping whenever steps sound in the corridor. If you *should* come, I have found a tiny villa for us, which seems to me almost perfect in its way. It stands alone in a small garden with terraces. It faces the 'midi' and gets the sun all day long. It has a stone verandah and a little round table where we can sit and eat or work. A charming little tiny kitchen with pots and pans and big coffee pot, you know. Electric light, water downstairs and upstairs too in the cabinet de toilette. A most refined 'water-closet' *with* water in the house . . . The salle à manger is small and square with the light low over the table. It leads on to the verandah and overlooks the sea. So does the chambre à coucher. It is very private and stands high on the top of a hill. It is called the *Villa Pauline.* The woman (wife of the mobilier) who showed it me would also find me a servant for 3 hours every day. Yesterday I *ran ran* all day long to find something and saw such funny places. Every little street I came to there seemed to be an old woman in woollen slippers with keys in her hands waiting to show me 'votre affaire'. Oh, such funny experiences! But I have been very careful to go to each other whom I left in a state of uncertainty and to say I regret that I cannot take their particular treasure so that I shall not have to spend the rest of my days in dodging streets, houses and people as I usually do on these occasions. And they are neither heart-broken nor do they call me a 'sausage'—to my *great* surprise. It is a sunny windy morning with a high sea and dancing light on all the trees. The *vent de l'est* is blowing as a matter of fact, but it has no terrors for me now that I have my legs again. Do not, my reckless dearest, wire me now that I have found the villa that you *will* come for I have to give my answer tomorrow at latest and I don't think there is another. At any rate I think we had better have done with the idea and I will stay here for the time being.

Mlle. Marthe has just been although I am still in my peignoir. She is not a girl; she is a *sparrow*. It is so awfully nice to have your jacket mended by a charming little sparrow instead of a monster with icy hands and pins in her mouth and all over her non-existent bosom. But Marthe hops about, smiling, with her head a little on one side. She is a sweet little thing; I wish to goodness I could somehow adopt her for us.

My roses—my roses are too lovely. They melt in the air (I *thought* that in French where it sounds sense but in English it's nonsense). I have 23. I just counted them for you and if you turn these blue glass vases back to front so that you don't see the handpainted horrors on them they are very lovely, the dark red stems and a leaf or two showing through the water.

I didn't have a letter from you today or yesterday. I expect they take longer from marbil halls than they do in London. If only I knew how long you were to be there. Perhaps you won't get my telegrams . . . . Bogey,—*make* me wash and dress. I've lighted another cigarette now and in spite of my absolutely cold, calculating mind, my heart keeps on *perpetually* like this. 1 large vase of white and yellow jonquils in the middle of the table. Roses in the bedroom, some little red anemones on the mantelpiece. 'This is the place, Bogey.' A ring at the door. The man with your boxes from the station . . . . Now we are sitting down, hardly daring to look at each other, but smiling. Now you have unpacked and put on your corduroys and your boots. I am downstairs and you are upstairs. I hear you walking. I call out, 'Bogey, do you want coffee or tea?' We arrange to work every morning—have lunch —go out until it is dark, come home, have tea and talk and read and get our own supper—and then work. On our walks we will take that satchel you bought—for pine-cones and wood and oranges. Oh God, this place is as fair as New Zealand to me, as apart, as secret, as much a place where you and I are alone and untroubled. But so I dream—and do not take my dreams too much to heart, my very dear, for you know that when I know you are not coming I shall be all right and come up again smiling and pin our colours to the mast of another little boat and put out upon another sea.

I love you. Now I am going to get up. I've got some *awful* toothpaste. It is called Isis and it has funny woodeny birds on the tube. It has all come out the wrong end, too, and it's *much too* pink.

I don't want any more books, my heart. Thank you, please, for all your dearness and sweetness to me.

The black pin and the white bear send their love.

But I send you everything I have got—yes, yes, even this throbbing sweet anxiety that beats in my forehead and makes my hands so cold and my heart intent and ready.

Always your own

Tig

Wednesday night,
(December 29, 1915)

I am like that disciple who said: 'Lord, I believe. Help thou my unbelief'. As I was dressing and your letter was already sealed, the

heavy steps really came along the corridor—the knock at the door—
the old man with the blue folded paper that I scarcely dared to take and
having taken—could not open. Oh, I sat by the side of my bed—and
opened it little by little. I read all those directions for the sending of
urgent telegrams and telegrams in the night . . . . At last I said: He is not
coming and opened it and read your message. Since then I have never
ceased for one moment to tremble. I shall never be calm again until I
am on your breast. I felt 'Now he is coming that villa is taken' and I
ran, ran along the quai. One day I shall tell you all this at length, but it
was not taken until I saw the woman and took it. I went through it
again. It is quite perfect in its way. It is always what I felt there was
somewhere in the world for us—in Spain or Italy. And the people to
whom it belongs who live next door are such good, decent, honest
folk, eager to have us, eager to make us comfortable and happy. 'Je
suis toujours là. Vous avez seulement de frapper si vous auriez besoin
de quelque chose.' The sun shone in every room and on the little stone
verandah danced the shadow of a tree. Is this true? Is it coming true?
I have to sign the agreement and pay a month in advance tomorrow.
Then to order the coal and wood and see my femme de ménage who
has already been found 'pour 3 heures le matin et pour faire mes
petites courses, n'est-ce pas?' All the rest of the day . . . I do not know
how I have spent it—such a lovely wild day brimming over with
colour and light. I have found the shortest way to our home by a road
you do not know, through fields of jonquils and past the olive trees
that blow so silver and black today. There are high walls on the road
and nobody goes. I thought: 'We shall stand here and kiss each other'.
Then I thought: 'But if we do, I think I shall faint for joy'.

Yes, I have found a lovely way—And I have made out a list of our
modest provisions that I shall buy on Friday. In fact I have made out
more than one list. For I can't even write or read. This evening in the
salon somebody said that already there was conscription in England.
Oh God, is it too late? Are you coming?

I have loved you before for 3 years with my heart and my mind, but
it seems to me I have never loved you *avec mon âme* as I do now. I love
you with all our future life—our life together which seems only now to
have taken root and to be alive and growing up in the sun. *I* do not love
you, but love possesses me utterly—love for you and for our life and
for all our richness and joy. I have never felt anything like it before. In
fact, I did not comprehend the possibility of such a thing. I seem to

79

have only played on the fringe of love and lived a kind of reflected life that was not really my own but that came from my past. Now all that is cast away. Oh, my soul—if you come now we shall realize something that it seems to me never has been—such warmth and such richness and such virtue there is in you and in me. Is it too late? . . . You are *really* coming?

This morning I went to the little Church and prayed. It is very nice there. I prayed for us three—for you and me and Chummie. It was so gay and yet solemn there.

Bogey, come quickly quickly. My heart will break.

Thursday,
(December 30, 1915)

I must be brave so that you will not be afraid and make the officials suspicious. I shall just go on believing and believing in God and preparing a place for you. Your letter on Xmas day has come—with that about the horrid woman in the shop—'There is no doubt that I hate life.' My dearest, my darling, I will stretch a lovely rainbow wing over you and not let them make you hate life. You must not really hate life. I promise you if you come here I will not let you hate it. I will always talk to all the uglies and you can talk to the nice ones. For there is no doubt that I love life. And now that I have cast away for ever that dark shell that I used to creep into in London I will face anybody and I am not afraid. The only thing that frightens me is that you cannot come.

Money doesn't frighten me a *bit*. We'll be 2 little silkworms and live on mulberry leaves. If you come here we shall both write poetry—a mutual book which we will publish together. Also we shall both write a kind of 'paysages' and we shall both write—well, I shouldn't be surprised if we both wrote *anything*.

The little house is there, waiting for us. Its eyes are shut until I open them. The sun touches the verandah and warms the place where your hand will rest. Tout bas, tout bas mon cœur chante: 'Cinquante kilos de charbon de pierre—cinquante kilos de charbon de coke et des poids pour allumer pour cinq sous—c'est presqu'un sac.' I have such a lot to do today. I must go out soon. Again I am not dressed, but idling here with your adorable letter beside me. Bogey, I hardly slept at all. I shan't sleep again until I have your head upon my shoulder and your burnt gorse hair sous mon nez. Goodbye for now. You are on your way? Will you send me a wire from Dieppe with just 'all serene'? Are you in Paris tonight?

Midi. This morning I went to the woman who introduced me to the villa. She is a Spaniard from Barcelona—and we are *really sincerely* friends. She is a dear creature—and at first I know she didn't like me but now really we have jokes together and she laughs, showing her pretty teeth. She tried to find me a femme de ménage but could not, so her daughter Marie, a dark-eyed Spanish beauty— a really fascinating creature with a fringe, big eyes and bright colour is coming instead. But do we mind 'cuisine espagnole?' 'Pas du tout.' Then I went to the church for a minute—I feel I must keep in close touch with God. They were dressing the altar with white and yellow jonquils—a sweet savour must have mounted. I prayed that my prayer was heard at the same moment and that God was pleased. Then I went to the station to ask what trains arrived and then to our villa by the path that you are coming. The door was open. The owner was inside hanging up saucepans. So we went through the inventory together, and she said she would give me tea-cups and a tea-pot—because we were English. Also she offered to take me to any shops when I wanted to buy anything. I then went over the villa again. There is the loveliest green water-pot like you admired. We must find something to fill it with. Then I went back to her house and together with her husband made out a lease, signed, paid, and put the key in my pocket. A friend came in and we sat talking a little. They told me not to buy flowers for your arrival. They had enough in their garden—and she said she would come in when Marie arrives on Saturday and show her how to make the fire. I walked home with the key in my hands.

I kept thinking—where is he now? Are you near Folkstone? . . . I simply don't know how I shall wait till you come. Every time I see the telegraph man I run out of his way in case he has a telegram for me 'Impossible to come'. What should I do? I feel we simply *must* be here together. I feel it's absolutely necessary.

It has been a dark morning, but as I write a pale sun is over everything. The clouds are white as marble. Tomorrow I shall buy stores and settle everything. On Saturday morning I shall go there and stay there. But I simply don't know how to exist until I know if you will be here Saturday or Sunday . . . .

Now it is late night. I have been playing games in the salon with 3 men and a woman from Avignon. Playing games that one only plays at school. Oh, I wish we had played all night long for I shall never sleep. You are arriving in Paris if you are on your way. That is all I can think. All the evening I have hid my joy and my heart has said 'Now he is dans le même pays,' but I am still so frightened that my breast hurts me to breathe. I shall know for certain tomorrow because if you have not come there will be a telegram. And I know you will telegraph me from Paris, my love—tomorrow. So courage—courage. In quelques heures I shall know. But I am in a fever.

Friday: noon. No telegram yet. I asked this morning at the post. They said that a telegram from Paris took perhaps one or two hours only. And yet if you have not left I cannot but think you would already have let me know. Now I am just waiting. I have ordered the little stores and the wine and the wood. All the windows are open—all the doors—the linen is airing. I went to the flower market and stood among the buyers and bought, wholesale you know, at the auction in a state of lively terrified joy 3 dozen rose buds and 6 bunches of violets.

I arrived in Bandol on January 1st and we lived, very happily, at the Villa Pauline until mid-April. The two following letters were written in March, when Katherine went to Marseilles to meet her sister, who was coming to England from India.

	Hotel Oasis,
The Same Afternoon.	Marseilles.
Dearest of All,	(March, 1916)

I got through to the 2nd and had a very comfortable journey. I nearly fell out of the train at the last moment looking for and then at you. But no, you walked away. It was rather awful—wasn't it? The country on the way here is so lovely. Where there used to be pink heath there is gorse now and white and red trees everywhere. Cook's weren't much consolation but they referred me to the P. and O. people, rue Colbert, (opposite the Post Office) and I found out from them that the *Sardinia* is definitely expected at 8.30 a.m. on Thursday morning. Also I explained my situation and obtained from them a card permitting me to go on board. So I must stay. It's a good thing I came. She 'moors', says my card further, at MOLE C—Bassin National. I shall find it. Cook's will tell me the way. The P. and O. people were *not* inclined to over-amiability. Then (very hungry as usual when en voyage) I went and bought my bag for 13 francs. It was expensive, but it was just what you would have bought. (Oh, how she flatters him!) Darling, it's a lovely bag, though, *mouse blue*, well finished and strong; and with or without a handle, AND the shape you said, AND deep enough to hold my passport. But my things somehow don't belong, don't quite belong to me now until you have seen them—and they've spiritually passed through the customs. Until you've more or less put a little white chalk squiggle on this bag, it isn't quite mine, though I'm very pleased with it. Then I came here and was remembered—but it was 'Eh, comment va Monsieur?' from Monsieur, Madame and especially that rather nice slatternly maid who was very friendly and shook hands. I have the same room (I'm in it now), the same flowers on the wall paper (that came out and bowed when I had fever). Only the couch has been 're-covered' in large yellow and black 3-eyed beetles. The same little chap has gone for my bag, because it is pouring with rain and has been ever since I set foot. A nuisance—for I don't feel I *can* buy a 3.75 umbrella. However, the rain is warm, and smells of Spring. I don't really mind it, but my boots do—and they wouldn't be protected with an umbrella anyway—I had two mingy eggs cooked in margarine, a pot of tea and one lumpish little roll for lunch, 1.70. Two eggs are 1 *franc*: tea 60 c,— bread 10 c. It was at the place we always went to. I protested, but was told a long story. Everything has augmented. I was very angry— especially as I couldn't eat the eggs for all my hunger. Our cooking spoils one for anything else. I bought 2 penny packets of note-paper, a pen, a bottle of ink, a *Daily Mail* and *Radical* and tabac. So here I am waiting for the baggage—as usual.

Madame Ferrand was at Cassis station; in the corridor of the train we met, and she did *not* acknowledge my bow. Why are people so *horrid*?

I'm glad you've not come. What could you do here? And there's not the ghost of a *home comfort*. But it isn't horrid and I'm quite all right and shall be very careful of the money. I hope to be home on Thursday night, but I will wire you again after I've seen Chaddie. Make no preparations. But look after your darling, darling self. Oh, Bogey, how *can* you be such a darling? I shall sit here and write all the afternoon. I feel so 'settled'. It is because of our love. I feel so rich and my heart is quiet—you know that feeling?

Always your own
Tig

Marseilles,

My precious, (March, 1916)

Even though I hope to be home soon after this letter I will send you a 'Bon jour'—I'm smoking my after breakfast cigarette. This morning I am going to find my way to the Bassin National in preparation for tomorrow. Cook's could not explain exactly; they advised me however, to take a cab (!); it is about half an hour's drive. Très, très bien. But the man here says I can go by tram from the Vieux Port all the way. This I'll find out by trying to do it this morning. Bogey—I had a funny night. All my fever came back. I shivered and my blood buzzed as though bees swarmed in my heart—and the lilies came out and bowed. Also it was rather late before I went to bed AFTER locking the door, fastening the bolt, etc., and to my Horror just as I began to fall asleep I heard SOMEONE turning the handle. Then the door was gently rattled. Then came a KNOCK. This is all true. I called out 'Qui est là?' No reply. So I leapt out of bed, threw my kimono on and, arming myself with a pair of scissors, I opened the door. There stood a horrid creature in his night-shirt who began mumbling something about the wrong door—but he *leered*. Oh I *slammed* the door in his face, and walked up and down my room—furious—I was not at all frightened.

Today it is very warm (so far) and sunny. The trams roll up and down, and clatters and squeaks fly up. Now I have had a scrupulous, cat-like bath and washed my ears beyond words. I feel we are about 15 today—just children: you and I don't live like grown up people, you know. Look at the way we soap each other's backs and hop about in the tops of our pyjamas and scrabble into bed, winking our toes, and I keep seeing in my mind's eye, your back view as you go down to the *cave* for wood—and then your front view as you come up with your arms full . . . .

Life isn't half long enough to love the different things about you in. I shall die in the middle of a little laugh at some new funny thing that I adore you for. Now I must go out and stop writing love-letters. Perhaps I didn't quite know until I came away what these months have brought, or how they have changed everything.

(Don't think I forget the army. I don't, but I simply feel it *is* a false alarm. It must be. But I know how you feel about it and, my love, don't think me unsympathetic. For I'm not. It's only I can do

84

nothing from here and ∴ we've got to wait. But it won't catch you, Bogey.)

Always your girl,

Tig

We lived in the Villa Pauline until the beginning of April 1916. *It was, without doubt, the happiest time of our life together—one to which we looked back, with love and a certain incredulity, in the after years. We could have written, like R. L. Stevenson: 'Happy? I was happy once—that was in Bandol'. It was not by any effort of will that we ignored the war, which was then at one of its blackest periods—the carnage around Verdun. We did it spontaneously, and without a tremor of conscience. Whether we deserved our happiness is not for mortals to decide. But we had it, and it was precious. And in that experience were laid the foundations of a conviction which has grown more solid with the years—that the only power which will ever put an end to wars is love between individual men and individual women. Only in that relation is the fundamental egoism of men and women really overcome.*

Katherine wrote the first draft of 'Prelude' at the Villa Pauline, and I wrote a book on Dostoevsky. We wrote on opposite sides of the table.

We might have stayed at the Villa Pauline longer than we did: but we knew from the beginning that our felicity must have an end; and when we had finished our respective pieces of writing it did not seem to make much difference whether we anticipated by a month or two the end that was certain. A much more comprehensive classification for national service was shortly to be introduced, and those, like myself, who had been rejected when there was plenty of better physical material to choose from were now to be drawn in the net for non-combatant services. It seemed much better to return to England betimes rather than wait to be fished out ignobly. Moreover, Lawrence for whom we had a deep affection was pressing us to return and live with him and Frieda in Cornwall.

So we returned to England early in April and went down to Zennor. Katherine was a prey to misgiving. The South of France was, ever since she first lived in it, more congenial to her than any part of England, which was always my country rather than hers. The South of France was much more like New Zealand which had been her home, and which had now become the home of her imagination also. Furthermore, though she was fond of Lawrence and Frieda, she was at this time deeply averse to the idea of community living, even on the modest scale which Lawrence proposed; and since our own experience of happiness in love, she was more than ever liable to be shocked by the violent

85

explosions which at this time were part of the normal texture of the Lawrences'
life. I must confess that these explosions terrified me; they filled Katherine with
horror.

I have no happy recollections of our time with the Lawrences at Zennor;
and Katherine soon became acutely miserable. I have done my best to describe
the strange situation which arose between the four of us in 'Between Two
Worlds' (Chapter XXVII). It was soon felt to be intolerable on both sides,
and in May we moved to the south coast of Cornwall, into a cottage at Mylor
on the Falmouth River.

Katherine was not much happier there. She found it impossible to settle
down to work and as often as she could afford it went away. She visited Lady
Ottoline Morrell at Garsington, and stayed with the Campbells in London. In
July I was called up for medical examination at Bodmin and advised by a
kindly colonel to try to get a job in London if I did not want to spend my time
navvying in Cornwall. I bestirred myself, and was taken on in the Military
Intelligence.

The first of the following letters was written to me during one of Katherine's
visits to Garsington. The following four while I was job-hunting in London.
When I received my appointment to the War Office we moved to London, and
for a time shared a house at No. 3 Gower St. with Dorothy Brett and Barbara
Carrington.

	London,
My dear Bogey,	Wednesday, (July 1916)

This morning I received a book and a note and a shilling on page 50.
But the letter to which you refer has never come. Perhaps it is just
delayed, but I don't see why. So your note was a little difficult to understand. I suppose the letter explained the book. I'll read it (the book) on
my journey to Garsington.

You could not have given me much less news of you. Not a personal
word nor half a phrase. So I suppose you don't want any from me, and
I'll not give it.

You are a funny boy, and you *do* rather offend me.

Tig

Ever so many thanks for the 1/-. You should not have sent it.

Mylor,
Very late Friday night,
(August, 1916)

My own,

I shall not be able to post this letter until I have heard from you where you are going to sleep after tonight. Nevertheless I must write and tell you. . . .

That it only dawned on me this evening that perhaps you will not be here again for a long time . . . that you won't see the dahlias of this year again reflected in your mirror and that the lemon verbena in a jar on my table will all be withered and dry.

As I thought that, sitting, smoking in the dusky room, Peter Wilkins [a black kitten] came in with a fallen-all-too-fallen leaf in his mouth, and I remembered that the Michaelmas daisies were out and, lo! it was autumn.

Is it just my fancy—the beauty of this house tonight? This round lamp on the round table, the rich flowers, the tick of the clock dropping into the quiet—and the dark outside and the apples swelling and a swimming sense of deep water. May brought me this evening some of this year's apples. . . . 'Good to eat.' They are small and coloured like pale strawberries. I wish that you were with me, my love. It is not because you are absent that I feel so free of distraction, so poised and so still. I feel that I am free even of sun and wind, like a tree whose every leaf has 'turned'.

I love you tonight beyond measure. Have I ever told you how I love your shoulders. When I hold you by your shoulders . . . put my arm round you and feel your fine delicious skin warm and yet cool, like milk, and your slender bones—the bones of your shoulders . . . .

Goodnight, my heart.

I am your own girl.

Mylor,
Saturday Night,
(August, 1916)

Darling,

Your girl has been so 'down' today, so appallingly 'low'. I knew I could not expect a letter—and cannot until Monday. Monday is 11,500 miles away. . . . How I loathe being here alone! It gives me nothing really. This place is only tolerable because of you, and even then it never inspires. . . .

87

Mrs. Hoblyn called and asked me to come to a Sale of Work on behalf of the Seamen's Mission. Her thread glove *squeezed* my hand. . . . Her father was vicar here forty years . . . she is a Whidow. . . . A girl called and asked if I felt inclined to subscribe to the Red Cross. . . . Little Keverns and parties from Kevern . . . 'Please, Mrs. Murry, can I go through?' . . . And then a Mr. Watson with a boat for sale . . . £9 with a centre keel, etc., etc. . . . And that grocer and the oil boy . . . and Mary has broken the Primus. . . . And Mr. Mustard says we use more than our fair share of water from the pump. That from *him*!

Then came your telegram which meant evidently that we'll be in a state of suspense until Thursday at earliest and dear only knows when I shall be in London. Do you want me? Would you love to have me? I want to reach out my hand and take yours and say, 'Oh I *should* have come. What is £2 10s. to us?'

Soon the Army may have you and then not all the £2 10s. in the world can give us each other. What *can* Goodyear know? If only you had *made* me come, wanted me so that you couldn't let me stay here!

Oh, I could cry, I could cry, tonight. I'll write no more.

My dearest heart, I am

Tig

PLEASE SEND ME NO MONEY.

Mylor,
Sunday Night,

Dearest, (August, 1916)

This evening I watered the flowers and went into the orchard and into that 'walled garden' where you cut down the nettles—on your birthday, wasn't it? I am simply prostrate with misery. I can do nothing. Are we *never* to be happy—never, never? We haven't had any 'life' together at all yet—in fact it's only on the rarest occasions that we have any confidential intercourse.

The day is dying—very grandly. I can hear the water lapping and I can hear some sheep on the hill. It's ages since I really talked to you, for when Goodyear was here—no—you *wouldn't* respond. But it's all of little account. What misery I have known! If it goes on like this, I'll make an end to it in October. I can bear no more.

Tig

88

Mylor,
Dearest Jack,   Tuesday, (August, 1916)

I am going up to Mylor to post this. I'll send you a wire from there, too—to cancel if I can my horrid letter of yesterday. But I could not help it. Now I shall write fully in answer to yours of this morning.

If they do accept you provisionally, would that be sure enough for you to decide finally to leave Cornwall for the present? If they don't accept you, are you coming back here? Heavens! I am really very much in the dark! And won't you have to find some place to live in in London as soon as possible? The whole affair seems to me so dreadfully in the vague.

But I'll get down to earth.

If they accept you provisionally, I shall wind up here—pack your clothes and my clothes—and travel up to London on Friday morning. As to what books and papers you want—as you have said nothing— you must leave it to me. I'll do my best. I shall stay the night in London and come down to Garsington by a train which (I think) leaves Paddington at 2.30.

If this is all O.K. wire me to Charing Cross, where I'll go for a telegram *or* letter *poste restante*, in the name of Bowden, in case I have to produce my identification disc. I'll call for letter or wire on Friday evening and Saturday not later than twelve o'clock. Then, *if* all this happens we may have a moment to talk things out and arrange our plans. I can't stay much after Monday at Garsington.

Salute Lady Ottoline for me.

Always, dearest,

Tig

Cheque for £1 5s. od. enclosed. K.M.

The following letter was written to me while we were both at 3 Gower Street.

(3 Gower Street,)
Afternoon.
My dearest Boy,   (? January, 1917)

I have just come in and smoked a cigarette, staring out through these dirty windows on to the dirtier windows across the way. I am awfully tired and exhausted—not physically, but mentally. The business of entering an agent's office, the sight of those huge unwieldy books being turned over and thumbed, the agent leaning back in a revolving chair and toying with a pencil as he talks, the little boy clerk who is told to see if 'the key of No— is out or in'—all these things are so revolting to me now that it's only by the greatest effort of will that I pass through that pinging door at all. I feel, don't you know? like a professional flat-hunter; all my requirements are stated so pat—all my questions are so intelligent and inevitable.

The first blow was that the tenants of the maisonette on the Parade have decided to continue their lease; the second that there simply are not any flats in St. John's Wood under £100 a year, and that the maisonettes at from £75 to £85 are always *lower* maisonettes i.e. entrance floor and basement. Each agent had the same story to tell. All the houses at a high rent were vacant; people were clamouring for flats —were even prepared to pay a large premium for the privilege of moving into one etc. etc. I took some addresses for maisonettes at £75 in Abbey Road and Finchley Road, but they were hideous. Rather worse than those we saw in Alexandra Road, with the same preposterous proportions etc. Finally, I went to Elgood's in Vere Street and inquired if they had any of their flats off the High Street, in Henry Street, to let. Yes, they had one at £95 and one at £48 a year—payable by the month. But 'the great thing about our flats is that we make the strictest possible inquiries about our intending tenants. We have some very nice people indeed in occupation and you quite understand, Madam . . . . Of course, if one wants the other kind of thing,' said this lunatic, warming his bottom before an immense coke fire, 'one goes to Maida Vale. But in *our* flats every tenant is known to be strictly correct!' *Très bien.*

St. John's Wood, my dear soul, is absolutely 'off'.

Now, I'll be extravagantly frank. I think, seriously, that we ought to stay on here until June and ask Barnicoat to let our house furnished or unfurnished if he can. We ought to save money against the end of the war, and, if we start moving again you know we shan't have a penny between us. If you were in the Army we *could* not move. In a way you *are* in the Army—I mean you are engaged all day long, you have no personal life, you are very uncertain as regards the immediate future because this immediate future is not in your control. You could not really enjoy your flat until the war is over—and the journey down to Cornwall, the moving of the furniture, the buying of all those extra things that we should *have* to buy would cost us every penny of £25. And then it is impossible for us to rent a flat of the size we need for less than a 3 years' tenancy—and that seems to me madness. What do you intend to do after the war? You must be your own master. That means that you will probably not earn more than £3 a week at most, and the high prices will continue, so your £3 will be more like 30/-. It is no good worrying about money and feeling the awful burden of not being able to do what you wish,—because you must pay away what you earn. No, we know that is torture. It's only a sweet dream to imagine that we can afford £60–£65 a year for our rent, and live like a little married pair, and me to take a studio in addition. My darling, we can't, and I have not the courage to face the prospect again. No, our experiences in the past have absolutely robbed me of my courage in that respect. When I am really faced with the practical prospect I draw back and shiver. Do you remember as vividly as I do ALL those houses, ALL those flats, ALL those rooms we have taken and withdrawn from. My valiant little warrior, have you forgotten the horrors? In their time they have broken me and I must live from week to week and not feel bound. Let us try and think of some other solution.

Isn't there one? Do help me. Whenever I try and talk this all over with you my positive horror of hurting you always prevents me from really speaking my mind. My one overwhelming feeling is that we both must be free to write this year, and that even our full life together must mark time for that. I'd far rather sit in a furnished room in an hotel and work than have a lovely flat and feel that the strain of money was crippling us again. Time is passing, and we cannot afford to waste another year. Do not be impatient with me. I hate to write all this.

You know I love you.

Tig

I found the work at the War Office very exacting. It consisted in reading mountains of German newspapers and writing a political report upon them. Since my slender German was very rusty I had, for some months, to work to all hours in order to keep up with my task. I must have been a very dull companion. After making a vain attempt to find a comfortable flat (for I was now, for the first time in my life in receipt of a regular salary) in the spring of 1917, Katherine and I agreed to live apart. The rumour went around that Mansfield and Murry had separated. It was nothing of the kind. We took rooms as near as we could get them to one another—Katherine a little studio at 141a Church

Street, Chelsea, I two rooms at 47 Redcliffe Road. I went every day to Katherine's studio for my supper on leaving the War Office, and then went on to Redcliffe Road to work. It seemed the best arrangement while I was living my half-life in the War Office. The first of the two following letters I found in my rooms when I returned from a weekend. The date of the second is doubtful; but I think it belongs to this period.

Saturday Night,
May 19th, 1917

My darling,

Do not imagine, because you find these lines in your private book that I have been trespassing. You know I have not—and where else shall I leave a love-letter? For I long to write you a love-letter tonight. You are all about me—I seem to breathe you, hear you, feel you in me and of me. What am I doing here? You are away. I have seen you in the train, at the station, driving up, sitting in the lamplight, talking, greeting people, washing your hands . . . . And I am here—in your tent—sitting at your table. There are some wall-flower petals on the table and a dead match, a blue pencil and a *Magdeburgische Zeitung*. I am just as much at home as they.

When dusk came, flowing up the silent garden, lapping against the blind windows, my first and last terror started up. I was making some coffee in the kitchen. It was so violent, so dreadful I put down the coffee pot—and simply ran away—*ran ran* out of the studio and up the street with my bag under one arm and a block of writing paper and a pen under the other. I felt that if I could get here and find Mrs F. in, I should be 'safe'. I found her and I lighted your gas, wound up your clock, drew your curtains and embraced your black overcoat before I sat down, frightened no longer. Do not be angry with me, Bogey. *Ça a été plus fort que moi* . . . . That is why I am here.

When you came to tea this afternoon you took a brioche, broke it in half and padded the inside doughy bit with two fingers. You always do that with a bun or a roll or a piece of bread. It is your way—your head a little on one side the while.

When you opened your suit-case, I saw your old Feltie and a French book and a comb all higgledy-piggledy. 'Tig, I've only got 3 handkerchiefs.' Why should that memory be so sweet to me?

Last night, before you got into bed, you stood, quite naked, bending forward a little, talking. It was only for an instant. I saw you—I loved

92

you so, loved your body with such tenderness. Ah, my dear! And I am not thinking now of 'passion'. No, of that other thing that makes me feel that every inch of you is so precious to me—your soft shoulders—your creamy warm skin, your ears cold like shells are cold—your long legs and your feet that I love to clasp with my feet—the feeling of your belly—and your thin young back. Just below that bone that sticks out at the back of your neck you have a little mole. It is partly because we are young that I feel this tenderness. I love your youth. I could not bear that it should be touched even by a cold wind if I were the Lord.

We two, you know, have everything before us, and we shall do very great things. I have perfect faith in us, and so perfect is my love for you that I am, as it were, still, silent to my very soul. I want nobody but you for my lover and my friend and to nobody but you shall I be faithful.

I am yours for ever

Tig

My dear Jack,   (1917)

I got up at that moment to re-read your article on Léon Bloy. The memory of it suddenly *rose* in my mind like a scent. I don't like it. I don't see its use at all, even artistically. It's a *Signature* style of writing and its *appeal* is in some obscure way to me—mind me: I suppose only to me—indecent. I feel that you are going to uncover yourself and quiver. Sometimes when you write you seem to abase yourself like Dostoevsky did. It's *perfectly* natural to you, I know, but oh, my God, don't do it. It's just the same when you say, talking to Fergusson and me: 'If I am not killed—if *they don't kill* me.' I always laugh at you then because I am ashamed that you should speak so.

What is it? Is it your desire to torture yourself or to pity yourself or something far subtler? I only know that it's tremendously important because it's your way of damnation.

I feel (forgive fanciful me!) that when certain winds blow across your soul they bring the smell from that dark pit and the uneasy sound from those hollow caverns, and you long to lean over the dark swinging danger and just not fall in—but letting us all see meanwhile how low you lean.

Even your style of writing changes then—little short sentences—a hand lifted above the waves—the toss of a curly head above the swirling tumble.

It's a terrible thing to be alone. Yes, it is—it is. But don't lower your mask until you have another mask prepared beneath—as terrible as you like—but a mask.

K.M.

Forgive me for not telling you frankly when you read it to me what I felt. I was wrong.

While living in the studio Katherine re-wrote 'Prelude'. Up to this time it had been called 'The Aloe', and had been conceived as the introductory chapters of a novel. Now Katherine decided to make it independent and submitted it to a drastic revision. My contribution was the new title.

Although it had at least this admirable consequence, I think our separation during the spring and summer of 1917 was a mistake. When we lived together, we did at least keep an eye on each other's health. Now we both neglected it. In October 1917 I fell ill. The doctor said I was threatened with tuberculosis and I was sent away from the War Office on two months' sick leave into the country. Lady Ottoline Morrell generously took me in at Garsington. Katherine was to visit me at the weekends. It was, I think, on the third of her weekend visits that she caught a serious chill. It was a bitterly cold night and when she got out of the high dog-cart in which she was driven from the station, she said she felt frozen. For the time she made light of it. She stayed in bed, however, all next day, during which we talked of our plans for the immediate future. She had decided, she said, that we must not live apart any longer. She had got all she needed out of her life in the studio, and she was going to try to get rooms in the same house as me, in the Redcliffe Road. After settling this, she returned to London.

A day or two after she wrote that she had had to call in the doctor. It was an attack of pleurisy. Rather worried, but not unduly alarmed, I went off to London to see her. The next letter was written on the following day.

Sunday,

Dearest,   (November 4, 1917)

It was not until you had gone yesterday that I realized what a great wind was blowing. I hope you kept tight hold of the strap of the railway carriage and were not wafted in and out of window on your way. . . . What strange first moments those are when the train has gone and the one who remains walks backward, as it were—into *the same city?* . . . They must be remembered. I must 'register' them.

Your telegram for which I waited about 365 hours, heart-beats and sighs, didn't—after one blissful second—perfectly satisfy me after all. Was it quite understood between us that you were not on any account to write 'first chop' just to 'comfort' me? No, now I have begun waiting for your letter. So do not forget to post it, my precious, beloved boy.

I am thankful that you are away from those cursed rooms. If you knew how I hate them, how I feel the very soles of my feet burning up the cocoanut matting on the stairs! As to that bedroom, with that green gaunt bed[1] so infernally high out of water—the dog howling outside the window and the linen hanging below in the yard—it always terrified me.

By the way, isn't *Furnished Rooms* a good title for a story which plays in the Redcliffe Road? I can't resist it. Come and look over my shoulder. The meeting on the dark stairs—you know, someone is coming down and someone is coming up. *Is* someone there? The 'fright', the pause—the unknown in each other glaring through the dark and then passing (which is almost too terrifying to be borne). Then the whole street. And for backcloth, the whole line of the street—and the dressmakers calling to the cat, the Chinamen, the dark gentlemen, the babies playing, the coal cart, the line of the sky above the houses, the little stone figure in one of the gardens who carries a stone tray on his head, which in summer is filled with flowers and in winter is heaped with snow, the lamenting pianos, and all those faces hiding behind the windows—and the *one* who is always on the watch. I see the heroine very small, like a child, with high-heeled boots and a tiny muff of *false* astrachan, and then the restless despairing hero for whom 'all is over'. She cannot understand what is the matter with him. Does she ever know? And what happens?

It is the extreme coldness of my room and the brown paper wagging over the sooty fireplace which gives me such a *veine*. Nothing will go up the chimney while this tempest lasts. And I begin to feel 'the blighted Mongol' stir and clamour in me.

It was a good thing that you did not step next door with me last night. Heavens above—a party! M. 'Bourrelet', Mrs Bustle, Major Jardine, Miss Francis etc. etc. etc. And 'Thank you so much!' and 'Should we play German music during the war?' and 'Do you ever get

[1] An old-fashioned wooden bedstead which we had bought for one shilling at a sale in Cornwall, and painted green.

anonymous letters?' and 'Will it, can it last another year?' M. Bourrelet's voice was true *bourrelet*. Instead of stopping a hole to keep the wind away it let the wind in. I was very unhappy and felt a strange, unreasonable desire to pretend to be a German and cry 'Wunderbar!' after the French songs. There was a boiled fowl for dinner and such great tumblers of cold water that I more than suspected a goldfish of flicking through mine. But Heron[1] pulled me through.

12 o'clock. I must go and make myself something hot. L.M. is still in bed—dreaming of Webb,[2] I expect, and saying that she never, never could be kissed on the mouth but did not mind the cheek.

Do not forget to take care of yourself—to go slow—to drift—to eat —to sleep—and to keep warm. Do not forget how I love you, and write me more than one line.

I am going to turn into a female Balzac, this week—house-hunt by day and write by night.

Goodbye for now, my soul.

Tig

Thursday,

Cher et charmant jeune homme,   (December 13, 1917)

You must not be so agitato, though indeed I well understand the state of mind. But you can't afford to feel in the least shattered. Take a long breath and think of the sea at full tide and a little boat riding in ever so slowly—to a little bay with white sand and wild cherries growing nearly down to the water. No, that's a silly recipe. It don't calm me. *Au contraire*, down I run to the water's edge with my heart beating like a drum.

Your song is very lovely indeed—exceedingly lovely.[3] So wild and shy and ardent, and the measure of it beautifully fitting. One line brings me up sharp:

White is her hair

I don't like that a bit. I know that it is not your meaning and I know I am an upstart, but '*unbind*' or 'bind up' or 'unbraid' all seem to me 'easier'. And as light hands are tending her, I think one of these wouldn't be out of place. I (1) simply don't feel her hair was ever white—it does

[1] This is the first mention in the letters of The Heron (or Heron Farm) which was the dream house we planned for ourselves after the war.
[2] The foreman at the munitions factory where L.M. worked.
[3] In *Cinnamon and Angelica*.

96

away with the ageless beauty idea (2) I feel a little crack where this line joins the others; it's not really part of them. I may be quite insolently wrong. I'd *bracket* the line if that was a help. What do you feel?

H.L. has[1] not been near again, has not mentioned Christmas. If she don't, I shall stay here, and you there. For I want to begin moving as soon as I can. I wrote to Fraülein Palmer last night about Mrs J's flat, which I've seen and like enough to take. It suits me, and then you can dine with me every night and go up and work after—and I am on the spot if you want me. We mustn't start houses or big flats. Beaufort Mansions has nothing under £80 and then only ground floor. We should be bound to live differently and spend more. This is best, for then we *are* so free to fly.

Johnny[2] came yesterday. He was so very particularly nice, measuring his drawings with a little compass and saying 'Yes, it looks pretty good to me.' Have you ever heard him refer to a person's state of health as 'one foot in the grave and the other on a banana skin'? Oh, that does make me laugh so. Please *do* give his address to Lord H.[3] I made sure I said so, and I have a feeling that he was immensely cheered by the idea. H.L. says she'd like a portrait. I told him yesterday. Of course, he said *No*. (Burn this letter. Burn it to bits, please.) The fact that you had put on 2 lbs was 'as it should be'. 'That's what's wanted.'

I loved the little drawing. Don't you think that you and I draw very well? Or is it just my fancy? I think we both have a real talent. But then I always think I can do everything, don't I?

The doctor is coming today. I have felt such a fraud—dancing about and eating every leaf and blade within sight. He'll put me in the army, I should think. However, I will keep a page clear to tell you how he turns up his eyes and admires me.

I am still feeling *prestissimo*. In fact, I can't sleep for a nut. I lie in a kind of *furious bliss,* and the room in the firelight looks like some encampment, with the stairs for a sort of *chemin de mouton*.

Ma Parker yesterday went to my heart. She said suddenly: 'Oh, Miss, you do make the work go easy!' What could be a sweeter compliment? It's one I could pay to you and J.D.F. but nobody else alive.

L.M. is simply loathing me. Here I am, supposed to be ill and bristling at every point with independence, and *hard* where I should be *soft,* and

---

[1] Her Ladyship, that is Lady Ottoline Morrell.
[2] J. D. Fergusson; but the quip was the late James Pryde's.
[3] Lord Henry Bentinck.

snorting when she says: 'I woke up this morning feeling a little blue and heartsick'. . . .'Ah, Putney!' I cried and knew I was horrid—but she exasperates me *trop*.

Goodbye for just now. I shall come back later.

———

That man has just been—the doctor—and thumped away. He says I must lie very low for a week. I have taken it beautifully in time and *all is well*. He is so fearfully nice *and* kind *and* has read Tolstoi. What a pearl to find in these oceans of sillies! I feel an atom bit dashed, I confess.

Knock! Now I really *am* dashed. Two loathsome females have come to look over the studio FROM MISS WRIGHT. Is that legal? I thought only 6 weeks beforehand. I'm jiggered! They made my floor filthy— said it was a quaint little place!! but not big enough for *real* furniture.

Oh, Hell! How I loathe these English!

Courage. Keep calm, Wig. It ain't so bad, but I feel a snip furious, I must allow.

It's all right. I'm angry, but not in the you-and-me country. There all is radiant. If I shut my eyes, will the train carry me away? No. So keep them open and try to be sensible. But it was a push in the face, I must say.

Let me end on a clear note—a real note. *Con amore*. My darling boy,

I am

Wig

Friday,

My darling boy,   (December 14, 1917)

My temper is serene again. I am so sorry that I let fly yesterday, but it did and *does* seem to me a bit steep *de la part de* Miss Wright. I have a lot of 'things' to say . . . . Miss Palmer came here last evening. I have taken that flat for a year for 11/- a week. She is having it colour-washed, cleaned, swept, painted where necessary. Not badsome. She was very nice and decent. *Je suis très contente*. I don't know just when I shall move my bits of things, for I want to have the floors and curtings done, and the kitchen-dresser painted etc. before I do. However, it is amicably arranged. I like the place. I feel so free there . . . I have *adored* this cubby hole, and that is a fact. I'm not ungrateful to it, even now, but it is plain to see that it is over.

About the South of France—please don't mention it, Betsy. I just *couldn't*. I am not in the least seriously ill. It would be a pure joke to pretend I was, and I am a little lion as you know most times. The South of France must *joliment attendre*.

But this is exceedingly important. Don't you DARE come back here until you have to. You'd undo all the good you've done and worry me to death. I should have to spend all my time collecting food for the Xmas season and so on, and where you are all is so simple. *Oh, my love, please be reasonable for just this one Xmas.* P'raps I'll come down *or* I shall stay here, but this idea that you should post up simply horrifies me. I implore you, most seriously, to be wise about this. When I think of your coal, housekeeping during the holidays, shops shut, etc. etc. I feel quite hysterical. I should be tortured. I, of course, here have got coal. L.M. and Chaddie and Belle[1] have stuffed this place with food for me. I eat like a warrior, and drink pints of milk a day. But if I have to feel that you are neglecting yourself in your rooms, I shan't bite another crust and I'll throw the milk down the drain, my temper will be vile. Bogey, stop torturing me *at once,* or I'll tell.

I feel much better today except for this worrying idea. In fact, I feel simply dandy. I ate nearly ½ lb of steak last night and I've got 9 new laid eggs, 1 lb butter, dates, filletted haddock, cream etc. etc. in the larder. I shall be as fat as butter and as brown as a Maori, if only you will behave. But of course you will—darling.

× × × ×
× × × ×

I have an idea that your hair will never grow until you take it to New Zealand. Then it will sprout up and wave in the breedge like a little fern-tree—all one lovely crinkle. I feel that if Mother were only to pat it with her tiny white hands and frown at it, there would be no holding it. I hope that is true.

What a nice letter from Milne! He is a rare nice boy. He must come and make a long stay with us when Sullivan is there too. There is something *shy* and *loving* in this letter which endears him to me—and he is 'serious'. Thank you for letting me see it.

I send you a kind of cabbage from Anne—bless her!

I did not do any work yesterday. That was another reason why I felt jumpy. But today I am going it and shall have to make an effort to be nice to Brettushka. H.L. hasn't been here again. I wonder what has happened to her? She seems to have quite disappeared.

[1] Katherine's aunt.

99

It's a nice day here. Very quiet and warm. Even the milkman crying milk seems to me like a bird trying its note—a funny sort of big bird, you know—a bird penguinian. The clock ticks on tiptoe and the yellow curtains wave gently. I love such a day. It's such a rest—not having been outside for these days. I love to be out of the streets and buses—out of the nudging crowds. Oh, I must work. The very shadows are my friends. Don't forget to weigh yourself again when the week is up, and if you are not heavier you must melt a horseshoe in your next glass of milk so as not to disappoint me.

Dearest of all, I am your loving, cautious playfellow

Wig

Saturday,

Dearest Boy,   (December 15, 1917)

I am spending an idle day in bed. Ribni sits by me and I have made myself a sort of Pirate cap which I think, hope, nay am sure, will startle the doctor's young eye. It's all sunny outside and I am bored. After he is gone I've a mind to throw away my wings and go off for a frisk. But I won't. I am almost terrifically well again. H.L. has asked me for Xmas, so I'll come—and if you don't get your usual paralysis down there and I my usual feeling that I ought to be in the little room, we may have some fun. —— came in last night and wanted to whisk me off to her house for a few days. Oh, what a dread prospeck! The amount of whisking that people want to do with me and a-wrapping of me up in bundils is quite terrifying. I said I was being superbly looked after by old Mrs HARRIS who was a very good cook—a woman I had known for years and couldn't be more comfortable with. Oh! what fun! Do you know who I meant? Sairey Gamp's friend. I laughed so much inside that I thought she would hear the laughs running up and down in me. Even to write it makes me laugh again, and Ribni stuffed the ends of his neck-tie in his mouth, stood on his head and waved his feet when I told him.

I wish I had more time to work though. You see L.M. is nearly always here at the weekends, and Chaddie is coming this afternoon and Johnny this evening, and then there is such a fearful lot to eat in this house that it does take time to get through with it. L.M. is so hopeless though well-intentioned. One has to issue directions all the time. A plague on it!

I wish you and I were away. Oh, I long to be away—just we two. Weren't we happy in our Pauline? Do you remember? And do you remember the drawing you made on a big stone? Your feet were bare and very pink from standing on that flat rock. Oh, Jag, we must *go off*— you and I—again. I am so frightened that the idea rather fills you with horror, and that you cling to this little island. Tell me the truth, and don't spare me. There is a fragrance on the wings of your play which fills me with childish longings. It sounds to me a heavenly play.

Now I must call you to account. If you don't like the other Aloe bud I sent you,[1] or if you can't read the (I confess) awful writing—well, tell me. I won't be offended. That I promise you. But majestic silence or 'Wait a bit' I can't stand. I don't mind what you say, but *do say something*. Look at me. I criticize you like a shot and never keep you waiting. You know I am *most impatient*. And I almost expected a peal of bells at least.

I'll finish this letter after that man has been.

Later. Really, I am nearly in love with this old doctor. He *is* such a find. No, that's not my feeling. What I do feel is that he's the sort of man we might all be talking to in a café in the good Paris days. I don't have to alter my vocabulary or pretend a bit—and, ah! you know how rare *that* is. He is coming again on Monday. So you can see how careful he is. He says I am much better and look much better and I've no temperature at all—but I must still go a bit slow and not go out. I think he thought I was a pirate. Yoho! Yoho! So don't you worry a bit. I am almost 2 lively and gay.

Oh, here is L.M. who wants to post this letter, my precious darling. Excuse the funny writing but the bed is all hills and valleys.

I am always your own

Wig

Monday,

My dear precious one,   (December 17, 1917)

I am writing fully tomorrow. This is just a note to say what my wire said—that all is well. Yes, I sent you the Aloe bud on Tuesday for a surprise, and where it is the devil only knows. I don't. But for some extraordinary reason I can't take in the fact that it is lost—or even going to be lost. So don't you worry, either.

---

[1] Another part of *The Aloe,* of which *Prelude* was part. I have a hazy memory that it was eventually recovered and formed the opening pages of *At the Bay.*

Your poem—ah, your poem is simply wonderful. Yes, it is really great. Don't hesitate to believe that. It is simply thrillingly good.

My own, I can't come for Xmas. That is what I want to write about fully tomorrow. The doctor says I would be so very mad to travel— even in a car from this door to that—and won't hear of it. So let my other letter stand and *believe me* that to know that you are there and fed and warm is the greatest possible relief for me and just makes me well. If you came here, I should worry my life out. The doctor is awfully nice and sensible. He says I am better. I *am* indeed, but I must be very careful of this wing.[1] Belle saw him today and she asked if she could take me to her place, *de luxe*—fur coats and motor-cars from here to there, but he still said 'No! So you see!

Rib and I must hang up our stockings. Half the world is keeping me supplied with eggs and fish and everything—and crowds are looking after me. It is absurd. You just stay where you are, Bogey, and believe that your Wig is doing every single thing. These silly people have kept me from writing to you today. That is why this is such a breathless rush. Don't worry, my precious own. Take care of yourself. We must turn into giants—this is preposterous. I will write freely, fully, tomor- row—a huge big letter.

But none could carry more love than this one to you from

Wig

I will write Ottoline and everybody, too, tomorrow. Oh, my Treasure, you just be all jokey and when we meet again we shall crinkle up our eyes and laugh at all this silly affair. I am writing this in a sort of *telegraphic* way that you and that I understand—a sort of signal to say Yes, the flag is flying. So full report tomorrow, Sir. But I want to write miles about *Angelica*.

Friday,

(? December 21, 1917)

How shall I begin this letter? All the love-names in the world are not enough. But you are to feel, as you read these lines, as though I held your head in my hands and were looking at you—a long, long look, before we kiss each other. It is absurd to say that I love you *more*. How could that be? And yet I do love you more. My precious one, love like ours hath no equal on this earth. I could not love you more; I always love you more . . . .

[1] Katherine's name for her lung.

A letter from you by this afternoon's post. I am only praying that you have got one from me by now. Curse these posts; they are hopelessly disorganised and we must expect them to be more so at Xmas.

'Something' in your letter worries me. You say you *dread* this Christmas at G. so much. Did I over-urge you to stay? And yet, if you come up, how shall we go down together again? Can you stick it without hating it too much? Can you swim over its head? Please tell me this. I cannot bear to think that I have begged you to endure something intolerable. I think it is always understood that you keep aloof.

And now, darling, about your having paid this rent in advance for me. I shall have to pay you back by degrees. You know I will. When I am well I shall save *by pennies* simply, but save I mean to, and you shall have it. You know my feelings about money. It is appalling that I should cost so much just now, but believe me I will repay you in the not too long run, my own.

I shudder at the thought of your journey. God! what a terror it must have been! Was there no fire in the waiting-room? Or couldn't you have sat in the tea-room? I suppose you were on the *qui vive* for the train and didn't dare to. I should have liked the country lad better if he had carried his suit-case quite alone; your rucksack was quite enough. But the walk must have been, in its way, wonderful.

Mrs —— brought me her boy for tea yesterday. She left him with me. I think it is the first time I have spent an hour alone with a thoroughly modern enlightened child. I found out that the method practised on him had been to treat him exactly like a grown-up *on a small scale*. You can imagine the result. I sat and gaped at him. He had brought with him a dairy farm from Heal's—exactly like a real dairy farm *on a small scale*. And of course he did not play with it because he can't play. He ran it as a little going concern and I bet he made it pay. God forbid that any child of mine should fall into modern ways. I was thankful when his mother took him away.

I have spent nearly the whole day lying on the sofa fast asleep. I can't think *why*—but I just got up, wrapped in a rug, lay down again and would be sleeping still if the boy from André, Sleigh & Angus hadn't woke me up. They charged me 10/10 for those two little blocks.[1] I was staggered. I had thought they would have been 1/6 each.

It is cold and quiet here, but I feel so much better for that long sleep.

[1] The blocks of two designs by J. D. Fergusson on the cover of certain copies of the original edition of *Prelude*.

Pleurisy has just the same effect as fever. It tires you out almost without your knowing it.

Are you walking again in your enchanted country? That is what I long to hear.

I am like you in your dislike of people. But the mania is more advanced. I think we shall live, a long time, one day, absolutely alone. That's my idea of Heaven.

I am yours for ever

Wig

Dearest,   (December, 1917)

Now that you have been here, everything seems quite simple and straightforward again. You were, in every possible and impossible way, *too* lovely and never was I happier than then. I do only hope that you were not over-tired. Weigh yourself again and don't forget to let me know the result.

I really ought to be seeing about my passport straightaway, oughtn't I? Because it takes ages. I will ask the doctor for the certificate on Sunday, and then you tell me what to do. You can find out from Brett, can't you? I feel hopelessly vague about what must be done, but I *do* think it ought to be put in hand without delay. Chaddie came yesterday. I did up your present in white paper and tied it with violet-heart-stamped ribbon. She was enchanted. She brought me an IMMENSE apple-green padded silk dressing-gown from Belle—big enough for at least three Wigs great with child. The ugliness and inappropriateness of it was a severe blow. I shall have to change it somehow. And Johnny spent the evening. He was very depressed and subdued. We talked about places. He says you *can* get little houses down there at about £10 or £15 a year.

I feel so stupid and bald in the head and lie here wrapped up, falling asleep over *Dombey & Son*. That man strapped me up so tight yesterday that, the wind out of my sail, I am too becalmed for words.

My love, if only you will get better still, stronger and fatter! Go on with the treatment, won't you? I would kiss H.L's hand for all that she has done for you. What rare luck it was that you went there!

This letter is so feeble and dull that I must put the cosy on it. Forgive me, dear love. I am longing to hear from you. And, Ah! my dear Bogey, I am for ever

Your Wig

Dearest and Wonderful Boy,   (December, 1917)

Your letter with the poem came today. I simply pray that you have got some of mine by now. The poem is extraordinarily good. It has such ease. Something has changed so in your work. You do seem now so to 'begin and somewhat loudly *sweep* the string'. Yes, that is just, just what I mean.

Every new thing that you send me seems to be surer to be more absolutely *poetry*. Ah, God! why can't you simply give yourself up to your power *now*? Why must your bird be still chained to your wrist when it is so ready for flight? But, my soul, it won't be for long, and nothing can stop you. I feel, with quite a new, 'special' feeling you are a *poet*. You have, finally and for ever, taken me up to the top of a hill and shown me your kingdom, not wreathed in mist, not with the promise of towers and fountains, but all touched with that strange, infallible light of dawn . . . .

What these few weeks have meant to you, and how they have taught me far more about you! My heart could fly out of my body with pride of you. The world is only the water that flows under the bridge. It may rush and roar, but we are two shining children leaning over that arc of light and looking down undaunted.

I love you.

It is not so cold today, and I feel a great deal better. I will tell you what the medicine-man says tomorrow. I am sure he will be surprised. I feel quite different—rather quiet still—rather like a doll that has been mended, but put on a high shelf to dry before it can be played with again.

God above! How I do love you!!

I can't send any presents this year, Bogey. Does it matter? I can't get out to buy them, and I don't trust L.M. I will try and write a sketch for Brett and perhaps for H.L. and p'raps for you. Anne, with rare sense, has sent me a big FAT FOWL.

Johnny is going away for Christmas to Fisher White. That is a relief off my mind for then I know he will be fed. Sullivan comes tomorrow. I think J.D.F. too, and I pray *not* ——. For though I like her so much, oh, why don't she talk more quietly, and why does she roar?

Here is L.M. waiting for this letter AND interrupting me as I write. A fool today beyond words. But she has brought me a flower or two. That is a comfort.

Here she is. I am quarrelling with her, too. And she keeps saying it is because she is always sleepy. One in the eye for me.

Lovely one—dearest

I am your own

Wig

NO L.M. ON ANY FARM.

Sunday,

My dearest,   (December 23, 1917)

Here is the certificate which the doctor has just given me. Is it alright? He says that left lung of mine that had the *loud deafening* creak in it is 'no end better' but there is a SPOT in my right lung which 'confirms him in his opinion that it is absolutely imperative that I go out of this country and keep out of it all through the future winters.' It is *evidemment* rather a bad 'un of its kind—at any rate it would become so if I did not fly.

About Oxfordshire. He says it is far wiser that I stay here until I am well enough to travel and don't attempt the country; that was even when I explained about the hot pipes and glasses of hot milk on trays. The programme seems to be (if I don't want to do this mysterious crocking up) to sit tight, pack and make for the sun. See? What do you think?

Although I am still snapping up fishes like a sea-lion, steaks like a land-lion, milk like a snake (or is that only a 'tale'?) and eggs, honey, creamb, butter and nourishing trimmings galore, they seem to go to a sort of Dead Letter Office. However he has given me a Tonic today which will put that right. Of course, I feel that I've only to get into the sun and I'll simply burst into leaf and flower again. It is this old place that does it for me, and I keep sweeping out *our* house with a branch of acacia tree, picking a rose to tuck into my bodice, and then hurrying off just in time to catch the train which tumbles you, my treasure, in my arms. And I keep going into that room and putting my arm round you and saying: 'Look! there's that diamond of light in the shutter!'

I know quite well, I appreciate absolutely, that you must be faithful to England. Hell it would be to know you were away and felt its call. But, all the same, you will have to have two homes, and we shall have to have all our babies in pairs so that we possess a complete 'set' in either place.

Je t'aime! Je t'aime!!

This man is coming again on Thursday to unstrap me and overhaul me. In the meantime I think that the passport affair should be got under way and the Hôtel Beau Rivage written to—to make sure—don't you? I thought: Tell them Madame will be there for two months at least, so she will require *une belle chambre avec vue sur la mer et beaucoup de soleil*, and to reply immediately. You, who write so much better than I, had better send that letter, and don't forget your *name problem*. But don't mention LUNGS, or they will take fright: you know the French. They'd imagine I had come there to gallop away.

Should I forward you my old passport? Tell me. I shall send *this,* and if you need it, *that, registré* of course. I was so glad of your wire this morning. It put a flower on my Sunday.

These my present letters are really such self-engrossed dull matron(?) affairs that I groan to think about them after they are gone. But you see I feel that life has changed so, and it has all happened so quickly— all my plans are altered, all my future is touched by this—all *our* future rather. It's like suddenly mounting a very fresh, very unfamiliar horse —a *queer, queer* feeling.

As to 'working', I can't just now. However, I have heaps to read and to think over against the time when I shall get down to it again. What is so difficult to realize is that this has happened to *me* and not to *you* . . . that seems just nonsense. And, oh dear! what a serious talk I shall have to have with you before I do go, about taking care of *yourself*. It's almost funny in a way, isn't it? One thing—which must be your *idée mère*—is: Don't you worry about me. Keep happy! We can afford to be happier than anybody, you and I. And just think how I shall write. I wish we could have been married before I go—but it don't really signify. (*Burn my letters.*) You are so grown into my heart that we are like the two wings of one bird.

Goodbye for now, my own. Have you weighed yourself again? I am sorry to plague you, but you know how one feels. And don't dare not to tell me the ABSOLUTE TRUTH.

I am ever your own

Wig

P.S. If the certificate is not right, I think you had better write to Ainger direct. Tell me if you do. I notice, for one thing, he has left the date out.

Ribni says 'Happy Christmas', and he's going to take off his kimono and hang up one of the sleeves tomorrow. And he says we've got two oranges and 2 tangerines and nuts and flowers in this place—see? *And* you are not to forget him, or he may creep into your pocket next time you're here and give you an awful fright. *And* 'Tell that old Mousey that I like him.'

Christmas Eve, 8 p.m.,

My precious love, (December 24, 1917)

A knock at the door and the postman hands me your Sunday letter and a card saying my G's are no go. If all my letters lie in Carsington . . . . For I have written to you every day. AMEN. And L.M. does not eat them (strange!) and I am sure she posts them in live letter-boxes. It really is *simply* awful. But perhaps by now they do lie in your bosom I can't bear the thought of strangers looking under their wings. *Aren't* my G's all right, really? However, I'll never make another. Boge: 'Hum! Ha!'

Fergusson is away just now, and when he comes back he has some special work to do on a big picture that will keep him busy pretty indefinitely. He is thinking of going up to *Leeds* after the New Year. He is *porte close* absolutely. Please tell H.L. *Who* sent me the most exquisite pink silk eiderdown—you know the sort of padded silk quilt *qui fond sur le cœur*. It's perfect for now and ever. I can also see myself wrapping up future generations in it and hurling them in a pink parcel to you in the meadow below. (But 'not a word to the wife' about that!) It is, at any rate, a staggering gift. I thought she'd send me some mittens.

You are an appalling bad boy to send me a jacket. Stop it! It has not come yet, and I know it will be perfect, but you MUST not buy me anything more or pay any more for me. Save, my lovely one, please! You have simply covered me with presents lately, and I've given you nothing. L.M. gave me a petticoat—rather like raspberries and currants. Very nice. I let her. It must have cost a lot, I suppose,—but perhaps it didn't.

The *food* in this studio makes me reel. I ought to get heavy again if I only bite off a corner of it, but at present if you charcoaled my bones I should be a very useful anatomical specimen.

At 10 o'clock this morning, just as L.M. went out, the lad Sullivan turned up. He was playing the wag, I think, for he said he had not got a holiday, but might he spend part of the day with me? All this *dead* serious, as though there were already a posse of police in the front garden. He was awfully nice to me and made up the fire and all that and went out for a bottle of wine . . . . At four o'clock (I sent him away for lunch) he went back to Watergate House. He really is immensely anxious to join us, and I rather think he will—that we will let him. But I was so tired after he had gone that I fell asleep.

I feel much better tonight. But a funny feature about this sort of illness is one's temper. I get so irritable, so nervous that I want to *scream*, and if many people start talking I just lose my puff and feel my blood getting black. Perhaps that's just because one is a bit weak. I only tell it to you to put in your symptom book.[1]

Julian has sent me such a dear little Kalendar Buch. I shall write her and H.L. I wish you could have eaten half my steak and stout tonight. That *is* the thing.

One is very peaceful here—and very independent. You know I feel that I have got written on my chest: PLEASE DO NOT FUSS! If the doctor says I may begin to go out at the end of this week, what shall we do? Do you feel inclined to come up for another day? That's so expensive unless we think it necessary. And do tell me all that must be done about my passport and *when I may expect to get it through*. It ought not to be difficult. I posted you a registered packet today.

I am a brute about L.M. who is really being amazingly good and kind.

Love, these are only dull jottings. Read them as such. Ribni is all bound up with gold ribbons, and he has got the postman's Christmas box ready, and the dairy boy's.

I love you. I am your woman.

Tig

[1] This irritability became very marked, particularly in Katherine's relations with L.M. But I am quite certain that I never had any first-hand experience of it. The nearest I came to doing so must have been the incident described in Katherine's *Journal* for September 20, 1918.

'My fits of temper are really terrifying. I had one this (Sunday) morning and tore a page out of the book I was reading and absolutely lost my head. Very significant. When it was over J. came in and stared. "What is the matter? What have you done? Why, you look *all dark*." He drew back the curtains and called it an effect of light, but when I came into my studio to dress I saw it was not that. I was a deep earthy colour, *with pinched eyes*.'

My ignorance of these fits of irritation, caused by her disease, made it peculiarly difficult for me to understand what was happening when Katherine described them in her letters. For lack of first-hand knowledge I could not easily comprehend the seriousness of a condition so alien from my experience of Katherine. In consequence I failed to understand her desperation at the end of a prolonged period of irritation, notably in December 1919 and January 1920.

Dearest,

This letter could not be registered yesterday, so I am adding a word. Also, as you see, I am sending you the passport. I do hope all this will not take too long. As I am going, I have a great longing to be ready—and I feel absolutely strong enough to travel. The spiritual fact *qu'on voyage vers le soleil* is such a staff!

Sullivan came last night. He was particularly nice. And he told me a story about you which is so *frightfully good*. Do you know it? Allan's remark about you? I'll not repeat it in case you do.

Sullivan and I talked mainly about music—Beethoven chiefly—and why these people fail in art. Then Sullivan left and J.D.F. and I had a long talk. Dearest, Bentinck went to see him, bought his *best* picture, and is going up to Leeds to see his others. Isn't that perfectly stunning of him? You can imagine Fergusson's quite extraordinary pleasure that this had happened 'and, between you and me, just at the right moment: It meant a great deal!' Of course, his pleasure was doubled because Lord Henry chose his best. That proved him the sort of buyer that he delighted in having. Fergusson wants to show you and me his work—all that he has got there. I have a sort of idea he is going to give you summat. If we can manage to get to the studio before I go, we must. But I wish you could get into touch with Lord Henry—*really* into touch.

No letter today yet—it will, I fondly hope, come later—and no parcil from H.L. I am writing this in bed, the bath is running. I had a devilish night and feel as though during the night I had slept in a furniture van. Also L.M. said, in the middle of *my* wakefulness and *her* sound sleep: 'It really was a delicious tapioca pudding. But I really do prefer elderly men. Funny, isn't it?' That gave me quite 'a turn'.

I have just seen Miss Wright about letting my place. I am going to have a board put up immediately.

L.M. is now doing the floor. My spirit faints. I must go.

Darling, I am

Wig

I was now well again, and returned to London for Katherine's last week before she left for France. Secretly, I was rather frightened by the strange and ironic turn events had taken. In coming to visit me who was supposed to be threatened with tuberculosis, Katherine had caught the chill. Now I was well, and she was the threatened one. It was a sinister turn, and I was uneasy. But Katherine was so confident that she would get well in the South of France that I suppressed my malaise. Indeed, she seemed very much better. On December 28 we went to Harvey Nichols' together to change the voluminous dressing gown, and she was happy and gay. It is impossible to say, but my feeling has always been that, if she had not undertaken this ill-starred journey, she might have recovered completely.

In the main the letters from January to April are self-explanatory. At the last minute the authorities refused L.M. permission to accompany Katherine to Bandol. That should have decided us against the venture; but it did not. Katherine's confidence was entire. She left London on January 7, 1918, and arrived in three days. Her still more appalling return journey took three weeks!

In the previous autumn, after six years' delay, Katherine's husband had divorced her. We planned to be married on the earliest possible day, April 17, 1918; and it was agreed between us that she would return for this purpose at the beginning of April.

The contrast between her suffering in Bandol and her happiness there two years before was tragic in its irony. Under its impulsion she wrote 'Je ne parle pas français' and 'Bliss'. The letters which culminate in that of February 3, 1918 are, I believe, of crucial importance to an understanding of her work.

Perhaps it needs to be stated that it was entirely beyond my power to go to her help. At this period of the war there was no possibility of my obtaining permission to leave the country. It is to be remembered also, in order to understand Katherine's financial situation, that the exchange at this time was 27 francs to the pound.

Paris: 5.30 p.m.,
My precious darling, Wednesday, (January 9, 1918)

I shall not be able to write you a 'proper' letter until I arrive in Bandol. It is so difficult to get calm, and I have spent an immense day rushing after my luggage and to Cook's (who wouldn't 'arrange' my affair for me) and to the P.L.M. However, it is all done now and I am in a café near the station with my *grande malle registrée*, my little 'uns at le consigne, writing to you before I go to that Duval where we went, to get some dinner before the train goes.

Everything on the whole has gone wonderfully. It's not a nice journey nowadays, and it was immensely complicated this time by the blizzard. We left Southampton at about 9 o'clock and did not arrive at Havre until after 10 next morning. We anchored for hours outside

Havre in a snow-storm and lay tossing and pitching and rolling. . . .
You won't believe me when I say that I enjoyed it. I did. For one thing
I had a splendid supper when I got on board—a *whack* of cold, lean beef
and pighells, bread, butter *ad lib.,* tea, and plenty of good bread. Then
I took a nip of brandy and went right to bed, in a little cabin, very clean
and warm, with an excellent stewardess in attendance. The upper berth
was a general's widow (more of her later)—except for her imitations
of a cat with a fish-bone in its throat I was divinely comfortable and
slept and woke, slept and woke, but did not move until we reached
Havre. Then I tumbled up on deck to find everything white with
snow. I shall tell you nothing in detail now, for I mean to write it all.
It was too wonderful to miss.

We had to spend the day in Havre. So I took a bedroom at a hotel,
had breakfast and washed and went to sleep until late lunch. The food
in France is simply wonderful. *Bread* that makes one hungry to look at,
butter, sugar, meat, 7 kinds of cheese for lunch and 7 hors d'oeuvres.
Then we started for Paris at 5 to arrive at 9.20. The carriage was packed,
*un*heated, with a broken window and the snow drifting in. This was
very vile. But a Red Cross old party took me in charge and rubbed me
and cosseted me and finally made me eat a dinner which cost 6 francs!
but saved me, as we did not arrive until 2 a.m.! Then a plunge into the
pitch dark and snow, as all the entrances to the *Terminus* were shut,
except the one in the street. God! how thankful I was that I had reserved a room. Crowds were turned away. But I staggered up a palatial
staircase, through ball rooms, reception rooms, *hollows* glittering with
chandeliers to a yellow and blue brocade bedroom which seemed to be
worth £50 to me. I slept like a top and got up early—*L'Heure! Liberté!
La Presse!*—saw about all my affairs. It is snowing hard. The streets are
all ice and water—and so slippery *qu'on marche comme un poulet malade.*

All the same I am unreasonably deeply happy. I thought I would be
disenchanted with France this time, but for the first time I seem to
recognise my love for it and to understand *why.* It is because, whatever
happens, I never feel *indifferent.* I feel that indifference is really foreign
to my nature and that to live in a state of it is to live in the only Hell I
really appreciate. There is, too, dispassionately speaking, a wonderful
spirit here—so much humour, life, gaiety, sorrow, one cannot see it all
and not think with amazement of the strange cement-like state of
England. Yes, they do feel the war, but with a difference. But this, too,
I must write about seriously.

My treasure, this is not a letter. It is a kind of intake of breath before I really begin to tell you all. Ah, how I love you here! The spring of my joy is that we belong to each other and that you and I are lovers and wedded to each other.

You are mine, and I am yours for ever. I can't 'get over' that. It simply fills my being with a kind of rich joy—which I know I shall *express* marvellously, marvellously for you and through you.

Ribni—our little John the Baptist—kiss him for me!

As for you, you are my own, and I am for ever yours.

Tig

Hôtel Beau Rivage, Bandol,

Friday (January 11, 1918)

This is one of the truthful letters we promised each other, my precious one.

My dearest Bogey,

My enthusiastic letter from Paris has been in my mind ever since. *And* mocked me. I took it to post; it was dark by then, piercing cold and so wet underfoot that one's feet felt like 2 walking toads. After a great deal of bother I got established in the train (no pillows to be had nowadays) and then the fun began. I liked my fellow-passengers, but God! how stiff one got and my feet hurt and the flat-iron[1] became hot enough to burn the buttoned back against which I leaned. There was no restaurant car on the train—no chance of getting anything hot—a blinding snow-storm until we reached Valence.

I must confess the country was exquisite at sunrise—exquisite—but we did not arrive at Marseilles till *one* o'clock. Good! As I got out a pimp getting *in* to hold a seat for some super-pimp gave me such a blow in the chest that it is blue today. I thought: 'This is Marseilles, *sans doute*.' Feeling very tired and hungry I carried my baggage 3 miles to the consigne, and finding that the train left for Bandol at 3.30 decided to have a snack at the buffet just outside—that place under a glass verandah. It was rather full, so I sat down opposite an elderly lady who eyed me so strangely that I asked if 'cette place est prise?' 'Non, Madame,' said she, insolent beyond everything, 'mais il y a d'autre tables, n'est-ce pas? Je préfère beaucoup que vous ne venez pas ici. D'abord, j'ai déja fini mon déjeuner, et c'est très dégôutant de vous voir

---

[1] Katherine's name for the burning sensation in her lung.

commencer car j'ai l'estomac délicat, et puis. . . .' And then she raised her eyebrows and left it at that. You can judge what I ate after that and what I thought.

At 1.30 I went to get my baggage registered, waited for one hour in a queue for my ticket and then was told I could not have one until my passport was viséd. I had that done, waited again, carried my luggage to the platform finally at 3 o'clock *juste*, and waited there in a crowd until four. Then a train came in at another platform, and the people swarmed in just like apes climbing into bushes, and I had just thrown my rugs into it when it was stated that it was only for *permissionaires* and did not stop before Toulon. Good again! I staggered out and got into *another* train on *another* platform, asked 3 people if it was the right one, who did not know and sat down in the corner, completely dished.

There were 8 Serbian officers in the compartment with me and their 2 dogs. Never shall I say another word against Serbians. They looked like Maiden's Dreams, excessively handsome and well cared for, graceful, young, dashing, with fine teeth and eyes. But that did not matter. What *did* was that after shunting for 2 hours, five yards forward, five back, there was a free fight at the station between a mob of soldiers and the civilians. The soldiers demanded the train—and that *les civils* should evacuate it. Not with good temper, but furious—very ugly—and VILE. They banged on the windows, wrenched open the doors and threw out the people and their luggage after them. They came to our carriage, swarmed in—told the officers they too must go, and one caught hold of me as though I were a sort of packet of rugs. I never said a word for I was far too tired and vague to care about anything except I was determined not to *cry*—but one of the officers then let out—threw out the soldiers— said I was his wife and had been travelling with him five days—and when the *chef militaire de la gare* came, said the same—threw *him* out— banged the door, took off their dogs' leads and held the door shut. The others then pressed against the connecting door between the carriages and there we remained in a state of siege until seven o'clock when the train started. You should have heard the squalling and banging. They pinned the curtains together and I hid behind them until we were under way. By this time it was pitch dark and I knew I should never find the station as a terrific mistral was blowing and you could not hear the stations cried—but as we came to each stop they pulled the window down and shouted in their curious clipped French to know which it was. Ah, but they were very nice chaps—splendid chaps—I'll not

114

forget them. We reached Bandol at 9. I felt that my *grande malle* was gone for ever, but I seized the other 2 and dashed across the line. I could not have walked but happily the boy from the Hotel des Bains was at the station and though he said 'qu'il n'était pas bon avec le patron', he brought me.

When I arrived the hall was rather cold and smoky. A strange woman came out, wiping her mouth with a serviette . . . . I realised in a flash that the hotel had changed hands. She said she had received *no* letter—but there were plenty of rooms—and proceeded to lead me to one. My own was taken. I chose finally the one next door which had 2 beds on the condition that she removed one. Also it was the cheapest, 12 francs a day! The others have had *de l'eau courante* put into them and cost 13! The big stoves were not lighted in the passages. . . . I asked for hot water and a hot water bottle, had some soup, wrapped up to the eyes, and simply fell into bed after finishing the brandy in my flask. For I felt that the whole affair wanted thoroughly sleeping over and not thinking about. . .

In the morning when I opened the persiennes it was so lovely outside, I stayed in bed till lunch. *Ma grande malle* really did turn up. Then I got up, and after lunch went into the town. The Meynets are gone for the present. The *tabac* woman did not know me and had no tobacco. Nobody remembered me at all. I bought writing things and a few bull's-eyes—about a penny for two, they were—and suddenly I met Ma'am Gamel. She, too, did not recognise me until I had explained who I was. Then she was very kind. 'Ah! Ah! Ah! Vous êtes beaucoup changée. Vous avez été *ben* malade, n'est-ce pas? Vous n'avez plus votre air de p'tite gosse, vous *sa*-avez!' I went with her to the shop which is just the same and saw the old mother who was most tender about you. I bought a tiny pot of cherry jam and came home—to find my room not yet done.

You can see, love, I am depressed. I feel faible still after ce voyage, but I shall get better and I shall arrange things here as soon as I have la force nécessaire. The place is, even to my blind eyes, as lovely as ever, glittering with light, with the deep hyacinth blue sea, the wonderful flashing palms and the mountains, violet in the shadow and jade-green in the sun. The mimosa outside my window is in bud. Don't worry about me. Having got over that journey and that Paris thaw, I shall never fall by the way; and when my room is ready, I shall *work*. That I do feel, and that is what matters, Bogey. I am not even very sad. It has been a bit of a bang, though, hasn't it? And I'll tell you exactly what I feel like. I feel like a fly who has been dropped into the milk-jug and fished out again, but is still too milky and drowned to start cleaning up yet. Letters will take a long time—perhaps 6 or 8 days—so do not worry if you do not hear.

And take care of yourself and *love me* as I *love you*. Ah, this is not the day to start writing about that, for my bosom begins to ache and my arms fly out to embrace you. I want you. I am lonely and fainting by the way, but only for now—you know.

Always your own woman
Tig

Saturday,
(January 12, 1918)

Bogey,

You are to write as often as you can at first—see? Because letters take so long, so long, *et je suis malade*. I have just got up and am sitting wrapped up in all my clothes and my woolly coat and your geranium jacket over and the Kashmir shawl over that and Ottoline's pink one round my legs and the rug folded on the floor. The fire is alight, but it will not burn unless I keep the iron shade right down!! The old, old story. It is bitterly cold, and a deep strange grey light over the sea and sky. I have got up because I *must* work and I can't in bed. If I am going to languish in Foreign Parts all alone, I must have a great deal of work done, or it will be no use. Please, Bogey, write me warm letters—*tellement il fait froid. . . .*

Ah, do let everything be lovely 'chez vous'; that would be the greatest joy I could have. That *you* are well and comfortable and that you think of me and work in the evenings.

You can't get any cigarettes here; nothing but cigars. There is a 'crise' in tobacco, too. This hotel is so quiet. There are only four uglies in it. I wonder they keep it open. I shall write to Madame Geoffroi tomorrow.

If L.M. was here, she could blow up that fire.

My little precious. My love, my child playfellow. Didn't we wave to each other a long time that day?

Say you want me back in April. Tell me I *must* come back then.

Your
Wig

116

le dimanche   Sunday,

My precious,   (January 13, 1918)

I got so cold yesterday that I decided, willy-nilly, to take a small walk and try and 'warm up' before the evening. So I made myself into a bundle, and started off. First I went to the Mairie to be registered. The old secretary was there at one desk in his braided cap; the drum stood in a corner. He was very solemnly engaged in cutting a Spanish beauty's picture off a card and gumming the same on to the back of a pocket-book, breathing like a grampus. The Mayor did not (as usual) want to have anything to do with my passport. However, I persuaded him that it really *was* necessary, and when he did make up his mind, he went very thoroughly into the affair. Result. I am written in the book as *Kadreen Bovden, fille d'Arnold Beauchamp et Anne Dysa de Nouvelle Zélande,* etc. I could not make him get anything more accurate, so I just let him go on.

Then I saw that the Meynets' blind was up and went in. M. only was there. He sat on a stool stitching a long red leather boot more × eyed then ever. Didn't remember me. Madame is away, but he expects her back. 'Marie est allée à Marseille il y a deux mois, et puis—elle n'est pas revenue! Voilà!' Did I want a villa? And he began to press villas *de quatre pièces* on me, but I felt a bit sick and went off. I then decided to go and see Ma'am Allègre. The afternoon was very cold and grey and just going dusky. The sea was high and made a loud noise. When I passed the vineyard where the two little boys used to work I realised quite suddenly that I was suffering—terribly, terribly, and was quite faint with this emotion. Then came at last the road with GRAVIER 2K written on the post. And then came our little home in sight. I went on, though I don't know how, pushed open the Allègres' singing gate, walked over those crunching round stones. The outer door of our villa was open. When I reached the stone verandah, and looked again upon the almond tree, the little garden, the round stone table, the seat scooped out of stone, the steps leading down to the *cave,* and then looked up at our pink house, with the swags of shells painted over the windows and the strange blue-grey shutters, I thought I had never, in my happiest memories, realised all its beauty. I could not get any answer from the Allègres', but I felt certain I heard someone moving in our villa, so finally I knocked on our door. You remember how hard it was to open. It tugged open, and there stood Ma'am Allègre in the same little black shawl, lean and grey as ever.

'Vous désirez, Madame?' said she. I just managed to say 'Bonjour, Madame. Vous m'avez oubliée?' And then she cried, 'Ah! Ah! I know your voice. Come in, come in, Madame. I am just airing the villa. Come in to the little salon. Comment ça va? Et votre mari? etc., etc. etc.'

I crossed the hall; she opened one half of the persiennes, and we sat on either side of the table, she in your place, I with my back to the fire in mine, and had a long talk. She remembers us well. Many times her husband and she have talked of us and wished to have us back again. Her husband always wondered what had happened to us. We were like 'deux enfants,' said she, and it was a happiness to them to know that we were there. Her son is wounded, and is on the Swiss frontier in a post office. They went all the way to Paris to see him. I asked her what has happened to the flowers; for there is not a single flower—not a jonquil, not a geranium, not a rose, not an orange—and she promised they would all be here 'plus tar', plus tar'. C'est la faute du mauvais *temps*, vous sa-avez!'

But oh, as we sat there talking and I felt myself answer and smile and stroke my muff and discuss the meat shortage and the horrid bread and the high prices and *cette guerre*, I felt that somewhere, upstairs, you and I lay like the little Babies in the Tower, smothered under pillows, and she and I were keeping watch like any two old crones! I could hardly look at the room. When I saw my photograph, that you had left, on the wall, I nearly broke down, and finally I came away and leaned a long time on the wall at the bottom of our little road, looking at the violet sea that beat up, high and loud, against those strange dark clots of sea-weed. As I came down your beautiful narrow steps, it began to rain. Big soft reluctant drops fell on my hands and face. The light was flashing through the dusk from the lighthouse, and a swarm of black soldiers was kicking something about on the sand among the palm-trees—a dead dog perhaps, or a little tied-up kitten.

It is so quiet today. I remember Sundays like this, here. Not a hint of sun. A leaden sky. A sea like oil. I almost think I may reasonably expect a letter from you tomorrow. I had a very bad night, coughing and sweating so that I had to keep sponging my face, and kept thinking, 'It *must* be five o'clock,' and finding it was only a quarter past one. Oh, these long, long, lonely nights when one is ill! They are unforgettable! But after breakfast this morning I slept till eleven o'clock. I heard all the noises in the corridor, but still I *was* fast asleep.

Good God! I have just remembered it was only last Sunday that I came to you—and we were so happy and you cut my bread and butter and we kissed each other—Be still! Be still!

This will all pass and I shall get better and spring will come—and it will be warm and you will write to me and we shall be together again. Lord, I believe.

Your child

Wig

Read this first   Monday,

Boge,   (January 14, 1918)

The Lord took Pity on me today and sent me a letter from you. As it was only written on Wednesday I thought that very good. I had been told letters took 8 days at least! I read it from beginning to end and then from end to beginning, upside down and then diagonally. I ate it, breathed it and finally, fell out of bed, opened the shutters and saw that the day was blue and the sun shining. So your Wig put on her clothes and went for a walk round by the Golf Hotel. It was very exquisite, cold in the shadows, but warm in the light. I still have an appalling cold, cough and flat-iron, but your letter was the best medicine, poultice, plaster, elixir, draught, I could have had. Bless you for it.

A word more about this place. There is a destroyer anchored here, close to the Quai, and sheds etc. erected for the sailors. Who spend their time $\frac{1}{2}$ in the urinals, $\frac{1}{2}$ flirting with the girls. Quantities of black soldiers everywhere. I saw that woman whose husband was in Salonique yesterday. She is quite changed, very made up, but pale and impudent —and horrid. I realized yesterday she is a type for negroes. You remember the lovely geraniums in this garden. They are little scrubby bushes now with broken bottles and bits of lead piping chucked among them. These hotel people are no good. A widowed mother and two Bragian daughters. And now there are only two people here beside me. However, I can't leave. *Je n'ai ni la force ni l'assurance.* It may improve. Certainly the weather has. I shall be back now, when you get this, in 14 weeks. Then I am going to somehow or other *faire un enfant*—so that when you ever should want to rush away from me, *je ne serai pas seule.*

My precious darling. Try and get inside the buses while the cold lasts.

Wig

119

Wednesday,
My own,   (January 16, 1918)

I had a very gay letter from Marie today including one from Mr.
Kay to her, which says that 'heaps' of letters are waiting for me at the
Bank. Well, he's got my address by now, so I hope they are on their
way .... Don't forget my papers—will you? Of course I simply devour,
believe and eat up every word of the *Paris Daily Mail* in the meantime.
Its latest scare is that the Germans are going to try marching on Calais
again and that the Channel passage will be cut off for aye.

It is a very grey misty day. After that one fine one it has relapsed into
winter again. A plaintive wind howls in the corridors. I shall light my
fire this afternoon and sit tight. Oh, dear! a panier of wood only lasts
me 2 days, try as I may to economise.

The post here is much better than I had been led to believe. One
hardly dares to say so, in case it snows again or more troops pour into
Italy, but Marie's letter was only posted on the 12th and today is the
15th or 16th—I'm not sure.

I still feel far from as well as I did when we went to Harvey Nichols'
together. I lie in bed all the morning until 12 and go to bed again as
soon as dinner is over. The *interval* I spend in going for a very small walk
and in working: I have begun, thank God, to work a bit. But my back
hurts horribly and I cough an awful lot. However, I did not compose a
single farewell telegram last night in bed, so that is *one up*.

Our butcheress isn't there any more. The pig-faced woman is, and an
old man. The pâtisserie where the girl was always eating is closed, sadly,
with big official notices plastered on the windows. The shop with the
funny smell where we bought our *charbon de pierre* is now the Municipal
Food Depot. I went round by the Golf Hotel yesterday, and just as I
got to the place where it says you are responsible for your own *dégâts*
and *frais,* the sheep with their little lambs passed by. God! what a
woeful company. The sheep with just a saddle of dirty wool on their
backs, their bellies shaven, many of them with swollen feet, limping
pitifully, the lambs tottering past—but *they* were pretty—there was one
ginger one that managed to give a hop or two. Between them went a
shepherd who was half a dog, I think. But he whistled to them in a way
I had forgotten.

There are 2 submarines in the bay and a black steamer with a big
white cross on her bows. The officers take their meals here. Their talk

Katherine Mansfield   February 1915

and grouping, etc., is pure Maupassant—not Tchekov at all, not deep enough or *good* enough. No, Maupassant is for France.

I read Wordsworth's sonnet beginning:

'Great Men have been among us: hands that penned. . . .'

Look it up and read it. I agree with every word. There is a change of front, if you like! Whenever I am here, I seem to turn to William Wordsworth.

My precious Boge, your real Wig lies on Ribni's bosom, so clasp her there. This old sort of pen-woman with a croak and a sad eye is not really me. Still not a cigarette to be had in all the land. 'It is sad.' Please try and send me a book, a Dickens would do. I have read *Barnaby Rudge* twice. What about *Our Mutual Friend*? Is that good? I never read it.

This letter goes like one of those sheep I saw. But by the time it reaches you, you must feel that I *love, love, love* you amen and that I am for ever your own

Wig

Tell me you are taking care of yourself for me.

Friday,
My precious darling Bogey,   (January 18, 1918)

I jumped out of bed this morning as though a bull had brought me your telegram on his horn, tied and buttoned myself, and blew off to the Post Office to wire Geoffroi to wait till he heard from me. Whether I was in time or not, I don't know. My spirit faints with horror that I wasn't. If that little chest of drawers does turn up, I expect he will carve me in a dozen bits and have done with me for ever. And THE EXPENSE! No, I shall *never* tell you the truth again, for you become violent. I should not write like this if something extraordinary hadn't happened.

Last night I didn't feel very much better. I climbed into bed and fell asleep and had a marvellous dream about you. You came rolling at me in your way, and you said in the 'boy' voice that always overcomes me 'Wig, I've grown a beard'. And you had. I never saw such a nice one. I held up a finger at you, and (we were in a big house full of people) I suddenly felt that every single soul there loved us—loved us with their whole hearts. I was wearing my Spanish shawlet, and you were in your corduroys—very much so. You took me by the hand and we looked at each other and I thought the tears came rolling out of our eyes, and we began to laugh. Ah, that sweet laughter! I woke and quite forgot my foreign bed. I found myself, for the first time since I left you, laughing, and though I realized it was a dream, the laughter fled, nevertheless, it has made the pain so much less . . . . Today, for instance, it is dark and very windy and cold, but 2 letters came from you, and then my dream, and I am clasping you—close—close to my breast, my beloved, and kissing the top of your darling head and calling you some of my hundreds and thousands of names for you . . . . Love me. Love me as I love you. When the cloud has lifted from both of us we shall be like 2 little rays of light dancing over the daisy fields. I had better get well alone. Don't send Lesley. I can stand it, and if I do get worse I will tell G. I have written him all about myself now and asked his advice from afar, so that is best.

I really am better than I was. I sleep more and the pain is a different one. I believe I have turned *another* of those corners, just managed to turn it, you know, as though I were learning to ride a bicycle round it. I heard from L.M. today too. She sounded very gay and 'sitting on the floory'. Boge, your letter was only writ on Monday, and today is Friday. God, I thank thee for thy merciful Posts.

Oh, my love—

> 'I could not wish
> Any companion in the world but you;
> Nor can imagination form a shape,
> Besides yourself, to like of . . .'

Shakespeare knew our love—what it was like. Yes, love, I took away my copy. I looked up that out of *The Winter's Tale*—the end of Camillo's speech. It is extraordinarily 19th century.

Is it safe for me to send MS *registré* to you, or should I keep it? I'd *like* to send it so it would be typed and you could read it. Please remember to tell me.

We must get rid of Madame votre femme de ménage when I come back. I shall start from here *the 1st week in April* at latest. And meanwhile the wind moans, the sky is purple and the sea boils up . . . 4.15. it is already nearly dark. My bluff old watch that you bought me ticks away and away. I often feel inclined to dip him in things, like jugs of water and cups of coffee, but I don't, darling. You shall have him when I come back. *When I come back, when I come back*: that is all my heart says. It doesn't see *this,* or hear *this.* It is fast asleep in my bosom except when I write to you. Oh, I can just see far away a most lovely poem coming out of that—not that exactly. Love as a sleeping baby, and when she bends over him and whispers his father's name to him, he stirs and stretches and opens his eyes and laughs—but she must let him sleep, must hush him and let him sleep. I see it. This is just a lift of the idea that I give you. Perhaps I can write it in prose. Now I am going to shut the shutters and work. I shall post this tomorrow.

Saturday (January 19). 5.20. I had just got that far when Victorine poked in her head: 'C'est une dame qui vous demande en bas', and suddenly I heard steps, and there was Madame G. 'Ma chère amie, j'avais l'idée que vous étiez paralysée'. She took me into her arms and I wept and she wept and I wept all over the collar of her impossible coat and she wept. Then I tried to explain how I had wired, and *she* that your telegram had come the evening before. She had been travelling to get to me since 8 that morning and was worn out. It was a *bit awful*. We both went on explaining and chère amieing each other until I thought I'd simply fall (?) down like Slatkowsky[1]—and finally she understood and she said she would write you that I had très bonne mine and was pas plus fatiguée parceque ce pauvre enfant votre mari—doit être a la folie etc. etc. etc. She said her husband *never* practised and at any rate he is the Mayor now. Voilà! And kept saying that I must eat and put on wool and eat—abundantly—and wants me to go to Carpentras in March until I leave for England.

At last the gong went for dinner, and we dined together, and then she came back to my room and sat till 11.30! talking about le Swinburne, Mistral, d'Aubanel, le Keats—le silence qui a pris pour sa maison la maison d'Henri Fabre. Finally, she left me and I simply groaned into bed. At 8.15, my dear—figurez-vous—she was in my room dressed, ready pour aller envoyer la télégramme à ce pauvre M. Bowden. Good! We did that. Afterwards she sat and talked of literature with me until *lunch.* Then I took her to the 1.15 train, which did not arrive until 5 *moins quart*! It poured with rain; it was utterly cold and cheerless; and she poor creature will not be home until tomorrow—Avignon 2 heures du matin. God! what a pilgrimage of love on her side! And how *I* bore the conversations I have no idea. I simply died with them and rose again—died and rose again—and I am sure that there is not a poem unturned in the whole of the Provençal literature after that. She is gone,

[1] Slatkowsky was the proprietor of the Russian Law Bureau, where Kotelian,sky worked. He was a comic quasi-legendary figure in our circle.

confident that she will reassure you, and my left lung aches and aches so as I write that I must ask Jeanne if she knows of a doctor here just to tell me *what* this ache can be. It is like an appalling *burn*. Sometimes, if I lift my arm over my head it seems to give it relief. What is it?

The Times and *The Nation* came today. Thank you, my love.

25 to seven. Saturday. I love you so, I love you so. The wind howls and the shutters squeak, and this old deserted hotel seems to be on an island—far, far away. But I love you so, I love you so. I am absolutely all yours for ever.

My precious, please don't ever send me a *penny* of extra money. That is very straight dinkum. Save it. Put it away. We shall want all our pockets full for later. I shall save all I can and *faire des économies* as far as I can. *Trust me.*

And again I implore you, take care of yourself. Don't sit in wet feet—eat—keep warm—sleep. Think of how I adore you—of how I can't bear a hair of your head should be harmed. You are all perfection to me—but guard yourself, cherish yourself for your little wife.

Tig

Sunday,

My own Precious,   (January 20, 1918)

I LOVE YOU.

I AM EVER SO MUCH BETTER.

I AM COMING BACK IN APRIL.

BE HAPPY MY DEAR LOVE.

ONLY WRITE TWICE A WEEK.

OR YOU WILL BE 2 TIRED.

MY MONEY IS QUITE SATISFACTORY.

There is the bulletin. Oh, Bogey, I *wish* that I had not told you the truth, for your two sad letters today, the one when my awful remark about 'malade' jumped up and down the typewriter, and the other, wrung my heart this morning. It is quite true. I have been *bloody ill*, but these last 2 days I feel ever such a great deal better and quite a different child. Chiefly because I know I am not going to get worse and that we shall be together again. I really *did*, at one or two times, think I would 'peg out' here, never having had a Heron or a Heronette, and that simply horrified me. But now, though the local pain is still there, everything else in me is against it and not for it. I feel *hungry* and I keep making plans i.e. I shall bring him, in my old biscuit tin, ½ a pound of mountain butter, a little pot of cherry jam, a tiny handful of sweet dried figs, and in my box I'll pack 4 of the biggest fir-cones I can find.

It's the 20th of January today. By the 20th of April we shall be married and sitting among our children I expect in some flowery field making daisy and bluttercup chains. *If* I don't break off into a thousand pieces for love of you before then. My mother sent us great and little blessings today—to 'you and Jack'. She has a feeling that 'a happy future is unfolding for you both', though of course our letters haven't arrived yet. She told me a way to make bread which sounds very easy for our farm. She says after the war she is going to do the cooking in their house and Father is going to do all the washing. Father bought the entire library with that house, which sounds a pearl. He has just finished reading *Robinson Crusoe*.

My grandma Beauchamp is dead. She had a stroke and died.

Aunt Li has never recovered from her stroke.

Bee's husband has hanged himself in an outhouse.

As mother says, we seem to be all on strike or on string out here.

I had a nice letter from Ainger today, asking me to tell him how I got on, and I had a letter from Belle, and Chaddie. In fact I had 11 letters. But they might have all gone down that wind. Yours were the only ones I really coveted—devoured.

Oh, my cherished one, I wish I could somehow tell you *here* and *now* that I am inclined to lie on my back and play with Ribni. If we were together, we'd make some coffee and a bright fire, and sit and talk, curled up in one round.

Next month, I shall go to Marseilles for 2 days to see Cook's and to get some books—to see Cook's about all that one has to do to get back, so as I can be ready.

It is dark and very windy today—the sea is all teeth and fury. It rained all night. But I would not be surprised if the sun came out next week. I feel I have lifted up my head again and all my petals have spread out ready to catch a ray. But I wish I had a pigeon to send this letter more quickly.

It's Sunday, and some strangers came here for lunch. We had bouillabaisse. I wondered what you had.

Yes, I am not one but *two*. I am *you* as well as myself. You are another part of me, just as I am a part of you.

Goodbye for now, my Bogey.

Yours ever, Wig

My own Boge,

I am only going to write you a note today just to say that I still feel better. The weather is 1000 times rougher. Never, not even on shipboard or in my own little country or anywhere, have I heard such wind. And in the night when one lay quiet in bed and listened, God knows how many Ancient Mariners cried in it or how many lost souls whirled past. I thought then what agony it must be to be wife to a fisherman. How could a poor soul comfort herself and to whom could she pray when such a wind and such a sea fought against her? . . . I thought, too, it must have been just such a storm when Shelley died. This morning at red dawn a destroyer and a submarine tried to put out to sea, but they were obliged to return. I despised them for that and thought no English sailors would not have mastered it. But you know, for all my big talk, I never believe the Frenchies can sail a boat, or throw a ball, or do anything at all which is a patch upon the English. . . . If you could see this sea today heaving and smoking like a herd of monsters run mad . . . .

Last night my little maid brought me a present, of rosebuds. Two green jars full of them and some yellow *soleils d'or* besides. She had been for a walk in the country, she said, and a friend had made her a present. She came to the door with them—so pretty—wearing a black woollen cap, and her cheeks were red. Shortly after, the Madame came to ask if I would like some hot wine at night for my cough. 'Je ne savais pas que vous avez été si fatiguée.' Well, though it's a bit *tard* for remedy as I'm such a much better girl, I said Yes to the wine—and it was a rare fine posset. 3rd, the submarine captain, having heard me try to get tobacco, presented me with a whole packet of Maryland—not cigarettes but tobacco—so I feel people have been unusually winning. . . .

My precious heart, as I write the sun thrust his head through a positive monk's hood of a cloud and blesses you and me upon this page. I thought this morning: In February I shall be able to say that I come back the month after next. And February is a very tiny little month, too, so that after it is gone and March has blown in, there will only be a few weeks before April. Does this comfort you as it does me?

I shall be awfully well—and all hung with presents for you, with 2 candles that can't be put out—in my eyes. You'll have to discover me like a Christmas Tree. Then we will wave and wave as the train carries us towards each other and then we'll be in each other's arms. I fully expect Rib to be with you, in your green overcoat cut down very small, with a feltie on.

Does this letter make you feel that you are the most loved and cherished Bogey in all the world? If it don't, it's none of mine—but it must. Now I am going to the post—then to have lunch, then to come up here—light my fire and write.

I am always your own

Wig

TAKE CARE OF YOURSELF.

The old man with the dog just brought it [a telegram from J.M.M.]. I think *he* thinks I feed on telegrams—like silkworms on mulberry leaves.

Tuesday,

My love,   (January 22, 1918)

I cannot write to you as I wish until I know that this cruel barb that I plucked out of my bosom only to drive into yours has been withdrawn. Oh, that I should have hurt you so. No, I never will cry out again. The bears can eat me first. I'll *never never* forgive myself.

I will just tell you, so that you may know how I am taking care of myself. I stay in bed every day until lunch. Then I dress by a fire. If it is fine I go for a small walk in the afternoon, then I come back to my fire. After dinner, at about 8.30 I go to bed. The food here has got much better since the submarines have taken to lunching and dining here. It is now very good and they have begun giving me portions so big that I think they suspect me of at least twins *sous mon cœur*. I set sail across tureens of nourishing soup, stagger over soft mountains of *pommes purées* and melt in *marmelades*. So you see how well I am looking after *myself*.

Now tell me about you. My love, my dear heart, my own. If you knew how all my being turns towards you, and is always anxious and wondering a little. I was always thinking when I first came here 'We have never had a *real life together* for only now are we grown enough in each other's sight to understand what that means and how it can be enjoyed.' It *must*, it *shall* be ours.

But tell me when you answer this letter if you still feel hungry—if 'The Good Intent' is still satisfactory and what you have for lunch. Do you get milk enough? These things are most important as you know.

Unless you want me before I shall now stay here until the first week in April as I said yesterday—then my ship will point for home. Great God! what is any country or richness in the world to me where thou art not. Until then I shall work and become a very strong girl, write to you, husband our money, and if I know that you are content—that you, my life, do not worry but can work and be at peace in the evenings —and perhaps get from my love a refreshment that will make your vile office a little more endurable, then I will be as happy as I can be— lacking you.

For quite seriously I adore you.

I have decided to risk the post with my work. I shall always send it registered and always keep a copy, but I want you to have it as it comes off my pen.

This, Bogey, is whispered, very privately. Rib can hear because he's ours. We shall have an English Heron even if it's only one stout room looking out upon nibbled downs and sheep. I am as firm in that as you.

When I have heard from you in answer to my wire, I'll write very fully.

Do you write twice a week, but as I don't spend any money on cigarettes (oh, we are babies) I can afford to write once a day. I've the time and until you tire of—just my fond embrace, even—just taking off your ring, kissing your finger and putting it on again—I will write every day.

The wind still blows a hurricane here. In the night the rain joined in but now the sun beats in the air like a kite. It is like living on a ship. The hotel is all bolted and barred up, the big doors closed and a strange twilight in the hall. People go about in shawls and coats. If a window is opened the seas of the air rush in and fill it. The great palm trees have snapped like corks, and many a glittering plume trails in the dust. They say it never has been known before. I have begun to like it. Were I to feel that you, my life, were put out of worry, I should enjoy it.

Yours, yours for ever—every part of me

Wig

Wednesday,

My dear life,   (January 23, 1918)

Here is your letter of Friday night under my hand—the one in which Rib rolled over and laughed. I have an idea that our children will use us just so. They will adore us, but our love will make them *laugh at us,* in just his careless, infinitely confident way. Oh, don't let us ever forget Ribni. He must always be with us and our babies must only be allowed to sit next to him and perhaps stroke down his fringe with their tiny brown hands.

Last night, when I had finished capturing all I could of this wind and rain and cold, it ceased, and this morning the sun came out. There is still a stiff breeze, but it's warm in the sun and indescribably lovely. Every mortal thing looks to be sheathed in a glittering beauty. It began, for me, with your letter. There was a pulse in your letter that set my heart beating.

I got up at about eleven and went out to buy myself *une canne avec une frique.* The disagreeable shop has become amiable. I bought a small stout one for 1.25 and then walked up the road behind the front, past Ma'am Gamel's, to the top of the hill and a little way further. The sky over the sea was like an immense Canterbury bell, darkly, transparently blue. Towards me came walking an old woman in a pleated black dress with a broad straw hat tied under her chin with a linen band and she carried a pack of jonquils. Then there came a butterfly, my little sister, weak in the wing, and staggering a little, but *basking.* The cats lay on the window sills. In a field against the sea a man and a woman were digging; the olive trees blew silver and the sea, very wild still, embraced the shore as though it loved it. As I came back I saw an old man sitting in a corner of a field, some wine and bread in a basket by him. He had a pair of breeches on his knees that he was carefully darning. They looked awfully forlorn as though he had just given them a beating.

But how can all this have happened in a night? Yesterday—mid-winter. I walked to the post wearing your wadded coat, my woollen one, my great blue one over all and was perished. I staggered home, and decided that I must ask you to send me an anchor, a small one, shaped like a crab, perhaps, with whiskers, that I could draw behind me on a string, to keep me from blowing (*a*) into the sea or (*b*) over *le grand cerveau*—and here's today come to mock me. *On a vraiment chaud.* By the way, my precious, my wadded coat has been and is a perfect treasure. It keeps out the draughts like nothing else. I wear it every day and sit up in bed in it and—enfin—it is just what I ideally wanted.

Oh, the washer-girl came today while I was in bed. You remember her? How fine she was, always so *gauffrée*, with frills over her hands and gold rings in her ears and very expensive sparkling eyes. Now, poor wench, she's so changed. There can't have been a soul in Bandol with *pyjame de laine* at 2.50 the washing since you left. She has shed all her brightness, *jusqu'à ses pieds*, which were covered in lovely red kid slippers. I hope it will *monte* again. She charged me 3.50 but it was not a 'swin' really.

I must tell you my little maid is becoming more and more friendly. She looks like the girl you read of who spreads the linen to dry in the orchard while the young boy up the ladder fills her apron with red pears. She was saying yesterday that she did not like the hotel to be so empty. We sit together, said she, there's nothing to do . . . 'Alors, nous nous regardons—nous causons—mais, c'est triste, vous savez, ce n'est pas si gai que la service!' What do they talk about and where do they sit? I began to wonder . . . .

I am thankful that the studio is let and off our hands. *No*, don't send the £5. Put it in the bank. I'll cry when I am empty but, being very well trained, not before. I am doing all I can to live without spending, to wear my old clothes and shoes—we shall feast and array ourselves when we are together, and 'fleet the time carelessly as they did in the golden world'.

My adored one. Now that you know I am so much better you will tell me all about yourself and you will take care of yourself.

> And this is not a boon.
> 'Tis as I should entreat you wear your gloves
> Or feed on nourishing dishes, or keep you warm,
> Or sue to you to do a peculiar profit
> To your own person . . . .

Warmly, warmly, passionately, eternally, I love you.

Wig

Please can you send me my old mended shoes. I do need them so and L.M. says she gave them to you . . . If it's not a bother.

Thursday,
Dearest of all,   (January 24, 1918)

I did not have a letter from you today. Perhaps you have already heard from me about the 'twice a week' idea. Of course, my fond heart said: 'Has there been an air raid?' But then I heard at length from Johnny and he would have told me. It was Sunday coming between.

Yesterday I took your letter with me and we walked our old familiar way—along by the coast and then inland. . . . Well, I suppose we looked as though we were walking, but, good God, my spirit never kept worse time with my toes . . . . A sea like quilted silk, the lavender bushes growing among the rocks all in new leaf. Such air as you and I have drunk together, and a whole flock of little winds to shake every perfumed bud and flower. The almond trees, if one stands close and looks up, are thick with white and red buds; the lanes have a thick border of white and yellow—wild candytuft and small marigolds. The mimosa is coming out over the gate of our house,[1] which is still sealed up—still as remote, *more* beautiful, *more* desirable than ever. This place is so full of our love that every little walk I take is a passionate pilgrimage. There is the villa—*allons-y*. Here is the field where we saw all the anemones, here the wall where the lizard lay basking. One could hear everywhere the voices of people in the fields—one could see, through the blue fresh-painted gates, women bending to the earth and rising up again—with the old leisurely grace. They passed me, the dark people we know so well with their little loads of olive branches—*or* a squeaking barrow of manure—and as I came home, I went by the Villa Pauline, and saw over the wall the geraniums in leaf and bud. (Ah, I did of course go in, and while you put the kettle on I took out the flowery cups, put our honey biscuits in a dish, and we sat down, faint and warm and smiling we knew not why). These incredible people who avant-hier were wrapped in every inch of fur or wool they could find were yesterday dabbling their legs in the water down on the shore . . . .

I had a lie down when I came home and then I worked. When it grew dusky I opened the windows to close the shutters. The moon was up. The sky over the sea faint rose, and there was a strange bright glitter on the palm-trees. After diner in the hotel library I found a copy of *Martin Eden* (which Orage always thought a famous good book) and a large shabby tome—Tissot: *Littérature Française*. No, a little Shakespeare makes one's nose too fine for such a rank smeller as Jack London. The other is *rare* meat. It is examples of French literature from the 9th century to the end of the 18th. And it is followed by a *Revue* of the state of the whole world at that time—each country taken separate— very excellent amusement. And too there are hundreds of the little engravings and fantastical letters that we love. I shall guard this in my room and bury Jack London again.

[1] Not the Villa Pauline, but a small and beautiful cottage in an olive yard, about a mile away.

I heard from Geoffroi yesterday *and* she included *une poème*. I send you both. By my passport I shall not be permitted to stay at Carpentras, you know. But I'll tell her that, later. It would kill me. After the war, with you to fly to, I will—but alone to sustain that 'parfaitement, Madame—justement—mais bien sûr' for more than half an hour would turn me into a parrot for life.

When we do have a house here, I think I'll try and get this maid to come. She's just *our* style, but **I** wish she wouldn't give me a fresh bouquet more than once a day. Five vases of flowers are enough. The last is feathery mimosa. My own, I write to you thus and tell you all because you *must* share it. This is the news which comes from your country which I am visiting on your behalf just as much as mine. For the present, my love, you are the King in his Counting-House counting out his money, and I am the Queen in her parlour eating bread and honey. Ah, God! that there *wasn't* a door between us. All my joy here is half yours. It is my love for you which puts all the sweet breath into this. As I write, as I think of you, I feel that I am love—nothing else. Oh, I could weep like a child because there are so many flowers and my lap is so small and all must be carried home to you.

Farewell, my heart,
Your
Wig.

Dear Love,

Thursday,
(January 24, 1918)

I *must* add this to today's letter. I have chuckled over it for hours. As I went out this afternoon I met the widow hurrying up from the town, *très pandaresque,* and all a-flower with smiles. *Justement* she had come to look for me. One demanded me at the Mairie, and the Mayor waited. I said that I had better get my passeport first, and she agreed. I told her I was already registered, but she said they were very strict now. She had *no* idea (mark that!) what I was wanted for, but *enfin—voilà!* Off I went. In that office of theirs the Mayor, his deputy, and old Drum waited for me. The Mayor wore white shoes with blue strings and his cap back to front and a *bout* of cigarette in his mouth, *mais il était très sérieux.*

'You are, Madame, the lady to whom these papers refer?' (The papers I had filled for the hotel.)

'Yes, Monsieur.'

'Bien! Will you follow me, Madame, to the Salon du Conseil?'

'Très volontiers, Monsieur.'

My spirits mounted with every step of the stairs. *He* is lame and had to get up them like a pigeon—you know, both feet on one step before he could reach to the next. Came a black door, heavily gilded, hugely labelled SALON DU CONSEIL. This was unlocked, and I had a glimpse of a chambre sich as my irreverent British eye has never twinkled on before. A black paper with gold stamping—a huge table covered with a heavy black cloth, fringed with gold. A few trunks of dead men, coloured, on brackets round the wall, and one of those portraits with a striped glass over, so that if you looked at it from your side it was La Liberté, but if you looked at it from his, it was—*je ne sais pas*. There were also an immense number of bundles covered in black cloth—dead mayors, I think. We sat down on a couple of velvet chairs with gold fleurs de lys so heavily stamped on their seats that if you had any chance *vous pouvez montrer à votre ami une derrière—mais vraiment chic*—and he produced a perfect mass of papers . . . .

'Connaissez-vous, Madame, un certain *M. Parquerre?*'

'Non, Monsieur.'

'You are not expecting a gentleman to follow you to France?'

'Non, Monsieur.'

Then, of course, 'I saw it all'. It was *Baker*. He had heard from the British Consulate at Marseilles that a lady had tombéd gravement malade at Bandol. Was there such a lady? Her friend, *M. Parquerre,* prayed for permission etc. This was, I think, the first official statement he had ever received from the B.C. He could not get over it—its importance—the whole affair. Then I explained. We had a lot of chat. Then, said he 'But do you want the lady? I can arrange it. C'est vite fait'. That is so like the Midi. And I said 'No' without hesitating—just like that. Are you surprised?

Dabord, none of us have the money unless the affair is urgent (2) I feel she ought to stay at the factory. She is simply bound up in it really and would be wretched here. What could she do? But the money aspect is the important one, n'est-ce pas? I did right, didn't I? I hope she will understand. *Also*—this is strictly confidential—it is far better she should not come. She has been an angel to me but in our new life she has not a great part—and she realizes that. It would be very painful. I left the Mayor, his deputy and old Drum preparing the answer to this document—trying pens—stamping the rubber-stamp on the backs of their hands to see if it would work etc.

BUT: there was one unpleasant fly. He says *le crise de chemins de fer* will last—will grow worse with the spring—and at times the railway will be, as now, absolutely closed to civilian traffic. So he warned me, if I wanted to get home, to choose a moment well in advance. How awful it would be if I got stuck here, Boge! Wouldn't it?

Goodbye for now, my soul. Oh, my 'mark that!' The mayor said the widow had read the paper and knew all about it.

Friday 25th. Not a word before I have greeted anew your poem in *The Nation.* It is supremely beautiful—an achievement that 'traces on your brow their secret mark for ever'. In a word, Bogey, it is *first chop.* Oh, my boy, do you *know* how lovely it is—how far away and clear—now it rings across the water even to the shores of that other country. Great God! to think that this lovely voice still sings in England—that you're alive, twenty-eight years old—and that you're to be—who could doubt it for one instant after this poem?—the Great Poet of our time. I sit here smiling, but the tears press on my eyelids. I whisper 'Oh, my *wonder*'. After the war is over, we must cover our pennies in silver paper if they are not bright enough and you must forget everything *except this—this treasure that is yours.*

My own, the letters were late arriving. Your Saturday letter came today and you had not yet heard that the weather has changed. I had no fire at all yesterday, and today I have pulled down the iron screen. So *paniers* of wood *are* not any more for the present. You did not send the money, did you? I received a *Lit. Sup.,* the *Daily News* and *The Nation.* I read your poem. All the others are to be browsed on *plus tar'.* I heard from L.M.—rather melancholy. I must write to her. No, love, it is much better that I remain alone now. I am really (except for one local funny 'spot' of pain about which I wrote Ainger yesterday) such a well girl. I hardly cough. They go on giving me wine at night and with my café au lait a jug of milk that must be a *whole goat,* and two fishes in place of anybody else's *one*—and the weather is if possible lovelier than ever. I sat on a warm stone this morning until my neck got burnt. The two windows of my room are wide open. It is much warmer, incomparably more exquisite than I have ever known it here. The sea is so clear (and every shade, blue and green and violet) that one can see, like a map outspread beneath you, a whole new uncharted country with little lakes and forests and bays. The coast is pink like the flesh of a peach, and everybody is out fishing—[a drawing] you know, hanging over the end of the boat and spearing the fish. . . .

I had today a portrait of Mother sent me. I want you to see it. But I must wait. Whether it's like or not like, there is all that I knew or imagined of her in it and it seems to me that if you saw it you'd agree with me that it's rare to see a more *fascinating* woman. I am very glad to have it to show to you.

Dear love, I shall be so relieved when you know it's warm here—and you do know now that I am coming back first week in April—don't you? Just reassure me.

They are mending and tarring the boats outside my window—you can hear the little hammers and a whiff or two of tar breaks across the mimosa. *La Ciotat: Marie-Réjane*—the boats we know.

Another week (month) has nearly gone. Six more days and it is gone Then comes little February,[1] then March—but I shall be making my preparations in March and then—I shall be in your arms again. You must not think I am a nuisance—will you? But, dearest, you will tell me, won't you, when you have a cold—if you hurt a finger or a toe—do not sleep well—feel shiny in the head. True, it is a kind of anguish to know these things but it is a thousand times greater *not* to know. When I don't know, I imagine every possible thing—at certain hours.

Don't you think when this is over we must agree never to part again? I shall never come so far without you again (unless it's you that flee me). It is unbearable to live in our divine childish way and to be out of hail.

(And do you ever think of getting married?)

Now goodbye until tomorrow. Yes, I think we were well out of the studio, and the other flat. I can't bear that you should have to spend the money you earn so painfully.

Oh, if there is a God, he must simply devote his time to watching over you until I come back.

Your

Wig

[1] Can't you see little February—waiting and pleased? 'I can't stay very *long*.' [K. M.'s note.]

My precious,

I seem to positively *eat* writing paper, but here's a bit of my old studio days at last. Today I had from you the letter with the £5, i.e. a Monday letter, and your *Sunday* one with the 2 Dickens. So yesterday's and today's posts seem to have got very mixed. About the £5. Well, by now you'll have my letters asking you not to send me money till I say. I'll cash it, of course, and hoard it. As a matter of fact, if my Kay money don't come on the very, very first I shall not have any left. So thank you, my heart.

You have a cold. Oh, Bogey, take care of it; and tell me if it is better. I hope you have not been too gay over the warm weather and run to the office without your coat. *Be sure to let me know when you answer this letter how it is.*

Our letters crossed again about L.M. I heard from her today, and I too felt callous, cool, and retired into my shell. She *is* a ghoul in a way. She does blossom out and become a brick *only* when the other person is more or less delivered up to her. That's what I can't stomach. That's why I don't want her here. As long as I am to be massaged she's an angel, for then *c'est elle qui mange*; if I am not in the humour, out pours 'Mr. Webb and I' and 'Why don't men . . .' etc. etc. She's all hungry fury, then, beating against my shores and trying to break down my defences. That's why I used to get so furious at the studio, for there she ate me before my eyes, and I really *revolted*.

Of *course,* I did see and read what was inside the envelope. Do you imagine I don't always turn the envelopes upside down and breathe into them and shut one eye and stare up at them and shake them, always thinking one of your eyelashes or perhaps a tiny twinkle out of your eye may still be there. Oh Boge, I like the Wordsworth story: it makes my heart warm to him.[1]

---

[1] The story is contained in the following extract from my letter:
'He [my brother] told me a story about Wordsworth—where he can have got it from I don't know. It's stupid, but characteristic, and it makes me love the old fellow rather. One day Wordsworth was dining with a friend. Some rather aged, yellowish peas were served. The friend, in order to turn it off, said to W., "Forgive me, but I forgot to send these peas to Kensington". "To Kensington?" says W. "Why, pray?" "Because that is the way to Turnham Green". W. thought this a very good joke, resolved to remember it, and to let it fly at the first opportunity. It came very soon. He dined with a friend whose peas were also rather passé. He turned to the lady of the house. "Madam, I am afraid you forgot to send these peas to Kensington." "To Kensington, Mr. Wordsworth? Why, pray?" "Because that is the way to make 'em green". And he roared with laughter.'

It is a different kind of day today, *il y a un peu de vent*. But with the bright sun it makes the sea an incredible almost violet colour. I went for a walk yesterday and got lost—you know how one can. I couldn't find either the path to the shore or the main road inland. And it kept getting on for sunset and the shadows great appeared before I was found. You should see the *swerves* I take past the dogs. They really are Bragian upstarts and their bold eyes and lifted lips terrify me. I thought What if *I* had a bulldog of my own. Would that help? But then I would always be frightened that it would wait until we got to a lonely bit and then turn on me. No, the only thing would be a very awful imitation dog—one that I could make smoke come out of its eyes and fire out of its mouth when it passed one of these mongrels. Look out for one for me.

As I sit here, I want you—I want you. I want to be at home with you. —anywhere. You're my country—my people—my whole life is bound up in yours. Come awfully close to me and let us hold each other tight a minute.

Ah, Love, Love, when I come back—we shall be so happy. The very cups and saucers will have wings, and you will cut me the only piece of bread and jam in the world, and I will pour you out a cup of *my* tea.

Why aren't you here, *now*, NOW. But I am coming, Bogey—and I am all your woman

      Tig.

                                Sunday,

French blotting paper don't blot, curse it!   (January 27, 1918)
Pas de courier pour moi.
   Si! (see page 4)
Darling,

Letter paper—except by the box at 7.25—has run out of Bandol and so I am forced to use this *papier de commerce*. I am just up. It's ten past eleven. What are you doing, I wonder? It is also the last Sunday in January which does bring me nearer you—and is therefore blesséd. It has been a dead quiet golden morning and I lay in bed feeling as quiet as the day, thinking. I decided to tell you as far as I could—*how* and of *what*. ... Something like this.

Why don't I get up now and sit at the table and write before lunch? No, I can't. I am too tired. I have overdone it these last perfect days and walked too far and been out too long. For when I come back at 4 o'clock in the afternoon with three absolutely undisturbed hours before me, I get into my room—lie on the bed—'collapse'—and then get up, light my fire, sit down at the table, leaning on anything I can find, leaning on my *pen* most of all, and though I do write—it is only a matter of 'will'—to break through—it's a sham and a pretence so far. I am so tired I can only just brush my fringe and get down to dinner and up here again to bed. Ah, how devilish it is! I am so tired I can't think of *anything,* and really can barely read. Still, my lass, this won't last. Don't walk so far or so fast. It's months since you really have walked, and your legs are bound to turn backwards. But if only I had the Stickleback[1] to lie on! These little chairs are for mean French behinds and they make me ache. However, none of this is serious. 'Twill pass. I'll go on *grinding* until suddenly I throw away the stone and begin to really create something. It's no use being peevish . . . . Are you sure this is not hypochondria? You are not getting ill here? Supposing you had a string kit and 10 little children? Oh, I'd sit in public houses and on steps. No, it's a feeling of confounded physical weakness— preparatory to great physical strength, I'm sure. It's the change: and then I get so fearfully excited, and that exhausts me. Keep your head. You'll be all right in a week. . . .

After this consoling homily, I put my legs out of bed and dropped after them and got into the basin for a bath. But it is true. I have written 2 *Patrias* (they are the pink cahiers) full here, and whenever I re-read the stuff, I can't believe it's mine. Tame, diffuse, 'missed it'. Don't blame me. I shall perk up, dearest, and I shall go slower till my legs get more *wiry*! I know what I want to do as soon as I can do it. I have no doubts or false alarms at all.

My own Boge, you know what I feel just at this moment? Rather dashed because I have been such an *enfant gâté* and now the old post has nothing for me. It's these trains again. Even if I had the money, I would not travel about here, you know. Yesterday I saw a train come in here all boarded up, all the carriages locked, full of soldiers, and those who wished to get out and 'go to the base', as Marie calls it, had to fling themselves through the windows and back again. A few poor civilians who were at the station were well jeered at by these braves. . . .

I left off there and went down to lunch. I stood on the terrace a moment in the sun wondering why French dogs and cats are so very

[1] K. M.'s name for a small sofa she possessed.

unsympathetic and suddenly there at the end of the palm avenue sparkled the brightest jewel—the postman. Yes, a letter from you and a paper. I sat down and read your letter on one of those old brown chairs. My heart's dearest, don't suspect I wouldn't write because you had missed. Of course, I wouldn't. What—to *you*? No, I'll reserve those tricks for the rest of mankind—*you* won't know them in me. What a curse this food problem is! (See, I am answering your letter.) When I come back we must cook meat and make dripping, and I swear your bregglechiks[1] won't be insipid. I'll arrange something fine. You *must* be fed in the morning.

Yes, the tinge of depression did come through just as I know a tinge of fatigue and depression is in this letter and I can't get it out. Your letter, though, has brought you—oh, so close to me. Every letter of yours is like a wave that brings you a ripple nearer—you in your boat— to me. Bogey, I want you *terribly* .... Of course, I will keep your poem. I had already cut it out and put it in my little case.

This *country, quâ* country, is really ideally beautiful. It is the very most exquisite enchanting place—yet I am very sincere when I say I *hate* the French, once I escape from a purely superficial interest in them. As *animals* they are interesting monkeys, but they have no heart—no heart at all.

I heard from H.L. today—very insincere. But she mentioned your poem—and said what a fine poet you were. I read between the lines almost a *shocked surprise* that you were so fine. We must not make her an enemy—but oh, she is *corrupt—corrupt*.

When I am at HOME and we are living together, perhaps you won't feel so depressed. I will be there, and in the evenings we'll sit at the table with the lamp between us and work and then we'll make something hot to drink and have a small talk and a smoke and do a little planning. You know we are going to be quite different. We are going to be simply absorbed in each other. While this awful war goes on you must just fling yourself at me—and feel I am always there at the end of the day—and the beginning—to make it a little bit lovely for you if I can. I am there to see about things and look after you. In the day I'll work like billy-o, but I shall have time to do everything for us. You must believe that utterly because it's true. Just till April, darling, look after yourself for me, and then give me the keys and don't you bother.

[1] Bregglechik: breakfast, in K.M.'s private language.

139

Goodbye for now, my blessed one. I live for you—you have all my love.

Your

Wig

If your cold gets bad (worse) see Ainger and ask about injections. He's so sensible and we trust him.

Sunday night,

My love and my darling, (January 27, 1918)

It is ten minutes past eight. I must tell you how much I love you at ten minutes past eight on a Sunday evening, January 27th 1918.

I have been indoors all day (except for posting your letter) and I feel greatly rested. Juliette has come back from a new excursion into the country, with blue irises—do you remember how beautifully they grew in that little house with the trellis tower round by the rocks?—and all sorts and kinds of sweet-smelling jonquils. . . . The room is very warm. I have a handful of fire, and the few little flames dance on the log and can't make up their minds to attack it. . . . There goes a train. Now it is quiet again except for my watch. I look at the minute hand and think what a spectacle I shall make of myself when I am really coming home to you. How I shall sit in the railway carriage, and put the old watch in my lap and pretend to cover it with a book—but not read or see, but just whip it up with my longing gaze, and simply make it go faster.

My love for you tonight is so deep and tender that it seems to be outside myself as well. I am fast shut up like a little lake in the embrace of some big mountains. If you were to climb up the mountains, you would see me down below, deep and shining—and quite fathomless, my dear. You might drop your heart into me and you'd never hear it touch bottom. I love you—I love you—Goodnight.

Oh, Bogey, what it is to love like this!

Monday (January 28, 1918)

Your Wednesday and Thursday letters came together this morning, darling. In the Thursday one you said you had not had mine. Bogey, I write EVERY day and post always at about the same time. I shall continue to write every day until I am home, so if you do not get my letters they are stolen or strayed. I will never disappoint you. I will try an article for Richmond[1] as soon as I can. How many words does he want? Thank God that you do feel you want to write every day. I shut my teeth hard when I said twice a week, and ever since then I have kept 'wondering'. For the day does not begin for me until the post has come. Will he be late? Or perhaps early? Is this Juliette with the letter—or no? Underneath everything that I do or think there is just this *attente*.

I have not been out yet today. I am going now, and your letter shall go with me and be posted on my way home. Tell me about Sullivan's friend. I have an idea that all his friends are rather *small beer*. Boge, have you read *Our Mutual Friend*? Some of it is really *damned good*. The satire in it is first chop—all the Veneering business *par exemple* could not be better. I never read it before and I'm enjoying it immensely, and Ma Wilfer is after my own heart. I have a huge capacity for seeing 'funny' people, you know, and laughing, and Dickens does fill it at times quite amazingly.

As I write to you I am always wanting to fly off down little side paths and to stop suddenly and to lean down and peer at all kinds of odd things. My grown-up self sees us like two little children who have been turned out into the garden. There we are hand in hand, while my G. U. S. looks on through the window. And she sees us stop and touch the gummy bark of the trees, or lean over a flower and try to blow it open by breathing very close, or pick up a pebble and give it a rub and then hold it up to the sun and see if there is any gold in it.

As I write I feel so much nearer my writing self—my 'Pauline' writing self—than I have since I came. I suppose because what I said about the children had a 'little atom bit' of Kezia in it.

I have enjoyed *The Daily News* very much. A course of *The Paris Daily Mail* makes one grey with anxiety. I see us *all* in the trenches for ever, and the Germans victorious. But the D. N. really seems to smell Peace. It has been reading *The Nation re* Austria.[2]

Now, my own, I must go for my small run. Will it be Thursday when you get this letter? I hope Chaddie will not be a bother. I am glad you are seeing her because of my family, you know. It's politic. But I wish I were there to help. I have written her today.

Here is a flower for you and a spidery bit for our Rib.

Oh—'by the way', I won't go to Marseilles till the end of *March*. It's

[1] Sir Bruce Richmond, then literary editor of *The Times*, had invited some articles from K.M., and I had passed on the invitation.
[2] I had written an article in *The Nation* on the peace-feelers from Austria.

not a necessary expense, and we can't afford it. What I ought to do is to write to Cook's there and get all particulars about the journey, and then wait here for my April money which will see me home, and start off then. Is that right?

Please answer this.

Don't go to the Corner House more than you can help. Please spend pennies on yourself. If it is too late for The Good Intent go to the Italian place where we had our little dinner. Oh, how I see the Japanese wall-paper, and you in your corduroys . . . . I was so happy. I must go back there with you.

Yes, dearest of all, do remember even on the tops of buses that I *adore* you and that no man living is as loved as you and never will be.

Your

Wig

Tuesday 29th,

My dear Bogey,   (January 29, 1918)

I feel greatly upset this morning because I realize for at least the millionth time that my letters to you are *not* arriving. I have taken great pains to write the address plainly on the envelopes. Are they safe when they arrive at the house? Do they lie in the hall, long?

This has been brought home to me by your letter of last Friday in which you enclose Geoffroi's. You say you never heard from me that she had been here. Well, of course I wrote.[1] And then I really cannot imagine that a great many other letters have not been lost. Did you get one with a telegram and a flower in it? You see I have no *notion* which letters of mine have arrived, so I am quite in the dark as to whether you know it is warm here now. Your letters appear to turn up here quite safely, but mine obviously don't. However, I shall go on throwing them into the French dust-heap—but with—I assure you, *beaucoup de chagrin.*

I have indeed tried to make you a little happy by writing to you at length and as neatly as I could. But it is, I suppose, another of those innumerable mean dodges of which Life seems more or less composed that—it don't come off.

Well, well—I wish I wasn't such a baby. The sun shines. It is almost hot. But if the sun were a reliable post-office I should much prefer it and would dispense with all its other devoirs.

[1] The letter dated January 21. It arrived some days late.

Thank you, dear Bogey, for telling me you do manage to get food. I hope that continues. What about porridge when the bacon is quite unobtainable? Could Mrs. H. make it? That 5-minutes stuff isn't half bad. And can you eat Quaker Oats? These things do warm you before you plunge into the early morning street, and that's the time you catch cold, I think. I do hope your cold is better, darling.

(This affair about the letters has given me such a *turn* that I can't get over it. It aches in my throat.)

I went for a walk yesterday, a little one. I can't take big ones yet. I do feel *assez vaillant,* but plenty of the *assez.* I got very much thinner those first days I was here and I haven't recovered my lost weight yet. Of course, I shall. I could not be more comfortable than I am here now, and absolutely private and remote. My room feels miles away from the rest of the hotel and I sometimes feel that Juliette and I are on an island, and I row to the mainland for my meals and row back again. I keep on with my fires.

Jag-Boge. You have a cold in your poor head and I have a cold place, a little iceberg suddenly knocking about in my heart where all was so warm and sunny. I will get it out before tomorrow. But, looking out on to the blue sea, the blue mountains and the boats with yellow sails, I feel full of *hate*—hate for this awkward, hideous world, these terrifying grimacing people who can keep one's letters back. I can't help it.

Wig who loves you.

Tuesday Night,
My very dear,   (January 29, 1918)

I sent you a changeling today and scarcely a letter. Since then so much seems to have happened. I went out and walked, and it was lovely, but I was tired, besides which I had my heart on a string and it kept catching in things. When I came home, Juliette met me, quite excited. She had managed to get a demi-litre of methy. She heard that it had come to the Dépôt and rushed off. That pleased me awfully, for now I can make coffee in the afternoon, and that will make a huge difference to one's fatigue—to have something between midi et 7 heures. It was an awful price: 5 francs, but as she had bought it, I could not object, and even at that it will in the end come cheaper than coffee at so much a whack.

Also, she had gone another of her excursions and returned with a cane armchair with a cushioned seat and back. This is so grateful that I feel like a cripple in a Dickens novel who has been given it after 65 years of doorstep. Then the brazen wash-girl came, gave me my washing, and lifted 50 centimes off me while she said it was 'si bon dans ma chambre—tout était si joli.' That made me furious of course—and this has been a heavy day for expenses. But all the same my heart feels a little bit lighter. There is a sailing boat moored to the quai. It is called *Les Trois Amis*. All the same, Boge, I miss you too much, you know. Something in me *pines*.

Wednesday (January 30, 1918)

No letter and the post has been. Two *Daily News*. Pas de lettre? Pas de lettre! So I suppose there's another gone, or perhaps Geoffroi's composition exhausted my poor boy. They are very trying efforts; I made one yesterday, and shuddered to re-read it. It is a very warm still day. Not a breath of wind, and a warm haze over the opposite coast. In the yard they are beating carpets: the sound 'fits' somehow. The sous-marin has just sneaked out of the bay. They are ugly brutes.

Darling, I do in a way live here. I see a great deal, am very solitary and quiet; lead the life I tell you of—never speaking to anybody except bonjour and bonsoir—and yet in a way it is all absolutely unreal: it is all a dream. My mind seems to do nothing but build and build and try and try that bridge that brings me home. I get into *panics* that I shan't be allowed home; the offensive will stop it, France will run out of coal. No, you would laugh at my fears. But life, as it is at present, is too terrifying to be endured alone. To be cut off, like I am here, and then to think of all that can prevent me being joined on. And then *air raids—colds*—about a million of these things rattle their skeleton bones at me. I can't really and truly enjoy it, you know. I am doing it for my health—et voilà! But though it is exceedingly lovely, and those first days were enchanted days, I'd rather live above a public-house in the Mile End Road and near you . . . . I can't *help* it. My heart is never free from anxiety and never can be while I am away from you and a war is on. That is why even one day without a letter is sufficient to start me off like this. Do you feel the same?

And I look out and think: if he were here, this would be Paradise—Paradise.

Tu sais, mon chéri, je t'aime *trop*.

Your girl
Wig

Late Afternoon   Wednesday,
My dearest,   (January 30, 1918)

I am not going to make a habit of writing to you *deux fois par jour*—but just on these days when there is something 'out of joint', I must—I must.

I decided when I went out this afternoon to buy the little coffee-pot and the coffee. But first I walked in the direction of the Hotel des Bains. Yes, it was beautiful, very—silver and gold light—old men painting boats, old women winding wool or mending nets—young girls making those gay wreaths of yellow flowers—and a strange sweet smell came off the sea. But I was homesick. I went to the paper shop to exchange a smile with someone—and bought for 3 sous *le Paris Daily Mail and* a smile. A commercial traveller with a wooden leg was in the shop taking orders. 'Toujours pas de chocolat?' said Madame. 'Mon Dieu, Madame, if my poor leg était seulement de vrai Menier, je serais millionaire.'

Ha, ha! Very good. Very typical. Very French. But I am faint with homesickness. Although it is so goldy warm, the tips of my fingers and my feet and lips and inside my mouth—all are dead cold. And so I walk along until I come to the public wash-place, and there are the women slipping about in the water in their cluttering sabots, holding up those bright-coloured things, laughing, shouting, and not far away from them a travelling tinker with his fat woman sits on the ground beside his mule and cart. He has a little fire to heat his solder pan and a ring of old pots round him. It makes a good 'ensemble'. The washer-women bawl after me 'T'as remarqué les bas!' but I do not care at all. I would not care if I had no stockings on at all.

And here are those villas built up the hillside. Here is the one whose garden was always full of oranges and babies' clothes on a line. Still is. Also there is a dark woman in a wide hat holding a very tiny baby to her cheek and rocking it. The road is all glare and my shoes make a noise on it as though it were iron. I feel sick, sick, as though I were bleeding to death. I sit down on a milestone and take out *The Daily Mail*. I turn my back to the shimmering sea and the fishers all out in their little boats spearing fish.

'Air Raid in London. Between 9 and 10 and again at 12.30. Still in Progress.'

That's all . . . . He would have had his dinner and be on the way home. Or if he escaped that one he was in bed. Today is Wednesday. It happened on Monday. It is no use wiring.

A cart comes up full of chunks of hay. An old man in a blue blouse with great bushy eyebrows holds up his hand and cries 'Il fait beau au soleil,' and I smile. When he passes I shut my eyes. This must be borne. This must be lived through.

Back back again along the bright burnished road and all the way composing useless telegrams: 'Heard Raid Is All Well' and so on and so on. Varied with letters to the B.C.[1] in Marseilles saying urgent family affairs compel me to return at once. Will there be any difficulty?

Shall I come back now and not wait? Answer this, my own.

Thursday

My dear love,

The facteur has just been and brought me a letter from Kay but there is again not a *line* from you. It is not as though the English posts were delayed then; there must be another reason. I do most earnestly IMPLORE you to wire if all is not well. You know what this suspense is like. It is quite dreadful. I cannot write any more until I hear again, for I am too uneasy.

For God's sake never spare me. Always write at once or wire. You can think what I felt when that bloody postman came to my door and left me empty-hearted. Oh Jag!

Wig

IMPORTANT

If you can afford a wire before you answer this letter—just the word AGREE if you do agree—it would be Heaven.

Wiggie

Dearest,   (February 1st, 1918)

I have made a resolution tonight. I mean to come back next month, *March,* as soon as Kay has sent me my money. I can see, from all signs, that if I don't get back then, I may not get back at all—the difficulties of transport will be so great. Tell nobody. Of course, a wangle will be necessary for the authorities. But the King of the Nuts at Havre told me that if I had any 'urgent family affairs' I would of course get back before 'my time'. Therefore, do you send me after the 1st of March a telegram saying 'Mother worse come back as soon as possible Bowden' and I shall have that to show.

I can stick this anxiety until then but no longer. *Don't send me any*

[1] The British Consul.

146

money, of course. I have plenty. And tell me just frankly what you think of this. I have headed the page 'important' so when you refer to it, say you have got the important letter and then I'll know which one you mean. By that time I shall be as well as I ever shall be during the war and—and—oh, I must come. I can't stick it out for longer. But tell me very frankly 'vos idées'.

Your woman

Wig

Friday,

(February 1, 1918)

Dearest Bogey,

This morning I got your Sunday night, Sunday morning p.c. and Monday night letter all together, and they all seemed to be knocked off by such a steam engine that I wonder they didn't arrive sooner. I could feel your hurry and haste post haste in every curl of your 'y's' and I felt that by the time the letters had touched the bottom of the post-bag you were up to your reine claude eyes again.

However, it is very reassuring after my Days of Panic and Homesickness to feel that it's all going on and it's silly to worry. The *D.M.* yesterday said it was the worst raid London had had, but perhaps that is my eye.

I have also with great joy received the papers: they'll be a feast.

I am rather diffident about telling you—because so many sham wolves have gone over the bridge—that I am working and have been for two days. It looks to me the real thing. But one never knows. I'll keep quiet about it until it is finished.

Blast your old cold. How rotten that the fine days didn't cure it! What extraordinary weather you have been having. As for today, here, at a quarter to nine it was hot in the sun, for I got up to pull the curtain over my dresses, thinking they would fade. The sea is like a silver lake and the exquisite haze hangs over the coast. You can hear the fishermen from far, far away, the flash of oars and their talk to one another. Where there were 20 flowers there seem to be 20 hundred everywhere. Everything is in such abundant bloom. We never knew this place so warm. One could walk about in a cotton dress and old men survey their villa gardens in cream alpaca jackets and swathed sun-helmets!

My wing hurts me horribly this morning: I don't know why. And I don't care, really. As long as I can work—as long as I can work.

147

Good God! There's some reckless bird trying over a note or two! He'll be *en cocotte* within the hour. I simply loathe and abominate the French bourgeoisie. Let me put it on record again. There are a round dozen of them descended on this hotel, and all, after a day or two, in each other's pockets, arms round each other, sniggering, confiding internal complaints and 'elle m'a dit' and 'mon mari m'a dit'—and the gentlemen with their 'Passez, mes-*dames*'—God! how I detest them. I must show it in some way. For they avoid me like pison, only breaking into the most *amused* laughter after I have passed (you know the style) and staring until their very eyes congeal while I take my food. It is the ugliness and cruelty which hurts so much, beneath all one's cool contemptuous manner. But I suppose a great part of the earth is peopled with these fry, only as a rule we don't see them. I do feel though that the Frenchies must be the lowest.

When you can afford it, would you send me *Nicholas Nickleby*? (I am not reading Dickens *idly*).

The quiet day! The air quivers and three tiny flies have performed a very successful and highly intricate dance in my window space.

I bought such a nice little coffee pot. It will do for hot milk at home. It has a lid and is white with blue daisies on it—in fact it's charming and only cost 65 centimes. I do hope Lesley has helped you to get really tidy. (No, darling, the shoes never came.)

Give my lo᷉ ᷉ to your Mother when you see her again. Did you ever take her that French muslin blouse?

Goodbye for today.

I am your own
Wig

Sunday morning,
Dearest,   (February 3, 1918)

It is early for me to be up, but I had such a longing for a cigarette, and as I sit here in my pyjamas smoking a very good one I'll begin your letter. There was nothing from you yesterday and the facteur hasn't been yet today. However—

I really feel I *ought* to send you some boughs and songs, for never was time nor place more suited, but to tell you the truth I am pretty well absorbed in what I am writing[1] and walk the blooming country-

---

[1] *Je ne parle pas français.*

148

side with a 2d. notebook shutting out *les amandiers*. But I don't want to discuss it in case it don't come off. . . .

I've two 'kick offs' in the writing game. *One* is joy—real joy—the thing that made me write when we lived at Pauline, and that sort of writing I could only do in just that state of being in some perfectly blissful way *at peace*. Then something delicate and lovely seems to open before my eyes, like a flower without thought of a frost or a cold breath—knowing that all about it is warm and tender and 'ready'. And *that* I try, ever so humbly, to express.

The other 'kick off' is my old original one, and (had I not known love) it would have been my all. Not hate or destruction (both are beneath contempt as real motives) but an *extremely* deep sense of hopelessness, of everything doomed to disaster, almost wilfully, stupidly, like the almond tree and 'pas de nougat pour le noël'.[1] There! as I took out a cigarette paper I got it exactly—*a cry against corruption*—that is *absolutely* the nail on the head. Not a protest—a *cry,* and I mean corruption in the widest sense of the word, of course.

I am at present fully launched, right out in the deep sea, with this second state. I may not be able to 'make my passage,' I may have to put back and have another try: that's why I don't want to talk about it, and have breath for so little more than a hail. But I must say the boat feels to be driving along the deep water as though it smelt port (no, darling, better say 'harbour' or you'll think I am rushing into a public house).

After lunch.

My Boge,

I have just read your Tuesday note written after *another* raid. You sound awfully tired, darling, and awfully disenchanted. You are overworking . . . it's too plain.

(Curse my old shoes. Keep them for me. Don't worry about them any more.)

Yes, I agree with you—blow the old war! It is a toss-up whether it don't get every one of us before it's done. Except for the first warm days here when I really did seem to almost forget it, it's never out of my mind, and everything is poisoned by it. It's *here in* me the whole time, eating me away—and I am simply terrified by it. It's at the root of my homesickness and anxiety and panic, I think. It took being alone here

[1] This a reference to a beautiful poem in Provençal by Henri Fabre, the naturalist, telling of the withering of the almond blossom by the cold.

and unable to work to make me fully fully *accept* it. But now I don't think that even you would beat me. I have got the pull of you in a way because I am working, but I solemnly assure you that every moment away from my work is MISERY. And the human contact—just the pass the time away chat—distracts you—and that of course I don't have at all. I miss it very much. Birds and flowers and dreaming seas don't do it. Being a biped, I must have a two-legged person to *talk* to. You can't imagine how I feel that I walk about in a sort of black glittering case like a beetle . . . .

Queer business . . . .

By the way, I dreamed the other night that —— came to you and asked you for money. She 'knew you had some'. She bullied you into giving her £5. I woke terrified lest this might happen. Never let it. Your money is really earned with your blood. Never give it away. You need it; you must have it. PLEASE, please!

I wonder what you will say to my 'important' letter, and if you agree will they let me through? Can they keep me out of my own country? These are a couple of refrains which are pretty persistent. They say here that after March this railway will probably be closed till June.

My own precious, I love you *eternally*.

Your
Wig

Sunday Night,
(February 3, 1918)

My precious,

I don't dare to work any more tonight. I suffer so frightfully from insomnia here and from night terrors. That is why I asked for another Dickens; if I read him in bed he diverts my mind. My work excites me so tremendously that I almost feel *insane* at night, and I have been at it with hardly a break all day. A great deal is copied and carefully addressed to you, in case any misfortune should happen to me. Cheerful! But there is a great black bird flying over me, and I am so frightened he'll settle—so terrified. I don't know exactly what *kind* he is.

If I were not working here, with war and anxiety I should go mad, I think. My night terrors here are rather complicated by packs and packs of growling, roaring, ravening, prowl-and-prowl-around dogs.

God! How tired I am! How I'd love to curl up against you and sleep. Goodnight, my blessed one. Don't forget me in your busy life.

Dearest, (February 4, 1918)

No letter from you today. I had one from Ida written on *Friday*—so the posts have got a real grudge against you and me. . . . I am posting you the first chapter of my new work today. I have been hard put to it to get it copied in time to send it off, but I am so *exceedingly* anxious for your opinion.

It needs perhaps some explanation. The subject, I mean *lui qui parle,* is of course taken from —— and ——, and God knows who. It has been more or less in my mind ever since I first felt strongly about the French. But I hope you'll see (of course, you will) that I'm not writing with a sting. I'm not indeed!

I read the fair copy just now and couldn't think where the devil I had got the bloody thing from—-I can't even now. It's a mystery. There's so much much less taken from life than anybody would credit. The African laundress I had a bone of—but only a bone—Dick Harmon, of course is, partly is—

Oh God! Is it good? I am frightened. For I stand or fall by it. It's as far as I can get at present; and I have gone for it—bitten deeper and deeper and deeper than ever I have before. You'll laugh a bit about the song. I could see Goodyear grin as he read that . . . . But what is it like? Tell me—don't spare me. Is it the long breath as I feel to my soul it is— or is it a false alarm? You'll give me your *dead honest opinion,* won't you, Bogey?

If this gets lost, I break my pen—

I am only, at the moment, a person who works, comes up to read newspapers, AND to wait for postmen, goes down again, drinks tea. Outside the window is the scenic railway—all complete—and behind that pretty piece is the war.

Forgive an empty head. It rattled all night. I can't manage this sleeping business.

Goodbye for now, my heart's treasure.

Yours, yours only for ever

Wig

Monday Night,

(February 4, 1918)

Tuesday is different. Just cast a beamy on this and then climb down the ladder. [A long line leading to the Tuesday portion of the letter.]

Oh, Bogey,

It would be heaven if I were to get a letter from you tomorrow—not *too* tired a one and one that brought me 'near'. Heaven knows, my precious, that ain't a complaint. But I *am* so tired tonight that I'd give anything for *you, you, you*.

I decided after I posted your letter and MS today and had my walk to try and forget work for an hour or two. So I have repacked and re-sorted my box, gone through all my possessions and generally behaved as though this were my last night on earth. Even to the extent of writing my address c/o *you* to be communicated with in case of need, in French and English, in my passport case.

Now, all is fair .... What a fool I am!

The worst of REAL insomnia is one spends a great part of the day wondering if one is going to bring it off the coming night. Can I stand another last night? Of course, I suppose I can. But must I? Not to sleep, and to be alone, is a very neat example of HELL. But what isn't? Ah, there you have me.

Tuesday,

My precious love,   (February 5, 1918)

I never had such a direct answer to prayer. Two letters, *real* letters from you about our cottage and all that—a Wednesday and a Thursday one. This of course has given me the *salto mortale*—and I am a changed child. Also, I did manage, by eating myself to death at dinner and only reading curly poetry afterwards and taking 10 grains of aspirin, to get to sleep. So + and + and +.

God! what it is to count on letters, so. Now about us living on very little after the war. You know I am as determined as you about that. You must take the saddle and bridle off Dashing Off and we must watch him *bolt away* for ever. We MUST live in some remote place and all our food must grow on trees and bushes. No cities, no people. And of course we must have a good servant. I'll not do housework again or cook, even though I shall long to because I think I do it so well. Least I mean I won't *be* the cook again—nor will you sweep the stairs. As to clothes—I'll never need them any more.

I had a red-wine letter from Marie today *re* your dinner. Oh, what a point it was! I am delighted you did it. She was quite swept away and described you in a thick brown suit, orange hanky, woolly weskit, hair just the right length—I sent the letter to Mummy today: I could see her 'lapping it up'. After we are married, I want to know your Mother differently. I *can't* before. I wonder if you understand that? . . . Oh, my darling love, how these letters have refreshed me! How that glimpse of the cottage has 'lightened my darkness'.

(By the way, I had better tell you: I am a MISER.)

I have worked 3 hours already today: it's midi. If you knew the time it does take to steep and steep myself before I am anyway near content. My own, I love you. Your letters are HEAVEN and I fly about in them like a gold and silver

Wig

Yes, a letter. A 'fog' letter.   Wednesday,

My own precious,   (February 6, 1918)

Four years ago today Goodyear gave me *The Oxford Book of English Verse*.[1] I discovered that by chance this morning . . . . Do you know how much this (the cheapest paper here) costs? One sou the page! Isn't that a revolting swin?

I knew the weather was awful with you. How vile! The only thing to remember is that it isn't and *can't be* November. Is that a consolation when one is in the foggy spot? I'm afraid not . . . .

Dearest, can you send me your financial statement one day soon? You know you promised you would. I should feel greatly relieved to know just what you had in your wild thyme bank. And don't think it will make me ask for a ta-ra-ra, because you know I am more of a miser than you. But I would greatly like to know.

By the way I think cultur*al* (one of ——'s words and a great one of Kennedy's[2]) a vile 'un.

I passed 'our house' again yesterday, and it looked so heavenly fair with the white and red almond trees and the mimosa attending that I went into a field hard by where they were gathering the flowers and asked for information. A big dark girl, with a great sheaf of flowers on one arm, and the other arm raised, keeping her face from the sun, said: 'Ah, Madame, c'est *une mauvaise maison*. Non, elle n'est pas louée. Le propriétaire habite Marseille. Mais, vous savez, la maison est *ben* mauvaise; elle se casse toujours. On a fait de grandes réparations, il y a un an, mais personne n'est venu pour la

[1] For Frederick Goodyear see *Journal*, March 1916.

[2] The first name is indecipherable. J. M. Kennedy was a friend of Katherine's in her *New Age* days.

prendre. Et, main-ten-ant, elle est à moitié cassée encore. On dit de cette maison, qu'elle n' aime pas les gens.' And then she bent over the flowery fields again . . . .

On my way home from my walk yesterday I met le père de Marthe. We shook hands. He was very nice—you remember, in a patent leather cap, rather like a drawing by Gus Bofa. Marthe is married and lives in Toulon. 'Son mari est à Gibralte.' Yes, he was the young man who used to walk with her in the garden on Sunday. I said, 'When you write, please remember me to her.' Said he, 'J'écris *tous les soirs*. Vous savez, elle était *ma seule fille*.' This, of course, warmed my heart to an extra-ordinary degree, and I wished Chaddie hadn't given me my furs so that I could have sent them to Marthe, etc., etc.

I worked a good deal yesterday, but I slept too. It's fatal for me to work late at night, when I am alone. I never realise unless I stop how *screwed up* I am. Last night, *petit enfant très sage*, I made myself another little 'front' out of material I bought here—you know the kind [draw-ing]—and it sent me into a fast sleep.

The widow here actually gave me 2 bunches of white hyacinths yesterday. What can it mean? They smell simply divine, and then Juliette still makes a garden of my room. I have to put the flowers on the window sill at night; ils sentent si fort. In the early morning when I wake and see the row of little pots so gentiment disposés I feel rather like the heroine of a German lyric poem. We must grow all varieties of jonquils.

I am still in *a state of work*—you know, my precious: dead quiet and spinning away. I feel rather today, and felt it yesterday too after your letters that I ought to stick it till April, that people will be so cross if I come in March, and that I ought to wait and then come *bang* in April. I wonder. If you think so, well, you will say so, I know.

Have you got your meat card? Of course, I think the meat cards will stop the war. Nothing will be done but *spot*-counting, and people will go mad and butchers and pork butchers will walk about with bones in their hair, distracted. Talking of hair—do you know those first days I was here I went a bit GREY over both temples. Real grey hair. I know—I feel the very moment it came, but it is a blow to see it . . . .

Another thing I hate the French bourgeoisie for is their absorbed interest in evacuation. What is constipating or what not? That is a real *criterion* . . . . At the end of this passage there is a W.C. Great Guns! they troop and flock there . . . and not only that . . . they are all victims of the most amazing Flatulence imaginable. Air raids over London don't hold a candle to 'em. This, I suppose, is caused by their violent purges, and remedies, but it seems to me very 'unnecessary'. Also the people of the village have a habit of responding to their serious needs (I suppose by night) down on the shore round the palm trees. Perhaps it's the sailors, but my English gorge rises and my English lips curl in contempt. The other day one palm tree had a placard nailed on it *Chiens Seulement*. Was that funny? It provided a haw-haw for the day, here. But on my life, I'd almost rather, like that English lady, not know whether my husband went to the lavatory or not, than be so unbuttoned. No, this world, you know, Bogey, this grown up world everywhere, *don't* fit me.

You do though, you fit me. Oh, my darling boy, what would life be without love? I don't think I'd stick it out: I'd jump over something.

I adore you (that's your reflection in me[1])

Your own
Wig

Thursday,

My precious one, (February 7, 1918)

The Aged brought me your wire last night. How it can have got here with such unspeakable rapidity I *can't* imagine, but there it was. But, dearest, I don't WANT any money. I shall have Kay's and that will be more than enough. If you haven't sent it, please don't. If you have, I'll tell Kay not to send his, because I must not travel too rich. I don't know what to say about your wire. I want your letter so, with vos idées in it. I still, in my heart, feel just the same, but I *could* and *would* stick it till April and chance getting a train back if you thought (having thought it over) this would be better. Please 'note that'.

Today I haven't got a letter from you, but a *Westminster* has come and a *D. N.* Thank you, love. I am still *at it*. Oh, when can I hear about that MS and *what* are you going to say? Now I'm up, now I'm down, but I am awfully frightened. The rest of the world can take a 99-year lease of all the houses in Putney—but—what do *you* think?

I must write to H. L. today or she will take great offence and I don't want to have her my enemy. It's too nauseous. But, to tell the truth, it's difficult, very, to keep it up: the 'atmosphere' at —— (which is now

---

[1] There is a wavy flourish under 'you'.

explained . . . one knows where the smell comes from, so to speak: it's her false relation with ——) does offend me unspeakably. I don't feel I *could* go back there. I am always underneath so acutely uneasy—not at my ease, I mean, and I do so hate dragging the Poets into such a pool. I'm so tempted to say, coolly and for all: 'Pray keep *Keats* out of this . . . .' You know? She *is* bloody interesting—the fact she doesn't know she's poisoned, *par exemple*, but I really have got all I want from her (down to the shawlet!!). Still, one mustn't let her 'turn', I suppose.

Bogey, I have such a passion, such a passion for life in the country— for peace, for you lying on your back in the sun looking up through wavy boughs, for you planting things that climb sticks, for me cutting things that have a sweet smell. Once the war is over, this is ours *on the spot*. For we shall live so remote that the rent can't cost much—and then you become dreadfully idle with long curly hair like a pony that has been turned out to graze in a speckled field.

IF I do come in March, you will keep the secret, won't you, and not let people know? I'll just turn up . . . and of course this is *tremendously* trains permitting.

This place does seem to launch me. I am simply packed with ideas and ways of writing which are important ones as I see it . . . . But the more I think the more astounded I am at the immense division between you and me and—everybody else alive. All the 'writers' whose books I see reviewed—did you ever! —— and —— and Co.

It's lunch time and the bell has gone and judging from the smell of fish the lunch is about to play the Mahomet's mountain trick on me. I'll to *it*.

Goodbye for now, my soul.

Your woman,

Wig

Friday,

My dear Heart,   (February 8, 1918)

A postcard and your Sunday and Monday letter today. Yes, the posts are MAD. But Bogey, we won't go flying off again when this is over, will we? Otherwise, I'd buy a pigeon today and begin to train it. Oh, oh, oh, your letters! My sails begin to flap, I am at the mercy of the sea and the tide and all the winds great and small, if there is not one aboard. They are simply *everything*. I cannot imagine how letters can do so much. Why, when I read you 'cooked a herring like a genius', do I simply roll over, squeeze the pillow, *hug* it and smile to every toe? But I do. And as I write this, I love you that you must feel the tips of your fingers beginning to tingle.

I can see your and Sullivan's gloomy little snack . . . . 'Unless they would marry a gallows and beget young gibbets I never saw two men so prone.' But Bogey, isn't it miraculous how our minds *cross*? You are feeling the war again just as I am and just at the same *time*.

Funny you should have seen Cannan too, when only yesterday I mentioned the Gillyflowers and the Wallypoles . . . .

(God! I am smoking the most infernal camel-droppings: 60 centimes a packet of 40 grammes. But it's all that's to be had.)

It's in the air today. I feel as though I were blowing back to you—on my way.

Juliette is like a double stock—tufty, strong, very sweet, very gay. Yesterday she helped me wash my hair. Every service she makes a kind of 'party' of. It was *fun* to heat and stagger in with two huge pots of water—to warm towels and keep them hot in folded newspapers—and the success of the operation was hers, too. She rejoiced over one's dry hair and ran away singing down the corridor. She sings nearly always as she works, and she has a friend, Madeleine, who pegs the linen on the line between the mimosa trees. When J. is doing the rooms M. calls from the garden, 'Juli-*et-te*!' And Juliette flies to the window. 'Ah-hé! C'est toi, ma belle!'

What an enormous difference it makes to have her about rather than some poor foggy creature—or some bad-tempered one. But she could never be transplanted. She rises and sets with the sun, I am sure.

I worked away yesterday, but I'm almost frightened. My leg-wings are bearing so beautifully and make such spiral dives and looping loops. . . . But it's all for you to see.

Here is a note from Eric.[1] It's like the little chap. Can't you feel there's a touch of him in it? And I like him for not pretending he's been in the thick of it. You must see him when he comes back. The pa-man sent me a letter the other day—to say he was 60. *Very* bitter about —— (to my wicked joy).

Oh, my own, my love, my life,—you know I could pray to the Lord to make me wise and good and 'big' enough to serve this love of ours. Don't let me ever be little, God, or mean. Don't let me ever forget the wonder and the glory of *this*. All the poetry of the world *ours* and you a

[1] Eric Waters, the original of Rags in *Prelude*.

poet and me a writer. Both of us not only equipped but more and more able to do what we will. Yes, we'll have the press, and we'll cut down our expenses to the last potato, and print our books.

Oh, Bogey, I have positively to pin this letter down: it flies like a kite. Catch it. I can't hold it a minute longer.

Yours amen

Wig

Tell Rib I'm 'coming soon now'.

Saturday,

My own,
(February 9, 1918)

The postman brought today a roll of papers from you but no letter. It will come tomorrow, p'raps. I was just brushing my fringe when I heard a clumpety-clump in the passage that my heart seemed to recognize long before I did. It began to dance and beat. Yes, it was the Aged with your ADORABLE telegram. 'Sthry receivid mafnifiient Murly' I read and of course this bowled me over so much that the pins won't keep in my hair and my buttons pop like fuchsia buds and my strings all squeak when they are pulled. Well the only response I *can* make is to send you the next chapter which I'll post, as before, on Monday. But oh dear, oh dear! you have lighted such a candle! Great *beams* will come out of my eyes at lunch and play like searchlights over the pommes de terre and terrify these insect children.

Now, of course, my only faint fear is: 'Will he like the next chapter as much?' Well, I must 'wait and see'. I must say when I wrote about the *tea* [1] last night—that's a funny little typical bit—I came all over and nearly cried those sort of sweet tears that I've only known since I loved you. I say, Boge, haven't I got a *bit of you*? Funny thing is I think you'll always come walking into my stories. (And now, of course, I see future generations finding you in all my books: 'The man she was in love with'.) No, dear love, I must wait until I've had lunch before I go on with this letter. I am too much of a 'gash balloon' altogether.

1.15. Well, I wish you had eaten my *tournedos*; it was such a good 'un. The great thing here is the meat, which is superb. Oh, but now I am turned towards *home* everything is good. I eat you. I see you. And my heart (apart from my work) does nothing but store up things to give you—plans for our life—wherever it is. Shall we really really next

---

[1] See *Je ne parle pas français, Bliss* p. 103 sq.

month curl up together on the divan and talk with Rib sitting in the fender playing on a minute comb and paper? I'd die without you. 'Hang there like fruit, my soul, till the tree die!' The tree *would* die.

I have just looked at the *T.L.S.*, read your Sturge Moore article which tickled me—the last sentence is perfect—and noted that Mr. M. M. had an article of really high quality in *The Quarterly*.

How *damned* depressing and hideously inadequate that Versailles conference has been! But what I do feel is—that handful can't stop the dyke from breaking now (is that true?). I mean, there *is*—isn't there?—perfectly immense pressure upon it, and L.G. and Co. may put their hands in the hole (like the little boy in *Great Deeds Done by Little People* that Grandma used to read me on Sundays) but it's no use. Oh, I *don't* know. When I think that I am not coming home and that 'all is over'—when that mood gets me, of course I don't believe it ever will end until we are all killed as surely as if we were in the trenches. Not that *love* and *you* falsify my feeling about it, make it less terrible,—but they do fortify against it. Yes, that is too true!

Now I am waiting for a letter from you tomorrow—Sunday. The post will be late and hundreds and hundreds of imaginary Juliettes will come along the passage to my door before the real one comes. But I can bear *that* as long as the real one *does* come.

I am yours eternally,
Wig

Sunday,
(February 10, 1918)

I write in this callous-sounding way because my heart *won't* believe it. My darling precious,

I am out of breath (1) After your telegram yesterday I decided that I could contain this story no longer and wrote and wrote at it, with it, and finished it today for you.

(2) Your answer to my Important Letter came.

(3) A MOST MYSTERIOUS TELEGRAM which *so* horrifies and bewilders me that I don't dare to let myself think of it. I must wait. It says: 'Am coming leave this afternoon Baker'!!! Of course, I thought immediately of you. Something had happened. She had come to tell me. Half of me can believe nothing else. Half of me refuses to countenance such a thing. God wouldn't let it happen, and even if he did

you would never leave it to that great monster to tell me. But oh! I am so terribly worried really. Of course, I shan't know a moment's rest till she comes. And I could bear anything to have happened to anybody else—only you, *you*. Can she be the ghoul made for this? Bogey, Bogey, Bogey. I shall (if all's well) of course come back in March. This is *unbearable*—this separation.

If I had not had this telegram I should have been feeling almost happier than ever before in my writing life—yes happier than ever before because I know I have not shirked it and I have finally set my hand to something and finished it and it is an achievement of our most blessed love. But all the while I write this you must know there is this great mountain bearing towards me. What does it mean? What is she bringing?

I will write again the moment she comes. But God! until then I have this to copy and send you and I must keep quiet. I can after all do nothing but wait and wait....

Your own true love
Wig

Hullo, Jag!   Sunday still and Monday after,
My own,   (February 10 and 11, 1918)

I am just going to ignore this wire from L.M. until I hear further. If I really did give way to it, it would do neither of us any good—and it CAN'T be bad news. So there, and you must understand. £10 is *more* than enough. I'll get no money for March from Kay. *When I feel the hour has come I will wire: how is* MOTHER? *And then you will reply: Mother worse operation necessary come soon possible. See?* (But it won't be before March.)

That's not mad, is it? I have ample, ample money. I shall take care of myself *because* of you, *for* you. I'll wire from Marseilles and from Paris.

I have just put up in an envelope the rest of our story. Again this *fusion* of our minds. You talk of love-poetry. All I write or ever will write will be the fruit of our love—love-prose. This time, for instance, as I went on and *on*, I fed on our love. Nightingales, if you like, brought me heavenly manna. Could I have done it without you? No, a million times. You can see us, can't you, sprouting on every page? Even Rib had a part. I don't want to exaggerate the importance of this story or to harp on it; but it's a tribute to Love, you understand, and the best I

160

can do just now. Take it. It's yours. But what I felt so curiously as I wrote it was—ah! I am in a way *grown up* as a writer—a sort of authority—just as I feel about your poetry. Pray God you like it now you've got it all.

I *dreamed* a short story last night, even down to its name, which was *Sun and Moon*. It was very light. I dreamed it all—about children. I got up at 6–30 and wrote a note or two because I knew it would fade. I'll send it some time this week. It's so nice. I didn't dream that I read it. No, I was in it, part of it, and it played round invisible me. But the hero is not more than 5. In my dream I saw a supper table with the eyes of 5. It was awfully queer—especially a plate of half-melted ice-cream. . . . But I'll send it you.

Nothing is any good to me—no thought, no beauty, no idea—unless I have given it to you and it has become the property of these wealthiest little proprietors in the whole world: Wig + Bogey and Bogey + Wig. Assistant: *Rib*. En cas d'absence: *Rib*.

I have asked you to wire when you get this second packet, my own, because of the sous-marins. Bogey, I have MOUNDS of money. I shall arrive (without my March allowance) with a great deal. So don't worry, please—and, dearest darling precious love, guard yourself for me. Oh, *keep safe for me!*

See, I ignore this black foreboding telegram. I feel that is what you would have me to do until I know why she is so awfully coming. I will keep this letter open till tomorrow's post has been.

Monday. But the bloody thing kept me awake all night. I didn't sleep an hour, I suppose. Now, with this morning, comes your Wednesday letter and the 2 books, my heart. Did you read in my other letter I could not come till March? It seems to me my case is stronger with the authorities if I have been longer here—and the days will go by. Oh, please, please, don't worry, my own—and don't worry about my wire *till* you hear from me *as* arranged on p. 1. I feel so calm about it now it is decided. All this, of course, is subject to 'all being well' and the mystery explained. What horrifies me further is I received from L.M. this morning 2 hysterical mad screams. 'Oh, my darling, make the doctor let me come' . . . 'Oh, my darling *eat*' . . . . If she comes with news of you that you're ill—you want me—something has happened—I shall understand. If she comes for any other reason, I've done with her. But what could her other reason be? I have asked her *not* to come on my account. Oh, it's a circle: I *must* keep calm.

I wrote and finished the dream story yesterday and dedicated it to Rib. I knew I would not write it at all if I didn't on the spot, and it kept me 'quiet'. Otherwise, apart from this black ghoulish thought, all seems ah, so fair. I am coming. I've done some work. I am turned towards home. We are going to live in a biscuit box—and be the most charming biscuit-crumbs together. No, Beaufort Mansions is tempting, but London is not our home. We only have a sort of biscuit tin there. Our home is a cottage with a gold roof and silver windows.

I can expect HER tomorrow night. Not before. Well, I must work and bide her coming.

Yours, yours—every day and hour and breath I'd say

I am more your own

Wig

Monday 8 p.m.
(February 11, 1918)

No L.M. tonight. I thought she might arrive by this evening's train. Every sound from outside is *her—she*. What the HELL *does* it mean? What *can* it mean?

I am mad to begin another *big* story, now that *Sun and Moon* is ready to send you, but between me and the difficult and desirable country looms this misty peak. Perhaps your letter tomorrow will lift the veil.... Bogey, if all is well with you—and yet it's so strange. Like our own Rib, I cannot believe that all is *not* well with you, even though my mind can find no other earthly excuse for her.... I simply can't listen to my mind. No, my heart won't hear it. My heart is an enemy to it. But the suspense! I walked and walked it this afternoon after I had posted your letter and the MS recommandé. I was like a blind shepherd driving a flock of—I know not what....

This note (so neat, isn't it? such little stitches!) is to say that I love you eight hours more than I did when I said it before.

Wig

With All the Flags of Love Flying.   Tuesday,
My precious,   (February 12, 1918)

Your Thursday letter and the page explaining L.M. has come, and your Friday letter about my story.

My heart was right. Rib was right again. This relief is boundless and yet I *knew* it. There was just this 'panic' like there always is. And, my own lover, be calm. Don't feel the strain. See? I am very calm about coming back. I will manage it—beautifully. Don't be frightened. I feel so strong. (I want to write about your Friday letter bang off first, but I'll just finish with L.M.) Bogey, I have done with her. I ASKED her NOT to come; said I didn't want her, and then she wired me 'Leaving'. That ends it. She's a revolting hysterical ghoul. She's never content except when she can eat me. My God!! But I shall keep great control. As she has come I of course must see her, and she must be here, but I can't stop working, for her. Till I get back I shall not alter my programme in the smallest particular for her. She's done it; very well—she must suffer for her infernal hysteria. I don't think it will make it more difficult for me to get back because it's not until March that I'm coming and I may travel with her, but I shall ignore *her* object in returning. She'd *like* me to be paralysed of course—or blind—preferably blind. However I shall keep cool and explain that I only can see her at meals and a walk in the afternoon. All the mornings I always keep my room. After lunch I write or read till 2. When I come in at five, it's my *great* time to write till dinner, and after dinner I read. She must find some occupation. I *loathe* her so much for this and for the drivel and moaning of her letters to me that I shall never soften. If I did, bang would go my work again. *Finis.*

Now about your letter about the first chapter. I read it and I wept for joy. How can you so marvellously understand and so receive my love offering. Ah, it will take all of the longest life I can live to repay you. I *did* feel (I do) that this story is the real thing and that I did not once (as far as I know) shirk it. Please God, I'll do much better for us—but I felt: There, I can lay down my pen now I've made that, and give it to Bogey. Yes, I did feel that. But, Christ! a devil about the size of a flea nips in my ear 'Suppose he's disappointed with the second half?' . . .

I'll send you *Sun and Moon* today, *registré, but of course* don't *wire* about *it*. And, unless the Mountain arrives here and milks me of money, I must tell you I have a surprise for you on that score, which will make you happy. *To tell your fortune I do not pretend,* it sounds like. You know that machine we stuck a penny in. Yes, I'm sure I shall be able to manage it. You know the programme? *Wait* for my wire: 'How is Mother?' That is the signal. Then wire: 'Mother worse operation necessary return soon as possible.'

I don't think there can be a big, big battle before March because the ground's not hard enough. (That sounds like Rib speaking.) Now I know about this woman, I am myself again. She will have to look after herself. But she's nicely finished my (really, on the whole) odious friendship. My new story is signalled. And I love you. I adore you. To eat in a kitchen with you is my ultimate wishing ring.

Your own woman
Wig

Tuesday Night,
(February 12, 1918)

My precious,

At about six o'clock *loud steps, special knock* (that special knock!!), black velvet head to follow familiar voice 'May I come in?' And she was here. She seems to have got here all right, completely hysterical about me. I debated as to whether to hold over my feelings and intentions or to be sincere, and was (but not horribly, not *hatefully*) sincere. Told her just what I thought and so on and established my relation with her. I *can't* like her; in fact, I am so shut away that she's a perfect stranger. She brought me some squashed *babas au rhum* from Paris. Why did that make me almost angrier than anything? However, all is *out,* and she took it all right, and I have told her my programme. I think, now she *is* here, she'd better stay till March and we will travel back together (if she can get back). Don't think me a cold-hearted friend; I am not. But really she has persecuted me and if I didn't put up a fight, she'd ruin all our life. That's what she wants to do. 'If there wasn't Jack'—that is what she says,—and that I really CANNOT STAND from anybody. But don't let's talk about her. I am not going to think about her any more. We shall feed together and walk together. The rest she must manage. If it's a toss-up between work and L.M., work wins—and it *is* a toss-up. What she can't stand is you and I—*us.* You've taken away her prey—which is me. I'm not exaggerating. Well, you have. So there, and now she knows it. *Finito.*

I lay down today under a pine-tree, and though I spent some time saying 'The wells and the springs are poisoned', they were not really. I began to construct my new story. Until I get back to you and we are safe in each other's arms, there is only one thing to do, and that is, to *work, work, work.*

God! how I want you! There are no words for this. It's just longing. ... But I can't help feeling the wind is in our favour somehow and I am blowing home. Until I come I shall *reste* as *tranquille* as I can and try and get a great deal done. This is just for to let you know she is here. Thank you for the book, my love. No more books now please. I have plenty to last me. Goodnight! Ah, when shall I *say* that and *seal* it?

Your
Wig

Wednesday,
(February 13, 1918)

No English post today, my darling, but I am not really worried, only —as usual—a great piece—the living piece of the day falls out, especially as the postman came singing all along the corridor, knocked and handed me a letter from an old woman who crossed over from England with me and who is in Paris. Any letter that is not yours I have such a grudge against that I don't want to open it even—I mean when it comes unaccompanied by one of yours.

When you have got this far, break off, look at Rib and say 'She loves me most frightfully today', and Rib will screw up one eye at you and say 'I know. It's burning me from right over there'.

I put all the unfinished MSS I had brought with me here in a row last night and, sitting on my Peggy,[1] I reviewed them, and told them that none of them were really good enough—to march into the open. (Ugh! No—I can't even in fun use these bloody comparisons. I have a horror of the way this war creeps into writing . . . oozes in . . . trickles in.)

Until I go from here I live in a sort of rainbow—wondering, Will it be brighter? That's my hope, and you are the little pot of gold. It's such a warm day today I sat in a basin of cold water and had a bath like a sparrow in a fountain. I *love* you, I *love* you.

There is a new sort of jonquil here that I must find the name of. We must grow it. It's so lovely—and the green is very deep, the flower being starry. You see, our future is so miraculous—so delicate—so heavenly, that how can one keep from trembling and feeling terrified, when this great blast roars between us and it. How can we possibly even try to pass it and escape it if we're not simply clinging to each other?

But I am coming.

Your Wig

[1] Alas, I do not remember what her Peggy was.

165

Thursday,

My own,   (February 14, 1918)

I had 2 letters from you today—your last Saturday letter and your
Monday letter. No Sunday letter at all. Your Saturday letter is the one
in which you speak of my staying longer and taking a villa perhaps now
L.M. is here. However long I stay, I would *never* do that. I can keep
apart from her more or less here, but any other form of life would be
quite intolerable. As it is she goes on just like Mrs. Nickleby and nearly
makes me die with fury at meals. Still—schweig! I am as strong as I
shall be ever *here*. I shall be careful *there*. *Unless you feel I ought to stay
till April, when I will without a word,* or that it would be better, I'll make
a dash for it in March. If you think it would be better for me to stay
till April *for one moment,* of course I will. She of course would go back.
As it is, it is: 'Oh dear, I wonder what my little foreman is doing etc.
etc. etc.' Do please never again reckon upon L.M. in my life. When I
get back I part from her—and she pretty well knows it, and if she were
honest (impossible!) desires it too. But remember if you think I ought to
stay till April, I stay—and risk the offensive and the sous-marins without a murmur. Put 2 little lines to your answer to this like I've made
and I'll know that you *have* answered.

Voilà! My health won't improve by being here: it's as good as it ever
will be—to her rage, disgust and chagrin, of course. Oh, you should
have seen her face drop when she said, 'I thought you were very ill.'
My blood turned ice with horror.

If I do come in March I will come with her. Frankly, that *is* a relief:
to feel I have someone to help me. I am not much good at this travelling
alone. Now you have my honest answer.

I went a great old walk yesterday, came in, screwed my head tight,
and thought myself nearly black in the face, but got very little down.
Trouble is I feel I have found an *approach* to a story now which I must
apply to everything. Is that nonsense? I read what I wrote before that
last[1] and I feel: No, this is all *once removed*: It won't do. And it won't.
I've got to reconstruct everything.

I hate to talk like this when you are so fiendishly tied and bound,
but, my heart, my own, I do feel so that I shall be able to relieve the
strain a bit when I come back. I shall? Shan't I?

Family News. M. is coming to England and bringing me maple sugar

[1] *Je ne parle pas français.*

166

which Chaddie is to hand over. *Do* see that we get it. You know how good it is.

I have got a fit of the war very badly today, darling: this is why this letter reads so hurried and strange. You know, I feel it like a black cloud pulling over. And I feel you overwork horribly! But there! Take me into your arms and I am well again.

Oh, Bogey, Bogey, Bogey!

Your own
Wig

My darling,   (February 14, 1918)

Please give your mother this little hanky with my fond love—will you? If you think it is fine enough. *And* please give her this receipt for brown bread—will you? It is *my* mother's and she says it is most awfully good. It sounds to me rather funny because of the bran, but mother says that is quite right and everybody who comes to our house walks off full of it, a kind of human pincushion. Of course, I long to 'knock up a batch' as they say. But do ask your mother to try it. And remember to give her the hanky—won't you?—just to prove I remember her and do think of her.

Your own
Wig

BROWN BREAD

Mix 2 cups of white flour with one cup of bran and 3 teaspoonfuls of baking powder. Add 1 dessertspoonful of golden syrup. Mix to a soft dough with a little warm milk and water. Bake in a greased cake tin for $1\frac{1}{2}$ hours.

Friday,

My dearest dear,   (February 15, 1918)

No letter today. Oh dear! How I did want one, too. The papers came registered, but I had not slept and I was most enormously in want of *you*. So I signed for the papers and though they are full of meat . . . still —you know!

I'm dull today. My story has got a bone in its leg—a big one. I may and I do (except for meals and a walk) ignore the Mountain, but she do cast a considerable big shadow. You see, there is no lesser word for it: I *hate* her so much—her insincerity, more her falseness—and you can

167

realize that she pays me back in pretty heavy copper, when I *do* see her. Still, it can't be helped.

I haven't a puff in my sails today, Bogey. You never saw such a head as mine must be within. . . . Nothing less than a letter from you will do. . . . It's also because I didn't sleep, see? and couldn't find my place in the bed and looked for it all night—*lashed* about in a hundred beds, I should think, but no, didn't find my place to curl in.

Yesterday behind the hills at the back, I struck 3 divine empty houses. They have been empty for a long time, and will be (till we take one). I cannot tell you *how* lovely they all are, or how exquisitely placed, with gardens, terraces. Ours had also a stone verandah and two particularly heavenly trees embracing in front of it. In the cracks of the stone verandah little white hyacinths were all in flower. A sunny bank at the side was blue with violets. There was a baby tree that waited to be hung with a poem. And the approach! The approach! The colour of the house was a warm pink-yellow with a red roof, the shape [here a drawing of the house]. Oh, I can't make it, but it was, I think, flying with little loves. It *faces* the city beyond the hills, which yesterday was bathed in light. But all this—without *you*—it is such mockery, such mockery. I look, I see, I feel and then I say THE WAR and it seems to disappear—to be taken off like a film and I'm sitting in the dark.

My own, forgive this very tame little girl of yours today. Her heart is—ah, you know her heart—but it is looking for a letter and all the rest of her is empty.

Your own
Wig

Saturday,
Dearest of all,   (February 16, 1918)

No letter again today: that is 3 whole days. Isn't it simply *too* cursed! The *D.N.* for Tuesday came, but I simply *long* for a letter—and it won't come. I had a moment, just after the post, when I wondered if you thought now L.M. was here it wasn't so necessary, but that was unworthy of me. You'd not think that.

Yesterday, your dull girl went for a dull crawl, got back, and in two T's a terrific squall had sprung up, it was icy cold, raging wind. Shelley was drowned again. The wind went on all night. Now it has dropped and it is SMOKING. I am writing to you with a pair of pale lilac hands and cheeks to match.

Such a fight goes on with my old work, too. The Mountain *will* sit on it. Though I stick so faithful to my programme, meal times and walk times are quite enough to exasperate me and lash me into fury beyond measure. 'Katie mine, who is Wordsworth? Must I like him? It's no good looking cross because I love you, my angel, from the little tip of that cross eyebrow to the *all* of you. When am I going to brush your hair again?' I shut my teeth and say 'Never!' but I really *do* feel that if she could she'd EAT me. Still, I shall use her as a walking-stick to help me to get home on—because I am *not* any good at travelling alone. I always seem to slip through the cracks in the floor like a pin and people do bang into me so. *Steps* at my door . . . .

They were the Aged with your wire. Wasn't that a bit of luck? It has just come at the right moment. Now I know that all is well and now I'll just go on expecting those old letters tomorrow. You must have got my babies[1] as well as the other! Thank you, my darling heart, for wiring so soon.

I was thinking in bed last night of being with you, in some little strange town it was, and we suddenly touched hands. I thought then how the feeling of your hand is such a wonder to me, such a comfort. It *fits* me so—and I thought: 'Their hands were *quick* with love'. That just expresses it.

I am homesick today, Bogey. I saw Ma'am Gamel yesterday, and told her I'd want to take some butter back. They will let me bring a pound of that butter, I suppose? I can see you undoing the parcel. I can see you—see you—I don't see anything *but* you. Nobody else exists for me. I can't write letters and 'keep up' with people. A note perhaps to Johnny[2] (because I feel he in a way knows about us) but everybody else—don't count.

I can never know real peace or rest away from you: I freely confess it. Because I leave my heart with you—and all my desires.

It is very cold and pale outside: and I can't help thinking about that Versailles business. It's at the back of my mind all the while I write.

Ah, love, take care of yourself for

Your own little

Wig

[1] *Sun and Moon.*   [2] J. D. Fergusson.

READ THIS CAREFULLY TWICE
THEN SHOW IT TO RIB.

My darling Heart,

The Lord saw fit to remove the shadow from me this afternoon and
I began to write free again, and was just in it when Juliette brought me
a letter—a miracle by an afternoon post! It was your *Monday* letter,
but you said on the envelope it was Tuesday (oh, yes: I understand). It
was the letter about L.M. and the money. If you *had* paid for her, I
think I'd have *had* to kill her. It would have been more than flesh could
stand. I won't give a sou or spend a sou: I save. I am mean, if you like:
but I save like a miser and account for every penny—so that I shall have
some to add to our pot-au-feu when I get back. *You are not to think for
one second that there will be the same old corvée after the war.* Please God,
we'll get a press. I agree absolutely: think with you, feel with you,
understand. My serious stories won't ever bring me anything but my
'child' stories ought to and my light ones, once I find a place. I am sure
I shall always have enough from Father to keep US in a cottage with
penny packets of seeds to feed us, and our fires we shall gather and our
water we'll get in a well. All you have to think of is that it cannot *not*
come true—it's so utterly simple. We shall live on honey-dew and
milk of Paradise; we shall be happy and free immediately. There is not
a moment to lose. Ah, my soul, if you doubt *this*; if you feel for one
instant that the big stone could fall on your head then love is not what
I think it is. Consider. Let's be practical.

In a real cottage, deep in the country, £150 would keep us at first—
apart from a penny you earn or I might. Bogey, what can I say? It
makes me so unhappy when you doubt it. I want to wring my hands
and run up and down. We know each other and our wants and ways
are plain to us. We shall always be 'little gentlefolk' wherever we live.
We've got furniture, books, a lovely doll. Don't you want to be my
mate and live with me in a tiny cottage and eat out of egg-cups? How
can you torture me by thinking anything else is possible? During this
bloody war it's true you're a prisoner. But how could I live knowing
you were in prison for one day after the war? If you really think you
will be and that we can't live on my money, then I shall die. For I
won't live any other life—no, I won't. We'd better both take poison.
Oh, how awful this is!

Of course, you can't ask people. You can't hate them like *I* do. I would put them all on a toasting fork and let them frizzle if I could. But who wants to ask?

Bogey, you can do whatever you please, but you are not to take a little hammer and bang at my heart because it will break. It's not a rag heart, or a calico untearable one even—and when you gave it *knock, knock, knock* by doubting our future this afternoon, it hurt terribly. Yes, you are to unburden yourself, but you are not to doubt the very stuff of our love, which is our freedom to work.

The press is bound to come. You haven't a Bee in your bonnet, or if you have, keep it and we'll start a hive with it. Why am I not with you? I cannot keep away. Oh that bag you run up the suburban stairs with!! Goodnight, my tired Boy. I will finish this tomorrow. But do remember all the heaven there is before you and your Wig.

Sunday. Your Tuesday letter about the herring is here. I wonder if we were always alike or if we've grown so. *Or*—and that's true, I suppose—we are become one person—a new one. Because I somehow get almost overcome by your letters, which say to me so absolutely what I *feel,* how I *reason,* how I *think* . . . . Of course, your 9 letters put me to shame. I haven't yet written to H.L. and each day I dislike her a bit more.

Chaddie wrote yesterday saying —— was here. If she asks you to meet him, say you don't feel you'd ever get on with him: he rubs you up. She'll understand. But *do* mention the maple sugar!!!

What a superb chap Wilson is! I think he's a bit unpopular over here. They prefer L.G. Dang their eyes.

The sun is out today, but it's still very cold. I am writing in my pigglejams and blue cape, and look as though these were my last words from a house on fire—espèce de tiptoe pour flightisme, you know, darling. I am sorry you have to go to the ——'s I don't like them, either. They are *smelly.* But there you are!

Oh, please, please, shut your eyes a moment—open them—rush into *our* garden and see the first smoke coming out of *our* chimney—rush in again and put the kettle on—and kneel on the floor by me and have a warm up . . . . Dear Love, we've got sort of through tickets to this place. It's only the frightful journey getting there—but it IS THERE.

Now I must get dressed. L.M. is getting so fat that she will be commandeered when she gets back. She eats portions for $2 + \frac{1}{2}$ lb. of dates at a time + slabs of chocolate + anything else between meals. I hate fat people. I shall always be able to play on my bones.

Goodbye, dearest dear, for now. Give me a little small hail. I'll come back with every penny I can hoard.

Your own
Wig

Monday,

My darling Heart, (February 18, 1918)

I have just read your *Wednesday* letter, and it makes me feel that it is high time you had that ½ bottil of champagne. We will—in April. Oh, if you knew my feelings towards Watergate House[1] . . . and all it means. But Bogey, I do feel L.G. had a bit of a downfall in the H. of C. *and* the German offensive (expected 2 days ago) hasn't given a sign. And then of course there is that eagle of a Wilson. All these are little rays of gold light on the shutters—aren't they?

I am up early copying MSS for you. When I get back I'll work as regular as you (tho' with what a difference) but I do seem to have broken through once and for all somehow, *and* I think there may be, if you hold me up by my heels and rattle me, some pennies in me. Don't you? At last? On my table are wild daffodils—Shakespeare daffodils. They are so lovely that each time I look up I give them to you again. We shall go expeditions in the spring and write down all the *signs* and take a bastick and a small trowel and bring back treasure. Isn't that lovely where Shelley speaks of the 'moonlight-coloured may'? . . .

It's still (I think) very cold and I am in my wadded jacket with the pink 'un round my legs. But the sun is out and I'll go for a big walk this afternoon and *warm up*. I saw old Ma'am Gamel yesterday. She is a nice old dear. The way she speaks of you always makes me want to *hug* her. Yesterday she said I must pass by her before I go back as she would send you a little souvenir—and then she looked up at me and said, her blue eyes twinkling, 'Il a toujours ses beaux yeux, le jeune mari?' 'Allez! Allez! On n'a pas honte?' called Thérèse, who was measuring biscuits for L.M. I also saw (looking for a bit of pumice stone: bought a bit for one sou!) the old woman from the droguerie. She's got a new cat called Mine, 'un grand, un sauvage, un fou avec des moustaches which would make a man pleurer d'envie.' In fact, she says, he is

---

[1] The office of MI7d in which I worked.

'presqu'un homme—il *crache* absolument comme un homme—et le soir il est toujours dans les rues.'

I've just made myself a glass of boiling tea, very weak, with saxin. It's good. I drink it on and off all day. Do you remember that funny sort of scum that used to come on the water here? It still does. I have to take it off with the point of my paper knife.

It's very funny (something about me) I was thinking in bed this morning: I can't think how we should have got on if we were *not* going to be married in April. It seems impossible to me. I feel that it will make things so easy—all sorts of things—and the feeling will be quite, quite different. Now, do you feel that? Apart from thousands of other things I know I shall take the most childish delight in speaking of you as my husband after you really are. But perhaps that is too babyish even for you. I would even like to roar it at the —— tea-table and see their look of horror at my dreadful Bragian boldness. 'I *do* think that is going a little *too* far. . . .' But God forbid I should find myself there.

Oh, I love you so—I love you so! I said that out loud just now—and now the watch is ticking it.

I've nothing else to say. Oh, Bogey, when that train slows down and we wave. . . .

Wig

Tuesday,
February 19, 1918

Your Thursday and Friday letters received.

Dearest,

I want to tell you some things which are a bit awful—so hold me *hard*. I have not been so well these last few days. Today I saw a doctor. There happens by an extraordinary chance to be an English doctor here just now, and L.M. got him to come. Look here! I can't leave this place till April. It's no earthly go. I can't and mustn't—see. Can't risk a draught or a chill, and mustn't walk. I've got a bit of a temperature and I'm not so fat as when I came—and, Bogey, this is *not* serious, does *not* keep me in bed, is absolutely easily curable, but I have been spitting a bit of blood. See? Of course, I'll tell you. But if you worry—unless you laugh like Rib does—I can't tell you: you mustn't type it on the typewriter or anything like that, my precious, my own—and after all Lawrence often used to: so did, I think, Belle Trinder.[1] But while it

[1] Katherine's aunt.

173

goes on, I've got to be most enormously careful. See? I've got this doctor and I've got the Slave—so I am provided for, and determined to stick it out till April and not come back till the first week of *then*. It's agony to be parted from you, but it would be imbecile to get the March winds, as I am so parky—and everybody would be so madly cross—and I couldn't stick in bed in 47. I'd only be a worry. So here I stay and work—and try to bear it. I've *ample* money for everything and my journey money fastened up with a pin and locked away.

I can do all this and everything as long as I know you are taking care of yourself and that you don't worry about me and do *feed* and don't over-work too dreadfully. I am afraid it must be done. Before the doctor came (you can imagine) I was so frightened. Now I'm confiding . . . it's not serious. But when I saw the bright arterial blood, I nearly had a fit. But he says it's absolutely curable—and if I sit in the sun till April, I'll then come back and see a specialist and Papa will pay for that. He can look at my wings with his spy-glass and decide. Of course, this man says this coast is my eye because it's not bracing. Still, now I am here, here I must stay, and he is looking after me and I am to have injections of strychnine (?) and other stuff, I don't know what, and more food still. So it's a good thing L.M. came (even though I feel in some mysterious way *she has done it*. That's because I *loathe* her so. I do.) Still I'll use her as a slave.

As I shall be here a whole month longer I can get a lot of work done and that may bring pennies. Oh, I can bear it—or anything—so long as you are well. And tell me when you feel a boiled haddock—don't disguise anything because I won't disguise things from you. See how I tell you *bang out* because our love will stand it. My money is splendid—and I shall *work work work*. In April there can't be the same chance of a snow-storm or a wind that might make *pas de nougat pour le noël* for us both. I think it must be. And then, please God, we'll be married—and see how lucky I am. I can work!

I had your letter about the 2nd part of *Je ne parle pas,* and I feel you are disappointed. . . . Is that true, and if it is, please tell me why.

This is a silly old letter all about wings. Forgive it, my love, and answer it as soon as you can. Oh, my own precious, don't work too hard—and love me, love me till April.

Your own little
Wig

I feel much better today and the haemorrhage is—hardly at all. Can't work much, or think very sensibly, but I am ever so much better than I was. *The* worst of all this is *this*. I have such a longing for you. I feel that once *you* had me I'd get well. Once we ate together the food would go to the right spot. If I was in bed with you I'd sleep. And this is a sort of *deep deep* conviction. I cannot help it. I *pine* when I am away from you just like ladies do in old songs and all my efforts seem to be in vain. However, I am making very great ones to be a strong girl for April. Oh, I *do* want to be home so. The absence from you eats at my heart.

I didn't have a letter today but I didn't expect one really. I had two such recent ones yesterday. The *D.N.* came and said Eat pulses instead of meat. Hadn't you better buy a first-rate porridge saucepan and eat it with *grated maple sugar?* As I write that for some reason I felt a sort of small twinkle in my eye. I *see* you.

Now that I've denied March it seems a long long way to April. Hurry it up, Bogey. Put paper wings on the weeks. Let us be together again—quickly—quickly!! And then all will be well.

Since this little attack I've had, a queer thing has happened. I feel that my love and longing for the external world—I mean the world of *nature*—has suddenly increased a million times. When I think of the little flowers that grow in grass, and little streams and places where we can lie and look up at the clouds—Oh, I simply *ache* for them—for them with you. Take you away and the answer to the sum is O. I feel so awfully like a tiny girl whom someone has locked up in the dark cupboard, even though it's daytime. I don't want to bang at the door or make a noise, but I want you to come with a key you've made yourself and let me out, and then we should tiptoe away together into a kinder place where everybody was more of our heart and size.

You mustn't think, as I write this, that I'm dreadfully sad. Yes, I am, but you know, at the back of it is *absolute faith* and *hope* and *love*. I've only, to be frank like we *are*, had a bit of a fright. See? And I'm still 'trembling'. That just describes it.

Tomorrow, my own, I shall write a gayer letter. Oh, just to forget me for a minute, do you remember or have I mentioned how the Fool in *King Lear* says: "Twas her brother who, in pure kindness, *buttered* his horse's *hay*.' I thought that was a good phrage for nowadays. 'It is hardly the moment to *butter* the horse's *hay*.' Isn't it? Pin it in *The Nation*.

I hate to ask you to spend on me, but now I'm staying, can I have another Dickens some time? *Bleak House* or *Edwin Drood*? If you can get them in a 7d., do. If you feel you cannot afford them, I understand. Mrs. Gaskell positively fascinated me. I think she's an extremely good writer. The 2nd story in the *Cranford* book, 'Moorland Cottage', is really a little masterpiece. *We shall read it at home*. Now I am quite cheerful again and can leave you with a smile and a wave instead of almost turning away like I had to on page 3.[1] And, oh my own lover, you just go on looking after yourself for me and I will go on looking after myself for you. Eight more days and this month is over—and then there's only March.

Yours, yours
Wig

Wednesday Night,
(February 20, 1918)

Dearest and most Precious one,

That doctor is coming tomorrow, so I'll tell you what he says. He is a most awful fool, I am sure, but still I suppose he *is* a doctor, and that's a comfort. One thing he says, this south coast is no use for me—too relaxing—and I ought to have sat on a mountain. Fatal to stay here later than March. Well, that's perhaps true. I think it is, for every time the wind blows I shut up all my petals—even if it's only a breeze. . . .

I feel *chirpy* tonight. I don't care *what* happens, what pain I have, what I suffer, so long as my handkerchiefs don't look as though I were in the

---

[1] i.e. the passage of the letter ending 'into a kinder place where everybody was more of our heart and size'. It is impossible not to compare this passage with one in a letter of Keats (February 16, 1820) shortly after his haemorrhage—a passage, moreover, specially marked by K.M. in her copy of Keats's letters.

'How astonishingly (here I must premise that illness, as far as I can judge in so short a time, has relieved my mind of a load of deceptive thoughts and images, and makes me perceive things in a truer light)—how astonishingly does the chance of leaving the world impress a sense of its natural beauties upon us! Like poor Falstaff, though I do not "babble", I think of green fields. I muse with the greatest affection on every flower I have known from my infancy—their shapes and colours are as new to me as if I had just created them with a superhuman fancy. It is because they are connected with the most thoughtless and the happiest moments of our lives. I have seen foreign flowers in hothouses, of the most beautiful nature, but I do not care a straw for them. The simple flowers of one Spring are what I want to see again.'

176

pork-butcher trade. That does knock your Wig *flat, flat, flat*. I feel as though the affair were out of my control then and that it's a nightmare. Last night was like that for me. Then this afternoon, when I sat reading Keats in the sun, I coughed and it wasn't red and I felt inclined to wave the fact to the whole world. And when L.M. said she woke at 3 a.m. this morning and felt very melancholy—'Perhaps one doesn't see things in their true proportion then'—and would I mind if she tapped at my door then if I had a light and she just *told* me, I said 'I don't dare a damn what you feel if you're not ill. You've no right to feel anything except "Thank the Lord I'm fat and strong".' I really feel that about her. Oh, I do *detest* her personality, and her powerful broody henniness—and her 'we' and 'our'. .... I even go so far as to feel that she has pecked her way into my lung to justify her coming, which *is* cruel, I know.

No, Bogey, to be in England, to see you, to see a good lung specialist —that's my affair and no other. But to be on alien shores with a very shady medicine man and a crimson lake hanky is about as near Hell as I want to be.

Thursday,
(February 21, 1918)

'Pas de lettre encore. Rien que le journal.'

'Merci, Juliette.'

Well that often happens on this day. Perhaps I'll get 2 tomorrow. It may be those bloody raids which I see have been on again. Boge, I feel ever so much better again today and *hungry*. I should like us to have a chicken *en casserole* and a salad and good coffee. It's a bit windy today, so I'll take the air behind a screen of my daffodils and not rush forth. Do you remember, or have I mentioned lately, that poem of Shelley's, *The Question*? It begins :

> I dreamed that as I wandered by the way
> Bare Winter suddenly was changed to Spring. ...

I have learned it by heart since I am here; it is very exquisite, I think. Shelley and Keats I get more and more *attached to*. Nay, to all 'poetry'. I have such a passion for it and I feel such an understanding of it. It's a great part of my life.

I can't but feel a brute if I write about my own work too much while you must sit with folded wings. ...

But each new *D.N.* I get I feel that the days of the Northcliffe press and the L.G. reign are numbered. There has been a big loud recognized crack. . . .

Once the war is over, all our woes are over for ever, I think. Then comes in the sweet of the year for you and me.

You won't worry about your girl, will you? Truly she is better again and today the crimson lake is back in the paint-box and there's not a sign of it.

If you only knew how I love you at this moment, you'd give a great jump for joy.

Later. I've just had lunch. They give me *pounds* of fish now. I had one today with lovely violet bones: I wish I'd kept one for you. Goodbye my own for now. A letter must come tomorrow, mustn't it? And keep your big umbrella over your *darling* head when the bombs come.

April! April!

> Your own
> Wig

Friday,
My life, (February 22, 1918)

A Horn of Plenty! Your Sunday letter and postcard and your Monday letter. Oh, *how* I have devoured them. The Monday one, which was written with smiling twirley letters, made me a bit sad; it was in answer to mine saying *March* was definite, and now, alas! our plans are altered and I can't come before the swallow dares. But oh, knowing this—all the same—let us try and be happy. We *must* try and be happy, looking forward to April.

I feel marvellously better today. *No* temperature—*vegetarian*[1]—and on the mend again flying down the road to you. But, Bogey, I have more than my share of alarums and tuckets, don't you think? Great big black things lie in wait for me under the trees and stretch their shadows across the road to trip me. You'll have to keep shouting, 'Look out, Wig!' when we walk together again. The doctor has been and says: If I use all his remedies, I'll be a well girl. (I think he is such a *ponce*. Oh, I could write you reams about him, but I'll *tell* you.) However, his remedies are sound, I think—injections of some stuff called Goneol and another called Kaikakilokicaiettus as far as I can make out—*and* a tonic *and* fish to eat—whole fishes—fish *ad lib*. If I am torpedoed on the

---

[1] i.e. no longer 'in the pork-butcher trade', see p. 177.

178

way home I expect I shall burst into fins and a mermaid tail as I enter the water and swim to shore.

Je t'aime, je t'aime. The Ghoul is of course doing all her possible. It's good she's here, after all. I don't see her more than I can avoid. I don't let her *touch* me. . . .

I will send you some more work as soon as I can copy it. But I am a bit *slow* just now—just for a day or two. Oh, if only you were working. . . .

But, dearest dear, how I shall make it all easy for you as soon as this war is over. All you've got to do, then, is to say 'It's *my* turn', and I'll fly.

That was a nice letter from Sullivan. He's a good chap; I'm glad you see him. I wonder if you escaped H.L.? She has become to me now a sort of *witch*. I can't write to her. When I put my pen on the paper it begins to tremble and make crosses and won't go further. . . . I see you lunching with Brett much as you would lunch with a mushroom. . . .

There's a bit of wind today: it's a $\frac{1}{4}$ to 12. I'm just up. L.M., I believe, ranges the mountains all the mornings. She comes back and I meet her at lunch, rosy, with bright eyes and an Appetite which makes the hotel *tremble,* and after having devoured the table-cloth, glasses and spoons, says, 'What I miss is the puddings. Don't you *ever* care for currant duff, *my dearie, or*—?' and then follows about 100 puddings as fast as they can tear. She keeps them all flying in the air like a conjuror, and still like a conjuror, eats 'em. What a strange type she is! But good to travel back with—yes, good for that.

You can feel from this letter that I am loving you today and that I am a very much stronger girl and inclined to tickle Rib. *Don't overwork, my darling.* Remember I shall come back with a penny in my hand for our store. I'm taking every care of myself for you. Please never post your letters while the guns are going. I hope the little boy upstairs is better— poor little chap![1]

Bogey, Bogey, je te baise, je t'adore.

Wig

Saturday,

My life,   (February 23, 1918)

The papers came today in a bundle. I am very glad of them, but no letter came. It will be here tomorrow. I have a sort of doubt in my

---

[1] A little boy in the rooms above me who had pneumonia.

bosom today as to whether I should have told you about my last attack or not. I have such a perfect horror (if you knew *how* strong!) of worrying you, of adding to your burden. And yet we must be truthful to each other in all things and at all costs. That, too, I believe. *I'm much better*; it's as though the last affair had never been, again, now—and I'm going slow and eating and trying to collect flesh at least. I'm not a bit an ill girl—just a very slightly 'faible' one; but that I'll always be till we're free and at rest. How *can* one be otherwise in the midst of all these horrors? War and anxiety and you imprisoned there and us parted. It's stuff for an L.M. to fatten on, but not Bogeys and Wigs.

Yesterday the woman at the paper-shop gave me a bouquet of violets. Here are some. And Juliette has filled my vases with yellow goldy wallflowers. God! how I love flowers.

After all, my own precious, my coming back is only delayed by a little more than three weeks. That's what I cling to for consolation. Then I *shall* come back, for I can't stop here any longer. Even the doctor says not to stay here after March. So I must come. Hooray! Will my Rib be at the window? What a throwing about he will get! Does he ever walk up you? Never? Do you ever read who made him on his tummy? Never? *Attend un tout p'tit p'tit p'tit beau moment,* as they say here, and he'll know these joys again. . . .

I'll have to get food cards, won't I? I'd better wait till we have thrown this old name away, and then it will be easier. I am going to get Belle to give us a fat fowl a week. I think it is a good idea. It would make such a difference.

On Monday, P. G. I'll post more manuscript to you, darling. Would *The Nation* publish *Sun and Moon*? If they publish that rubbish by —— I think they might. Have you read any reviews of Yeats's book? And did you see the pompous ass's remarks on Keats? There was a good story agin him (though he didn't know it) in a quote I saw. He dreamed once 'in meditations' (!?) that his head was circled with a flaming sun. Went to sleep and dreamed of a woman whose hair was afire, woke up, lighted a candle, and by and by discovered 'by the odour' that he'd set his own hair ablaze. This *he* calls sort of prophetic. I think it's wondrous apt. It's just as far as he and his crew can get—to set their hair afire—to set their lank forlorn locks a-frizzle. God knows there's nothing else about them that a cartload of sparks could put a light to. So he can jolly well shut up about Keats. If you should ever have the chance, dearest Bogey, pull his nose for me, as well as Conrad's.

But oh! how *ignorant* these reviewers are, how far away and barred out from all they write. There was a review of Coleridge in *The Times* —so bad, so ill-informed. But then, of course, I feel I have rather a corner in Coleridge and his circle. In fact, you and I are the only people who can write and think and whose opinion is worth while.

The sea is breaking restless and high on the coast opposite—so are these waves and waves of love breaking over you

Your
Wig

Saturday Night,

Dearest Bogey, (February 23, 1918)

I wish I knew where you were, what you are thinking and doing. It is just 9 o'clock. I have been sitting by the fire. L.M. came in after dinner for a few minutes with her knitting, but now she's gone to bed, thank God! It is impossible to describe to you my curious hatred and antagonism to her—gross, trivial, dead to all that is alive for me, ignorant and *false*. I spoke about the war to her tonight—about the meaning of it—and, like a fool, told her how it was at the back of my mind all the time—was a sort of sea, rising and falling, but never, never still. . . . And then I said how *sick* this new offensive made me feel, and so on. Said she (knitting a grubby vest) 'Roger has got four teeth. Does that interest you? It *is* interesting, my Katie. And the gardener says that little black kitten is the *child* of the grey *lady* cat.' I felt exactly as L. must have felt with F.—exactly. You remember the feeling L. had (before he was so mad) that F. wanted to destroy him; I have— oh, just that!!! We must go off at the station and she must go her ways and we must not meet for a long time. Don't soften to her; don't feel grateful. She's *so* happy to feel that she was right after all about coming. . . . Until I am rid of her I shall always see myself in a kind of desert and she hovering above on broad untiring wing ready to descend the moment I stumble over a grain of sand. . . . Enough about her. I *had* to get rid of that.

Yes, I was sitting this afternoon round by the Golf Hotel watching the waves. They reared very high and loud and as they fell came those bright 'golden windows' that you and I so loved to see—and I realized again that they were *nothing* to me—that the sound of them was like a bombardment and all their roaring only said 'Danger! Danger!' God,

181

how I want you tonight. We would fold up close in each other's arms and perhaps talk softly or not at all—but I would feel your heart beat in my bosom and I'd rest. . . .

All over the hotel (it is full now) I can hear people going to bed, talking, pouring out water, dropping their boots in the red tiled corridors. A little dog yelps and the bells ring and the tired maid runs up and down. What am I doing among these people? Je me demande, *or* 'I fondly ask'. But it's only for four weeks more or at most five. If I leave here the last week in March. . . .

I shall not write any more until the morning. As the night deepens it drags my courage down with it, and I've no right to cry to you then. If a *letter* comes tomorrow. . . . Goodnight, my love. We are aliens and strangers in this world, and when we are alone we are very lonely. Goodnight, my soul.

PLEASE READ TOTHER FIRST: LETTRE MINEURE.
It makes me nearly *laugh* today because I am *so* in love and confident.

Sunday,

My dearest love,   (February 24, 1918)

I have written II on the other letter because it was one—is one—oh, you'll see why. I needn't explain.

Today there came two letters from you: one contained Father's, said my wire had come. I simply fix my eyes upon April. March has *got* to be weathered—*got* to be borne. It only has four Sundays.[1] There are only five Sundays more before I'm home. I *won't* think of March. Only your disappointment, my darling heart—that I hate. I have never known children so positively *chivvied* as you and me. We can't go out for a minute by ourselves without something happening. But once we are together we won't let the chance occur—not till you positively run away from me. And then Rib and I and two babies hanging out of one window will call so loudly that you'll come back for shame.

Now about the Pa man's letter. I'll be frank. It amazed me. I thought it very possible he'd have an attack of *gravel* or *stone* and write about 'Duty'—or 'as a practical man of affairs', or 'one cannot live on mulberry leaves like a silkworm', or something like that. Also, knowing how extraordinarily shy and reserved he is, and how horribly difficult it is for him not to shut up like an oyster, I consider the letter an

[1] In fact, it had five.

amazing tribute to yours. For one thing he put *On Tour* on the top (which is a family joke) and the preface had a twinkle in its eye, and I thought he put that bit about worldly considerations and my allowance very well. Yes, darling, knowing the Pa man, it is extremely satisfactory. I wish you *would* reply. Just a word when you are in the mood, saying how relieved we are, and that you read his Bank speeches, p'raps, and if you could make a very small little joke—just a sort of preliminary hop—it would *chauffe* him. He's *far* shyer than you are even. I think Mother will write for sure. I have had no letters yet from them. Kay is steaming them at the Bank, I suppose.

God, the afternoon is so fair! Your letter about *our* work, the fusion of *our* work, simply dropped into my heart and opened there like a rose and every breath I draw, its fragrance is upon me. Five more Sundays, and then I'm HOME. Next week, I'll write Four more. Like that, it don't seem so long. Especially as I think I'll cheat a Sunday at the last moment and come back at a gallop. Five more walks in your corduroys, and then, if you'ld have me you will carry me in your pocket and we'll try and look in a curiosity window at a teapot, and we'll come back very slowly and put the kettle on and take off our hats and lift our arms and drop into each other's bosom. I am bringing back a small flower-basket. I think it would do so well for sanwitches, don't you? I'll put a pound of butter in it. I must bring figs, too. They are delicious and very cheap—one franc a pound. What about *dates*? Can you get them? Shall I bring some? It will be nearly March when you write.

I am still better; so that old ugly one has gone back to his lair after a final growl. I must write to Geoffroi and say this hotel is full (which is true). She *is* a jingo, but all the French I know or hear of are. What they can't stomach is *paix sans victoire*. Who wrote 'Washington and Versailles' in *The Nation*? And wasn't ——'s poem ridiculous? It was like a dead earwig.

Mais, tu sais, je t'aime *trop*.

Your loving, longing, faithful, hoping—*hoping*

Wig

Monday,
My own precious, (February 25, 1918)
The *D.N.* and the French Book came today but no letter. I shall hear tomorrow. I wish it wasn't always such a disappointment, but it *is*. You know the feeling. . . .

183

Isn't this nice paper? A biggish block of it costs 65 c. I shall bring you one. There's fresh nougat here, too. I must put a great lump of it in my box for you. You see where *all* my thoughts turn to. Yesterday, *par exemple,* it was as warm as summer. I sat on a bank under an olive tree and fell a-dreaming. . . . Now I came back as a surprise and just sent you a wire to the office: 'Look here she's back Rib,' and then I lighted the lamp and arranged the flowers and your presents were on the table. And at last your steps—your key in the door—'Wig! Bogey!' *Or* I came again as a surprise and phoned you from the station. 'Is that you Jack? I've just arrived,' I sat there thinking like this until I nearly wept for joy. It seemed *too good to be true.* Will it *really* happen, Bogey— really and truly?

I managed to send Sullivan a sort of Broken Meat note yesterday, and I have tried to put off the Geoffroi. She + L.M. would drive me quite dotty. As it is, L.M. has pretty nearly finished me. I mean not quite seriously but I live in a state of the most *acute exasperation* and black rage —yes, it's just like L. and F. I try to put up a fight against her but it's like trying to sing against the loudest thunderstorm in the world. She would, if I lived with her, send me out of my mind—just like L. *is.*

Oh, Bogey, I'm so subdued today. I expected N.Z. letters and got none, and it's very windy and cold, and my work is *thick,* absolutely *thick,* for the moment. Under it all—is: Will the offensive prevent me coming back? Will the Channel be closed? You know this mood. Your letter tomorrow will start the wheels going round again, and I'll be a gay girl and write more. But I don't seem to have seen anything to tell you of. I feel in a sort of *quiet daze* of *anxiety.* I tell you so you will understand the tone of this letter. *All is well really.* But I'd like to call out your name very loudly until you answer—and I begin to run.

Take care of yourself for your

Wig

Tuesday,

My darling Heart,   (February 26, 1918)

I have a *Gorgeous Letter* from you written on Thursday (Chummie's birthday). You remember the one. It was about Love and War . . . and our future and 'not by a long chalk'. That's given it to you I expect. But oh, it has done me so much *good,* real solid *good*—just as if I'd been with you and we had broken bread together and this *ache* were past.

But when I read about —— being carried shoulder high, I felt quite *sick*—for such a silly, an incredibly stupid thing. How humiliated he ought to feel! It would be for me like if I was a burglar and was caught after having burgled the potato knife. I expect if he goes to Prison he'll get immensely fat in there: in fact, he's so blown already that I shudder.

Mother has written to you. It may or may not be a nice letter. She said in hers to me that she had lain down and recited silently to herself a polished oration but since then 'my brains have gone and I can't find them. What will Jack think you spring from?' I wish her letter to you would come. Jeanne sent you this note and the Pa man wrote delightfully to me. I'll send you his tomorrow. I like especially what he says about always having longed for a remote existence in the country, but 'man proposes, woman disposes'. That is so like him.

Last night after a full moon and a sea like velvet a huge thunderstorm burst over the town. Rain, bright lightning, loud wind. I was sitting up in bed writing, for thank God! I've managed to stave off the werewolf a bit, and the storm was wonderful. I had forgotten what it sounded like. But just in the middle, while the rain drummed, I saw you lying asleep—all your youthful slender body that I love so, your black, round head, your hands and feet—and I *longed* to clasp you—and to curl up in my place, which is there.

Trust L.M. for knocking then—a low ominous knock. I think she hoped I had been struck by lightning. (I always feel her dream is to bury me here and bring back a few bulbs from Katie's grave to plant in a window-box for you.) She asked if she might lie on the floor (you know these *tile floors*) till it was over, as it was so very agitating.

Boge, we must have plenty of gillyflowers in our garden. They smell so sweet.

> How shall we spend the day?
> With what delights
> Sweeten the nights?
> When from this tumult we are got secure,
> Where mirth with all her freedom goes
> Yet shall no finger lose,
> Where every word is thought and every thought is pure;
> There from the tree
> We'll cherries pluck, and pick the strawberry. . . .

Don't you like that—darling mine?

I shan't go out today because it rains. I'll read *Le P'tit* this afternoon and *Nausicaa* and write you about them,[1] and I'll make no END of an effort to finish this story called *Bliss*. I hope you'll like it. It's different again.

I was thinking last night that I must not let L.M. obsess me. After all, she is a trial, but I must get over her. Dosty would have. She adds to the struggle, yes, but the struggle is always there—I mean if one don't feel very strong and so on. But they have nearly all had to fight against *just this*. So must I and so will I. I hope I've not been a coward in my last letter or two. At any rate, my loins are girded up no end today, and I spent the morning in bed full steam ahead.

Queer the effect people have on one. Juliette is a positive help to writing. She is so independent and so full in herself—I want to say 'fulfilled', but it's a dangerous word.[2] I love to feel she is near and to meet her. She *rests* me positively. She'll make some man tremendously happy one day. Yes, she's really important to me. As to all the other *swine* with which the hotel is full—well, they are swine.

> Unhappy! Shall we never more
> That sweet militia restore
> When gardens only had their towers
> And all the garrisons were flowers;
> When roses only arms might bear
> And men did rosy garlands wear?

I *keep* (as you see) wanting to quote poetry today. When I get back I shall be like a sort of little private automatic machine in the home: you wind me up and a poem will come, I've learned so many here while I lie awake.

Now, darling, I must write to Kay and get my next month's money —*at once. Money is splendid,* and I am keeping it fast. I have more than enough for every need.

I shall make Rib a wedding-dress of blue jersey, sailor-knot, full blue trousers and p'raps a very tiny *whistle* on a cord—if I can find one. What about your food cards? And ought I to apply for first week in April and onwards?

I adore you, Bogey, and I am

Wig

[1] Stories by P. J. Toulet.
[2] I.e. because much used by D. H. Lawrence in a special sense—sexually 'fulfilled'.

My own darling,

Your Saturday letter has come—the one about the Eye and about my wings. Now I am being an absolute old *coddler* for your sake and doing *everything* and feeling ever such a great deal better, so do you do the same. Please see a specialist about your eye if it's not better. We are the most awful pair I've ever heard of. We'll have to pin notices in our hats and on our chests saying what we've got and then get a couple of walking sticks and tin mugs if this goes on. . . . But though I write so lightly I am really worried about your darling eye. Can you knock off for a day or two and just rest it. Oh dear, you oughtn't to look at anything smaller than a cow. . . . But you know the *great necessity*: *don't* neglect it. See Ainger and get him to tell you who to go to. He *is* a decent chap. And what about a week-end with the Waterlows? Can you stand it? It would be a rest perhaps. I don't mention —— because its 2 vile.

Bogey, March is nearly here and then I'll begin to count the days. I'll make you out a list of them, too, and cross one off each night. Don't strain your other eye if you tie up the one. Now, Bogey, that really would be silly—wouldn't it? Now I won't say any more about it in case it has gone or you'll get cross.

I feel simply spanking today: it must be 'La Faute des Poissons'. I'll live on fishes when I get back and all will be well. . . .

Don't forgive L.M. I can't bear to hear you say you do, even. My feeling at present is that I'll never see her again after I get back. I *do* manage to work in spite of her, but if I did not I think I'd really go *insane* with exasperation. She *is* F. II. . . .

I have read *Le P'tit*. It's *very* good—very well done. I think it's got one fault, or perhaps I am too ready to be offended by this. I think the physical part of Le P'tit's feeling for Lama, is unnecessarily accentuated. I think if I'd written it I wouldn't have put it in at all—not on his side. On hers, yes. But never once on his. Am I wrong, do you think? Yes, of course, I agree it's well done, that part, but I would have left it more mysterious. Lama must do all she does, and Le P'tit must say: 'Si tu savais comme je t'aime!' But 'lorsqu'un spontané baiser dàns l'affolement furieuse de l'instinct chez le jeune homme . . .' that I don't like.

But the 'way' it is done, the 'method', I *do* very much. *Nausicaa* has got something very charming, too. If he wasn't a Frenchman, he'd be a most interesting chap. But I do find the French language, style, attack, point of view, hard to stomach at present. It's all *tainted*. It all seems to me to lead to dishonesty—Dishonesty Made Easy—made superbly easy. All these *half* words—these words which have never really been born and seen the light— like 'me trouble'—'tiède'—'blottant'—'inexprimable' (these are bad examples, but you know the kinds I mean and the phrases and whole paragraphs that go with them)—they won't, at the last moment, *do* at all. Some of them are charming and one is loth to do without them, but they are like certain plants—once they are in your garden they spread and spread and spread, and make a show perhaps, but they are *weeds*. No, I get up hungry from the French language. I have too great an appetite for the real thing to be put off with pretty little kickshaws, and I am offended intellectually that 'ces gens' think they can so take me in.

It's the result of Shakespeare, I think. The English language is damned difficult, but it's also damned rich, and so clear and bright that you can search out the darkest places with it. Also it's *heavenly* simple and true. Do you remember where Paulina says:

> I, an old turtle,
> Will wing me to some withered bough
> And there my mate that's never to be found again
> Lament till I am lost.

You can't beat that. I *adore* the English language, and that's a fact.

> Your eyes be musical, your dewy feet
> Have freshly trod the lawns for timeless hours,
> O young and lovely dead!

There's a man who can 'use' it!

That is all very badly put. But do you agree?

Having got so far, I am so seized with the wonder of the English tongue—of English poetry—and I am so overcome by the idea that you are a poet and that we are going to live for poetry—for writing—that my heart has begun dancing away as if it will never stop, and I can see our cottage and our garden and you leaning against the door and me walking up the path, and now you say 'All those seeds we planted are *well up*. Come and see!' And we go and see. Oh I'd die if this wasn't all before us. But it *is*. (We must have a garden table under a tree with a bench round it).

188

Now I'll stop for today.

Darling, darling Heart, it is really on its way you know. I can *smell* the land even if we can't see it yet.

And how I love you! Ah—you'll never know.

Wig

Thursday,
(February 28, 1918)

My darling Heart,

It's three o'clock. I've just finished this new story, *Bliss,* and am sending it to you. But though, God! I *have* enjoyed writing it, I am an absolute rag for the rest of the day and you must forgive no letter at all. I will write at length tomorrow. Oh, tell me what you think of *our* new story (that's quite sincere). Please try and like it, and I am now free to start another. One extraordinary thing has happened to me since I came over here! Once I start them they haunt me, pursue me and plague me until they are finished and as good as I can do.

You will 'recognize' some of the people. *Eddie* of course is a fish out of the —— pond (which gives me joy) and Harry is touched with W.L.G. Miss Fulton is 'my own invention'—oh, you'll see for yourself.

No letter today. That's because of England's Sunday post. I'll get one tomorrow.

I walked to a little valley yesterday that I longed to show you. I sat on a warm stone there. All the almond flowers are gone, but the trees are in new leaf and they were full of loving, mating birds—quarrelling, you know, about whether to turn the stair-carpet under or to cut it off straight. And the trees were playing ball with a little breeze, tossing it to each other.

I sat a long time on my stone, then scratched your initials with a pin and came away—*loving* you. I am really spankingly well again and have absolutely NO NEED of any money. So don't you talk about it, but keep it tied up tight—but use it for your darling eye.

You can feel I am wheeling this old letter along in a creaking barrow. My head is *gone.* I'll send a long one (letter not head) tomorrow.

I love you beyond all measure and for ever and ever I am your own girl.

Wig

I'll pay back these wires because it's not fair but they do make such a galumptious moment.

My darling Heart, my dear Jack Murry,   (March 1, 1918)

Your Saturday, Sunday and Monday letters all came together today, and I *feel* that you are ill and you have said not a word about your eye. Yes, of course, you must write to me when the world hangs like a large cloud over your head. I can bear it; I do the same. (And yet I feel that if I were true to myself I'd have it from you but I oughtn't to come to you on my own account.) Still, as you know, I do.

My faith, my hope, my star is that this is our last month apart—that on April 1st I shall be on a strong wing back to you and we'll just catch each other in each other's arms, and all will be well—with Rib playing on the flute a composition of his own called Welcome-Home-No-More-Away. Now, I am going to be jet frank about myself for a minute.

I am simply 1000 times better and stronger—can *walk, eat, sleep*— am not so thin—guaranteed to twinkle all over at the sight of a Bogey. Simply *bursting with love*. You will be so beautifully taken care of next month. Not fussed over—don't be frightened—but there will always be little surprises happening—and, oh God, I write like a child—I feel like a child. We are the only pair who are walking hand in hand. But that is not quite true, for I met another yesterday trundling along, not saying anything, neither much bigger than Ribni, and he (who had been sent to buy bread) was having a small nibble off a loaf nearly as big as him on the way. (At the back of my mind I am worried about your eye. *Please* tell me *exactly* about it.)

Yes, dearest love, nearly all the world is vile, and we are the wrong size for it. But why do you say you were hanging saucepans for the Heron 2 weeks ago? As though the Heron were not any more? *That* gave me such a shock that I am going to wire you today just to say it is.

I am so glad that Richard sees you. He's a very good lad and he's going to be a great deal in our lives. Won't he be nice to our children?

Oh, Jag-Bog, my precious own, clip me tight. I must hug you, warm you, put my hands on your breast, see you look down and smile at me and call me a worm. It is so sweet to be called a worm.

I feel very strongly that Mother has come bang over to our side and loves us. She keeps saying to me 'Your Jack'. Her heart was very warm when she wrote, didn't you think? And when she said her second to you wouldn't be so cramped for conversation, as though there you were in that little book of hers where she makes notes.

Must write to children.

Must write poor old Lizzie Fleg.

Must write K's Jack.

She always has small notebooks like that, and a very professional absurd way of crossing out the used ones—you know—by $\sqrt{}$ and $\sim\sim\sim$ and $\backslash\backslash\backslash\backslash\backslash$. Which all have different meanings.

Look here, if I love you any more, the top bit of my hair will blow off with a pop like a champagne cork. I'll be home in 4 weeks—4 weeks—only four more Fridays! And then the fun we'll have. Say to Rib please from me: 'Rib, what larks!' and see him blow out his sleeve and bang it with the other hand as though it were a paper bag!

Kiss your darling little Mother for me. I'm going to start a new story today. If you knew all the poems I have learnt to recite to you in bed—when we wake early!

It's a calm calm day. I am going out. Do you know I believe my last attack was coming on ever since I came here, and now it's over, it's sort of *cleared the air*.

Here is a gillyflower for you. There are the goats passing: I hear the bells, and that lovely fluty whistle.

Oh, tell me about yourself *always, always,* and about your eye—and if you feel strong or weak (it sounds, love, like coffee.) And until I see, you, *God* keep you. He must. He must keep us for each other, for we really are lovely in our way, and look at the fair place we are going to make.

All, all—every bit of my heart is yours for ever

Wig

I am delighted with the books and papers. Thank you, my own.

Saturday,

My dearest Life,   (March 2, 1918)

I sent that wire yesterday, but when the Mayor asked to translate 'Hay for Heron' I was rather up a tree![1] So I said, 'tout va très très bien.' That was true, wasn't it? But if the wire *is* stopped, what a roundabout I and the censor would sit in before I explained!

It is so Bitterly Cold today that no amount of clothes, food or fire

[1] The telegram was 'March First Hay for Heron Home April Darling.'

can stop spider-webs of ice flying all over one's skin. Juliette says I am like a little cat, and I feel like one, because I am always by my own fire or, as I go along the corridor, purring round any stove that is lighted there. And there was 'pas de poste aujourd'hui'. (What I want is my wire to arrive on Saturday *pour vous chauffer un peu le dimanche, mon amour chéri*.) I didn't really expect any letters. Look here! Did you know you sent me 2 copies of *Master Humphrey's Clock*? It was in the back of *Edwin Drood* as well as in the separate volume. I thought I'd just tell you.

What an old wind-bag G.K.C. is! His preface to the Everyman book is simply disgraceful.

I must talk a bit about the Heron. We must find a place where it is warm and at the same time *bracing, i.e., abrité* and yet rather high. But, to be absolutely frank, I am beginning to change my mind about this place for the winter. I won't come here again. If it is calm, it is perfect, but there is *nearly always* 'un peu de vent' and that 'vent' is like an iced knife. One would be much snugger in a thoroughly snug cottage with doors and windows that fit, a good fire, etc. *And* I don't want *to have two homes.* No one can. If we have the money and the desire we shall always be able to cut off together for a bit *irgendwohin*. But one home, with all the books all the flowers, is enough and can't be beat. Also we can't afford another arrangement, I don't think.

If I talk about my own physical health—well, I know I ought to be in the air a lot. Well, if we have a garden, that's what I call being decently in the air, to plant things and dig up things—not to hang pegged on a clothes line and being blown about like a forlorn *pantalon*. Also, I want to range about with you, BUT ALWAYS with our own cottage to come back to and its thread of smoke to see from far away. *That's* life, that's the warm South, wherever it is.

My God! how we shall talk when I get back, planning all this and saying, 'Yes, I think so, too'.

I don't think I *can* wait much longer for a garden—for fruit trees and vegetables. The thought of knocking the lumps of earth off a freshly pulled carrot fills me with *emotion*; 'je suis tout émue,' as these crawly froggies say, at the idea. Another—plums with the bloom on them, in a basket—and you and I making jam—and your Mother coming to stay with us—and—and—everything—with you, like the Cupid on top of the wedding cake, giving the whole thing its meaning.

(How is my precious darling's eye?)

Please when saying you've got this letter say 'Your *Heron* letter' and I'll know.

L.M. has made me perfectly *sick* today. She's skittish. 'Dearie, I'm very proud. I remembered the word for candle—*bougie.* That's right, isn't it? I'm not really very stupid, you know. It's only when I am with you, because you are so many million miles ahead of all the rest of mankind—' and so on. I *squirm,* try and hold my tongue, and then—*bang!* and again I shoot her dead, and up she comes again.

I've begun my new story. It's nice.

Du reste,—je t'adore—and I'm eagerly looking—staring towards the land—towards you. You must picture your girl all wrapped up, always rushing up on deck to see if that is a cloud or a piece of coast or a grey feltie in the distance. For that is all she does till April first.

Your
Wig

3 more Sundays only

My precious darling,

Sunday Morning,
(March 3, 1918)

Another *jour glacé*—so cold indeed that the country might be under deep, deep snow. It's very quiet, and through the white curtains the sea shows white as milk. I am still in my bye, for I have just had mon petit déjeuner. It *was* good. I made it boiling in my tommy cooker. I really think that Maman must have gone to see a fire-eater or been frightened by one before I was born. Why else should I always demand of my boissons that they be in a 'perfeck bladge' before I drink 'em? And now I am waiting for the courier.

Alas! the same light quick steps won't carry it to me any more—for Juliette is gone. She came into my room last evening in an ugly stiff black dress without an apron. I noticed she had her boots on and that she was very thickly powdered.

She leaned against a chair, looking at the floor, and then suddenly she said, with a fling of her arm, 'Alors je pars—pour toujours. . . . J'ai reçu des mauvaises nouvelles . . . une dépêche . . . mère gravement malade viens de suite . . . alors! eh ben, voilà . . . i'y a rien à faire'. And then suddenly she took a deep sobbing breath. 'J'ai bien de la peine!' I was so sorry that I wanted to put my arms round her. I could only hold her warm soft hand and say, 'Ah, ma fille, je le regrette, je le regrette de tout cœur'.

She lives on the coast of Corsica. The idea of the journey, of course, *terrifies* her. And then she was so happy—'si bien-bien-bien-ici!' and the *beau temps* is just coming and she did not know how she could pack her things, for she came here 'avec toutes mes affaires enveloppées d'un grand mouchoir de maman.' But she'd never saved and always spent. 'Il me faut acheter un grand *panier sérieux* pour les emballer.'

Of course she thinks she'll never come back here again; she's in the desperate state of mind that one would expect of her, and she wept when we said Good-bye. 'Qui vous donnerait les fleurs main-ten-ant, Madame, vous qui les aimez tant? C'était mon grand plaisir—mon grand plaisir!' I saw her in the hall before she left wearing a hideous hat and clasping her umbrella and *panier sérieux* as though they had cried 'To the Boats!' already.

I must not write any more about her, darling Heart, for after all, she can't mean much to you. She *has* meant an enormous lot to me. I have really loved her—and her songs, her ways, her kneeling in front of the fire and gronding the *bois vert*—her rushes into the room with the big bouquets and her way of greeting me in the morning as though she loved the day, and also the fact that she distinguished your letters from others. 'Ce n'est pas *la* lettre—malheur!' Goodbye Juliette, my charming double stock in flower. I'll never forget you. You were a real being. You had *des racines.* (L.M. is sea weed, if Juliette is double stock.)

This morning it was Madeleine, the laundrymaid, Juliette's friend, promoted, who brought *mon déjeuner. Très fière,* in consequence. With her fringe combed down into her big eyes, a dark red blouse and a scalloped apron—I could write about these 2 girls for ever, I feel today. Yes, I'll write just a bit of a story about them, and spare you any more.

You remember writing to me in your criticism of 'Je ne parle pas français' that Dick Harmon seemed to have roots? It struck me then and the sound of it has gone echoing in me. It's really the one thing I ask of people and the one thing I cannot do without. I feel so immensely conscious of my own roots. You could pull and pull and pull at me—I'll not come out. You could cut off my flowers—others will grow. Now I feel that equally (it goes without saying) of you—and Johnny has roots—Sullivan (I think)—Richard, I am sure—H.L., never—L.M. never. In fact I could divide up the people with or without them in a jiffy. And although one may be sometimes deceived—sometimes they are so clever, the bad ones: they plant themselves and look so fair that those two little children we know so well stand hand in hand admiring them and giving them drops of water out of the tin watering-can—they fade at the going down of the sun and the two little children are perfectly disgusted with them for being such cheats, and they *hurl* them over the garden wall before going back to their house for the night.

Well, well! The heap of dead ones that we have thrown over. But ah, the ones that remain! All the English poets. I see Wordsworth, par exemple, so *honest* and *living* and *pure*.

(Here's the courier.)

Good God! Bogey. Your Tuesday letter, and I read 'Wordsworth—so honest and so pure.' And remember my letter yesterday about our little house, and here is yours in answer—just the same! We *are* one. Well I suppose I ought to accept this—but oh, the sweet sweet shock that goes through my heart each time it happens!

Yes, you are quite right, my precious shipmate. I *do* laugh at your preparations for this voyage of ours. I laugh so quietly that not even a harebell could hear—I laugh with every drop of my blood—and two tears laugh on my eyelids. You see—I am doing *just the same*. How many times have I lighted the lamp, wrapped up in my shawlet, sat down on the floor at your knees and said 'Boge, you read first'. How many times has *Cinnamon and Angelica* been published by us—have we leaned over each other's shoulders looking at it—have you said in a rough soft voice 'It looks pretty good'. Now Ribni has begun walking all over the cushions with a walking-stick and a broad hat, or pretending he is fetching in our cow. What an imp *he* is!

Why, I've just remembered I did a drawing of our house yesterday.

Oh, our divine future. The mists of morning are still upon it, but underneath it sparkles ready—waiting just for the sunrise—and then we shall catch hold and *run* and run into its garden, and I will put the key in the door and you will turn it, but being small ones we'll walk in together.

I must get up, darling Heart, and make myself a pretty girl for Sunday. I feel *simply immensely well today*—skipping and hopping and never never stopping[1]—don't cough at all—don't know how to—madly hungry and my hair in the most lovely little curls of bacon out of sheer crispness.

And its March 3rd and next month Mrs. Middleton Murry will arrive—which ought to excite you.

How is your EYE?

[1] This is from a music-hall song.

You know, you feel how I love you. Now I am this moment as you read running into your arms and having a small lift up while I *hug* my darling Bogey until he can't breathe. Yes, underneath of course I am serious—but

Oh God! what a joyful thing it is to have a true love!

I have given myself to you for keeps for ever.

Wig

Monday,

My own precious darling Bogey, (March 4, 1918)

I am writing to you, as yesterday, after my early breakfast, and still tucked up. Immensely tucked today, just a fringe and 2 fingers showing because outside it is all white with SNOW. And icy cold within. These houses are not made for such rude times. There seem to be a thousand knife-like airs that draw upon each other and do battle even unto th' extremities o' the floor.

Jag: Wiggie, you are very silly.

Wig: My breakfast crumbs have gone to my brain.

But it is very silly of the *Lion* to come in like this. I expected him to be a rough rude tumbling monster, but not with a mane of icicles!

Bang at the door. 'Une dépêche, Madame.' Cinq sous for the Aged. I open it. . . .

Hurras for April Bonie Murry! What *is* that word? It may be Boge —it may be Love. It is a very funny one. And, my dear darling, how can this have arrived so soon? I only sent yours late on Friday afternoon.

God! God! How I love telegrams!

And now I see you handing it across the counter and counting out the pennies. But the telegraph form, feeling awfully gay, flies off while the girl hands you the change, and begins to buzz and flap round the gas-jet and against the window-pane—UNTIL, finally, you have to make a butterfly net out of a postman's bag on the end of your umbrellachik and climb on to the counter and on to that iron rail (a Lovely Fair holding your grey woolly ankles the while) and do the most awful terrifying balancing feats before you snare it. Then you go out, quite exhausted, saying, 'I shan't have time for any lunch now!' But at that moment Wig appears riding on a cloud with a little heavenly hot-pot tied up in a celestial handkerchief. . . . No, Bogey, I must put this letter away to cool until the postman has been. . . .

Later, but no calmer. A Wednesday and a Thursday letter came. Quick March! is the best joke of the year, I think. I shall never never forget it. Now about the food cards. I am so glad you have got bacon, because it means fat. I had already decided to try and persuade you to let us feed at home le soir while the war is on. I'll go out with a bastick and buy things and make scrumbuncktious little dinners for us. It will be 100 times as cheap and awfully good for I have gleaned many hints here—and *essen muss der Mensch* and I should always be black with fury if I gave up a cowpong and did not get what I thought *a fair cooked return*. The sugar, of course, I will save too, for jam. Saxin just as good in coffee. That kitchen is so 'to hand' that we must make use of it while the war is on and save, save, save. See, I'll be mobilised too. I won't do it after the war but I will while the war is on. And Mrs. H.[1] would be no good. We'd hate her ways, you know, because we are such a chic little couple and so dainty.

Were I to live long with L.M. I should eat *nothing*. While she was at factory I could in a way understand, but here she eats *all day* and has even gone so far as (in fact always does) two large plates of soup as a kick-off for dinner. God, I must not talk of her.

I am very shocked that such a pirate as you profess to be should not have seen my skull and crossbones! I'll bring you the dates and figs and butter if I can and pine cones.

(But these 2 letters of yours written with the most lovely pale blue ink are so sweet that I can't stop hovering over them. I read and re-read them!) Oh, I've got that coat-collar changed. You know it *was* big and now it's little and furry up to the chin. Great improvement. But I shan't have the money surprise for you after all, for the Chemist + the Doctor have snapped it up. It was money Pa sent me for Xmas. Still, there it is and it's good I had it to pay these ponces with. I'll have to leave here on the 26th I think, for L.M. and I can't manage otherwise. However, there is time enough to talk of that. Of course, I told you not to tell people about the marriage and of course a light lager sent you popping off.[2] It's no matter: I like you for it. But what, ye Gods, don't I like him for? love him, adore him?

Wig

[1] The lady who 'did' for me at 47 Redcliffe Road.
[2] I had told Sullivan of our impending marriage.

Monday Night,
(March 4, 1918)

Love, it is very late. The winds are howling, the rain is pouring down,
I have just read Wordsworth's poem, *To Duty,* and a description in a
N.Z. letter of how to grow that neglected vegetable, the Kohl-rabi. I
never heard a wilder, fiercer night: but it can't quench my desire—my
burning desire to grow this *angenehme* vegetable, with its fringe of
outside leathery leaves, and its heart which is shaped and formed and of
the same size as the *heart* of a *turnip.* It is of a reddish purple colour, will
grow where there have been carrots or peas. Of course, I can see *our*
Kohl-rabi—the most extraordinary looking thing—and Wig and Jag
staring at it.

Do you think it ought to look like that?

No. Do you?

No. I think it's done it on purpose.

Shall I show it to somebody and ask?

No. They'll only laugh.

And as they turn away the Kohl-rabi wags and flaps its leathery leaves
at them. . . .

Tuesday, (March 5, 1918). Thunderstorms all night and today
torrents of rain, and wind and iciness. It is impossible to keep warm—
with fires, woollies, food or anything, and one is a succession of shivers.
The DRAUGHTS are really infernal. How I despise them for not being
able to fit a window! or a door! And how my passion for *solidity* and
honesty in all things grows. I feel the time has come when you and I
have put everything to the test. *We* are all right: we are dead honest.
Our house must be honest and solid like our work—everything we
buy must be the same—everything we wear even. Everything must
ring like Elizabethan English and like those gentlemen I always seem
to be mentioning: 'the Poets'. There is a light on them, especially upon
the Elizabethans and our 'special' set—Keats, W. W., Coleridge,
Shelley, De Quincey and Co., which I feel is the bright shining star
which must hang in the sky above the Heron as we drive home. Those
are the people with whom I want to live, those are the men I feel
are our brothers, and the queer thing is that I feel there is a great
golden loop linking them to Shakespeare's time and that our Heron
life will be a sort of Elizabethan existence as well. If you knew what
a queer feeling I have about all this as I write. Is it just because I

am so steeped in Shakespeare? I can't think of jam-making even,
without

> And if you come hether
> When Damsines I gether
> I will part them all you among.

And you know, if ever I read anything about *our* men, you should see
how arrogant I feel, and how inclined to say, 'Child, child!' I positively
feel that nobody has the right to mention them except you and me!
And dreadfully inclined to say to the poor creature who makes a mild
observation about *my* S.T.C. 'You really must not expect to understand!' Yes, Bogey, I am a funny woman—and a year or two at the
Heron will make me a great deal funnier, I expect.

Richard is very real to me, by the way, and part of our life. He is
going to 'fit', isn't he? I want us to have him and give him a rich true
life right from the start, with no false alarms.

Pas de courier. Only a *D.N.* It's lunch time. I must get up. Tomorrow,
D.V. I'll get your first of March letter. I hope nothing will happen to
this letter while L.M. takes it to the post—that she won't, in a fit of
absent-mindedness, eat it. That's a dash about the *courier*. I wanted to
warm my hands and lips and heart at one of your adored letters, oh—
as well as every other sweet name that ever blossomed on the tree of
love—my *friend*.

I do long to see you again and talk BOOKS. For your Worm is the
greatest bookworm unturned. It grows on me. I always was a bit that
way, but now—and with the Heron before us—well—Do you feel the
same? My Shakespeare is full of notes for my children to light on. Likewise the Oxford Book. I feel they will like to find these remarks, just as
I would have.

Goodbye for now, dearest dear. I am writing you with a cold, cold
hand—all stiff.

> I love you.
> Wig

Wednesday,
Dearest of All,   (March 6, 1918)

I ought to have known that having written to you as I did yesterday
your next letter saying you have bought Ben Jonson's plays would
arrive today. That *you* should write about books and the Elizabethans

and Keats—that *you* should talk of the Heron as I did! You see, we do seem to be in some utterly mysterious fashion two manifestations of *the same being*. We don't echo each other, for our voices are raised at the same moment. But it *is* damned queer that it should have reached such a fine intensity. . . . For God's sake buy Lamb.[1] We'll love to have that book. My mouth waters at all those new treasures that I so soon will fondle.

Oh, Jag, Jag! G—— is here with her husband—and she is nearly doing for me. I can't *think*—or write—or escape. She *is* a dear and generous and all that but a most APPALLING bore and I haven't the physical strength for her. I feel as though all my blood goes dead pale, and with a slight grin. When she goes on Friday I shall spend Saturday in bed *with the door locked*. I hate people: I loathe G—— unlimited, tearing, worrying G—— saying the same things—staring at me. If only I were *bien portante*, I suppose I should not feel like this at all—but as it is, wave after wave of real sickness seems to ebb through me and I dissolve with misery. She and my ghoul would have me *fixée* if it lasted long. I can't say her nay. 'Nous sommes venus exprès pour vous voir.' And she brought me books and *berlingots pour Monsieur,* etc.

It's not the slightest use pretending I can stand people: I can't. I hate L.M. so utterly and detest *her* so, that she's torture enough, but + this *grande femme, forte et belle, me parlant du Midi—des poèmes ravissantes d'Albert Samain . . .* ET *de Keats!* and Monsieur who dogs me saying what I ought to lick up 'pour me donner les belles joues roses'! I said faintly, clinging hold of a rosemary bush finally, and aching to cry, 'La santé est une question de l'esprit tranquille chez moi, Monsieur, et pas de bouillon gras,' and the darling rosemary bush squeezed my hand and left its fragrance there and said, 'I know—my dear!'

I am sorry, dear love, to make so loud a moan—but *you know—don't you?* No escape till Friday. *Alors, en plein Enfer jusqu'à le vendredi soir. Une lettre!* Send me a letter and I'll wear it over my heart and try and keep these big grown-up *mangeurs* away. You should see L.M. under their directions alimenting herself avec le potage. No, my gorge rises.

Aid me, ye powers. Oh, my poets, make a ring round little me and hide me. Oh, I must find a daisy for an umbrella and sit under it, but then, down would come L.M.'s shoe just for the pleasure of raising up 'cet*te* plante, si frêle, si délicate' once again.

No, you must wear me next to your heart and never let anyone

---

[1] A copy of E. V. Lucas's edition of Charles Lamb's Letters.

know I am there. I'll lie ever so lightly and only creep up and kiss you from time to time. Everybody is too big—too crude—too ugly.

Goodbye, darlingest heart. I don't want to seem depressed—but till Friday—till they go—I want to be your gay Wig, only your adoring one.

She has asked me to send you these cards pour vous donner une impression quoique frêle etc. etc., in this treacle tongue. But the house[1] is nice, isn't it?

> Thursday, Quick March,
> (March 7, 1918)

Draw this when you answer this letter and I'll know which it means. It's a spring chicken.

My dear Love,

This is my little moment of quiet before I am thrown to the Three Bears again. (Fancy *Southey* being the author of the Three Bears!) I am in bed. It's ten o'clock. The post hasn't come, but at break of day the Aged brought me your telegram, a particularly nice one, and so with that smiling on my knee I feel almost as though I'd had a letter. . . . It's a blue and white day, very fair and warm and calm. The sort of day that *fowls* enjoy, keeping up a soft faraway cackle—you know the kind? Were I alone I should dive into my new story. It's so plain before me. But I don't dare to. They'd see me: they'd look over the fence and call. No, darling new story, you'll have to wait till Friday night.

Poor old Carpentrassienne! If she knew how she offends me—how the sight of her binding up her balloon-like bosom preparatory to 'la fête de la soupe' makes me *frissonne*! If she mentions another book that she's going to make me eat when I go and stay with her, I think I may—fly into bits! And this French language! Well, of course, she always did caricature it, but in my clean, pink Elizabethan ears it sounds the most absolute *drivel*! And poor old L.M.'s contributions! 'En anglais mange les poudings c'est très bien.'

Hours and hours and hours of it! Are you wondering where Wig has left her sense of humour? Oh darling, my sense of humour won't take his head from between his paws for it—won't wag his tail or *twirk* an ear.

It's a comfort that the bloody cold has gone again *pour le moment*. I

[1] Henri Fabre's house.

201

hope it has in London, too. Here today it feels very quick March indeed.. *We shall have to send our telegrams all the same,* you know. The man at Havre said: 'Of course, if you have urgent family affairs which recall you to England before the time is up, it can, doubtless, be arranged.' I think he meant that I should do wisely to have *evidence*—like a tele-gram. So, unless you think the How is Mother telegram with its answer, 'Mother is worse operation necessary come soon possible,' too extreme, that will be the one we shall send. I think it is all right. I'll be *most awfully frightened* till I am on English shore. And even then, dearest heart, it will be no good for you to attempt to meet me because the trains are hours late—or perhaps nearly a day late, and we'd both suffer *too* cruelly. You know what I'd feel like thinking you were waiting and I couldn't get out and push the engine. No, I'll have to (*a*) phone you at the office, (*b*) go home by taxi if it's not office hours. Voilà!

My poetry book opened this morning upon 'The Wish' by old Father Abraham Cowley.

> Ah, yet, ere I descend into the grave,
> May I a small house and large garden have,
> And a few friends and many books, both true,
> Both wise and both delightful, too!
>
> Pride and ambition here
> Only in far-fetched metaphors appear;
> Here nought but winds can hurtful murmurs scatter
> And nought but Echo flatter.
> The gods, when they descended, hither
> From heaven did always choose their way:
> And therefore we may boldly say
> That 'tis the way, too, thither.

5 p.m. Dearest darling, two letters came—Saturday and Sunday—heavenly ones, full of rashers of bacon and fried eggs and casseroles. Oh, I love what you write to me. I *long* to know if your and Johnny's eyes popped when you 'lifted the lid as the hedgehog did'.

Ignorant Boy! Haven't you ever heard 'Sing hay'—for something—and then you have to sing 'Ho!' after.

Sing hay! }
Sing ho! } isn't that familiar?

Well, I sang 'Hay!' and waited for Boge to sing 'Ho!'. But he stood with his hands behind his back and said, 'I don't know what Hay means'.

OFFAL is a filthy word: but I have read about it in the *D.N.* and it seems a useful idea. One can get kidney and brains, sweetbreads, liver, heart—all that without getting one's coupong snipped. (Can't you hear Gordon Campbell?) *Très utile.* No, I don't think I'll write to that Food Depot. Because it will be so vilely confusing when I change my name again, and I'd have to register as Bowden etc. etc. *So* I'll bring 1 lb. of butter to last me till der Tag and I'll eat fish to your meat. You know I never eat bacon in the morning. That's my best idea. Then we can start 2 square after the 18th.

This gaiety is the result of absolute desperation. I've such a headache that everything *pounds,* even the flowers I look at, everything beats and drums. I feel all over absolutely *bled white* and it still goes on till to-morrow evening 8 P.M. Insufferable monsters!!! L.M. and she have just snapped up a whole half-pound of biscuits (2 francs) bought by L.M. for me (I *said* a ¼!). 'Oh, I am so sorry, Katie!!!' In consequence, I never touched one, and watched them dip the ½ lb. in their tea—'les sucreries de la guerre épouvantable'. My knees tremble, and where my little belly was there is only a cave. If they were not going tomorrow, I'd leave, myself, with a hand-bag. *Or* die and have L.M. plus the G.'s at my *pompes funèbres.* 'C'était une femme telle—ment douce!!!' No, madness lies this way. I'll stop and try to get calm. Oh God! these monsters!!

On Saturday D.V. after a whole day alone I will be again at least a gasping Wig—not a Wig in utter despair.

DAMN PEOPLE!

STILL IN PRISON and being tortured by
P.G.
R.G.
L.M.

Friday,
(March 8, 1918)

My last day of Three in Hell and Hell in Three.

My dearest dear,
In bed. Breakfast over. The window open, the airs waving through and a great beam of sun shining on a double stock. . . . But I'm blind

till tomorrow. The G.s go by a train at 8 o'clock tonight and tomorrow I'll be myself again. So I'll really be rid of two of my vampires at least and the third I can at least keep out of my room and not see except at meals. After these other two she seems a mild vulture, almost, but perhaps it's only that they subdue her and she has not had occasion to VENT the factory on me as she does otherwise. I feel horribly weak and frail and exhausted and if they stayed a day longer should take to my bed. But once the *great pressure* is gone, I will perk up, as you know, ever so quick again. But don't ever worry about not replying to the G. and don't feel under the least obligation to her. She's so blown that not even the ox could brake her belly—and she's a damned underbred female. All that she has done or wants to do for me is the purest fat conceit on her part, because I am English and you write *pour Le Times* and we have been innocent enough to flatter her vanity. She said yesterday: 'Mais, qu'est-ce que c'est, mon amie! Même quand vous n'êtes pas très bien portante, c'est seulement avec vous que j'ai le sens de la vie!' And I thought of L.M.'s 'Even if you are nervy, Katie, it is only when I am with you that I feel full of life.' And H.L.'s '*So* strange—the divine sense of *inflation* that I have when I come near you'. Oh Jag, if you are a little warrior in times of peace, *do* keep me from harpies and ghouls!!!

I write those three remarks out of horror, you understand, because they do terrify me. . . .

The lines of the poem I quoted were, alas! not mine, darling. They were writ by Thomas Randolph (1605–1635) and were part of an ode to Master Anthony Stafford to hasten him into the country.

> Come, spur away.
> I have no patience for a longer stay,
> But must go down
> And leave the chargeable noise of this great town:
> I will the country see. . . .

And the verse ends with this line:

> 'Tis time that we grew wise, when all the world grows mad.

It's altogether a most delightful poem. I wish I knew what else he had written. There's another line charms me:

> If I a poem leave, that poem is my son.

I feel he is a man we both should have known—that he is, most decidedly, one of the *Heron Men*.

And did Sir Thomas Wyatt write a great many poems? He seems to me extraordinarily good! Do you know a poem of his: *Vixi puellis nuper idoneus*? My strike! Bogey, it's a rare good 'un. (I don't know why I keep on saying 'poem'.)

Oh, how I do thirst after the Heron and our life there. It must come quickly. We must indeed start LOOKING for it—spying it out, buying maps of England and so on and marking likely spots as soon as I get back. Sundays will be Heron days. You shall go slow, my very dear, and sleep in the afternoons an' you will. At any rate we'll lie on the sommier and smoke and plan our real real life, and that will—please God—rest my tired boy.

4.40 p.m. I have escaped for a moment after giving them tea as usual. (Oh, here comes L.M.!!) Darling dearest, no go. Till tomorrow. Here's R.G. as well. *Dead again*. Wants me to read Keats's Grecian Urn to her en Anglais!!!? Well, she goes tonight.

Your
Wig

Saturday,
(March 9, 1918)

Dearest Love,

A cold wild day, almost dark, with loud complaining winds, and no post. That's the devil! None yesterday, none today! I should at least have had your Monday. I am very disappointed....

However, the Monsters have gone. A darling brown horse dragged them away at 8 o'clock last night. For the last time I, shuddering, wrung Monsieur's little half-pound of swollen sausages, and Madame's voice rang out, 'J'ai eu entre mes mains *cinq mille* lettres de Mistral,' and then they were gone, and I crept up to my room, ordered a boiling coffee, locked the door and simply sat and smoked till midnight. I'll shut up about them now. I feel better physically already. Isn't it awful to mind things so?

Oh, why haven't I got a letter? I want one *now, now*—this minute—not tomorrow!! And I believe it's there and the Post Office just won't deliver it, to spite me. I believe that *quite seriously*.

'By the way' *re* President Wilson. Monsieur G. says he is not at all liked in France. And why? . . . It's all very well for him to stand on a mountain and 'dire de belles choses'. *He's* never suffered. He only came into the war because he saw that the Allies were going to be beaten and realised that if they were, Germany would attack America with fleets and fleets of 'sous-marins puissants'. America's entry and 'retard' were both on purely commercial grounds. Wilson held out to collect as much war-profits as he could—came in to avoid having those war-profits taken from him by Germany. So *the* men are L.G. and Clemenceau. They *do* understand that you can never 'traiter avec ces gens-là', that we must go on until—'bien sûr'—England and France bleed again, but equally 'bien sûr' Germany is in the hands of whoever is left 'en Angleterre ou la France' to do whatever they please with. Their pleasure, of course, being to make strings of sausages out of the whole country.

'Gôutez-vous! Ce sont les Boches. Pas mauvais!'

Later. I told you how vile the day was. Terrific wind and cold. I went down to lunch to find L.M. had asked the *patronne* for her dinner in a paper to eat it on the rocks, as (she explained to the *patronne*) she preferred to do this so as not to be late and to keep me waiting!!! It's the sort of day when you'd ask the fowls to come under cover to feed— and here's this fool done this and sits, I suppose, shivering on a rock eating dates—rather than RISK being late for lunch and 'upsetting' me. . . . I could push her into the sea for this sort of idiocy. Now it's raining. Not being made of stone, I can't ignore the fact that she does these things—but nobody—not even you—could make me not believe that she does them to torture me, to keep my attention engaged with her at all costs.

God! if you knew how sick to death I am of all this and how I long for home and peace. I'll not stick this much longer, Bogey dear, and I shall very soon ask for news of Mother. . . . They will kill me between them all.

Tomorrow I'll have letters and I'll be a merry Wig again. Forgive this dull little toadstool.

(Found a word in Shakespeare I liked—'writhled': means wrinkled or furrowed. Henry VI, Part I, Act II, Sc. iii. 'this weak and writhled shrimp!' And another word which interested me was 'peise'. 'Lest leaden slumber peise me down tomorrow'. French *peser*, I suppose.)

Jag: But, Wiggie, I know all this. You are so dull today.

Wig: Yes, I *am*, Jag. Please forgive me and love me for I do love you.

Wig

Bytwene Mershe and Averil
When spray beginneth to spring
The litel foul hath hire wyl
On hire lud to synge

I can see her out of my window on a branch so fine that every time she sings it bends in delight. Oh, it is such a sweet sound. It is an early morning Heron bird. . . .

And now you must wake up and leap and fly out of bed. There is a smell of coffee from downstairs and I run on to the landing and call, 'Mrs. Buttercup! Will you please put the breakfast in the garden.' And I come back to find you dressed already and a *staggering* beauty in corduroy trousers and a flannel shirt with a cramoisie necktie! And then Richard comes up from the field with a big bright celandine in his buttonhole. And you say as we go down, 'My God, there's a terrific lot to be done today'—but not as if you minded. While I pour out the coffee you cut up the bread, and Richard says, 'I say, Jack, couldn't you make a fine woodcut of the house from here with the sun on it like that'. And just at that moment Mrs. Buttercup hangs a strip of carpet out of an upper window which gives it the finishing touch. We are going to drive over to a sale today in our funny little painted cart to see if we can buy some ducks and we have to call at the station on the way back for a parcel of paper. . . .

Knock: 'C'est la blanchisseuse, Madame. Je suis très matinale. Il fait beau, n'est-ce pas?'

Well, it's a good thing she did come. I might have gone on for ever. . . .

But, dearest love, was ever wine so potent as this Heron brew? A sip, and I am completely bowled over—'knocked out', as you say,—and when in addition I think that in a fortnight's time I shall be winging my way home and—instead of writing to you—talking to you, looking at you, hearing you, holding you—well, then, my pen even begins to dance and says 'Lay me down and let me be until the post has come'.

My love, my own, your Wednesday letter is here. I've just read it, and if you remember what it was about, you'll understand that it has simply added fuel to the flame. It was all about the Heron. The most divine, heaven-kissing letter that ever any woman received. 'For what we *have* received (and are about to receive) may the Lord make us truly

207

thankful' as I used to say with my eyes shut when I was a tiny. Well, as you say, our life is built on it! It is the fortress and the hiding place of our love—the 'solid symbol'.... Heavens! what would the world think if they looked through a little glass door into my head and saw what sweete madnesse did afflict my brayne. The miracle is, of course, that we are at the Heron already. We have found it—we are children of the Heron and no other home. Little exiles, everywhere else.

Funny you should have mentioned a cow. I was *worrying madly* over a nice name for a cow in bed last night. I wanted first to call it 'Chaucer': then I thought 'Edmund Spenser'—and only after I had ranged up and down for a long time did I remember that a cow was *feminine!!* and would kick over the pail and give you a swish in the face and then stalk off if she were so insulted.

Butter we must make with a stamp cut by ourselves. Oh, darling! I feel the whole world is homeless and 'makeless' except us—but wilfully so. How can they ever understand?

Now I must get up. Kay has sent my money. All is well. *Keep* yourself—for me. Take care of yourself for 2 weeks more—and then—Wig and Bogey will fly into each others arms.

There is a certain little white pink, striped with dark red, called 'sops-in-wine'. *We must grow it.*

I have also a feeling too deep for sound or foam for all kinds of *salads*.

Tuesday,

My very dearest,   (March 12, 1918)

L.M. has heard from Gwynne's. She is to come back as soon as possible. That being so, and I wishing to travel with her, I wired you as arranged today. I shall not be able to tell *when* we start, until I hear from Cook's as to what sort of chance we have of getting places in the Paris train. But, of course, I'll wire you as soon as anything definite occurs.

I feel (as you may imagine) on the wing already—oh, ever so on the wing!! And as to the letters—as you say they are flying. Your Friday 8th and Thursday 7th letters came together this morning. And now just having sent your telegram and been to the mairie with it and so on, I feel very empty in the head, and it's hard to write. I'll calm down and be more fluent tomorrow. But to have really despatched my pigeon! Pretty thrilling, Bogey! Don't let Rib answer. He'd say '*She's* all right,' and do us in the eye. I hope Rib does post me a card. I rather see him tagging along the Redcliffe Road with a ladder to prop against the pillar-box made of dead matches.

That sounded a vile raid. So many houses were destroyed. But I do somehow feel you will take care. You could not be so cruel as not to. I shall be *extremely* interested in your Rousseau. I feel you are pleased with your operation on him even though it had to be hurried....

Oh, I *am* coming, yes, really coming, Bogey. There goes a train which isn't *the* train but is at all events one of the trains before. And I have ordered nougat (*specialité d'Ollioules*) for you and Richard, to be ready in *quelques jours*. I had a Tragick Letter from H.L. in reply to my *un*-written ones. She sounds very 'sombre' and is raging round to seek someone to devour. 'My passionate desire for *vivid life*. I have been up in London and saw D——'(!) S——has gone to the Holy Land. (With a hay down, bough down.) That reminds me of old Goodyear. I'd like to see his father's letter. Send the sonnet. I wish you had time to write a sort of memoir. And see we get the book—won't you?

(By the way, I am afraid the English colour 'maroon' was a corruption of the French *marron*. I've just thought of it.) However, that is no reason why it should not be orange-tawny. But the English maroon—I had once a maroon sash I remember, and it was not gay.

It's such a vile day here—cold, dark, the sea almost red, very sinister, with bursts of thunder. And dogs are barking in the wrong way, and doors bang in the hotel, and all that is pale looks too white—blanched. I must get the idiot to give me a handful of wet leaves or so to light my fire with. And then I must try not to pack and re-pack my trunk for the rest of the evening (in my head, I mean). But you know the feeling. Think of it! No, I just can't. I wish the Channel wasn't between us. I am very frightened of being torpedoed. I'd be sure to sink, and oh, until I have been potted out and grown in a garden, I don't want to be either drowned or otherwise finitoed. So wear something crossed over your heart for a good omen. No, Bogey, I can't write today. My heart is wrapped up in that telegram. I feel almost serious, too—anxious, you know—and don't dare to *think* of my happiness if all does go well.

I am your own girl who loves you.

Wig

Wednesday,
My dear Love,   (March 13, 1918)

No post today. Well, I am not surprised. It could not have gone on

209

at that rate. I am writing to you, for the first time depuis mon arrivée, in the garden in a summer house, which is thatched with a pretty, delicate thing rather like—not very like—a honeysuckle. L.M. sits by. As long as I am out of my room she always does. *Elle est très forte, très vaillante aujourd'hui* and has nearly knocked me down. If I hadn't the telegram at the back of my mind, I *should* be flat. *E.G.* 'Of course I will come back to '47' with you in the taxi and unpack—even if Jack is there. You will be bound to want somebody to look after you *decently* after the journey.' And if you saw her eyes rivetted on me while she says that 'decently', you'd know why I hate her. That's a *bite* to her. She's drawn my furious blood and she knows it. She's made me feel again *weak, exhausted* with rage, and so she's happy. I don't exaggerate. I grant I have an L.M. complex—but to hate any one as I hate this *enemy*. . . of ours. Please, darling love, for my sake don't forget never to give her a loophole. And never, never must she walk into the Heron.

There's such a sad widower here with four little boys, all in black—all the family in black—as though they were flies that had dropped into milk. There was a tiny girl, too, but she was not fished out again soon enough, and she died. They are *silly*, so *stupid*: that's what makes me sad to see them. Like a Dostoevsky 6th floor family to whom this has happened. The man can't quite make up his mind whether his little boys can walk or if they must be carried, so he does half and half, and sometimes during meals he feels one of them and dashes up, his eyes rolling,—dashes out of the *salle à manger* to get a coat or a black shawl. . . .

I read in my *Daily Mail* today that the double daffodils are out in English gardens and red wall-flowers. I have been to Gamel's also today and asked her to put in reserve for me 1 lb. of butter. That makes me feel *presque là*. The tulips are coming out here, but I shan't dare to bring them because of the journey.

Oh God! this pathetic widower! One of the little boys has just begun to make a sort of weak sick bird-piping and to jump up and down—and he is *radiant*. He is sure they are well already.

Dear precious one—that's all for today. Tomorrow I shall hear from Cook's, I hope, and then I'll feel more settled. You know, I am already 'on the wing' and have been making up my *marvellous accounts*—you know, pages and pages where everything is reduced and then turned back again—and the simplest sum seems to be thousands.

Addio, my darling love,

Your Wig

My Precious,

Thursday,
(March 14, 1918)

I have just received your Sunday letter. It was very noble of you to do as you did and so beautifully keep your promise about my story.[1] You're of course, absolutely right about 'Wangle'. He shall be re-sprinkled mit leichtern Fingern, and I'm with you about the commas. What I *meant* (I hope it don't sound high falutin') was Bertha, not being an artist, was yet artist manquée enough to realize that those words and expressions were not and couldn't be hers. They were, as it were, *quoted* by her, borrowed with . . . an eyebrow . . . yet she'd none of her own. But this, I agree, is not permissible. I can't grant all that in my dear reader. It's very exquisite of you to understand so *nearly*.

You know (seriously) I don't feel as though I have really written anything until you have passed your judgment—just as I should never feel that I had had a child—even though it were there and screwing up its fists at me—until you had held it and said 'Yes, it's a good kid!' Without *that* I am just in a state of *attente*—you understand.

I have, of course, kept all of your letters ever since my arrival here, knowing that they will be of use to us one day.

All that you write of the Heron and of our 'departure' is so true and clear that I can only look at you and smile and say 'Yes, Bogey!' You see the Heron is the Miracle. I can't write about it today. Very soon we shall talk—for ever—and as we talk we shall become more and more at peace and wisdom from on High shall descend upon us.

I hope Lamb arrives in time to go home with me as fellow-traveller. (I will make a cover for him so that he shall come to no harm.) And I *don't want* the £5, dearest love. However, if you send it, I shall just keep it. I heard from Cook's this morning. There is evidently great difficulty in getting places in the Marseilles-Paris *rapide*. But otherwise all seems more or less plain. I think I shall leave the middle of *next week*. Though I write that, I don't feel it. Somehow a curious *numbness* is beginning in me about this journey, *or* a sort of feeling that it is all going to take place in the pitch dark—with no thought of place or time. Rib must be a little crusader and sit with his feet crossed 'for luck' all the while I cross the Channel. I am still terrified of that part of the journey. I keep thinking myself into a little boat with a bundle or not a bundle on my lap and the cold sea-water round us and you and the Heron, you and

---

[1] *Bliss.*

211

the Heron—all my solid earth and all my Heaven far away. But it's silly of Wig.

It's a gay sunny day and the tamarisk trees are *blowing* into leaf. Tomorrow I half expect an answer to my telegram. Did it surprise you awfully?

Goodbye, shipmate
Wig

(March 15, 1918)

This begins on Thursday—and continueth into Fri-i-i-day

A
A
A
MEN.

Dearest Love,

I received your telegram this (Thursday) afternoon. I had also a letter from Cook's today saying that one must engage a place a week in advance for the *rapide*. So I am sending Ida to Marseilles tomorrow (Friday) to spy out the land, and she will get the seats for as soon as possible. In the meantime I will wire you my delay. I must try *at all costs* to get across before Easter. That means, however, that I' can't possibly leave here before the 20th at earliest, and it may be a day or two later. It will be as soon as I can. I shall have much more to go upon once L.M. has been to Cook's and if possible to the Consul's. Your telegram, of course, made me feel I must *rush* even tonight.

I was amused because it had been *opened, read* and translated by these people (for it was still *wet*) and they gathered in *force* to see me receive it, with their hands and eyes all ready to be lifted proper. You see your little Briton casting a moonlight beam upon it and saying, as she read, 'Voulez-vous me monter un thé simple à quatre heures, s'il vous plaît?' They were very cool upon that. So was the tea. From a sort of 'ice to ice' principle, I suppose.

Saturday—no, Friday,
(March 16, 1918)

Charles [Lamb's letters] came and a perfectly heavenly letter which simply *bore* him on rosy wings to my bedside—also the papers that bound him. I am going to make him a very thick coat with a velvet

212

collar and ten buttons a side for the journey. For I cannot resist such a companion across France.

Bogey, dearest love, your letter has made my coming *real again*. It keeps flashing in and out, now light, now dark, like a revolving light-house (not your letter—my coming). Sometimes I do see—but some-times there's nought but wavy dark.

L.M. is gone. A great mistral is roaring. It's a *brutal* day, and my room is only just done, 4 p.m., and I spent the night hunting and hallooing after a flea. I saw it once—a pox on it!—sitting on the edge of my navel and looking into that organ through a telescope of its front legs as though it were an explorer on the crater of an extinct volcano. But when *I* hopped, *it* hopped and beat me. Now it is still roaring in this room somewhere. It was a very wild savage specimen of a monster—the size of a large China tea-leaf—and tore mouthfuls out of me while I slept. I shall hang out a little sign tonight: 'No butter, no margarine, no meat.' But I'm not hopeful.

The Sunday Evening Telegram, which was Lamb's undervest, as it were, gave me a Great Shock. In this little time, and even with *The Paris Daily Mail* occasionally, I had almost forgotten that appalling abyss of vulgarity . . . which does exist. I had to ring for a fork and have it took away. Did you read Lamb on Rousseau?

Oh, oh, I *burn* to read your article. It's going to be wonderful!!

What idiot wrote that leader on Morris, I wonder?—and there were *good bones.* And how shockingly ill the novels are reviewed! The 'Stevenson: 2nd Thoughts' was interesting.[1]

So you have got Thomas Wyatt. Well—I suppose that is quite natural. The poem I meant begins

> They flee from me who sometime did me seek
> With naked foot stalking within my chamber. . . .

and what especially caught me was the second verse which I can't now read calmly. It's marvellous, I think.[2] I could say why, but I must take this to the post before the wind blows *too* loud and *too* cold.

[1] These were articles in the *Times Literary Supplement.*
[2] The first two verses of this beautiful poem are:

> They flee from me that sometime did me seek,
>   With naked foot stalking within my chamber:
> Once have I seen them gentle, tame and meek,
>   That now are wild, and do not once remember
>   That sometime they have put themselves in danger

And I am, dearest, on my way. Oh Bogey—just a moment before I shut this letter up and it is carried away from me. I love you—love you —love you—and you are all the secret of life for me.

Wig

(No letter today)   Saturday,
Dear Love,   (March 16, 1918)
    I must tell you just how matters stand, and you must help me please, if you can. L.M. saw the Consul at Marseilles yesterday. *She* can return without any trouble, but my telegram *re* Mother will not do at all. It appears that everybody who came to the Riviera 'for fun' this year has been recalled by the same sort of thing, and the French authorities will not allow it. It is absolutely insufficient. What I have to do is to *write* to the authorities at Bedford Square asking their permission to return before my time is up *i.e.* before the END of April. They, having looked into my reasons, communicate with the Consul at Marseilles, and either grant me a permit, or do not grant me one. The Consul at Marseilles says he has no power over the matter at all.
    So this, you see, will take a most confounded time, and I have had to cancel my wire of yesterday by sending you another today. I am, as well, *extremely* anxious not to travel without L.M. as she'd be such a help to me on the journey.
    My plans, then, are as follows: I shall endeavour to obtain from the English doctor here a chit to the effect that it is no longer advisable for me to remain on this coast, and that, if I have to go to England, it *is* necessary for me to have a companion. As L.M. is practically forced to return *now*, that means I have to be 'let through' with her. This chit he may or may not give me. I can't see him until tomorrow afternoon (such is the press of illness at Bandol) and then it depends very much in what mood the man is. He is so exceeding shady and suspicious that he may have a lively fear of signing his name to anything; on the other

To take bread at my hand: and now they range
Busily seeking in continual change.

Thanked be fortune, it hath been otherwise
    Twenty times better; but once especial—
In thin array, after a pleasant guise
    When her loose gown did from her shoulders fall,
    And she me caught in her arms long and small,
And therewithal so sweetly did me kiss
And softly said, *Deare Heart, how like you this?*

hand, he may do it just for that reason. If he *won't*, I'll write to Bedford Square and state this same case, and I thought I might also plead that I wish to re-marry on the 17th of April and wish to return to make preparations. I can't tell whether that is wise or not. I'd give anything for your advice on that point. Indeed, I really think I will not mention this marriage until t'other has failed. If I can reinforce my plea with the chit, I think there will be no difficulty. Otherwise, there will be. . . . L.M. of course, will stay for the present, and as long as anything is unsettled she will stay. Yes, I am now brought so low as to be thankful.

It is all very vile and unlooked for. This new 'strictness' has only been established during the last fortnight on account of all the false reasons people have given. I do not think I *could* wait here for another whole month—I mean, until May. The idea almost frightens me. I feel there is a plot to keep us apart—and then, *our marriage*. . . .

I suppose you can do nothing from your side—*influence* nobody— ask nobody? In case you can, I give you the number of my passport: 177256. You see, dearest Bogey, I write in this *numb, dumb* way, because at present I know nothing, and the idea that the war can do *this* in addition to all it has done to us *strikes* me and lays me low for the moment. I'll get up again. I'm only speaking 'spiritually', but at present, after I had packed and taken my tickets (transferable) I should cry if I wrote any more. I feel I can't *bear* this absence a great deal longer—and yet . . . they *will* torture me.

If any change occurs, I will wire you, and do you wire me if you can think of anything I ought to do, or anything that *can* be done. What about that friend of Pierre MacOrlan? Any use?

I sit thinking and thinking. Curse this doctor—he's either the victim of a big bottle or a little 'un and not fit to be seen today—and he's the only person who can help me—a little sot with poached eyes who bites his fingers.

No, we must comfort and sustain each other *a great deal*. Comfort me! Put your arms round me! It's raining here—too, and the rain is all over my floor, and it's blowing and cold and I feel so *far, so far*. And oh, how my homesick heart *faints* for you and you only. Love me.

Wig

But harder to bear than anything is *your* disappointment. That's what hurts—oh! like sin!

My precious Love,

Your wire this morning simply *smote* me in two. ½ of me was pain for your watching at the window, you and our darling valiant cabin-boy, watching for the boat which isn't even *remotely* allowed to leave the harbour yet by these *cursed* war officials. Half of me was agony at the thought of the letterless days I must endure before you write again And never never have I so wanted the support of letters!

God! why didn't I say that it might be a difficult process—that there was, 'enfin', a *risk*. But you knew there was, didn't you, my precious darling? And of course you knew I'd have taken *every possible precaution* that a letter of yours should not be lost, but should be returned to me. I lay in bed with that gay beflagged little telegram on my heart and felt *it could not be*. Why, Bogey, must we have this new trial—and this new agony? Why is it so dreadfully—difficult? And then there came the last letters I shall get for a while, I suppose—and the one where you waited for my *wire* from *Paris* and my telephone message. Heart dearest! it's far away still. Don't wait—don't wait so ardently. They won't let me out yet, and while I know you wait 'like that' my lamentable state in this prison is like to kill me. I could *break through*, and yet I can't....

Just try and keep calm and keep *confident* and know how I am fighting and then I'll get strength from you. Otherwise I feel a sort of desperation and 'I can't get out, darling!' feeling which won't help. I have delayed writing to you today in the hope that the doctor would have been as he promised. L.M. went to remind him this morning, but now it's 5 o'clock and there is no sign, so I suppose he is 'hors de combat'. I paid his bill a week or two ago (which he didn't acknowledge) and asked him not to come again unless I sent for him—and I am afraid he is *fâché*. I have not told you about him, and it's not necessary to go into details now, but he's shady—and unreliable—to say the least. This being so, IF the storm has abated at all tomorrow, I shall go to Marseilles tomorrow and try and see a man there and get a chit from him. But, you understand, this *all* takes time—*days* and *days*—even if I can bring it off. So turn from the window and don't wait for me just yet. Only know that I am doing every single thing I can, and so is L.M.—that every drop of blood I have is sick for home and that your letters—your adored confident letters—have made it seem almost impossible that I am NOT coming. Our telegram the consul at Marseilles merely laughed at. 'It's the telegram they *all* send when they wish to return. It won't do, dear lady, it's too old. You must apply through the London office. It may take ten days for a reply.' So, until I come, I shall be doing nothing and thinking of nothing except the ways and means. All we have to do is to try and keep calm and weather the storm and win through. I'm strong enough if I feel your umbelella[1] is over me. Oh! once I really *am* under it, never let me forth again.

I say nothing about Charles Lamb while *this is on.* But he has been an immense comfort, even though I read him in that mingled fever, dread and dismayed impatience that one must feel in a tumbril, I should think.

Now I must put my arms round you and kiss you and lean against you, and do you kiss me. And then I must [let] go again for a little. It's still a great wild storm here—rain and cold and wind. Tomorrow I'll have my try at Marseilles and wire you from there. These wires are not an extravagance. I feel you must have them. But do you try not to worry, and remember how hard I am trying to—to keep calm and not to allow myself to be overwhelmed.

Your small but fighting
Wig

Marseilles: Café de Noailles.
Monday,

Dearest, (March 18, 1918)

Everything seems changed. My whole life is *uprooted,* and living in Bandol, even with the G.s and L.M., feels like *calm* compared to this violent battle. I arrived here, very late this evening, too late for the Consul or for Cook's: the train was 2 hours en retard. And so I got a room at the Hotel de Russie, had some food, and here I am. I must bring you up to date with this Battle of the Wig.

Last night after I wrote you I felt desperate and sent L.M. after Doctor Poached Eyes, even though it really was rather late. He was at

---

[1] This comes from a favourite rhyme of Katherine's.

> Come along, Isabella,
> Under my umbelella.
> Don't be afraid,
> There's a good maid,
> Come along, Isabella.

dinner—fatal time!—but promised to turn up. Whereupon I set to, turned L.M. out of my room, dressed in my new frock, and a black swanny round my neck, *made up,* drew chairs to the fire, and waited for this little toad. If you could have come in, you would have been horribly shocked, I think. I have not felt so cynical for years. I knew my man and I determined to get him by the only weapon I could and that *he* could understand. He came *far* more than 3 parts on, and I sat down and played the old game with him—listened—looked—smoked his cigarettes—and asked finally for a chit that would satisfy the Consul. He gave me the chit, but whether it will I'll not know till tomorrow. It could not be more urgent in its way. I dictated it *and* had to spell it *and* had to lean over him as he wrote *and* hear him say—what dirty hogs do say. I am sure he is here because he has killed some poor girl with a dirty button-hook. He is a maniac on *venereal* diseases and *passion.* Ah, the filthy little brute! There I sat and smiled and let him talk. I was determined to get him for our purpose—any way that didn't involve letting him touch me. He could say what he liked: I laughed and spelled—and was so sweet and soft and so *obliged.* Even if this chit fails I think he can get me through in other ways. He has, for all his shadiness, a good deal of very useful influence in high quarters in Marseilles and Toulon—and it's all at my disposal. So I'll use it.

Oh dear, oh dear! I feel so strange. An old, dead, sad, wretched self blows about, whirls about in my feverish brain—and I sit here in this café—drinking and looking at the mirrors and smoking and thinking how utterly corrupt life is—how hideous human beings are—how loathsome it was to catch this toad as I did—with *such* a weapon. I keep hearing him say, very thick, 'Any trouble is a pleasure for a lovely woman' and seeing my *soft smile.* . . . I am very sick, Bogey.

Marseilles is so hot and loud. They scream the newspapers and all the shops seem full of caged birds, parrots and canaries, shrieking too. And the hags sell nuts and oranges—and I run up and down *on fire.* Anything—anything to get home! It all spins like a feverish dream. I am not *un*happy or happy. I am just as it were in the thick of a bombardment, writing you, here, from a *front* line trench. I do remember that the fruit trees on the way were all in flower and there were such big daisies in the grass and a little baby smiled at me in the train. But nothing matters till I have seen the Consul. I am staying tonight at the Hôtel de Russie. It is clean and good. I have *Elle et Lui* to read. But this is all a dream, you see. I want to come home—to come home. Tomorrow I'll wire you after I've seen the man. Under it—above it—through it I am yours—fighting and tired—but yours for ever.

Wig

Marseilles: Café de France,
Bulletin du Front   March 19, 1918

I advanced to the Consul and gained a local success, taking the trench as far as Paris. I expect to advance again under cover of *gas* on Saturday. The enemy is in great strength but the morale of the Wig is excellent.

Please explain this to Ribni and make him salute.

Dearest of all,

Well, as far as I know, the 'wangle' has succeeded. At any rate I have leave to go as far as Paris and try my luck there—and I don't think, having got so far and pleading as I shall, they can withhold their consent to my going further. Especially as L.M. (lunatic attendant) has permission. The Consul here was *not* agreeable about the affair, but whether that was just a formality or not, I don't know. I rather think it was. After having been there I went to the police and had my passport viséd again and then to Cook's to take the ticket.

It is still a divine day—a sort of *anguishing* beauty of spring. Wonder if you know what I mean. I mean something so definite. I have bought myself a bottil of *Genêt fleuri* (which I can't afford) so that I shall be a little perfumed bride (*if* I get back). I think I shall today. Oh, how much I could tell you. I have lived through lives and lives since I last wrote to you in calm. That night at the hotel *par exemple*—but *that* I have written at four o'clock this morning. It's pretty good, I think. This city seems to me to be stranger and stranger. Does one always have fever here? And are these things here to be seen, or are they all 'dreams'? Buds on the trees—so big—so fat—flowers to sell, lovelier and more poisonous-looking than flowers could be—and the beggars who are like the beggars of the 14th century (Wig, that is swank). And then the blacks and the women with white faces and pale pale gold hair and red dresses and little tiny feet—women who seem themselves to be a sort of VICE.

L.M. has of course just been like an immense baby without a perambulator. I have carried her everywhere, paid for her, ordered for her, arranged for her bath, showed her the cabinet, and answered all the questions which my Grandmother used to ask my father when *she* came from Picton to gay, wild, evil Wellington.

219

I go back this evening, pack tomorrow, and leave by the early Thursday train. In Paris on Friday—start for Havre Saturday (all being well) and I suppose at that rate England on Tuesday, or perhaps Monday. But that is still dark. At any rate the lighthouse throws a beam as far as Paris. Oh, my *lean* purse. Its *bones,* its *stringiness.* But all is well. I am so full of black coffee that if you see at the station a dark copper coloured little Wig, don't despise her.

Now I must go back to the trenches and go over the top to the station. Goodbye—breathlessly—with all my loving heart.

Wig

Hôtel Beau Rivage, Bandol,
Wednesday Night,
(March 20, 1918)

Packed and sent to station.

Darling Heart,

Just in case I don't arrive as soon as I hope to, I'll go on writing. Because I know what it feels like not to have letters. (No earthly *vague* reproach intended). Much more because it's a habit I can't break when I am away from you. Pray God it's a habit I *shall* break very soon.

I arrived back last night and your two wires were here—about the £5. As I had just been really wondering about money, I was terribly glad. (All the same I shall have a bright penny for you, I hope.) I wired you then and ever since I seem to have been 'en voyage'. *Figs* I have for you, and *nougat du pays,* and chocolat for you and little brother, and a big pine kernel and safran and carnations (these last a present). The nougat is the thrilling present. It is made at Ollioules of the very almond trees *here,* and I feel that when you eat it your eyes will crinkle up. Shall I *really* give you this—really feel your arms round me—really be a child with my child playfellow? . . . Oh, Jack—if I dare think [it] my heart would break for joy. I have said goodbye to everybody like a good girl, and they like me—in their way, I suppose. And all who knew you ask to be remembered to 'your jeune mari'. They always seem to think we were so very very young at the Villa Pauline—playing houses —going to bed under the table for a minute with the cloth pulled down for a blind—calling out 'Morning!' and getting up and eating each a most lovely fried marguerite daisy for breakfast. . . .

I leave by that early train. If God loves us I shall be home on Sunday and perhaps you will come to the station and wait for me with your casserole in a hanky and sit on a bench there and eat it (the inside only) if the train is late. But no, it *blinds* me. I can't see so bright—into such heavenly brightness. And our Rib—our little tiny one—will you tell him you are going off to bring me home? Oh, Jack, Jack, Jack. My love, my darling Heart! I can't write. Everything even in this room seems to move and breathe and have being because I love you and I am turned towards the only home I long for. God keep us for each other till Sunday. Amen.

Wig

At the Café Noailles, Marseilles,

Thursday,

Darling Heart,   (March 21, 1918)

The train goes tonight at 7.5.

Tea, orange-flower water, fever, a pain in my stomach, tablettes hypnotiques ('ne pas dépasser huit tablettes dans les 24 heures'), sun, dust, a great coloured—a dreaming swaying balloon of balloons out-side—yellow, red orange, purple. (A little boy has just had one bought for him and he's terrified of it. He thinks it means to carry him away. What's the good of being cross with him? But she *is* cross. She shakes him and drags him along.)

L.M. has lost all her luggage, but *all*, and has had to buy it all over again with a rucksack to put it in. She can't think how it disappeared. 'Will you see about it at Cook's for me *and* write to the hotel and explain?' I've done that. But she is good otherwise, quieter now that she is *en voyage*, and she has bought, oh, such *good* figs. . . .

I feel so bloody ill—such a belly ache and a back ache and a head ache. The tablettes hypnotiques cost 7.50. What do you think of that? But they are the same things that good old Doctor Martin gave Mother to give me when I was 13 and knew myself a woman for the first time. That being the case, I bought them, just as Mother would have, and felt a *mysterious well-being* all through me as I swallowed one. I couldn't have gone off tonight if I had not bought them. I should have had to go to an hotel and lie there.

Cook's seemed to take a perfect joy in giving me the £5, and long *beams* of light came from my fingers as I took it and tucked it away.

It is so *hot,* so very, *very hot.* One feels as though some fiend had seized one by the hair and peppered one all over with dust and sand. (*Rotten sentence!*)

I had an omelette for lunch—2 francs—and then thought some cauliflower, because it was only 20 c. and very harmless. So I had that and then some stewed fruit. God! The cauliflower was 2 francs instead! And you can buy whole ones at Bandol for 35 centimes! Can you see my face? And L.M. comforting me: 'It's not as if it is for every day but only for one day.'

Paris tomorrow, and then the offensive at the Consul's. Shall I arrive before this letter? And will Rib make fringe papers of it under my very eyes—what he will call 'les petits frissons'? Or does it mean I am going to be torpedoed and that's why I keep on writing? Oh, I *hope* not. I am very frightened of the journey on the sea, because my wings are so sinkable.

(Deux limonades—deux! That gives you the day.)

Oh, darling, have you got my wire tonight? And do you know I am on my way and are you holding thumbs?

This place seems to me *infected*. I mean in the fire and brimstone way. It ought to be destroyed and all the people in it. It is a filthy place. And the actor next to me, who is holding out the promise of a part to a poor little woman *while* he eats her sweets and drinks her chocolat—on him I would let fall the biggest brimstone of all.

God help us!

                Yours, yours for ever.

                    Wig

Katherine arrived in Paris on March 22, 1918, the very day, I believe, on which the bombardment of the city by Big Bertha began, though it was not realized for some days what was the cause of the regular explosions. She was not able to leave Paris until nearly three weeks later, on April 10. By this time she was very seriously ill indeed, and the effect upon her of her physical and mental sufferings during this period can be imagined. The peculiar horror of these days was that for many of them all communication—postal and telegraphic included—between London and Paris was suspended. While I eventually received nearly all Katherine's letters, she received very few of mine.

                                    Paris,

                                    Friday,

Dearest,   (March 22, 1918)

They won't let me through till they have obtained permission from the office at 19 Bedford Square. That will take *at least* a week, and having to stay in Paris a week—it means I must notify the Commissaire of the Police in the quarter in which I intend to reside, and he will give me permission to leave France in 8 to 10 days—not before. So I must really count on ten days here. What a more than B. curse! They were very decent at the office here, but absolutely immovable. They could do nothing via Bedford Square except by letter, and I am told to write as well and crave permission to return. Otherwise I must stay in France until May!! I am now going to Cook's to postpone all the remainder of my ticket. I am also going to wire you and to ask you to write to me at Cook's as I have not yet found a hotel. *Please, John, I don't need any money.* I will tell you if I do, but PLEASE don't send a farthing until I do ask. I have more than enough to last me here and get me over. And more would only be an awful curse. The hotels we have known here have become deadly swindles. Cheapest room at *Odessa* without déjeûner 7.50. Cheapest room at *de Loire* 6 and *filthy*. I have just been to the *l'Univers* where they may have something tomorrow. L.M. will wait with me. I shall send her to Cook's every morning for a telegram or a letter from you, and I beg you to wire me here just to say *all is well*. I shall get a cheap room tomorrow and stay in it and work till I do get back. I have a great many formalities to arrange with the police—military permit office here—etc., and at this moment my head is quite empty, after the journey and getting about, and the disappointment and fatigue of this looking for rooms. Also, the fact that I have not heard from you for days is *dreadful, dreadful*. I might be in China. I have made careful arrangements for all your Bandol letters. But, God, can't I have news? Please wire just a word, dearest. Oh God! it *is* a blow. Ten days more. This journey—it never ends. I seem to have been trying to get back from that moment we stopped waving. Now I must dash off to Cook's. I will write again tonight. Bogey, write soon and at length to your wandering child.

Wig

My address. I will not change it.

Select Hotel,
Place de la Sorbonne,
Friday Night,
(March 22, 1918)

My precious darling,

At last I am *free* to write to you again, even with this horrible ten days delay between us. I mean my spirit is free. You know, somehow at the back of my mind I couldn't altogether believe that I *would* be home on Sunday. I saw you preparing, and yet I had to keep on writing you letters in case it didn't come off. Oh, I am so glad I did now, even though they were silly ones. They will keep you in touch and you will know what happens more or less while it is happening. . . . It is not the worst that has happened. That would have been to be tied up in Bandol till May. I think, from the manner of the man at the Military Permit Office today, that there is no doubt the 19 Bedford Square people will give me a permit. The only trouble is the time it takes and the horrible worry it entails here with the police. For Paris is guarded against strangers with hoops of steel. However, all can be arranged. And having written and sent my doctor's chit to No. 19 and gone to the Commissaire for permission to remain here and permission to depart as early as possible, I must just see it through.

This has been a *bad* day—looking for an hotel all day—with 'Do let us take a taxi, Katie!' and strange desires on L.M.'s part to go to hotels at about £1,000 a bed and £500 petit déjeuner. Finally, late this afternoon I was passing along the Boulevard St. Michel and saw this, at the end, next door to the Sorbonne. It is very quiet—trees outside, you know, and an extremely pleasant chiming clock on the Sorbonne *même*. Also next door there is the best looking bookshop I have ever seen—the best set out, with exquisite printing on all the window cards and so on. The hotel seems just what is wanted. Six francs for my room with déjeuner—a big square room with 2 windows, a writing table, waste-paper basket, two armchairs, de l'eau courante, a low wooden bed with a head piece of two lions facing each other, but separated for ever, kept apart for eternity by a vase of *tender flowers*. There is also a white clock with three towers. It stands at six. But this is a fine room to work in. Immediately I came in I *felt* it and took it.

The people are quiet and simple, too, and the maid is pretty. The two armchairs, I have just observed, are very like pug-dogs, but that can't be helped.

Very well, until they let me come home I shall stay here and write. All the back of my mind is *numbed*. The fact that this *can* happen seems to me so dreadful, and I feel we must never go apart again. Getting back is too difficult, Bogey—and oh, so tiring and wearing. Now you and Rib are nearly in my arms. Now they tell me—'No, that is not the land you see. Those are clouds. . . .' Oh God, better not think. And I *can't* write properly any more until I have heard from you. *One certain* thing is send NO money, please. I have enough and more than enough. And oh, dearest, while I fight this through, take care of your darling self for me. It is very warm here—just as warm as Bandol and the chestnut trees are in leaf. It is the early May. If there are bad raids I will sit in the caves and try and hold a door over my head.

Oh, Bogey, I want a letter so much that my heart can hardly beat any longer without one. On Monday there ought to be a wire at Cook's for me. If you want to write to me *here*, I am sure it is quite safe. It would be a very lovely surprise to get a letter. I am just going to sit under my working umbrella now till I start off again—that is all—and go on making notes about Charles Lamb and George Sand and wandering in that shop next door to see if I can find a present for my love.

Goodnight, my soul. Oh, Bogey, *do* hold me tight and *never* let me go again.

Wig

My letters lately have been so hurried and written with such a feverish pen. I want to tell you how I love you—now—very gently kissing you, my soul. Oh, I long for you so: it is rather hard to bear these extra days. But, Bogey, I love you so immensely tonight. . . .

Tel.: 'Selecotel'

Select Hotel,
1 Place de la Sorbonne,
Paris.
Saturday,
(March 23, 1918)

My precious Bogey,

I am afraid I shall have to wait until Monday before I hear from you. I've never been so long without news. It is simply horrible, but it can't be helped and I must just go on, trusting that they will finally let me through. . . . I have written to Bedford Square, applied to the Police for permission to return and now there is nothing to do but wait.

This place is in a queer frame of mind. I came out of the restaurant last night into *plein noir*. All the cafés shut—all the houses. Couldn't understand it. Looked up and saw a lovely aeroplane with blue lights— '*couleur d'espoir*', said an old man, pointing to it—and at the door of the hotel was met by the manager and made to descend to the *caves*. There had been an *alerte*. About 50 people came, and there we stayed—more than long enough. It was a cold place and I was tired. At eight this morning as I lay in bed—bang! whizz!—off they went again. I washed and dressed and just had time to get downstairs before the cannons started. Well, *that* alerte *n'est pas encore finie*. It's now 3-45! Most of the shops are shut—all the post offices. The shops that are not quite have a hole in the shutters, and you put your arms over your head and *dive* through. The *curse* is the post office, as I have to register my letter to Bedford Square, and now I've lost a whole day. I have gone out, between the showers, to the police and fixed all *that* up, thank goodness, and now, as soon as I can post this other—there will be *rien à faire qu'attendre. C'est joliment assez!*

I look out at the lovely hot day and think 'I might have been at Havre by now!'

Does this letter tinkle far away? I feel it does. It ought not to, but oh Bogey it is so very long since I have heard from you and tu sais comme je suis un enfant gâté—*and* I hardly know where I am myself until I know that you know. I am not *found* until you have found me too and taken my hand and walked away with me. . . . If I had a letter. Yes, a letter—that's what I *need* so. I am getting so very, very impatient. Also, I want to see a medicine man and ask if there is any divine reason why I have never seen Aunt Marthe *since that Sunday afternoon*. I shan't hope a bit till I have asked him. But I had to tell you: it's on my mind, rather. This *waste* of life, here. Why should the Lord treat us so? It's not fair. Oh, Bogey, a letter—a letter—to revive a parched, fainting, little

Wig

Mother's Birthday. Paris,

Sunday,

Bogey, my precious, (March 24, 1918)

What *is* the good of writing anything—except that I love you and I can't get through yet, and I would be home by now if all had gone well and here I am in this cruel town, waiting for the bonté of the Military! There's nothing else to say. I want a letter or a telegram—*something* to break this silence. News of any kind from you. It is incredibly long since I have heard, today. Has Rib forgotten me? Given me up? Oh, Bogey, I do my best, but you know it is a most awful obstacle race. The only grain of comfort is that I am here and not *là-bas*, for I *am* nearer. Once they let me start, it won't take long. Please don't despair. Please keep on hoping for me: it's awful, Boge.

And then, this battle and this bombardment of Paris. I don't know what the English papers say about it. All I care is that it holds up all communication with England—no telegrams get through and letters are delayed. I thought, this morning, I'd tell you a bit about it—but you don't want to know. There it just *is*. This afternoon I went to the Luxembourg Gardens. The spring this year seems to me *hateful*—cruel—cruel like pigeons are cruel—all the leaves burst into claws. But p'raps it's just me. And then the people in black, with made-up eyes and red lips and black embroidered handkerchieves. And then all the young men—still in light overcoats—wet brushed hair—stocks—pincé at the waist—boots with light uppers—still going. I feel that corruption and destruction are in the air—and we may just survive. The world is *hideous*—and we are apart, and I haven't heard of you *since your letter of Wednesday week*—Ah, God!

As soon as I hear again, dearest love, I will write differently. But at present I *am* not. I am fast asleep until my little knight wakes me. What are you doing *now*? We are so near—really. Paris—London: it's nothing, yet between us there are swords and swords.

Bogey, you must go on loving a great deal your wandering

Wig

Paris: Café de la Source.
Monday,
Darling,   (March 25, 1918)

There is still no word from you at Cook's. I went first thing this morning and last thing this evening. Nothing. The rest of the day is just—nothing, too, in consequence. I am simply a sort of 'vide' until I get a letter, and I feel at moments—just despair, as though I shall be kept here and ages and ages will pass before I ever leave Paris. . . .

At one o'clock this morning I got up and wrapped up in shawlets and went down to the *cave*, and sitting on a heap of coal on an old upturned box—listening to the bloody Poles and Russians—it all seemed a sort of endless dream—oh so tiring, so utterly fatiguing. I've caught a cold, too, and that makes the life in the *caves* so beastly. They are like tombs. I have nothing to say—nothing—nothing. L.M. is simply awful again—again she is one of the G—— family—poor creature—and doing her best to kill me—but it can't be helped. Perhaps THEY *will* let me through. As long as I hear from you, I can bear it—

227

but this silence! And 'writing' is rather difficult because of the bombardments. You see one *can't* stay out of the *caves* when they are near, and they were yesterday, to put it mildly, *extremely near*. I am sending L.M. to the Consul tomorrow to ask again for me and plead my chill and this life in the tombs for a further excuse. You see all the posts and police affairs are held up. They told me at Cook's today perhaps you hadn't yet got my telegram. When they said that—well, I felt in despair.

Far, far away, I expect those two little children are standing at the door of the Heron trying on tiptoe to reach the knocker.

But oh, my love, my life—it is so long since I have heard from you. I am weary. All I *can* do is to go on. I have not missed a day. You *at least* must have news, and perhaps tomorrow I shall have a letter too, and the world will change. As it is I am nearly *starving* and all is dark because I haven't heard.

Jag, Jag, Jag—

I am your little

Wig

Bogey,

Tuesday,
(March 26, 1918)

I have just been to Cook's and there is nothing again. Now I have come back by tram and I am sitting in the Café Mahieu—an *old spot* of mine. It's not really a cold day, it's cloudy and strange, but I am bitterly cold, trembling with cold. This long silence really has begun to frighten me at last. The only consolation that I have is that, please God, *you* hear from me. It's not a silence on both sides. God! how dreadful it is. Will it ever be broken again? I had moments yesterday when I almost gave up, and I saw myself living here for ages—till the end of the war—and never getting a letter—not a single letter or word—again. I had moments when I felt that you and Rib were tired with the waiting and had not only turned from the window but given me up. I walk—walk —walk and go into cafés and try and get coffee hot enough and go back to the hotel and stare at my room—in a sort of stupor of fatigue and anxiety. And each time I go out I seem to buy another newspaper. It is like 1914 over again.

L.M. has gone to the Consul today to tell him what a bad thing it is for me to stay here and live in these *caves*. It was my idea that she should go and tell him of my chill. I don't suppose it will help, but at any rate it means we keep in touch with the office and are not forgotten.

As I write I can hear the patrol planes booming away, and out on the boulevard all the shops are being protected with strips of paper over the windows—in all sorts of patterns.

But this is *not* Paris: this is Hell, and L.M. who walks about with me —stopping in front of all the shops and murmuring 'I should like one day to see your little hands covered with *fine rings*'—is a sort of fiend-guardian.

Well, well—now I must pin my faith (it only needs the tiniest pin) on to tomorrow and hope for a letter or a wire or a *sign,* then. If it *don't* come, I suppose I shall go on till the next day—and so on—for ever.

I must say *darling* before I finish this letter: *darling, darling*—you haven't forgotten, have you? to keep the door open just a crack and just a speck of light burning for your child who has such an awfully long walk home.

      Wig

Dearest,
                               Tuesday Night,
                              (March 26, 1918)

I have just sat down to a tea, as that seems the best value and the hottest. It is most infernally cold—impossible to keep even moderately warm and the charbon question leaves (as Charles Lamb would say) the hotels cold! As I am nearer tomorrow and ∴ nearer the possibility of a letter or a telegram, I feel a little bit more cheerful. But the *waste* of this!—this appalling cold, the rushing from bed into the tombs—but why do I put those silly things first? They don't really count. But I feel the things that *do* count you accept and know as I do—the *silence* into which I am fallen as though I had fallen into a lake—something without source or outlet—the *waste* of life, of our love and energy—the cruel 'trick' that life has played on us again—just when we timidly hoped— and timidly stretched out our longing hands to each other. Well, I suppose it has some sort of meaning (I don't suppose any such thing). I wish to God I could stop my suffering with those endless comfits that L.M. can suck. But I can't. It's the devil. . . .

I have been to Cook's again this evening. I thought there'd be a telegram, and the idiot took out a wire, handed it across and then said 'That's not the name, is it?' No, it was not the name. After this, I felt very inclined to sit down on the pavement and put a shawl over my head and *stay there*.

L.M. returned from the Consul, but he says there is nothing to be done until we obtain the permission from Bedford Square—and as these letters were practically thrown into the cannon's mouth, God knows if they will ever get there.

I am *sure* that Rib understands and waits. You do, too, don't you? If you knew how I hate life at this moment—all these Parisian dogs and their b——s. What a set! How vile they are! Oh, who will come and take me away? Nobody—not even a telegram. I am so tired of this anxiety—this lack of sleep—that I am beginning to get a sort of *dulled feeling*—and I don't think I shall mind anything soon. What the hell is the good of putting up a fight? Why should we, who are good and loving and wise, be treated so?

My soul is full of hate—but if you were to come, all the clouds would roll up and the sun would come out and shine on the far far away Heron windows.

Goodbye, my darling

Your

Wig

BYRRH

Dearest Jag,

Wednesday,
(March 27, 1918)

This is a funny little café where I am come to write you my forlorn, forlorn letter. I have been to Cook's—*Rien de rien encore*—so out comes my little flag, so small now that it can hardly be seen, and I must pin it on tomorrow. This is just a hail, my darling, faraway, silent one, just to prove that I *do,* faithfully, faithfully, come up to the top of the hill every single morning and look into the direction of the empty sea and wave as long as I can—just in the hope that *one* of these days I'll see a speck there and it will turn out to be a boat.

It's very cold and foggy. There's such a pretty girl in this café—a girl whom you would admire—and the man and woman who keep it, too, are *your sort*. There are also some red carnations, a white dog, and a yellow basket covered in a red and white fringed cloth. It would be very beautiful if I were in the least alive. But I am not.

Goodbye, darling Boy. I'll write tomorrow. Tomorrow the telegram at least ought to be there. But who knows? . . .

I am always for ever your own Wig who loves you *utterly*.

Darling Heart,

Three letters came from you today, two Saturday and one Sunday; one of the letters had £3 in it. I have received no wire at all. This is the first news. Upon getting it I wired you rather at length: because my letters have been depressed and I wanted to get near you if I could a bit quickly. But they say at the *poste* there are at least 48 hours delay for telegrams in England—so God knows when this will arrive. *I do not want any money at all.* Please keep this secret. Mother sent me some money to make myself a lovely girl the day I was married, but she said I was not even to tell Chaddie, as it was her 'secret funds'. This money I am spending and it will see me and the Mountain through—that is, provided we are allowed to leave France. One can't say anything for certain with this battle raging and the whole infernal upset—here and everywhere. I have lost confidence, for some ghastly reason. I go on, do all there is to do, make all possible efforts, but my heart don't pay any heed. *It's gone quite dead.* I feel I suffered and hoped and tried to pull through unendurably before the moment. Now the snail simply can't put out its horns again for the moment. It will, of course, mais. . . .

And topping it all this long *inevitable* wait for letters . . . and this great half-idiot woman at my heels always, with 'Katie, what shall we do now?'. . . . God, what Hell one does live through!

The Military Permit people, though they will not let me through without having heard from Bedford Square, are not the Great Brick. It's the police.

Any person who stays longer than 48 hours in Paris must obtain a permit to leave France. This *sauf conduit* takes from 8 to 10 days to obtain, and is, even then, uncertain, as to one day or another. Have you had any dealings with the French police? They are like the Russian police rather in Dostoevsky's books. I don't want to discuss them here. I went again to the office yesterday, but they laughed in my face at the idea of my getting a permit sooner. In fact, my anxiety seemed to amuse and delight them so much—and the fact that I was *une Anglaise* in a predicament—that I did my case no good, I fear.

I hope Sydney's man helps: it sounded a good idea.[1] I was infinitely relieved to have letters from you after so very, very long, dearest, and the lovely little poem. But I can't help it—to be sincere, *je suis très*

[1] Sydney Waterlow was in the Foreign Office, and I had begged him to use what influence he could.

fatiguée aujourd'hui. Nothing serious—only I am *tired out* and everything seems so far away. As though you were in London and I were passing Cape Horn.

You won't send me any money will you? I have 300 francs. That is enough to pay both our bills, HER food etc, all the extra booking expenses. I've worked it all out.

Here is an Easter card for Rib. *He* mustn't be a sad one: he's my brave little boy who looks through his telescope every morning and comes down and blows in it and shakes it out as though it were a trumpet and says 'I think I can see something'. . . .

    Goodbye, darling
        Wig

If you were not there, I'd really die, you know. I only live, I think, *with you.* Without you, I'd give up.

Friday,

(March 29, 1918)

In case this letter is opened or detained I append my name and address:—

    Bowden, Select Hotel, 1 Place de la Sorbonne, Paris.

Recd: A wire at this address *and* a letter written on Monday night.

My own darling,

Not very good news today—in fact as damnable as can be. I don't know why I am dropping into L.M.'s 'preparations for a shock'. They don't suit you and me. Cook's told me this morning that all civilian traffic is cancelled for 8 days at least and that no letters will either go to or come from England. This latter fact I shall ignore. I don't believe it. The former gave me a *new blow.* I had just pinned that unfortunate, quivering frightened little faith of mine on to Tuesday and Bogey's holiday week—and all this agony over. Now I must undo it again. You will have your holiday without me. (Ah, try and make it one, my own. Try and let us forget just a tiny bit our present misery and read and rest.) There is no explanation given of this new order and my faith in it is *un peu vague!* 'Eight days for the moment, Madame!'

I went to the Military Permit Office this afternoon to ask for further news, but found it was *closed.* Nobody there except one rather fishy-eyed Frenchman and a notice stating that the service was suspended.

This gave me a most unpleasant feeling, and as I came out, *Bang*!—
'what a burst!' as Matthew Arnold so dreadfully says of the nightingale
—the big gun had started again!

All this upon one of those heavenly blue and white and tender green
afternoons—those afternoons that almost make you weep. I stood at a
corner, thinking this out and trying to 'get over it' enough to walk
home—and in a blue pool of sky a tiny cloud came to the edge to
drink—a 'little lamb, who made thee?' cloud. And at the same moment
a lobster in a bowler hat rushed at me and shouted 'Ne vous attendez
pas, Madame! Rentrez! C'est le canon qui a commencé encore'—and
then he waved his arms and cried 'L'obus!' What does it all mean?

What does everything mean?

Well, one must just go on. Your letters, my precious, are *healing* me.
Each letter seems to be another sort of divine protection against this
bitter life. When I was without them I suffered so that I grew almost
numb. Now all the tenderness comes back and I can breathe and look
up and whisper 'Oh, Bogey, my darling' and weep. . . .

I cannot go on if you are not there. It all becomes then the nightmare
that it is. You must know—you do—what this further disappointment
is to me. We have to bear it and go on, I suppose. But oh, do not let us
ever again leave each other. It has been too bad a time and I am still
very terrified.

I can't stay in the *caves* while the bombardment goes on, but in case
of air attacks of course I shall. My cold is much better. I wired you this
afternoon about my April allowance from Kay. You see—it is due, and
I thought he, being a banker could wire it across or get it over somehow. I don't want any other moneys. You know, also, what it is like
for me to feel that I seem to eat up your money as fast as you make it—
your *divine, sacred* Heron money. But that will not always be so. I will
explain when I get home—if, dear love, I get home.

Do remember every single moment how I love you. How I long for
you—how hard it is for me to be here and in danger of being, I feel,
swept by a great broom further and further away from *all* my world,
all my life, *all* my heaven—which is you.

If my letters ever seem cold or dull it is because I am tired or
frightened—those are the only reasons.

I simply live for you and in you and in our future. I still believe we
shall be together again and all this will be over—but whatever does
happen, my own darling, you're my whole life—amen. Keep on writing

until I let you know. Let's risk the ugly world getting the letters rather than you and I being without.

And now, at this minute, stop and say 'Wig', and hear me say 'Jag'—but I cannot, for, fool that I am, *je pleure*.[1] I am not always so faint-hearted. It's only, I think, when I write to you that I feel it is unbearable and that we have been treated too badly. (Oh, Bogey, these are tears—and kisses, too. Wipe them away and don't let anyone know that I have been crying, not even the little Rib.)

Goodbye for now, my soul, my life, my darling.

God bless us both!

Wig

Saturday,
(March 30, 1918)

My darling Heart,

I *should* have been home nearly a week by now—and I'm still far away. But yes, this is better than the far distant South, for as soon as a train or a boat can go, I will be on it. I have been to the M.P.O. this morning. They have not received our permission from Bedford Square. The whole office was in a vague state of unquiet, and the official to whom I spoke seemed to think that, while this battle raged, civilians would be held up i.e. that eight days was all too hopeful an idea.

L.M. is going off to the Consul this afternoon to try and get work.

I suppose the blockade has started, for no post has come today here or at Cook's. It is raining fast, and the bombardment is—frankly—*intensely* severe. The firing takes place every 18 minutes as far as I can make out. I won't try and tell you where the bombs fall. It is a very loud ominous sound, this super-*Kanon*. I am not frightened by it even though I have been extremely near the place where the explosions have taken place, but I *do* feel there is a pretty big risk of being killed by it. You see, there is no warning as to where the next shell will fall, neither is it frequent enough to make one stay in the icy cellars. Also, one *must* go about to Consuls etc. and try and get away. If it were not for you I should not care whether I were killed or not. But as you *are* there, I care passionately and will take all the precautions you would have me take, and I you in the same straits. Today, people are frightened—quite otherwise to what they have been before. And the ghastly massacre in the church has added very much to their feeling.

[1]At this point the letter is blotted with tears.

I tell you all this. I can't keep anything back from you. But I am *not at all* frightened. And so I want to add—Don't worry about me, my own. But that is absurd. For I worry about you, too. No, rather—think about me and tell me in your next letter that I shall at least be home for the 17th and I shall believe that. Ah, I can't say what store I set on that day. It seems to mean such an infinite thing to us—a sort of blessing from on high will be visited on us when we walk out of the place into the street, hand in hand, and telling everybody by our smile that we have just come fresh from heaven. Rib must be there too. I shall carry him, and he shall have one grain of rice in one hand shut up tight and one piece of pink confetti in the other.

Now you are smiling—are you, my own love? I want to put my arms round your neck and pillow your head on my bosom. I just want to hold you and kiss you and *never* let you go.

After all, I have fallen into this old war. I felt that one of us would. But, Bogey—Oh, God! I thank thee that it is I and not my beloved who am here. That, from the bottom of my soul. Goodbye, my own, for now.

I adore you and I am for eternity

Your own
Wig

Easter Sunday,
(March 31, 1918)

Darling Heart,

I received today your letters of Wednesday and Thursday. I am sure that no letter has gone astray. The only thing I have not had was a wire you sent to Cook's. In your 2 letters you are feeling like I was just at about that time. Now, thank God, at least I am getting letters and I pray that mine are arriving, too. . . .

Yesterday, the lady called 'Long-sighted Lizzie' became so violent that I got a bit jumpy and decided at any rate it was no use simply sitting here and waiting for the 18 minutes to be up before another crash came. So L.M. and I went off to an underground *cantine* at the Gare du Nord for soldiers and refugees and got taken on—to start today at 1-30. It seemed to me the best thing one could do—to be underground and so busy that you'd no time to think. . . . I went today —but, *of course*, I shall never go again. It was too hard work. When I came off duty at 7, I couldn't speak for fatigue and even now (though

235

I could tell you a lot about it—oh, no, it's not interesting) I am pretty dished. No, I must stay here and keep down low when the gun-fire is violent. I am keeping notes of the kind of thing people say about it— some *terribly* good things. L.M. will continue to go to the *cantine* because it feeds her, too. We'll have to take the risk. It's not a great one. Do you remember where we saw those little children *skating* one year? All that is destroyed utterly. . . .

I don't know why. I feel—for all my fatigue—*hopeful* tonight, as though at the end of eight days they may—let me through. God knows why I feel this, for as a rule a sort of deadly fatality seems to be in my heart, and it's all just—oh, a chance—a chance. But, Bogey, I feel I *must* come. If they go on keeping us apart, what will become of us? I suppose Brett has no influence? I thought she might have helped—but again I suppose not.

Queer thing: I am for the moment *dead* off my family—the result, I think, of a gay 'Cheerio' card from Chaddie, which came so damned inappropriately last night. On the other hand, Jack darling, I *love* your mother. Don't you think, after the 17th, she might adopt me as her daughter and that I might find some name for her that wasn't Mrs. Murry?

If I get back I want to make her very happy and Richard of course. I long for us to keep him very near.

Oh God—as I write—this all seems like a tremendous—impossible nightmare. I look round this room and think of all that divides us—see the copy of *Paris-Midi*, read again L-G.'s ominous message, and my heart goes dead with fright. If you can convey to me what is happening in England, I beg you to.

My Bogey darling—oh, my love—please try for my sake to eat, to sleep—not to get too lonely. I am, thank God, nearer than I was in the South. If God is kind, in less than eight days I shall see you. At any rate I'll try and believe that, and so live in faith. But in reality—I live on nothing but your love. That's all. I am all yours for ever and ever.

Wig

My darling Heart,

Easter Monday,
(April 1, 1918)

I wonder if your holiday has begun today, and if the weather is fine. Here is April—our longed-for April—the month in which we mean to get married. I felt this year that April was simply made for us, and that it would be such a glory—such a Spring as never had been known before. And now—all I think is—when will the boats start again? When shall I be able to get through? It is idle to tell you again (yet I must tell you again) how simply boundless my longing for you is. I feel I *must* see you soon with my own eyes and hold you and be held. What perils we have gone through and are going through! And to think that those fruit trees are in flower in the Heron orchard and all the flowers are open to the sun and our children walk about with handfuls of tired little violets. . . .

There is no post today. I suppose that means there was no Good Friday post in England. Cook's is shut and the Consul's, so nothing can be done. I'll visit both tomorrow. I am, thank God, alone, as L.M. has gone to the *cantine,* and won't be back till late tonight. It has just struck 3, so beautifully and calmly, with a kind of sunny langour, and my silly childish heart said: 'Darling, shall we go for a small walk?' And away we went, going slowly, me on your arm, and talking very quietly, just for ourselves, you know. And occasionally you gave my hand a squeeze and said 'Wig!'. But no, these dreams are too sweet: I *can't* dream them while I am so far away. Shall I be home next Sunday? What do *you* think? Oh, Bogey, I *must* be on my way home at least. The boats must start again and they can't keep people away from their own country. If only we had influence! I asked for Sydney's man at the M.P.O. but was met with the coolest stare: 'Don't know him. Major Knight is the head of this office.' So *that* was *not much good!*

At that moment a knock came at my door and the maid opened it, pushing in front of her a tiny little boy in a white pinafore and white socks with red shoes. *Very* small, just two years old. He was eating his goûter—a bit of bread—and he staggered in, and when he saw me, turned his back. She said might she leave him a moment, and when she had gone I remembered that I had a little piece of chocolate in my despatch case. When I mentioned it he was so moved that he sort of— waded 100 miles over to me and about 200 more to the cupboard, and there he stood, beating time with his toes as fast as possible while I got the chocolate out. He was so very nice I held him up to the glass, and he gave the other little baby first a crumb of bread and then a taste of the other, and when the maid came for him, being anxious to kiss his hand, he kissed the bread instead and waved it at me. How fine and lovely little children can be! While he sat in my lap I felt a moment of almost *peace,* as though the Sodom and Gomorrah world had stopped just for an instant. But now he's gone again. . . .

Every taxi that stops at this hotel, stops at my heart, too. I know how utterly absurd that is. But I feel—by some miracle. . . . and I wonder: Would they 'phone me from downstairs, or should I just hear steps along the passage?

So far there has only been one shot today, but few people are out in the streets and it is not gay.

Goodbye, my own darling. God keep us both.

Your own
Wig

Tuesday,

My darling Heart,   (April 2, 1918)

No letter again today, but I hardly expected one. I mean by that that I knew that the English post would be disorganised for Easter. To-morrow, perhaps, I shall have 2 at least. That's what I look for today.

Since yesterday the 'lutte', as they say, has continued. Gunfire last evening—and at 3-15 this morning one woke to hear the air *screaming.* That is the effect of these sirens; they have a most diabolical sound. I dressed and went down to the *cave.* Everybody else was there—the place was packed with hideous humanity: *so* hideous indeed that one felt a bomb on them wouldn't perhaps be so cruel, after all. I don't think I can go to the *cave* again. The cold and agony of those stone dusty steps and these filthy people *smoking* in that air. I crept back to bed and woke to a perfect deafening roar of gunfire. It was followed by the sound of people running in the streets. I got up again and went to look. Very ugly, very horrible. The whole top of a house as it were bitten out—all the windows broken, and the road of course covered with ruin. There were trees on both sides of the street and these had just come into their new green. A great many branches were broken, but on the others strange bits of clothes and paper hung. A nightdress, a chemise, a tie—they looked extraordinarily pitiful, dangling in the sunny light.

One thing which confirms me again in my dreadful feeling that I live wherever I am in another Sodom and Gomorrah . . . this. Two workmen arrived to clear away the débris. One found, under the dust, a woman's silk petticoat. He put it on and danced a step or two for the laughing crowd. . . . That filled me with such horror that I'll never never get out of my mind the fling of his feet and his grin and the broken trees and the broken house.

I have just posted you a book because of the pages on Dostoevsky. The woman, Sonia Kovalevsky, is awfully nice; her friend, Anna, is a b——h, I think. But perhaps that is because I can't stand women, Bogey, who 'pretend' to friendship.

I am writing to you in the Café Mahieu. It is a divine, warm day. I keep thinking and thinking only of you, my darling, and wishing and wishing—you know what. I went to Cook's this morning. The man seemed to think the boats would start again at the end of this week. But no, I don't dare to hope until I have been to the M.P.O. tomorrow.

On my way home I fell in with an accident. A man on the pavement said he had broken his ankle. A large crowd collected, but nobody believed him. Two policemen nearly *swore* him away, but as he groaned and sweated a great deal they decided to take off his boot and sock and see. After *pulling off* the boot—I said: 'Cut the sock! Don't drag it!' and really it is just a fluke I wasn't arrested. You should have heard the 'Taisez-vous!' that was flung at me, *and* the rest. So they pulled it off, and the ankle was all broken. His whole foot was at right angles—pale green in colour, with black nails. 'When did you do it?' they asked him, and the fool said 'Pas aujourd'hui'. At that the whole crowd began to laugh—looked at the foot and laughed. He had evidently been going about for days with this foot, and I should think it will have to be amputated. But, God, what a joke it was for these Parisians!

Bogey, the dreadful beauty of this spring terrifies me—and Bogey, darling heart, I keep wondering if your holiday is begun. Where are you? Have you seen any flowers or bees?

What can I say? Nothing, except that I am far from my own and all else doesn't matter. Perhaps tomorrow—that is my only cry. Tomorrow—tomorrow!

Oh, please don't give me up, and don't shut your heart to me. Keep it very warm and ready, won't you? *My heart* is such a frail one now. It beats so fast if I look at the letter-rack, and hardly beats at all when I look away.

God help us!

      Your own
          Wig, who loves you *terribly*.

My darling Bogey,

I had a note from you written on Sunday. That is the first sign I have had from you since a letter written on Tuesday—so the other letters of the other days (for you must, knowing my trouble and anxiety have written) have all been lost. However, I am thankful for this note after the long and painful silence again. If you knew the *fever* I live in—the constant strain and agony of mind—and trying to arrange my affairs *and* L.M's affairs here. . . .

I went to the M.P.O. today. They have heard from Bedford Square saying we can go back. But of course it rests now with the question of a boat. At present there are none. So in the meantime and while most of my life is spent in trying to get home—oh, please write fully to me about anything—only WRITE or my heart will really break!

I go to Cook's, to the M.P.O., to the Consul—then to a café. I make up sums. I walk about. I read the awful papers and it seems such a risk as to whether I ever get back that I feel half frozen with fright—and I LOOK for letters—nearly always in vain. Risk losing them, Bogey, but for God's sake don't leave me without them. If you knew with what fever I tore this open and found the 2 middle pages empty!

My life, I assure you, is very painful here, and I am so helpless. I can do nothing but wait for the broom to sweep me home or sweep me away.

That's all.

Goodnight, my dearest. My little boat feels awfully knocked about tonight, and I've had to creep into the cabin and hide my head—for I am tired and I weep. Please, please don't leave me in silence.

Wig

Friday,
Darling Bogey, (April 5, 1918)

As usual—I might say—there is no letter from you either here or at Cook's. I have been to Cook's and the M.P.O. this morning, but as yet they have no news at all about a boat sailing. So I must go on and somehow bear + all my other appalling anxieties, this silence. You know I hardly sleep at all, I am so *restless*. Work is absurdly out of the question. I simply seem to spend my days asking if there is a letter or a boat, and there is neither. I have got the police permit and the Consul's

Katherine Mansfield   1916

permit. As soon as a boat *does* sail, I am ready, But when will that be? This is, you can understand, can't you? almost a maddening question if one is *alone* in a *foreign* country, with absolutely *nobody* to talk to—*no* influence—a woman dependent on you who can't speak the tongue.

If the whole affair has worn you out and you feel you have nothing more to say then you MUST wire me on receipt of this letter: *Can't write just now.* You must not leave me without letters unless your heart has quite absolutely changed to me—for I cannot bear it. But if I know *not* to expect, then I'll arrange otherwise. But without a sign from you, and when I know that English mails *do* arrive, *are* delivered, my days are intolerable.

Can't you imagine them darling?

You at least are in England. And you have a person or two to speak to and you are *chez vous*—but I feel I may be swept away any minute, and I need you as never before. And yet no letters come.

Jack, do give a sign, or you will kill

Your Wig

TO RIBNI

Friday Night,

My Tiny,   (April 5, 1918)

When I came in tonight a Miracle waited for me in the pigeon-hole where key 30 hangs. Your little father had managed to send me another paper boat—and only launched on Tuesday night, and for a sail oh! such a lovely poem by you both. . . . Such a lovely poem that I don't know how to live another moment without you both. There is the poem, you see, rocking in my bosom, but it's not an awfully calm sea, my little man.

Oh, my Ribni, our small door-keeper! watch him when he goes out in the morning, and wait for him when he comes home at night. Be ready to wave to him. Walk all over him and kiss him for me. Tell him every way you know that I am coming as fast as the Uglies will let me come. When he sleeps walk up and down by his pillow and keep guard and see that the Lions and Tigers do not tear up our letters but that the Doves carry them swiftly guarded by Eagles. I languish away from you both. I have no little laughs, no one calls me a worm, no one is my size. You are both my size.

But Rib, old fellow, I trust you. I can trust you utterly, can't I? to

241

look after him? You know don't you? that he's all I want. He's mine, and I am his, and I shall never be happy again until all of us are sitting together, looking at each other, holding each other tight. Don't give me up. Please keep on sweeping the doorstep with a feather and putting out the tiny lantern at night. For I am tired, my little tiny doll, and I want to be home with him and with you. It's dreadful being here. But all you've got to do is to keep him for me, *see?* Oh, Ribni, curl up in his heart and kiss him for every beat. My heart's nearly broken with longing.

Saturday,

(April 6, 1918)

A boat is supposed to go next Wednesday.

My darling precious Bogey,

Thank God! a registered letter came from you today. It was written on Good Friday and Saturday, so it was a very old man, but still, oh! how I clasped it. I jumped out of bed and gave the postman 6 sous. I felt inclined to kiss his hand. And then I jumped into bed again, and though the letter was very short and a sad one, it was *news, news* of you That's all, and that is everything.

They say today that a boat sails for England next Wednesday. But it is not quite definite. The Consul advised me not to wire. I have been everywhere twice—morning and afternoon, I mean—to Cook's, the M.P.O., the Consul at Rue Montelivet and the G.W.R. office where you left the 20 francs a hundred years ago. I *do* hope, and yet I am too afraid to. No, the game has now been played so often that it don't take me in any more. I'll wait. I'll even wait to hope. For every edition of the papers that comes out may make one's return absolutely impossible—and Wednesday, with this second attack just beginning, might simply not exist. It might be blown away by the *obus* or swept over by the German troops. I have carried your last letter in my bag all day—as a sort of mascot. When I waited for the Consul this afternoon, two such exceedingly nice people came out of the office, arm in arm and nearly bursting with happiness (especially him) and then the doorkeeper stuck up on the wall a card to say that the Consul had just married them. His second name was Longweight, and her name was Lily, and she was a music-hall artist. . . .

This almost broke through my blind numbed anxiety. Otherwise I

242

am half dead. Although I write like this about Wednesday of course in my heart all my faith is pinned to it already, and already I see my Rib dimpling. But oh! my treasure, if ever I do get back into your arms again—I don't think I'll even talk or laugh or cry—I'll just *breathe*. That's all.

I want desperately to know how you are—if you eat, if you sleep.

But I have such a perpetual crying need to know everything about you that it's no good. No questions will do.

Kay's money came today. I wired its arrival to him. That makes me all right whatever happens.

But what does it all matter? What does anything matter? There is only you and my jealous, furious, passionate, longing love for you. There is nothing else on earth. Give him to me and me to him and let us be. Never disturb us again. Shut the door on us, and let us sit in our own lamp-circle of light and rest.

For in you alone I live.

Wig

Precious, dearest, darling Heart,

Saturday Night,
(April 6, 1918)

I am so hopeful tonight. Two letters came from you today—one written on Tuesday evening and one on Wednesday afternoon—and they bring you so . . . tremblingly near. I had a 'phone message from Sydney's man at the Embassy today, too, went to see him and he said I would *definitely* get across on Wednesday. He gave me a card to the M.P.O. telling them that it was urgent. I shall go. (He was a great ponce.) And the M.P.O. still say that a boat will go on Wednesday, though Cook's say it is most uncertain. I think it is absurd *not* to regard it as uncertain, for it is a race between Wednesday and this second battle, and those vile Germans are still marching on.

But everybody and every tree and every person and every breath seems now to *incline* towards Wednesday. If that again is just a big black hole and again there comes the uncertainty and the waiting, I don't know what I *shall do*. I am glad Kay was decent. Kiss your darling little Mummy for me. I am so glad that I am going to be her real daughter-in-law, and oh! how I want to see the little brother again—the dear lad. But all these things come after.

First of all, there is just YOU. L.M. has just lifted 150 off me; she can't help it and it's all right, of course. I've plenty and she'll pay me back.

243

But I wish she was not dead drunk as the result of one Dubonnet. She is, and can only (as she says) 'giggle'.... If you knew....

The Bombardment has gone on again today, and it's 8-30. I've had news. I'd better get back as soon as possible. But there is still a good quarter of an hour. I haven't had any *bread* since this new rule came in. I do want a crust. As to butter, it doesn't exist.

Do you know, if ever I do get back, it will be just a week before our wedding, and your mother must ask us to tea. We'll say it's the anniversary, for she must *never* know, and we'll take her flowers—lovely ones—and be very gay children. Shall we? Shall we? Is it all before us? Not all swept away?

I spend my nights now playing Demon patience. I sit up in bed and play and play. This morning at 3 o'clock a mouse jumped into my waste-paper basket and began to squeak.

But I can hardly tell you these things. Wednesday begins to more than loom. Again I think: I must take him back a pepper-mill, and another of those red and green cups and saucers. God! if ever I do get back—then I feel our trial will be over for ever.

But the German army and the big gun and the raids and all this vast horror still rolls between.

Bogey! hope *for* me. I've been so tortured that I must have someone to *help* me *hope*. Your letters are my salvation—but that you know.

Your own
Wig

Sunday,

Darling Heart,   (April 7, 1918) 8-30 p.m.

This has been a perishing cold *dead* day, and I have not been very great shucks. I'm in bed now. I've been playing Demon nearly all day. Tomorrow I have to be at the M.P.O. at 10—so I wanted to rest a bit today. I'm awfully exhausted by all this. All day—all day—I have thought of you, and so often of your darling little Mother. You can't think how I love her just now. I feel as though she *must* love me, too, and take me for one of her children. Will she?

During the afternoon I looked down and saw your ring—such a Bogey-Wig ring—on my finger, and I *kissed* it. When I went out for lunch, dearest, I saw something. A *poilu's* funeral. A very grey day with big clouds in the sky—the plain hearse covered with the solemn flag—

the cheap flowers—and, walking behind, a tiny boy in a black fur coat, carrying his father's rifle. He twinkled along with a handful of soldiers, and it was very hard for him to keep up. It made me cry.

Tomorrow my week of *hope* begins—in four hours it begins. Oh, child! playmate! help me! Wave to me! You and Rib, and this time, please God, I will come.

When I read your letter—how you had walked down the Tottenham Court Road *without me,* I felt as though they had tortured me so, I'd never recover. But I know at sight of you I would recover in an instant. Only I must have that sight.

Goodnight, my precious own, and God help us!

Your own

Wig

Bar Monaco, Tuesday,

Dearest Love,   (April 9, 1918)

I am simply *desperate.* I had your two wires today—one at the hotel and one at Cook's, but you can never have got a wire I sent immediately after my Friday letter, saying *Let's hope on it's all the best.* No, you can't have got it. And there is a letter from you today referring to things I know nothing of, that you have already written about. This letter was written on Friday: it's the one about the letter-press. Oh, Bogey, will it never end?

I have spent the day *rushing* from the police to the police. Now, it all seems finished and I've only to pack and try and get back tomorrow. I keep on writing, you know why, and now of course it's in case the boat is submarined. I think I should keep on writing even under the sea.... Yes, of course I should. I have bought 2 *quarts* of butter, and am going to try to bring them, but that's all I can afford *cette fois.*

We leave at 7 tomorrow. You know that though. I am speechless with anxiety and hope. I will write to you in Havre tomorrow, darling, more leisurely.

Oh God! this Friday letter has something of you in it which carries me straight into your heart. It's a letter so like you. Oh, my darling heart, I do love you so—and I too am terribly timidly just beginning to think of a bud of hope—ever so tiny a one.

I have simply everything to tell you—everything—and I can't help today telephoning—endlessly: 'Put me through to Mr. Middleton Murry.... Is that you, Boge?' And then I can't say any more.

Can you think what I feel like, my treasure? My courage is just about mouse-high, and I am nobody but your tiny, timid, loving

MOUSE

Give the Worm a kiss and show him my new passport photograph.

Katherine arrived in London on April 11, 1918. She was haggard and frightened. The hardships she had suffered had given phthisis a secure hold upon her. She stayed with me in my two ground-floor rooms at 47 Redcliffe Road for the next five weeks. We were married on May 3, 1918, at the Kensington Register Office, Dorothy Brett and J. D. Fergusson being the witnesses.

We agreed to get a house in Hampstead, if we could, as soon as possible. But what were we to do until we found it? It was obviously undesirable that Katherine should remain where she was, though that was what she really wanted. Not only were the cramped quarters unsuitable; but I had to go to the War Office every day, and there was no one to look after her or prevent her from overtaxing her strength. My memory of these five weeks together is an unhappy one. Katherine wanted to ignore her illness and to keep house for me as though nothing had happened. I was desperately anxious to get her away into the country, into a place where she could be looked after until we had found a house to live in. She, on the other hand, believed that it was better for her to be with me.

However, she gave way. Anne Estelle Rice, who was staying at Looe in Cornwall, found a place for her there. Katherine left London for Looe on May 17, 1918.

Headland Hotel,
Looe, Cornwall, Friday,

My dear husband, (May 17, 1918)

I have been sitting in a big armchair by the *three* open windows of my room wondering how I shall group or arrange events so that I may present them to you more or less coherently. But I can't. They *won't* group or arrange themselves. I am like a photographer in front of ever such a funny crowd whom I've orders to photograph but who won't be still to be photographed—but get up, change their position, slink away at the back, pop up in front, take their hats off and on. Who *is* the Most Important One? Who *is* Front Middle Seated?

The morning with you was quite unreal—another dream nightmare. When I kissed you did we wake? No. When you kissed my hand I did feel a kind of thrill of anguish. (Will you understand that?) But it was all a part of this racing, vile dream. Let us try and shut our eyes to it and go on as though it had not been—at least for the present—at least until the—the plaster is off your finger and the place healed again. . . .

I had a very comfortable journey. The country in the bright swooning light was simply bowed down with beauty—heavy, weighed down with treasure. Shelley's moonlight may glittered everywhere; the wild flowers are in such a profusion that it's almost an agony to see them and know that they are there. I have never seen anything more solemn and splendid than England in May—and I have never seen a spring with less of the *jeune fille* in it. God! why are you caged up there? Why is our youth passing while the world renews itself in its glory.

I must confess, of course, that, standing in the middle of the goldy fields, hanging from every tree, floating in every little river and perched on top of every hill, there was a Thermos flask filled with boiling coffee. I have so often seen people in trains armed with these affairs, *appearing* to uncork them and pretending that real steam and real heat flows out, but—but I've never believed them until today. At Plymouth I got out and bought two wheat-meal bigglechiks from the scrupulously clean refreshment room (fresh hot meat and potato pasties still for sale!) and made an excellent tea. But indeed I had such constant recourse to the bottil that some soldiers in the carriage could not quite believe my exquisite signs of satisfaction were tout à fait sober. But 'twas nectar, darling. And, of course, we shall never be without one again. Only think for a moment. One need never want again for a cup of tea at one of those 'odd' moments which always come on journeys to us.

Anne and Drey were at Liskeard. Anne just as I had imagined, *bronze*-coloured with light periwinkle eyes carrying a huge white bag bulging with *her* Thermos flask and a vest of Drey's (I didn't find where *it* came from or how) and a box of paints and a handful of hedge flowers and 'the most beautiful lemon'. Drey was awfully kind: he did everything. We featherstitched off to Looe. It was very hot—all glowing and quiet with loud birds singing and the blue-bells smelled like honey. The approach to Looe is amazing, it's not English, certainly not French or German. I must wait to describe it. The hotel buggy met us driven by a white-haired very independent boy who drove the horse as though it were a terribly fierce ramping white dragon—just to impress us, you know. We drove through lanes like great flowery loops with the sea below and huge gulls sailing over—or preening themselves upon the roof tiles, until we came to this hotel which stands in its garden facing the open sea. It could not be a more enchanting position. The hotel is large, 'utterly first-class'—*dreadfully expensive*. It has a glassed-in winter garden for bad weather with long chairs—a verandah—the garden hung between the sun and the sea. Anne had taken for me a really vast room with three windows all south; the sun comes in first thing in the morning until 3 in the afternoon. It is clean as a pin, gay, with a deep armchair, a bed with two mattresses—just across the corridor is a 1st class bathroom with constant hot water and a lavatory so superb that it and the salle de bains might be part of a sanatorium. For everything (except the cream) for four meals a day served in my room, breakfast in bed, the extra meat and so on, it is 4½ guineas. There! I know it's dreadful. I can't possibly live here under £5 a week alors, and I've only just four. But I think I ought to stay here at least till I'm strong enough to look for another, because for a 'cure' it could not be better.

The old servant unpacked for me, gave me hot water, took away my water bottil just now on her own and filled it. In fact, Bogey, it *is* a sanatorium without being one—as it were. The manageress gets the butter—so I am sending mine back to you. You see, it's included here. And will you please send my *sugar card*? She'll get me that, too. I think it's easiest. She says she'll give me butter at each meal and ½ pint of milk at each meal—a ¼ of butter every two days!! Don't you think I ought to stay here, just at first and get a stronger girl? I know it's hugely dear, but I feel it is right—that I will get well quicker here than elsewhere. All is so clean and attended to. Anne had arranged everything of course and filled the room with flowers. She has just walked across to say Goodnight. She really *is* wonderful down here—like part of the spring, radiant with life. It's ten o'clock. I am going to bed. My room has all the sea spread before it. Now with the blinds down there floats in the old, old sound, which really makes me very sad. It makes me feel what a blind, dreadful, losing and finding affair life has been just lately, with how few golden moments, how little little rest. But I am not across the water, and you are coming down for your holiday—*next month*. It is agony to be away from you, but what must be must be. Forgive me if I have been—what was it? I find it *so* hard to be ill. But ah, if you knew how I loved you and am for ever

Your loving
Wife

For dinner there was:
Soup
Fish cutlets
Mutton chops
Greens
Pancakes with cherry jam
Cheese and biscuits
Coffee
Butter
½ pint milk.

10.30 Saturday morning. In bed
(May 18, 1918)

Having 'slept in it' I am convinced that this place is what the South of France should have been—so still and warm and bright. The early sun woke me pouring into the room and I looked out and there were the little fishing boats with red sails, and row boats in which the rower *stood*—in the familiar way. Rib was wide awake. He looks such a grub down here—poor darling—after his long dip in filthy London.

The old woman who looks after me is about 106, nimble and small, with the loveliest *skin*—pink rubbed over cream—and she has blue eyes and white hair and *one tooth*, a sort of family monument to all the 31 departed ones. Her soft Cornish cream voice is a delight, and when she told me 'There do be a *handsome* hot bath for eë,' I felt that I *had* given a little bit of myself to Cornwall, after all, and that little bit was a traveller returned. I had the hot bath and nipped back into bed for breakfast. (I should have brought Charles[1] rather than Dorothy.[2])

Breakfast was—porridge, a grilled mackerel—most excellent—four bits of toast, butter, home-made winter-crack jam, cream *ad lib* and coffee with ½ pint hot milk—all on a winking bright tray—

So there!

I shan't get up till 12 any day, and then I shall just sit in the sun and read. The Three Windows are wide open now—one is almost *on* the sea.

This is only a note, darling. Do you know what guelder roses are? Big sumptuous white clusters with a green light upon them. We must grow them.

[1] Charles Lamb's *Letters*.   [2] Dorothy Wordsworth's *Journal*.

Yes, as far as *I* am concerned and except for the expense, all is as well as it could possibly be. But there is a great dull ache in my heart at the thought of you—a prisoner in that vile city. I see you—so pale—always half dead with fatigue—exhausted. But you *will* rest more now the infernal worry of me is gone, won't you? If only I could feel you were a little bit *easier*. Why aren't *you* here? You want this just as much as I. You *will* tell me the truth about yourself and *not* spare me because I am 'ill '. That, Boge, I couldn't forgive. And do, darling heart, try and rest a little—read a little poetry—lie down on the Stickleback and think about the Heron. And give me any books to review. I can do them well here. Thank God, I am not across the water.

Goodbye for now, my precious.

Dear Love,

Sunday Morning,
(May 19, 1918)

Your wire came yesterday and made you feel near. Now I want a letter—of course—for I am *un enfant trop gâté*—yes always.

When I got up yesterday I sat in my long chair in a kind of pleasant daze—never moved—*slept* and really did not wake until tea when I opened Dorothy Wordsworth and read on steadily for a long time. The air is heavenly, but don't imagine I walk or lift anything or even move more than I need. I can't even if I would—for the least effort makes me cough, and coughing is such fiendish, devilish pain that I'd lie like a mummy to avoid it. However—the divine sea is here, the haze and brightness mingled. I stare at that and wonder about the gulls, and wonder why I must be ill. All the people who pass are so well, so ruddy. They walk or run if they have a mind, or row past in little boats. Perhaps the curse will lift one day.

This place is very good *just now*. You see I am going to stay in bed all day—not going to move—and all is done for me—so pleasantly—by the old 'un. She came in early and threw open my windows at the bottom, and said the air was better than medicine—which it is—and yesterday she patted my cushion and said I must try and gather up a little *harm*ful of strength. I am always *astonished, amazed* that people should be kind. It makes me want to weep. You know. It's dreadfully upsetting, Boge. What! Can it be they have a heart! They are not playing a trick on me, not 'having me on' and ready to burst their sides at my innocence?

Anne and Drey came in last evening with an armful of those yellow irises that grew in the Marsh near Hocking's Farm.[1] They had been picnicking in the woods all day among the blue-bells and were very burnt and happy. Anne must be doing *some* kind of good work, for I can feel her state of mind—a sort of *still* radiant joy which sits in her bosom.

There pipes a blackbird, and the waves chime. Would that you were here! Yet—perhaps—better not. I try you too much. This is God's final joke—that even I should weigh you down—fall on you—like a dreadfully incredibly heavy sparrow, my darling, and take still more of your precious life and energy.

Try and take care of yourself and see Johnny now and then. He—I know—loves you.

Yours for ever

(May 20, 1918)

Monday. A gorgeous day. I really might be *on* the sea.

Dear Love,

Certainly yesterday had a Big Black Cap on it, but here is dawning another blue day and I feel better—really better. Yesterday this *pain* was very dreadful and then I had the most trying fits of weeping. I was simply swept away by them. I think it was the fever made me so feeble and wretched. Just as I had written you another *farewell* letter A. came in, with a picture for me. And she, thereupon, took charge, and soon the whole hotel seemed to be off. My bed was made, boiling bottles appeared, hot milk, a shade out of an orange bag she put on the gas, and sent for the doctor—all in the most ideal cheerful manner.

The doctor came at 11 p.m. The whole place shut up of course. He is —or appeared to be—about 19, but I am sure 19 times as intelligent as Longhurst. A wild Irish boy with curly hair and eyes which still remember what the world looked like at 9. He spent about an hour walking over the worn old battlefield with his stethoscope and saying, like Gordon, '*Wait now*'. Finally decided my left lung is *pleuritic* again for the present and that is what gives it the pain. I must stay in bed, but I could not be in a better place. A man came down here in precisely my condition and in a month he had gained a *stone* and was a changed creature in every way.

[1] At Zennor in Cornwall.

251

Anne, poor darling, was waiting downstairs to hear the verdict. It was midnight before she left, and the manageress left me the Thermos flask full of boiling milk for the night. In fact, they are one and all amazingly kind. So here I am, in bed again, but breathing the sea and the sun and *Anne*. The baby doctor is coming again today. He made me feel like an old writing woman—a sort of old George Sand tossed up by the tide last night. Once I can get over this attack of pleurisy I know I shall get really well. I feel it, and I keep hearing about all the wonders in the woods and fields. . . .

This is an appallingly *dull* little note. But you know what one feels like. My skull and crossbones effusion of yesterday I have destroyed. But my head is a pillow-case until I have heard from you. As soon as I am well enough I am going out sailing with these fishermen that I see from the window. So different from France. Here one longs to be *on* the *sea*.

   Yours for ever
    Wig

I have still got the feeling that this place is absolutely marvellous even though I haven't seen it.

You know the last three days I was in London I had pleurisy. This doctor says I have got over the worst of the attack and have only to lie still today and tomorrow and I shall feel *much better* again. I believe that.

               Monday,
            (May 20, 1918)

Darling little husband,

Drey has brought me your Friday letter—and it is a sad one. Yes, you feel—oh, like I do—and what—of all other things—seems so hard is how we swore *not* to let each other go again . . . and then how soon . . . we were gone. Yesterday, thinking of all this in the afternoon, I wept so. I could not bear it: I thought I must come back and *die* there rather than always this living apart. But now that I am stronger today I feel that all may *yet* be well, and the Heron, now I am away from London, is so clear and perfect. Try and look after yourself for my sake. Try and *eat* and try and *be happy*.

I opened this letter to say Anne and Drey have both been here, and the doctor, too. He says I am getting on all right. I must stay in bed for the present, and I must take cod liver oil and iron mixed!! He is just like a student in a Tchekhov book. But he promises me that as soon as my left lung calms down I can go out and drive—and sit on the beach. Oh, such glorious prospecks! Anne is being perfect. I am *eating* all I see and milk 4 times a day *and* butter *and* cream. Bacon for breakfast: new laid egg-wegs. The food is excellent.

Your own wife.

But you know, Bogey, *I shall always be homesick.*

Wig

Tuesday Morning,

Dearest Love, (May 21, 1918)

I am to get up today, and I feel there is going to be a letter from you. (How dangerous these glad feelings are!) Yesterday I found in a copy of *The Western Morning News* that there had been a raid. It made me dreadfully uneasy—it does still. I shall never conquer this *panic* I feel if you are near danger. How can I? I can only implore you to take every care—that's all. You *must*—you know.

I am incredibly better really, for all this complete rest and food and sleep. I must have slept more than I've been awake by a long chalk. Tomorrow, the little young larned gentleman, as the old 'un calls the doctor, says I may go for a drive with Anne, and see all the butterflies and the hedges. Oh, she brings me bright bouquets that take the breath! We must have our Heron soon. Darling, you have no idea of all the treasure that still lies in England's bosom. But even while I admire it, it's an effort not to *pitch* it out of the window because you are not here. It's just the same about everything. What you can't have, I don't want. I keep looking out at the sea and thinking: Thank God, that don't separate us! There is not that to cross. One just gets into the train *this* end and tumbles out into the other's arms. I am not taken in by this silky, smiling, purring monster outspread below my windows.

Darling Heart, I am giving Drey the bit of butter you sent me down with (I can't write English today.) Souse it well in cold water and salt. Leave it in a pan of cold water and salt overnight, and 'twill be as good as new. *Then* eat it. I eat everything. So you must not fail me.

Queer—I can't write letters any more. No, I can't. We have written *too* many, you know. Oh, Bogey, I think it is *infernal* that we should be apart, and yet I bring you nothing but anxiety and sorrow—so we *must* not be together. What an impasse! Sometimes, I am so bewildered—

253

utterly bewildered—as though I were caught in a cloud of rushing birds.

But I understand Wordsworth and his sister and Coleridge. They're fixed—they're true—they're calm.

And there you live, wearing yourself out in that bloody office, wearing yourself out in your rooms—spent, exhausted. No, it's *unbearable*. Don't send me any money until I ask, will you, precious? That is our compact. I can only beg you to try and keep well, and to get your holiday as soon as you can, and to let me know the moment it is fixed.

Your true love

Wig

I have opened this letter to say the post has just been. I am *intensely* worried and surprised to receive nothing but that milk chit—not a *word,* even on the envelope—not a line! What can it mean? I had a letter from L.M. written on SUNDAY—so that means you have been silent 2 days. I must telegraph. You can imagine opening that envelope and finding not a word—not even Love from Boge. Yes, if you *could* help it, it was cruel. But I am sure you couldn't. No Bogey, I'll have faith till tomorrow and school my unquiet heart.

Tuesday afternoon. (May 21, 1918)

(See that 't'. It means it is dancing.)

My dearest Own,

I sent that wire after seeing how awful the raid had been and then this afternoon came your two letters, your gay ones—and I am in touch with you again. My pen—it's as though the ink flows through its veins again—just that. I will stay here then for the present. It is truly ideal—perfect room, bed, food, and all arranged for me and served so decently and punctually—perfect attendance. Also I think my young doctor is about the best I could possibly get anywhere. He's absolutely *our* generation, you see, tremendously keen on this business, and takes my case so intensely that A. now feels he's the only man who *could* have such a grasp of it. She won't let me move or open a window without just running round to the surgery and asking. . . .

I confess I feel better today than I have for MONTHS and I can breathe more easily. I have been up and out in the sun for half an hour. As soon as I am well enough the doctor is going to take me driving, on his rounds. But he won't let me drive at all yet or do anything but sit in the sun. 'Wait now!' he says. 'I can see the kind of woman you are. There's nothing but a pain like a knife that will put a stop to you.'

This place out in the sun today was a miracle of beauty. The sea and the coast line remind me curiously of New Zealand, and my old servant is like an old woman down the Pelorus Sounds. (My dream N.Z. and dream old woman, of course.)

A. has just brought me oranges and caramels and smiles and such a lovely flower picture.

'My dear', she said. 'The idea just came to me—*sharp,* like a bite in a plate, you see—This is the place for Mansfield!' Can't you hear her?

I have given Drey the butter. Now I am going to answer your numbers.

(1) No, my precious. Don't send me the money now. I'll ask when I want it. I hope I shan't want so much. It's just *like you* to give like this.

(2) It will be quite all right about the sugar.

(3) Don't send Lamb. But if I could have any anthology of English poetry, p. ex. *A Pageant of English Poetry,* or any other. *At your leisure. No hurry.*

(4) I burn to review books. I shall do them well and promptly here and post the books back to you.

(5) I'll write every day, of course, and tell you more when I see more. I have only really opened my eyes wide after reading these two letters of yours.

(6) I won't climb a hill without a permit.

(7) Rib sends a kiss and if you can find him some orange and white striped bathing drawers, he'll be obliged.

(8) Would you take cod-liver oil and iron if I sent it you? Twice a day—after breakfast and dinner? It is better than malt. It's superb for the nerves, and is just what you need. Don't forget to answer this. Did you send Anne a prospectus?[1] I so want her to see one.

I suppose Harrison won't take my story.[2] Wish he would.

As to the Armenian cushion—I shall be known by it. I feel I'll never go out without it. It's so dark and bright and perfect. I can see people at the Heron taking cushions into the garden and our children saying, 'No, you can't take that one. It's *hers. He* gave it to her.'

There is a haze on the sea today from the heat, and a slow rocking

---

[1] Of *Prelude.*   [2] *Bliss.* He did.

swell. The fishing boats have hung out the fine tarred nets between their two masts. They look very exquisite.

You see I am just like a plant revived by your letters. I have just had *tea,*—thin bread and butter, gooseberry jam, cream, and two fresh buns with SUGAR on the top. I must ask these people where they got the tea-pot. It's very beautiful.

Yours for ever,

Your wife

Wig

Wednesday,

Dearest,   (May 22, 1918)

I think your Saturday letter came today—because yesterday's seemed later and yet you don't say a word about the Awful Raid. *This* one contained perfect letters to Papa and Janey[1] and the account of the Bush Fire, which I hadn't seen. Pretty powerful! I am extremely glad to have this paper.

Yes, the letters to N.Z. are quite perfect. I am sending them back to you this morning.

Another tropical morning: all the fishing boats out. I feel *extraordinarily* better, grâce à cod liver oil and iron. (You've got to take it, you know, or *I* shall stop.)

I had a nightmare about L.M. last night. You know she *does* terrify me. I have got a 'complex' about her regard for me. I suppose I shall get over it. She isn't a werewolf—is it? Are *you* sure?

The people here, the 'management', are really awfully decent to me, Bogey. I mean far more than they need be. I give a lot of trouble (well, it's true, I pay for it) but still—that don't account for their thoughtfulness. Coming in every morning at about 7 to open my windows wide, and heating my last glass of milk at night, and always leaving me biscuits. The old 'un made me feel about *four* last night, when she said, as she put my hot water down and I was going to bed, 'Come here while I unbutton eë.'

Anne and I have been sitting outside, she talking about the spring. She can't mention the flowers without her eyes just *cry over*, as she says. She brought me masses of pink lupins—terrifying flowers, but beautiful. This garden is so gay with real purple columbines and gillyflowers and marigolds and early roses. At night a procession passes along the coast

---

[1] Katherine's name for her mother.

road of fine old sailors, each with an enormous cabbage under his arm
—it looks to be a *sea* cabbage—grown on their new allotments. They
are beautiful, hale old men.

[A drawing of a boat.]

She has just come outside my window. I wish I could draw her. She's
a little beauty. See that queer kite-shaped sail? Oh, God, how I love
boats!

Darling, this is just a note, sent with the letters. Eat all that extra
ration of meat—eat *all* you can—as I do. God! this darling boat—
swinging lazy with the tide. Give Fergusson my love. We *must* have
a boat one day. Tell me as soon as you know about your holiday and
try and eat fruit while the warm weather lasts—and remember what
you are to me. It's no joke. My love seems all to be expressed in terms
of food.

Everybody has a boat here. Little babies leap out of their mother's
arms into sail-boats instead of perambulators.

Goodbye for now, my darling Bogey.

Wig

Thursday,

In bed. 11 a.m.   (May 23, 1918)

The old 'un has just brought your Monday night letter 'right up'.
Your letters all arrive perfectly now. My wire was sent really—in a
panic, because of that *cursed* raid, which you evidently in the 13th
Corinth. manner 'winked at'—the raid, I mean. I don't worry. But
for God's sake *don't* keep anything from me so that I shan't worry. That
is too appalling to think of.

Today I am going for a walk—down to the Surgery to be weighed.
The weather has changed. It rained in the night and this morning the
light is so uncertain—so exquisite—running silver over the sea.

An idea....

Are you really happy when I am not there? Can you conceive of
yourself buying crimson roses and smiling at the flower-woman if I
were within 50 miles? Isn't it true that, now, even—though you are a
prisoner, your time is your own—even if you are lonely you are not
being 'driven distracted'. Do you remember when you put your
handkerchief to your lips and turned away from me? And when you
asked me if I still believed in the Heron? Is it true that if I were flourishing you would flourish ever so much more easily and abundantly

without the strain and wear of my actual presence. We could write each other letters and send each other work and you would quite forget that I was 29 and brown. People would ask 'Is she fair or dark?' and you'd answer in a kind of daze 'Oh, I think her hair's yellow'.

Well—well—it's not quite a perfect scheme. For I should have to hack off my parent stem *such* a branch—oh such a branch that spreads over you and delights to shade you and to see you in dappled light and to refresh you and to carry you a (quite unremarked) sweet perfume.

But it is NOT the same for you. You are always pale, exhausted, in a kind of anguish of set fatigue when I am by. Now I feel in your letters this is lifting and you are breathing again.

'She's away and she's famously "all right". Now I can get on.'

Of course, L.M. would keep us one remove from each other. She'd be a help that way. Did you reckon on that when you were so anxious to keep her? For, of course, as you realize, I'd have given her the chuck for ever after the Gwynne affair if it hadn't been for your eagerness.

You are simply, incredibly perfect to me. You are always 'in advance' of one's most cherished hopes—dreams—of what a lover might be.

But whether I am not really *a curse*. . . . I wonder.

Mrs. Maufe's letter was most lovely.

Goodbye for now, dearest Bogey.

Wig

Thursday afternoon,

Dear Bogey, (May 23, 1918)

This is just a note on my tomorrow's letter, while I remember. Please don't send me any money at all until I ask—this is of course including the £8 for June. IF I want that £8 I will ask. But don't send it otherwise. Stick it in your Bank. But the £1 for the belated *Times* review, please send that to my Bank when you get it and tell me when it has been sent so that I can reckon on it being there. Also, in writing for cash, how do I *address* the Bank—inside and outside the envelope— and do I cross a cheque I send them—'Pay Self' do I cross that?

I haven't got the *Times* book yet: I'd be very glad to do it.

I have just had, by the afternoon post, your Wednesday letter. That's good going—isn't it? I note that the Elephant[1] is still on the carpet though still couchant. You won't finally fix up without a last word to

---

[1] The Elephant was the name we gave to the house which we eventually took in Hampstead. 2 Portland Villas, East Heath Road. It was tall and built of grey brick.

me, will you? And you talk as though I intend staying here until the *late Autumn*. But I don't—dear—I never had such an intention. For one thing I couldn't bear this coast in summer—far too enervating. However, that don't matter yet a while, as Anne would say.

It's a windy *fluid* day. I can't walk in it, but I have started working—another member of the *Je ne parle pas* family, I fondly dream—It's a devastating idea. However, I am only, so to say at the Heads, at Pencarron Light House, with it, yet—not even *in* Cook's Straits, and they look par-tic-u-larly rough and choppy. Goodbye till my letter tomorrow.

I have just had a note from L.M. I feel profoundly antagonistic to her —and now she's *waiting her hour!!* It's in every line—but 'Don't you be too sure, my lady,' is what I want to say.

Friday morning in bed. Drey and Anne came last evening and we sat up late talking of Anne's life. She has had a great deal of rich variety and change in her life—far more than I'd known. You know she is an exceptional woman—so gay, so abundant—in full flower just now and really beautiful to watch. She is so healthy and you know when she is happy and working she has great personal 'allure'—physical 'allure'. I love watching her.

It's such strange weather—not warm—with big sighing puffs of wind and the sea a steely glitter. At four o'clock I got up and looked out of window. It was not dark. Oh, so wonderful. I had forgotten such things.

The old 'un has just brought the morning post—letters from C. and M. and W. D. I expect yours will come this afternoon. I didn't expect it this morning. God! I feel so hard-hearted. I don't care a button for Chaddie's letter and yet—it was so charming. In fact, I only want to *drop* all those people and *disappear* from their lives—utterly disappear.

I am so keen Bogey that you don't send me any money. You see I do want to live absolutely on my own money if I can and even ('Ha! Ha!' chorus of Ravens) earn a bit rather than have it from you. As it is my illness has cost you an incredible number of armchairs and stair carpets and corner cupboards—almost, I should think, a hot water supply. Well, work as much as you like without over-tiring your darling yourself, but work for the Heron but not for the *poupée malade*.

I must get up. I am afraid there are no flowers in this letter, dearest. I haven't any. I'm shorn of them today. When I 'see' again, I'll show you, too. I feel extraordinarily better and stronger with no pain at all.

But I can't write you the letters I should like to, because my 'vagrant self' is uppermost, and you don't really know her or want to know her.

I wonder what *is* going to happen—if the war will end in our lives. But even if it does end, human beings will still be as vile as ever. I think there is something in the idea that children are born in sin, judging from the hateful little wretches who 'play' under my window, somehow—horrible little toads—just as evil as slum children—just as mean as French children. I believe if they were left to themselves the strong ones would kill the weak 'uns—torture them and jump on them until they were flat! Well, that's excusable in grown-up people, but in children ... !

Oh, people are ugly. I have such a contempt for them. How hideous they are, and what a mess they have made of everything. It can never be cleared up and I haven't the least desire to take even a feather duster to it. Let it be and let it kill them—which it won't do. But, oh (without conceit) where are one's playfellows? Who's going to call out and say 'I *want* you. Come and see what I've made'? No, one must have an iron shutter over one's heart. Now I *will* get up.

À toi
Wig

Saturday morning,
Dearest Bogey,   (May 25, 1918)

When I got into bed last night, the wall paper, the lace curtains and double washstand were all covered up by the dark. The iron shutter went up and oh, my darling, I began to think of you so tenderly—and to *sehne nach Dir*. Were you awake and perhaps thinking about us? It was about half past eleven. I felt towards you as I often feel when we are in bed together—when we are curled up together, close and warm, and one of us says (it's always me) 'What do you see behind your eyes?' ... You know?

Yesterday on my way to the post I met Pagello and went off with him to the surgery. Such a queer place, so absolutely 'Russian'—I mean as Tchehov has described. It will walk into a story one day. It was warm windy weather, I made a 'tour' of the town. I pretend to Anne I like it, and I do in so far that it satisfies my literary sense. It is very compact—ugly—the side streets are concreted over. There is a sense of black railings, and out of that *dear* little white house with the flowers comes a female voice: 'You stop thäat or I lay a rope across eë.' Which is just what I expect of Cornwall. But I'll stay, I am determined to stay here for the present, until the end of June at any rate. And then I shall only go off to some other country place, perhaps—*certainly* not to London.

I do hope you agree about the Elephant. Oh, I DON'T want it or L.M. in it, melting bits of butter in glasses of milk and following you out on to doorstep. 'Oh, Jack—you do still believe me—don't you?' I can see it—hear it.

I shan't stay at this hotel after my fortnight is up. Anne and I are going to look for two rooms. For many reasons. This place is perfect when you are ill, but it's frightfully *bald* when you are not. It's too ladylike for me, too, and I'm not a lady. And I want a sitting room. I can't work, can't concentrate in this bedroom. It's too big and too glaring. Also that great blue gape at the windows don't mean anything to me. Perhaps it would if I looked at it from my cottage door. But Anne says (she agrees with me) there are excellent rooms to be had with women who cook extremely well, etc. I shall go looking this next week. This place has been perfect for its purpose, but *j'en ai assez*. I want to WORK and it's too hard here. Each time I light a cigarette I feel a refined shudder come over this hotel. I will find something first chop, sunny, with a view over the snug little town as well as the sea. It would be worth staring at—this little town. . . .

Now you see why I don't want your £8. I must do this, and it's right, and my *diet* goes on just the same—so there's no 'break'. But if I were taking money from you I'd not feel quite free. I'd feel you had given it me for this place and no other etc. etc. True, I shan't need it in any other—which is all to the good—but that is not my primary reason for leaving here, *je vous assure*. And as you've no faith in me, dearest, I'll agree to take no place that Anne doesn't approve of. She, being American, is 'up to everything'.

Here comes the post. A blue envelope—you, *enfin*.

Yes, your Thursday letter. Where HAS this idea come from that I am to be here 4 months? I cannot grasp it. That funny sentence was me laying down your letter and simply shouting that in my amazement!! But our ideas have 'crossed' as usual—and I am thankful—oh, more than thankful—that there is a chance of getting out of the Elephant. Don't let's have the Monster. I hate the idea. I DON'T WANT IT AT ALL. Don't let's ever have a house in London.

I am sure the whole idea is wrong. I will wire you again this morning.

No, what is best for us both is for us to stay as we are. I shall, as I said before, stay here till the end of June or July, then go to some more bracing place—wander about, *enfin*—and when I do come back to London I take a furnished place in Hampstead. It is idiotic, I think, for us to be together when I am in the least ill. Waste of energy. I realize that. And really—you are like a new being already. But, for God's sake, WORRY me if there is anything worrying. I am not a cow—I can't be a cow—and worry *kept* from me makes me feel just like a mental. Don't 'hate to worry me'. It's awful to read that.

Now for this last piece of paper, I'll let all the rest go hang and to blazes and tell you I love you—that you are the most adorable darling boy who ever walked or rather rolled over the earth. There is no other creature in the desert of darkest Africa like you. And I adore you. Your poem with the decoration of life-belts of love is perfect, *you're* perfect. Consider yourself kissed and hugged—and held and squeezed and half killed by Wig. In *this* world there are no houses—no wings—no war—only Wigs and Boges and other cherubim.

Goodbye, precious one.

Wig

Saturday Evening,

Dearest Bogey, (May 25, 1918)

This is a final fling from me before we land the monster.

Would it perhaps be better to cry off? To tell the agents I have been sent to a sanatorium—'suddenly worse' and—until we have the Heron —to live like this—I to take 'provisionally' furnished rooms in Hampstead where you could always come for the week-ends. Such things are not too difficult to find. I should take them with attendance, of course. Then, when I wish to go to the country or the sea, je suis *absolument* libre.

Moving, all we must buy, will completely exhaust our Heron money. Of that there is NO doubt, and we cannot be in the least certain of getting it back. It will and it must be an infernal strain.

L.M. will certainly cost £2 a week, but apart from that I really am frightened to take her for better and for worse. My love for her is so divided by my extreme *hate* for her that I really think the latter has it. I feel she'll stand between us—that you and she will be against me. That will be at its worst my feeling. I don't mean 'simply' against me. I mean, of course, absurdly, nonsensically, abnormally, subtly.

The other arrangement leaves you at 47 for the week, but then you only sleep there—and it is quiet in the evenings for your work. The week-ends we could always share. Then we are really saving for the Heron—not touching Heron money. I feel the Elephant will be '47 in the kitchen' over again, in some degree, *with* L.M. *J'ai peur*. Don't you think perhaps it is the Heron or nothing? You see, your QUITE INDEPENDENT IDEA that we should be separate until the late autumn 'frees' me in thought. I think it is the right idea. I'll wander away this summer—and when I do go back, I'll establish myself in rooms in Hampstead.

Please reply to this fully, darling, and *don't* hate me for it.

Wig

But of course I am ready to be persuaded. I write this because I must be honest. I *feel* it at the time—very strongly. Do you be dead honest too. Then we'll understand.

Sunday,

Dearest Bogey, (May 26, 1918)

I had a wire from you yesterday. Funny French it was by the time it reached here, too. But it was awfully sweet of you to send it and you are not to feel your cœur declinéd. Now how can I prevent that? Prevent it I must. Look here! I'll go on writing truthfully to you because I can't 'pretend' (you *do*, a bit) but if my truth is melancholy and you feel gay, just pretend it is all my I and pay it no serious attention. But I can't dance *s'il ne joue pas*—and you wouldn't have me just keep silent —or would you? Tell me, darling.

It's true the melancholy fit is on me, at present. But, as I told you in the S. of F. (seemed always to be telling poor you) that to be alone (*i.e.* without you) and to be utterly homeless, just uprooted, as it were, and tossed about on any old strange tide, is utterly horrible to me and always will be, even though I were twelve stone and a prize-fighter—though I own my horror would be a bit ridiculous then. However, I fully, freely acknowledge that it's *got to be* for the present and my only salvation lies in drowning my melancholy fit in a flood of work. Which ain't impossible.

But what about Anne? you ask. Oh, yes, of course I see Anne occasionally, as much as both of us want to, for an hour at a time perhaps; but you know it's all on the *awfully jolly* surface. I can't really talk to Anne at all. Still, it's nice to have her here and she's a distraction and 'too kind for words. . .'.

Passons oultre.

It's Sunday. Cornwall in black with black thread gloves promenades on the edge of the sea: little tin bells ring and the Mid-day Joint is in the air. Pas de soleil. Low tide and the sea sounds to have got up very late and not found its voice yet.

Damned queer thing. I have dreamed for two nights in succession of the name of a street *rue Maidoc*. 'Not rue Medoc,' says Chummie, 'but rue Maidoc'. There is an exhibition of pictures there and Chummie is showing 3—'two landscapes and a portrait by Leslie H. Beauchamp'. We idled down the street afterwards arm in arm. It was very hot. He fanned himself with the catalogue. And he kept saying, 'Look, dear,' and then we stopped, as one person, and looked for about 100 years, and then went on again. I woke and heard the sea sounding in the dark, and my little watch raced round and round, and the watch was like a symbol of imbecile existence. . . .

There is a circulating library here. Not quite bare. It's got *In a German Pension* and *Eve's Ransom* by Gissing. I took out the second yesterday. Although, like all poor Gissing's books, it's written with cold wet feet under a wet umbrella, I do feel that if his feet had been dry and the umbrella furled, it would have been extremely good. As it is, the woman of the book is quite a little creation. The whole is badly put together, and there is so much which is entirely irrelevant. He's very clumsy, very stiff, and, alas, poor wretch! almost all his 'richness' is eaten up by fogs, catarrh, Gower Street, landladies with a suspicious eye, wet doorsteps, Euston Station. He must have had an infernal time.

I'll send you back D. W.'s *Journal* in a day or two, just in case you have a moment to glance into them—to refresh yourself with the sight of W. sticking peas and D. lying in the orchard with the linnets fluttering round her. Oh, they *did* have a good life.

Well, I'm going to work now till lunch. Goodbye, dearest.

Toujours

Wig

P.S.—Boge, please don't forget to tell me the moment Harrison sends my story back. Back it will come, of course. But I want to know *at once*.

While you read this feel that my arms are round you and your head is hidden—and I'm telling you it all—with every part of me.

My dearest own,

I think, reading your three letters this morning, I suffered every atom that you suffered. Nay more, because it was I who inflicted it on you—you who came crying to me and saying 'This is what you have done to me! This!' Even now I can't get calm and I am all torn to pieces by love and hideous remorse and regret. I must try to explain all this away and it's so difficult—so difficult—with these great clumsy words. I could do it were I to see you in a moment—in a breath. Only *one thing*. Never, never have I ever said to myself 'Shut up shop and take your love away'. If you ever feel that, don't tell me until you DO take it away. It really nearly killed me. The sky—the whole world—fell. Before I begin to speak—you must know that you're all life to me. God! haven't my letters said just that? Hasn't all my suffering and misery been just because of that—because of my terrible—exhausting—utterly INTENSE love? But you must have understood that. That was the whole why aud wherefore.

You see, I was in the S. of F. from December till April. What was it like on the whole? Just HELL. As you know it nearly killed me. Then I came back to rest with you. All my longing, all my desires, all my dreams and hopes had been just to be with you, and—to come back to my home. Bien! I came. Heard how ill I was, scarcely seem to have seen you, except through a mist of anxiety, felt that *all* your idea was for me to get away into the country again. Well, I understood that—although, please try to realise the appalling blow it was to me to uproot again—and so soon—with hardly a word spoken. Please do try and realise that. Plus the knowledge that I was more ill than I'd thought, and that all my precious 'privacy', my love of 'self-contained' life, doing all for myself in my own way, doing all *enfin* for YOU, was to be taken away from me, was 'bad' for me, *enfin*.

However, it was only for a month or six weeks that I was to be alone. Then you came down for your holiday and we went back together. I arrived, and found I was to be here (without a word explaining why this change had been) at *least* 4 months, until the *late* autumn. No word of your coming, no word of anything else. It was a sort of ultimate *comble*. It knocked me back on to my own lonely self. I was in despair, as you know, and I saw Life quite differently. I felt that if all I had oh so passionately pleaded and protested without shame or fear about my love—my longing for married life—as soon as possible—was to be just delayed, not understood—I could endure no more, and I fell into the dark hollow which waits for me always—the old one—and I wrote from there. I felt he has not this same great devouring need of me that I have of him. He *can* exist apart from me. I have been in the S. of F. nearly four months and here is another four. He will never realize that I am only WELL when we are 'together'. All else is a mockery of health. I depend on him as a woman depends on a man and a child on its little playfellow, but he, as long as he knows I am all right, he can play 'apart'. Now, do you see a little bit? Is it a little bit clearer? But there is more to say.

Our marriage. You cannot imagine what that was to have meant to me. It's fantastic—I suppose. It was to have shone—apart from all else in my life. And it really was only part of the nightmare, after all. You never once held me in your arms and called me your wife. In fact, the whole affair was like my silly birthday. I had to keep on making you remember it. . . .

And then—all the L.M. complex is—taking the reins out of my hands. I am to sit quiet and look at the country. I can't—I can't. Don't you know that LIFE—married life with you—co-equal—*partners*—jealously alone—jealous of every other creature near—is what I want. I am jealous —jealous of our privacy—just like an eagle. If I felt that you and she discussed me even for my own good—I'd have to fly out out of the nest and dash myself on the rocks below.

My little Boge-husband, you don't know me even yet. I adore you and you only. I shall not take my love away ever—not even long after I am dead. Silly little button flowers will grow out of my grave with Bogey written on the petals. . . .

Do you understand now? (Maintenant, c'est moi qui pleure.)

There is my answer for ever to you.

Now about the Elephant. Get it if you can, and we will make it a Singing Elephant with all our hearts.

As I wired you this morning, I am not going to leave this hotel after all. I cannot explain to another landlady that my lungs is weak. Also the fag of wondering what I shall order to eat would mean I'd order nothing. Here, it comes, and one eats it, and it's over. And they know me here, now, and are more than kind to me. The old 'un, Mrs. Honey, is 'pure Heron'. Bless her! I can always hear her and my Gran'ma talking as they put the linen away. So here I shall remain, and I will take your money, please—unless it leaves you short. I will take it from you. You must try to come here, as we did once arrange, even for a week, and we'll have a sail-boat and go 'whiffing for pollocks'. I am working hard and Pagello says I have made remarkable great strides.

So now, please God, let us be calm again. *I will not be sad.* Let us be calm. Let our love keep us quiet and safe—like two children in a great big quiet field—sitting there hidden in the flowers and grasses.

O thou who hast all of my heart. Accept me.

I am simply for ever and ever your own little

Wig

I have told the manageress I am staying for the whole of June—*at least.*

The books came and the cigarettes—thank you, love.

Tell me all the practical things. Don't spare me. Tell me all the worries. They are my RIGHT. I must have them and discuss them. You are NOT to have any worry *un*shared.

Tuesday,

Dearest Bogey,   (May 28, 1918)

I don't expect a letter today—or at any rate not before this afternoon and it's very difficult to write before you've had yesterday's letter explaining. . . .

It's windy this morning and sunny and there's such a loud noise of gunfire: it sounds like a bombardment: the house is shaking. I wrote a great deal yesterday. I'm fairly out at sea with my new story. The same difficulties plague me as they did before, but it certainly 'goes'. Darling, will you please ask Johnny for *Je ne parle pas* and put it with my other MSS.? He don't want to read it. Why should he?

I had a TREMENDOUS letter from H.L. yesterday, begging me to go down there and stay in the top flat of the bailiff's house—to have the woman to 'do' for me—and to be absolutely 'free'—only if I did feel I must talk there was Brett and she. If you chose to come for every week-end, it was *entendu* that you did not have to 'even see them'—This completely took me in and I longed to do it. I felt I *could* ignore them—the food problem was solved—we'd have all our week-ends together.

But no—I'll stay here for June and accept no bounty from them. But she can write the most *brilliant convincing* letter. If you hadn't known her—after reading it, you'd burn to know her—to be her friend—her champion against everybody. For five minutes I am completely overcome—but not for more than five.

God! I do want to know so much that I can't know yet. About the Elephant, about your flat. How soon is it to be taken over? What will happen to our things? How can I wait to hear all this? If you are not too tired, try to tell me all, won't you? But don't tire yourself, my precious Boy. Go slow.

I sat up in bed last night writing till after one o'clock. This new story has taken possession, and now, of course, I can't go out without my notebook and I lean against rocks and stones taking notes.[1] I expect I shall be arrested in the course of a day or two. I think these people have an idea that darling Anne and I are spies. And you should have heard the postmistress yesterday asking if the word were *Elephant*.

Attendez! Bogey, I love you this morning with absolute rapture. It's a good thing you are not here. I'd be a perfect plague. But are these feelings the result of a hot bath, a big pink rose I'm wearing, a grenade (the strongest cigarette—heavy-weight Spanish champion—I've ever smoked) and a sunny wind? For in the course of this letter I've got up and now I'm wearing Feltie and just off to the post.

Ah, je t'aime. Je t'embrasse *bien bien* fort.

Wig

Wednesday,

Dearest of All, (May 29, 1918)

Your Tuesday letter written at the office is here. I have just exchanged my breakfast tray, with a poor little sole's bone on it, with the old 'un for it. (Here's pretty writing!) I don't know what to say about it.

> 'If you read it once, you must read it twice;
> It will make *your* heart smell sweet and ni—ice'

as the lavender gipsies just don't sing.

Re health (as Papa would say) I am really bonzer. I went for a walk yesterday—really a walk—and today I feel better than ever and am going out in a boat. Are you coming down here at all? For a week? The manageress would board us, bed us, light us and clean our little

---

[1] I believe, but cannot prove, that this was *A Married Man's Story*.

shoes for £6½ the two of us. That is a monster room with a balcony. Well, just say. And you have not told me how to write to my bank, so as I am extremely short I shall have to ask you for the June £8 by wire. You see I've had a chemist's bill as well as all these old extras.

I *want* that old Elephant now. If it falls through we must try for a flat —but there are no flats, are there? And—yes, if we can get another person clean and honest, they'd be better than L.M. I feel, [*Marginal note: No*, see page 3] because, you see, we can't treat her just as a housekeeper—and I *have*, I must say, this horror still, even though I know it's 'wrong'. I have to tear a delicate veil from my heart before I can speak to her—and I feel I oughtn't to tear it. Is that nonsense?

Darling love, this is absolute Heronian weather—and I think our Heron must be somewhere near here, because it is so amazingly open— and healthy. And now that the black monkeys have folded up their little tents (I see *and* hear them) I am beginning to feel like Anne does about this place. Also, now that I *can* work and look over the walls—

Forty-nine sailing boats sailed 'into the roads' yesterday. I counted them for you. There they all were, skimming about. . . . This place is 4 miles from Polperro, 10 from Fowey. You can go across country to Fowey in a Jingle. Anne and I mean to do it one day.

But now, before I finish this letter, I talk to you seriously and at length about 'our plans'.

Grand Sérieux!

If we do not have L.M. one bother will be the moving. We shall absolutely need HER for that. She's the only person to be trusted to pack all that is at 47 and to understand *where* that all shall go at the other place. Also, tied as you are, there must be a second person who can see to ALL sorts of various things, like measuring for curtains, buying the 'odd' things, ringing up the builders and so on. The *so on* is really very important. It is absolutely impossible for you to attend to this and your work. No strange woman could. She's the only one. But if we took her at all like that, it would have to be for ever. We could not say: 'Leave your factory. Do all this. Then find us a housekeeper and decamp.' So what I think is this: Now you and I know just *how* we want to live— just *how* we think about all of L.M. and you know what a jealous woman I am. I think that if we can overlook 'all the other things' we ought to regard her as God-given and take her, and if she don't like her position as a 'housekeeper and friend', well—she can chuck it. But we shall find no one like her for the first months. Phone her. See her.

Tell her my letter to her is cancelled—and explain, will you? *She* will understand. The devilish thing is that now I have told you *all* I feel about her, I feel that nothing could be simpler than for the three of us to live together in Harmony.

Tak! Now how long will you be at 47? What do you intend to do? And try, precious, in your *rushing* life (I know how few minutes you have) not to be done by the agents. They generally leave us roasted— oh, such a brown.

I have heard from Virginia who dislikes the drawings very much. So does Leonard. Well, they would, wouldn't they? It's their press. I suppose they'd better not use them. Just a plain blue cover, with *Prelude* on it. To Hell with other people's presses! I'll send you her letter, however—and I'll write to her and ask her to send you a proof of the cover. I don't want Roger Fly on it, at any rate. (That 'Fly' seems to me awfully funny. It must be the sun on my brain.) Don't bother to type *Carnation*. Let it be. You've enough to do. I am, of course, in heaven that you liked it, cos I did too. And you 'understood'. I meant it to be 'delicate'—just that.

Has a parcel from Lewis, with two little pantalons of mine, turned up? Oh, will you please send them to me.

Oh, my Boge, my precious own darling—

Anne is painting me and old Rib. Rib, of course, is violently flattered and keeps flattening down his fringe at the thought. He is getting very brown. He is going to bring a tame shrimp HOME, please, he says.

All my letter is just one thing. I love you—in every way—always— for ever.

   I am yours eternally
      Wig

Give Johnny a big hug from me.

             Thursday,
Darling,   (May 30, 1918)

This weather can't go on. It will stop just before you come. That's my awful fear. I've *never* never known anything like it. And then I feel so well—eat, walk—went out to sea yesterday with an aged boy in a blue jersey and a straw hat with some sea-pinks round the crown. His name was Pearrrrrn. Rib, of course, when I got home started walking on his hands and bursting with laughter. 'What's the matter, Ribni?'

'Your nose is peeling now,' said he. It's true. I am as brown as a half-caste. I do wish the Elephant would take our bun that we're offering it so awfully anxiously, don't you? Why does it go on waving its trunk in the air? (I LOVE you) Blessings on thee, my beast. Do let us go for a ride on you,—I with what the old 'un calls my red silk *parachute* hiding us both from the world.

I had a letter from L.M. today—extremely sensible—and just carrying out exactly what I wrote *you* yesterday.

If you do come down here and I do meet you at the station I think the Heavens will open. I don't want to think about it. No, I hide the thought away, and just occasionally open the door a tiny bit, just enough to let a beam of light out. But oh, even *that's* so blinding. You see, we'll go for picnics. Yesterday, I saw you, suddenly, lying on the grass and basking. And then I saw us sitting together on the rocks here with our feet in a pool—or perhaps two pools.

I'll do Gus Bofa and Paul Margueritte on Sunday and post them on Monday. I can't go out on Sundays because I haven't a Prayer Book and Hymn Book to carry. The people would stone me.

Did I tell you they are building a lugger here? To the side of the bridge? To be launched in July. The carpenter and the carpenter's boy think I am so funny, that now when they see "tis herr again,' they become comedians and pretend to pour tar on each other's heads or to swallow immense long nails and then take them out of their ears—you know the sort of thing. But this boat-building is always a sort of *profession d'amour* for me. It's your boat—*our* boat they are building, and I am just keeping an eye on the workmen until the King comes down in a jersey and he and the Queen and Ribni the Infanta sail away with a silk carpet for a sail.

There is a saw mill here, too, which maketh a pleasant noise.

I hope I see Anne today, for last night, after I came in, I wrote 4 of those 'Poems' for our book. I've discovered the form and the style, I think. They are not in verse, nor vers libre, I can't do these things. They are in prose.

    (1) To a Butterfly.
    (2) Foils.
    (3) Le Regard.
    (4) Paddlers.

You would like them. They are very light. Like Heron feathers, so to say.

God! God! This sun and air and Love. What is one to do with it? The walls of the Heron are so warm. But the pantry is very cool, and the milk stands in a shallow pan. I went in there just now. How *can* there be a War Office and MI7d? I must get up and go out.

I've found a little tiny horse shoe which I am going to nail on one of our doors. Shall I send it you? No.

Sugar, please.

I love you FAR more than ever.

Toujours

Wig

Friday,

Dear Darling,   (May 31, 1918)

No post. Bin and gone. I understand *why* there's none, all right. I got your Wednesday letter yesterday, see? But all the same. . . . Oh, it is so *hot*, too. Why aren't you here? Why didn't you arrive last night, so that we could have a pig-nig today. These are not real complaints, you understand, only laments for the impossible. Anne and I are going off for the day, she with her sketch book and I with my writing book— and our *flasks* and sangwiches. She is going to bathe. The people here even are bouleversé by the weather and lovely day.

[A long wavy line across the page.]

That is one immense wave which lifted me right up into the sun and down again. Mrs. Honey brought me a letter after all! And the moment when I got it and saw your black writing on the blue—oh dear, does anyone know the meaning of rapture but me?

My adorable Bogey, I'll send the first long chapitre of my story this week. Your letter has so *fired* me that I know I'll write like billy-o today. It's just for you, for you. (But I seem to have said that before.)

I must answer your 'news'. I sigh still for a Definite Elephant. They ought to let you know this week.

Do please send me Frankie-boy's[1] letter. I like him for that. But then I don't *hate* him at all. Now that I see all round him, he astonishes me, and I like and pity him—and he does enormously feed one's literary appetite. How he beats that man in *Raw Youth*, par exemple, and yet what a man he'd be in that espèce de livre!

B—— is terribly conceited. When he was *not*—before he was spoiled —he was very nice. I mean, as a boy.

[1] Frank Harris's.

272

You'll have to see Landon, of course (another subscriber to the HP.) I am glad he wrote you. Oh, they'll find out, you know—all of them. I'll be delighted to have Duhamel.

Now I've answered all. You know what I think about L.M. I am *for* her—definitely, in her defined capacity.

The £8 are extremely welcome. I just take them, like that, but you know my feelings about them, and like the Reaper in Longfellow's poem I mean to 'give them all back again'.

I met Palliser père yesterday—and had a long talk. He says there's no place like this for my complaint. It's absolutely *the* spot. And he knows. He is a very very fine chap—what one would call—and sincerely—'a glorious fellow', I think. Anne don't see it at all. She doesn't even admire his appearance. But of course the fact that he and the pa-man were boys together does influence me. Queer when he called the pa-man *Hal* yesterday. He has three terrific gardens here, one on the cliff cultivated in the S. of F. manner. It is a most wonderful sight. I hope I see a great deal of this man. He can teach me a lot for the Heron. He says the climate about this region is superb in winter even, too. It is cold, but it is bracing, and if there is sun, the sun is here. I woudn't be surprised if Looe was our nearest town! Yes, you and Johnny and Palliser would hit it off, sitting idle and talking about boats and flowers.

It's such weather for Love. . . . And my room has a balcony looking over the sea. I simply LONG for you. Precious darling boy, try not to overwork.

I am getting so dreadfully young—a sort of Pelorus Sound Wig. Rib and I seem about the same age again. He is wearing my coral necklace today.

There is my bath coming. Mrs. Honey says I must get up.

Ah, que je l'aime—Do feel my love all about you—on hundreds of little fanning wings.

Ta femme
Wig

Saturday,
Bogey darling, (June 1, 1918)

It is another day the spit of yesterday. I think it is the end of the world —but not a Sullivan end. No, the planet will fry rather than grow cold. . . . Nine o'clock. The room is bathed in sun. I've just had bregglechick and I am *so hot* that I pine for a *cold shower*. Is it hot like this in London?

Yesterday Anne and I took our lunch and tea and went off for the day. We found an ideal beach, really ideal. And the flowers on the way! Every blade, every twig has come into flower. Right down by the sea there are the foxgloves, sea pinks, dog daisies—I even found violets—and yellow irises everywhere. It was really almost too hot—exhausting. I crawled into a cavern and lived there a long time. Then I went among the deep sea pools and watched the anemones and the frilled seaweed, and a limpet family on the march! By lunch time our sangwiches were frizzling, and Anne kept wishing her Thermos flask had a great platter of ice-cream in it, *my dear!*

We had intended to work and we tried to, but it wasn't possible. All day, like a refrain, my heart said 'Oh, if *he* were here!' This is the most astounding place. Where we were was absolutely deserted—it might have been an island—and just behind us there were great woods and fields and may hedges. I got fearfully burned and tired, too. I simply had to lie down with a stone for a pillow at one point; but in the cool of the evening when we came home I felt refreshed again. Only I wanted to come back to a cottage and to say 'Bogey, would you cut a lettuce for supper?' instead of a big hotel. It was still light, pale, wonderful at ten o'clock last night and *very* warm.

This heat—in this place, you see, the water and the country—is absolutely the ideal weather, I think. And, as Anne says, that terrible dust you get down South isn't here. All is *intensely* clean, dazzling, the sea-gulls glitter even when you are close to them down at the ferry, and all the old men are clean and fine as sailors are.

Old John Lewis's pants came in their fair box, thank you darling, and the Duhamel. I read the book last night. I thought it would 'help' me with Gus Bofa. And it has. He (Duhamel) is the most sympathetic Frenchman I've ever read. I think he is really *great*. Well, that's not a very illuminating remark. It's his *dignity* of *soul* which is so strange to find in a Frenchman—you know that I mean? (Why don't the post come? I am sure those were his steps ten good minutes ago, but there is no Mrs. Honey with what I call my second breakfast. I won't write more until she comes.)

Later. I have just been to the post with a wire for you to catch you definite this morning—my own. First, your adorable letter!! 'There's nothing to say.' Second, I hope you go to the country just to fill your reine claude eyes with the himmelsche grün. Third, Elephanitis. Bogey, there is a snag somewhere. Why did they—so *absolutely* definitely—tell us that *all* would be done? Why did they tell me it took a few DAYS to reach the other Trustee who was abroad, and now—paraît-il—he's in India? Why did they say the house had just been sold and the new owners were prepared to do anything. 'They owned a great deal of property in Hampstead and money was really no object; they wanted a good tenant' This was told me definitely. Nobody nowadays is prepared to pay £90 for decorations and *then* be tied by a long lease—or even £50. It's ridiculous in the highest degree. It's a pure case of bringing pressure to bear on you because they see you are keen.

I am sure, with every ounce of Father's brain, that this is a *swin*. And further—I am extremely anxious that you shouldn't take cash out of the bank. We never know in these days when we may really dreadfully need it—and you cannot grind yourself to powder you know, darling, darling boy. (P.E. Suppose Hampstead gets dished by air-raids and we can't sublet when we want to—we should still be liable, etc., etc.) This whole affair is disgraceful, I consider.

I propose—

That I accept H.L.'s offer of those top rooms in the bailiff's cottage—for July or longer—and you come down for week-ends. We talk it all out. I am close at hand. We discuss it at leisure. C—— and Co. go hang. We can afford to ignore them. They couldn't touch me. I don't care a whistle for them all. I feel I could get into the very middle of a Bloomsbury tangi and remain untouched. The great thing for these two children to do is to go slow—keep their tiny little heads—hold hands—not walk into spider's webs and always have a small sit-down before they decide to walk into parlours—see?

Well, that's what I think.

Anne has just been here to ask me to go whiffing all day. But I can't stand another of those days just yet. I am sitting on the balcony all day now under my parachute, feeling tremendously well and fit and eating away and getting browner and browner—and I want to 'work' today. She of course says: 'If you've got your health and you feel good, to Hell with art!' But, elle est plus simple et rude que moi.

What about this Billingsgate trial? Is it going to topsy-turvy England into the sea? What ultimate cinema is this? It is nauseating. I feel great sympathy for Maud Allan. But I have not seen much of the trial. Only the *Daily News* without tears.

I am eating all my rations here—and beginning to sleep even above well—which is a triumph for me. *Mais tout de même c'est pas l' même chose, tu sais.*

Goodbye for this moment, dearest of all. Just before I go, embrasse-moi encore. I feel like nothing—nothing but a force of love. I feel the air round me quivers with love as the air outside quivers in the light.

Du *reste* je t'aime.

Ta
Wig-wife

P.S. This letter is badly written and expressed: it's the dancey light. Forgive it.

P.P.S. I won't post it until I have an answer to my wire.

4.30. No answer yet, so I must let this go, dearest. I've not moved from my balcony all day. If you could see the water—half-green, half a tender violet—and just moving. It is unbelievably exquisite. But it has changed my morning love into a sort of late afternoon love—something more thrilling and tender and ——

My precious Boge,

Sunday,
(June 2, 1918)

Voilà encore un! Il fait plus chaud que jamais, et je suis décidée de ne pas sortir. Je reste alors sur le balcon. Ayant pour amie intime ma vieille tante Marthe (première visite depuis le mois de janvier—grande enthousiasme—de la part d'elle *seulement*). Si je savais, mon chéri, que vous étiez à la campagne—même à Garsington! Ce n'est pas du tout le jour pour chauffer la casserole—et je sais comme vous détestez Redcliffe Road. Bogey, avez-vous l'idée de venir ici? Dites-moi. Parce que, depuis votre télégramme, vaguement, chaque soir je vous attends, et quoique je peux attendre pour toujours, tout de même, c'est inquiétant de ne pas savoir vos projets.

I don't know why I am writing pidgin French: perhaps because the English in the dining-room sounds so *remote* from any tongue of mine. It's a cursed nuisance. Since this hotel has filled a bit, they cannot serve my repasts, except breakfast, in my room, and I have to descend to the common feeding ground. Dead serious—there's not a single person there under 65 and the oldest and most garrulous is 84! A more revolting, loathsome set of old guzzlers I can't imagine. Not only with their blown-out old bellies and clicking false teeth have they the appetites of proud, fierce lions, but oh! and oh! and oh!—I'd better not talk about them.

I sit at a table pushed up against the window, and try not to look on or to HEAR. They'll make a good story one of these days, but that's grim comfort. I can *smell* them all up and down the passages now. But they are just as bad as the Frenchies were, in the room next to mine at Bandol. In fact, they are just exactly the same, and in the same state of pourriture.

I've reviewed *Pour toi, Patrie* and copied out the first chapter of my brief story. I'll send it you tomorrow—*both* in fact in the big envelope —registered.

Oh, these old *horrors* downstairs.

I know what they are like. They are exactly like blow-flies—but exactly, in every way. They have unsettled me so. It is so infinitely hard for me to go among them, don't you know? and of course, being the particular kind of silly that I am I cannot help but listen and look. Instead of splendidly ignoring them, I simply quiver with horror.

Late last evening I went off to the village to look for (vain quest) an orange or an apple or any kind of fruit. Neither are there any cigarettes except 2/1 for 25. Darling, will you send me a few cigarettes or (better) ask L.M. to get another box of those Grenades? They are very good really.

I *hate* Sundays. One thing, I always miss you twenty times worse and I feel the need of a *home* more and I hate being tossed from hotel to hotel worse—if possible—on Sundays. *But do please let me know if you can whether you are coming here.* That is très important. I am still in favour of Garsington if the Elephant turns away. . . . *Don't* let's be apart. It *is* such torture really. What is fine weather and what are columbines without you?

No, I am not what you call a good girl today. But please don't let it make you unhappy. I'm an awfully loving one. Only I am sad. I have seen another *horror* this feed time, and I can't quite *fly,* after it, but have to hang on a flower and try to forget it before my wings will spread again.

God knows I adore you—and am for ever thine,

Wig

Enclosed a letter from Rib

Honourable Parentchik She is alright only missing you see? She

keeps snatching me and crying O Rib I do want him frightfully. Your
sonchik Rib.

June 2, 1918

Sunday afternoon,
(June 1, 1918)

Are you writing to me today? You are in my mind so—in fact, I'm
so filled to the brim with you—with the extraordinary (mild, silly

word) thing that is happening to us that I can't write. No, my pen refuses. Have you been living through what *I've* been living through these last few weeks? I know you have. . . . There is everything here—heavenly weather, birds shaped like the ocean, slow clouds, tufty flowers,—but you're not. You are never to enjoy anything without me —*never*. In fact, when I go away from you I shall tie Ribni's sash over your eyes.

    I am yours
     Tig

I've two great big letters   Monday,
1 lb. sugar   (June 3, 1918)
Frankie's and Virginia's.

 I'll answer first. No, before that even I shall just tell you that your letters are quite enough to turn any woman into an angel. They are the most celestial, glorious, inspiring, adorable letters that ever were penned. Rib says he's going to make a raft of one and punt off to London to fetch you—no, paddle off—with an old tooth-brush for paddle. 'Only see where the hairs have been nicely *finished off.*' (I suppose he gets that from his father.) So if you *should* look out of window and see your darling winky one bobbing down below—haul him up, please. I *note* that you intend coming on the 21st. This note is such a bright joyful one that it keeps on echoing and sounding among the hills of Looe. . . . 'You'll be glad to have him in your bed again,' said Mrs. Honey. I think the telegraph here thinks I am a 'booky' with elephants for 'starters'. (Is that right?) I hope we shan't find Sir Andrew Fripp saying (see Billingsgate case) that interest in the large animals is a sign that one ought to be put away. This case is a pretty exhibition. According to it Dostoevsky should be burned publicly in Trafalgar Square.

 Oh, I must not *run on*.

 Your calculations were so superb, so convincing, that I had to send a wire in case my letter of Saturday in the slightest degree shook your enthusiasm. If we can take it on those terms and more or less live within that margin nothing can stop us. And we shall have Brett's fowls and Rib will have a little cart with 2 chickens harnessed in it and go and meet you at the station and perhaps be allowed to drive your fountain pen home with him—or perhaps a 1d. bunch of flowers for me. In that case, of course, the cart would be so full he'd have to sit on the shafts. (I am very silly. I can *not* be sensible today. It's your fault, too: it's these letters, Bogey.)

I am sorry to say I don't care about D——. She don't interest me, somehow. I even feel her refusal was a kind of vanity. P'raps this is wrong of me—but there is something wrong with her face—a kind of *set pride* which is not the right kind of pride. But she's very young and I should not be intolerant. I've noticed the same fault in her dancing, too—the wrong kind of arrogance. Do you feel that?

Anne keeps asking me to do things I can't do. That picnic was a mistake—deadly tiring: I'll never go another till you come. . . .

Frankie's letter (save the P.S. which was really very stupid and wrong of him to write) won me. Yes, it really did. He *does* know good poetry, and if someone says 'that beautiful poem of Middleton Murry' I cannot help but lay down my sword and clasp his hand and ask him to come in and eat with me and is there anything I can do for him? I know, too,— curious it is—that Frankie did appreciate that poem in the *right* way.

Oh, about *Prelude*. I really think they had better print both kinds. Would it be an insult to Johnnie? I don't want not to have the designs at all—after the prospectuses. But please decide this for me. I shall abide by what *you* think. I don't want to hurt Fergusson. But perhaps he wouldn't care.

Re CAT. Please buy a *wire* cover at the Stores big enough to go over the milk jug and the meat and butter. It's a most useful thing for all times. And get Johnny to explain his butter-cooler, will you? Oh, we *must* have a house. You can't go on like this. Think of standing at the foot of the stairs and calling 'Tig!' and me saying 'Hullo!' and then me running down and you running up and us meeting like two comets. Why comets? They are positively the only things I can think of that meet.

That's all for today. I am going to trust this non régistré because it's too hot and I am too fatiguée to walk to the Post. So if it does not arrive it will be a Tragedy—a black one. If you have not sent the cigarettes, don't bother, dearest. Virginia sent me some today.

And now all my love again—ever so many more branches and flowers and leaves of it without end—

From your own
Wig

Dearest of All,

This is just a line because I feel lonely and want to talk. It is 'close on dinner' as Mrs. H. says, so I'll soon have to sit among the fuzzies again. I've solved the tea problem, which I really could *not* stick (tea en famille: one big pot). I give my flask to the cook and then she pours mine in and leaves it for me to descend for. I feel awfully like a spider going down for a fly and tearing off to eat in solitude. But it is a great idea. I could not see those awful old claws among the bread and butter again. Why do I *mind* uglies so? Mrs. H.—funnily enough—seems quite to understand that I do, and talks as though she 'tended' them in their cages. Well, I wish she did. My bregglechik in bed has become a kind of gay feast— without 'em. I saw Anne today who wanted me to go out, but no, I've spent the day up here resting in my chair and look-ing at the sea which has got quite rough. Now you can hear the boats *creaking* in the roads and the waves sound eager.

Oh God! Suddenly it sweeps over me again. We are writers! You are a poet and I write stories. But how this knowledge makes me *ache* for us to be together.

I wonder what it meant—your telling me the story of Strawberry Heart.[1] For me it was something like this. We lay down together and it grew dark, and while we were there we wandered away to that country you told me about. But, curiously, there were moments when this wandering was almost intolerably painful to me. I wanted to implore you to stop. I felt I'd *faint* if you went on, and you went on and on. I lost absolutely all sense of time and place until it was like dying, like the years one must go through before one dies. . . . And then quite suddenly the front door came back, and there stood an old sniggering crone with long, long grey curls, curls past her waist, fumbling at the keyhole with a bunch of keys and come to *spy* on us.

GONG.

Well, that's over, and I waylaid the waitress and took my coffee up here. P'raps they think I've got a deserter sewed up in the mattress. And now it's cloudy and almost cold and all the ships have gone.

No, I'll write no more tonight. *I want you* and I want to pull up the tent pegs. I don't like this ground any more. *Something smells.*

Tuesday. (A New Nib.) If you could have known what an inspiration

---

[1] *Cœur de Fraise,* by P. J. Toulet.

your little 'chit' was. The post was late. I 'argued' that I couldn't hear from you this morning, and then down this fluttered. I had been awake nearly all night, too. It was all so noisy and at 2 o'clock my French windows burst open—out popped the candle—the blinds flapped like sails. As I rushed to the rescue I thought of that Appalling Moment when Kirillov rushed at Pyotr Stepanovitch.[1] There's a big Gale blowing this morning, but it's sunny.

But please don't say even in jest, my darling, that you are not coming down. I'm only staying here because you are. Otherwise, I'd leave next Monday morning, and if you threaten again I certainly will.

For some curious reason (I can't explain) this is 'over' for me. I mean, my being here by myself. It's finished, done with. It don't interest me a pin. It's a marvellous place really, an incredible place, but I've got cold to it again. And this continual uncertainty about the Elephant! Not that I want it hurried. Good God, no! But I do wish they would say Yea or Nay. I want to put myself in it, and I'm afraid to, in case they throw me out. By myself it's understood that I mean US, with every single one of our possessions.

Note. (*a*) Need we *rush* into stair carpets? Foreigners don't. Champ-Communal's stairs were delightful in their bones.

(*b*) Why buy a geyser? A big sort of stock-pot with a tap on a gas ring (like those things in *Lyons'*) would surely cost a deal less and do the job.

(*c*) You're not to buy things without ME, and please, oh please, don't let L.M. choose ANYTHING. Her idea of me is so utterly absurd: it's always humiliating.

Jag: 'Wig, are you disagreeable today?'

Wig: 'No, Jag, but I feel that I am shut behind so many doors. And I'm sad and exasperated—and the wind throws everything about. Everything is flapping, even my thoughts and ideas.'

But if we get into a quiet place—a rabbit burrow—or creep under a giant rhubarb leaf, I'll lie still and look at you, and you will find I am really warm and loving—only tired of being away from the sight and touch and look and sound and breath and ways of you.

Ich *sehne nach Dir*

Wig

[1] In Dostoevsky's *The Possessed*.

P.S.—Has Harrison returned *Bliss*? I bet £100 Massingham won't print *Carnation*[1]: that's just 'by the way'. I *know* he would hate my mind.

Mittwoch. Die Hitze ist zurückgekommen.   Wednesday,
Dearest,   (June 5, 1918)

Your Monday night letter and ½ oz. from Tuesday afternoon and the Immensely Good Chinese poems.[2] (We ought to have that chap's book, you know. I think it's notwendig to the Heron!)

The oranges will be positively thrilling. It's very lovely of you to send them: I do only hope they are not shudderingly dear. One really sighs for fruit here and it's not to be had. Strawbugs are on the market—but teuer and they're no fun without sugar and cream.

I'm much less depressed today, Bogey. Oh God! I *do* get black. I simply go dark as though I were a sort of landscape and the sun did not send one beam to me—only immense dark rolling clouds above that I am *sure* will never lift. It is terrible—terrible. *How* terrible I could only 'put into writing' and never say in a letter. This afternoon I am going to Polperro with Anne and we shall 'boire du thé sur l'herbe fraîche.' She came up to see me last night. She has quite the right idea about the country and living in it. I explained to her last night what I meant by *religion*. I feel awfully like a preacher sometimes, I really have a *gospel*: this seemed rather to startle her.

Last night (this letter is like kalter Aufschnitt, please forgive it) I read *The Well-Beloved* by Thomas Hardy. It really is *appallingly bad, simply rotten*—withered, bony and pretentious. This is very distressing. I thought it was going to be such a find and hugged it home from the library as though I were a girl of fifteen. Of course, I wouldn't say this about it to another human being except you—c'est entendu. The style is so PREPOSTEROUS, too. I've noticed that before in Hardy occasionally —a pretentious, snobbish, schoolmaster vein (Lawrence echoes it), an 'all about Berkeley Square-ishness,' too. And then to think, as he does, that it is the study of a temperament! I hope to God he's ashamed of it now at any rate. You won't like me writing like this about him. But don't you know the feeling? If a man is 'wonderful' you want to fling up your arms and cry 'Oh, do *go on* being wonderful. Don't be less wonderful.' (Which is unreasonable, of course.)

[1] He did.   [2] Mr. Arthur Waley's first book of translations.

This happened yesterday.

(Wig gets up from the table and is followed by old white-bearded monkey, with bruised eyes and false teeth.)

Excuse me Moddom, is thaät a New Zealand stone you are wearing?

W. Yes.

O. M. Do you come from New Zealand, may I ask?

W. Yes, I do.

O. M. Reely! From what part, may I enquire?

W. Wellington.

O. M. I know Wellington. (Shows false teeth.) Do you know a Mr. Charles William Smith, a cousin of mine, who was residing there in 1869?

W. ....

O. M. But perhaäps you were not born then.

W. (very faintly) No, I don't think I was.

Voilà for my grey hairs!

Oh, how lovely these Chinese poems are! I shall carry them about with me as a kind of wavy branch all day to hide behind—a fan.

I hope H.L. turns up trumps. I feel *fond* of her, just now. Go down if you can, my precious, and refresh yourself. Dear Brett will keep the bad things away.

It's good, I think, that I didn't meet Massingham, who, I am sure, will not print *Carnation*. And please don't forget to tell me when *Bliss* comes back. I feel it is come. That's why.

Goodbye for today my dear love. If you go to Garsington, don't forget to let the Woolves know *and* try to catch the Sunday post (if it's not a bother) for then I'll get the letter on Monday. But if you'd rather rest, I understand, my precious, and will be happy to know it.

Your

Wig

Was the review all right?

Thursday,

Dearest and Best of All,   (June 6, 1918)

As I write that the 'worm'[1] who hears everything my pen says takes a sort of little pinging guitar out of his sleeve and begins to play—striking an attitude, you know, and rolling his eyes at me. He is a ribald, wanton worm and badly wants a beating *by* you.

[1] Ribni.

284

I have just eaten a juicy, meaty orange—an orange that *hasn't* riped among soup squares and blotting paper like the ones down here. And they're not only food for the body, they positively *flash* in my room, a pyramid of them, with on either side attending, a jar of the brightest, biggest, vividest marigolds I've ever seen. (Yesterday on m'a fait un cadeau from Mr. Palliser's cliff garden of Spanish irises and marigolds—a boatload full.)

It's *very* warm. I have a letter from you saying the Elephant seems to want us,—as did your telegram. (God, how I love telegrams. I could live on them, *supplémenté par* oranges and eggs.) But I have so much to say that I *can't* begin. Let me dance my way through the flowery mazes of your letter again—until I get to (what's the place called in the middle of a maze, where you stand on a little platform and look round?) Well, I'm there now and standing on the top.

(1) They say there are superb *sales* here. We might jingle-bells off to them when you're here. Chairs, *par exemple,* eh?

(2) I saw Pagello yesterday, who gave me more cod and iron. He's satisfied with me and he says I'll always be a Light Weight Champion. So don't expect me, darling Boge, to be a Heavy One. Jimmie Wilde is more my size than Jack Johnson.

(3) Rib is glad you liked his letter. He was very incommoded by a pen. He writes with a brush made of mouse's whiskers as a rule, but you can't get them while the war's on.

(4) Nice look-out for Art when Billing is pelted with flowers and Lord A. D. our conquering hero. I feel very very sorry for poor Maud Allan.

(5) Which is a very nice age. I LOVE you more than ever.

I am sending you some of my notebook today. Please let me know what you think of it. I've been keeping it since I was here. Do you think *The New Witness* might. . .? Or am I getting a little 'fresh'. Here's a letter I got from Virginia, too, which is nice. We must try and find out who that man Edwards is.[1] Useful.

Well, yesterday, Anne and I went to Polperro. It's all my I, you know, to go to places like Étaples and so on while these spots are here. Polperro is *amazing*, a bit spoilt by 'artists' who have pitched garden-suburb tents in and out among the lovely little black and white and grey houses—houses that might have been built *by* seagulls *for* seagulls. But you must see this yourself. You'll *not* believe it. I didn't, and can't

---

[1] One of the first subscribers to *Prelude.*

even now. It was a divine afternoon, foxgloves out everywhere, AND we found the most SUPERB fresh strawberries.

A. was a darling yesterday. You can imagine both of us at finding these—our excitement. We each bought a basket and had a basket put by for us to bring home *and* arranged for the carrier (for 2d.) to bring us fresh berries 3 times a week.

Wig (feverishly): Will they last till the 20th of this month?

Strawberry Woman: 'Why, bless eë, they be just a coming on.'

They are grown there in gardens overhanging the sea. A. and I took ours and ate them on the cliffs—ate a basket each (½ lb., 8d.) and then each ate and drank our propre thé and became 'quite hysterical,' as she says. We could hardly move and stayed much longer than we had meant to. The whole afternoon in my memory is hung with swags of strawberries. We carried home our second baskets (just having 'one more occasionally') and talked about raspberries and cherries and plums, and tried not to say too often 'When Murry comes'.

Looe is much more beautiful than Polperro. Polperro smells—like those Italian places do, and the people (families who have been there since the Armada: that's true) are dark, swarthy, rather slovenly creatures. Looe is brilliantly clean. But, dearest, it really is, you know, a place to have in one's inward eye. I saw Hugh W.'s cottage, but went no furder.

As I wrote that I have kept up a running fire with Mrs. Honey. *She* says I ought to have children. 'It might maäke eë a deal stronger, and they do be such taking little souls.' I agreed and asked her to order me a half-dozen. The other night her husband 'waited' for her outside, and she asked me to 'come and look at him on the bal-*coney*'. A fine, neat old man, walking a bit shaky. She said, 'He don't look his age, do eë? He wur a rare *haändsome* lad.' There is still love between those two: that's what attracts me to Mrs. Honey.

Oh, don't forget to bring a bathing-suit. The beach here—the beaches, in fact, are perfect for bathing or you can take Pengelly's boat and bathe from that. At any rate, you've got to bathe. I must ask Pagello if I can, too. Otherwise, I will sit on your cricket shirt under my parachute and wave a lily hand at your darling sleek head.

I wonder if you feel how I love you just *here, now*—I wonder if you feel the *quality* of my love for you. I am carrying you with me wherever I go, especially as I lean over and look at the new boat or read the names of the other boats. (There is one, pray tell Johnnie, which is

called *The Right Idea*). But they have such lovely names: *Harvest Home,*
A Ring of Bells.

Tomorrow fortnight. It will be a real holiday, won't it?

(Don't tell L.M.) I eat marmalade puddings—all kinds of boiled
puddings. They are delicious. And these people give me *plenty* of sugar.

I ADORE YOU

Oh, what *can* I do—how *can* I tell you? Well, here is your

Wig-wife

Friday,

Darling Heart,   (June 7, 1918)

All the morning a thin fine mist-rain came spinning down and the
only people on the *plage* were the sea-gulls. I saw them (when I got out
of bed for my cigarettes) standing on the wet lovely sand in rows
waiting for the waves that came in, heavy and reluctant and soft like
cream waves. I never had such a bird's-eye view of voluptuousness. . . .
Then Anne came with some berries for me and sat on the bed and
smoked and talked about hospitals in New York, and the helpless feeling
of the patient and the triumphant sensation of the nurses being a question of ANGLES. The patient being horizontal etc., etc. *Then* I had a hot
bath and dressed and went across to East Looe and bought a shady
chapeau (Feltie is too hot). The little hand-glass had an emerald bow on
it; it looked exactly like a cat. When I heard myself explaining to the
girl—'the hat must appear to be painted on the head—*one* with the
head—an ensemble—not a projection as it were'—and saw her Cornish
eyes gazing at me—*horrified,* I walked out, feeling very humbled.
Everything smells so good—oh, so good—and two men are lying on
their backs painting the belly of *The Good Fairy*—they are wearing
green overalls and they are painting her bright red. The ferryman says
we're in for another three months' spell of fine weather. You will like
him. His boat is called the *Annie*. He is particularly handsome and fine
—though he has only one eye—and only one good 'arm' and that one
ends in a thumbless hand. (He was blown up in that explosion. 'Oh,
yess!') All the same he don't look in the least mutilated.

It is very warm, now—'soft', you know—Cornish weather—and the
sea is half green, half violet. I had a very large, commodious, tough old
mutton chop for lunch while everybody else had a teeny little bean cutlet.
This caused horrible bad blood.

Ladies: 'I wish I had thought to apply for *extra* rations. I could have, quaite easily, with may health.' I pretended of course that it was divinely tender—melted in the mouth—and I tried to waft the choppiness of it in their direction.

No post today—not a sign. Mrs. Honey promises there shall be one this afternoon. She has confided in the manageress: 'It's in my heart, and I must out with it. I *dearly love* my little fine leddy'. . . . Oh, if only she could be at the Heron with her 'little maidy' to help her! She's only got one tooth and she's small with these rose cheeks and big soft blue eyes and white hair, but how fond I am of her!

Now the tide is nearly high. I've just been on the balcony. I heard a boat *hooting*. It's a queer little lugger with one orange sail and a tiny funnel. A man has put off from it in a boat—not rowing—standing up and—sort of deep-sea punting along. The lugger is called the *Eliza Mary* and she comes from FY.

People have such funny names here—there's a man called Mutton and another called Crab. You must please take me into *The Jolly Sailorman* when you come down. It's so lovely—I *must* see inside.

The post has come. There's only this. 'Tis a book. Oh, dear, it had a letter in it. This was simply *heavenly*. But why hasn't my letter come? I have been infinitely careful about the $1\frac{1}{2}$d. It's just delayed, my darling love. But I know what it means to start the day without one. I am a sort of hollow cave until the letter comes. All day I've waited for this. I shall talk over The Elephant on a separate page and you must say Yea, yea and Nay, nay as you will. It's just suggestions. Talk them over with me, won't you? You know—oh, well, I'll talk of that on the separate page.

One of my suggestions.

Shall I come up today (Friday) week and discuss Elephant in all its bearings, going as I know now how to go—*dead slow*—and then shall we go to the bailiff's cottage for your holiday? And I stay on there? We save a lot of money and a lot of mental energy this way—but, on the other hand, you don't see Looe. And I don't know which would be more of a holiday for you. But this is well considered before it's written, so don't FAIL to answer it.

Goodbye for today, my Bogey

Wig

If you agree to my 'suggestion', wire—will you, love?

SUGGESTIONS FOR THE TRAPPINGS OF THE ELEPHANT

I think front door, windy frames and gate a bright green. A house must be handsome to support blue—and green seems more in its period. But not a cooked-spinach green—an 'emerald' green.

Kitchen and garden-room and basement generally WHITE with all the woodwork and dresser a bright light BLUE—what they call *hyacinth* blue, I think. China and glass and food and fruit look so lovely with these 2 colours. P'raps its Wedgwood blue. Do you know that I mean?

All the rest of the woodwork in the house is best WHITE, don't you feel? One can always paint a fireplace with flat Ripolin if one wants to, later, but I think coloured woodwork, unless one is going in for an immensely intensive colour scheme looks patchy. We'd better, I think then, put as it were, a *white frame to the house* inside. This applies to the staircase, too.

For the hall and staircase-walls I suggest a good *grey*. Yellow ties one in the matter of a carpet, and altogether grey with a purple carpet and *brass stair rods* which give the grey the 'gilt' it wants, and drawings with a gilt frame or two. *Or* one could have a blue stair carpet (lovely with grey). Grey is so kind to you as you come in, don't you think?

With all our furniture in my eye, I really am inclined to say *grey* again for the huge big two-in-one studio. I don't know exactly why, but I am a bit 'off' yellow walls. I feel yellow wants introducing in curtains etc. but one can use purples, blues, reds and greens with grey, and especially, as you are so fond of *chintz*—it's the best background for it. However, if you incline to yellow for the studio—c'est entendu. Again, books are good against grey, and inclined to go a bit muddy against yellow. Does that seem nonsense?

I'd like my two rooms to be WHITE—quite white. Both of them.

I suggest for L.M. who, of course, must choose for herself, GREEN—the green of my sponge bag. All her bits of Rhodesian fur and every-thing would be lovely with green—all *tawny* colours—and the wash-stand set, par exemple. She ought not to have white, I am *sure*. No—stop it. The room faces North. A really *deep* yellow? It's not a big room. But that's for her to say. I'd *still* say green.

Why not have a little delicate flowery paper for your bedroom? If not, I'd have *pink* with white paint, like we had at Acacia Road. Oh, that would be lovely, wouldn't it? With coloured, much-patterned, 'fruity' curtains—and your workroom I'd have a deep cream (with engravings of the poets against it.)

I hope this don't sound dull. But I have, and so have you, a horror of *patchiness*. People are so *patchy*. And I think we must carefully avoid smacks in the eye. A cushion, or a bowl, or a curtain are pleasant little flips, but a door, skirting board and mantelpiece are positive *blows*. I feel that the body of the house enfin ought to be *spring*—real spring—and we'll put all the other seasons in it, in their time. But this [is] absolutely nothing but suggestions. You tell me, dearest, what you feel, and say if you think me a very dull little puppy.

Don't forget the kitchen range is broken.

My precious Bogey, Saturday,
(June 8, 1918)

I had a divine letter from you this morning writ on Thursday night. No, dear love, God knows, my 'blackness' does not come from anything in your letters. Truthfully, I think it comes from my health: it's a part of my illness—just that. I feel 'ill' and I feel a longing, longing for you: for our home, our life, and for a little baby. A very dark, obscure, frightening thing seems to rise up in my soul and *threaten* these desires ... that is all. I know this will recur and when it is there I cannot put it away or even say: This is *temporary*, this is just because of so and so. ... No, again I am enveloped and powerless to withstand it. So please try and understand it when it comes. It's a queer affair—rather horrible. ...

You will not always be a 'failure' even where the world is concerned, because we'll change the world. Fancy believing that and feeling as I do —all this hatred and contempt for human beings—all this desire to cut absolutely off from them! And of course I don't mean that we'll change *The Daily Mirror* world—but *a* world—*our* world and the world of Duhamel is there and waits for us to give a sign. I believe that, profoundly. When we are in the Heron and of it there will come such a brightness and such a sweet light from it that all sorts of little travellers (young ones) will draw near. You see we have not shown ourselves yet—that's why we're unrecognised—shown ourselves in our completeness, I mean, and in our *strength*. That's it. In our *strength*—that's what I mean. We have shown them our suffering (you have at any rate) but that is too hard for them yet. We have to show them our strength and our joy.

Bogey, my whole soul waits for the time when you and I shall be withdrawn from everybody—when we shall go into our own undiscovered darling country and dwell therein. That is the whole meaning and desire of life for me. I want nothing but you—and by you. I mean our home, our child, our trees and fruit, our flowers, our books—all our works for they are all contained in you and when I embrace you—all this treasure is in my arms. Oh God, that is so profoundly true. As I write, my happiness brims up. Do you feel it? You are everything, everything—and you are mine and I am yours.

After I had read Duhamel yesterday I went for a walk along the beach. My only thought was: 'What can I *send* him for his little child? I must send him something.' And then I picked up a tiny, exquisite shell—glittering with water—and that seemed the perfect thing. Then as I dreamed along, Duhamel and his wife (she is *very* cloudy; I left her out—with her parents) and his boy came to stay with us at the Heron. And we three sat smoking and talking on the terrace while the little Duhamel walked about the garden with Dickie Murry and pointed to things and said 'Ils sont beaux' and Dickie said—a bit off-hand because they were all his '*I* like them'. This vision made me feel quite faint. I sat down on the shore, looking over the water—and I saw it all so plainly and my heart trembled for our child. And I saw him a tiny baby—*very* serious—just awake and you leaned over him and after a good look at you, he gave a funny smile—and waved his feet at you by mistake instead of his hands.

All this is true—true—as true as our love—as *infallible*. It will come to pass just as the Heron will come to pass. That I do *utterly* believe.

Later. I have just been to the post and sent you a 'quite unnecessary' telegram. I *had* to, otherwise my heart would have flown away. My room feels awfully quiet, but the worm has gone off for the week-end with Anne. She fetched him this morning. She is doing a Still Life of him surrounded with marigolds. It *ought* to be lovely. She thinks he is 'too perfect for worlds, *my dear*'.

And we are to have a sketch. Of course, Rib was so flattered that he left me without a pang. He's coming back on Monday. Anne is more than good to me, Bogey, brings me fruit, flowers, and this morning a bottle of cider, and last evening some very superior chocolates that Drey had sent her. She is infinitely generous, too, in looking after me.

Just remembered. It is her birthday on the 11th, on Tuesday. Do you think you could send her a wire? She'd appreciate it tremendously—if it wouldn't be a trouble for you, my darling. Tie a gnot in your handkerchief to remind you. Oh, I wish we were together this Saturday afternoon. I wish it DESPERATELY. I am so tired of not having you. Oh, it's awful to want anyone as I do you. As of old, in France, I feel I *pine* for you today. It's a divine day, too. But you must be here to share it.

My darling Heart,
> I am your
> ## Wig-wife

Sunday,
(June 9, 1918)

Please read directions on the other side first.

This letter is not to make you sad. I expect my tomorrow's will appear absolutely to deny it. But it will not really. This *does* stand for all time, and I *must* let you know.

Precious darling,

I have just been writing about Gus Bofa. Now I want to write to you. It all feels so different today; it's been raining and 'tis loövely air, as Mrs. Honey says. No sun—rather cold—the curtains blowing—very, very desolate and far away from everybody—11500 miles away at least. . . . Oh, dear! I wish I were in London (but you'd be angry). I wish I could have some tea (but you wouldn't let me go into the kitchen.) In the middle of last night I decided I couldn't stand—not another day—not another hour—but I have decided that so often—in France *and* in Looe, and have stood it. 'So that proves,' as they would say, 'it was a false alarm'. It doesn't. Each time I have decided that, I've died again. Talk about a pussy's nine lives: I must have 900. Nearly every night at 11 o'clock I begin wishing it were 11 a.m. I walk up and down, look at the bed, look at the writing table, look in the glass and am frightened of that girl with burning eyes, think 'Will my candle last until it's light?' and then sit for a long time *staring* at the carpet—so long that it's only a fluke that one ever looks up again. And, oh God, this terrifying thought that one must *die,* and may be *going* to die . . . the Clovelly Mansions, S. of F. 'writing a few last words' business. . . . This will sound like exaggeration, but it isn't. If you knew with what feelings I watch the last gleam of light fade! . . . If I could just stroll into your room, even if you were asleep and BE with you a moment, 'all would be well'. But I really have suffered such AGONIES from loneliness and illness combined that I'll never be quite whole again. I don't think I'll ever believe that they won't recur—that some grinning Fate won't suggest that I go away by myself to get well of something!! Of course, externally and during the day one smiles and chats and says one has had a pretty rotten time, perhaps, but God! God! Tchehov would understand: Dostoievsky wouldn't. Because he's never been in the same situation. He's been poor and ill and worried but, enfin, the wife *has* been there to sell her petticoat, or there has been a neighbour. He wouldn't be alone. But Tchehov has known just *exactly* this that I know. I discover it in his work—often.

I have discovered the ONLY TREATMENT for consumption. It is not to cut the malade off from life: neither in a sanatorium, nor in a land with milk rivers, butter mountains and cream valleys. One is just as bad as the other. Johnny Keats' anchovy[1] has more nourishment than both together. DON'T YOU AGREE???

However I'll cling to the rope and bob up and down until Friday week, but not a day later. Look here! dear. Do please give me every bit of your attention just to hear this. I MUST NOT BE LEFT ALONE. It's not a case of L.M. or a trained nurse, you know. It's different.

But that really IS a cry for help. So do remember.

Your

Wig-wife

Monday,

(June 9, 1918)

Dearest Bogey,

Here's my *third* letter. I've torn up one attempt, kept another as 'interesting evidence', and this one I'll send. It's a process of clarifying ... you know.

Truth is—it is one of my très mauvais jours, as bad as can be. I'm jetty black. But what's the use of saying so? No use at all. It only 'confirms' me though in my determination not to spend another day here after you are gone. I could NOT stand it. That's as much as I'll stay. I'll stay. I'll try and stick until Friday week, and no doubt I shall. But not a day more!! *Tak por tak!*

I think a letter of yours is lost. Here is your Friday letter (postmark Sat. 5.30 p.m. W.C.) and a 'note' from Sunday. But you 'pass over' my wire and my note book and the p.c.s. Or are all these things delayed your end—or hadn't you time—you were too tired? Oh, there are a thousand reasons. And, enfin, the note book wasn't grand' chose

[1] Katherine had made a mistake. Keats's anchovy—part of his starvation diet in Rome—had no nourishment.

—postcards are a waste of money and the telegram was unnecessary and out of the air. Still, I would just 'like to know'. Also would you try and remember to tell me if my review was all right?

That's very superb about the £13. Especially the recovery of last year's.[1]

No, darling, I shan't buy anything on my own. No energy. I shall buy a bottle of Beaune, however, because I feel I must take some stimulant regular, plus the milk, cod liver oil, iron, etc. Wine that maketh glad the heart of man. What heavenly words! Are they true, do you think? Then I shall be a drunkard. But they are not true.

Addio. I am in despair, you see. Laissez-moi. Let me wave my jade-white hand and go. I love you *un*speakably—with a strong stress on the first syllable today.

Tig

Tuesday,
(June 10, 1918)

See page 5 first. All this is stale now the 2nd post has come.

Dear Bogey Darling,

It is quite obvious upon this morning's showing that *several* of my letters have been lost in the post and especially (1) the one with the tour of the Elephant interior in it, (2) my (I'll confess) rather precious 'Note Book', of which I don't possess anything like another copy.

What has happened, at its very brightest and best, is—that the post has been—that these treasures have been perhaps 'overweight'—there's been, therefore, a 1d. to pay and—naturally—no one to pay it. So the postman has chucked them away. On the other hand, some person in the house, either tops or bottoms, may have stolen 'em. That's just as possible, in fact, very much more so.

This 'sort of thing,' familiar, oh, ever so familiar as one *is* with it, is still devilishly wearing. So if they *do* turn up WILL YOU PLEASE LET ME KNOW.

I mourn the Note Book. Yes, I *do* mourn that.

Perhaps you will understand *if if if* you get my letter this morning why I sent my so unreasonable wire. That was the only explanation—Impatience. A profound dismay at the idea of holding out so long, a feeling that I'd get cramp or the waves would go over my head too

[1] An unexpected refund of income-tax.

often or the rope would break. So, though I *know* and do absolutely realise you're hurrying as fast as your boat will sail you, I yet—simply couldn't help lifting up my cowardly little voice and saying, 'Oh please do try to come faster'.

You see a *fortnight* in London is so broken up into little bits so shaken and scattered that it can be gathered up and held tight in the smallest little bag.

(*Bolo:* 'What, Monsieur, is a million? A little pile like that!')

But a fortnight in MY world (into which, dearest dear, you never will enter—even loving each other as we do) is a thing quite without beginning or end. You see 14 nights or 12 nights or 2 nights *can* be up the gathered meadow of Eternity and down again.

There are hours, moments, glimpses, when one can't face it when one wants to stand with one's face in one's sleeve and just WAIL. . . .

But. However. Having received your dear wire and your darling letter, I'll make the effort and succeed and on Friday week nous nous rencontrons à la gare.

I note, *cher* (how much more real Stepan Trofimovitch is than—Johnny for instance)—I note, *cher,* that you 'dined with the Wolves'. Do forgive my dreadfully persistent question. Was there any sign of a blue cover? I hate to ask you—for your tiredness comes in a great sigh of weariness through this letter, my own precious, and I do—oh God, I do—hate to add a jot to your present worry. So lay down your pen and *don't* answer captious Wig.

I fully, completely, absolutely understand about your holiday. Consider my wire *unsent. Don't*—oh, my perfect one—*don't* try and come faster. Come as you have arranged and we will be quiet together and look at—you at the boats and I at you.

Mrs. Honey. There's another telegram come. Oh, now I wish I had delayed this morning's wire until I had your Monday night letter which won't arrive until tomorrow —— might if a cherub was about to be wafted me by the afternoon's post—but *im*probably. I am so afraid that you'll take this—my morning wire—as an answer to your Monday night letter. Will you understand that your Monday night letter can't have travelled so fast. One of your chiefest charms is that one never knows *what* you are going to understand.

Doesn't Johnny know a woman who would tidy you while Mrs. H. is ill? Make L.M. come across, too. She ought to be keeping an eye on you, for me. She is behaving *rottenly.*

(What a brilliant success I am to be married to!! Curse me.)

Now I am going to read the *Nation* and finish this after the 2nd post —*just in case* there's something I must answer. (There is, of course. Your wire says you are waiting for an answer).

1.30. I've just had lunch *and* a glass of wine '*to it*' and have read the *Nation*. Your *Civilisation* review is excellent. I, personally, think your article on Gaudier exceedingly, extremely good—very valuable, too—very well written—*discovered*: that's the word I want. But—*warning*. You have mentioned his poverty and that he did the house-work for his sister. She is in London. By all accounts she is a very dangerous horrible woman of the B—— type—and she may feel, you see, in her jealous, almost insanely jealous way that you'd no right to open that particular door to the public eye. THEY are not to know that he did the housework. See? So don't be surprised if she hits out. But *don't* answer her and *don't* see her. This is important, I am sure.

I have torn up and chucked in the waste-paper basket all the work I have done these last few days. It was *hectic*.

Mrs. Honey brings me the afternoon post. Hides it behind her apron and says, 'I thought you'd be wanting a caändle,' and then suddenly just like a girl shows me the letter. 'There's nought so good for eë.' Well, I agree with you and my wire of this morning will 'stand', will 'fit'.

Your letter has brought you near and lifted me from under the appalling umbrella. Now, I'll just turn to Friday week—and live for it and believe in it, and you are *not* to hurry, not to rush, *not* to worry. Take your precious time. I can't write today. I am going off to the plage to watch the waves. (That's your letter, again.)

I am glad you got the Note Book and glad you saw the Woolves. Would the *Nation* print the Note Book. Much more likely than *Carnation* (which they *won't* print). But you *can't* offer another. Let it all be.

Oh, yes, at this moment, you're wonderfully near. I feel 'better' today physically—much. No, we'll sit tight and on Friday week you will come. The Colonel[1] helps the Heron, too, at present.

Goodbye, my own love

Wig

[1] My chief in MI7d.

Mittwoch   Guten Tag mein Schwartzköpfchen!   Wednesday,
Dear Darling,   (June 12, 1918)

No letter by this morning's post, so the day sets in very quiet. It's rather like waiting for a clock to strike. Is it going to strike? Is it *not* going to strike? No: it's well past the hour now. . . . Still, 'thanks be to Fortune,' I've the afternoon to look forward to—two chances a day: that beats France.

Re Jam. Mrs. Honey has got a nice little lot of gooseberries coming soon—they are called 'golden drops' and do make handsome jam. She's keeping them for us. BUT do you like gooseberry jam? I do, awfully, if it's home made, and yet it's not (which really *is* a point in these days) *too* alluring. I am become, since I arrived here, a Gluttonous Fiend sur le sujet de marmelade d'oranges. It really does seem to me one of the superb discoveries, eaten early in the morning—and so prettie withal.

Yesterday afternoon, on the rocks, among the babies and family parties (*too* near me for my taste), each of us with our tea and trimmings and cigarettes, Anne and I sat. And SHE talked and I added:

'Anne!'

'Really!'

'How extraordinary!'

'Yes, I can imagine it.'

ringing the changes on this little chime, which somehow wonderfully was enough to bring *all* her thoughts rushing to me in a little urgent troop until I really (if you will please conceive of me now as a kind of little warm dim temple) couldn't have held another.

But oh—they *really* were—some of them—no end 'interesting', Bogey. You were there, par exemple, sitting next to 'a rather big girl with round eyes and a cream complexion' while Johnny and Anne (who were to meet you next night) looked on. . . . That was at the d'Harcourt.

Passons. I am going to spend £1 before I leave here on pottery—blue pottery—which seems to me exquisitely lovely. We shall choose the shapes together—a high fruit dish—a bowl—some flower jars. £1 will cover them all. There is *such* a shop here. I keep placing these things in the Elephant—the clean pale delightful Elephant.

Why didn't I have a letter!

All the same I am a nice little thing this morning. If you were here I think you'd like my ways.

I fell fast in love with you last night at about 12.30. I was going to bed, dropping my velvet coat and velvet shoes on the bank before I took a header in what I prayed was going to be a dark little pool and suddenly I saw you in the 'garden room' making something, with a packing case, a hammer, a plane, nails. . . .

'Wiggie, hold this for me.' I held it, and you banged away.

'Half a minute, Jag. I'll just put a paper down to catch the sawdust.'

And later you put a little pot of glue in a saucepan of boiling water, where it *bumped* away while it melted.

This was so Ineffably Heavenly that I tied a love word to the leg of my very best and fastest pigeon and sent it off to you, to perch on the end of the grey bed and give the top of your precious head the gentlest possible peck so that you'd wake and get the message. . . . Did you?

I must go out out out in the world.

Goodbye dearest love

Your own little

Wig

Bon soir, Tête Noire!

Thursday,

My own darling heart,   (June 13, 1918)

I shall not write much today. I am too worried about you. You *can't* go on. I am going out to wire you to see Croft Hill. This you really must do. He will, I hope, order you immediate leave and you must come here *as soon as possible* and rest absolutely.

I had no letters at all yesterday though I waited ever so. Now this morning your Tuesday and Wednesday letters are here and I feel that the case is immensely urgent. You can obviously stand no more. If you don't do this, you may break down very seriously. I implore you to take all the care you can of yourself.

(Of course, the main cause is my INFERNAL coldness, heartlessness, lack of imagination in having written as I have lately. No more of that, though, or the pain will be too great and I'll cry out.)

Try and forgive me—that's all.

Re Elephant. Are you 'legally' free to sign the agreement in view of the fact that you're an undischarged bankrupt? I saw some man was fined yesterday for some offence or other and it made me think—

Hadn't I better sign? As your wife with independent means? Don't risk anything. But, above all, for God's sake, take care of yourself.

Your own
Wig-wife

Friday,
King of the Turnip Heads!   (June 14, 1918)

I hasten to throw this letter into the wall to tell you (in case you do 'see your way') (and my *D.N.* says there is a 'glut' of them au moment présent dans notre Londres) my way to make Strawbug Jam. As far as I remember it's like this.

¾ lb. of sugar to each
1 lb. of fruit.

Put the fruit and the sugar in a pan overnight. Turn, before leaving, ever so gently with a wooden spoon. (Turn the fruit, I mean. Don't *waltz* round it.) By the next day the berries will have 'sweated'. Boil, without adding any water, (gently again) for ¾ of an hour. And then apply the Saucer Test. (During the ¾ of an hour, Christian, you must *not* seek repose.)

God! as I write I freeze, I burn, I desire, with a passion that is peign, to be there all in my little bib and tucker.

'Yes, Rib dear, you should have a taste on your own little dish! . . .' But I think this receipt is right.

Queen of the Wigglechiks

The time for boiling given here is for a lot. Perhaps it needs less for a little. That's a point I have never yet decided.

If you feel there ought to be water added—well, you know our high courage on former occasions. And it's always been triumphant.

A Week Today   Friday,
My precious Bogey,   (June 14, 1918)

Wednesday evening when L.M. came and brushed you and Thursday morning note are come.

Also, just as I had tied two lovely bows on the shoulders of my chemise came Mrs. Honey with such a sort of sweet piece from the comb that I am still tasting it—your telegram despatched this very morning as ever was, saying you are 'chirpy'. (When you use that particular word my heart always overflows. It's such an exquisitely *brave* word from you—and my 'Hurray!' in return has a little catch in its voice.)

You shall have strawberries, love, in this happy land three times a day and I don't see why we shouldn't take back a great basketful for jam, too—and do the Government in its cruel blind eye. Oh, the Picnics! We shall have almost perpetual picnics—whole or half day ones. There is a river here, you know, which I've not yet been up. Waiting to explore it with you. Then we shall, even if we don't buy a pin or a curtain ring to it, adorn the Elephant here and plan it and plot it and mark it with E and put it in the oven for Bogey and me.

Rib: 'She's in one of her worse moods. Look out, parentchik!'

But it's all your fault, as Wilkie's girl says.[1] You ought *not* to be so enchanting.

Oh, darling Boge, wings or no wings, even if I become a sort of baby pelican with a bright eye, *I* must be the one who looks after you—until the Heavens open and we behold the Lord with the Heron on his right hand. It's not fair—hopelessly not fair—that you should have to drag me in a little cart after you to the office and then drag me home again and that I should fall over every time I'm 'propped'. No, I refuse —for ever and ever—amen.

(We are to have a couponless poulet to take back.)

Now I am going to talk to you about what you ought to bring here. If it means the large suit-case—and it's not too great a nuisance—bring it, for an odd corner would be most welcome on my return journey. This hotel is a . . . 1st class English Pension. Awful if you had to fraternise, but as I have established a squirrel reputation (only descending to seize my nut or two when the gong goes and then simply flying back into the branches again) it's quite all right. But what I mean is—one *changes* in the evening, and though I don't expect you to join the boiled ones you'd be happier if you had your—say, blue serge—I think, to get in after you have been out all day. You'll need, of course, your slippers, too, and some cricket shirts if you have same. Socks, ties, hanks and spunk bag. Also, a belt for wearing when we row away and you throw your coat at me—for not even oriental embroidered braces will do. Corduroys, of course, would have you in the lock-up in $\frac{1}{2}$ an hour and a jersey would have the fishing boats after you.

S'pose you'd better wear a straw hat, hadn't you?

[1] In Wilkie Bard's sketch *The Night Watchman.*

And don't forget pigglejams.[1] You will, of course, be met with a jingle—Rib driving.

I thought you'd wear your white silk shirt in the evening with a bow tie. Is that a possible combinaison—or do I rave?

These are just hints. If you want to throw them away and arrive with your ruck-sack—well—you will, of course!

Pagello—*galanuomo*—was here last night and made a tour of the battlefield. There is no sign of an *advance* by the enemy—they are still more or less there in force on our left wing—but the moral of the Commander-in-Chief is excellentissimo today.

This long letter is because Sunday comes in between—a dull old day —no post.

But you must understand it has Love Love Love enough to fill all the letter boxes in the world. It will, my own, if only you hold it to your warm heart a minute, keep alight until Monday.

Oh God! How she does *love* him! Is it possible? What can she do to express it? Go to the town and buy the ferry-man some tobacco? Yes, that's what I'll do.

Give the old boy a hug from his sister.

As to what I give YOU—and Rib throws up his arms—

Yours for ever
Wig

Do *please* send me *Colour*. Cigarettes are excellent, thank you.

11.30 a.m.   Sunday,
My Dear Love,   (June 16, 1918)

I feel I have such a great deal to write to you today. Perhaps it won't all (it certainly will not) get written: some will have to 'bide over till eë come'.

Firstly, the brown paper note came yesterday morning and I thought paid me almost *too* well for my own wisp. But then Mrs. Honey brought the telegram on a silver charger. Tomorrow I shall know all that Crofty[2] said, but the fact that he has ordered you injections and a half-holiday a week proves, darling, that I *was* right. Doesn't it? You grant me that. I'm awfully anxious to know just what he said—and whether he was 'intelligent'. It seems that he must have been. Thank Heaven your tiny holiday is before you, and the Elephant, too. You

---

[1] Pyjamas.   [2] Dr. Croft-Hill who was a good friend to us both.

must NEVER be left in such an impossible situation again. No wonder *you* loathe the Redcliffe Road. (I confess I have 'turned' against —— and couldn't greet him. He's a coward and utterly selfish. Feel inclined to write to him: 'You do your share of the work, my lad, and don't worry about the planet getting cold.')

You do everything that Crofty tells you—or Rib will beat you terrifically—see? I think I'll put Pagello on to you, too, as soon as you get down here. *He* (Pagello) is leaving Looe—going back to Dublin in a month's time. But before he goes he's going to give me a sort of programme to live by which will be very useful. I have not told you my weight this week because I am not going to the Clinic until next Wednesday to ascertain it. I've been trying a special diet and Wednesday will 'give it a chance'. What a curse! The weather has changed: it's really more lovely than ever, but showery—immense clapping showers of rain, castles and mountains in the sky and reflected in the purple sea, the air smelling of elder flower and seaweed. But alas! for my bones. It's brought on a devilish fit of spinal rheumatism, and I walk like little Nell's grandfather—and spent until four o'clock this morning—literally—wondering whether people my age could have paralysis. If not, how account for being cold-stone to the knees and so on and so on. The pain is devilish, devilish, devilish—but I am *not* down-hearted, so don't you be.

Yesterday morning I went into Looe and met Mr. P. and had a talk about chickens, tulips and boats. He is a *huge* man, a positive Titan. I came home to find another huge bouquet from his garden—mixed sweet williams, superb great velvet flowers. My room looks *full* of them and Ribni's dark head shines out of velvet bows. Anne has made such an exquisite painting of mon fils chéri *and* given it to me.

She came yesterday afternoon—strangely happy and *stout*-looking, and said, standing by the bed and smiling 'Je *crois*—je ne suis pas certain —mais il y a enfin un retard d'une semaine—je crois que je suis en-ceinte!' But, of course, it is a *deadly* secret. As I watched her I 'recog-nised' her expression: women, saying that, have always looked 'just so' —it's extremely beautiful to behold.

And then Mrs. Honey brought me another letter from you. I am glad L.M. has been decent. Make her *pack* for you and look after you all this next week. Use her, dearest.

After today Friday will feel ever so much nearer. I am not going to meet you at Liskeard. It means such a waiting about and though, God knows, I'd wait about for ever for you, I feel that it is *défendu* until I am a bit more of a lion.

This morning when I woke up Mrs. Honey was particularly honeycomb. Dear old soul—in her black Sunday dress. She said 'You've not slept. Thaät's bad. I'll see to it that you haäve your coffee right hot.' And she brought me boiling coffee and 'a fried egg with bacon fried for a relish'. When I had done up all my buttons and was having a small sit down she said, looking at me with her kind old eyes, 'Shall I recite you some verses I learned when I was a girl? Will eë haäve *The Death of Moses* or *A Mother's Memories?*' I said I'd have both. Down she sat. Each had, I should think, about 40 verses to it. She never hesitated for a word. She folded her hands and on and on went her soft old voice, telling of the 'crested waves'—telling of 'the lion the King of Beasts' who sat under the mountain where Moses was buried and 'forgot to roar'.

> 'Yea, from the monster's golden eyes
> The golden tears dropped down. . . .'

I listened and suddenly I thought of Wordsworth and his 'faith' in these people—and again, Bogey, in spite of everything, I believed in England. Not only in England—in mankind. You will understand me when I tell you that I wanted to weep, to cry, Father, forgive them, they know not what they do.

Oh,—Love—the Beauty of the human soul—the Beauty of it—the Beauty of it. Don't let us *ever* forget!

You and I know it. Duhamel knows it. There will be others. We will build an altar.

No, I've not written half that I meant to, and I *can't*. My back has got the upper hand. I'm off back to bed with a hot-water bottil. It's no good, Betsy. But don't worry. I'll be better tomorrow. It's only *body*, *not* heart, *not* head. These are all I've got intact, and all yours for ever. Dearest of all and best of all, you are coming *this week*: and by Friday I'll try and be dancey. Make L.M. look after you—that's all. Phone her.

Goodbye for now, my precious. What a silly I am to be so stiff! Oh so stiff!

Always, always your own

Wig

Dearest Love,   Monday,
                                                            (June 17, 1918)

Your telegram, which arrived at break of day, found me *toute émue*. It just stopped me from being in the least disappointed when the old post did come—and—gave me you to eat with my frügglestück. J'ai bien mangé.

I do feel today that Friday is—oh, so near. I keep making preparations . . . and speculations. Will my flowers last till then? Shall Rib wear his new dress or the old one his father loves?

I feel ever so greatly better today (can't write or spell tho'). I had a good night. Oh, a *good* one! A. came early and began the great painting —me in that red, brick red frock with flowers everywhere. It's awfully interesting even now. I painted her in my fashion as she painted me in hers: her eyes . . . 'little blue flowers plucked this morning. . . .'.

The second post has just been with your Sunday afternoon letter on its horn. I am delighted at Crofty's news—but what's all this about 5 guineas? Don't shame me so. Think what you have spent on me, precious. It made me blush to read that. But p'raps you were only making fun of me. Crofty is the right man for you *evidemment*. Stick to him and let him fortify you with iron bars against the time. . . .

The reason why I have been so very quiet about my weight is I was only 7.10 when I weighed last, so I didn't tell you. For I had lost a couple of pounds. I know when and why. It was when I had one of my blackest moods—I felt very dreadful; but by next Wednesday I ought to have found them again and I will wire you the good tidings. . . . Bother—wasn't it?

No precious love, don't bother about pumps. Crab-shells will do— one for each foot—slippers will be high perfection. I wish you would whisper Chaddie to send me ½ lb. of good chocolates. I *pine* for that sweet toothful, and there is nothing here just now but chewing gum. Everybody in this hotel has told me how much better I am today than I was yesterday—which is very naice of them.

I say—what about *Thursday*! I told Rib who became a shocking boy on the spot, absolutely too much for any woman to deal with. I threatened him finally with the Children's Court and said I'd tell the magistrate he was incorrigible. But he pays no attention, only asks the empty air: 'Well why does she keep on kissing me while she says all this?'

You're not to think I bullied you about this large suit case. (You do.) Really and truly I have only gone into the affair in such detail to make you feel comfortably disguised—camouflaged—in the presence of the chimpanzees. For, tho' they don't bite, their chatter is the hell of a bore, don't you think? You must not bring anything but a coloured hand-kerchief and a tommyhawk if you don't want to.

Now take care of your darling self. Your letter has brought Friday—rainbows nearer

Your
Wig

My own Bogey,
Tuesday,
(June 18, 1918)

It is as cold as Winter, grey with white horses, solemn boats—a pale light on everything—a feeling of great 'uneasiness' in the air. I think I may have a letter from you by this afternoon's post—none came this morning. *Colour* came. I shook it, held it up by its hair and its heels, but it hadn't a message. The reproductions are very beautiful. I have had a good long look at them. . . . You know 'Poise' is extraordinarily fine, but having gone so tremendously far as Fergusson *has* gone, I don't think the *mouth* is quite in the picture. It is—it is more 'in the picture' than most of his other mouths are—but I think it might be more *sensitive* . . . more 'finely felt'. Of course, I can hear his 'To Hell with rosebuds!' but I won't be put off by it: it's too easy, and begs the question any way. To exaggerate awfully (as I always do) he really seems sometimes to fit women with mouths as a dentist might fit them with teeth—and the same thing happens in both cases: the beautiful indivi-dual movement (mobility) of the face is gone. Looking at 'Poise' again this mouth seems more nearly right than any other. Perhaps that's what sets up the irritation in me. I must say as a picture it properly fascinates me. . . .

The magazine as a whole is VILE. Nothing less will do. The article on J.D.F. is such pigwash that I cannot imagine how he allowed it. There is not a hint of even low ability in one word of all the writing from cover to cover. It makes me want to start a paper, frightfully, but not a soul would buy our paper. We'd have to make our cow subscribe and all our little new born chickens and ducks would be presented with life-subscriptions. The birds that sang above the Heron I am sure would gladly pay a feather a copy, too, but then in the case of swallows, for instance, it would be such a *job* posting theirs on to funny strange addresses in Africa and Italy. No, no paper. Books.

Bogey, the north wind doth blow. It has found out my bones again and is playing a fine old tune on them. I should like to come into your room, light a big fire, put a kettle on—and then both of us curl up in two big chairs. The doors and windows are shut—tight—there are books and I'll make coffee and we'll talk or be quiet. This ain't a day for hotel bedrooms. If I hadn't FRIDAY nailed to the mast. But I have— I have—Thank God!

I think you'd better bring down your woolly weskit, darling—to be ready for weather like this. But the Lord may turn his face to Looe again by then. He just must.

I am a silly, dull girl today. I had a *nuit blanche* and my brain is still, as it were, empty with it. But Friday is in this week and, thank God, you have not to cross the water. Let us make a solemn vow—never—never to let the seas divide us.

Be careful not to lean out of the train window. Have tea at Plymouth —but don't miss the train while you are blowing on it. Cut yourself a large huge sangwich for your lunch. It's better to have too much food when you are travelling. I didn't have half enough on my way down here and I had to keep on buying snippets. Above all—keep *warm* and remember you're looking after yourself for me as I do for you.

Your own

Wig

P.S. Look here! I have just taken a room for you. Does that sound awful? It's near to mine. It won't cost any more than if you were in this room with me—but it will give you *Platz*. You needn't sleep in it if you don't want to. We are 'side by side', and as I have bregglechik in bed I thought you would perhaps prefer to dress and so on in your own room. It will cost just the same as this room. I feel we'll both *rest* better like that. It's a nice room—tiny, though.

Wiggie

Before I gets up.   Wednesday Morning,
My own Boge,   (June 19, 1918)

Your Monday evening and Tuesday morning letters have come, after a jour maigre yesterday. What should I do if Friday wasn't Friday? It would *have* to be. Vous êtes horriblement fatigué. You must just be taken care of and we'll get an old sea salt to pull us up the river while you sit tight and just dabble your fingers.

I had a really bad old day yesterday. They made me a fire and brought my food into my cage and I wrapped up in my pink quiltie, but it was snow use. My rheumatism was so ghastly that I could *not* write. I tried, time after time, but, oh dear me, my bones played such Variations Symphoniques that I had to give over. So, having no book, I watched the hands go round my watch and wondered why the Lord has cursed me with this *vile* ill health—I who love and long so to be well. It's queer.

Evening. Anne came. Very welcome. She stayed and we talked. I showed her *Colour,* and on her own she remarked that F's 'mouths' always troubled her—in fact she entirely agreed with me about them. This, from her, was a relief to me. Drey told her that 'everybody' is talking of your wonderful article on Gaudier—*tak por tak.*

It's sunny today, but very uncertain. The clouds are pulling over again—a plague on them. When you come, it *must* be fine for you. As for me, personally, I would not care if it snowed as long as I had you to look at and to listen to, but I care, for you. You have to turn a lovely brown and you have to paddle and swim and eat your tea *out,* as they say.

Dearest, *what* is the page of accounts you refer to? I never made one out, and certainly did not send you one intentionally. It must have been an odd sheet which got into your letter by mistake. I don't want any money at all, thank you, Mr. Millionaire. My finances are quite satisfactory, and you sent me £8 for this month, you know.

I am so glad you are taking the old boy to see Charlie Chaplin. I wish you were taking me, too, and Rib, who would give us imitations afterwards to the life.

'One more letter—one more letter to Jordan': that I'll send tomorrow and then—well look out for me on the station, for I shall be there.

Yours yours yours
Wig

Later.

I've just come from the Clinic, where I was weighed—7.11. very good—and also heard that 'another of our leading townsmen' tried to cut his throat from ear to ear last night, after (he being over 40) he had received his call-up notice. The doctor of course couldn't help *thrilling* rather: I think it must be his first affair of the kind. But there's a pretty state of affairs *here*—about this tribunal business. I'll not write it.

My glass was bedeckt with your telegram, darling Boge. Thank you for sending it me. Do you mean no letter from the Agents, or none from me? I gave *mine* to you to a maid to post yesterday and she says 'Oh, *yes,* she did', but if the stupid wench caught the post or not (she'd only an hour and a half to catch it in, and the box is ½ a minute from the kitchen door)—that I don't know. I don't depend on people or believe in 'em—but I couldn't get out yesterday. I had to trust to them.

The day has now got very lovely and the ferry-man (with whom I would be very much in love if I had any to spare) has just been particularly attractive—and Friday is still coming nearer.

Wig

Thursday,

Bogey darling, (June 20, 1918)

This will catch you before you leave. Don't forget to leave our addresses—for 'Mansfield' as well. And provide yourself with food. Suggestion: Travel in your little grey felt and pack your straw with the spunk bag inside it. The weather is so funny.

Tomorrow, tomorrow, tomorrow. That is at full gallop.

The wardrobe 'thrills me through and through' (to be sung con amore).

Don't fall out of the train. Perhaps you had better tie a label on your top button. I don't trust you *at all*.

Rib says: 'Parentchik, I shall be there to meet, on the stopping of the chariot, the August Emergence.' He says he is going 'to write a book now called *Fan Tales*'.

Now. Oh, *please* hurry. But *don't* rush. And don't forget that I shall be, once with you, simply . . . *too* excited.

Your

Wig

I spent a week with Katherine at Looe, and we returned together to my rooms at 47 Redcliffe Road, where she stayed until we moved into 2 Portland Villas, Hampstead ('The Elephant'), I think on August 26, 1918. Shortly before this, on August 8, Katherine's mother died. Katherine loved and admired her deeply. There are three memorable pictures of her in Katherine's stories, as Linda Burnell in 'Prelude'; as Mrs. Sheridan in 'The Garden Party'; and as Mrs. Hammond in 'The Stranger'. 'She was', Katherine wrote in a letter, 'the most exquisite, perfect little being—something between a star and a flower—I simply cannot bear the thought that I shall not see her again'.

The household at Hampstead consisted, eventually, of Katherine and myself, L.M. and two maids, Violet and Gertie, who, as so often happened, became devoted to Katherine. Katherine lived there continuously for the next twelve months, and came under the care of Dr. Victor Sorapure. In October 1918 she was examined by two independent specialists, both of whom pronounced that her only chance of recovery was to go into a sanatorium. Perhaps it was so in theory; but it will not be evident to the reader of these letters that the discipline of a sanatorium would have prolonged her life. Probably in order to profit by such a régime she would have had to be of a different composition.

But the question whether she should enter a sanatorium or not lurked in the background throughout the year; it was postponed rather than settled until, in the summer of 1919, Dr. Sorapure, whom Katherine trusted more completely than any other doctor who attended her, definitely advised her against it, on psychological grounds.

In October 1918 Lawrence came to London, and frequently visited Katherine. For the time the misunderstandings and quarrels of the past were forgotten. 'For me, at least,' Katherine wrote, 'the dove brooded over him, too. He was just his old, merry, rich self, laughing, describing things, giving you pictures, full of enthusiasm and joy in a future where we became all vagabonds —we simply did not talk about people. We kept to things like nuts and cowslips and fires in woods and his black self was not'.

In January 1919, I was offered the editorship of 'The Athenæum' which was about to be revived. After talking it over together Katherine and I agreed that I should accept it. She entered into the project enthusiastically and we gave up the idea of leaving England in the spring. The new opening seemed to come as a godsend, for our financial difficulties were considerable; and the new interest lifted Katherine's depression which had lain heavily upon her through the winter.

Nevertheless, it is questionable whether we did wisely in accepting. Katherine worked very hard, reading and reviewing novels, collaborating with Koteliansky in translating the letters of Tchehov, and helping generally. That was a great drain upon her energies; it left too little over for her own proper business of story-writing. On the other hand, when 'The Athenæum' began to publish short stories, Katherine was sure of a market for them, and the stimulus was good for her.

In the autumn of 1918, 'Prelude' was published by the Hogarth Press as a blue paper-covered volume. In July 1919, 'Bliss' was published by 'The

*English Review' and attracted a good deal of attention; and in the same month
my brother and I began to print 'Je ne parle pas français' on a handpress.*

*At 2 Portland Villas we had a cat called Charles Chaplin, through our
ignorance that she was a female. Two of her kittens, Athenæum and Wingley,
became important figures in Katherine's life and letters.*

*In August 1919 it was finally decided that Katherine should go to the
Italian Riviera. She wrote to Lady Ottoline Morrell on August 17 :*

Here's an absurd situation! My doctor strongly urges me *not* to put
myself away, *not* to go into a sanatorium—he says I would be out of it
in 24 hours and it would be 'a highly dangerous experiment'. "You see,"
he explained, "there is your work which I know is your life. If they
kept it from you you'd die—then they *would* keep it from you. This
would sound absurd to a German specialist, but I have attended you
for a year and I know." After this, I with great difficulty restrained my
impulse to tell the doctor what his words did for me. They were
breath, life—healing, *everything*. So it is the Italian Riviera after all.'

*In her new hope Katherine had entirely forgotten her past experiences of
the horror of separation.*

My dear Jack,   (October, 1918)
   I confess that these last days my fight with the enemy has been so
hard that I just laid down my weapons and ran away, and consented to
do what has always seemed to me the final intolerable thing i.e. to go
into a sanatorium.
   Today, finally thinking it over, and in view of the fact that it is not,
after all, so much a question of *climate* as of régime (there are very
successful sanatoria in Hampstead and Highgate) I am determined, by
my own will, to live the sanatorium life *here*.
   (1) Father shall have built for me a really good shelter in the garden,
where I can lie all day.
   (2) He shall also give us two good anthracite stoves.
   (3) I shall buy a complete Jaeger outfit for the weather.
   (4) I shall have a food chart and live by it.
   (5) This new servant releases Ida, who has consented to give her
whole time to me, as a nurse.
   (6) Sorapure shall still be my doctor.
   I shall have a separate bedroom *always* and *live by rule*.

You must have a bed in your dressing-room when the servant comes.

(7) I shall NOT WORRY.

You see, Jack, for the first time, today I am determined to get well as Mother would be determined for me. If we are depressed we must keep apart. But I am going through with this and I want you to help me. It CAN be done.

Other people have done this in Hampstead. Why not I?

Anything else, any institutional existence, would kill me—or being alone, cut off, ill with the other ill. I have really taken my courage up, and I'm not going to drop it. I *know* it's possible.

Your own
Wig

Friday,
(March 7, 1919)

My Own,

At about 4.30 this afternoon there sounded the smallest possible knock on the door—so faint that nobody but Ribni could hear it. He waved his fan at me, presented arms with it, and said DOOR. So I went.

Opened it, looked

down

down

down

to a minute young gentleman whose boots were just seen, who was, as it were, extinguished under a stained glass halo. I realised immediately that this was an angelic visitation. (The darling had 2 very small *black* wings sprinkled with diamonds and stars.) But when he handed me the bouquet, I nearly picked him up as well.

Jack—you never bought them. Such flowers are never seen except by lovers, and then rarely—rarely. I have put all in the big jar, and they are on the table before the mirror. You will never, never know what joy they have given me. What is the good of sitting here at my writing table? All my little thoughts are turned into trees and butterflies and tiny humming-birds and are flown off. Now and again I take up the lamp and follow them.

Were they like this when you bought them? Or did the lovely act of your buying them cause them to put on this beautiful attire? Oh me, I don't know.

But please remember that when my heart *is* opened, there will be: *item,* one bouquet of Anemones presented by her true love, March 7th, 1919.

Thank you for Ever More

Your

Wig

Noon

Darling,   (March 7, 1919)

This letter from L. has just come: it is *very* nice, I think. And he could do the ' a bit old-fashioned style' very well.[1]

The sight of you with the rucksack has unsettled me. I want to be off with you—fair weather, broad hats, stout little shoes. 'Let us sit down at the next fair place we come to and have lunch'—and down swings the rucksack. . . .

There'll be time for it.

I had a heavenly letter from Pa. You must take him to Hornsey Lane[2] in June. I'll come too.

It's raining—raining—with a queer pinkish sky outside and very significant shadows in. I hear L.M. and Charles[3] playing bo-peep on the stairs. Blessings on thee, Charles! Thou receivest without the flick of a whisker much that might be lavished on my stubborn head.

Enjoy yourself. Forget all the Horrors. I am *glad* that you are going away out of your *vie de chien* for a little bit.

Your

Tig

Saturday,

Dearest,   (March 8, 1919)

It is a lovely day here—very 'cool and clear'—a mother of pearl day really. I want to go out for a walk on the Heath, but must wait for the Piano man. This morning when I had gone to the P.O. to wire you, he turned up, asked for *me*, and said he would return. Alas, my knees are

---

[1] This refers to proposed contributions by D. H. Lawrence to *The Athenæum*.

[2] The Beauchamp family lived in Hornsey Lane at the beginning of the nineteenth century.

[3] Charles Chaplin the cat, mother of Athenæum, April and Wingley.

dissolved and I fear the worst.[1] But I must see him. More of that after he's been.

Sullivanoff turned up yesterday and spent hours over the fire. We talked about (1) you (2) him. His admiration, 'deference' and interest for and in you are reinforced now by affection. 'I am grown so *fond* of Murry.' This is a subject capable of infinite variations—and the subject I enjoy—so I *did* enjoy it. I think his personal life worries him, poor old boy, but that is his affair.

The *D.N.* has sent you B.R.'s new book. No, I won't post it on to you.

Sorapure came yesterday. Did I tell you? He thinks I lead too sedentary and too quiet a life. 'Tubercular patients ought to enjoy themselves.' This I almost wept to hear. It's true, too, but what can one do? Il faut attendre le beau temps pour sortir. I felt most woefully that he really despised me for sitting in my quiet room—and I so despised myself I wanted to *wail*. However, all can be arranged, and I shall not take to horse-riding or anything, dearest love, before Tuesday.

Can't you stay a little longer? Will such a tiny rest do you any good?

Richard came last night. His face is still his active enemy, but he was very nice. He had supper and then talked to me—très content.

Charles has his box in your dressing-room, and has sat in it—solid all the morning. He is a most satisfactory animal. I confide in him. L.M. confides in him. Why the mixture doesn't kill him I don't know. How it must fight!

L.M. and I are peaceful parties. She sings 'Pale hands I love', but I am a good child and say nuffin.

Take care of yourself, dearest of all. I am going out. The pianner man can't be coming after all. Of course my idea is he has gone off to fetch a police force, handcuffs and Black Maria—and I have already thought: 'What a good thing it was I bought a nail-brush today.' I am sure one must live on nail-brushes in Holloway.

Give my love to Ottoline.

Do not forget—and do not store away in some dark place—but *remember* and *count* on all my heart. It's yours.

Tig

[1] Katherine's trepidation over the piano-man was due to the fact that she had purchased a piano under a hire-purchase agreement in 1910 and had not completed the payments.

To Wate.

Top Floor,

Ring 3. (If Bell out of Order Please

Sir,   do not Nock)

A highly Respecktable Party who as known the Best of Everythink in er Day and is ony come down in World threw no Fault of Same but Illness loss by Death an Marridge etc. would be greately obligded if Groun Floor dark Gent would *lend* Same for Reading only Essays by Wal. Pater.

No chilren and is Agreed Book Shall not leave House.

I Am

Yours Faithfully

Geo. Mungrove

On September 14, 1919, Katherine, L.M. and I left England for San Remo. Ostensibly, Katherine was to stay abroad for two years; but it was privately agreed between us that I should fetch her home in the following May. In the meantime I should try to find a house in the English country in which Katherine could live all the year round. This was to be 'the Heron'. It was the symbol of our faith in the future. Hence the recurrent concern with its furnishings.

It may seem difficult to reconcile Katherine's ardent longing to get out of England to the South with her still more ardent longing to settle in a home in England. It is equally difficult to reconcile her affection for and dependence upon L.M. with her passionate hatred of her. These contradictions, undoubtedly, had their roots (as she often suspected) in her disease; they were the forms taken by the fearful alternation between confidence and despair which are characteristic of the phthisic patient.

After a fortnight's search in and around San Remo, the only villa that was available to us was a little one on the hillside overlooking Ospedaletti. After seeing Katherine and L.M. installed in the Casetta Deerholm, I started to return to London on October 2, 1919. I was held up in Paris, and in Folkestone, by a sudden railway-strike.

3.30 p.m.   (October 3, 1919)

Darling,

Your card has just come. Figurez-vous my happy surprise. I am disgusted that you had the extra bother but *much* relieved to think you will be comfortable in the first-class express (or moderately so). Of course you couldn't have waited and then travelled in such a caterpillar. There is Felti[1] in the hall. Signs of you are everywhere. I jealously gathered your clothes and sent them to the donna bella this afternoon, making the list *myself*, so that no other hand should touch them. By this same post goes Swinnerton[2] to the office, written in spite of the flies. I hope it is all right. After you had gone, I coo-eed when I saw you on a part of the road which was visible—then, when I saw you at the station, I ran up to the bonne's bedroom and, remembering your old eyes, waved a *chemise!!* I felt sure you'd see.

No sign of water. I sent L.M. to phone. The agent says the people are *here* working but deep in the mountain like gnomes, and we may expect them to appear above ground tomorrow and the water the day *after*. No Mr. —— or Miss; they are frauds, and I've received their bill. They charged us 2.50 for those custards with our own eggs and milk. Oh, a plague on human beings, only you and I are really the right kind. Here is a letter from Rendall. Kot's parcel came today with a cheque for £1. The parcel contains sheets and sheets of translation to be 'ultimately published in book form in America'. What a bother!

L.M. refused lunch today, but only tore a piece of bread, she said she was not hungry. I did not get angry and later discovered her *having her lunch*. Proved at last! She *is* a silly. I'll not mind her, though. The sea is white, with silver fishes of light in it. The waves say Boge—Boge—as they come in. Yes, find the house. Yes, the 28 weeks will pass. Then comes our month of May, and after that our home. Eggs are to be had in Ospedaletti, good ones, and figs and mutton cutlets.

The good things that happen to you, you may leave untold if you like, but you are to tell me *all* the bad things that happen. Then I feel secure of your confidence and I don't worry, see?

I am going to start bang in on Mackenzie and Gilly[3]—so that I shall be a bit ahead. So send along some more books soon, please.

You will be in London when this reaches you and at home. Give it to Wing to sit on for a moment. Oh, darling Heart, *how* I love you. All must go well. I want to know about the house and Violet,[4] and if she really does all you require in the way you require. It's so hot. The

---

[1] A large grey felt hat which we possessed in common.
[2] A review of Frank Swinnerton's *September*.
[3] Reviews of novels by Compton Mackenzie and Gilbert Cannan.
[4] Violet and Gertie were the maids at 2 Portland Villas.

flies are eating me up. Oh, Bogey, you come up the steps, carrying the pail, a geranium in your waistcoat pocket. You are more loved than anybody in the world by your

Wig

Saturday,
(October 4, 1919)

By the time you get this it will be nearly the beginning of the 27th week.

Darling Bogey,

No letter from you yesterday. So far I've just had the two cards from Vintimille; I do hope for a line to catch on to from Paris, perhaps, this evening. The evening post goes *out* here 5.45, comes in after *six,* so I can't tell you whether or no I shall hear. *No* —— yesterday, of course, and *no* workman at the water job to-day; it is getting damned annoying. No locksmiff either. I think there are disadvantages in the Granville type.[1]

I am sitting outside in the bastick chair; it is a mild cloudy day. This morning was quite chilly—so was last night. Talk about the bounding horizon. . . . As I sit here I have to throw everything I write against it and it seems to me the pink geranium beats me out of hand. It is a lesson in humility to write *or* think with that sky there.

Where are you?

How are you?

When I know those things, and how you found everything, I shall feel really settled, but while you are en voyage I'm restless. You understand that? Augusta, the maid, has disappeared. She must have seen that furniture arriving.

L.M. has broke

(1) the big fruit dish
(2) our plate
(3) a saucer

all at one go, from leaning on the sideboard. I shall buy crocks here, but put them in your suit-case against the Goldene Zeit. And the worst of it is I always feel she thinks it 'so nice and homey' to occasionally smash a thing or two. You must keep me from getting overstern, overtrict and overtidy. It's an obsession. I realized it this morning. Even

[1] The publisher of Katherine's first book, *In a German Pension.*

316

out here I had to rearrange the pick, the shovel and the rake before I could do a thing—even though they were behind me. I hope I won't say to our darling little boy: 'As long as your mud-pies have *form*, darling, you can make them. But there must be no slopping over the mould.' He will like you best. You know how, when we get hungry, we are at least even unable to play Demon for wanting the hash-hammer to sound. That is precisely my state of mind *re* a letter from you to say you are at home. Once I've got it, sat down to talk with it, fed my soul on it, eaten every single scrap with all the appetite in the world, I fire ahead with other things. But you do understand, don't you, darling, that especially as affaires are si graves I am very specially anxious. We got perfect filet today for 2.75, a whack of meat with a bone attached and a kilo of peaches for 1.50. Your figs on the footstool are still there. I'll never eat them.

> My ros-ary—my ros-ary
> Each fig a pearl, each peach a prayer etc.

Forgive a silly. But I have decided to steal two of these wooden stools when we go home—one at each end of my big box. Be happy. Keep well. Tell me everything. Never spare me. Remember at odd moments how I love you and how happy we shall be. My very darling of darlings.

Wig

Sunday,

My own Love,
(October 5, 1919)

Still there is no news of you later than the 2 p.c.'s posted at Vinti-mille. This means you cannot have had the time to send me a p.c. in Paris, and yet that seems to me *queer*.[1] By the time you have this letter I shall have heard from you and my present anxiety will—please Heaven—be over. But since last evening when the last post brought nothing my anxiety has run away with me and it will not stop until I see your darling handwriting again. It seems so horribly mysterious. Not a line from you. There was a storm all last night, and today is strange and passionate. I can do nothing but wait. No further post today—none until tomorrow—and it's only midday here. Don't worry about this. You know how one feels. I live for letters when I am

---

[1] There was a railway strike in England, and I was stranded first in Paris and then in Folkestone.

away from you—*for* them, *on* them, *with* them. It's as though you had gone to San Remo, and train after train passed and I go out and lean over the fence with the cotton plant and wait to see my darling at the bottom of the hill, and he isn't there. But don't remember this. Only remember how I shall rejoice and be made new again when your letter comes.

Sunday today. Now there are only 27 Sundays. Oh God! send May along quickly. I can wait *perfectly* if I have letters, but I tremble when you are en voyage and silence falls. It's no good saying 'Wire me'. I know you realize my anxiety and that's all. I'll write about other things when I've heard. All is well here outwardly. I keep my anxiety hidden —but there it is. No good pretending it isn't.

Your longing wife
Wig

Casetta Deerholm, Ospedaletti,
(Monday, October 6, 1919)

Your postcard from Paris has just come. Why it has taken so long God only knows. I felt certain you'd have sent me one from there, yet yesterday I gave up all hope of getting one—indeed of hearing at all until you were back in London. I feel quite different with this postcard. When I die, just before the coffin is screwed up, pop a letter in. I shall jump up and out. . . .

L.M. has broken my thermometer. *Good.* I got another for 12 francs, which seems to play the same tune, though the notes are not so plain. 'I was pulling your cupboard away from the nets and it just rolled on to the floor.' I suppose in Rhodesia you just have notches on a bamboo or a tchetchetchetche branch.

I have been out since 9 o'clock. The sea is divine. It's very hot. All last night I chased the midges Buzzing in the nets afar Each one bearing, as it kindled, Message of the open war. (Macaulay) It's perfect except for the 'afar'. They are a scourge here, now; in hundreds. On dit that they will go when the fruit goes, and that flowers in the house are fatal for them. Well, what a silly country!

I started a big story yesterday. I don't think it's very good, but I am going straight on with it, whatever it is like, just for the practice and for getting into my stride. . . .

My Boge,

I have just had an interview with a bonne who does not speak 1 word of French—a pretty, nice, awfully nice girl with pearly teeth. What *she* said, what *I* said, I really don't know.

Me: La lettiere nonne arrivato attendre duo giorni venuto Bordighera?

She: Si, si, cuisino.

Me: Oh, dear, what a bother!

She: Si, si, dimano-sabbato.

I finally gave her a letter in French for the woman at the dairy to translate, and off she went. When (to make it plain) I showed her the empty room with two coat-hooks and a sheepskin in it, she seemed to think it was superbly furnished. 'Bono, bono, molto bono!' A sort of Maori haka! Wise old Feltie, listening in the hall, is still shaking with laughter at your Wiggy.

I think she is just the person—young, strong, pretty, with black, laughing eyes, a bit grubby, but only *de la terre*, a kind of Italian Marie[1] of a lower class. She gave a little half curtsey when we parted. What will come of it? She also wrote on a bit of paper, *Da muni vineri si.* Whether that means she is coming or that she is fond of wine I am still not certain. . . .

It's a lovely morning. I am working and very happy. It's hot—grilling. I think I shall have a pet lizard here. L.M. said a *sissida* (cicada) was buzzing round her electric light all last night. What do you say to that?

Sitting here, I have had your most disturbing p.c.[2] If only you had some money. Isn't this just our luck? I shall be more than eager for the letter saying you are safe home. Oh, Bogey, you'll borrow from Valéry, I hope—you'll not go without. Wish I knew more.

I had a letter from S. today which really boxed it. I mean, he said it was only my 'indomitable will' (!) which kept me alive this last year, and he is sure I shall now get absolutely well and 'grow into your dream of achievement'. This, of course, makes me feel *cicatrisé* all over and also rouses my pride. I *will*.

He also says he has been at our house twice and got no reply. Kot said the same. When I read that I felt very suspicious of Violet and

---

[1] The bonne at the Villa Pauline in 1916.　　　　[2] About the strike.

319

Gertie and that they have played us false. It can't be true. Is it? I had a horrid moment when it seemed so.

We got excellent butter today from Ospedaletti and fresh haricots verts and figs and two perfect whacks of mutton (2.50). There is a vegetable and fruit stall there which seems to supply all needs. No sign of Mr. or Mrs. ——, no cart 'with the other things'—no water. L.M. is going to phone as she posts this. I expect he is in prison. That's always my idea. I have been out all day and feel burnt. That table is excellent for writing. Oh, I do wish you were home and settled in. Then I shall be at rest about you. Take care of that precious self of yours. The sea dances, the olives dance with tiny flickering leaves. . . .[1]

Tuesday,

(October 7, 1919)

The pages are rather groggily numbered because I am outside and I haven't any blotting paper. Kiss Wing for me on his head.

My own,

A workman has come who says they will have finished their part of the job today and after that it's only a matter of quelques jours before the water is turned on here. Wonderful people! It's another summer day. As the waves break they are full of gold, like the waves we saw at Bandol. This early morning (6.30) the sea was *pink,* pale pink—I never saw it so before—and it scarcely breathed. . . . The washer-woman brought home your clothes last night (yes, the change of subject isn't a really absurd change. I'd think the pink sea all the lovelier if it had a boat in it with your blue shirt for a sail.) I have just put the clothes away among mine—and the carnation sachets. There are tiny false links in your cuffs which impressed me greatly. Here they are waiting for you.

The insect plague is *simply awful.* No nets or veils will keep them out. I am bitten to death. The tiny, almost invisible ones, who are so deadly, the laundress tells me are called 'păpĕtechīkŏs.'

(Zuccinis are not cucumbers. They are a kind of elongated pale yellow marrows. L.M. bought one yesterday. I don't at all see why we should not grow them in Sussex.) I am longing to get out of the garden and make a small tour of Ospedaletti. Every day a new shop seems to arise; and the butcher is evidently a fascinating man. But I

[1] The remainder of this letter, written in poor ink, has become indecipherable.

shall stick to the garden for the present and get my cough down. I feel
wonderfully better, wonderfully stronger. I feel myself walking about
like a normal person at times—quite lightly and quickly. Soon it will
always be like that.

The olives are ripe and beginning to fall.

Shall I have a letter today, Boge? No, not till tomorrow, says my
sensible head, but *Wig* says Perhaps. I hope I'll get more novels quickly,
for the last 2 go today. They make very excellent *pasta* here—very
fresh. I think it's much better for shopping than San Remo. It's not
cheap to feed very well, and I think it will cost us 30/- a head per week
for food. That is really dearer than London. Of course, the amount of
butter and eggs and milk is not normal. If one were well, one could do
it on 25 fr. each, but not. . . .

I keep the strictest accounts so that we shall know for another time.
All the while I keep wondering how you are—and the house and
WING and the office and the weather and Violet. Are you warm enough?
Do you feel hard up? How is Richard? Give the old boy my love; he's
part of our family—not yours, not mine, but our special family tree

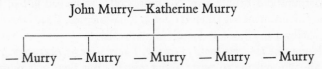

John Murry—Katherine Murry

— Murry — Murry — Murry — Murry — Murry

(Oh, Wig, how stupid!) No, I'd like that. They would be so useful in
the garden. . . .

Corporal Love-in-a-Mist is coming out in that place in the garden.

You have all my heart and I am yours.

A week today. 27 weeks to go.   Wednesday,

My own,   (October 8, 1919)

Ida had to go to town late last night and returned with your first
letter from home. *This was breath of life to me,* to know that your
journey was over. Was Pa's account of the revolution all my eye? For
how did you get to Hampstead? It's puzzling. I am very interested in
Betts[1] and his garden-Bett (joke!) I believe every word. My speciality
will be Italian tomatoes and Italian things like marrows. They'd sell in
England, you bet. (Oh dear, *no,* not again!) 'My lord, she hath been
eating honeycomb.'

[1] A steward who put me up for the night in Folkestone.

Precious little Wing! Keep him. I shall see him again, after all; and all the tears I shed for him here were in vain, bless his nose! I see him grubby and a bit hungry. But I grudge his whole little derrière on your letter.[1] He must only write with the tip of his tail. You sounded tired, my darling. Was there food for you? Was the house in good order? Fancy Violet not having my letter. You mean tho' my last letter, not my Sydney one, don't you?

It is awfully hot here—as hot as when we came. The insects are *simply awful*. It's a good thing you left before they got really bad. My leg is so swollen I can only hop today. It is maddening because otherwise I feel so well and strong. Curse these confounded countries!! We have double nets, powder, bathe in verbena, oatmeal, milk, salt water, fresh—but nothing cures them. I think they make the idea of a life in this country absolutely insupportable. Enough of them.

I took the revolver into the garden today and practised with it: how to load and unload and fire. It terrifies me, but I feel 'like a new being' now that I really can handle it and understand it. I'll never give it back. They are fascinating things; one is childishly fascinated. I almost understand old Brontë *père*. No more coffee to be had in San Remo. The Government has taken it over as it has the rice. Dear knows when we shall get any more. It doesn't matter really.

Please send me some books to review. I have none for next week. Dearest of all, you tell me to write about myself. But then you must write about yourself. That is only fair. I want to know about YOU.

L.M. waits to take this to the post. I am going to look at my plants. I found some lovely roots in the lower garden which, like the wedding-guests, are being put up higher.

Look here! I am so much better that I feel like your old goblin girl. In spite of the bites, my S. of F. hunger is coming back again. So you must take care of yourself and be my goblin Boy.

Love, dearest heart—all my love for ever.

Wig

Friday,
(October 10, 1919)

I wish Wing could write letters. I should set him papers of questions and give him prizes for full answers. The weather is marvellous, like

[1] Wingley had been lost before we left England. He was sitting on my note-paper when I wrote, so I wrote my letter round him.

silk—very hot and still. People are bathing below. It's so clear one can see their legs and arms, almost their toes. This house is rather like a fairy house. It is an adorable place to live in—and then the garden—and the view of Ospedaletti is exquisite. The view is for ever subtly changing. It's far more beautiful and remote than Pauline. The fact, too, that one is for ever conscious of this huge expanse of sea. . . . God knows I don't want to live here, but for a place to get well in, it could not be more ideal.

L.M. is off to San Remo to see if she can find a *litre* of fine muslin. Just as I thought, she loves that jaunt in, and 'You don't mind, Katie, now you have your revolver, do you?' No, I don't. . . .

Later
There is *no* letter from you today. I expect with luck there will be *something*, at any rate, tomorrow. One came from —— for my birthday containing her *wishes* and that's all. So you needn't bother to say what I would like. Ida has returned from San Remo and is making tea. The workmen have gone and *water flows*. A man climbed on to the roof and the deed was done. The sound of the plug is rare music. I have been walking up and down the garden, having a rest from work and thinking of you. My morning letter to you was scattered. Forgive it. All the while, as you know, with my daily life, but running deep and true and silent is my life with you which is the *living* part of me. If I fly from one odd thing to another you must know the other is still there and depend on it. For it is my religion and defence and all that keeps life possible. Love, dearest Love, only you and I know what it means. The letters from other people who are in the other world and never have known ours jar me so—and at the same time they make me feel how wonderful we *are* and *have been* and shall be. You, my noble angelic Boy (I am sincere)—how could I love you enough. I could not —not if I had fifty pairs of lungs.

Still later. I have opened the letter to say:
Ida went to the Banque d'Italie today with another letter from me. They have been told nothing—so they must be given up. She then went to Benecke with £1 to cash for herself: they gave her 40 francs. She took my £5 to the Italian Bank, at the corner of the Via Colombia, who gave her 41 francs for each £1. Last week Benecke gave 39 to the £1 and this same bank 40. What am I to do? I must have this decided

pretty soon because my purse begins to show its lining. Advise me please, my little lawyer in chief. Isn't it a bother? I have decided what to send you by ———some of those chemises de Byron OR polo shirts you liked so. The extra 5 lire will be the first egg in the nest for the Heron.

   Darling
    precious
     Boge

     No. 5 Tuesday letter and Wednesday morning letter
         both received and this is only
             Saturday,
My dearest,   (October 11, 1919)

Just a line more. I've got three letters this afternoon: it's a perfect festa today—those before my Swinnerton review fetched up. Would to G. I had some books. But I'll write something for this week and post as usual on Tuesday.

(1) I long to know about the house (*two words indecipherable*)

(2) I am very glad you saw Pa. I send you his letter. Please note *re* Bank of Italy. What is this game? In future I shall do as you advise and get Kay to send my money per registered insured post. I wouldn't mind if he came for a fortnight. I can always plead fatigue and do my work.

Don't go to ——— unless you can help. You'd be miserable. They are not *ours*.

I'd love to see Dent's old ladies—love to any time. Please tell him. I am beginning to feel so dreadfully affectionate, just en l'air. Not for any one I know particularly—but just that I'd so like to be very nice to old ladies from Nice.

Tell Tommy[1] we have small and big flies by day—that the mosquitoes are of various kinds—some really poisonous. They raise a great swelling, others big blisters. It's just as bad as his old place. Give him also my love.

This was to have been just a line. I had a sweet letter from Violet,

---

[1] H. M. Tomlinson.

telling me about the cats and you, asking whether you'd like anything special in your saucer.

> Dear Bogey,
> Dearest Bogey,
> Darling precious Bogey,
>   Yours for ever
>   Wig

Treasure brought to shore today. Monday night's letters No. 3, No. 4 Lytton's letter.   Saturday,

My precious own,   (October 11, 1919)

When I got up this morning, I put on my hat first and as soon as the food had been arranged, went out for a small walk. The day was so— what *can* one say? there isn't a word, perfect is not enough—that I had to go. First thing I saw was a large daisy at the bottom of our steps, in a pinafore—you know the kind, a Wingley flower. Then I walked along the Boulevard which smelled of pines, gum trees, heliotrope, geraniums and a dash of the sea, and really had a look at Ospedaletti. But Bogey! I hadn't the faintest *idea* of what it was like. It's just a fairy tale; that's all. And the country above and beyond it—these immense romantic glimpses! I sauntered along, gripping Mother's walking-stick. My heart was bursting with happiness. The sun had his arm round my shoulder. The sea made a sound you would have liked. There was a breeze that filled one's mouth with pleasure like wine does. Hardly anybody about. A small scene from an opera being enacted at the one cabstand between two lovely girls carrying baskets of fringed linen on their heads, a boy in a blue undervest eating a loaf of bread, and the cab-driver in white. That was all.

Then I keep coming to these glimpses of the old town, seen between the trees, and then to pine trees with rose-red geraniums climbing up to their topmost branch. The only work being done was gardening. One heard people gardening and felt them gardening, and that was all. By the time I got to the Poste I knew something very good was going to happen, and three letters were handed across. You know that row of darling little oleanders [a drawing of one]—little trees like that. I sat on a bench beneath and read them and then walked off clasping them very hard and stopping occasionally and saying to a bush or a plant, 'Darling!' very quietly.

325

Really, when you come in May I dread to think of what we shall do. When it's Spring here, as well as everything else. You see, we shall trundle off with our *filet* in the morning, and then we'll come home ravenous like I did and see this little house as I did perched on the hill half in sun, half swept by the dancing shadow of the olive-trees. And there will be flowers everywhere.

I didn't feel in the least tired. I stopped at the drug store and bought four bottils of St. Galmier: it wasn't a luxury. I think one needs to drink here, especially while the skeeters are so skeeterish. Such a nice woman in there, extremely pretty, and awfully nice jujubes on the counter. Blow! everything was awfully nice. Beams came from the toothbrushes. She says it is like this all the winter except for an occasional day of wind or rain, just as hot, and people who come *pour se reposer* go away on wings. Cherry pie grows in trees in the jardin publique at Ospedaletti. Did you *see* that wonderful park-like place with all its flowers? Lawrence was working in the garden with a handkerchief round his neck.

Well, Bogey, *I* don't know—but really we seem to have found the most ideal place we could have found. I can *whistle* again.

Look here! Won't May be perfect? Remember May. Hug the thought of it: it's going to be our new life.

(1) I am so glad about Violet.

(2) As you face it,[1] the left-hand back leg is the one to prop with a match-end and a French stamp folded small. Both front legs must be off the ground.

(3) I think much the best plan is to come home early in the afternoon. I wish you would. Then you can change, and put on your slippers, and have a good fire and tea, and not feel you have to go out again. . . . See?

(4) Everything is now done except the lock on the door. —— came yesterday with still more linen. We shall lie in fair sheets in May. He will persist in wanting to bring *more* carpets—a set of *lovely* blue china ornaments, tapestry etc. 'I feel I can't make it nice enough for Mrs. Murry.' He's a good soul after all. I've turned again.

(5) Augusta has disappeared. Half the town is looking out for another. There's no hurry: it keeps L.M. quiet, but she's a most rotten cook. However, she *learns*. Perhaps it is because I am always hungry—even had to eat bread and butter in bed last night.

[1] Katherine's Shepherdess clock.

Please send me BOOKS, and if you don't do something about poor little Wig's money soon, she will not 'have a bean left'. I'm still at the long story. It makes me *groan,* but I must do it. It's a form of practising to get back.

Must start a new page after all because I wondered if you would ever publish a column 'From a Note Book'. It is going to be called 'From the Casetta', and it's a kind of day book about things like flies or a certain light or a fragment of talk over a table or workmen going home in the evening. . . . I want to write a whole book—ready in six months—of these . . . *observations.* I quite understand if you don't want them, dearest.

Wasn't Lytton's letter a nice one? Queer how some people seem to *see* things: I thought that a *bad* review. Oh, Bogey, it is cruel to say how warm it is here. I never saw anything like the shadows in this house cast by the delicate trees outside. I have already noticed 5 different grasshoppers. They are great favourites of mine as insects: they are such *characters.* As for the cicada, every night he is here. I can't tell you how good the stove is here. It is a gem, now that it is accustomed to go. Yesterday, when L.M. was out, I made my tea with about 2 leaves and a twig and the whole kitchen felt so warm and lived in.

Forgive a drunken girl who loves you and you alone. I am so glad you are finishing *Cinnamon and Angelica.* Please let me know if you have other plans.

A warm warm hug. A big kiss—love enough to last all the winter through.

Your own

Wig

Tell Wing how much I love you. See he doesn't catch cold after his bath. You ought to buy him a tiny Jaeger woolly.

Sunday,

My own Bogey,   (October 12, 1919)

I am sitting in the Bastick chair covered with the Jaeger rug, as although the sun is hot the air is chilly (it's about 4.45 p.m.) It has been a marvellous day here; I've not moved except for meals. I've been reading and writing, and after lunch I fell asleep from the general *shipboard* atmosphere. Speaking of ships, such a small jewel of a sailing ship passed the house today, riding close enough in to see the men on board.

She had two small sails at the bows, one big one at the stern, and a medium *very* movable one amidships. The sea is my favourite sea, bright, bright blue, but showing a glint of white as far as one can see. That lift of white seen far away, as far as the horizon, moves me terribly. In fact it is *the very thing* I would like to express in writing: it has *the very quality*. Here comes another most interesting little steamboat —a very small trader, she looks, painted black and red, with a most ridiculous amount of smoke coming out of the funnel. [A drawing of the steamer.] No, I can't draw her.

From where I sit, I cannot see any ground below the balustrade. That is threaded through with sea. One would think it was a sheer drop from there into deep water. What a place, eh, Bogey?

I had a nasty jar last night. As there was no water last week, the laundry was put 'out' and it came home exquisite, covered with a white net with a rose on top, carried by the nicest old body on her head, who seemed to take the greatest fancy to me, as I did to her. *Long* conversation. 'Comme vous êtes bien ici,' etc., etc., etc., etc. And under all this a bill for 37.85!! This, of course, after the old 'un had gone and the rose had been smelled admired and Wig had thought how *much* better, after all, they order these things in Italy. L.M. did not really 'think it very heavy. I don't think you could have expected it to be less, Katie'. This with her overall 4.50 and an immense white petti-coat 3.85! As to serviettes at 1 lira apiece, 'Oh well, my dear, that's not quite sixpence if the exchange is still at 41 for £1. It's about . . . let me see . . . hardly fivepence,' and so on and so on and so on. How I should beat her if I were married to her! It's an awful thought. She thinks I'm made of money. That's the worst of it! On her last but one journey to San Remo she bought *one* hecto of coffee for 4.50 from '*such* a funny little shop' and when I protested she thought 'the parcel was small for the money, but the beans felt very tightly packed'. Could you believe it? However,—let her go. And I shall never shoot her because the body would be so difficult to dispose of after. One couldn't make it into a neat parcel or put it under a hearth stone, and she would *never* burn.

Every day I love this house more for some new grace, and every day I hold a minute review of the garden, and there is always some-thing fresh and wonderful. Then there is the wild hill, never the same, *satisfying* one's deep love for what is living and ancient in literature. I look at the hill, dearest Bogey, and because I have not had a classical education, it seems to me full of the spirit of those old boys—the wild fig and olive, the low-growing berries and the tufts of sweet roots. . . .

This is a place for lovers. (Hullo! there goes a swallow.) Yes, it is made for lovers. You know, don't you, how even now I am preparing it for you. I look at it and think: I shall put net curtains here—and the baskets under the verandah shall be flower-baskets and——. It's enough to keep me busy until May, my very own. Another Sunday. That's two gone—now there are only 26.

Yours for ever and ever amen

Monday,

My Precious, (October 13, 1919)

The weather has completely changed. It's chilly with a thick, thick fog and heavy downpour of rain. The sky is grey. It's like living inside a pearl today—very lovely, for a change.

The October 10 number of the paper I have just gone through. Good Heavens! How good it is! What different eyes, different hair to the little measles that came out all spotty while you were away. *This one simply thrills me.* I'll have to get a flagstaff in this garden and when I've read my copies through, fly them—just out of pride. The leading article was excellent—it went so well. I think one ought to begin by—not knocking the reader down exactly but by showing him 'who is master of the house', as Wilkie's girl would say. Scott-James, too, is admirably to the point, and it's a very good article to have. Sheppard is one of your most valuable men, I think—an excellent mellow quality in what he writes and, altogether—just what the *A.* can publish so well.

I wish the first letter from America had not been so particular. It's first-chop to have secured it, but we don't really care so passionately about Mr. Kreymborg—do you think? I do so love a general *survey* or at any rate an ordnance map—before I visit the various paths and farms. Now and again this chap gives me the idea he could write very well.

Most excellent letter from Italy, I thought, and awfully good dramatic criticism of Tolstoy—so *fresh.* In fact, the whole appearance, contents, everything has form and substance again. You are evidently a genius as an editor—nothing short of that: a perfect genius. I adore working for you, but I do *wish* you'd send me some novels. I am sending an article tomorrow on some novels here, in the bookcase, but it's a bit steep to be left without a single one.

Yes, the paper is a noble paper, my son: it most certainly is. I don't know what to do. I am so damned proud of you, you little marvel. I feel, if only I had some books here I *would* write a review, and that's what all your team feel, I believe. What about Ripmann?[1] Have you ever thought of him again as a possible contributor—an article on languages, or the *production of books,* He is a very great nut on printing and so on.

L.M. has surpassed herself today. At 1.30 I staggered in to ask where the lunch was, and it was *not.* She had *no kindling,* and the olive root won't burn with just paper. After all these days when every afternoon she is up in the hills, roaming the pastures wild. *Then* there were no eggs—then she boiled the coffee in the water she had prepared for spaghetti—reeking with *gros sel.* I got a bit fierce, but I apologised at once, and really I don't get upset by her at all now. I think she is *very queer,* though. You know that lovely room of hers with that view. . . . I asked her yesterday why she didn't make it nice, and she said she hadn't unpacked 'as you are sending me away in April and at any rate my room is just a passage—isn't it?—to the lavatory'.

Visitor last night. A *very* nice one. While I was waiting for the beans, I saw two honey-ball eyes looking at me from the hall. (The front door was open.) When they saw me, they *flashed* away, but I immediately said as much Wing language as I knew and went quietly to the door with my soup plate. A perfectly lovely tiny cat came in, *gold, white* and *black,* with a body rather like a rabbit. It simply bolted the stray pasta: then I gave it some milk, and it simply more than bolted that. Then it purred more loudly than any cat I've ever heard. Its purring machine must have been wound up until that moment. It sat under a chair singing like this for a little, and then fled into the night again. In my mind I called it 'Genêt'.

I have just looked up. The fog has rolled away. The rain has stopped. The air smells of the geraniums. Tomorrow the gardener comes for the day; the ground will be just right for sowing. There are carts going by. *Yip-y-y-y-ip-yip,* say the drivers and the bells go *tring-tring-tring.* The sea sounds as though it were somehow exquisitely refreshed by that mist; all the grass-blades are bowed down by a diamond. Oh dear, I'm awfully happy. It has been so lovely lying here in the rain. I feel renewed, too, and bowed down with a diamond, too, I love you. I love

---

[1] Walter Ripmann who, as Professor at Queen's College, had influenced Katherine greatly.

you. Shall I have a letter by the late post? Oh, Bogey, look at the new leaves on the rose bushes—bright red. Were they there yesterday? There is one hidden frog here; he croaks every evening. He shall be invited to the festa in May.

Isn't this rotten paper? It's oiled in places, and you can't write on both sides really.

After all a birthday present came from —— and ——. An ordinary small 1d. match-box, enamelled yellow and painted (very badly) with an ugly little Chinaman. Oriental Department 1/11¾. 'To our darling Katie with our united love and best wishes.' They couldn't have said more if it was a carpet. I shall keep this match-box for ever and measure the size of their hearts by it.

Goodbye, most precious.

Bites are still going strong. Does Tommy know a fly—just like an ordinary house-fly in the face, that stings? *It is here.*

And now I hug you tight and hold you a minute.

Wig

No letter. Weekly Times. A for October 3 and the 10th, Narina fetched up.

Monday,
(October 13, 1919)

My precious little Husband (This title is reserved for State Occasions)

It is not only that the spoon is the most exquisite perfect little spoon, a spoon that faeries might go to battle for—a spoon that fascinates—that just to hold and turn and balance and feel is a joy—it is over and above these things a sign between us—a secret message from our real house. It is come from the tea-table on the southern terrace, where we sit, idle, drinking tea, and there it lies winking bright in the late sun. And it shall be the spoon our own little boy shall eat his first strawberry and cream out of, standing by you, clutching your knees while you prepare the marvellous dish and make eyes at him. Ah, the darling! Ah, *both my darlings!* All this and more the little spoon brings.

October 14th. No. 6 Wednesday No. 7 Birthday letter Thursday both here.

My precious,

You see that spoon came a day early even though it was registered—just to please us. It won't happen again. These are two Letters Extraordinary from you. Letters with icing, candles, marzipan, cupids and sugar Wingleys on them with angelica eyes. They *are* my birthday. Next one—where shall we be? We shall be in our own home, eating off Italian plates, drinking out of honey-coloured fluted cups. But stop! You are nice enough. Don't be any sweeter, more adorable, more Bogey-like, more precious, more cherished than you are—or I shall fly off into a shower of stars.

I *note* the saucepans. It was high time we had them. I hope they were not 2 dear. Violet will give them a mother's care, I expect, and not leave them to cook themselves only. Fancy Sydney being there.[1] May fortune favour the arrangement! See that you both eat enough. Do get home to tea as often as you can.

Fancy 2nd the Moults to dinner on Wednesday. That thrills me. I see you at the top serving or *not* serving or serving with your own spoon and then licking it afterwards, and Wing under the table playing a tune on Sydney's shoe-laces. Oh dear!

I send what I have penned. But I cannot make up every week. Where are the novels? How disgraceful it is! Conduct an inquiry! Have some menial burned!

You ask me how I am.

Oh, first, about my other birthday presents. Told you about the 1d. match-box, didn't I? That curve over 1d. is a *fling* of disdain. Thank heaven, I've scratched a bit off the Chinaman's hat already. Then L.M. gave me a bottil of *Genêt fleuri*. Wasn't it remarkable? The chemist had it *here*—same bottil and all. It must have cost an awful lot. Well, I've given her the money for this month—and it's a heavenly scent—and that's all I got. Father sent me a communication not mentioning it, so all my fervour has gone to nothing so far. I thought my opinions on the Labour Crisis were good for a fiver—but *no*. He gave Marie £10 on hers. Isn't it *awful minge*? Never mind. . . It is a brilliant glancing day.

You should have seen after the rain was over yesterday, little old men appeared from nowhere in peaked hats, crawling over the wild hill looking for snails. They carried coloured handkerchieves which *frothed*. Flowers are coming up everywhere on the hill. I just went for a glance today—not more than five steps high, and there were 8 kinds there.

Caterina came yesterday (the pretty one from the laundry). She brought me vivid pink carnations and two eggs in cotton wool for a

---

[1] Sydney Waterlow now lived with me at 2 Portland Villas.

present. But I felt she could afford to. All the same, she was fearfully nice—laughing, gay, beautiful, *healthy* creature. She says May here is magnifique beyond anything. The whole place is covered with flowers, and all the little kinds *pour les distillations* are out—tiny hyacinths, violets, small roses.

Well, now I'll tell you about myself. I feel marvellously better. All that remains is my cough. It has bad moments still, but that terrible boiling sensation when I can't stop, I haven't had *once* since you left. Nor have I *once* had a temperature. I get short of puff if I cough, but my lungs don't hurt at all. The pain in my joints is—well, it's not outwardly better, yet I feel it is. So it is evidently on the mend. Think of last October 14th. Sydney Beauchamp came,[1] and at night I had fever in that North Room and thought I was going to die.

Here's Ida for my letter. She's off to San Remo for supplies. Tram waiting.

> Yours for ever
> Wig

> Wednesday,
> (October 15, 1919)

No. 8 Saturday letter. Two books, *Weekly Times* and *Nation* all here.

My Blessed Bogey,

I am in the middle of a review of Brett Young[2] which I will post tomorrow to the office unregistered. I had just ready for the post an article on a non-existent novel called *A Fine Day,* by Emilia Lanteri, published by Paolo Littardi, Milan—but these books came and did the trick. I'm thankful to have them. The Brett Young is interesting, too, from the reviewing standpoint and the other has an interesting preface —so that's O.K. The Banca d'Italia acknowledges me—so I can get money. Also good. I don't want *any* of your old money—not a crumb. Never dare to send it me. I am very glad that K.M. is liked a bit. She wishes she was more worthy. That's *sincere* from my soul. But whenever I'm praised I always want to fall on my knees and ask God to make me a better girl. It just takes me that way.

I saw and shuddered at the *Lit. Sup.* campaign. Very fierce. And how awful about *The Mercury.* You bet we won't be asked. But it means a pull, doesn't it? I'll send you extras as soon as I can for my part. I wish

---

[1] Katherine's second cousin, a lung specialist, who examined her then.

[2] *The Young Physician,* by F. Brett Young.

we could do the Drama together. I feel there we could collaborate and be perfect wonders. I LONG to see your notice. Fancy you and Richard sitting there watching it; it's so lovely where Portia and Jessica meet their men at the end. I want an order form for your book; every copy tells. So please tell Richard to send me one immediate.

That Wing! What a fellow he is! I wish you could bring him in May, but he would eat his way out of a suitcase just as you were in the Customs office. How I would love to kiss him! It's only L.M. who had a bad influence on Athenæum; he'll be all right now.

Yesterday ended in such a blazing glory of a sunset that I was quite frightened. It really was the most superb day, and at night (all the windows open) the sea sounded like an immense orchestra; I could truly hear violins, especially, and great rushing passages for the wood-wind. The skeeters drank my blood last night, and I'm awfully bitten today—but to death—both hands, one face, and one leg.

You know, I can't write letters here—only to you. Other people are not when I'm away. I am very glad you are going walking with Eliot; perhaps you'll tell me about it. And what kind of food do you have? And how are the household bills? And won't you and Sydney share in a dinner wine? The Australian Wine Company's address was on my table; it's so good in winter to drink wine at least once a day, and you need it. You have no vitality to spare, as you know, and you bolster up the lack of it with your WILL, which is a big strain on you. Health, darling, as we BOTH know is really cheap at any price.

Food here is much better. I am dead nuts on *pasta*. We eat it once a day, and for 2.50 to 3 lire we get quite good meat. Is that a great deal of money, do you think? Z.b. we get two veal cutlets for 3 lire; that seems to *me* reasonable. Last week my bills were huge, but then net for a new mosquito net and £3 for L.M. and the laundry came in, but even with all this I shall manage admirably on [my] money *and* save. So that when you come there will be a lovely nest egg ready for spending—you and I together.

I wish I was more of a stoic about under-linen, perfumes, little boxes for a toilet table, delicate ribbons and silk stockings. But the older I grow, the more exquisite I want to be, *fine* down to every minutest particular, as a writer, as a talker, in my home, in my life, and all my ways—to carry it all through. Even now sometimes, when I write to you, a word shakes into the letter that I don't mean to be there, an old windfall, you know, from a tree in an orchard I've long forsaken. . . .

334

Do you know what I mean? It is my illness which has made me so bad-tempered at times. Alas! one can't fight without getting battle-stained, and, alas! there have been so many occasions when I've never had time to wash away the stains or renew myself, but have come to you just as I was. You must forget these *melancholy, melancholy things,* my own precious darling.

A year ago I thought I was going to die, and I think I *was.* And now I know we are going to live. Don't let's forget how Sorapure has helped. I really think I should just have died in that room upstairs if he had not taken me by the hand, like you take a little girl who is frightened of a dog, and led me up to my pain and showed it me and proved it wasn't going to eat me. That's what he did.

I must go on with my review, my own. I am glad Sydney is there now; it 'makes a difference' to hear another step on the stairs and to have someone at meals. How soon can you get any anthracite?

Bogey, I am getting *absolutely well*; there's no doubt about it, no doubt at all. You see I live in the open air all day long and at night I practically sleep in it. I shall see Ansaldi next week and tell you what he says. But don't even have the ghost of a worry about me. Dismiss me as a worry.

Oh dear, on the wild hill today I found thyme and rosemary—it reminded me of Bandol in the early morning. Very large astonished daisies are beginning to flower everywhere, even in the gravel. The cotton-pods are huge. Exquisite pale yellow butterflies flutter by. The Marygolds unclosèd are.

Goodbye for now. I love you more than ever now I am 31.

                                                                                Wig

A huge fawn-coloured rat just ran over the verandah. Tell Wing.

Did you see the easy chair advertised in *The Nation* to be bought of Waring and Gillow for £4 10 0? It seems that prices are going down.

26 weeks only. No nuffin.   Thursday.

My own Precious,   (October 16, 1919)

My review is just finished, too, thank goodness. L.M. is off to post. There was no letter today. I have been so spoilt lately that I expect one every day and then the post punishes me.

It's bitterly cold, pouring with rain, a hard, heavy wind blowing and the sky like an iron shutter. 4.30 and the light is on. I went outside this morning but was blown in again, and I've been writing at the dining room table. My little table is too small. I am so thankful after all that I brought really warm clothes. *On a besoin.* Today—thick jaegers, jersey and cardigan, and deux pantalons.

That cat I made such a fuss about got in the larder last night and stole our meat. It sprang in the window today again and looked like a devil when I shooed it away. I shall have *no* cats here. And *she* has broken our glass jug. Well, well. First thing I saw was the fragments outside the back door. It can't be helped. She said, 'It was very frail from the beginning.' I suppose one would make the same excuse if one dropped and broke a baby! I hope my review is all right. I feel far away when I am writing—as though I am being confusing, you can't *hear me.* It makes me anxious.

Heavy thunder prowls round the sky. Now it is sunset, and the shutter of the sky lifts to show one bright band of gold. I am just a little bit tired; it is the weather—the thunder and sudden intense *heavy* cold like lead. Oh, what a good idea! I'll drink a glass of wine. . . . Getrunken. Really, England is never colder than this today. Now it is hailing, enormous hail. I'd like to be in Sussex, Bogey, and very, very *snug.* But don't think I'm depressed, my own darling Boge; I'm not—only *so* parky after such a long taste of heavenly fair climate. And very angry because in spite of the cold the mosquitos and gnats persist; both my hands are bandaged today. Why don't they die? L.M. caught one today and put it out of window instead of killing it! I expect they've passed the word round that this house is an *asile* for them.

Give me a very tight small hug and then hold me close till I am warm. Until tomorrow, my treasure.

Your
Wig

Friday,
My own Precious, (October 17, 1919)

The four pounds and letters (that is your Sunday letter) both arrived last night and filled me with warmth and light again. I ate a large dinner, went to bed with a hot bottil, and had coffee, bread and honey there *ad libitum.* Today the sun is shining in the sky: it is real winter again and, though the sun is warm, the wind blows in it and through it and you have to wrap you very lively. I think winter has come for

good. I've a feeling it has, at least as much winter as we have here—
and I am sure it will be cold whatever they have told us.

Last night's letter was just—just the letter I wanted. It told me
everything—all about Violet and the house. I *lapped* it up. Zuccini is
good to look at *and* good to eat. You remember it? What we called
cowcumber and even saw the seeds. When it's not cooked it's about
twice the size of a cowcumber and it's pale yellow. We have got our
sugar all right. I wish we could get rice, but it does not exist. The other
foodstuffs seem abundant, though; the butter here is excellent. I find
the Bank of Italy charges 1 lira in every pound, so I shall do as you
suggest—get £25 a month from Kay. It was like you to send that £5.
And what a picture of you, running out of the office, trying to hide
twenty books all in a pile, like a conjuror's boy, tripping on the stairs
or bumping into Bernard Shaw, and then buying half a pair of blankets!
Oh, dear, how *nice* you are, Bogey! My eyes have gone all bloodshot;
I am resting them today; it's trop de soleil—nothing. So I am looking
at the flowers instead—just for a change.

And I love love love you

Your

Wig

Friday,

Dearest of All,   (October 17, 1919)

I had just given your letter to L.M. to post, I had put on my cape,
and after walking through the rooms and thinking how delicious
apples and pot au feu smelt when they were cooking ensemble, I went
to the door to see the sunset. Up our steps came Caterina with a
gardener in tow. (Caterina has established herself a kind of guardian
here. She it was who brought me the eggs in cotton wool and the pink
flowers and who tells L.M. where to get things.) Alors, she had found
me this gardener; she talked as though she had just picked him up
somewhere on the path. He was very nice—a big grey kind old dog in
a cap. Caterina was very cold. She had her hands tucked in the cuffs of a
small grey woollen jacket; her nose was pink, charmingly pink, and
her eyes sparkled. 'Do you mind work on Sundays? He can come on
Sundays?' Not at all. 'And he will bring you plants. Would you like
quelques geraniums?' At that I held up my hands, and I saw Caterina
was having a joke, too. So I asked for violets, and he said he would

bring them, both savage and mild—little blue growling darlings and white meek as milk ones. He says they *poussent comme rien* here.

All roses flower in le mois de noël. It is just time for jonquils, narcissi, tulips,—rather late in fact. He will also bring roses. But when he asked me if I wouldn't like some little palms, and I said No, I loved plants with flowers, I saw by his shrug and his *moue* that he rather despised me. 'Ah, ces femmes avec ces fleurs!' was what I felt. Then he asked if I'd like a lily that grew about the size of the villa— *enormous*. By the time you came you would have had to hunt for me and the house among the lily leaves and the big white flowers. You would have said, 'There they are!' and then 'No, that's a snail!' because on such pasture the snails would grow large too.

This rather frightened me. I said if he had a smaller one, I'd have it please, but not 'those of the Lar-gest size'. Then in the late pale light with Caterina and the gardener outlined against the olive, the deep blue sea and the red sky, we had a little talk. The gardener meanwhile spat very splendidly over the olive boughs. He was greatly impressed by his performance.

(*Enter L.M.:* 'Katie, do you mind if I put the pot au feu through the sieve?'

Me: 'Terribly.'

She: 'Oh, I am so sorry. I was only thinking how beautifully it would have gone through. It was just an idea. Do you mind? I won't interrupt again.')

Now it's dark. The big daisies in the vase on the table have shut their pretty eyes. The shadows are wonderfully quiet. The sea sounds as though it were sweeping up hollow caves. A dog is barking: a bell tinkles on the road. Now it sounds far away. Through the window I see an olive tree growing in a room just like this one and a girl sits at a table under its branches writing to her love.

Ah, to love like this!

Wig

No. 10 received. The new schema noted and approved.

Saturday Afternoon,

My Very Own Bogey,   (October 18, 1919)

First, I will answer your cherished letter which arrived by the noon post. Why I thought London was *une ville morte* was because Pa more or less conveyed: There are cannons in Langham Place; all the life of the place is at a standstill; starvation stares us in the faces in a few days!

I am delighted to hear of the books. I do not like Virginia's woman; she is as clever as you like, but frightfully pretentious and precious and like a foreigner who knows her Paris—*from within*. But it's an interesting book to review.

Please always tell me at once of the faults in my reviews. Haul me over the hottest coals. It is only kind. I expect you to do this. I respect your opinion, and I want it. If anything is all right—let it be; but otherwise, do please beat me. Elizabeth Stanley[1] is sending 2 poems on Monday; she wants to hold them over till then. One longs to write poems here.

Dearest, that Samuel Butler! We knew it, didn't we? The ironing-board and the sewing-machine—they are in *all* his books—he gave them to himself as well—was an expert in the use of both really. What a surface he puts on things! What little crisp frills! How neatly turned! *How beautifully, enfin, he 'got up' other people's washing.* As to the sewing-machine, the 2nd half of *The Way of All Flesh* is all machine-sewn. I wish I could see the woman's[2] letters; I'd *dearly* love to.

This afternoon I have been to San Remo. A great Ausflug—the first since you went away. We took the tram and went first class—velvet seats, very fine, but iron seats in velvet gloves alas! as the journey progressed. It was a beautifully light gay afternoon. I don't feel in the least tired, I feel *rested*; in fact, I went partly to rest my eyes. Oh dear, if I could tell you *all* I saw! But the very very thrilling thing was that I went to our china shop and bought another plate, (I am beginning our collection with ½ dozen soup plates: they are a late *dowry*, darling), and the woman said at the end of this month she will have cups and saucers in this ware *all* sizes, from large café au lait downwards, also teapots and jugs. This is of international importance, isn't it, Bogey? I *shuddered* with joy, seeing the large fluted cups, the sun on the breakfast table, honey in the comb to eat, Bogey one end and me the other with three each side with their cups tilted up to their noses. But seriously, isn't it Great News?

Then I bought 2 lbs. of honey, curry powder, tea, medicine, toothpaste (German: but in an Italian wrapper. Calve *said* it was German), peaches, apples, brioches, letter paper—*and* heard from the market

[1] Elizabeth Stanley was a pseudomyn K.M. used for her poetry.
[2] Miss Savage, the original of Alethea Pontifex.

woman she will have baskets of large freshly dried figs next week
—I hope in time to send them to you by ——. This also thrilled me
greatly.

The money flew out of my purse—but it was worth it. Then we
caught the tram home. L.M. carried the parcils, and soon the kettle
was boiling and we were having Tea. That is like the end of a 'composition', *Describe an Outing*. The villa trembling in the late sun and
shadows was beautiful to return to. It *is* so beautiful. If only I did not
get so bitten! Worse than ever—both my arms and hands.

I heard from —— today written on my birthday. *All* wishes—a
Panegyric on the matchbox she sent me—'so *like* me—it would fit in
so beautifully with your belongings—so *Eastern*—we know how you
appreciate "things Chinese".' It is really very funny. I am going to send
it back to them, say I've had a little patch-box given me which fits my
bag better and I would so love to think of them using it among the
Indian rugs and brasses. Alas, says she, there were not so many rugs as
she had thought—not enough in fact. So *ours* have gone. They are
made for a comedy. I must write it here. This match-box business is the
comble; it is almost perfect.

Take care of that cold. Please nurse it and tell little Wing to wrap
you in blankets and bring 2 saucers of mustard and water for your feet.
But I am really serious. You will—won't you, darling—treat it as
though it were a Roaring Lion or the Dragon with Seven Bellies?

San Remo is all in readiness for its visitors. Every second shop a cake
shop: little cakes about the size of a cup for 3.50, and *Victory* with her
car full of chocolates—you know the style—two sugar horses with
silver wings, and little loves holding, staggering under, the bonbons,
and then the stern, majestic, helmeted figure with her sword upraised,
standing in a chariot of bouchées!

How strange human nature is! An English clergyman and his waife
in front of the postcard shop.

'My dear, that view, I am share, was taken from our window!'

'Oh, do you think so, Arthur?'

'There is no question of doubt.'

'Well . . . perhaps so.'

'Perhaps? What do you mean by perhaps? Why should I be so
positive if it were *not* so?'

'Yes, I see what you mean now.'

And they walked away, poor silly creatures, and he said '*Niente*,

niente!' to a boy crying newspapers who was not for a moment crying them at him—and remarked 'These Italians are famous Beggahs!'

Do please send me *Art and Letters*. Does my story [*Pictures*] look bad? I feel rather anti-Johnnie and Howard de Walden, and it was not I, it was *you*, who interested Bentinck in his work. I did nothing.

I weighed myself today: 7 st. 1 lb. 3 ounces—just exactly the same. But that is good, I think. It takes, I am sure, a month to settle down to a place before one begins to put on weight. I certainly have *a perpetual appetite* and we feed very well. Dinner tonight is:

Filet de boeuf aux vignons
Pasta. Sauce Tomate
Salade
Haricots verts neufs sautés
Gebäckte Apfeln

My own darling Treasure, think of those cups and saucers and the plates and everything we shall have. There will be *no* holding us.

Goodbye. Heaven bless you.

Wig

25 more Sundays
Bogey darling,

Sunday Morning,
(October 20, 1919)

The Gardener is here; he arrived at Aurora's heels, thumping his tail. I think he has done wonders but oh—-I feel inclined to cry to the garden like I do to you when you've been to the barber: 'Why did you let him take off *so much?* When will it grow again?' My cotton plant has lost its curls—a ruthless chopping of them; the roses that had all started what I thought were the most exquisite promising shoots are cut down to the bone and told to try again. (I must plant sweet peas immediately.) And he is so *delighted* with his work; his good face beams; he shows me all stones he has taken out—it sounds like an operation—and there on the path lie the pink geraniums. *O Weh! O Weh!* I feel there's an awful moral to be drawn out of all this—Except ye can bear this to be done unto ye, ye shall not bring forth. At any rate some old Gardener or other has been doing it to us for years, and God knows we've had our naked shivering moments. So now I shall *fill* this garden with flowers. I shall make it to blaze and shine and smell ravishing and look celestially beautiful by the time you come, just to point the moral further.

341

The wind with light, faint footfalls walks over the sea: the water
rings against the shore, like a bell, striking softly.
[Later.]
No letters today, my darling. L.M. has just returned from the post.
She went down to see if there were any by the 3 o'clock, but the post
was shut. I knew it was—Sunday, but she made the effort. She has
broken my medicine glass. It grieves me. Ever since you 'noticed' it at
the Flora I've had a feeling of affection for it. But each fresh breakage
confirms me in my determination *not* to have our new plates used until
you arrive. Then they will all be on the table.

The gardener has gone; there is a smell of blue gum: that means the
tea kettle is on. After tea I am going for a walk up the road behind the
hill. It's a marvellous day, warm and yet *refreshing*.

198 received. (*No* 199)[1] Books received: Benson and Weyman.

Monday,

(October 19, 1919)

Oh, Bogey, why are people swindlers? My heart *bleeds* when they
swindle me, doesn't yours? This gardener—he promised to come and
put the garden in order for 10 francs and bring me some little plants too.
It was to be 10 francs a day *with* the plants. And now his wife has come
and explained the plants are 10 *francs more*. And he only came for half a
day yesterday, but she says he spent the other half of the day looking
for the plants. So they between them charged me 30 francs. It isn't the
money that matters, though I felt ashamed as I gave it them and could
not look at their eyes,—it is that *they are dishonest*. That hurts so! Yes,
put the wall round the house. Why will people do such things? I'd
rather they turned and beat me.

The sun streams through the folded clouds on to the sea in long
beams of light, such beams as you see in picture-books when the Lord
appears. It is a silent day except for the sound of his *false* pick as he digs
up the little beds. L.M. is in San Remo. I have to hide from this old
man now. I wish he'd go. His wife was all in grey, with big black
hollow places where her teeth had been and she said *firmly*, 'C'est moi
qui viens tous les soirs arroser votre jardin pour vous.' When I said
'No,' her 'C'est bien' was like *steel spittle*.

Well, I've cried my cry to you. But, my dear love—this vileness—
this snail on the underside of the leaf—always there!

[1] My letters were numbered according to the number of days to Katherine's return.

199 is lost—is roaming in the wilderness. Perhaps I shall still get it. It's awful to miss letters. This today—Mrs. W. seems established in the house. Oh, I HOPE not. Its what I had feared. Can't you send her away? She mustn't be there long. No, that's childish, You know what is best from where you are and you will do it. But *another woman—it hurts.*

Still, be sensible, Katherine. Don't mind! What does it matter? She goes and comes on the stairs. She waits in the hall and I expect she has a key. I *knew* it would happen, I *knew* it. She pulls the chairs forward. It makes me feel exactly as if I were dead. She talks to Violet, and would Violet mind doing this instead of that? Oh, curse my heart—curse it!! Why am I not a calm indifferent grown-up woman . . . and this great cold indifferent world like a silent malignant river and these creatures rolling over one like great logs—crashing into one. . . . I try to keep to one side, to slip down unnoticed among the trembling rainbow-coloured bubbles of foam and the faint reeds. I try to turn and turn in a tiny quiet pool—but it's no good. Sooner or later one is pushed out into the middle of it all. Oh, my enchanted boy, I am really sadder than you, I believe. At any rate if they weighed us both in the scales, we'd both dip as deep. . . .

Two books have come—Stanley Weyman and Stella Benson. Good. I'll do them. Stella Benson seems to me just to miss it; she reminds me of Colette in a way. But I've only *dipped* into her book. A very attractive creature.

Father wrote to me: he is only coming as far as Nice or Cannes. Guaranteed no infection, I suppose. I shall go on writing away to him so as to be sure of my position. L.M. is at San Remo buying butter. This week I hope to work more. My hands are still poisoned by the bites and my eyes are not Dorothy Wordsworth eyes. It's a bore.

Shall I send this letter? Or write another one—a gay one? No, you'll understand. There is a little boat, far out, moving along, *inevitable* it looks and *dead silent*—a little black spot, like the spot on a lung.

Don't mind me. I am very foolish and ought to be punished. Even as I wrote that the little boat is far away, there have come out of the sea great gold streamers of light such as I never before saw.

Your own

Wig

198 received; *no* 199. Benson and Weyman received.   Monday,

My dear Heart,   (October 20, 1919)

199 is evidently roaming in the wilderness—strayed: I do hate missing letters. This today—tells me that MRS. W. is also established in the house. It's what I had feared. When I read your letter telling me I wrote you one on the spot which I don't send.[1] No, it's not fair to you to send it. *I simply must not mind*—that's all. You do whatever is best: I *knew* it would happen. Pinchey's girl again,[2]—on the stairs, in the hall, moving things and talking to Violet. Oh, well, I must bear it. I wish I were a calm indifferent grown-up woman. *Why* do things hurt so? There's no answer.

The gardener has just gone. He swindled me. He promised to come for a day for 10 lire and for that to bring me some plants. His wife however came this afternoon 'parceque mon mari ne parle pas bien le français' and explained it was 10 lire for the day *and* 10 for the plants (a basket of roots worth perhaps 50 centimes from his garden). She was all in grey with a mouth of black teeth and she said firmly: 'C'est moi qui viens tous les soirs arroser votre petit jardin pour vous, ma—*dame*, et mon mari vient tous les dimanches—alors come ça vous aurez. . . .' When I said *No* to both, she folded her dirty spotted hands and said 'C'est bien'. It hissed out like steel spittle. I don't mind the money so much; I mind the shame and the longing to cry out that I felt when I knew they were swindling me. Oh, it is agony to meet corruption when one thinks all is fair—the big snail under the leaf—the spot in the child's lung—what a *wicked, wicked* God! But it is more than useless to cry out. Hanging in our little cages on the awful wall over the gulf of eternity we must sing—sing.

Father wrote to me he has been ill. You wouldn't just look him up, would you? Or send a note? He is not coming further than Cannes or Nice—guaranteed infection-proof. I shall go on writing to him, however, for *my reasons*.

I had an extraordinarily nice letter from the dear old Boy. Bless him!

This week I hope to work more. My hands are still very poisoned, but my eyes are better.

L.M. to say she must go to the post.

---

[1] This was the previous letter, which was sent after all.

[2] This refers to an episode in 1912 when Katherine was outraged by the familiar behaviour of the fiancée of an acquaintance.

Goodnight, darling, *all's well*. It's grey here and raining, but *all's well*.
Heaven bless you for

Wig

199 fetched up and 197 with cheque.   Tuesday,

My little Lion,   (October 21, 1919)

I hope by now your cold is better; it sounded like one of your *specialités de la maison* and it's not only unfortunate, it's horribly disgusting that you had so much extra work to do while it was ramping. If only you could find someone for the routine work: it is ridiculous that the editor should have to peel the potatoes as well as squeeze the white and pink icing over the puddings *and* be responsible for the savoury and the *plat du jour*. (It's just after lunch: this is *too digestive*.)

About that O.K. sauce—I was always reading that bit about it taking the place of fresh fruit and vegetables. W.L.G. should have it on a paper wrapper or done into Latin for a motto perpetual for the House of George.

I'd like to have heard you and E. about minds. I miss talk.

L.M. (brightly and lightly): 'Wouldn't it be awful if one hadn't got hands and one lived in a place where there were a great many flies? Wouldn't it be simply dreadful?'

That is *no* substitute.

It's a queer day here, all greys and purples and very chill. The sea seems to be growing bigger and bigger, pushing further and further out. . . . People shout as they pass, against the wind. Two exquisite birds have been walking in the garden. They had long, narrow, pale-yellow bodies, little jackets in black and gold, very long silver-grey tails. Happy tiny creatures, quite unafraid, walking over the gravel and having a gay, gay little talk.

I have a feeling, Bogey my darling, that my letter yesterday did not *ring* properly. Please blame the insects. My hands feel as though they were on fire, all swollen and inflamed. They will be better in a day or two. It's so strange the insects should persist, for it's really *very cold* at times, as cold as it was in Marseilles. Yet in the evenings, even with the windows shut and powder burnt, out they come. Bother them!

I finished Stella Benson last night. I thought I might do her with Hope Mirrlees—two women, both protesting in the preface that their books are out of the ordinary. But no bridge could be thrown from

345

one to the other. Miss Mirrlees lives in another world, and her world would *shudder* at Stella Benson. I don't. On the contrary. They are two interesting problems, *very* intriguing. I hope I manage to say what I want to say. . . .

Oh, how dull this letter is! And yours were so wonderful—they had their hands full of wonders. Oh, my own Bogey, I love you beyond all the dreams of man. I want this letter to warm you—to creep into your heart and blow very gently—until all is tiny flames. Let us think for one moment of our *own home*. Early autumn say, evening, our first fire. We are curled up in armchairs before it: and all the world is shut away. It is no dream—it is all at the end of this voyage, isn't it? I couldn't *not* believe it. Now I'm going in and I'm going to ask L.M. to make me a tiny fire in *my* room. Mr. Parky is certainly spending the day. *But all is well, my darling heart*—perfectly. I expect I've got a mild attack of poisoning from these bites: that's all. I wrote Ansaldi yesterday just for him to report how much better I am. I hope your dinner with Pa is not too tiring.

Please give Wing a foursquare kiss from me and Athenæum a *plain* (non-currant) kiss. Richard spoke of my four brothers—you, he and the cats. We sound like a fairy family, don't we?

Love, love, love
Wig

Tuesday,—no, Wednesday,
(October 22, 1919)

My own dear Love,

I owe you a small explanation. The truth is I haven't felt quite well these last 2 days (since Sunday) and I think that's why I have been such a dull mouse. See? Nothing on earth to worry about, I am sure. One can't have a disease and be O.K. all the time—can one? My head's been aching and my cough going and yesterday after I'd written your letter I just went bang to bed with hot water bottles and had a good rest. I organized L.M. and made her give me good food—twice as much as she would have given me—whipped-up egg-wegs and meal broth and hot milk and honey. There I lay and rested. My temperature went up a bit, but it went down after a few hours and this morning it was normal. I also took *Guiacol*: so you see how sensible I was. Couldn't have been more so. Having no doctor makes me awfully wise and careful. Thank God for Sorapure. I just follow his instructions and cure myself. Ida rang up Ansaldi last night, but he's not back for 3 days. Not that I want or need him: I DON'T. I think it was just a bit of a chill or p'raps, because of my head-box, a touch of sun. Anyhow I EAT, and I got up this morning and came straight outside, and here I am resting in lovely weather—repairing. So don't you worry. I'm a kind of doctor, you know.

Doctor Wig
At the Sign of the Fig.

Now, that's off my conscience. I won't write any more till I see if a letter comes from you. Galsworthy came last night and another parcil I didn't open and can't get at just now because L.M.'s out and I am so *enveloppée*. I'll tell you plus tard.

Afternoon. My dear Treasure, and luck was with me. 196 arrived and the *A.*, and the *Nation*, and another whack of books. Now I have food for weeks and shall get ahead so that you have articles in hand. Now, about your letter. Your letters are *changed* this time: they are almost too much for me: they make me feel breathless and as though I must face the sea and say: *How shall* I tell him how I love him? The little waves come in, fold upon fold, folding up my love for you. It seems to me, Bogey, when we have our own home—when we are *safe home at last*—that we shall really turn into fairies and disappear from sight of man.

When you say 'By the way, old girl,' I just have to wave my hand at eternity and smile. It's as though you've known me and I've known you ever since those queer trees grew that we looked at in the garden of Villa Flora. I'll do that about *Sons and Lovers* and incidentally get a whack in—a perlite one—at the Bloomsberries. I won't send you any more of that notepaper: it *felt* like mottled soap, too.

If you write that novel you've got to have a chapter called 'The Birth of Wingley,' don't you think? I have, as I always have, a sort of sweet scent in the air, a sort of floating mirage of your novel. But I feel one would be torn between tears and laughter all the while: everything would be in rainbows. Already long before your child is born I see the light above its head, a ring of light—so lovely. Would it have cats and flowers in it, and could B. wander there, wearing old Feltie, and Wing wave at him from a high window? There would be pain in it, too, *agony*. Would there be a description of *the house* after they were in bed —the fire dying in their room—the cat on the stairs—the moon coming through the window and shining on to the Shepherdess clock

347

—on to her gay little dreaming figure sitting on the hill with her basket of fruit—and then his dark head on the pillow? Do not be cross with me. I am only dreaming to myself of what the book might be. . . .

I pray God I am not 'heavy-fingered', dearest Love. . . . Don't call me a genius—*you* are: it makes me embarrassed when you say it of me.

This copy of the *Athenæum* is really excellent—*full* of interest. Your Shaw is most admirable, and your *Merchant of Venice*—putting Moscovitch in his place—could not be bettered. How very fortunate there should be *your* Shaw against ——'s! There's an orange and a lemon for the public to choose from. I bet they will come on to our side after that. All the paper, I feel, has been through your hands. Sullivan and Huxley are different creatures—so tightened up. I haven't read it all yet, because I have not had the time. L'Hôte is a great acquisition: a most interesting chap—and so alive to himself as a painter and so free from *c'est moi qui vous parle*. Dent also I like very much this week. I feel it is the *Athenæum* way of writing about music. S. might call it superficial, but it's not. I long to tuck into all these books and do my best with them. I shall, darling. Please, if you get a letter that might interest me, would you send it over? Like that American's, par exemple, and any letter which says you're a great man. I can stand any number of them.

It's a marvellous day—the flies appreciate it as much as I do: they are appalling. I've just sent L.M. off for an extra supply of milk. I don't care what I spend—*well I will be*: that's how I feel—and since Sorapure wrote me that letter, which was really a kind of diploma: (This is to certify that K.M. has passed the examinations and is fully qualified to look after herself), I don't feel as though I *could* get really ill again. L.M. is stupidity personified, but I am learning just to take it quietly and make her re-do the thing that's wrong—and not do it myself.

I wish you were here, just for a little minute—with me. I'm in my room, lying down, the door and window open. The wind, thinking the house is empty, is taking a quiet *look through,* humming to herself. The shadow dances from the olive and there's no sound except the sea. Ah, my precious one,—to have you here just for a moment, to hold you, *look* at you, hear you call me 'Wormie'. . . . But the boat has only 196 waves to ride over and then there's the dazzling shore!

I dreamed last night that I had come home (a fever dream—horrible) and it was still October, dark, foggy, bitterly cold. And I was ill. I sent a note to Sorapure, who came. I was still in my travelling clothes: a black velvet cap and my peach-coloured shawl for a coat. He came and did not speak to me: you and he started talking about a new tobacco to be bought by the *sheet*: he had some to show you. Then you said 'Well, I'd better go,' and left us alone. And Sorapure wiped his glasses and said, very dryly: 'Well, I'm afraid you've broken something more than your journey.' I said: 'Oh, but I'm leaving for Italy again next week.' He put his glasses on again. I said: 'Doctor Sorapure, I can see you'd rather not attend me any more.' We shook hands and he walked out—and I saw the greenish fog in the window . . . and knew I was caught. To wake up and hear the sea and know I had not done the dreadful thing—that was joy.

Boge, I feel much better now—more normal. If it were anybody but you I could not say this, but really the gardener's wife had something to do with it. I felt her in my lung. Perhaps the truth was I was feeling weak, and she stabbed.

What about the house Duncan spoke of? Have you made any plans at all for week-ends, or has this extra work made you put all aside. It's a pity really you can't take the old boy into the office and train him. He would save you and know how to do it. Goodbye for now. Tell Wing to send Gan'ma a message.

Your own
Wig

No letter yet   •   Thursday,
My Bogey,   (October 23, 1919)

I wish you could see this glass of flowers on the dining room table— daisies and roses. Field daisies, but larger than English ones, and very wide, with the fringed petals dipped in *bright* crimson and crimson roses from the wild garden at the side of the steps. I have just gathered the third rose and remarked hundreds of buds which will be blowing in a week or two. The sea is very pale today; small boats go sailing by. I don't suppose I ever see a little boat on the sea without thanking Heaven you are not in it—just as I never read the Shelley story without thinking 'There but for the —— of God goes Wig and Bogey'. I was out in the garden all the morning: now I've come in to write. Don't you find it very difficult to work without a large table and four walls? I try everything, I work on a tray—on a chair—on a book—sit up high and arrange the ink and papers on Table Mountain, on the verandah . . . but *no*, at the last I have to come in. In our Sussex house we shall have a real table and a real chair and a real 'abri.'

349

Except for my head today, darling, I'm well again. I again went to bed after tea yesterday, rubbed my lung with Capsoline, ate a very nourishing dinner, and then had hot milk and egg later and really I am cured. I'm very glad to have had the experience: it makes me feel so secure. I should have had a doctor in London pour sûr, but here I did without one, treated myself and cured myself. This makes me feel so safe in case we should ever find ourselves on a desert island—just in case. If there are cannibals there our lives will be spared because of Wig the Healer, and if there aren't, they'll be spared pour la même raison. But please don't be cross. In view of the state of my *head* I am doing Galsworthy this week. I know what I think about him: I mean he has been in my mind for years and only wants dusting, bringing to the light and *proving* by this new book.

> (Oh why, why
> Did the Lord make the Fly?
> And when we die
> Shall we find them spry
> In eternity?)

To be *spry* in eternity seems to me particularly awful: eternally spry! I don't want eternity at any rate, so it don't signify. Now it will be ideal for L.M.—time for everything, time to get to know everybody and to wonder about 'this that and the other' to her heart's desire. She is, indeed, made for eternity—one of God's own, as you might say. But no—if the Lord will give me 30 years starting on May 1st, 1920, he can do what he likes with what's left of my bones and feathers after that. . . .

I send you Violet's letter just so that you may realize who is in the kitchen. What do you think of it? And what fortune to have found her! And would she and Roger come to the country with us? That is my dream now, of course—a little cottage for them or at any rate their own rooms in the house so that they may have babies of their own. You might *sound* Violet on this (leaving the babies out) one day—will you?

There are 25 more Wednesdays before we are together. Twenty-five more copies of the paper. Do you feel—as I do this time—that it's *not much*. It's just two months to Christmas, after that the New Year, and in February snowdrops—and they are the flowers of *our* spring. What are you doing about the garden, darling? Anything? Have you re-planted the bulbs? I am sure you'll want them next March. Please tell me if you do. Then I *see* you, but not as I did last year—from my window—thinking of all that was to come between—of the dark, dark bridge to be crossed before the flowers would be discovered. But this time from the terrace by the cotton plant.

I have 6 packets of cigarettes at 1 franc the packet, black soldiers' cigarettes, I should think, made to be distributed to dying Zouaves in hospital and—held over. But they are a great deal better than nothing.

Bogey, is there *any* life of George Eliot so that I can write an article for November 22—less than a month to do it in—or if you could send me one or two of her novels—*Romola, Adam Bede,* whichever are best? I feel I'd love to do something, but if there are other people on the spot more competent and with more material, *c'est entendu.* At any rate we mustn't pass her by.

Oh, that PAPER. *It simply fascinates me.* If only I were by your side, sharing the work more, discussing it more, seeing the people more, helping more. Next year we shall make it very living: we'll have Eliot down and Sullivan and Sheppard and whoever is *there*—subjeck to your approval.

Now I must finish my review. Goodbye, my darling Heart. Keep happy, keep well, keep warm. Don't work too much.

Your true love
Wig

195 Saturday 194 Sunday received.   Friday: le soir,
My own precious Bogey,   (October 24, 1919)

I can't understand why you have never received my letter about the spoon. I *can't* understand it; for I sent it, I thought, on my birthday; it is a blow if it's lost.

When you talk about Wing, I don't know what it is, something in all you tell me goes to my heart. I see him as he used to lie, in a kitten coma, while you kissed his nose. Never shall we have such an adorable kitten again. When he slept on our bed, too, and wouldn't settle down (you remember), *would* dive off and swim about under the cupboard and up the screen-pier. I do wish you'd take his pigglechur[1] and send it me.

(*Oh,* the midges!!! There are *three.*)

Your Sunday letter brought you and the house to me very, very clearly. It was wonderful how you conveyed the quality of the day— the one thing happening after another thing—in a silence. But I wish

---

[1] Picture.

you didn't always have a *duty* ahead—a horrid duty walking off that you have to follow, at such a round pace, after—just when you've put one in its stable, so to say.

No, I don't think you're like a deep dark pool: I think you're like a deep silent sea—with wonderful ships on it—wonderful ships—but there again, my own precious darling, you never have time, never, to sail where you will and how you will.

I know what you mean about *people babbling,* even though je ne suis pas une silencieuse, moi. But the *years* one has spent, sitting with a strained smile trying to appear *of* the party, *in* the know . . . what foolishness, what waste of time!

But on those rare occasions when you and I talk, I do—I do feel the heavens opening and our thoughts like angels ascending and descending. Time, peace, freedom from anxiety—these things must be ours. Time to be silent in and to talk in. But especially that last. The *strain* we have lived under! No one will know. Isn't it queer, my little brother, what a cold indifferent world this is really? Think of the agony we've suffered. Who cares? Who dreams? If we were not 'set apart' for ever before, this has been enough to do it. We could not, knowing what we know, belong to others who know not. If I can only convey this difference, this vision of the world as we see it! Tchekhov saw it, too, and so I think did Keats.

I am sending a parcel of books to Thorpe's tomorrow, and here are the names writ on a page for you to put in your pocket book. I have told him you will call for the money. That's best, don't you think? Anything else would be so confusing, and you don't mind 'passing by', do you, darling? But don't forget, mignonette, because it is real money and buys things.

Goodbye, my love
Your
Wig

Wing, my duck box,   Athy
let me kiss you.   a warm wave of the tail

193 and Tuesday received   Sunday on the verandah,
My own Precious Heart,   (October 26, 1919)

I am thankful you got my letter about the spoon. Could you imagine for a *moment* that I'd not have written? It was awful to have to wait so long, though. I was simply *dying* for letters today. None yesterday or the day before: the posts are really very uncertain. These two make me feel I've not been fulfilling my trust in my last letters: make me LONG to see you for a moment and tell you that *all* is *well* here. You simply must never worry about me; I am as safe as a rock. Just think of the seas that have washed over, and all the same I'm not only here—I'm getting better all the time. I repose myself absolutely and eat and sleep. The chill is *tout à fait parti*: and when I get some spegglechiks[1] my eyes will be A1 eyes. It IS cold, but look at the warm things I have. I simply rejoice in them and am sitting out now in the Lamb—with Jaeger underneath and on top, snug as can be. Then, when it's cold, my little room by virtue of its being against the kitching keeps a warm wall—and I don't stint firing a little bit, nor shall I. Nor do I deny myself anything, but eat butter and honey, meat and eggs as if they were provided by ravens. You believe all this, don't you? The insetti, I must say, are a real trial, worm. They make work really difficult. You can't get away from them. *They are a real pest.* But I suppose they will go. I confess they have awfully discouraged me at moments—these constant swellings and the heat of them—and then trying to write, waving off moustiques and moucherons. But you see what an external thing they are, aren't they? If they'd go, life would be 100 times easier.

Now I'll read over your letters and answer them. I am thankful you have sacked ——. I agree *absolutely* with you about him AND about a man like Orpen. One must have an open mind. It's so difficult not to find a *sneerer*. What's the good of sneering? I imagine what Strachey or V.W. would think of a writer like Brett-Young—but he's WORTH considering. One must keep a balance i.e. one must be critical. There's your mighty pull over your whole generation—and there's what's going to make the *Athenæum* what it is in your imagination. I'll look up Wilenski and tell you what I think tomorrow—and I'll carefully read his stuff next week. I'll tack the 6/- for Phillips on to my cheque for you next month.

Your cold is *still* there? Boge, please do see Sorapure. Why don't you get injected against colds? It can be done. You cannot afford to have them for so long. This is IMPORTANT.

Now your Monday letter. You are so overworked that I don't know what to say. A dramatic critic must be found. Does Strachey himself know no-one? In despair I even think of ——. My darling, try and slow down just a bit. You can't keep up this pace. You're running

[1] Spectacles.

353

the whole show—and then dinner is brown stew and an apple. Really, it's not good enough.

I *did* want to see my Pa—now—well I don't mind if I do or if I don't. I was careful to extend a pressing invitation 'for the sake of the firm' and to give —— one in the eye. I'm desperately anti-family now—you're my family. (You can have your own, too, if you like, darling: but mine doesn't exist.) We must form a brand new family with Mansfield and Middleton for family names. I'm very glad you have heard from Gogarty. Couldn't he put you on to an Irish correspondent? Or to some chap who might write an interesting article or two? You must try and get some time off. I hope you do spend a bit of time in the garden: I know you can't plant bulbs with your pen. The lemon verbena ought to come in: it's next to the scented geranium. But I expect both of the little dears are sitting in golden pots about the Throne of Grace ere now: frost kills them.

When you say forgive me for talking shop, that's all nonsense you know, precious. Bogey, you can't say anything which doesn't affect me. But I am worried that you have to work so dreadfully hard.

It's Sunday. The sun hangs in the dappled sky like an uncertain silver star. The wind blows over the calm sea and then traces rivers, creeks, little lakes and bays in violet on the blue. On the horizon clouds like white crumbling mountains. Five men down below are fishing, hauling the net into an open boat. Oh, I long to be *well*, quite well, and with the albatross off my neck and in Rhodesia. These are convalescent longings. Where are you now? Take me in your arms, darling Boy. This time we are not going to fail. All will be a success, and in May all will be perfect.

Your own
Wig

Monday,
(October 27, 1919)

Darling,

Here is your cheque for the rent and for Phillips. I made it up to £3 0 0. L.M. has just said *en passant*: 'And, Katie, I must order another load of wood today: there's only enough for another 3 days. It *does* seem to disappear so.' This is the kitchen fire only—80 francs a month! It's all gone. Remember when they put it in and Wig and Bogey said a good three months? What little optimists they are!

Wig

She has JUST realized about the draught.

'I realize it now, Katie. I have always left it wide open, and that's what makes the wood roar away so. . . .

'Never mind, Katie, it will go better now.'

Did—you—ever?

My Precious Precious Darling,

Monday Night,
(October 27, 1919)

This is most important. Bogey, listen to me—listen faithfully. Don't think of anything but what I am going to say.

YOUR LIFE MUST CHANGE.

Bogey, this partner of the Firm can't stand your goings on; she can't stand them. Her heart stands still with horror; she feels as if she were crumbling away. Your Thursday letter came: too tired to do the garden, you fell asleep—WORN OUT, and you woke up. 'I CREPT downstairs to a frugal meal, because I have to be very careful what I eat.'

BOGEY, I CAN'T BEAR this. I feel as though the South of France swept over me; it's raining, it's very cold, with a high wind and sea again. I persuade myself things will get better—may be better now but PROMISE me to see Sorapure AT ONCE, for my sake.

Think, Love, these six months are the most important of our lives. Your letter pulled me up—I swore cross my heart, straight dinkum, never to give way to depression again. I WILL not and I will KONKER my albatross and work and live on letters and be as gay as I can. This time we must succeed. But HELP me by not overworking, by eating, by seeing doctors, by resting. No, I'll not listen to the weather: I shall just work. Let us be very strong i' th' arm—two Indian braves making a path through the forest towards each other—188 trees to chop. Oh, my precious husband—thou dearer than life to me—feel my arms tightly round you, kissing those tired lips. Then I'll kiss your hands and the top of your head, your eyelids and your cheeks. Then I'll kiss the stud showing above or below your tie. *Now* laugh. *Now* say I am silly.

Your very own for ever

Adoring Wife

Terrible storm raging, bitter cold and rain and wind.

Nex Day.

A picture. *Figurez-vous* your Wig on the verandah in all the clothes she has, topped with the woolly lamb, and with her cherry sunshade

355

up, under a green fly-net! It is so perishingly cold today—a wind like *ice*. But for the first time I seem to have weapons to fight it with, and I am as snug as can be. As I walked into the garden wearing the woolly lamb, I leaned on the green gate which is my *confessional* and said to the daisy who remarked on it: 'Oui, c'est la jaquette militaire de mon mari qu'il a porté pendant les trois hivers qu'il était au front. Le khaki était affreusement sale; alors je l'ai ... etc. ...' If the daisy had been Catherina the same histoire would have been recounted: I am *fascinated* by these ideas sometimes. I saw you in this British-warm tucking your pocket-book away, pulling on immense gloves, and going off somewhere by motor-car. ...

Bogey, at break of day I went through all the paper and had a good read of it. The printers seem to get a bit scrimpy at times and will cut the noses off the words: it's very annoying. But—here goes. Your Butler, I think, is awfully good: the beginning paragraphs are first-chop writing. They are so free. But then I think you do show traces of fatigue: I am sorry you didn't say what his relations with Miss Savage were and how they failed. That 'quote' made me curious for more. However, I know how you felt. You've ticked him off before—*et voilà!* Who wrote *What is Bolshevism?* It's one of those reviews that begins with a bouquet and then gradually takes the flowers back again. And sentences like 'It is of course impossible to estimate the number of people, etc.' are footle. Of course, it is. L.M. might try. At the end the reviewer decides to give him back a stalk or two—but ... it's a bad style of reviewing, don't you think?

Bogey,

Tuesday,
(? October 28, 1919)

About the paper for the 24th. Can I go over it a bit with you? All I say I do say as you know dead sincerely and with all respeck to you who know the difficulties as I cannot and the ins and outs. I wish the printers would not be so scrimpy, cutting the noses off the words, don't you? Bren, for instance, and Lyn.

Santy[1] is full of the eyebrow this week. But it's good stuff to publish —awfully.

Your Butler, whatever you may think, is extremely good. The writing of the 1st column is first-chop; it is so free. True, I don't feel you spread your wings as you might have done, but then you'd said

[1] George Santayana.

356

all you had to say before. I always want you to *go on*, as children say, I always want to say: 'Take your time—please, please don't pull me past the doors. You know what's inside and you're the only person who has the key.' But that's this cursed Life which puts those horrible demands on you and makes it impossible.

'Our Welsh King' *must* have been by a B.A. My Aunts! 'Henry VII turns out the more we study him to be. . . .' I smell a B.A. there. *And* 'traits which *smack* of the Celt'. Take 3d. off *her* cheque for that. (It's a lady?)

I don't think Eliot has in the least justified your generosity in his review of Pound. I quite understand that you *had* to give him the chance, but it's lamentable, all the same, for there is no doubt that Pound is small beer. It makes Eliot look very silly, too, to be carrying cannon-balls for the prestidigitateur.

K.M. is tame, I think, and there is not enough shape in her review. She's not looking at it from above as well as all round it. 1/- off her cheque.

As to the Notes from Ireland—Oh! oh! oh! They begin like Fashion Notes *exactly*. And what about 'Much may be said as to the value of *wide culture* but if the *reading of modern literature* etc.' Back to the taypot, Mrs. H.T.S., je vous prie. Also 'when the curtain falls and we come to earth again'—oh!

Sullivan is all right, don't you think, but undistinguished. I always feel he's on the point of choosing *The Idylls of the King* as his great poem. But it's serious and interesting and the wires are quite well laid,—which is, I think, his part of the job in literature.

Dent gets better and better. Really, the Busoni is *famös*. It's excellent. It is indeed like a fine piece of pianoforte playing by Busoni.

The drama is, of course, nobody's child and it feels it. 'The Tempest' is just like a review of *The Tempest*. 'We left with the firm intention' is rather an awkward ending, isn't it? I *did* smile to find our song in your review. Oh Boge, do you think it necessary to put the names of actors in brackets? Good God! it's maddening. (Here I am, exaggerating again!) But I'm sure it's not a good plan—what can Mr. Percy Parsons mean in the criticism? I don't think *The Net* ought to have *been* reviewed. After all, *The Athenæum* goes to the theatre to say what *The Athenæum* has to say—to look at it very very specially from its own angle. These critiques—'The Tempest', for instance, is so like any review of *The Tempest*. You'd never let a book-reviewer say such

357

things as: 'She seemed to have but an imperfect control of her instrument of expression,' for that's been *cliché* for years and years. And the *way* in which *The Net* is seen. . . . No, I think the theatre wants a New Broom in it—not necessarily a Hard Broom, but a new one, who *speaks out* with wit and sympathy and gives the impression of a man of some learning who finds himself in the theatre for the first time. (I know what it means to find such a man, tho'.)

If you knew how I have this paper at heart! Turn down anything of mine you don't care for—but I am whacking in this week. I am sending 3 novels under one cover and a review of Stella Benson for you to use when you want to, and the little essay. It's a wonderful paper—wonderful, but too big to be carried by one pair of shoulders. I should be there to share the dog's work and make your personal life very easy and look after you. I shall be there after May. Can you stick it as long as that? In May I shall be well again and on the spot. Save yourself all you can till then but *keep it in mind, darling*. Won't Bertie[1] write some articles? Or some fabulous tales—an account of his journey to China and his discussions with the philosophers he met there? Am I mad?

Your

K.M.

Tuesday,

(October 28, 1919)

My precious Own,

Forgive this bit of paper; it's just a note I'm writing you because your 190 letter has come and you've got my Monday letter, and this of yours is about the kettle-holder I haven't got—you remember. It's a divine letter—a perfect kettle-holder in itself. Thank you, my darling of darlings. But I have determined after this—no looking back, no minding so dreadfully—the journey is too important. I'll not fail you again.

(*a*) I'll write to Sylvia Lynd

(*b*) and to Grant Richards.

Later on I feel that Richard ought to come into the office, don't you? I don't think Dicky C-S will last very long.

I shall be a week ahead with the novels this very week: I had decided already because of the uncertain posts. I *long* to do Waley. There is a flower out in the garden which is the first sentence.

[1] Bertrand Russell.

Half a stone is a terrible amount to gain in 2 years, isn't it? My little optimist. But then I'll always be in fear that you're going to break. I'll try my best not to let you know and to look the other way when you hang over precipices and lean out of trains and dangle out of boats—but it's a poor pretence. I'm never certain of you unless I'm hanging on to a handful of your jersey.

Ansaldi is due back in three days. I'll see him then just to see how things are going. I feel they are going well—yes, well. My cough is less frequent. I'm stronger. I eat *terribly*. My joints are still very painful, that's true, but I've no temperature again. There's my 'statement'.

I've just looked out of window. L.M. is at San Remo. There is going to be an *enormous* storm; terrible lead-coloured clouds are pulling over; the sea is almost silent—just a deep beat—and the wind has arrived to clear the court, as it were, for the Elements. The cold is immense here, Bogey, but I don't feel it at all as I did in the S. of France, thanks to all my warm woollies. But it's absurd to say this coast is warm *all the time*. Perhaps next month will be finer. Now I must work again and pray the house isn't struck by lightning. It's the moment to shut all the windows. You know that moment. Well, I've done it. I've also been into the garden, picked a rose, and brought in a bundle of kindling from under the verandah table, and I haven't coughed once or got out of breath. So I must be *furiously* better, really.

Goodbye my precious

Your

Wig

Wednesday,
(October 29, 1919)

My own love,

No letter today so far. I may get one this evening.

I have heard from Father at Menton. Poor darling! he was robbed at Boulogne of his wallet—all his money, addresses, papers, £50 in banknotes, a letter of credit for £500. This really wrings my heart. I can't help it. If he does mind so terribly about money, it must have been so *ghastly* to be *alone* among foreigners, having to keep up and be a man of the world and look out of the railway windows as though it hadn't happened. I really literally nearly fainted when this swept over me and I 'saw' him with a very high colour 'putting on' a smile. I do hope to God people don't suffer quite as I think they do: it's not to be borne if they do.

I am writing this in a hurry. I seem to have such acres to plough and the horse is going so slow. I wish I could change the horse, Boge. He just sits on his hind legs and scratches his ear and looks round at me when we're ½ way through a furrow.

It's icy cold, thundering, blue-grey with a flash of steel. I should think it was going to snow.

I will write to you again later, my precious, when this review is done, but I wanted to catch the post with this. Would you send me the *Times* review of Virginia? I'd *very* much like to see it or any other. I want to read the book,[1] but dare not so much as put my nose in till I've cleared off this accumulation.

Take care of yourself my *very own* Bogey. Love me: I love you.

Wig

Thursday,
My darling,   (October 30, 1919)

I am sending a review today and I shall send another tomorrow. Things have not gone as fast as I wished (as usual) but from now onward they will improve. I expect you wonder why, with such unlimited opportunity I do not just waltz through with things. Alas, up till now it [has] been—not so much my health, indeed, except for that chill and mal à la tête—not my health at all, but my domestic arrangements. Now I have discovered how I can live with L.M. It is by not speaking more than is necessary for the service of the house. Two nights ago we had a *crise* which made me realize it must be the very last, that if it occurred again I'd have to ask her to go, and to make other arrangements. This, of course, I don't at all want to do, so the other plan is adopted. I don't know what she thinks: I imagine she is furious, but I don't care. It's *such a rest*—you can't imagine. No shouting, no quarrelling, no violence, just quiet: I am basking in it. I can keep it up, too, by an effort of Will; I am *sure* I can. Otherwise there would have been no work done—nothing done—nothing written—for our hate had got to such a pitch that I couldn't take a plate from her hand without shuddering. This *awful relationship* living on in its secret corrupt way beside my relationship with you is very extraordinary; no one would believe it. I am two selves—one my true self—the other that she creates in me to destroy my true self. . Still, I'll write no more

[1] *Night and Day.*

360

Katherine Mansfield   April 1918

about it and try and think about it less and less so that the fire gets more and more covered. But that's what makes my work so hard and *paralyzes my mind*. It's just like a terrible fog; I'm lost in it and I go mad —just like L. used to. Here I have thrown things at her—yes, even that —called her a murderer, cursed her. Her three standing remarks: 'Give me time!' 'I'll learn by degrees, Katie' and 'You must first teach me, that's all' are to me too sinister. . . . I haven't the time to give. However, it's over. And I shall live in silence with her now and put it away. Better a thousand times be lonely than speak to her. But that is the real reason why I cannot work as I could—L.M., L.M. and L.M. So after this I'll do better, see?

No letters came today, none yesterday. I am longing for the post. There'll be two tomorrow, I expect. It's fine today though still bitter cold: I've been lying still in the sun all the morning—haven't moved. The sea is wonderfully beautiful—so deep and dark, yet with the light on it, moving and glittering.

I heard from —— yesterday. 'How I wish I could send you a great hamper from the orchard of nuts and apples . . .' it's a safe wish at this distance. One page was devoted—this is *dead true*—to the match-box: she knew it would appeal to me—so delighted it had fetched up safe, they both said 'K!' when they saw it etc. It made me violently jealous that they should have a house and nuts and apples. I *yearn* to beat them. I feel I shall buy all the china I can get here to beat their china, and, oh! if we had more money you could be looking out for oddments too. We must have our house, Bogey, next year. Is there any star on the horizon?

Chaddie sent me a photograph of myself at three years old. It was *a dreadful shock*. I had always imagined it—a sweet little laughing thing, rather French, with wistful eyes under a fringe, firmly gripping a spade, showing even then a longing to dig for treasure with her own hands. But this little solemn monster with a wisp of hair looked as though she were just about to fall backwards head over heels. On her feet she wears, as far as I can make out, a pair of ordinary workman's boots which the photographer, from astonishment or malice, has photographed so close up that each tootsie is the size of her head. The only feature about her is her ears which are neatly buttonholed on to the sides of her head and not just safety-pinned on as most babies' are. Even the spade she clasps with the greatest reluctance.

Now I must work. The hot water runs at last—for the first time yesterday. Oh, I do hope there is a letter tomorrow, darling, with news of YOU in it. I am anxious about this ghastly press of work. Otherwise all goes well here, and under my new regime it can only go better. Goodbye, my own precious Bogey. When you get this it will be November—2 months to the New Year.

Your Own
Wig

189, 188   Friday,
My love and my dear,   (October 31, 1919)

Two letters today: *the first since Monday.* Oh, how welcome they were! I had begun to think that L.M. made away with them. I often have a moment of doubt as to whether she's going to post what I give her or throw it into the sea. . . .

Your Saturday letter, darling, telling me your cold still hangs round you was a sad one. I know how you felt. Yes, one *has* a lonely furrow, and all I look forward to is *our home.* There is nothing else, you know, Bogey, absolutely nothing for me.

I sent a review yesterday, Boge. Before I forget, will you change the last sentence of all? Substitute another word for the word 'great' or 'farewell meeting between father and son it would be a great deal more'. I can't just remember how the thing went, but I woke up in the night with the Lord crying 'Samuel!' to me and saying 'Cut out that bit about a great novel!'

I am going to do my best to send another review off today. I am sending L.M. to San Remo *pour faire les commissions* on purpose. The sun came out this morning, took a cloud or two, did a little extremely high-class modelling on the grand scale—'The Banquet', 'Greek Warriors Resting', 'A Grecian Lady with a Bowl', and so on all along the horizon for the benefit of a tiny little sailing ship and me. Then it went in again and Heaven knows how many doors are between us. It is bitterly cold and windy with great puffs of dust rising. I wonder if it will get warmer again? I don't see why it should, and yet who would come for a *saison d'hiver* to get a blue nose and fingers. It's a mystery.

Your portrait of you and Wing gardening is one of the wittiest, most charming things *in the world.* Who are we? What are we doing in *this* world? We are the only original Babes in the Wood as has been played for the last—years. Life is the old woman in the bonnet who gets our engagements for us, waits for us in the wings and rubs the black stuff round our eyes. And Wing must have a tiny veskit painted on him and be a robin with his *own private* leaf to lay upon us.

Oh, my precious darling, *how* I love you. Let this be our last separation. I can't help feeling—in view of this intense cold—why didn't I go to Ventnor or some such place? Why go so far? It couldn't be colder in the Isle of Wight. Well, it only determines me never to do it again.

Peace still reigns supreme between L.M. and me. She talks to the bread instead, and it's a perfect listener for it lets her fill herself with it to her content and is made to be devoured.

My lung isn't exactly painful, but it creaks like a Sam Browne belt. I've no temperature. I go to bed every night after dinner and rest all day. Perhaps it is healing and that's what makes the noise. I am sending her to Ansaldi today to see if she can get news of him. Boge, could you send me that Italian grammar soon? I wrote it on your little list, you remember. You know I can't bother about a *soul* in England but you. They're just *gone*. Yet I am very lonely. But only for *you*. I am so glad you were in the garden, my darling.

Yours for ever

Wig

Friday,

(October 31, 1919)

Bogey,

L.M. is just back from San Remo. The chemist can no longer make my cough mixture for lack of this ingredient. He has tried for it everywhere. This is important, for my cough has got the upper hand still. Would you ask Doctor Sorapure to make me a new prescription or failing that would you have the medicine sent to me from a chemist? It is rather urgent. You might explain to the doctor if you see him that my cough is certainly no less troublesome than it was and at the slightest exertion I am very short of puff (such as dressing, doing my hair etc.) So I'd rather it was stronger than weaker, see? I am fighting all the time the most *overwhelming depression*: that I am sure is what keeps my cough going and keeps me feeling weak. I merely state this. I am determined to be 'gay', but I am *desperately* lonely and depressed. This is just medical truth.

Your own

Wig

363

a Blank Day   Saturday
My darling Bogey,   (November 1, 1919)

I had thought to have your Monday letter yesterday—but no: it
wouldn't come. You must throw them more quickly down the letter
boxes, darling, *hurl* them, send them *flying*: tell them that if they come
quickly there is nothing—nothing she won't give them. They can take
whatever they please, pull off her rings and put them on their thumbs,
peacock in her flowery shawl, eat all the honey jar at once. . . . Oh *no,*
they are not children: I won't have them children. Little children must
never travel. How could I have written so! It breaks my heart only to
think of them. No, they are just—birds to whom the journey is no
labour. Up they fly, out of sight, with one beat of a delicate wing. . . .
But birds are so heartless, alas!

It is a fearful day; long cold rain, a homeless wind crying at the windows, the sea like ashes. I am sitting in my little room in a corner,
wrapped up with a hot brick at my feet. I must work hard today. Thank
God for definite work—work that must be done.

Bogey darling, precious, do tell me when my reviews are not up to
the mark. Criticise them and *please* let me see the *Lit. Sup:* I really am
a bit lost without it over here. If you can't send it to me, then I'll write
direct. Just let me know. Couldn't I have the office copy?

November 1st. Six months to May. After that don't leave me alone.
I am not made to live alone—not with an enemy. Hating L.M. as I do,
I should have gone to a place like Mentone where I could sometimes
go for a small walk without a climb and *lift the shutter* that I live
behind. But work, work, work—simply to thy cross I cling. (Why
must it be a cross? Ah, why? What a question to ask at 31! But I *do* still
ask it.)

Six months. Bogey, let us look across them and sign to each other.
Only six months to cross. A mountain a month. Six mountains and
then a soft still quiet valley where no wind blows—not even enough to
fray the one o'clock dandelion—and we are there and hidden. *Love* me
You MUST love me—as much as I love you. Send me a very brave
piece of love to pin in my bosom.
                                        Wig

                                                                              Saturday,
Darling Heart,   (November 1, 1919)
No letter. Oh, what a disappointment. I have only heard once since

                                      364

Monday—true I got 2 then but I did at least hope for your 'Monday' letter today.

I am sitting in the dining-room. The front door is open, the cold salt air blows through. I am wrapped up in my purple dressing gown and jaeger rug with a hot bottle and a hot brick. On the round table is a dirty egg-cup full of ink, my watch (an hour slow) and a wooden tray holding a manuscript called 'Eternity' which is all spattered over with drops of rain and looks as though some sad mortal had cried his pretty eyes out over it. There is also a pair of scissors—abhorrèd shears they look—and two flies walking up and down are discussing the ratification of the Peace Treaty and its meaning *re* our civil relations with Flyland.

I am just sending L.M. to San Remo to ask the Hochwohlgeboren Doktor Bobone to come and see me. Curse Ansaldi! he'll never be back. I *must* know from somebody how I am getting on and what is the state of my left lung, *i.e.,* I must be cheered up. Ten years passed this morning as I sat in my darkish little room. I am now 41 and can't lose a moment. I must know. If my depression continues, my precious, I shall try to get out of here in January, because if it does go on, we shouldn't have a May here, we'd be flinging our daisy chains round the tops of cedar trees. But on the other hand if Bobone consoles me and so on, I may feel better.

It's being alone with L.M. Things have gone too far, you know; we positively *loathe* each other. It's such a complex with me that only fear of the consequences stops me from shooting her. I see myself at the top of the stairs and she at the bottom and then to know she'd never never stare at me again—

Later. L.M. is back from San Remo. She has been to the post again. No letters. I feel simply paralysed with dismay. Think! I've no 'negative tonic' here. There's my only link with Life, with reality, and in the whole week I've heard ONCE. Pray, darling, tell me not to expect them or for God's sake send them.

Bobone comes tomorrow at 9.

In bed   Sunday,

Darling of darlings,   (November 2, 1919)

I have heard from you twice this week—du reste, silence. If I do not get a letter today, it will be TOO dreadful. My mind is paralyzed with dismay and apprehension, and I am in bed with this horrible storm raging day and night outside. No one to speak to—like Robinson Crusoe: *he* lived alone.[1] Worse—ah, much, much worse——

I have just seen the Hochwohlgeborene Doktor Bobone. I did not want to wait any longer for Ansaldi. Yesterday was so terrible, Boge, in my darkish room, like a cave—unable to write or think—no news—no letters. I sent her to San Remo: because I felt I must at least have someone in touch with me. He stayed about an hour and most thoroughly examined me. I think he is a very good doctor indeed, scientific, dry, *German,* and as frank with me as if I'd been a student examining the case—with him. He says the fact I have so little fever is good—all on my side. 'So long as you have not the fevers you do not die. It is de fevers which kills.' I don't think he had at all a *great* opinion of me. On the other hand he said he thought I might go in to see him once a fortnight—go into San Remo! He says the apex of the right lung only is affected; the left is infiltrated to the third rib. He is giving me a medicine for tuberculosis. This I don't like. Sorapure said they were so often dangerous. This man said himself it is not one of the dangerous ones. 'It do nothing or it do well'. I suppose I must trust him, then.

This villa he approves of for fine weather, but when the weather is not fine he says I must stay in bed to be out of draughts and to be warm. Air, to live out in the sun, food, and no vorry, no fever, 'and you will not die. It is the fever kills the patient'. This was his one cry. But when I tried to tell him of my appalling *mental* state of depression he didn't even listen. . . . No one *listens* to a patient except Sorapure.

Now, listen. TRY to send me letters often or cards or papers from the office—anything. If I were there, you'd spend 10 minutes with me. Give me those 10 minutes here. HELP ME, HELP ME. If I veep I getta de fever, and I am veeping strong!! I have no negative tonic. I am tired. I can't always write or work or read. Then I have nothing but darkness. I live on this desolate hillside with L.M. munching by me. *But I can fight through all this* if I am in touch with you. If you are ill *Richard must let me know immediately*.

Reality, Bogey, is ALWAYS less than my dreams and apprehensions. If you will bear that in mind you will make life easier. SILENCE is the ULTIMATE BLACKNESS. I must stop crying and send this to post. Oh God! what an end of all my fine hopes—to be writing my S. of France

[1] These are words from a music-hall song.

letters because of these cursed posts! The weather is perfect hell: the sea roars: it's never never quiet—it eats away the air. The room is half dark and I'm alone all day all day all day every day every day. Mrs. Jones can do up a paper, can't she? But you are so pitiful. Have pity on me and WRITE.

      Wig

Nothing is hopeless. Nothing is lost. No new terror has been added, no new fear, really. But this loneliness is what opens the gates of my soul and lets the wild beasts stream howling through. I shall get over it. Let us keep firm. But write me AT LENGTH.

Monday,

My darling,   (November 3, 1919)

    I am sending 3 novels together this week so as to be ready for the new ones. As Madeleine and Virginia are evidently on a like tack (from what V. told me of her book) I'll do them together.

No letter came today, but the paper did. We had the devil of a great storm last night, lasting for hours—thunder, lightning, rain, and I had appalling nightmares. I think it must be the noise of the sea which makes me dream so: it excites one's nerves at night. One longs for it to 'lie down' . . . old age, I expect. After the thunder the day is very lovely, cool, but so *definite* and on *a big scale*. I began to write an article for the paper yesterday called 'Eternity'; I hope it will be finished today. If you don't care for it, please just keep it: it will go in some book some time or other. It's so nice to walk in this little garden. After tea yesterday I went up and down, up and down, thinking out things. It was then I hit on the subject for the article.

I've been out of doors all day, still am, in fact,—under a sunshade on the verandy. I feel quite all right, not a suspicion of anything is wrong with me, but I'm FLAT. It's the albatross round my neck. *Never* mind. She will be cut off in April and fly back to Rhodesia. But it's weary living with her, and never seeing another person. I come up out of my pool, and there she is on the side staring down into the water, glassy-eyed, to find me. Oh, I do *hate* her so. There's nothing to be done. A maid would not help matters in the least. Of course, nearly all the time I am working, but to come out of work to a person, the person whom you really *hate*—this is very horrible. No one can ever know what it is like, for the form it takes is so strange. Her passion for me feeds on my

367

hate. I won't talk about it, Bogey. I have only remembered it because it accounts for my *flatness*. Awful—isn't it?

However, let us put a penny in the box, let us have a tune. Let us nod and grin while the others get up and do our dancing for us, as we sit over here in the corner, waiting, waiting—for the bead curtains to jingle, to be pushed aside, for La Santé to come laughing, laughing in, running over to our corner, putting her arms round our neck and saying, 'My friend, my darling friend'. The garçon hovers by, biting his nails and shooting me a glance or two. I've read all *the* illustrated papers—*all* the comics. Suddenly he swoops forward and piles two chairs on the table next to mine. Good Heavens! it's really closing time! Why doesn't she come? Why doesn't she! . . .

I don't know why I am writing this. Please forgive it, my angel. And forgive me for not being gay. Forgive me for that. I always want to be like a little bell, ringing in our happiness when I write to you—but then at the same time I can't be insincere. It's such a predicament! And oh, my Bogey, *don't worry about me*. I'll get out of this. See in your mind's eye Wig under an umbrella much too large, thinking it's still raining, and open the window and tell her how silly she looks and how that policeman with his scythe is laughing at her.

Your life is so dreadfully hard, I feel. I ought to give you all that's fair. L.M. has gone off to 'look' at 'Bawdygerra' as she calls it and won't be back till evening, so I'm quite alone. Now I've come in to get out of the glare and am sitting in my room. Your spectacle case is on the mantelpiece. On the table with the Russian bottle and Ottoline's book and the green paper-knife is your spoon. I don't use it. I can't have it washed and polished here. I only eat fairy soup out of it. There's a strong eager wind blowing—very cool. I'll write about the *Athenæum* tomorrow, dearest, for I am giving this letter to Caterina when she comes up for the laundry—and here she is. Otherwise it will miss the post.

'Bon jour, Madame.'

'Bon jour, Caterina. Que vous êtes jolie, aujourd'hui.'

'Ah, c'est mon nouveau golfe!'

Goodbye my precious. I am for ever

Your own

Wig

Monday,

My darling Bogey, (November 3, 1919)

I got your Monday and Tuesday letters yesterday and they reassured me that nothing was wrong. In fact everything seemed all right: Sydney there for company and Eliot's poetry lecture . . . it sounds Gaierty.

The storm at present is hanging over: it has withdrawn to await reinforcements—a horrible lowering violet sky, a boiling sea like porridge, snow on the mountains. Fancy, with that, to get more air I had one side of the net up last night and I am bitten frightfully by mosquitoes. This is almost laughable. . . . Everything about this *Côte d'Azur* is lies. Why does one believe it? One might as well believe that London is a rich, magnificent city, or that the Midland Hotel, Manchester, is the most comfortable place in the world. Why believe *liars*? Everybody lies. I don't know: but there you are. Dostoevsky at least understands through and through. . . .

I feel a bit like the outside elements. At least I feel that they've had their way with me for the moment, and I'm now high and dry, on a rocky ledge looking up at the sky and simply vaguely wondering. I'M NOT ILL. No temperature today. I've taken it and written it down in my book. But I shall get up and go downstairs and lie in my little room. My joints won't stand any more bed.

I hope to get work done today; I long to—ah, so much!!! If that were possible I'd get back my *spirit*. When that goes (the power to work) then I'm nothing, just a straw before the wind. And I feel *one must hurry*. There are you and the paper—so important, so enormously important—your big number Nov. 12 nearly there. . . . Believe that I try ALL I can, every single bit I can. Nothing less than La Faiblesse (who is really the toughest old hag of them all) keeps me from the performance of my promises.

I had 2 letters from Father yesterday. He is ill, too, with the cold and, of course, terribly disappointed with the climate. Thinks it 'a perfect farce' . . . can't keep warm even in bed with a hot-water bottle and a Kaiapoi rug. Very anxious to know if my villa is adequately heated. I only pray he doesn't come here while this cold spell is on: he'd be so cross and want to make other arrangements and I could NOT stand that.

Good God! There's a little wavering gleam of sun on the wall— white, still. It makes everything look shabby and dirty. It's gone again.

Perhaps now I have encountered the whole troupe of fiends so early I shall get better of them and be at peace. I suppose anyone who has lived my life of the last two years is bound to have these moments. That is what I hope. When I am with you I am furious because you will not see 'happiness' in the future. Well, still, if we're together in our own home, living our own life, I *do see it*. Apart from that there is nothing: I mean there is just a living death or a dead one: it really don't signify. (Yes, it does).

But to walk, kiss the earth, run, laugh, go in and out of houses and rooms—if I could do any of these things!

'You are always an invalid—hein?' says Bobone, looking at me with absolutely inexpressive *red* eyes like an ox—no whites to them at all. 'Vot is your age? Dirty-five?'

'No,' I said. 'Dirty-one.'

'*Zo.*'

Well, well, well. Why do I feel like this about Dostoevsky—*my* Dostoevsky—no one else's—a being who loved, in spite of everything adored LIFE even while he knew the dark dark places?

Richard wrote me a little letter—so awfully nice. He is a very fine lad indeed. 'Jack seems happy in a quiet way and very keen on his paper.' He positively worships you. All his fineness is come from loving you. He is so young. You are in time to save him from so much that you suffered. There is no reason why he should not go straight ahead and grow into a *real man*. He put at the end 'Oceans of love'. Wasn't that sweet? Fancy *oceans* of love. Aren't they boy's words—such a fling about them.

Tell Wing Gan'ma has been a very pore girl and would love to see him climb on to her bed now and would make him a whole cake for himself with Wing written on it in mousetails of icing.

Well, my beloved Boy, goodbye for now. Perhaps this is partly due to the terrific shock of the cold and rain and dark—when one thought all was going to be so fair. It is well to look for reasons. I am always looking for reasons *why* my courage goes. But after all, here it is. I am not WELL—no good pretending I am. I'm bound to get these fits of depression I suppose. The only thing that helps is to feel that you are there, to know all about your life, which is my *real* life—not my sick life—and to WORK. We must stick to our six months. Last night I felt in the middle of the night L.M. must not turn us away from our month here: one must conquer that and not let her win. I shall try.

370

Remember always how long I've been ill and don't think hardly of me. I have been ill for 200 years.

Love me. I am your true love.

Wig

185 received; Hardy poem received.

Monday afternoon

Darling Bogey,   (November 3, 1919)

I think your poem is extremely beautiful. So awfully like you to have him him *dead* first. But Hardy beautifully understood, you say. Please do send me the letter you speak of. It has not fetched up,[1] but — then neither has *Art and Letters,* or *The Weekly Times,* or the American Letter, or the Italian grammar or the *Lit. Sup.* They all lie at the bottom of Bogey's head somewhere. . . .

Well, if you've had terrible weather, you have not had any worse than this place. Not a crumb worse. No one could ever convince me of that. And England has comforts—carpet, fire, porridge, coal, and so on that these parts have not.

I have heard from Thorpe; the books have arrived and he has credited me with 12/- which is quite good. Please get hold of it, will you? and do what you like with it. It's household money, isn't it? We decided that. Buy half a dozen serviettes or something like that.

I am longing to see the Paper. Did my Galsworthy get there? Was it all right?

I had a long characteristic most kindly letter from old Kay today. He said how Pa hated this coast and wished himself back in England. It was a really charming warm-hearted letter. I have sent Ida to San Remo today with a cheque to cash and the most extraordinary letter for the Bank Manager—all rubbish. I couldn't take the trouble to be perlite—curse him! So she's gone and I'm alone for the afternoon, thank goodness.

My breathing is much better today, so is my cough. Don't imagine I use up my new energy. Indeed, I don't. On the 11th of last month I walked to Ospedaletti. On the 18th I went to San Remo. But I've done *nothing* since and am going to do nothing but lie about and get up and go to bed. Don't imagine I exert myself physically, and I eat quite double what I did. I am awfully hungry—always.

[1] 'It has.' (Katherine's note.)

371

I've read your poem again. It is very noble and beautiful and it is so finely *tempered*, I mean, like steel is tempered. You will always write elegies, it seems to me. Even your lullabies are to deaders, small and great, and Love is the darling small house on the mountain of loneliness—*the house on the way*. Isn't it so? The human soul is very mysterious. Don't answer me. You *know*. Now I must work. Goodbye for now, darling.

Ever your Wig

Later. L.M. has just returned with your Thursday letter with Hardy's letter in it: I am more than glad you sent it me. It is a treasure. What a strange 'situation': how strange to acknowledge a poem on one's own death! How great the character that can so do: how different to us impatient creatures *craving* for life's fitful fever! Life, life! we cry. And Hardy writes so quietly as though he were already entering the quiet harbour, the sails furled, drifting in on a silent tide. You did very well to send them to him, unaltered. He is a man who, I am sure, would understand you very deeply. But after all, he is old, he has lived. He is a very old man. Perhaps with age, with long years, desire dies.

I can imagine you writing this very letter to a jeune homme of the next generation, in all its particulars, except your wife won't have a tomb. She'll have at most a butterfly fanning its wings on her grave, and then off.

L.M. returned from the Bank. By cashing cheques there I drop a deal of money: I can't afford to do so again, but Kay had taken such pains to arrange the matter (and as he said 'tickle them up') that I felt I couldn't start another plan. Sentimentality, you see, which costs me 22 lire. It won't do. I always feel people's *feelings* are being hurt: I suppose they are not really, and I'm very silly to imagine they have such hurtable feelings.

How dreadful—Sullivan away and Aldous away. You will have to begin slaving again. And then there will come my letters. Oh God, why do I write? Perhaps it would be better not to write letters. You'd be all right, and I'd pull through, or not—just the same, I suppose. Anyway I am not ill and don't *cry* today, which is a big relief!!

Goodbye precious

Wig

Chinese Poems and Monkhouse received   Tuesday,

My darling Bogey,   (? November 4, 1919)

The paper has just come and I am enjoying it tremendously. It seems to me to be an excellent number. The 'Preface' little essay[1] is good: I like R.L.S.' remark,[2] don't you? And Swinnerton is very sound.[3] That is a useful article from the *trade* point of view as well: good for the circulation. Who wrote 'Fatigue'?[4] I love that kind of article—with a frog in it, even though I pity the poor frog so I feel I *must* have him out of it. L'Hôte is really a splendid fellow, and I am ashamed I did not realize how good Dent was until lately—not only good, but such a personality comes through, something wonderfully unaffected, sincere, English and kind.

I wish J.S.[5] would do the drama. He's the man, don't you think? His Euripides is *famös*. It's just right. . . .

So we tickled Ambrose up. Why not get Mrs. Maufe to write defending something or other or at any rate telling us how it should be done? I was very sorry to see that arch-snorter, that fatuous old sea-lion E. blowing. I'll never forgive that creature a letter he wrote to Spender: it makes me utterly detest him. Besides, his letter with its 'tang, gusto etc'—What rot! murmured a stray lady in the crowd.

A funny foreign article in evening dress with kid gloves—a 'name day' bow on Couperus, but it has a deal of information. I must go through all the paper again at tea-time. I am just reviewing Romer Wilson and Stella Benson together for this week. 'A Real Book and an Unreal One'—the flowers go to young Stella. Romer Wilson is one of the ladies of fashion who are teaching us how to put on our clothes. But she's tremendously absurd. I have got her, as she would say, on a trident.

It was a fine morning. Now it is very hazy—milk-white. I feel *dead* emotionally and spiritually—just 'not at home', but mentally and physically I feel harder than I have since I got ill. You had better not pay much attention to me. Perhaps part of my awful depression *is real maladie*—sickness, poison, a real symptom of tuberculosis. I don't know.

[1] On Prefaces. By Bonamy Dobrée.

[2] 'It is best in such circumstances to represent a delicate shade of manner between humility and superiority, as if the book had been written by someone else, and you had merely run over it and inserted what was good.'

[3] *Author and Publisher,* by Frank Swinnerton.

[4] Mr. Geoffrey Keynes, I believe.   [5] Mr. James Strachey.

When I say dead emotionally, my own darling. I mean to all people except you—to all external things. You, Wing, Richard, our life is hidden away, deep—but all else I don't care a straw for. It's good to be in this air because it makes me better physically, but I wouldn't care if all the geraniums turned into cabbages. I don't want to look—NO. WORK, that's all.

Ever your own girl

Wig

183 with 10/- received
and Pa's letter
Wednesday,
My own Precious Bogey,
(November 5, 1919)

This Friday 4 p.m. letter has a bit frightened me. You are for certain keeping something back, what is it? Is it that I am not sending enough work? Is that it? Are things not going well somewhere? Are you fatigued with writing letters? I have read and re-read it; each time again I feel the *quelquechose*. It's true you drew a heart at the end, but then I felt you did that to disguise the other—to fill up some vacuum which you were conscious of. Do I imagine this, or is it true? I wish you had not sent me the book money. Keep it in future. I shall put this by and buy plates with it for our home. I shall do as you suggest henceforward with the books.

Be open with me, darling. What is it? You don't say to me 'I am in the best form'. That's not us. It's just your silly over-courage. I am thankful you have Sydney there with you—tremendously thankful. He must take the edge off the empty house—and then there is our precious little grub, trailing ash over the carpet.

I finished my Benson and Wilson last night and am tackling Dosty today, I can't go any faster just now. You must just give the overplus to others if I don't go fast enough. *I understand.*

It's warmer today, with a huge wind blowing and working up for rain—all deep greys. The wind *tugs* at the trees, *tugs* at the waves. It's a vile wind.

Yesterday a parson came to see me from San Remo and his wife— he a glazed old fish, almost imbecile—she a grinning nightmare, eating her veil as she talked. They said, with gay bridlings: 'This is our *January* weather.' How very nice! I smiled away. L.M. was out. I think she thought me very fishy. To Hell with her.

I wish the sun would shine, I wish it would—hot, bright sun day

374

after day. I've managed to get good porridge here, which makes all the difference to breakfast, and at last we can get *rice*. The food's all right; it couldn't be better really or more plentiful—unlimited excellent butter and so on.

Do you think, later on, you will be able to get away for week-ends? It's no good now, because the weather is too bad and you're too tired. You'd get colds. You ought to *rest* at home: but you never do rest. But later on, do you think? It would be wonderful to know of the house, even if we weren't there. Even Hampstead rests me to think of. It *is* my home. I *have* a home. I have every right to sit on the stairs and look at Wing come lopping up. I love 2 Portland Villas from here. I'd kiss the gate and the door. Often I go in and wander through and look out of the windows, with love, with love. My room was so beautiful—the long glass reflecting the books—the Black Monk[1]—the exquisite clock, and the brass scuttle. These things I expect you take in your stride. In my memory I caress them—they are beloved darlings. To turn that unwilling key in the Black Monk—oh, what joy! To curl up on the Stickleback and to have Wing climb up the outer shell and then walk over unimportant me! And my chest of drawers—the special one! Don't let us ever give up our things—truly I *couldn't*.

I don't like foreign countries or foreign ways or foreign houses. It's only the sun that tricks them out. When the sun goes it is as though the flesh were gone, and there's nothing to tell over but ugly bones.

Well, Bogey, my precious little husband, I'll begin working. Thank God, you found our Wing again: he must never be really lost. And will you tell me what the cream jug is like. Describe it when you have time. This is an ancient wind. In spirit I put my hands on you gently and kiss you—but not interrupting, not interfering. *All is well here.* Don't worry. We shall get through. We are winning, but the fight has been so long.

      Ever your own
        Wig. Amen.

                                Thursday,
My precious Bogey,   (November 6, 1919)

It has just stopped raining and is steamy, misty and cool. I'm out on the verandah: the sea sounds heavy, so is the air—one feels wonderfully

[1] The Black Monk, so-called from Tchehov's story, was a big cupboard which I painted black and yellow for Katherine.

tired. The *Nation* came yesterday but no letter. Father wrote to me. He is motoring over here next Wednesday—it will be all right, I suppose. It doesn't matter, anyway.

Not having heard from you I feel a bit dumb: I feel as though I were standing at a door waiting for it to open—or sitting up against it (more like that) just waiting. I wish I were a great deal more self-supporting. It's a thousand times harder for me to write reviews here where I have no one to talk things over with. I'm 'out of it' and see so few papers and never hear *talk.* I have to get into full diver's clothes and rake the floor of the unprofitable sea. All the same *it is my life: it saves me.*

The woodman and his mate came yesterday. I feel a bit sentimental about him, because last time he was here you were here. He looked at the picture of Berne. 'C'est à Londres, ça? Jolie ville. Londres est sur le lac de Londres, n'est-ce pas?' And finding it was also a mirror, he twisted his moustaches in it. How nice he is! I thought etc., etc., until I had the bill. Same amount of wood, same size—115 francs, and it is to go up again this month. He declared also it is défendu to take the wood from the hillsides now. Coal—does not exist for private houses, only hotels. This is all rather a blow considering the climate, but we shall have to manage. But now I think I must have the book money, darling—if you don't mind. It's 'odd money', isn't it? And I had not reckoned on this expense. What do you think? Oh, as I write, I *feel* the sun comes out in my heart at any rate—or in your heart and I am turned towards you. When I wrote that 'darling' I suddenly changed all over —even physically—as though you were here. I didn't feel blind and shut and sealed up any more—but your true Wig, loving life. It's not six months now before we see each other. I'll be here in this Casetta and you will come here.

Oh, God, let us try to make this our last separation. At any rate it will be. I'd never bear another. They are too terrible.

Give Violet my love. I will write her on Sunday and Richard too. But you have every single bit of me that is worth the giving, my own love.

181, 180   Friday,
My darling,   (November 7, 1919)

She came back with your Saturday night and Sunday letters (enclosing Butler). They heap coals of fire on my head. But I must tell you. Your Saturday letter when you spoke of us being lovers was like a credo, I believe to me. It seemed to bring the future, near and warm and *human*. At sight of it—of so much life—the birds drew back, flew up and away. And then you seemed to tell me so much of what you were doing, and it was home-like. Our tiny Wing, clean in patches!

Early summer morning—think of it—a day before us—in the garden and in the house. Peace. Holding each other, kissing each other, until we are one world.

It is all memories now—radiant, marvellous, faraway memories of happiness. Ah, how terrible life can be! I sometimes see an immense wall of black rock, shining, in a place—just after death perhaps—and *smiling*—the *adamant of desire*. Let us live on memories, then, and when the time comes, let us live so fully that the memories are no nearer than far-away mountains.

Richard sent me another of his letters: you and he eating sausages and mash. *Hug* the old boy for me—tell him he's my brother.

My 'Eternity' seemed perfect rubbish: I'll send it if you like. It seemed to go out as I wrote and I raked ashes. I'll send Butler back tomorrow. I'll send Dosty tomorrow. This isn't a letter. It's just a word again with you, my precious lover.

I've paid Porter.[1] It's all right. I wish you'd go, though.

Think of me as your own

Mouse

The Athenæum for Ever!!! Saturday afternoon,
My own Bogey, (November 8, 1919)

I will give this letter to L.M. to post in San Remo. I went out today and weighed myself and found in a fortnight I had gained over 2 lbs. I weigh 46 *kilo* 70 and last time it was just on 45. This is as you can see extraordinary. Now you will believe that I rest. I went then to the P.O. and found your Monday letter written after three awful ones of mine. What could I do? I could only send that p.c. *Now* I want to say I would really count it almost as fearful if you gave up the *A.* and came out here as if all were lost. It would in a way mean all was lost; it would mean scrapping our future. Never think of it; never do it. I can imagine nothing more horrible for us both than that. It would mean—looked at from whatever angle—that this thing had beaten us. Oh, it is just not possible to contemplate such a thing. I had rather live here the 2 years

---

[1] Katherine's dentist.

than that. That is the solemn truth. You see, I *am* getting better; my body is getting better. I have a theory that perhaps the creaking and pain I had were caused by the moist spot drying up in my bad lung. It's quite possible. Old Bobone would of course not know a thing like that. But he, good as I think he is, does not believe tuberculosis is curable; it's evidently a craze of his. I saw it, and he said as much. 'Quick or soon coma de fever'—

But never come to me or give up a thing or send me money or bind yourself, whatever I say *now or in the future*. Please my own precious, NEVER do. We must see this through *successfully*; not otherwise. If you will just accept the fact that I am not gay—see? I will try not to talk of my loneliness or depression nor of L.M.

It is a bright sunny day today and I am not in the least tired after my walk—only hungry.

As usual I thought I was going to have it all my own way—get well, be happy, the horror of my disease over (it *is* a horror), peace with L.M. and ease to work in. What a fathead I am! Out of those—I'll get well—and that's all and enough. Let the others wait. *Work* of course. Work is second breath. When you spoke of planting a tree of hope, I felt—oh, it was *you* to speak so. Plant it—plant it, darling—I will not shake it. Let me sit under it and look up at it—spread it over me and meet me there often and let us hold each other close and look up into the boughs for buds and flowers. No, there's no God. That is queer. This morning I wanted to say 'God keep you!' or 'Heaven guard us!' Then I thought of *The Gods,* but they are marble statues with broken noses. There is no God or Heaven or help of any kind but Love. Perhaps Love can do everything. 'Lo! I have made of love all my religion.' Who said that?[1] It's marvellous.

L.M. is ready to go. I shall have the place to myself. It's nice. Then I turn into a real Mouse and make as tiny a noise as possible—so as not to disturb the life round me.

We shall not get another sou out of Father, darling, not on any account. I wish you would send him a farewell note to the Hotel Westminster—just for 'the firm'—would you? It *does* please me enormously that he goes back to N.Z. enthusiastic about us. And he is. The worst of it is he keeps writing about us going there. 'Pray God the day be not far off.' It *is*; it's very far. I want Sussex and you and Richard and the cats—but only YOU.

[1] It is a line from a poem of mine.

(b) The Lit. Sup. received
(a) 178 received   Sunday,
Bogey,   (November 9, 1919)

Your letter was terrible but I knew it would be because of my
Hellish ones to you. It was the one in which you'd phoned Sorapure.
But by now you will know how things are and I swear I shall not fail
again, however long I stay here. Trust me once again.

The papers have come; I've been reading them. The ad. of the *London
Mercury* gave me a terrific knock of fright. Then I've read the ——. The
disgraceful dishonesty of it! The repellent log-rolling. The review of
Dostoevsky and the one of ——! My God! what has happened to this
age? It cannot have been like this before. Look here! we must be bold
and beat these people. We must be dead straight in our reviews. If they
don't care for what we say, it doesn't matter, but let us come bang out
into the open while we have the chance and say it. I confess the world
seems to me really *too* hideous. I felt after I had read the *Times* that it was
all like Mrs. Fisher's party (you remember, when we ran away). My
blood is up. Let's up and at 'em this winter. Send me as many books as
you like. I'll do them. I have got my second wind from all this.

Oh, my darling soul, how could I have cried out so? Blow me and
my depression. What does my personal life matter! Let it go. It's hateful. But *we* matter: we have a chance to stand for something. Let's
stand for it. Of course, I now see plainly that we shall never be successful writers—impossible. But let's be honest in the paper and give it them
strong. There must be young people who see through this crabbed malice.

If it were not so tragic it would be—no, it wouldn't. I am *all* for the
paper now. I am with you every moment in all you do for it. I am
your cabin boy.

Sweep me away, Bogey, sweep me away. Let's work this winter and
when we meet in the spring let us forget work. As regards the *Times*—
there has been no war. All is as before. What a crew! I only wish I were
with you. I could tell you what I feel. Besides, we could work together.
But we must do that from here. I have the Albatross against me the
whole time, which is maddening, but I must beat her, too. Let's just
win all the way round.

At the same time, I hate and loathe it all—these sets and dishonesties
don't you? I mean it is the stern daughter of the voice of God that make
one fight, not a joyful impulse.

I wish Sorapure had not seen my private note. That hurt a bit. I winced and hung my head and felt horribly ashamed. We must never speak of ourselves to *anybody*: they come crashing in like cows into a garden.

Love, believe me, I'll not fail again. Fire away, old ship—sail on serenely into the deep waters I shall never send another signal of distress —NEVER. And may my precious little Boge sailor whistle to the morning star. It's bright sun today with a huge wind and sea like thunder.

The grammar came. Thank you, darling. But the papers are a real godsend. Bogey. tell me you forgive me. I will never be ill again. Let us *fight* now and then lay down our arms and love.

Your own own
Wig the Warrior

Monday morning,

My own dear Love,   (November 10, 1919)

Here is another Monday. They do seem to come round so fast, like the horses we saw at the fair—no, the *roosters*—that was our one, wasn't it? Do you remember those little Princesses who went round for ever? They wore cotton frocks and tiny leather belts.

It's a chill, strange day. I breakfasted in Valhalla—cracks of lightning, thunder, tearing rain. Now I'm on the verandy and the clouds are immensely near and distinct like mountains.

Will you please say if my Dosty is all right? I sent it rather in fear and trembling, but I meant it. I am doing Virginia for this week's novel. I don't like it, Boge. My private opinion is that it is a lie in the soul. The war never has been: that is what its message is. I don't want (G. forbid!) mobilisation and the violation of Belgium, but the novel can't just leave the war out. There *must* have been a change of heart. It is really fearful to see the 'settling down' of human beings. I feel in the *pro-foundest* sense that nothing can ever be the same—that, as artists, we are traitors if we feel otherwise: we have to take it into account and find new expressions, new moulds for our new thoughts and feelings. Is this exaggeration? What *has* been, stands. But Jane Austen could not write *Northanger Abbey* now—or if she did, I'd have none of her.

There is a trifling scene in Virginia's book where a charming young creature in a light fantastic attitude plays the flute: it positively frightens me—to realise this *utter coldness* and indifference. But I will be very careful and do my best to be dignified and sober. Inwardly I despise them all for a set of *cowards*. We have to face our war. They won't. I believe, Bogey, our whole strength depends upon our facing things. I mean facing them without any reservation or restraints.

I fail because I don't face things. I feel almost that I have been ill so long for that reason: we *fear* for that reason: I mean fear can get through our defences for that reason. We've got to stand by our opinions and risk falling by them.

Oh, my own Bogey, you are the only one in the world for me. We are really absolutely alone. We're a *queer couple,* you know, but we ought to be together—in every sense, really. We, just because we are 'like this', ought not to be parted. We shall not be after May. I'll come home then.

Do you want to know how I am? Yesterday, upstairs in my room I suddenly wanted to give a small jump—I have not given a small jump for two years—you know the kind, a jump-for-joy. I was frightened. I went over to the window and held on to the sill to be safer. Then I went into the middle of the room and *did* jump. And this seemed such a miracle I felt I must tell somebody. There was nobody to tell. So I went over to the mirror—and when I saw my excited face I had to laugh. It was a marvellous experience.

Blessed little Wing! Kiss his nose for me and whistle in his ear and say 'Your gan'ma loves you'. She does. I wish he would have *one* kitten in May. Has he grown very big? And how is Athy? And how does the house look? Does it shine? And do you have nice food? Why can't we meet in dreams and answer all each other's questions? Our nights are wasted.

The sea is up to the brim of the world today.

Your own
Wig

Monday night late in bed,
(November 10, 1919)

My own Love,

Your Wednesday and Thursday letters have come and the note about the hydrobromic acid and Sorapure's note. About your letters I feel inclined to requote you, but only half the phrase: There's nothing to say. I can only wait and wait till Wing brings you my postcard[1]

---

[1] Of November 8. 'I have just weighed myself and have gained TWO POUNDS.'

waving his tail and you know that all is well. I shall get the cough mixture made up as soon as the acid arrives: it will be a comfort. But what a Fate that my cough should have been these last few days so much better! It's almost cruel to say that, because of the trouble you have had; the chemist is still unable to get *any* of the acid here or from any town in France or Italy. Darling, tell me what this has cost your pocket: I will send a cheque. Tell me, please!

No, you will know by now I shall not go to Menton: or mix up with Connie and Jinnie in any way. With all these my defences I can ignore L.M. I am not cruel. She goes to San Remo and spends her money on rank cake and is happy, I know. She thinks it is all my illness and bides her time. I am tired of cursing myself—tired of repenting. I can say no more and do no more. You will never have to forgive me again as long as you live. I WILL NEVER CRY OUT AGAIN. You make me feel like a vampire. I can't understand why you don't hate me. There was all your pressure of work and I chose the moment to crash. What a fool I was! How blind! It has been the lesson of my life. You are never to fear that again; *that* at least will not happen to us again. *Last moments* are always terrible moments. Those days here were the last moments of two terrible years: that is how they appear to me. All my . . . 'feelings' for the last 2 years went into them and I cried out, and of course of course of course dragged you in. Yes, I feel as though I drowned you. You almost make me feel it is unpardonable of me to feel better; that having made you suffer so, I should have justified myself by getting worse and worse. . . . Do you feel that? It's a bitter taste.

The *A.* is here and *Art and Letters* and *The London Mercury.* Let us talk about them a little. I am hugely relieved by seeing the lion after all the trumpets. —— is quite a big enough flea in his ear to keep him from doing aught by scratching. What a piece of *grocery prose* is the editorial! But the lack of style, poise, dignity—the boosting of his shop, the crying down of the wares of the gentleman over the way—Good God! His 'fungoid' writers and 'sterile' young men *and* so on. I take a deep malicious delight that his vulgar literary Harrod's should be so bad. I had thought it would be a great deal better. Really, his article on the 'Poet' and Nichols' mock opals *and* the tooth-comb run through Rupert's bright locks *and* the reviews—so undistinguished. But this makes me keener than ever on our own paper (*our* in humility, love; it's your hat, yes, I know). Bogey, —— is not up to much, is he? Can you get out of him? He can't write: he's *no* point of view. He hasn't a word to say about Fay Compton, yet there's nothing but her—and look at his prose: 'need we say', 'needless to say', 'needless to specify'. He's absolutely colourless.

The article on 'The Critic' is excellent, but of course the paper has only one gem. That is, I think, flawless. I feel I shall have to send you a telegram about it tomorrow. It thrilled me so that I had to run to the door and search the stars and the dark moving sea: I couldn't get calm after it. And all the while I felt how supremely good that Hardy should be so understood in his day—how supremely right that you should speak for this silent generation. We shall remember it with joy all our lives.

Oh, I feel our responsibility is so tremendous: I wish now I could take back my review of Stella Benson and beat it into shape. I shall write far better from henceforward. And I am so strong now. I can tackle any amount of work.

You are at rest again, my beloved. I hardly dare to ask. I shall send little Wing as my messenger: 'She says: is it all right?' And then he must come and tell me. 'Yes, he says it's all right but I don't know if he wants to see you.' 'Oh, Wing, go back and see!' He is gone. I'll have to wait.

It's midnight. The sea roars. I must lie down and go to sleep like a good girl. Today I have been gathering roses on the hill. The hedges are full of deep cream roses. But I can't tell you these things or anything until—Wing comes back.

Your love
Wig

It is the papers that solve the L.M. problem. That's why they matter so.

Tuesday. I wake up so happy, my darling love. I just want to say this. If you can make somebody else send me regularly the *Lit. Sup.*, the *Weekly Guardian* and of course *our* paper, I can go on here, *full of fire*. These papers have made me feel in touch with *the* paper. I cannot exist without mental stimulants, even though they are such that provoke my rage or contempt. They create a vacuum which is filled with one's own ideas. Is that foolish to you? But, you see, here they are society for me: my kittens, my acquaintances, all the talk I have, all the interruptions which send L.M. out of the room. Do you see what they mean? I will pay an extra 10/- a month for postage etc.

Two novels came today. No letter. I am doing Virginia for this week. Next week I shall do Hewlett, Stackpoole together, and the week after Monkhouse and Benjy. That finishes all I've got. I am on for *any* frisk you care to send me and have got (p.G.) my second wind.

Mistral blowing. Very cold here and sea like metal. But my room upstairs is as good as a verandy, and warm in the sun. Love to Violet and to Athy and to Wing (what is left over)

Wig

Salzman is quite a good chap, but he needs watching. 'A memory of pre-Pelman date' is a bit thick in the *A*. Aren't the *Mercury* reviews unthinkably bad? The vocabulary!! But we must get some poetry. Ou est Henri King? E. Stanley is so slight and thin!!

Good News!   175 received   Tuesday,

      Rutter received   (November 11, 1919)

My little mate,

(I shall answer your letter après). I have just had the extraordinary comfort of seeing a really first-chop doctor—the man Ansaldi. L.M. was at San Remo. It was getting dusky. There was a ring at the bell and I opened the door and nearly fell into the arms of a beaming, glistening Jewish gentleman mit a vite felt hat. I immediately decided he was a body-snatcher and said, most rudely, 'Vous désirez?' At which he replied 'Ansaldi' and abashed me very much. He came in—dark bright skin, gleaming eyes, a slight stoop—and said, 'Oh vot a nice little house you have here!' The *spit* of the music halls. It made me feel terribly laughy. I don't know: L.M. away, this solitary spot, this queer stranger with his stethoscope in a *purse* (it would be a purse) and me in less time than it takes Wing to pounce, sitting draped in my flowery shawl, with my discarded woollen coats strewing the floor like victims. He examined me before he saw my chart.

My bad lung he says is drying: there's only a small spot left at the apex. (When I was in London there was a spot the size of a hand.) The other has also a small spot at the apex. I told him my history to date and he says that I have gained weight and can eat are excellent signs. There is no reason (bar accident) why I should not recover. 'Never to be a lion or shoot the chamois or the hare'—*figurez-vous,* my darling, I'd rather feed them with rose leaves—but to lead a normal life, not the life of an invalid. The chances are, he says, 99 to 100 that I can do this.

He gave me no medicine, saw my prescriptions and said that was just what he would have prescribed. The fact of so little fever, my appetite, weight and that I can sleep are all in my favour. He says it will take two years to cure me but I shall be a great deal better by April and able to live at home, but never to be in London after September.

He was urgent about no mental worry, *very* urgent, but work—all you like and be in the air and walk, but never to tire yourself. Always stop everything before you are tired. I'll tell you the truth. He said I was not half warmly enough dressed. He was most emphatic on that, though I was wearing my jaeger and a jersey and a cardigan. He says this climate is admirable and especially here because the air is *balsamic* and positively healing, but one must take absolutely no risk as regards a chill. Never to go out uncovered and really never to know what it is to feel cold: he says that wastes one's energy—fighting the cold. This I am sure is sensible. But what was so good was his *confidence* in me: it made me feel so confident. He told me I had so much *life* even in my skin and eyes and voice that it was abnormal for me to be ill and that was my great 'pull' over other consumptives. He's coming again in a fortnight. But after closely examining my chart and reading *aloud* that writing we couldn't read, he pronounced a definite improvement. Isn't that really superb? (I'll not always be such an egoist.) Of course, he told me a chill or influenza might mean disaster, or mental worry—but I must try to avoid these things. And also he impressed on me that I shall never be a lion. That, of course, is bad, one wants to be a lion, but after these years to think I could lead a normal life is lion-like enough.

But here's a brilliant, clever, sympathetic doctor on the spot, see? When I go to San Remo I must please to call on him so that he may show me some little politeness (as though he had a collection of them I saw them, darling little tinies, sitting on his finger). Then like the bee, the lizard and the man in the poem 'he went away'. *I* went upstairs, put on an extra pair of stockings and a scarf and came down and had tea and ate four delicious fresh dried figs with it. Terribly good!

I won't spare money or fires. I'll be as good as gold and May will be *divine.* I shall spend the £2 10 0 on wood, Bogey, but now *keep* the book money. Keep little Wing and keep him warm.

385

Rutter is good.[1] I'll do it. But I've sent back Kurt,[2] so I must write and ask 'em for a copy. Fancy calling my writing *critical essays*! I saw you wink at Wing and Wing overcome turning a catherine wheel (with a K).

Do you know what time I go to bed here? 7.30 or 6.45. There is not a chair or a sofa to sit on: I am driven there. But it's a good idea.

Everything seems to me good tonight except you. You're BEST.

Answer me. It's so curious. I still feel positively shy of you. I can't ask you to kiss me even, after I 'broke down' so.

Bogey, when you have the time and if it is *easy* can you send me a woollen scarf? I'll pay you by cheque. (I *must*—you *must* let me—pay for things or I shall stamp and rage.) But I mean one of those soft blanketty scarves that goes round once and twice and covers one's mouth. Do you know the kind of thing I mean? Ask Richard. I feel he might be very practical about clothes. But it must be *woolly* and long and warm. I'll pay up to £2 2 0 for it and you can choose the colour— a grey-green, I should think, or purple—yes, purple—or whatever you like. This is just when you have the time. I expect Jaeger would have them. But I need it here. NOT fearfully urgent—just when you have the leisure.

Now goodbye, my One.

Your One, too
(a joke.)

Wednesday,

My precious own,   (November 12, 1919)

I got a telegram from you today—it was an extra luxury, a *great* joy —but it is not to happen again. A nice little boy literally *blew* in with it.

Strange, strange day! My party has just gone—Connie, Jinnie (admirable person) and Papa. They arrived at about 10.30 (I expected them two hours later). But it didn't matter. The Casetta seemed to turn into a doll's house. Pa couldn't even find room for his glasses. The womens' furs and coats and silk wraps and bags were scattered every- where.

Pa suggested a run into San Remo, which we took. I was, I am, just a little corrupted, Bogey darling. That big soft purring motor, the rugs

[1] Frank Rutter, editor of *Art and Letters*, had asked Katherine to contribute a review of some novels.

[2] Richard Kurt. By Stephen Hudson.

and cushions, the warmth, the delicacy, all the uglies so far away. We 'ran' long past San Remo: it was *thrilling* for me. I didn't dare to speak hardly because it was so wonderful, and people laughing and silly Pa talking Maori down the whistle to the chauffeur. Very silly—but very nice somehow. It carried me away. Then we got out and bought a cake and were, as they say, the cynosure of all eyes, and it was nice, too. I was glad the chemist saw me (see what a snob you married!) and then while Connie and Jinnie were at Morandi's, Pa and I talked and the sun streamed into the car and he said we were like a couple of hot-house plants ripening.

They have just gone. Jinnie left me a pair of *horn* spegglechiks of her grandfather's (the kind on a long black ribbon which suit me admirably). She took photos of the Casetta, too, and said, 'They'll do to send your husband'. I don't know what happened. They seemed to me so many. Father at the last was wonderfully dear to me. I mean, to be held and kissed and called my precious child was almost too much—to feel someone's arms round me and someone saying, 'Get better, you little wonder. You're your mother over again'. It's not being called a wonder, it's having *love* present, close, warm, to be felt and returned, And then both these women had been terribly homesick for their dogs, so they understood Wing. That was nice too.

Pa did not like this place, neither did they. They were horrified by the cold. Pa said that at Menton they have had *none* of this bitter wind. that it has never been cold like today. He seemed to think I had made a great mistake to be in such a thin house and so exposed. So, alas, did they. They said Menton was warm, still, with really exquisite walks, sheltered. I said I'd consider going there in the spring. But I won't. When the bad weather is over, here will be warm too. And I don't want a town. I don't want to uproot. At the same time I was a bit sorry it was so much warmer. I *fed* them and Pa left me five 3 Castles cigarettes!!! He made the running, talking French, telling stories, producing spectacles. (He had four pairs of them. Connie had three, and Jinnie had three.) At one moment they were all trying each other's on—in this little room. It was like a dream. [A drawing of many pairs of spectacles.] And here on the table are five daisies and an orchid that Pa picked for me and tied with a bit of grass and handed me. If I had much to forgive him, I would forgive him much for this little bunch of flowers. What have they to do with it all?

Wig

387

Thursday,
My own Love,   (November 13, 1919)

This is the third day without a letter. I believe the Post Office does it on purpose. I have a box there which I bought for 14 lire where all my letters and so on are kept so as to avoid any mistake, but they don't care.

I went to the Post today down the road past the railway station through a small *place* and up some steps. Did you ever go that way? I did not cough once all the way and came home past the shops and wasn't in the least tired. It is a brilliant day, bitter cold here, but on the level—gorgeous. There's no doubt about it, Boge, the Casetta is *not* a warm one. This morning, for instance, it was *icy* here, really perishing cold: even in my room the wind was so sharp. I went out and dressed in furs and a shawl and woolly coat and after ten minutes on the level was much too hot. There was no wind there, either. But coming back, as soon as I began to climb the steps, the wind could be felt. The two front rooms are, of course, unlivable till after lunch, but that shelter is as bad—even worse: it's a wind trap. I shall always, when it's fine enough to go out, walk in the mornings now, and then (as usual) write here in the dining room in the afternoon. But the difference of temperature between here and in the village!

Did you ever explore the village, darling? It is so lovely—more beautiful than Bandol. All is seen against the huge background of the purple mountain. It was silent today except for an old woman crying fish and the boys flinging a ball among the trees of the *place*; but it feels gay, rather fantastic. The air smelled of pines and of deep yellow roses which grow everywhere like weeds: they even climb up the aloe trees.

I can't describe (yes, I *could*) what real convalescence feels like. I decide to walk in the road, and instead of stopping, putting my stick off the pavement, then one foot, then the other, I take a little spring with all three legs and have to hold myself back from crying to an indifferent native: *Did* you see that superb feat? (That is not intended for a Pa joke.)

I am reviewing Virginia to send tomorrow. It's devilish hard. Talk about intellectual snobbery—her book *reeks* of it. (But I can't say so.) You would dislike it. You'd never read it. It's so long and so tāhsōme. By the way, my dear, I gave Connie the *Oxford Book of English Verse* to look at yesterday while she was testing somebody's specs and she said a moment after, 'There are some quite pretty things here, dear.

Who are they by?' . . . What do you think of that? I *should* have replied: Temple Thurston. Instead I pretended not to hear.

Look here! I want you terribly today. I want to see you—hold you, touch you, play with you, talk to you, kiss you—call you. I want to open one of those huge great cotton-pods with you and see what's inside. I want to discuss the novel with you and tell you what a darling of darlings you are.

Wig

174, 173 received   Friday,

My Precious Own,   (November 14, 1919)

These are the first letters I've had since last Monday and in them you say mine are not like stars appearing. What happens to our letters? If only one knew, there's some incredibly *silly* reason why they don't arrive, yet Pa said he got his regular and piping hot in three days. I loved your Sunday picture letter and saw it 'ever so' plain—you cross-legged, Richard reading and Wing discovering *terra nuova* in the chest of drawers. I am glad you have seen Brett. I feel about Lawrence—that I don't in the least know whether I want to see him or not. I do, and then there sweeps over me an *inscrutable* knowledge of his feeling about *you*—about you and me. He doesn't understand *us* or believe in *us*—and there you are. I can't do with people who don't. I am not one, individual, eternal: two in one, co-equal, co-eternal (or whatever it is). This, if people want me, they must realize. That's one reason why I *hate* L.M. She's always trying to make me 'one' again. But I must not speak of her. My life here with her must be between me—and nothing.

It's a bitter cold day, pouring rain, wind, fog, and air like acid. I am sitting in my room before the fire wrapped up snug with a hot bottil and Jaeger dressing gown over all. I am terrified of the cold and would go to any lengths to avoid it. Ansaldi's 'chill in your case would be a fatal disaster' rings in my ears when the weather turns like this. At the same time, God! what courage we have to remain apart, knowing that. It amazes me. But we could do nothing else, nothing else at all. It would be very wonderful to be rid of these melancholy thoughts, for them to withdraw into the forest and come out again for—say, fifty years. The fog and ceaseless drip of rain makes them very *impish*.

I wrote to Rutter saying 'Yes' and to Grant R. the day before yesterday. Now Sylvia Lynd is on my conscience. I'll write to her on Sunday. How I hate furrin parts today! I feel numbed when the sun goes in.

That's a great mistake—to think it a good idea to live facing the sea I've discovered it's a bad one. For this reason. When the sun is not out the sea is like a mirror without light. It simply *asks* for the sun far more than the land does. 'There's nothing to say, my heart is dead,' says the sea and goes on saying it in a loud keening voice. Another discovery is not to live alone and more or less tied to a house where the sea sounds so loud. If one broke up the noise with talk and kisses and walks it would be all right, but it has a frightfully depressing exciting effect if one doesn't. Sometimes I lie awake literally all night, so excited that I play Demon, *sing* and talk out loud to try to work it off. If there were a second person I don't think one would notice it. L.M. says she never does. These things one just has to find out.

I suppose, Bogey darling, there is not the vaguest hint of a house for us. Do you feel it's a great deal more difficult than you had imagined? I wish Fate would smile on our loves for once.

How awful about Marie Dahlerup! Yes, do please open any letters for me—or anything that may come. I much prefer you to.

L.M. is taking the train into San Remo to buy a few things for herself (???) No, I won't ask. But this letter shall be posted from there. It's almost too dull to send. Forgive me, love; it's the ugly weather and the COLD.

It's less than six months now before you come. And then we won't be separated again—no long separations—and we'll be AT ONE and together. If Virginia should not come in time this week, you've got Dosty, haven't you?

Goodbye, my precious darling. I am all yours and I love you for ever.

Wig

Let me see *Cinnamon* when you can, Bogey. How marvellous Hardy's love poems must be—these last. But the earlier one you quoted—*The Crucifix,* isn't it?

Dearest Own,   Saturday, (November 15, 1919)

I have just come downstairs and lighted my fire. Do you smell the blue gum wood and the pommes de pin? It's a perishing coal-black day, wet, dripping wet, foggy, folded, drear. The fire is too lovely: it looks like a stag's head with two horns of flame. I managed to get

390

Virginia off yesterday, but *not* without a struggle. I wanted to be sincere: I felt I had a duty to perform. Oh dear, oh dear! What's it all come to, I wonder?

This morning Jinnie Fullerton sent me a box of Khedive cigarettes. That was very nice of her. I admire her terribly. Pa sent me a letter. I feel that between them they are going to *move* me from here. It is I confess extremely cold and draughty here, but on the other hand—privacy, privacy, privacy. I won't go into a hotel or prisonette[?] or rooms where I'm not private. That's the *essential*. They (that is F. and his Co.) seem to think of Ospedaletti as a kind of rock that rears its awful form.

Oh, darling precious Jag Boge, isn't it nice when I write so small? I am taking very tiny little stitches with my pen and making eyes of admiration at myself. I wish the Albatross would produce lunch: it's nearly *one* and lunch is at 12 and I'm shaking like a leaf and trembling with want of it.

Now a fly has walked bang into the fire—rushed in, committed suicide.

Lunch.

Lunch over. Pendant ce repas L.M. suggested I should take the tram into San Remo and get another back in ten minutes, just to enjoy the sun. I would not drive a *strong* pig to market today: it's such a weed-killer. So this suggestion for me made me angry. She then said: 'Of course it is damp, the damp went right *through* me, but you do such funny things.' Now, I *don't* do funny things: I haven't for ages and I hate to be reminded. I came back and smoked a cigarette and got over it. On the cigarette paper it declares:

Qu'à aucun *moment* de leur fabrication, ni par quelque procédé que ce soit, aucune substance aromatisante, opiacée ou chimique, *en un mot,* qu'aucun *corps étranger* n'est introduit dans le tabac. . . .

One feels there must be snippets of sheik brûlé in 'em after that.

Did I tell you? When I was in San Remo in that motor I went to a bread shop, and there was a queer-shaped loaf which looked nice for tea. A kind of tea bread. So I said: Combien? and he said: I must pèse it, Madame. Will you take it? So I said Yes. And he pèsed it, did it up in a paper with a pink ficelle and said: Cinq-francs-juste-Madame! Now, what do you do then? I paid and took it and walked out—one living curse. But do the brave give it back? Which is the lesser humiliation? Have you ever decided that? I was awfully ashamed of myself.

Then I realised if it hadn't been for the motor, I would not have paid. It was the price of corruption....

All the same I read an article on small cars for tiny people (2 people, their luggage, a cat and its saucer and bastick) for 3d. a mile all round the world from door to door. Self-starter, electrical installation and a bag for the money to roll into when you come to the place where money rolls. That sounded to me the spit of us. I thought Wing as cleaner would be so good—in overalls, you know, wiping his little nose-box with a morceau of cotton waste. The trouble with those cars is they ought to cost 3d. to start with. It ought to be *all* 3d.—3d. all the way through. 'I'll have 3d. worth of petrol please, and a thrippenny horse to pull us out of this hole.'

By the way, *re* ——. She has been sending hampers of fruit even to Kay. Didn't you get one? Aren't they prize mingies? I have been silly enough for today.

I *wish* a letter would come. I'd like some good news to put in this room—no, to wear in my bosom. I am very well, darling love, with an old-fashioned face coming back, very bright eyes and a pink colour like Bandol. I hardly know it when I powder its nose.

Addio, my little mate.

Your
Wig-wife

Sunday, 8 a.m.,

My own Bogey, (November 16, 1919)

It was a fearful *blow* to get no letters yesterday again. I shall never understand it. When L.M. came back after the last chance, I *hid* for a moment or two upstairs, just to delay the 'No letters—nothing'. Perhaps my luck will turn today and the sea have a pearl.

Such a night! Immense wind and sea and cold. This is certainly no 'pensive citadel'. This morning the storm still rages. It's a blow. I long to go out and have a walk, but I daren't face the wind.

What is this about the novel? Tell me, thou little eye among the blind. (It's easy to see who my bedfellow has been.) But seriously, Bogey, the more I read the more I feel all these novels will not do. After them I'm a swollen sheep looking up who is not fed. And yet I feel one can lay down no rules. It's not in the least a question of material or style or plot. I can only think in terms like 'a change of heart'. I can't imagine how after the war these men can pick up the old threads as though it had never been. Speaking to *you* I'd say we have died and live again. How can that be the same life? It doesn't mean that life is the less precious or that 'the common things of light and day' are gone. They are not gone, they are intensified, they are illumined. Now we know ourselves for what we are. In a way it's a tragic knowledge: it's as though, even while we live again, we face death. But *through Life*: that's the point. We see death in life as we see death in a flower that is fresh unfolded. Our hymn is to the flower's beauty: we would make that beauty immortal because we *know*. Do you feel like this—or otherwise —or how?

But, of course, you don't imagine I mean by this knowledge let-us-eat-and-drink-ism. No, I mean 'deserts of vast eternity'. But the difference between you and me is (perhaps I'm wrong) I couldn't tell anybody *bang out* about those deserts: they are my secret. I might write about a boy eating strawberries or a woman combing her hair on a windy morning, and that is the only way I can ever mention them. But they *must* be there. Nothing less will do. They can advance and retreat, curtsey, caper to the most delicate airs they like, but I am bored to Hell by it all. Virginia, *par exemple*.

Here is the sun. I'll get up. My knees are cold, and my feet swim between the sheets like fishes.

Si tu savais com-me je t'ai . . . me! Oh Bogey, darling heart, I shall never reconcile myself to absence from you—never. It's waste of life. But be happy, my precious.

Wig

Cheque received   Sunday night,
(November 16, 1919)

Yes, my darling Love, your mood travelled to me unbroken, perfect, exquisite. It filled my heart, filled it to the brim so that I felt a great stillness and could scarcely breathe for joy. Oh, my own, I share, I share it all—your knowledge of how we have suffered, how we seem of all our generation to have been to the war, and your AND YET. I am looking at the letter as I write. Queer little fanciful things happen sometimes . . . each time you write AND YET these letters take a shape which is *like* you—they are a minute manifestation of you. The A walks, the Y is a man waving his arms, the E is someone sitting down

. . . oh, all this is nonsense, but all this is true, too. I remember at the Villa Flora sewing a button on your pigglejams and the button became a little image of you—a sign—so that I fell in love with it and kissed it and said to it 'Now stay there for six months' and I felt that it understood and felt very strong and determined every time you did it up. But your belongings are like that for me—they're sacred. When I see your hat, it becomes 'the only hat in the world' for me. Do you know how I love you, you strange little husband? Do you know how I dream sometimes that your darling dark head is beside me on the pillows? How often I've seen the dawn come into our top bedroom at Hampstead, waited until I could distinguish the figure of the man on the horse in the picture[1]—how often I have just touched you, sleeping, with my hand—or watched that dark beloved boyish head turned away from me? Mysterious Love!

Beautifully you say our suffering might pass away as a dream. When I am *really* with you it is gone. The day I watched you climb these steps, you had been to the fountain, you wore Feltie and a sprig of geranium. I watched you coming up towards me slowly, smiling, and something within me cried: 'Here comes my world!' We are like the twin doors of that *home* which is ours. *I enter it through you and you through me.*

This afternoon sitting by the fire in my room I suffered from desire as I have never suffered before. Everything seemed to become suddenly almost unbearably vivid and alive and lovely. It was a hot summer day —early evening—and we were in a big room like a studio with a great low divan. The shutters were shut: we were terribly, terribly happy. We looked deep deep in each other's eyes smiling at the happiness we were giving each other. You know that strange smile when the lips are so dark and the eyes gleam. . . . I can't write more about it even now.

Little Wing's telegram came this early afternoon. The postmistress must have known it was from him. She wrote Wing just as he would have done. It was a very lovely surprise.

I return the American letters. They are extremely gratifying. How nice the people sound. Of course you and I went to America and met them. '*Pleased* to meet you, *Mr.* Murrry.' She was charming. Now I'll go to sleep. Goodnight my precious.

[1] A Dürer etching.

Monday   Your Wednesday letter and the books received
My Bogey,

After the poisonous day yesterday it was calm here this morning and
I went to post. It was lovely in the village—warm as toast, I fanned my
wings many times and at the post I found this letter about the table and
the linen. I read it sitting under a tree that smelt of nutmegs—it was
full of great bunches of flowers and the bees were busy in and out. [It]
reminded me of old Dan Chaucer. I love to feel you are gathering the
feathers for the *new* perfect nest and an oak table is a very big feather
indeed. Oh, *what it means to get letters!* I wonder if you wrote me one on
Monday. It never came. Here at this moment comes L.M. with your
Thursday letter describing the dinner party and E.M.F. staying the
night and the cutlets. Violet is a treasure, Boge. It warms my heart,
chauffes it, to hear they are keen on the paper. Oh, I am so dissatisfied
with myself. You say lovely things to me and I feel I'll be better next
time and then, again I seem to *miss* it. You're right: I'm not a real
'cricket' at all and only sing on our private hearth really. But I do my
best and *thank Heaven if I please you.* But I feel such a fly beside you—
and I feel I ought to explain myself more. My review of Virginia
haunts me. I *must* improve, you know I just worship that old paper.
There it is, your ship. I stare at it, examine it, wonder at it. Thank you
for the cheque, darling. It's a grateful sight. I am so glad you have gone
to see Porter. He's good. He wrote me a nice little note here the other
day, hoping I was better. He's a *sound dentist,* too. The 4 books *all* look
deeply interesting. I'll try and do them justice.

It's a TERRIBLY cold day—really shocking. I have a big fire and a rug
and bottle and am wrapped up. The air is like ice—the sea like a sheet
of lacquer. Truly this is a cold spot, Boge. Yet I don't want to leave it. I
love Ospedaletti. I don't want Menton and a *band*. Here one works, lives
simply, is retired. If I got there people would call and so on, and it's no
good: I am not that kind of person. But I do wish it were not so cold.
Cold frightens me. It is ominous. I breathe it and deep down it's as
though a knife softly softly pressed in my bosom and said 'Don't be
too sure'. That's the fearful part of having been near death. One knows
how easy it is to die. The barriers that are up for everybody else are
down for you and you've only to slip through.

But this is depressing. Don't mind it.

Love me. I love you. We'll risk all, all—for our love.

                                                    Yours Wig

My precious,   (November 18, 1919)

First: I received your *Monday week* letter today (posted 10th arrived
18th) both the postmarks plain to see. Now how *can* that be? It had the
cream jug and Hardy in it, so thank goodness it wasn't lost. The cream
jug is a pearl. It's two dear little feet look as though it was skating on
cream or toboganning on cream. Heaven bless it and our Home!

Hardy's letter was most revealing. He's so frightfully *touching*. To say
that poem really happened. Oh God! isn't that like *you*! You seem to
me the next link in the chain after Hardy.

I received also your *Friday* letter and the paper and the *Lit. Sup.* and
the *Guardian*. A great feast. Your Friday letter frightens me about my
Virginia review. I missed it. Did I? Didn't walk round enough? I hope
to God you *won't* publish it if you feel that is true. I'd rather write
another, gladly, willingly, than that. What a cursed little creature I am!
Beat me!

The paper is simply *superb* this week. It's the best you've ever cooked.
'The tenderness and flavour, size and cheapness'—no, that don't fit—
but it's a perfect corker. I had to send a télégramme to say so. Your
review of Lewis is excellent—simply 1st chop, the Henry King poem
one of the best of his poems, and how apt it rang after Santy on
Experience. It's an amazing good number altogether. That *plus* the new
advertisements makes one feel that the child is 'getting a big girl now,
Eliza'.

Boge, it's a devilish day. 5.30 p.m. I'm just going to bed. It's too
parky to be up. The robber with the knife is everywhere—he's not even
afraid of the fire. No, darling, this climate is a *fool* of a climate—because
it's dishonest. It smiles and it stabs. Never again. Father is ill in Menton
—he has caught a chill. It goes through anybody. And you know how
hard it is to work in extreme parkiness. And one plays the old game,
pulling down the fire screen, hearing a great roar, pulling it up, meeting
a dead silence. But it can't be helped. I take as much care as a human
being could—that's all one *can* do. But if one has to go abroad again, it
must be der Schweiz *with stoves and windlessness*.

I keep pondering over our new Treasures—jug, linen and real
serviettes. We shall sit at breakfast table, delicately poised on our chairs,
like two butterflies hovering over a flower garden. Oh, that house! I
want to feel the walls, to smell the fire, to shut the door, to call you:

'Boge, come up here. There's a little room with a pear-tree in flower at the window.'

I can't write tonight, dearest. My back aches. I must go and lie down in a garden of hot water bottles. Nothing serious, only the cold. And yet there's so much I long to say, I long to talk over. *Your* letters are so marvellous.

Peake is the Oxford Street end of Wardour Street. I *think* '141'. He has a sign with his name on it from a first-floor window. As you face the street, it's on the left, about six doors down. DO GO. I feel I'd like you to sell all the office furniture bit by bit and put it into salt and pepper pots.

> Your own adoring
> **Wig-wife**

Wednesday le midi,

Dear Love, (November 19, 1919)

A most beautiful man has just been here to put the lock on the door— really a superb creature. He could *not* put the lock on the door so he spent his time explaining (1) how easy it would be for a person to come in at night (2) how unpleasant (3) how much wiser to trouver quelqu'un to sleep here seulement pour la bien garder. Just give them a morceau de paille in the vestibule and the thing is done. Locking the horse in the stable *en pension,* so to say.

It has not been cold today—temperate air. The result is I am a different child. I've been out for a walk and I'm tingling with warmth and my bones don't ache ½ so much and my lungs open and shut. The cold really *paralyses* me: I went to bed last evening and felt in despair about it. First one couldn't work because of moustiques and moucherons, then because of L.M., then because of the cold—a sliding scale. But when the day is fair one forgets. I climbed about the hill at the back of the Casetta. After you get up a certain height there's a perfect little promenade—quite flat, only used by the sauterelles, full of gay small flowers and insects. Below are pines and the sun shining through them makes them smell sweetly. I was so happy there. I thought how much more my kind these little boulevardiers were—the butterflies, the grasshoppers and the daisies—than the crowd at Menton, par exemple. How much lovelier to look at the wild thyme and the tiny honey-suckle than the shop fronts. I stayed up there (like M. Séguin's goat, I felt) all the morning, and below ever so far as I came round a bend I saw the Casetta with its foreshortened geranium bushes, looking a jewel.

Just as I left I said out aloud: 'Thank you very much, it's been lovely'—
But to whom? To the Lord who gave me consumption?

Just then lunch was ready—curried pasta, fresh bread, marmelade de
pommes and dried figs and coffee. L.M. is off to San Remo to buy
oatmeal and 'have a *little* look at the shops'. So I shall write my review
of Monkhouse and Stern and Stevenson. The sun has gone, clouds have
pulled over—soft grey ones with silver fringes—the wind is piping. Of
course, the locksmith man said they had never had such a year as this
year. The flowers are nearly spoiled with the gêlée, and snow on all the
mountains. . . . Why do these things follow us? Wherever I go they
never have known *such* a year. I take back my Thank you. . . .

Boge, the Irish man is a deal better. I smell he's a rank rebel and may
use the *A*. for code messages to prisoners—but it doesn't matter. He
writes decently and has a way with him. I don't think much of the Art
man—in fact I don't think anything of him—do you? He never gains
the attention. Dent is really top-hole, and old Sullivan was very readable
this week. An occasional *simple* article like that is very good for catching
new readers, I am sure. Clive's curtsey and retreat is always worth
reading. It did show a tiny little soul this week—but he speaks well for
himself. Your Lewis was, as usual, masterly. It was *fair* in a way fairness
isn't understood nowadays. It praised him, explained him, and *took him
a bit further on his way*. That's the difference between you and all other
critics: I feel you do it even to Hardy.

I have a suspicion that Eliot is finding himself as a poet in his analysis
(not quite the word) of caricature. I feel he is seeing why he fails, and
how he can separate himself from Sweeney through Sweeney. But this
may be sadly far-fetched.

Santy is the sweet little cherub that sits up aloft far from our con-
fusions and distractions.

I'm very glad you drew Heal. But he ought to advertise with us.
That's why I think an article on the subject of the first article and the
correspondence ought to appear. But who's to write it? And perhaps
you think there has been enough. Did you ever approach Ripmann in
view of the 'educational public'—modern languages and so on? And
have Forster and Lytton caved in?

This is a very tiresome letter. I'll stop it. I'm always thinking of the
paper and wondering about it. Wednesday is a kind of press day here:
I think of you and wonder how all has gone.[1]

[1] Wednesday was press day for *The Athenæum*.

Goodbye, my treasure. I must give this to L.M. to post in the town. I am so thankful about old Porter: his attentions may make your *hair grow*.

  Always, always and for ever
Your
Wig-wife

Thursday,

Dearest of All,   (November 20, 1919)

Your Saturday letter has come: when you are just off for the week-end, and you tell me O. has invited you there for Xmas. I strongly advise you to go. It's so comfortable and one always gets ideas for the house—from just being among those Spanish chests.

It's a very dull day here with wild ragged clouds and a cold halting miserable wind. My black fit is on me—not caused by the day altogether. Christ! to *hate* like I do. It's upon me today. You don't know what hatred is because I know you have never hated anyone—not as you have loved—equally. That's what I do. My deadly deadly enemy has got me today and I'm simply a blind force of hatred. Hate is the *other* passion. It has all the opposite effects of Love. It fills you with death and corruption, it makes you feel hideous, degraded and old, it makes you long to DESTROY. Just as the other is light, so this is darkness. I hate like that—a million times multiplied. It's like being under a curse. When L.M. goes I don't know what I shall do. I can only think of breathing—lying quite still and breathing. Think what you would feel if you had consumption and lived with a deadly enemy! That's one thing I shall grudge Virginia all her days—that she and Leonard were together. We can't be: we've got to wait our six months, but when they are up, I WILL not have L.M. near. I shall rather commit suicide. That is dead earnest. In fact, I have made up my mind that I shall commit suicide if I don't tear her up by the roots then. It would be kinder for us both—for you and me, of course I mean. We'd have no love otherwise. You'd only slowly grow to think I was first wicked and then mad. You'd be quite right. I'm both with her—mad, really mad, like Lawrence was, only worse. I leaned over the gate today and dreamed she'd died of heart-failure and I heard myself cry out 'Oh, what heaven! what heaven!'

Should I *not* send this? I must. I want you to know so that when the time comes for her to go, you will remember. The worst thing about

399

hate is that it never spends itself—is never exhausted and in this case isn't even shared. So you come up against something which says: 'Hit me, hit me, hate me, hate—feel *strongly* about me—one way or the other, it doesn't matter which way as long as I make you FEEL.' The man who murders from sheer hate is right to murder; he does it in self-defence. Worst of all is that I can't write a book while I live with her— I tried now for two months. It won't go. It's no good.

Does this seem to you just absurd? Can you imagine in the least what it is like? I feel I must let you know even though you wave the knowledge aside or think it is just 'Tig's tearing off at a tangent'. It's not. It is a curse, like the curses in old tales.

Well, that's enough 'in all conscience', as Mr. Salteena would say. I shall recover, darling, as I did before—I'll get over the positive imperative overwhelming suffocating mood of it and pass into the other. But oh, let this cup pass from me in April. It's TOO MUCH.

> Your (in a black cloud hidden away)
>
> Wig-wife

166 received   Friday morning 8.30 after déjeuner,

My own,   (November 21, 1919)

It happened rather luckily yesterday that L.M. and I reached a crise at tea-time and after that the frightful urgency of our feelings died down a bit. So I'll not say more about it. It ruined yesterday and made me so tired that I felt I could have slept days and nights away.

Here is your letter from Oare about the Waterlows' house. They are lucky, aren't they? Shall we really have such a house? It's not too late? We don't just make up dreams—precious dreams? It's not 'all over'? I get overwhelmed at times that it *is* all over, that we've seen each other for the last time (imagine it!) (No, don't imagine it!) and that these letters will one day be published and people will read something in them, in their queer finality, that 'ought to have told us'. This feeling runs exactly parallel with the other—the feeling of hope. They are two roads, I can't keep to either. Now I find myself on one, now on the other. Even when you tell me about the table I think How perfect! but at the very same moment I think 'Will he sell it? Of course not. He must have a table after all.' It's all part of what I've said before, haven't I? I say it so many thousand times over in my mind that I forget whether I've written it. Once the defences are fallen between you and

Death they are not built up again. It needs such a little push, hardly that, just a false step, just not looking, and you are over. Mother, of course, lived in this state for years. Ah, but she lived *surrounded*. She had her husband, her children, her home, her friends, physical presences, darling treasures to be cherished—and I've not one of these things. I have only my work. That might be enough for you in like case—for the fine intelligence capable of detachment. But God! God! I'm *rooted* in life. Even if I hate life, I can't deny it. I spring from it and feed on it. What an egoist the woman is!

And now, love, just supposing by a miracle the blissful thing should happen. . . . I don't remember where it was I stayed with the W.'s. It was near Marlboro' and the country was beautiful. There were forest glades—a beautiful forest. They took me for a walk that was miles too long: I remember that. I remember standing in a rank-smelling field and seeing them far ahead and waving very gaily when they looked round. . . .

But the country does not really matter a great deal, does it? As long as it *is* country and one can grow things (Oh, MAKE it happen!) But the money question is pretty dreadful. As to furniture, that we can always accumulate Eric-or-little-by-little, but I should think an anthracite range costs at least £30 or more—and alterations—we know what they run one into. I think we might do it by not paying down. We overdo the paying down, I believe. Other people never have their money in bags. But first we ought to find the house, take it and then consider. That is my idea. The house (like the Jew) first. (I never understood that text.)

Oh God! When you say we'll have to get a builder in, I suddenly dimly see a hall, a staircase with shavings, a man with a rule and a flat pencil measuring for a cupboard. I hear a saw and the piece of sawn wood creaks and tumbles (such a *final* sound). I hear the squee-quee of a plane, and the back door of the house is open and the smell of the uncared garden—so different to the smell of the cared one—floats through, and I put my hand on your sleeve and rest a little against you, and you say Do you agree? and I nod Yes.

But these dreams are so dear that they feel unearthly—they are dreams of heaven. How could they become reality? *This* is reality—bed, medicine bottle, medicine glass marked with tea and table spoons, guiacol tablets, balimanate of zinc. Come, tell me, tell me *exactly* what I am to do to recover my faith. I was always the one who had a kind of overplus of it; you hated it in me; it seemed to deny you so many of your more subtle emotions. You made me feel it was so crude a thing—my belief that couldn't be shaken.

Take this all *coolly*: it's all—what? Just add to my diseases a touch of melancholia, let us say, and REMEMBER how I adore you for so long as I live.

Wig

165 received
ACID from Roma received
Copy of *Eve*   Saturday morning,
My Precious Darling Bogey,   (November 22, 1919)

Per usual your adorable gay letter comes flying after my crows. I shall make L.M. wire you to ignore those two black things and forget them if you can. I can't help them, my darling, yet I know I ought to. If the others make you so happy you *must* have the others.

Find that house we must! I feel it's absolutely necessary. Then to ask Violet if she and her husband would live with us. Is that a good plan? I feel Violet ought not to be allowed to escape—and from what Chaddie says, with all her competence and Belle's, she can't get a soul. And I hope you do go to Bedford Square and see if there is anything for us there. There might be a lovely mirror *or* a chest (it would be too dear) and there might be an exquisite 'bit' which would grace a whole room like our bergère does.

It is a brilliant bright day. The flowers against the sea flash and quiver with light. This house is full of roses: every jar, pot, spare glass has its share. Even the sauce-boat has a little cargo with their heads over the sides and their leaves trailing in the mer imaginaire. I am going off to San Remo this afternoon if it stays fine just to have a look at the gay world and to take the acid to the chemist. I ought to unwrap it and take just the bottle for I want the box. On the other hand I'd like him to see the seals just for him to know what an important person I am.[1] . . . You're shocked?

I sent off a review on Thursday night. Is it all right, love? This copy of —— is really too degraded. I wonder if *Vogue* is like it. It is written *by* imbeciles *for* degenerates. One gets so fastidious—oh, I don't just

[1] The hydrobromic acid had been sent in the Diplomatic bag and the box was covered with Foreign Office seals.

know what it is—living alone on a wild hillside. At any rate, what they call the 'semi-demi' shocks me no end. I suppose there are a great many women who care for this sort of thing or it wouldn't be produced. It's positively *foul* and *filthy*. I do shrink from this world and its ways.

I had such a charming letter again from Richard. He is a little trump to write to me like this. I want you to see this letter, but I am nervous of sending it in case you leave it about and he finds it: he wouldn't understand. Shall I send it? And will you keep it in the file?

Yes, darling love, I *do* wrap up no end. I am more frightened of catching cold than anybody. It's a terror to me, in fact. And I can keep warm enough on the whole. The fireplace in this my small room is excellent; the others are no good—except the kitchen which is all right but wasteful, since we have a fire there all day. Woollen goods don't exist in Italy. Even Ansaldi told me that. Father leaves Toulon today for Naples. I've just written his farewell letter. He's had an awful shaking since he was here—has been in bed nearly all the time with a severe chill and a touch of congestion. We have had a rare tangi over this climate.

Yes, it's a beautiful day today, an opal. I am so looking forward to San Remo—to lose myself for a bit and watch the people and perhaps the china will have come. I long to send you the superb fresh dried figs. L.M. is making enquiries about them today....

Darling, I must give this to her for the noon post. Your marvellous letter is beside me. It *breathes* joy and life, you precious Boge. Take care of yourself. Try and keep the house warm. Have you enough coal? Does the house look shabby—or cared for?

With my meals I am drinking *The Winter's Tale*. It's again one of my favourites. It's simply marvellous.

Goodbye for now, my precious. *The flag flies.*

Ever your true love,
Wig

Cheque for Scarf enclosed   Sunday,
My darling darling Bogey,   (November 23, 1919)

I have just read your letter about the scarf. I wish I'd seen that girl asking you if terra cotta suited me and you wondering if I was fair or dark or a hazel-nut. I'm sure I shall love it.

The ACID is here: a bottle has been made up and it has a most superb effect. Très potent—the best I have come across. You did not see the bottle it was sent in, did you? A round glass-stoppered exquisite one, which the chemist is not to be allowed to keep.

I didn't go to San Remo yesterday after all. Got all ready and walked half-way down the steps, and the bells rang Turn again Whittington. I had no puff, my back ached. I felt it would only be going on my nerves. So I sent L.M. and lay down with the window open to rest a little. The bell rang. (The bell here when pressed rings and goes on ringing till you open the door, unscrew the top and stop it. This is a common habit. I never think of a bell that stops by itself now. It makes all visitors sound extremely urgent). *That* visitor was Catherina with her minute Gus Bofa dog—Flock. She had just given him a bath and was attired for the occasion in a kind of white robe de chambre, très décolletée, with bare arms, her hair just pinned up, her feet thrust into wooden pattens. In her hand she had a large *brush*. Flock, sitting in the garden, covered with what looked like prickles of black and white fur all on end, shivered violently and kept his eyes *pinned* on the brush! He *is* an adorable little animal—for sale—for 150 lire!!! But he's worth it really, he's such a personality.

Catherina had come to say three men were following her bearing in their arms a porcelain stove. When she and Madame Littardi had been discussing the *coldness* of the Casetta, Mme. Littardi had suddenly remembered she had this put away dans la cave and *they* decided it would chauffe toute la petite maison if it were installée in the salle à manger. Would I like it? It was un peu cassée, so Caterina had brought three admirers to mend it for me. Wasn't this very amiable? There must be a rat somewhere, but I can neither see nor smell it up till now.[1]

Presently three good men and true hove in sight bearing a small *terra cotta* crematorium. C., in her element, ordered them about, made them put it in the garden, sent them into the Casetta for a pail, a cloth, water for the cement, started them scrubbing, while she watched and Flock sat with an air of intense pleasure watching the sufferings of another while he still shivered and the blood showed red in the muscles of his delicate little hind legs. She came up today to have it put in the room. All my thanks were over borne with: Je suis si contente, si contente d'avoir trouvé quelque chose. And when I said Wouldn't she at least have a bouquet of boutons de roses? she replied seriously *Demain,* avec

[1] There was, see letter of January 22, 1920.

grand plaisir. Mais vous savez, Madame, I cannot walk carrying a bouquet without my shoes on.

After she had gone I lay down again, and between my book I heard the workmen whistling and talking, and then there was a new voice, a child's voice, very happy. It went on for about an hour. Vaguely curious, I got up to see who it was. C'était le petit de la poste qui porte les télégrammes, and he was beating up cement very firmly with a little flat trowel—in his *element,* a workman, in fact. When he saw me he paid no attention, and I just chanced to ask if he had anything for me? Si, Madame. And off came his little cap with a telegram from Father inside it! I went in to sign the slip and he followed, leaned against my table and suddenly, picking up the pig, pointed to the old letters underneath and asked for the stamps for his collection. Then he strolled over to the mantelpiece and looked at your photograph while I humbly tore them off for him.

I lay down again. The bell rang. A LADY, Miss Lionel Kaye-Shuttleworth, Villa Giovanni, San Remo, to call—a friend of Dent's aunt in Nice. Elderly typical, good family, dowdy gentlewoman with exquisite greenish ermine scarf, diamond earrings and white suède gloves. The combination suggested *arum lilies* to me somehow. I liked her very much. She knows a great deal about Italy; she was *gay, sociable,* full of life and *pleasant talk,* and she was a 'perfect lady'. (I *do* like delicate manners.) I made her tea as Ida was out. But you know this form of entertainment is quite new to me. It is like playing ladies. Are they playing, too? They can't be serious, surely, and yet. . . . I see myself and hear myself and all the while I am laughing inside. I managed to inform her: we were not related to the John Murrays. We spell our name without the A. Yes, from Scotland. . . . The A was dropped generations ago. (Do you hear the A dropping? Hullo! There's the A dropped. We can't put it back. It's broken to bits.) My *private* idea is that the ship's carpenter dropped it over the side.[1] But never mind. Also—that Papa *motored* from Menton to see me: that my relatives there had managed to find *four* excellent maids: that my *cook* in London finds shopping so much easier: that (this is the invariable final and always comes in as natural as you please) Elizabeth in her German Garden is my cousin!!! It is Butler's Montreal brother-in-law.

She was rather horrified at the Casetta: the coldness and the loneliness

---

[1] My great-grandfather and my grandfather were both ships' carpenters in the Royal Navy.

... the pity I was not at San Remo where 'we' could have looked after you if you had let us and at least introduced you to our friends. *What do you do when it rains, especially as you are not strong, etc., etc., etc.?* I am afraid I was a little brave-and-lonely at this. It's so nice to be cared for. . . . She is asking a few people to meet me at lunch on Wednesday, and I'm going. Do you wonder why? I will tell you.

People steady and calm me. When I am not working, when I'm in pain, and conscious every moment of my body, and when my heart indulges in what Sorapure calls disorderly action and my joints ache, I've no one to turn to. I can't forget my body for a moment. I think of Death: the melancholy fit seizes me. Nature helps me when I'm well, but if the weather is cold and I am ill Nature mocks and terrifies me. Then healthy people help *beyond words*. I've noticed this many times. L.M. doesn't help: she always makes me feel she is waiting for me to be worse, but if I see people, the strain of her even goes. I feel I've cut away a few hundred octopus feelers; I feel refreshed. Do you understand? Does it sound to you unworthy? I swear when Catherina has been here sometimes, just to be with her, to feel her health and gaiety, has been *bread* and *wine* to me. . . .

Bear with me. I had to explain. If I were well, you see, it would be utterly different. And then the past is so *new*: it's *not past* yet. Why, Bogey, on Thursday when the wind blew and I was not well I suddenly *relived* the afternoon you and Richard were in the kitchen—and I came down and you 'teased' me. 'Don't move. Sit still. Don't poke the fire. Be quiet. Stop talking!' And I felt distracted. I began to cry and cry. I saw Richard laughing. I didn't know what to do. It was like great black birds dashing at one's face. What *can* I do? I thought. If I go upstairs he'll say 'Don't climb the stairs!' and now he says 'Don't stay here!' And I heard myself cry out 'You're *torturing* me!' And the past and the present were one frightful horror. This is *sober truth*.

It's over now, done with. But I love you beyond words, your letters are *miracles,* and after I have failed you I suffer, suffer. I want to keep you happy. But I can't lie and pretend. So if I do see a few people you will understand why and not think I am neglecting my work. . . . This is so long. Forgive me. Put your arms round me. No one in the world would understand but you. My fear of death—you do understand it? And the fact that you have thought of me as dead and written as though I were and that L.M. is always preparing for that—you understand why, having been so near it myself, its made me terrified? As though I had nothing to help me fight it off except my own powers.

I am looking at the little ring you gave me—the blue stone with the pearls round it. I love it so. I feel you made it of a flower for me when we were children, and it has turned into pearls.

Glancing again at your letter I re-read the part where you say you'd drive anywhere for a good table. Oh! How nice you are. *Too* nice. Terribly. I thought you meant *food* first . . . 'to keep a good table' . . . then it dawned on me. It's the spit of you to say such a thing. But, my precious, be careful, if somebody asks you to 'take the chair,' they won't mean what you mean. I now see you answering an invitation that you'll be very pleased indeed to take the chair on Friday 20th, thanks awfully. How did they know we were short of chairs? And you will arrive at 8.30 as they suggest, with a small handbarrow. . . .

It has been the most perfect exquisite morning. I went into the village. There were no letters. The whole village is adorned with roses, trees of roses, fields, hedges, they tumble over the steps in a shower, children wear them, hideous middle-class women in chocolate-brown 'costumes' with black button boots and hard velvet toques pull and twist them from the stems. I walk about wishing I knew the name of that white beauty with petals stained as though with wine and long slender buds—those pink ones, round and curled—those red ones with *silver shadows*. Ospedaletti is an enchanting little village, and the village people seem very nice. The visitors are simply APPALLING. All the men are forked radishes, but their strut, twirl, stare, ogle, grin is so bewildering. And the women are all either chocolate brown or a colour I always think of as Belgian grey—a second-class-on-the-boat grey. They have cold selfish faces, hard eyes, bad manners, mean attitudes and ways. Serpents come out of their eyes at sight of me—I don't know why—and they draw the radishes' attention to me and then (*really*) burst out into a loud affected laughing. I, of course, don't notice, but I feel myself getting very *English*—but in truth, one's heart is wrung. How *can* they be like that with all these roses, with the air humming with bees, with the great white bunches of sweet flowers on the promenade—how *can* they? Divine weather—a crocus-coloured sea—the sun embracing one's body, holding one like a lover. . . . You know, people are *impossible* to understand. . . .

I think I only understand you of all the world. We *must* have children —we *must*. I want our child—born of love—to see the beauty of the world, to warm his little hands at the sun and cool his little toes in the sea. I want Dickie to show things to. Think of it! Think of *me* dressing him to go for a walk with *you*. Bogey, we must hurry—our house— our child—our work.

Goodbye for now, my own little mate.

Your
Wig-wife

Master of the Cats! Hail!   Monday,
My precious darling Bogey,   (November 24, 1919)

I've gone and gained another 2 lbs. I weighed myself and couldn't believe it and made the man weigh me as though I were beurre frais at least and still there it was—another kilo—that's a bit more than 2 lbs. Pretty good, for a young 'un, don't you think? Please whisper the news in Wing's ear. I now weigh 7 stone 4 and when I left home I weighed 6.13. Having found out this fact I phantasmagorically (see Miss R. Wilson) danced off to the post and found hymn number 163—the one hundred and sixty-third hymn (why do they always say that?) waiting for me. I read it in the public eye, but when I found you had not given me the chuck absolute for my Virginia review I lost my head and kissed it—looked up and saw an old female leaning on a broom watching me and smiling very broadly. This was awkward because I blushed and had to climb up a flight of steps so as not to pass her. Her broom by the way, was made of those great reddish stems that grow in the centre of palms with tiny dates on them—a very nice broom indeed.

Don't ever flatter me. Beat me *always* before you would beat anyone else. But God! to think that review was all right. I've been on the point of wiring my regret that I had failed you. That's enough to make a person gain 20 more. . . .

I burn for the next number. Hind's letter was *exceedingly* gratifying. How you wiped the floor with those old Oxford people. They must feel pretty silly. Really letters like this ought to go to the managers. Won't you send this one and the other American one? They *ought* to see how it is admired.

I am so glad that the precious cats have won Sydney. I sent them each a card yesterday. I *see* little Wing rabbiting on the stairs. They are blessed creatures and must have perhaps a whole tiny cottage of their own in Sussex. I see Wing leaning out of the window pouring a jug of water on to Athy in the garden below. Athy will get very 'pa' in his old age, don't you think?

The Ottoline furniture makes my mouth water. A *chest,* a *cupboard,* a *couch,* a delicious cabinet. I should like to have a cabinet—tall—you know the legs. Oh dear! Why aren't we rich? We want £800 a year *without* working, please, and just a few lump sums, that's all. It's not much to ask. If I ever went to Menton I might meet an old dying American there who for sufferings-nobly-borne might well leave me twice the sum. But I don't want to go to Menton, Boge. Terra Cotta, the new stove, has been installed today. It's a regular German stove with a flat top [a drawing of the stove]. It looks awful there. But that round thing is where the red shows and below is a sort of baby oving. I should think it would box it[1]—the cold, I mean.

You see I can't afford to go to Menton and live there. It would cost quite double this place, I am sure. No, if I see tumpany here and go into San Remo and see people, I think I can manage, and this place must be terribly healthy for me to have gained 4 lbs., stopped all my fever and planted in me a roaring appetite. And then—MAY!! I feel so well today that only to write that makes me almost unbearably excited.

I have to do the books for *Art and Letters* this week. It's a dreadful sweat having to *re*-read two, and *The Mask,* which I imagine I am supposed to admire. I dislike it intensely. It's a very vulgar ill-bred book with *two* climaxes where the little Jew is forced to expose himself. —— would think it a masterpiece: that's the exact measure of it, but I can't quite say that, though I'd like to.

I had 8 pages from Father at Toulon, written just before he left. You know how in the old days you used to *wring* my heart in letters—*all* the ghastly things that happened just to you. F. does it. If he manages to secure one egg on a journey, it's a bad egg. He loses things, people cheat him, he goes to a hotel where they won't give him a fire—he 'feeling very shaky'—he peels the bad egg, letting the shells fall into the crown of his hat so as not to make a litter, and the 'juice' spirts out all over the lining that he showed me with such pride the other day when he was here—and so on. Of course, he *has money,* but it makes no difference to him. He falls into absolute *pits* of depression and loneliness and 'wanting Mother'.

Talking about Mother, he told me such a typical little story about

---

[1] To 'box' something, in K.M.'s private language, was to settle it satisfactorily.

her in his letter. It was when they first took The Grange. He was at a
board meeting and was called away 'in the thick of it' to the telephone.
A voice said: 'It's Mrs. Beauchamp of The Grange speaking.' He
couldn't make out what was happening and thought she had wanted
to ring up the *office* to give 'a wholesale order'. But when she heard his
voice, Father said, 'All she said was "Hal dear! I'm at home. I love this
house. I simply love it. That's all" and rang off.' Can't you hear that?
I can.

I shall love to see Hardy's poems. It will be interesting to read
De la Mare on him, too.

It's a soft grey day with puffs of warm wind blowing. L.M. has gone
to San Remo. She's already borrowed 40 lire of her next month's £5.
What can she spend it on? I suppose she sends it away or something.
And she buys the most awful-smelling cakes, but you can't spend £5 a
month on cakes. It's all I can do *not* to ask.

(Miss Kaye-Shuttleworth had 40 lb. of sugar sent her this summer to
make peach jam with! I *don't* believe it.)

Clemence Dane will be sent tomorrow to be another odd review to
have by you. The *Times* notice of it was really too funny. I've made a
discovery. It's a very old book touched up. She's left some bits untouched which give away the show. But I think I've made it pretty
clear that she wrote it about 20 years ago.

Goodbye, darling Bogey. Forgive the soap paper. I'll get some decent
stuff tomorrow.

> Always yours.
> Your own
> Wig

162 received   Tuesday,
                                              (November 25, 1919)

New Version Boge (appassionato) We want a house!
             Wig   (con brio)   Garden and cows!
             Ath   (szorzando)   Not forget-TING!
             Wing (con amore)   For Athy and Wing
All (fortissimo diminishing to a pianissimo) MOUSEHOLE FOR MOUSE.

The paper has come. May I talk it over a little? And please remember
I am nobbut a cabinboy and you are the skipper.

I don't think S.W. brought it off with George Eliot. He never gets

410

under way. The cart wheels want oiling. I think, too, he is ungenerous. She was a deal more than that. Her English warm ruddy quality is hardly mentioned. She *was* big, even though she was 'heavy' too. But think of some of her pictures of country life—the breadth, the sense of sun lying on warm barns, great warm kitchens at twilight when the men came home from the fields, the feeling of *beasts,* horses and cows, the peculiar passion she has for horses. (When Maggie Tulliver's lover walks with her up and down the lane and asks her to marry, he leads his great red horse, and the beast is foaming—it has been hard ridden and there are dark streaks of sweat on its flanks—the *beast is the man,* one feels *she* feels in some queer inarticulate way.) Oh, I think he ought really to have been more generous. And why drag Hardy in? Just because he (S.W.) was living with you and is, I am sure, like certain females powerfully influenced by the climate of the moment. Perhaps that's unjust. But I feel I must stand up for my SEX.

V.W. does it very well. Aint she a snob? But she does it very well in her intellectual snobbish way. A Wyndham and a Tennant *no* aristocrat....

I think D.L.M.'s review is excellent, don't you? It's so informed, out-of-the-way, and direct—and Saintsbury I like *awfully.* I wish we could lay down a little piece of excellent vintage. But ours will be dandelion elderberry, cowslip and blackberry. (*Oh Bogey,* won't it be heaven!) I say: Who did Fisher? Do you altogether approve? I read bits of the book in *The Times.* He's a presumptuous, self-conscious, high-stomached old roarer. No doubt the Admiralty was at fault, no doubt everybody was a fool—but Fisher could have put nought right. And as for saying he was a great man. . . . Or are our sea-legs being pulled?? I was a bit sorry to read that.

I like the way Tommy keeps hitching up his trousers as he writes and just not yarning. He's always full of life somehow.

Lewis is extremely interesting I think. He hurls lumps of sentences at you, but that doesn't matter. I think you ought to give him a chance. You're *very* clever to have seen him.

R.H.W. is immeasurably more interesting this week. I don't know enough about Matisse to know if he's right—but he sounds very right. It's got ideas—that article—hasn't it?

Of course, Dent is as good as ever. And his remarks *re* the *Boutique Fantasque* are, I am sure, *absolutely sound.* That's what I like about the

A.—the way it *steadies* opinion. You do it supremely. We tag along after, putting our two feet down on the bit you tell us to and trying to stand very firm.

P.H., Bogey, frankly disgusts me. Oh, I wish that first paragraph had not appeared in the paper. 'Gave herself' in commas! Oh, the unspeakable journalist! Shoo him off! He simply revolts me. Apart from his vulgarity, he's got nothing but a very old newspaper in his head.

The Duchess of Malfi is a useful little article very à propos.

I suppose you had to publish 'Thomas of Duddington' to fill space. It's a pity you can't get better letters. I don't think one ought to publish irritated splenetic outbursts, do you?

The Duhamel is, of course, another eye-opener. The idea that they should surrender something of their personality . . . that started a terrific excitement bubbling in me. It's true of all artists, isn't it? It gives me another *critical point of view* about an artist and quite a new one. I mean—to find out what the man is subduing, to mark that side of him being gradually absorbed (even as it were without his knowing it) into the side of him he has chosen to explore, strengthening it, reinforcing it even while *he thinks* it is subdued away. Oh, that's frightfully vague. . . .

The Letter from Italy was *peculiarly* interesting to me—about the poet who had consumption and his 'fits of blackest depression'. It's a very good letter, too.[1] I wish that old Valéry would write again. I think it's time Lytton sent an article, don't you? Are you going to publish anything special at Xmas? A Christmas 'ode' by you? I *wish*, I *wish* you would write a Christmas poem.

It's raining, a heavy, misty rain—most beautiful. I went out to post in it and, after so long, it was thrilling to hear the fine rain sting the stretched silk of my umbrella, the sudden heavy drops drum on it from the gum trees. All the coast is soft, soft colour: the roses hang heavy: the spiders' webs are hung with family jewels. Aged men in pale blue trousers are sweeping up the dead leaves, and there is a succession of bonfires—puffs of white, fine smoke, with the old figures moving in it, sweeping and bending. The sea is still very full—faint to see—with

---

[1] An essay on Guido Gozzano by Guido de Ruggiero. The poet died at the age of thirty. The essay contains this sentence: 'His illness, with its violent alternations between hope and despair, its sudden bursts of exuberant vitality, followed by fits of the blackest depression, and above all the fatal knowledge of its steady inexorable course, plays a large part in this poet's lyrical world.'

dreamy lines upon it, and my two little royal birds are back in the garden.

Goodbye, my darling. Tomorrow I send some *menus*.

> Your
>
> Wig

Photograph enclosed. Don't let it drop out.   Wednesday,

My darling,   (November 26, 1919)

It's press day for you. How is the paper going? What's the day like? I am thinking of you. I have got our house on the brain as well as the heart. I feel such a frenzy of impatience, but that must not be. We must be wise children and hard to please, for this time it really is more important than ever before. This time we decide to live in the land with our flocks and our herds, our manservant and our maidservant and our two sacred cats.

All the same, I keep seeing *chimneys* in the landscape of my mind, so to say—chimneys that are going to be ours. Think of the first time we visit together, sitting on a step with our hats on our knees smoking a cigarette (man with a vehicle waiting for us somewhere round a corner) looking over the garden, feeling the house behind us, saying: We must have peonies under these windows. And then we get into the station cab and the man drives away and we hold each other's hands and think how familiar this road will become. . . .

It's a wild glittering day. I can't go to those people for lunch. The wind is like a great bird tumbling over the sea with bright flashing wings. I am upstairs in my bedroom sitting in the sun. The windows are open. It is very pleasant. One could make a charming room of this.

At three o'clock I woke up into the middle of a terrific thunderstorm. The thunder seemed to set one's bones vibrating. One heard the sea, not breaking regularly, but *struggling* and only now and again with a great harsh sigh the waves spent themselves. It is strange to be alone in such a storm. I kept feeling I must write this, I must write this; but it must be a man who feels it, rather an elderly man away from home, and something must happen to him—something, you know, which could not happen to such a man—and then the morning must follow, still, clear, 'poised', like it is after such a storm, and he. . . .

At 7 o'clock the front-door bell rang. A telegram from Father at Naples. (I had 2 from Toulon). This was to say Goodbye finally. You know I have a feeling that he may buy us a farm in the North of Auckland. Wouldn't it be *too awful*? I shall have, every letter I write, to accentuate the importance of your being in England for (at least) five years with the *Athenæum*. He sketched the kind of place that would suit us in his last letter, and it was so vivid that I hear him asking Mr. Bob Fenwick to keep his 'eye skinned for him' and let him know by wire if such a little farm comes into the market. Wouldn't it be tragic?

L.M. has gone to the post with my telegram of regrets. I should like a letter, a paper, and the scarf. But I'll leave this open in case the letter comes.

Later. Darling, a letter came from Jinnie enclosing this photograph for you. It looks like Wing's house, doesn't it? Nothing else came. It's afternoon. I've just had *another* caller. A woman who lives here in Ospedaletti with her Italian maid, her English maid, her mother, and I should think a few Spanish menservants. She asked me to tea on Monday. Her villa has a flat roof. She was swathed in fur, violent perfume, and I thought she was M. The spit of M.M.'s eyes, teeth, extravagance. *Chicken,* 18 *lire, butter,* 20 *lire!!* Did you ever! 'You must go to Algiers next year. Algiers is *perfect*.' She is, I should think, very rich and what they call 'fast'—plays golf, bridge, *our car*. No 'swank'. She has a house in the South of England. I had no time in this *race* (so familiar!) to ask where, but it was that which interested me. But I must have cards. Here are 5 people I ought to leave cards on. What an absurd predicament. Oh, how nice our name is! My husband bulks very large in these conversations. What a dark, romantic, brilliant creature he is, and as he need never see the people he is quite safe.

Boge, here are a few recipes. You see I don't know what the meat ration is or what's in season or anything, but they are sound—and I thought Violet might not know them. Are they at all what you want?

My God! the wind. It's blowing great huge guns.

I send Jinnie's letter just to give you an idea of her. She is a nice woman, streets above these *callers*. This woman has left rather a faded taste of white suède gloves in my mouth after all. She is unhappy, dissatisfied, like M. was. I don't know: one's work sets one *finally apart* from the idle world, doesn't it?

You must like the little photograph *very* much, please, and look long at it. Show it to Richard, will you?

Goodbye, my precious. This is a dull letter: I am waiting for one from you. You know that state. I want one *terribly*.

I love you, love you, love you.

Wig

Wednesday night,
My precious little Paper Boy, (November 26, 1919)

I don't want *The Times* as well as the *Guardian*. I didn't know the *Guardian* was going to be a regular: it's of course 100 times more interesting than t'other. (You see, I am answering your Saturday morning letter). About the 10 stories. They won't all bear reprinting, Boge. I can't afford to publish my early Works yet. If you don't mind I'd rather let them lie and deliver you the new goods in May. In any case I don't want —— to have any of my new work. We really *are* opposed. I know just how angry —— *et Cie* are with me. They ought not to be for indeed I tried my best to be friendly and erred on the side of kindness. If you read that book you would realize what I feel . . . its aristocratic (?) ignoring of all that is outside it's own little circle and its wonder, surprise, incredulity that *other people* have heard of William Shakespeare. Though what in God's name THEY find in Shakespeare I don't know.

The wind has been joined by the robber cold. Both are in highest spirits. There is a perfect uproar going on outside. It makes my room feel like a lighthouse. I seem to see you in another lighthouse. I see my beloved seated at a table, reading or writing or playing with his little cat. All the rest of the world is in chaos—but there is he. It makes every gesture, every movement of yours, *beautiful*—charged with a sort of solemn quiet. Goodnight my love.

Thursday. Hail, rain, wind, dark. The terra cotta in full blast, smelling dreadful as the plaster bakes dry. No, the point about this climate is its extreme variability of temperature. It's never a whole day the same. That's what puts such a terrific strain on one, I think, and that's what makes it truly preposterous for people who are not as well-covered and as solid as L.M. They may win through. But why have to fight so hard? Why have to use up one's energies in keeping warm? It's so wasteful. The sea sounds like a big old rake. I was awake more than half the night. At one o'clock I called L.M. and she went down and made some tea. Bogey, in my *home* I shall always have the things for tea in my room,

415

so that in the middle of the night I can brew a cup. Mr. Salteena's thrill for tea in bed I feel for tea in the middle of the night. Ten years ago I used to have tea and brown bread and butter every morning at half past two. I don't know why it should be such a gay little feast then. I long for somebody to *laugh* with. I think of such funny little jokes— minute little jokes. Wing would perhaps be the perfect companion of such revels: he *shall* be. I see him stuffing his paw into his mouth or the end of his tail so as not to laugh out loud and wake you.

Oh Boge, I hope I get a letter today or something. It's the *vilest* old day. However, I've *got* to stick it. There's nothing else to do. God! how lonely I am! You know, I sometimes feel a violent hate of Sullivan, Eliot, Tomlinson, all of them, because they have never suffered what I have had to suffer, and especially not THIS. It's just one of the many poisons, I suppose. But to have been *alone* here—that—even you will *never* know.

Here's L.M. for the letters. Goodbye, Bogey.

Wig

Friday,

My precious,   (November 28, 1919)

Forgive a note today instead of a letter. I must finish that review for *A. and L.* and it's the devil. The cold is back; it is paralysing, and I'm stiff as ever (!), and there were no letters yesterday or today. (*The Observer* came today for which I'm very grateful.) But I'll come out of my hole when this review is over and I've had a letter. The brick is the icy weather—one's whole energy is taken up fighting it: there's *none* left over for work. But I must work—so there you are. L.M. will post this in San Remo. She is going in for my cough mixture. If only this climate were not so *intensely variable*: it's never two days alike, it beats England. Now with a groan and a flick of a disconsolate paw I'll run away again. I'll come back and nibble a letter and then talk. But you know, old boy, I'm so *stale*. Oh for a 'weekend' or even a ciné or a theatre or the sound of music.

Your deadly dull
Mouse

Don't be cross with me. Even L.M. thinks it's colder than Hampstead.

My Beautiful Bogey,

Your Sunday letter is here—about —— and ——. Yes, I agree about
——. I have only met the sister once. I'd like to know her, she sounds
very attractive. How I envy you seeing people—and yet, of course, it
means nothing to you. I mean you are not, like me, *dependent* upon
contact with people. I am—yes, I am. By people I mean—not being
alone. I'd live all the rest of my life without seeing another human
being if I had you.

We had a severe earthquake last night at 11 o'clock. The little
Casetta gave a *creak* and then silently shook.

And today it is dead calm, airless, real earthquake weather. Wasn't
that nice about this week's review which I did early so as to have the
rest of the week for Rutter? I don't know—it beats me how she can do
these things. She said last night it was because her brain had gone rotten,
but that's nonsense. Well, I feel this last affair is not to be talked of. I'll
have to take my work to post myself in future; that's all.

—— comes this afternoon on his way to England: he brings you figs
—*figs only*. Boge, you'd better, I suppose, give him lunch and a cigar,
but be a bit on your dignity, will you? Tell you why. I feel he may ask
you for some money. If he does, make him sign a receipt to the effect
that it's part rent. You see, you are such a *child* in bad people's hands.
You are fairly safe with the lambs, but you must not ever play with the
lions unless I'm by.

I couldn't get to sleep last night. When I shut my eyes *gardens* drifted
by—the most incredible sort of tropical gardens with glimpses of
palaces through the rich green. Trees I've never seen or imagined—
trees like feathers and silver trees and others quite white with huge
transparent leaves passed and passed. My heart just fluttered: I scarcely
had to breathe at all. It was like a vision brought about by drugs. I
couldn't stop it and yet it frightened me; but it was too beautiful to stop.
One is almost in a state of coma—very strange. I've often got *near* this
condition before, but never like last night. Perhaps if one gives way to
it and gives way to it one may even be able to get there.... Oh, I don't
know, but it *was* a vision, not a memory. I am going to San Remo today
to try to get some tea plates for you. Those two items *don't* hang together.

Filippi sent his bill for that chit yesterday: 40 *lire*. I consider that an
absurd swin. But I must pay it. Don't you think it's too much?

No sign of the scarf yet nor of the acid that was posted here. Did I tell you I'd paid 8 francs for a box for my letters so as to have them secure. Now L.M. tells me it's 8 *francs par mois*!!! I thought it was for the season, for after all they won't deliver here: they refuse. Another robbery, alors, and I dare not quarrel with the gens de la poste. On the contrary L.M. takes the little box-faced girl bouquets of roses from Madame. If she'd like me to burn candles I'm only too willing. But Bogey, they do make one pay. This is a horrid letter. I'll be a nicer girl when I come back from San Remo. Goodbye for now, my darling.

Wig

My precious Bogey,

Sunday morning 8 a.m.,
(November 30, 1919)

It's a real Sunday, calm, quiet, with the sea practising over a voluntary while the verger tiptoes laying out the hymn and prayer books in the strangers' pews. There's a lovely piece of bright sun in my room—but, bother, it is moving towards great banks of unruffled cloud.

Your letter with the house and the horse has come, darling. Yes, I am a ～～～ but I do my best all the same. I'm *prisoned*. I'll never be right until L.M. and I part company. About the parcels. The acid sent to Rome has arrived: the other has not, neither has the scarf. But I believe the parcel post takes a month occasionally or even five weeks, so they may turn up. . . . I hope you have a whack at the Georgians. Is Nichols one? There was a most disgraceful article by him in the *Observer*.

I went to San Remo yesterday afternoon. It was *very* exciting. The shops are all prepared for the Great Fleece. A great many antique shops are open. I suppose they are all frauds. At any rate the prices would be appalling, but, by Jove! they have got some lovely things! There was a chair yesterday that can't be a fraud, covered in the most exquisite needlework on old ivory brocade. Figs and their leaves, pomegranates, apricots, pears, a spotted snake or two, all in most gay delicate colours, and then there was another great piece of embroidery, all flowers, with a little running border of wild strawberry fruits, leaves and blossoms. The shops are rather darkish. One looks in and one sees a flash of silver, a mass of copper, dark polished furniture, lace, a glass case or two of miniatures and jewels, and the old spider with a silk handkerchief over her head sitting quiet, on the watch. I'd be the first fly to go in if my purse were full.

I had to order some cards yesterday, but they can't cut me a *plaque* here: the wretched things have to be printed. Boge, *would* you send me out some decent ones? I must have them as soon as I can. No address—so I'd better not have many.

I went to the market. It was gay there. You remember where they used to sell fried cakes? Yesterday there was a stall covered with them and to one side on a charcoal stove women were cooking pancakes. A queer feeling markets give me. I feel that—once every hundred years or so—I walk about among the stalls, price the fruit, note that the new raisins have come, smell the fried cakes, and see the woman's gesture as she rattles for change in the money-bag at her side. . . .

Waiting for the tram —— came up. Well! He'll commit murder one of these days. If ever man looked like a murderer. . . He's a fascinating character, a *real* villain. Not a fool, not merely vague (*far* from it). He'll end by having a small hotel at a place like Boulogne or Calais or Dieppe, and he'll meet the trains wearing a straw hat and sand shoes.

It's autumn here now: the vines are red and yellow: the dark women carry pale chrysanthemums, and oranges and lemons are ripe. I came home, lit my fire, began to take my shoes off and fell asleep. When I woke up it was dark—the fire just burning—not a sound. I didn't know how long I'd been asleep. Everything was still. I sat there for about half an hour, then I heard steps outside, and L.M. came in, back from the village. It was nearly seven o'clock! I ate dinner, came up, got into bed, fell asleep again and woke at eleven, bitten to death by three *huge* mosquitoes in the net. Murdered them, went to sleep again and slept till seven! What a pa woman! Oh, Boge, find the house! I am *longing* for it. Christmas is near. *Shall* we next year really keep Christmas? *Shall* we have a tree and put it in a room with the door locked—only you and I allowed to go in and decorate it—and then have a small party on Christmas Eve?? We shall go out all wrapped up to the noses, with a pruning hook to cut holly and we'll burn a Christmas log. (PERHAPS!)

You know it's madness to love and live apart. That's what we do. Last time when I came back to France do you remember how we *swore* never again. Then I went to Looe—and after that we *swore*: never again. Then I came here. Shall we go on doing this? It isn't a married life at all—not what I mean by a married life. How I envy Virginia; no wonder she can write. There is always in her writing a calm freedom of expression as though she were at peace—her roof over her, her possessions round her, and her man somewhere within call. Boge, what have I done that I should have *all* the handicaps—plus a disease and an enemy—and *why* should we believe this won't happen again? We've said as sincerely as we can ever possibly say: 'It will not. This is to be the *last* time. We'll *never* let each other go again. We *could* not.' But the time comes and there's nothing else to be done, and before you say Jack Knife, we're apart again, going through it all again. Shall I be in Malaga next winter, or Algiers? Odious, odious thought. But really, I'd better get used to it. We are the sport of circumstances. It's obviously impossible for us to do anything. But how tired the dice get of being rattled and thrown!

Your
Wig-wife

I long to see *Cinnamon and Angelica*. I expect it will come today.

Weather report. Dead calm. Warm. Some sun.
Earthquaky. I had a proof of E. Stanley. Did you
like her verse?

Sunday evening,
My precious,   (November 30, 1919)
What a fate you should have published the Dosty the very week my review won't arrive. The Lord is *not* on my side. But to the extent of having let me have two of your letters today it is. One mentions the house. Is there really a chance for it? What is the rent? What is it like? Old—young? Garden—Fruit? Trees? I expect I would get very friendly with the Waterlows if I lived near them. Well, that's that.

Your Wednesday letter about the paper gives me such a glimpse of you—rescuing it. It is, though, an awful drag on you, isn't it? Aren't there many moments when you long to be free? What do you feel about running this paper? Do you feel the game is worth the candle? I often wonder. ON the other hand how are we going to make money? We can't live on ha'pennies: I mean we don't want to. You don't want to—do you? I don't. The days of washing saucepans are over. Of course, I'd do it *like a shot* if need be and be *perfectly happy*, but I think it's a waste of energy and time when we are together. No two lovers could possibly talk while they are cleaning the knives. No wonder you 'upped' with the bath-brick. (Oh, I *do* love you, Bogey.) If we took it you wouldn't come here for May, would you? But your letter says you're going to De la Mare on Sunday, so p'raps the house is 'off'. No, you *mustn't* go such long journeys: you're as bad as I am with your Thank you very much instead of NO. When—if—we are together for good, I'll always answer your invitations and you mine: then we'll be safe.

Old Rutter forwarded this letter today, together with a note from him asking where to send my cheque and would I send another story because people liked the last[1] so much. Very rash.

Yes, the Fake-ists quite overcome me. That *Observer* had *p.e.* a review of *Legend*. IF you read *Legend*!!! Humbug—deplorable humbug —rant—rubbish—tinpot provincial hysterics. But they couldn't have said more if Clemence Dane had written *The Tempest*. It makes me feel quite queer sometimes when I read that *Saint's Progress* is one of the great masterpieces of all time, and yet I never feel for an instant that I am not right. There can't be any doubt about such rot as *Legend*—and the *Times* RAVED. Perhaps when 1200000 people a year buy *Georgian Poetry* we shall be burned together.

At that moment —— and his babies came over and I gave him the figs for you, packed with my own lily white hands, wrapped in a linen napkin which is ours. They are the figs *of* Ospedaletti—dried here—in this very place—and sold by the *panier*. Chew them well, child, and don't swallow too soon. He promised me wardrobes and plants and ↗ ↗ ↗ (rockets). But do you think he is safe enough to convey a parcel for me? The thing is this. My cardigan that you gave me October 1918 is horribly thin. *No, no, no.* I don't want another. I *can't* just now. I've heaps of things I can manage with—really and truly. I stayed in bed all the morning and *slept*. Queer how I suffer from in-somnia and then make it all up by perpetual sleep. Last week I couldn't sleep. After my jaunt yesterday I have slept practically ever since. Oh, I do wish we were a bit rich, don't you? Money is a bore. I must get more wood tomorrow and pay old L.M. *She* is coming into some more money: £300–500. It's *hers*. And that other legacy was over £100. 'But that's all settled and out of my hands,' she said. 'I've spent that.' I feel a deep rage that it trickles away so—that the £5 a month I give her flows away and is not. Still, however I hate her, I owe her the money for all she's done.

There's tea. I must go and drink and eat it. Wasn't the sketch of the cats good? Wing is the spit of Wing. It was nice of the old boy to send

[1] This was *Pictures*.

421

it me so carefully—little trump that he is. Give him a squeeze from his Sissy.

It's getting dusky. The house is full of small shadows. I can hear the kettle having its lid taken off and then it's filled and now it's on the fire again—all this is very distinct. It's sunset. The windows are shut, the sea is pale. Oh, my dearest darling, my wonder, how dare I lean on you as I do? Do you feel I'm a weight? I want to lean so light, so light, and then suddenly I get heavy and ask to be carried. You ought not to have chosen me to travel with. Ah, I don't agree with that. We made the right choice, the marvellously right *choice* at any rate. *We've* done all we could. It's only the . . . Boss Omnipotent who's been so horrid.

Yours for ever and ever so long as I live and after that the flowers will come up small and starry with love.

Wig

The *A*. not here yet
    nor scarf
    nor acid.

Darling,   Monday,
                                                  (December 1, 1919)

I'm rather dashed today. I've got fever and that makes me frightfully depressed. Ansaldi came yesterday. Don't *count* on him. He's a charlatan. He owned yesterday that the reports he gave me were because 'I saw dis lady wants vot you call sheering up. Like de Irishman I told you you can trot and I hope you may be able to walk'. You observe the polite smile with which I listened. The whole interview seems to have been more or less of a fake. He said yesterday, for instance, *em*phatically that I could not winter in England next year or the year after: that I must have sun and warmth. In fact, he behaved precisely as all other doctors in the world but Sorapure do behave. Sorapure is the only man one can trust at all. This one wasn't like —— in the face for nothing. He *did* give me a good beating. And when I told him of my melancholia, he said it was part toxin poisoning and part because you are alone wiz nobody near you to love and sherish you. I tell my patients dat is better than medicine, *Mrs.* Murry, and so on and so on and so on and so on. And then he went away and I sat in my dressing gown and watched it grow dusk and then dark here, and REALISED how I had been taken in again.

Doesn't matter. What must be, must be. I am writing to J. today to ask her if I may come to Menton for a few days. But what's the good?

I couldn't go today. My temperature's 102. So one goes round and round and round like the squirrel in the cage. It's a cold, grey day.

L.M. is at San Remo getting money for me. When I 'get better' again though, I'll go to Menton for a few days. I think I *must*. I am *too* lonely. You, my own precious, don't grieve for me. It's just my melancholia. Tig's black birds. Kiss Wing and know I love you.

Wig

Wednesday,

My own,   (December 3, 1919)

Your wire came this early morning. How it could have arrived so soon I cannot understand, but there it was—THANK GOD. I am sending 2 reviews this week so that you have one in reserve again. I'm doing Couperus and Kuprin together as 2 foreign novels. I thought that the best idea. Here is also your darling Friday letter about the new linen for the house and Wing saucepan rolling. It all sounds so wonderful. I am better today—my temperature is lower and though I feel a bit like a fly who is *just* out of the milk jug,—ça va. Must have caught a chill, I suppose. I don't know how. It's a very ugly day. I am lying in my little room warmly wrapped up with a hot bottle and fire. L.M. has gone to San Remo. She dropped 32 lire on a cheque yesterday and as it was a 'mistake' I have had to ask her to go back with it today and see if she can get the extra. I suppose not.

Last night under the inspiration of a fever attack I wrote these verses. Keep them for me, will you? I feel a longing to write poetry. Don't forget you were going to send me Hardy: I feel passionately eager to read his poems. Did we mention the review in *The Times*? It was superficial, 'silly', and the snail under the nasturtium leaf again. That don't fit Hardy. Talking of snails, the *Nation* and the *Guardian* came today. Did you see the one in the eye Wayfarer gave me? He *had* his quarrel I own, but he was unfair all the same.

V.'s old gardener is outside—bless him!—sowing sweet peas. He's a dear old root of a man. He peers at me through the window and when I open it to speak makes the gesture of pulling his coat round him so that I'll keep covered up and mutters 'd'vent, d'vent' as though it were spelled *devant*. It's all right. I shall be better still tomorrow. It's always a comfort not to feel worse. But don't rush a house. Who knows that I'm not turned out of England by the Lord—that I'm not a wandering tribe, complete with lamentations? It looks jolly like it to me. But even if I am, *you* must have a house in the country. So go on collecting.

Goodbye for now, my precious. I LOVE you, LOVE you, LOVE you.

Your own
Wig-wife

Thursday,
(December 4, 1919)

My darling Bogey,

I am sending my review of Couperus and Kuprin today. Don't the names go well together! I feel a little better today. My temperature rose again pretty high last night tho' I went to bed at five. I expect it's that which knocks me out so absolutely, *morally*. It's pretty frightful—the loneliness, the noise of one's heart pounding away—and the feeling that this is ALL there is. I can't master it. I must just go on with it and take what comes. There is nothing else for it. I reviewed the whole situation last night.

The old gardener came again yesterday to sow sweet peas. We parleyed through the window—he roaring and I nodding. He wants to dig up the lower terrace and plant zucca, concombres, haricots, tomates, pommes de terre, kakis. And then he performed a pantomime of the servant-maid emptying jugs of water on to these delicacies and they growing round and fat—all by next spring.

I've never seen or heard from les dames de San Remo since I did not attend Miss Shuttleworth's lunch. That was the end of that. But it was an appalling day—impossible. Everybody seems to agree that the appalling cold this year has been quite exceptional and that the worst is over. It has not been so cold these last few days. I begin to think that even *with* it this climate is vastly better than England. The sun does shine; the air is pure. If one were not alone here and conscious of every tiny smallest change in the elements and in one's sick body even the cold would not matter so much. And there *is* sun.

Ospedaletti itself is quite the most beautiful little place I've ever seen —far lovelier than Bandol—and behind it that valley must be really exquisite. The cemetery bulks in my vision but then I'm an abnormal creature. If it didn't and if people had to come abroad, I should say come here. It's so small, there's no fashion, no parasitic life—the people are self-contained and pleasant—you and I in the old days could have been ideally happy here.

You know I am going to Menton I hope for a few days when I am better—to *break the iron ring*. I want to have a talk to Jinnie F. too. If I can be sure of getting better—absolutely sure—would you mind very much if I adopted a child? It's evidently on the cards I may have to spend a good deal of my life—alone—and I can't stick it. I think, I'm sure in fact, I could manage as regards money, and I want to adopt a baby boy of about *one* if I can get him. I cannot do it if you dislike the idea, because of course he would be always with us when we were together just like our own child—and you might hate that.

On the other hand, when I am alone, he'd keep me from utter loneliness and writing these agonizing letters!! I thought I'd ask Brett to be his guardian supposing anything were to happen to me. I think she would like it and that would free you from any possible responsibility should you not want to have him, and of course you couldn't if I wasn't there. If I must spend next winter abroad I can't spend it alone, and a nurse for him kills two birds with one stone!

But at any rate, my dear darling, I can't face life alone, not even for six months at a time. The prospect is unbearable. It can't be done. Neither can you and I live together. There's the paper. You CAN'T give it up. We must have the money. You can't earn money away from England and even if you could you mustn't leave England. That is obvious. Your place is *there*. It would spell failure for you to live abroad with me—I absolutely fully realize that. I can imagine what hours we should spend when I realized and you realized the sacrifice. And then there's the house in England which I could come to in the summer and perhaps after a year or two live in always. . . . But I'll never be sure that a moment of uprooting will not recur and this is what I cannot contemplate. I think quite seriously I shall go out of my mind if I have to suffer a great deal more. There's where the child comes in. I'd love him and he'd love me. We'd look after each other. But when you reply to this consider that he'd be always with me. I'd have to bring a nurse back to England. (She wouldn't cost any more than L.M. however.) But I want you to think of it and write to me as soon as you can for if I go to Menton I'll talk it over with Jinnie.

L.M.'s off to the village. I must give her this letter. Goodbye for now, darling Bogey. I hope O's sale was a success (for us I mean).

Ever your own

Wig-wife

Darling, please keep all these verses for me in the file—will you?
I'll polish them up one day, have them published. But I've no copies.
So don't leave them about—will you? Just thrust them into the old
file or into my cupboard. Wig

My darling,
Your Saturday letter telling me of your cold and your Sunday letter
are come. I do hope the journey to Penge didn't make the cold worse:
it seemed a bit like madness to go and risk waiting at the railway
stations—but—what could you do? Wing ought to be trained to
balance the paper weight on his nose, like Dora's Gyp did the pencil—
you remember? I have been wondering whether you marked the new
linen and how: it *is* so important to have it plainly marked and to see it
comes back from the wash. I expect Violet is careful though. Would
you put an *ad* of my story[1] in the *T.L.S.* I'll pay. I feel we must sell it
now it's been such a labour and that's the only way it will sell. But it
ought to be in before Xmas.

Don't overwork, Boge. I wish I could see your Georgian Poetry review, I tremble a little for you when you go 'eyes out' for or against a
thing. I always feel you don't quite get the measure of your opponent—
you expose yourself in your enthusiasm and he takes a mean underhand
advantage. But perhaps that is nonsense.

It's sunset, with a wide, wide pale yellow sky and a blue sea gilded
over. I feel horribly weak after this fever attack, but calmer—just now
—thank the Lord. My heart is so hateful. If you had such a heart. It
bangs, throbs, beats out 'Tramp, tramp, tramp, the boys are marching,'
double quick time, with very fine double rolls for the kettle-drum.
How it keeps it up I don't know. I always feel it's going to give out. I
think every day I shall die of heart failure. I expect it's an inherited
feeling from Mother. Oh—*envied* Mother—lucky, lucky Mother, so
surrounded, so held, so secure! Can't I hear her 'Child, you mustn't be
left here *one instant*,' and then she'd make miracles happen and by tomorrow she'd have me wrapped up and defied everybody.

But we are firmly held in the web of circumstance. We've got to
risk it—to see it through. If you were to leave there our future is

---

[1] *Je ne parle pas français.*

wrecked; if I came there, I'd die. No, once I am better I go to Menton and I'll return here later, in the spring when I'm stronger, with a maid so as to be ready for you in May.

L.M. is out to tea with some people in Ospedaletti—gone off with a big bunch of roses for them. The wind sighs in the house and the fire goes *chik-chik*—very small. My fever makes everything 100 times more vivid, like a nightmare is vivid. But it will be over in a day or two, I expect. A bad business!

Brett sent me some photographs. Will you thank her for me? I can't lash myself into any kind of a friendly cackle. I thought the photographs very weak, that's all—but she sent me a nice letter.

Can you get Lawrence's address for me? I should like to have it.

Goodbye, darling.

I am ever your own

Wig-wife

I am sure Menton will do wonders for my old depression. I've great hopes of it. Bogey, forgive me, all you tell me about the house—I can't help feeling it's all part of a hideous vile joke that's being played on us for les autres to read about in days to come. I *can't* see it except like this. I sometimes even get to the pitch of believing that subconsciously you are aware of this, too, and with colossal artistry are piling on delicate agony after delicate agony—so that *when* the joke is explained, all will be quite perfect,—even to a silver tea-pot for her.

THE NEW HUSBAND

Someone came to me and said
Forget, forget that you've been wed.
Who's your man to leave you be
Ill and cold in a far country?
Who's the husband—who's the stone
Could leave a child like you alone?

You're like a leaf caught in the wind,
You're like a lamb that's left behind,
When all the flock has pattered away;
You're like a pitiful little stray
Kitten that I'd put in my vest;
You're like a bird that's fallen from nest.

We've none of us too long to live,
Then take me for your man and give
Me all the keys to all your fears
And let me kiss away these tears;
Creep close to me. I mean no harm
My darling. Let me make you warm.

I had received that very day
A letter from the other to say
That in six months—he hoped—no longer
I would be so much better and stronger
That he could close his books and come
With radiant looks to bear me home.

Ha! Ha! Six months, six weeks, six hours
Among these glittering palms and flowers
With Melancholy at my side
For my old nurse and for my guide
Despair—and for my footman Pain
—I'll never see my home again.

Said my new husband: Little dear,
It's time we were away from here.
In the road below there waits my carriage
Ready to drive us to our marriage.
Within my house the feast is spread
And the maids are baking the bridal bread.

I thought with grief upon that other
But then why should he aught discover
Save that I pined away and died?
So I became the stranger's bride
And every moment however fast
It flies—we live as 'twere our last!

The effect of these verses upon me was shattering. At that time I did not
fully understand how uncontrollable is the mood of despair which engulfs the
tubercular patient, or how Katherine was from time to time possessed by it as
by a totally alien power. Nor was it possible (I suppose), even if I had understood the completeness of this 'possession' by despair, for me to have been so
detached that I could regard the verses as coming from beyond herself. They

struck me as a terrible accusation of myself—the harder to bear because it was unfair: for it was not of my own free choice that I stayed in England at my job. My livelihood and Katherine's depended on it, at the time.

I immediately began to make preparations to leave the 'Athenæum' for a fortnight, and to go and see her. She begged me not to come in repeated telegrams. Nevertheless, I persisted in my preparations. I arrived in Ospedaletti on December 16, 1919.

Friday in bed,

My dearest Bogey,   (December 5, 1919)

I was thinking over *Cinnamon and Angelica* in bed last night and you know I think you ought to find something else for that bit where Cinnamon comments on his nose and Mace says: "'Tis the Cinnamon nose' and tells him his grandfather was called Old Long Beak. For this reason. There have been so *many* royal noses, so many Long Beak grandfathers that the idea is too familiar to the ear. I am a perfect fiend about this play, aren't I? and I'm afraid I come, as Miss Dane would put it, 'savaging your Holy of Holies'. But you know how it is meant. It's what I want you to do with my stories. I feel you ought to have done it more to *Je ne parle pas*. Don't, because you're exquisitely tender, spare me. I'd rather not be *sporn*.

Your play suggests so much—that's the trouble—and I can't be quite sure that what you have imaginatively apprehended yourself has *got into it enough*. You know how, beyond a certain point, if one is deeply in love with a piece of work, it's almost impossible to say what is there and what's not there. I think too it might be more faëry: by that I mean have more *songs*. I think when Angelica is found with Carraway and Marjoram she ought to sing. There ought to be indeed to my thinking a song for the three of them—Angelica's song, with a line for Carraway here and a line for Marjoram there. . . .

Perhaps this is because I do *shy* a little at blank verse. It makes the *quality* you want to get very difficult. On the other hand, at Cinnamon's death, at Mace's account of it except for that (forgive my horrible cruelty) 'war, Mace, war,' you bend it wonderfully to your will. By mentioning that 'war, Mace, war,' I know that is precisely what you meant to convey. Yet it seems to me—curse the word!—reminiscent. I hear so many lovers saying with just that real feeling 'war, Mace, war,' but I don't on the other hand hear them saying 'My darling' nor read how they drooped and died.

At that moment I tried to *think* out what I wanted to see—and, instead, bending my mind to your play, I saw you instead—in all your innocence and beauty. I saw that you which is the *real rare secret* you. Oh, if only I could lift this dark disease from me. It did lift for the instant, but then I realized how dark it is and how it has poisoned me. It does not stop at your lungs; then it attacks your brain and then your heart. And I also felt I must make very very plain that I never want you here. Don't think that for one instant. I DON'T. You must stay where you are and I must get through this and find my way out, or not, alone. I feel that to the bottom of my soul. The time is past when we might have been together in such a case. Now it would only spell tragedy for us both. You feel that, too, don't you? Of course, that being the case, it is really not fair that I should tell you what I suffer. But the feeling is stronger than I. I can't know you and not tell. I don't write to another creature simply because I couldn't not tell them. It's all there is of me TO tell. Hideous, hideous predicament! I hope to hear from Menton today or tomorrow and as soon as I am well I will go there for a bit. I've still got fever but it is going. My temperature was only 100 last night. I'll get L.M. to buy a bottle of Cognac today for a stimulant.

Well, here's December. Does Richard remember the paper flowers we made last December and how we decorated the hall and stairs? *Darling Memory.* I was very happy. If I am alive next year, Bogey where shall I be? *Malaga,* I think; it sounds so peculiarly odious, full of the most beautiful *flowers* and *shops* and an English boarding house kept by a Mrs. Cooper. But she won't take anybody who is ill or who won't dress in *low* evening dress for dinner. That's one strange door that's fully shut then. Goodbye, darling. It's a pity this all happened. Alas! Alas!

Your own
Wig-wife

My darling Bogey,   Friday,
                                    (December 5, 1919)

Your after the sale letter has arrived and I think you did very well. What you say about *clocks* is quite true. No room is complete without one. And the writing table sounds exquisite. Will you put it in the hall for the present in place of that ugly? Or is not the right shape or size? What a lot of new things there are, even since my time!

430

Now about your talk at Delamare's on poetry. No, you're NOT too serious. I think you are a trifle over-anxious to assure people how serious you are. You antagonize them sometimes or set them doubting because of your emphasis on your sincerity. In reviewing again you cry sometimes, in your sincerity: these are the things which have been done, which have happened, to *me* or to *us*. I think as a critic that *me* or *us* is superfluous. If they must be there, then you must write a poem or a story. People are not *simple* enough—Life is not simple enough—to bear it otherwise. If fills me with a queer kind of shame; one hears oneself whispering in one's soul to you: 'Cover yourself—cover yourself quickly. Don't let them see!' That they think you are asking for alms, for pity, doesn't matter. That, of course, is just their corruption—their falsity. Nevertheless, though they are wrong, I do not think you are right. If you speak for your generation, *speak,* but don't say 'I speak for my generation,' for the force is then gone from your cry. When you know you are a voice crying in the wilderness, *cry,* but don't say 'I am a voice crying in the wilderness'. To my thinking (and I am as you know so infinitely, incomparably nearer the public than you) the force of either the blow you strike or the praise you want to sing is *broken* by this—what is it? Is it the most infernal modesty? Innocence? Do you see how all this which is non-critical in you proves and proves and proves and proves you *poet*. Heavens, child! You're quite capable of kicking off with

> My lips have sipped oblivion, I have known
> The golden hours chime through the charmèd day

while reading Mr. ——'s essay on ——. No, that is extreme; but there's a big *pearl* of truth in it. The trouble ∴ is that when a book really engages your passions you are dangerous. You can be trusted with other books but if a book stirs you to real anger then there's the fear that you will be all poet and miss it and—at the same time—what I call expose yourself.

You have of course worked about a million times too hard and too long. That *long breath* you never have time for. You're not crippled, your wings aren't injured (*real* wings now) but they are bound to you, bound tight, and until you've had time to really really spread them— to sail down a tideless breeze—you'll never really be the writer you ought to be. Whenever a little spell has come—the smallest—you have made these extraordinary beginnings of real flight—I mean *short perfect* flights as in some of your poems—but you must know your *freedom,* to be the poet you are. If it's not absurd to say so, you are capable of infinite expansion (see the Globe-Wernicke)—and ripe for it In fact I see you as a man *starved.* If we could—ah, if they would let us pull off the house idea, you're saved as well as I—you're saved as a poet. (Reading Hardy made me realize this). You oughtn't to *give out* except what's just overplus—you ought to *absorb* and receive.

I expect this is both dull and impertinent.

Later: Oh, your new book has just come. It looks *superb.* I want to burn all I've written here. I'll read it tonight. It looks terrific. And when I looked at the title-page and decided, No, he's forgotten, and then saw that TO MY WIFE, I had a moment of such *ancient bliss* you cannot conceive. Now, I'll go on with this. Really, C.S. has done you very proud. I mean it's so distinguished-looking, don't you think? No, that *To my wife, To my wife* is written on every wave of the sea at the moment. It's to me just as though I'd been going home from school and the Monaghans had called after me and you—about the size of a sixpence—had defended me and p'raps helped me to pick up my pencils and put them back in the pencil box. (I'd have given you the red one.)

I had by the same post an awfully nice sympathetic letter from Grant Richards asking me for a book. He can have *White Roses* when ready. I feel better today. The brandy was a great point. 'Very Old Pale Cognac' —one can't help pitying it. Yet that it should have such fire!! My temperature was only just on 100 last night. Now I've got to climb back again, curse it.

Bogey, about that scarf, would you gather the insurance. I think it's gone for good all right, and we can't just drop the £2 2 0. And if you get it, might I have it in notes to buy summat woolly here if I can? The post is obviously quite untrustworthy.

The sea comes rolling in—rolling in. There's not a sound but my pen. L.M. is somewhere out in the village. Catherina came to see me yesterday guarding against the infection de la fièvre with a shawl, but an *immense* shawl! which she kept held up to her lips till I made her smile and then forgot all about. I was asking her if she was going to help with the tea-room that Mme. Littardi is opening. 'Ah non, Madame, ce n'est pas mon métier, vous savez'—and here she flushed lightly and put her hands in her pockets—'je suis *née* pour le repassage . . . e—t puis . . . c'est ma passion!'

432

There's the secret of her charm.
Here's L.M. back. It's ¼ to six. Post time très juste.
Goodbye, my darling own.

Your
Wig-wife

Dear Editor,

Friday,
(? December 5, 1919)

I felt that this book demanded a review of its own. I shall send (cross my heart straight dinkum) Kuprin and Philpotts and Stacpoole on Sunday.

K.M.

103.4

I certify this girl has had a temperature this week and hasn't been able to do more
Doctor Wing

Priez pour Elle.

Darling Own,

Sunday,
(December 7, 1919)

I wonder what you are doing with your Sunday? And if it's fine or dreadful? It's very fine here—a little windy, that's all. My day has been like my last few days. I rise at *12* lunch lie on the sofa till 6, and then say, 'Are the hot-water bottles upstairs?' and go to bed. It's a small beat, but there is a large Policeman on it who frightens me a bit. My fever returned last night, I don't know why. It decided me to take a step. Your 'clock' complex is surpassed by my doctor complex, but my collection, unlike yours, never is reliable, never tells the real truth, or sustains or strikes the real hour—except the beautiful clock Sorapure. But I am going to call in another. I don't want to see Ansaldi again. What *is* the good. Who wants 'sheering up' only? And besides he repels me. But yesterday that Miss S. came here and though she was *far* too kind and concerned, she did implore me to see Foster, the Englishman. In fact, she asked me if she could go back and telephone him, and I said Yes, perhaps it's just as well. He comes tomorrow.

But I must get Richard to print off a decent little pamphlet entitled 'The Physical History of K.M. 1917-19—?' It's so wearisome, so—I don't know—like ashes, to hear myself recite my *one* recitation—a bird with one song, 'How the Fowler Trapped me'. Perhaps that's what all birds in cages sing. Next time you pass me, listen and hear it:

> I was flying through a wood
> A *green* wood,
> A spring wood,
> It was early, early morning. . . .

This afternoon I've been reading your book, but I can't write about it till it's finished. Thank goodness you're not going to De la Mare's tonight—all that journey. You must not do it again.

The fire is all right, but it's becoming a burning bridge with no heart—just an arc de triomphe. I can't get up and put it together, I am so wound round in my Jaeger rug. There *was* a purchase, Boge, my own. Oh, I DO love you. It's dusk here. My pen seems to make such a loud noise. The winds swing in the shadowy air. The sea cries. I love you and love you.

Don't forget how I love you. Remember pour toujours. How long since we've said that! I expect this week I'll get well again. I know why I have the fever today: it's my left lung—but not intolerable by any means.

Goodbye for now darling darling heart

Your

Wig-wife

Monday morning,
(December 8, 1919)

My darling,

It's warm and still. I've all the windows open—practically the *wall* open in my bedroom—and I'm looking out on to the hillside. There's just a gentle, gentle stirring of the trees—lovely to watch. Let's talk about your book.[1] I read it through last night. The quality that is ever-present and that makes the greatest impression on the reader is your *honesty*—your almost desperate struggle in a world of falsity to get at the truth. That is *very noble,* and the *imperative impulse* which urges you to speak for the sake of truth, whatever the cost,—not, indeed, counting the cost—is again a noble, noble impulse.

Nevertheless, it seems to me that the false world has wounded you— has changed your 'word' from what it should be to what it is. You

---

[1] *The Evolution of an Intellectual.*

434

ought not to have to say these things. It is wrong that they should have been forced from you. You see, I don't believe that the war has done these things to you: I don't believe you are maimed for life—that you *go on* certainly, but that you never can recover. (Your generation I mean that you speak for) I think these are the conclusions arrived at by thinking: granted such a war, granted such a *reception* of such a war, granted such falsity, indifference, squalor and callousness—their effect upon an intellect would be so and so. . . . But this intellectual reasoning is never *the whole truth*. It's not *the artist's truth*—not *creative*. If man were an intellect it would do, but man ISN'T. Now I must be fair, I must be fair. Who am I to be certain that I understand? There's always Karori to shout after me. *Shout* it. I've re-read 'The Question' and 'The Republic of the Spirit'. 'The Question' is very brilliant. But it's an *étude*—isn't it? *Tour de force sur les écharpes?* Isn't it? The other is the best essay in the book. I think it might have been written by a famous MONK. As I read, I felt: Yes, yes, yes, but now let me turn and kiss somebody and let there be music. . . .

Now I do not want you to think it's the female in me that wants to kiss somebody after these essays. It is not because I am incapable of detachment that they seem to me *un*-warm (in the sense that fertility is warm. I keep seeing a golden hen on her eggs). For you are not detached. If you were detached, you would not have been influenced in the same way by the spirit of the times. Yet it is not the *complete you* who is influenced: it is the intellectual you. The *complete you* rebels against the intellectual you at times and wrestles and overthrows it. Which wins out, after the book is finished, in the mind of the reader?

p. 19 'We are maimed and broken for ever. Let us not deceive ourselves.'

p. 86 'Tchehov's sense of the *hopeless indescribable* beauty of the *infinitely weary* pattern.'

p. 97 'And even that to such contemplation our own *utter* discomfiture is beautiful.'

p. 110 'Yet we feel that the effort to respond to the *Sursum Corda* will be as long and may be more terrible still.'

p. 110. 'A part, how great we do not know, of our soul is become *for ever* numbed and insentient. But with what remains we feel, and we feel no joy.'

p. 117. 'And while we reach back *timidly* into the past to discover the sequence of our wounds.'

p. 131. 'We are afraid to speak of it because we know in our hearts that the breath of the very word will find us *naked* and *shivering*....'

p. 156. 'The possibility which we had desired stood before us in the *frozen intolerable* rigidity of a law. Against it we might dash our minds but they would break.

p. 166. 'The impulse is almost overwhelming to withdraw into ourselves and discover in the *endurance* of our souls....'

p. 216. 'In a life in which the gold has dimmed to grey.'

p. 218. 'A menacing instinct warns us that we are somehow maimed.'

I have just copied these few things because though I know it is not all 'like that' they are there—and they are important. They DO give the tone. You know, Bogey, they seem to me deathly. They frighten me. I don't believe them—but that's beside the question. What I feel is that they cannot be the VITAL you? Were the world not what it is, that you would not be alive today. Whatever the world were, the you of certain of your poems—of parts of *Cinnamon and Angelica*—will always be there. It seems to me that the intellect only ceases to be a devil when the soul is *supreme* and *free*. I know that you have been naked and shivering, timid and frozen. Oh, that you should have known Love as deep as ours and still feel *like that*—*Love that is of the soul*.

I can't write any more today. These are just 'notes'. Please forgive them. They have been interrupted by the Wednesday letters. I hope your cold is better, my darling. DON'T send me a cardigan if you've not sent it. Because neither of us have any money at present. But if you have, SEND ME THE BILL AND POSTAGE. I shall carefully count my pages in future. I am sincerely, deeply sorry to have given you the extra work. I know how annoying it must be.

I had such a nice letter from Kot. Wing has charmed even him. 'Small and slender and quick-witted' he calls him. What a little *briseur de cœurs* he is!

L.M. is taking this to San Remo. Foster hasn't been yet. It's a perfect summer day. I feel a good bit stronger. I don't *fret*, darling. Fretting always seems to me tearing at the frayed edge of a feeling. I tear the whole feeling into great black bits. Don't know what that's called. I'm going to *flood* you with work this week and then have a holiday at Christmas.

No, Boge, don't send *A. and L. Sun and Moon,* if you don't mind. (1) They'd not publish it (2) I feel far away from it.

I think your Christmas present to me of that writing table is just perfect. I could not have one I like more.

Ever your true love
Wig

My dear Love,

All is explained. Foster has been. I have a SLIGHT attack of bronchial pneumonia. (I've often had them before you know when I was at my Doctor Sorapure's college.) As far as any one can tell at present it is not any fresh outbreak in the left lung—I mean any new tubercular trouble, but a local attack as [such] as any non-tubercular patient might get. This will keep me in bed of course and it accounts for my fever and for the unpleasant symptoms in my heart. I mean there is considerable nervous exhaustion which strains the heart (but no disease in it—'no reason why it should not last you out'.) He has given me a preparation to help my congestion and he advises me to take brandy at least twice a day—or two full glasses of Marsala. (Oh, the relief it is to *know*: to know I was not just giving way!) My situation in this villa with L.M. to look after me he said was quite satisfactory. He does *not* regard it as very exposed. He says those winds have been everywhere. No villa in San Remo would take me, or any hôtel. 'They've all got the wind up about you since you tried for the Excelsior.' That accounts for the fact that there were no villas for us! It's either this or a nursing home, and there is no present necessity for the latter and 'I certainly *don't* recommend it if you can be comfortable here'. This is also the reason why I can't get a maid. He says they won't come because they *know* about me.... Very nice! But 'can't be helped'.

He examined me thoroughly. His verdict was: 'There is serious disease in your left lung of long standing. The right is at present quiescent. You stand a reasonable chance.' He was quite frank and rather on the brutal side, which is pleasant and refreshing. He said, in reply to my question, that if I managed to 'pull round the corner this winter' I could return to England and live there, though for two years my life would be an invalid's life and I could only do it 'provided you lived in great comfort'. I said: 'Please don't for one moment be over-optimistic. I am just as prepared for a verdict against me as a verdict for.' And he said: 'Quite so, Mrs. Murry. Your first job is to get over

437

this pneumonia and then I can examine that lung better, but from a first inspection that is my opinion.'

He is going to notify me and I must sign that my sputum is disinfected and that my knife, spoon and fork are kept apart. How utterly repellent! But the Italians, according to him, have a perfect horror of this disease. He has told me my régime and you can judge the attack is not serious for he is not coming to see me again for a week unless I phone. I'll just keep here very still. It's a good room to be in bed [in]. When L.M. is out, she locks the doors and I have the loaded revolver so no one can come in and steal your Wig. No thief in his senses would, Bogey my precious. Well, I think that's all, my Darling. He seems quite a good serviceable dining-room clock—with an emphatic tick and a well-defined face. I'll keep him on the mantelpiece for the time being, at any rate—thankfully. He asks if old Vernon Rendall was still in the office. Does Francis still edit *Notes and Queries*? I don't know how he knew this. Sydney Beauchamp made no end of a difference. They were at Cambridge together!! Bogey, it is a funny world. Well, I'll take every care as you know and in a week I'll be better I expect. Tell Wing and hear him when he tells you I am all right. I *do* feel greatly better to know why I was feeling worse. Forgive me. I am for ever and ever

Your own little true love

Wig

Tuesday,

Dearest,   (December 9, 1919)

Your wire saying 'Will come for week Xmas' has just arrived. I beg you not to. I beg you to reply by wire that you will not do this. Please, please forgive me and remember it was only my pneumonia which made me so miserable. Now I am in bed, and quiet, and I'll get over it and be stronger. I know I have *driven* you to this by my letters. I don't want it at all. The idea is perfectly dreadful. We shouldn't be happy AND you wouldn't get back. I caution you most seriously on that point. You'd never get your passport from Genoa in time. You'd spend the whole week in getting ready to go. Yes, I know it's my fault. I have left you no other loophole, but forgive me and DON'T DO THIS THING. It's not only a question of the money. It's a question of the paper. The paper won't stand it—and, more important still, the journey is *preposterous* for so few days. You'd not get a week here. The doctor told me only yesterday that people can't GET here without a wait of DAYS in Paris. Xmas will be twice as bad. *Bogey, don't do this thing.* You've given me such a proper fright that I set my teeth again and will somehow or other get through. For God's sake wire me that you'll have a peaceful Xmas at Garsington. While I'm ill, it's no good. I can't bear it. No, save the money for later in the year. I've driven you to this. I don't want it. It horrifies me. DON'T COME, DON'T COME. Stay there. I'll be calm. I won't be such a vampire again. And consider carefully that, quite apart from 'us', there is the fact that one's passport now takes from a fortnight to three weeks to recover from Genoa. It would be a perfect disaster. I *feel* it. Don't do it.

In May I shall be better. All will be different. L.M. will be 'going'—not staying with me and you gone again. I really don't think I could stand that. Above all there's no need.

The idea is like you. Thank you from my heart, but please don't ever do it.

Wig

Tuesday night,
(December 9, 1919)

Will you change the last sentence of my Kuprin to: 'And what more has anybody said....'

My precious,

After sending you the wire, I want to send another—to say that I do feel stronger. I have spent the day you see dead still and the pain is *much much* less. Then to my joy the paper came.

Your Georgian review is FIRST CHOP. Wing must decorate you with the O.M.T.—order of the Mouse Trap. You couldn't have done it better, Boge. There's not a chink in your armour either. You have really wiped the floor with them—and I cheered you—to the echo (you know, on my thumb).[1] I had no idea you were going to bathe it in a kind of twinkling delicate light. I thought you were going to cry *Woe*. You have cried *Woe* but oh, with what arrows, to spear these sparrows, to their very marrows! I feel as though we'd been through a naval engagement and now drew away and heaved up and left them—tuned our fiddles, brought out the dishes of gold and the fishes' heads of pure jade with lamps for eyes. Bogey, 'twas a famous victory!

Swinnerton is very good and L'Hôte excellent. So is Dent. I must,

[1] I don't understand this phrase.

439

though, say the Christmas Supplement is bad, Boge, to my thinking: what do you think? It's simply *rotten* for trade. You can't make an ad. out of a single review, and then they are SO SLOPPY. Turner makes me burn in not mentioning a single book. But the women are simply squashed flies, though I say it as shouldn't. After all in a Supplement you're out to *sell*—I don't mean vulgarly—but you're out to let's say make a point. . . . And apart from that, R. 2½ columns on a 1/9 book that she dismisses—whew! I shuddered at the look of the publisher turning it over. . . . S. on Crusoe is not only so wrong in idea that the spirit faints—she writes as though she were baking a cake. Next year we'll do a Korker. We'll have an article on what children like and *should have,* and list of books and poetry books and reprints. The copy all in advance—a dummy ready to be taken round for the ads.

Later. L.M. has just brought the post—your Thursday and Friday letter and her income one. My own precious darling angelic little mate, you're working to your eyes, you've a cold in your nose, I've come down on you like a ton of bricks and away you smile. I must pray again—I must pray louder and longer and harder to my *cruel* God to make me not to fail. Oh, *you* MUST not come. It would be too awful!!

Tell me the price of the cardigan. I shall love it. But now I *don't* want a scarf. Ça suffit. Look at The Lacket[1] when you have time. Yes, I can easily do the work this week and send it off *easily* in time. You'll have Mrs. H.W. and Benjy tomorrow by the noon post. I've only a page more. Hewlett and Philpotts ought to be for Xmas.

Take care of that cold please for our sakes. Why don't you have a few inoculations against cold? And are your teeth perfect? Talk to me *only* about yourself—not a word about me. Don't worry about me. I'm here in bed, not moving, wrapped up warm, eating, all the windows open, my temperature descending 'by slow degrees, by more and more'. Another load of wood came today. The wood cupboard is full. It's filet for dinner. Oh, *cruel* God, help me not to sink into the pit again—help me to give him all the love I feel. For tonight I am just love of you—no more to me—and tonight I do believe. Bless me, my brother.

  Your
   Wig

[*Enclosed was the following. I was dealing with an income-tax claim of L.M.'s.*]

[1] The Lacket was a house in Wiltshire which had been suggested to us.

Sir,

       Re abatement and the questions in that clause
claimant does not remember
when it was
or
where it was
or
to what office her claim was sent
I advised her ∴ to leave all unanswered.
Was that right?
(Bet I don't get a sniff of that £7. She's *furious* with me!)

In the night,   (? December 9, 1919)

    I am awake and I have re-read your letter. It is stranger than ever. It is half an account of what I have done to you and the other half is all money. And you say I don't appreciate the seriousness of these your views about money. You do me great wrong. But I must not be kept in the dark. Have your creditors come down on you? But if they have it is since Ottoline's sale? For were the burden of your debts so imperative and terrible you could not have spent any money there. What are these terrible debts? I must be told them. You cannot hint at them and then say I lack sympathy. You are not a pauper. You have £800 a year and you only contribute to my keep—not more than £50 a year at most now. You write as though there were me to be provided for—yourself—and all to be done on something like £300. I know you have paid my doctor's bills and that my illness has cost you a great deal. IT WILL COST YOU NO MORE. I cannot take any more money from you ever and as soon as I am well I shall work to make a good deal more so that you have to pay less.

    But your letter frightens me for you. I think you have allowed this idea of money to take too great a hold on your brain. Either we must do nothing but pay off your debts or you must not care so greatly. It's madness to write like this to your wife and then to buy furniture. It's unworthy of our love to taunt me with my lack of understanding. How *could* I understand? I had no idea you still felt these crying claims: I thought all was going fairly smoothly. You must stick to the paper. I have never had another thought. Your being here is impossible from every point of view. I do not want it at all. I thought I had made that plain and about the paper—many many times. You say 'money is

441

fundamental to any decision you make'. Yes, of course it is. But I do not need to be told, and truly you should know that. I feel ashamed when I read that.

What I do beg you to do is to stay there, to live quietly and get the paper really going. *Live quietly.* I suppose you laugh. I have made that so impossible in the past. You'll have no cause to blame me in the future for it. I leaned on you—and *broke you.* The truth is that until I was ill you were never called upon 'to play the man' to this extent—and it's NOT your rôle. When you said you ought to be kept you spoke the truth. I feel it. Ever since my illness this crisis, I suppose, has been impending—when suddenly in an agony I should turn all woman and lean on you. Now it has happened. The crisis is over. You must feel that. It won't return. It's over for good.

And I don't ask you to 'cut off with nothing' or to sacrifice anything. All I do ask of both of us is to keep very steady and calm and by May we shall have recovered. But please be calm. You are not asked to do anything quickly—there's *no* decision for you to make.

However ill I am, you are more ill. However weak I am, you are weaker—less able to bear things. Have I really put on the last straw? You imply in this letter that I have. You make me out so cruel that. . . . I feel you can't love me in the least—a vampire. I am not. That is all.

I am not so hurried now. I want to talk more with you. God knows if I have managed to stop you. I can do no more.

Granted (and I grant absolutely) that I have sent you this 'snake? (though now I'm not talking of the verses but of my depression in general), granted that, are you justified in punishing me so horribly? I know when I write happy letters they make you happy. You ask me to write more and you say 'if you want to keep me happy that's the way to do it'. Listen. When I was in Hampstead with you were you always able to put all else aside and make me happy? Did you never come to me, depressed, fearful, uneasy, fatigued, and say 'You can't expect me to dance—or act up to what you want?' Did I ask you to make such an effort that your whole nature should change and you should be *really* happy, *believing* in happiness. You have even denied you *wanted* happiness—on the Heath by a broken tree. I did not think I had to make the effort; I thought you alone—you, the secret, secret you—would understand. The effort to keep perpetually radiant was too great. But you asked it of me. I did not *only* write to make you and keep you happy. That was important but not of first importance. Of first importance was my desire to be truthful before you; Love, I thought, could stand *even that*. Love could penetrate the isolation surrounding another, and lovers did not suffer alone. Not that I required of you that you should suffer with me. Never. Never. From the bottom of my heart I can say that. But I took you at your word: it seemed to me almost my duty to tell you all in the greatest possible honesty—anything less would not be *our love*. When you wrote: 'That's the stuff to keep me happy,' I was full of despair. I knew I could not go on giving it you. It was not as though you were ill and turned to me, strong and well, as a flower would turn to the sun, crying: 'I am in the shadow, shine on me!' Alas, I was no sun. I was in the shadow and when at times I came into a bright beam and sent it to you, it was only *at times*.

I keep thinking of Wing as I write this and of our love. Will it all come back, or have I, the snake, laid everything waste?

Peace! Peace! It could not be helped. If I have done this, it was a snake in my bosom—yea, in my bosom—and not I.

I will not receive your dreadful accusations into my soul for they would kill me.

But here is your letter and you tell me I have driven you nearly insane—ruined you, it seems—quenched your hopes even of getting your money affairs straight. You tell me again that you are a bankrupt. It can't be helped. No protestations now.

Remember how we've loved—remember it all, all, and let us not talk of *money*. It is not necessary to tell me, to hint that THEY will come after you and perhaps put you in jail for debt if you run away. I don't ask these things. I never asked them. I believed that the human being did not suffer alone. I showed you my sufferings—I have learned the truth. Do not let us talk of it again. Let us just go on. Let us bury the past, and go on and *recover*. We shall. Our only chance now is not to lose Hope but to go on and not give each other up.

Your devoted—yours eternally

Your wife

Wednesday,

My dearest,   (December 10, 1919)

Another wire has come this morning and I have just prepared the answer. You must please please obey me and believe me and not come.

The idea is more terrible than I can say. You must stay there till May. We break our resolve, ruin our future by such a thing. Stay away. Don't come. What in God's name would be the good? *What for?* To see each other? Why? we might even break with each other if we were to do such a thing. You'd 'forgive' me, but you'd owe me a grudge always and rightly. It would be a sign that we had failed—*ganz definitif.*

Waste of energy—waste of life—waste of money—a mad impulse grâce à moi yielded to—our *new* selves betrayed—the paper can't stand it, either. It's rocky still as we know. AND YOU WOULDN'T GET BACK.

My own love,

Thursday,
(December 11, 1919)

All day long I've lain waiting for the bell that should mean your answer to my telegram, saying you're not coming. Sometimes, for days, this bell isn't rung: today there has been an old woman and a child with grapes and a maid to inquire after Madame and a beggar. Each time the bell has rung my heart has felt *suffocated, fainting,* and the moment when L.M. went and did not come to me has been an age—an age. I *must* have stopped you! I think of you leaving home—the cold, the dark, your cold—all this vile terrible journey before you—your fatigue. I think of your making arrangements to leave the paper—working, overworking, at top top speed. I see you sitting in one of these loathsome trains, my tired boy and pale, longing to sleep, wrapped in your overcoat—the draughts, the rattle, and your uneasiness—your *state of soul.* Oh, can Love keep this horror from you? I'll wire again tomorrow if I do not hear. Be calm, be calm, wait for his answer! It *must* come. I see you with your passport bending over a table, explaining that your wife is ill. I imagine you held up here, unable to get back. If I can only save you from this by those messages. Tonight I would promise to stay here a year I think rather than you should come.

My love goes out to you—running out to you down a dark path saying 'Keep away! Keep away, Bogey!' Can you hear? Will you realize my relief when I know I've been in time? I feel it will make me well again.

God forgive me for what I have done. Those words Chummie spoke as he died. Ever since I have had your telegram they seem *mine.* Can

444

you forgive me? I lie here wondering. Oh my love, oh my love, stay in England.

> Your own true love
> Wig

Friday,
(December 12, 1919)

Jack, your wire has come saying you are determined to spend Christmas here. I have wired finally begging you not to.

There is no need.

Our compact is broken.

It's one of our old *mad* flings.

We haven't the money.

You'll not get back under three weeks at earliest.

We shan't enjoy it. I am not well enough to have fun with you. L.M. is here. You know how before you left last time we were all at near breaking-point.

I'd a million times rather you saw The Lacket and wrote to me.

Even if you have your tickets and visas I would not come if I were you. I can easily give you £5 to help with the expenses you have had. All goes well here. There is nothing to worry about in the very slightest. If you come I feel we have failed. I can now say no more but trust you to believe

> Your Wig

Friday,
(December 12, 1919)

My dearest Love,

I heard the front door bell. It's just after 8 a.m.: and knew it was a telegram. L.M. has just gone off to wire you. I am frightfully worried that you should have felt compelled to send it. Ever since I had that *crise* of depression, I have bitterly reproached myself for letting you know. Madness! Madness! I shall never do so again if I am in my right mind.

Let me try and be very plain with you. *All is all right* here. I thought in those first few weeks it was going to be 'happy'. It's not. But I have lost my capacity for happiness for the time. I am sure, even counting the climate, it is right to be here and to stick it out. I am lonely, very lonely. I somehow hadn't counted on that. It's like imprisonment. And

I find it inconceivably difficult to work. Work is an immense effort of will such as I had never dreamed of. Now I know what *your* will is like. Nevertheless, work is all I have. If I am not working I want to run up and down, just that. And I am fearful that my reviews are not what you want. It would greatly help if you would tell me. Would you? I am—seem to be—nothing but a great great drag on you—no comfort, no blessing, no help or rest. I just put out my hands and say: 'Please!'

It's not really so. *I'll make it otherwise.* Tell me though if you feel a grudge against me or if you want to shut the door in my face—enfant trop gâté, am I? Do you think like that?

It won't go on—my mental state, I mean. It will change. And physically I am really and truly much stronger. That's genuine. I'd like to see Sorapure and find out from him whether it 'showed'. That would be immensely comforting and a great spur. No other doctor is of the slightest use; he knows nothing. I *ought* not to be so unhappy. After all, I am able to——and there I want to make a line—able to—what? You see, it's like a kind of *blindness*. I only thought of Mentone because I thought there might be concerts there and music would help. I simply hate the sea. But *please* think and believe that physically I am better.

Then you have your paper and winter campaign. Oh, to think I should bind you. It cannot be. Will you please, after this letter, trust me not to do it again? And just plant your feet on a rock and say: 'Tig's all right' and so forget me. I mean forget me as a worry. Think of me as on a sea-voyage or something like that—not much use (no use) to you while she's there, but when she steps on dry land again all will be as it was before the blow fell. Nothing can take away from the fact that the blow did fall, you know. But I want to put myself away and think of you. For you are not to be worried. Do you FEEL that? Forgive me! Can you forgive me? If someone was being attacked in a wood you'd not be angry with them for interrupting, would you? It was like that. It's sunny today.

No! only forgive me, forgive me!

Wig

Saturday 7 a.m.,
Darling,   (? December 13, 1919)

I've been lying here while my dream ebbed away. I never have had such vivid dreams as I do here. Campbell in this came to warn me (we

446

were at 'some strange hotel') 'Mansfield, I'd lock your door tonight. There are two Chinamen downstairs, and they're very *predatory*.' He repeated this word while he made some small tentative golf-club-swinging motions, immensely familiar. Campbell belongs to another life, doesn't he? But so does everybody, every single person. I feel they're all quite gone. Even Hampstead and the tapestry in the studio and the sommier. They are not in this world—not for me. What is in this world? Nothing. Just a blank. It's fine this morning, sun and blue sea,—and I don't even care to look out of the window. How long was Dostoevsky in prison? Four years, wasn't he? And he came out and did his finest work after. If only one could rid oneself of this *feeling of finality*, if there were a *continuity*. That's what is so intolerable. The feeling that one goes on, just as the sea does for hours and days after a storm, presenting an appearance of agitation and activity, but *it's really all over*. Could it be possible that I am wrong? I think I'd better not write stories but only my confessions here, and keep them out of letters.

G.B.S. on Butler is very fine indeed.[1] He has such a grip of his subject. I admire his tenacity as a reviewer and the way in which his mind follows Butler with a steady light—does not waver over him, find him, lose him, travel over him. At the same time it's queer he should be (G.B.S.) so uninspired. There is not the faintest hint of inspiration in that man. This chills me. You know the feeling that a great writer gives you: 'My spirit has been fed and refreshed: it has partaken of something new.' One could not possibly feel that about Shaw. It's the clang of the gate that remains with you when all's over. What it amounts to is that Shaw is anything you like, but he's not an artist. Don't you get when you read his plays a sense of extraordinary *flatness*? They may be extremely amusing at moments, but you are always laughing *at* and never *with*. Just the same in his prose: You may agree as much as you like, but he is writing *at* not *with*. There's no getting over it: he's a kind of concierge in the house of literature—sits in a glass case, sees everything, knows everything, examines the letters, *cleans the stairs,* but has no part, no part in the life that is going on. But as I wrote that, I thought: Yes, but who *is* living there, living there as we mean life? Dostoevsky, Tchehov and Tolstoy. I can't think of *anybody else*.

Oh God! What wouldn't I give for a TALK. Well, it can't happen.

[1] A review of Mr. Festing Jones's *Life of Samuel Butler,* by Bernard Shaw, in *The Manchester Guardian.*

I did so love hearing about your walk last Sunday. To think of you in the open air and just walking and getting warm and refreshed, you darling, darling Bogey—and then sitting at the yellow table in your velveteens.

Don't move my shepherdess if you can help. I *see* her there so plainly: I'd hate to think it was another dream: she wasn't there at all, only a little carriage clock. She is the gentle little spirit of the room to me. I always, always until I die shall remember how we listened to the tiny bell striking—from a world of faery. Please don't put her away, Bogey. Think what she has meant. Put the carriage clock on the writing table—can't you? But she is everything to the room—the poet to the landscape. Have you moved her? Tell me.

Goodbye for now, my own darling. Keep happy and don't overwork. Keep warm. Is Violet all right and content? your comfort depends so much on her. I feel inclined to end this letter with the Browning quotation that *cross my heart* I have sworn not to repeat. I used to say it in fun: it was really I suppose a celestial warning. It's my whole life now and I used to play with it and throw it away. Queer business.[1]

Yours, yours for ever, every bit of me, with undying love

Wig

I was with Katherine at the Casetta for a fortnight, returning early in January. As far as I could tell, Katherine's physical condition had not deteriorated so much as I feared; and her depression seemed to leave her. We were indeed happy together, although I was not a very cheerful companion, because I had a violent and prolonged attack of neuralgia in the head—the only one I have had in my life. With the idea of sparing ourselves the worst of our torments we passed a sort of self-denying ordinance, limiting our letters to two a week. It was quickly abandoned.

We discussed the immediate future between us very thoroughly, and decided that I must redouble my efforts to find a suitable house in the English

[1] The Browning quotation was this:

> What so false as truth is,
>   False to thee?
> Whose the serpent's tooth is,
>   Shun the tree.
>
> Where the apple reddens,
>   Never pry—
> Lest we lose our Edens,
>   Thou and I.

country, where Katherine could live in comfort and so be spared the necessity
of going abroad for the winter. She insisted that she must part from L.M. and
wrote to an old college-friend to engage her as secretary-companion. Both these
plans were abandoned as the sequel shows. But a knowledge of them is
necessary to understand the letters that follow.

The Italian railway and postal strike which broke out in January 1920 and
in which Katherine was involved was a very serious affair with avowed
revolutionary intention. It was the precursor and excuse for Mussolini's
seizure of power.

My own darling Bogey,   (early January, 1920)

Since I have put such a stopper on my pen I feel as though dear knows
when I *shall* write—if to write is to be merry. Yesterday I realized to the
full the strangeness of a day when I didn't write to you. You know it's
for years that we have written to each other every day: I thought we
always would—for toujours. But I see and still hold to the foolishness
of it for people like us—I who can't *hold back* and you who can't bear. . . .
But should (God forbid!) the situation be reversed and you away from
me and unhappy, you will write to me? I am of that nature that I can
bear anything better than silence—

Ever since you left you have carried the sun in your pocket. It's
bitter cold, raining fast, *sleeting,* and an east wind. D. says he has
never known the glass so low. The cold is intense. One's fingers ache.
You could not believe this was the same place. And the sky seems to
have great inkstains upon it. I am working—all day—all the evening,
too. Your telegrams, my thoughtful love, were a great pleasure. But
you were a *day late,* weren't you? In arriving? I hope you are well at
home now and with your Wing and your friends.

The post office has struck—no one knows for how long. It just
announces a strike. The country is in a queer state. D. yesterday on
his way here met the men from the railway below who shouted 'You'd
better pack up your traps and go.[1] We don't want any more of you
English here. We're going to clear you out.' But 10 to 1 that is an
exaggeration. He is an alarmist of the very first water and sat here
yesterday suggesting that even at 3 o'clock in the afternoon no one
could hear my screams if I were attacked, and that a revolver for a person like me was ridiculous. *They'd* knock it away in no time. I have

[1] D. was an English visitor who called once or twice during my visit to the Casetta.

come to the conclusion that he's not only a *real insane lunatic* but a *homicidal maniac*. I thought the first time he was here he was a trifle insane, but then you liked him so and I felt you would laugh at me for always 'suspecting' people and for my 'horrible mind'. But I know I'm right. His glance, without any barriers, cruel, cruel like a man raving with delight at the sight of a torture; his *flat-sounding* voice, somehow so repressed and held back; his physical great stiffness and the shape of his flat head—real criminal shape. See him in profile, his eyes glittering. He's a *terrible* object. He is attracted to me because he realises my sensitiveness. I'm weak for him to terrify. It relieves him to sit in that small room and suggest that navvies will break in and 'slit your throat' while L.M. is in San Remo. Well—well. . . .

The new maid is here. If to be a maid is to drop the stove-rings on to the tiled floor, she's an excellent one, and very cheap at 5 francs a day. Dearest, I cut out this ad. just because I wanted to tell you I really didn't recognise the paper without the imprint.[1] It loses *tremendously*, I think.

I send a long Tchehov letter. If you don't care to use it will you please have it typed for me (at my charge) and send the typed copy to Kot for our book. I hope to send off another review tomorrow.

Take care of your precious self. I long for news of you: my dearest own.

If only this black weather would lift. The wind *howls*. Please give Sydney my love but my Wingchik *kiss* for me. All goes well here. I hope to hear from you tomorrow. I *work* and *work* and *work* and stay in bed until the sun returns. Heaven bless you my precious.

Your

Wig

Wednesday,

Dearest Bogey, (January 7, 1920)

The post office and the waterspouts are open again. Here's the *Athen.* the *Lit. Sup.* 2 novels and letters which are not from you and ∴ I don't want as letters and here is the bedroom flooded, water spouting through the window-frames, great watery maps on the walls, the continent of Australia (very true) on the ceiling. This plus a wild gale and a boiling leaden sea. And the *cold*. Is it within the bond to tell you I had rather a

---

[1] A medallion of the head of Athenê.

bad heart-attack yesterday morning at 8 a.m. and languished all day unable even to read? But today I feel better and I've written to Sorapure. He's my one remaining confidant. . . .

Zut . . . alors! I hate talking of this to you.

Bogey, I am really thankful you are at the helm again. Pages 12–13— the bit of poetry about the boarding house and 'Poetry for Babes' beginning with a capital I'VE (pretty, that!) and in my review 'swish' for 'swim' (malice?) made me shudder this week.[1] Don't I pray you leave the paper again. Sullivan appears to compose his pages after a 9d. mixed *hors d'oeuvres*. . . .

The review of your poetry in *The Times* was very intriguing. What I felt was they had to judge you by extra-ordinary standards and they felt it. This pleased me. The quotations, too—my word! what a jewel the second was! It gave me a deep thrill of joy. I think the reviewer was really very complimentary (properly so, of course) to you. I felt that tho' he didn't understand you, *he* felt it was because you were beyond him.

I note Grant Richards picked out the Firbank. At the risk of your shouting me down—*please* don't praise Firbank. He's of the family of Aleister Crowley—an 'Otter' bird—a sniggering, long-nailed, pretentious and very dirty fellow. As to *honesty*—the fellow would swoon at sight of such a turnip. Huxley is very silly and young sometimes— and watery-headed.

I wish you were not so innocent in these matters. Please forgive my 'impudence'. I've no earthly right to say these things—but, dear me, I can't suppress myself *entirely*. If I agree to suppress the personal me, t'other must come out.

I send you today to the office the first instalment of some autobiographical notes on Tchehov. Do you care for them? There are more to follow and they are *very* interesting. If you don't, would you have them typed (at *my* charge) and sent to Kot. I also send 2 parcels of novels. If you will send me the money they fetch it will help me to pay Arina.

I hope to send off a review by today's afternoon post and another before the end of the week.

The *London Mercury* is beneath contempt, but it is evidently as fat as can be—bursting with fatness, curse it. 'The Moon' is the flattest orb

[1] 'In the moonlight, the naiads, tired of water springs, come down to the lake to swish and sing.'

451

that ever sailed the hevings. This doesn't mean I don't enjoy seeing it (the paper, I mean).

Oh, the acid has come today—sent 5. 11. 1919, as the parcel states. This is a record, I should think, even for this horrible country. I shall get up again as soon as I behold bright Phœbus in his strength. All's well, my darling. *Write to me as often as you can and love me.* For I love you. I am afraid to tell you how much I love you. Write to me even if it's only a note you jot down and post. Well, here's black January. I hope it is better with you.

Goodbye my precious love.

Ever your own
Wig

(about January 10, 1920)

My precious darling,

I have just received your Monday letter explaining about Wing. I had been so uneasy about him: now it's all right. I DO love you—this adorable generous letter calling all things OURS. You are a wonderful lover. I shall be terribly proud of you. I feel your book is going to have a great success. Did you see Goldy's letter in *The Nation*? It pleased me *terribly*. Print his poems—ask him to dinner—do anything: he admires my Bogey.

Now my precious please forgive what I am going to say. And do not think you came here all for nothing or anything dreadful like that. It's just my peculiar fate at present which won't leave me. I must tell you, but there is no action for you to take—nothing for you to worry about in the very slightest. I don't ask you to help or anything and God forbid I should make you work harder. Just go on as you are and I shall manage what I have to manage.

Bogey, I must leave here. The doctor has been today. He says I must go—there are no two opinions. I have been ill this week with my heart —and very nauseated by food and unable to sleep or rest with these fearful fits of crying. I have fought and fought against it but it is all no go. Today he came and I told him. He says I am suffering from acute nervous exhaustion and can't afford to stand any more. My *lung* is very improved but my heart is not and this causes the depression just as the depression, he thinks, has caused the heart. I've had too much to fight— so he says. I asked if it was within my power to conquer this and he

452

said: 'No—absolutely impossible.' In fact he was kind and did not seem to think me a coward—so *you* must not. I have known these last few days that I was at the end of my tether—but we won't discuss them. Well, I have written all about it to Jinnie at Menton. The doctor thinks this much the best plan. If she can't find me a place there I shall go to the nursing home at San Remo and send Lesley to Menton and look round. She (L.M.) does understand at last and has been kind.

It is not feasible to believe. She was away one day this week, and I was alone. It was evening. I had a heart-attack in my room and you see there was no one to call. I had to wait till it was over and then get upstairs for the brandy—and I fainted. Well, this, you see, isn't good enough. Yet he says when I do get away I shall get better quickly—just as I did when you were here. When you were here, my cough nearly stopped, I was always hungry, I slept all right. Now, don't think that means I regret you are not here now. It does not. All it means is that I must not be alone. I will wire you when I do go. It will be by motor of course. But don't worry dearest love. ALL IS WELL. This has of course thrown my work out utterly. But I've sent the one review this evening and another shall go with this letter tomorrow.

Your letters are meat and drink. I think everybody but you is not to be trusted with the paper. S. and A. would have it ruined in a week. The Shestov! . . . did you ever! But you are just a little marvel. Oh, our Wing too late for your train! Did you kiss him *enough* to make up? Kiss him again for me.

> Your true love
> Wig

The carol was lovely. I am so glad about the Hardy. Richard sent me a really wonderful letter—don't be cross with the dear old boy! Give him a hug from me and tell him I'll write as soon as *I possibly can*. But my pen is very *lourde* at the moment. My love to Sydney and to Violet. *Did Gertie get my present?* Please ask Violet. Don't forget about chestnuts boiled, put through the sieve and then made the consistency of mashed potatoes.

Monday,

My dearest Bogey,   (January 12, 1920)

I received your wire yesterday Sunday and am sending by the first post registered this day (Monday) a story called *The Man without a*

Temperament. The MS I send is positively my only copy. I cannot possibly repeat it. May I beg you to see that it is not lost? I have asked Rutter to send either (1) the story to you if he doesn't want to use it or (2) the proofs to you in case he does. But if he does send it to you, I would most earnestly intreat you to have it copied for me (at my expense) as it is one of the stories I am giving to Grant Richards and as I have not so much as a shaving or a paring of it wherewith I could reconstruct its like. I hope I do not exaggerate. If I do—forgive me. You know a parent's feelings—they are terrible at this moment. I feel my darling goes among lions. And I think there is not a word I would change or that can be changed so would you examine the proofs with the MS?

That my novel review did not arrive on the Tuesday proves that Friday posting is not early enough. You'll have no more of that worry, I promise you.

I have just sealed up my story. I am sorry to say I am nervous about its safety. If you could wire me the word *arrived* when you know it has arrived you would give me very great relief.

Goodbye darling for now

Wig

Take care of it for me: PLEASE, PLEASE.

My dearest Bogey,

Tuesday night,
(January 13, 1920)

Thank you for your letter today and for letting me see the two poems; I think they are exquisite and could not be improved on. I return you them.

I return also Nevinson's letter. It is an outrage; it made me feel quite sick and faint—the spirit of it seemed to get into the room . . . and to go on and go on. It is a really revolting letter.

I am enclosing a letter to Marie Dahlerup which I want you please to read before you send it to her. I am very much afraid that the contents will surprise and anger you. Will you please try to be patient with me while I explain? Bogey, I am so sorry—when I have anything to explain to you now I have a kind of premonitory shiver. I see you turn away so quick and sharp. . . . But you *really must* please be patient with me now.

454

I do not want Marie any more. Ever since you left here this time—since this last 'illness' of mine (what the doctor called acute nervous exhaustion acting on the heart) my feelings towards Lesley are absolutely changed. It is not only that the hatred is gone. Something positive is there which is very like love for her. She has convinced me at last, against all my opposition, that she is trying to do all in her power for me, and that she is devoted to the one idea which is (please forgive my egoism) to see me well again. This time she has fed me, helped me, got up in the middle of the night to make me hot milk and rub my feet, brought me flowers, *served* me as one could not be served if one were not loved. All silently and gently too, even after all my bitter ravings at her and railings against her. She has simply shown me that she understands and I feel that she does.

Am I right in feeling you would never have disliked her had it not been for me? How could you have? I look back and think how she tried to run the house for us. She failed—but how she TRIED! I think of her unceasing devotion to us, her patience with me, her trying to help you and to efface herself when we were together. Who else would have done it? Nobody on earth. I know she loves US as no one ever will. She thinks (STILL thinks) it would be the ideal life to be near us and to serve us. In Hampstead she was in a false position. She cannot be a servant—a nurse—a companion—all these things. But to overlook—to help—to keep an eye on OUR possessions (precious to her because she knows what we feel about them) there is no one like her. My hate is quite lifted—quite gone; it is like a curse removed. Lesley has been through the storm with us. I want her to share in the calm, to act Marie's part for us in our country house. Do you agree? I feel I cannot do without her now. Here is some one *tried, trusted,* who understands, who is really bound to me now, because of what she has done here for me. I think I would have died without Lesley these last terrible times. You know she has such an affection for you, too, deep down. 'Jack is JACK.' I know she is not perfect. I know she sometimes will annoy us. God—who won't? And who will leave us so utterly free and yet be *there* in *thought* when we want her. I confess that now I do lean on her. She looks after me; she has become (or I see her now in her true colours) the person who looks after all I cannot attend to. It was only when I refused to acknowledge this—to acknowledge her importance to me—that I hated her. Now that I do, I can be sincere and trust her and of course she, feeling the difference, is a different person. Her self-respect has all come back. She thinks *for* me and seems to know my ways as nobody who had not been with me for years, ever could.

This great change will, I am sure, astonish you and, I am afraid, anger you. I think my hatred must have been connected with my illness in some way. I cannot explain it—only tell you, and, though I am afraid, I must trust that you will believe me. Will you please tell me what you think? You must realize that now we are at peace I am never exasperated and she does not annoy me. I only feel 'free' for work and everything.

My dearest, I am still waiting to hear from Menton. It is still early to expect an answer. Foster comes again tomorrow. I got up for an hour or two today, but now I am in bed again. Did I tell you we have had an alarm here at night? Some men very late ringing and ringing the bell until finally Lesley shot out of the window. It was so queer—like a siege—very dreadful, really. Lesley did not take off her clothes all night.

Thank you for sending me the Tchehov. I will do my very best. It is awfully good of you to let me do it. Tell me about *yourself*, will you? My darling, remember how I love you. If you knew what your letters mean to me!

Be happy. Fare well. I am your devoted

Wig

My dearest,

Wednesday,
(January 14, 1920)

Just a hasty note enclosing the letter I have received from Jinnie. I have replied saying I will take the room at 30 francs a day and Ida is to go to the pension at 15. It seems to me to be really ideal. I have asked whether it will be possible to go next Wednesday. Of course, I must take a car. It costs £6 but I must do it; there is no other way. And once I get there to such a place I shall be able to do a great deal more work and earn the extra money. I can't really imagine a kinder letter than this and she must have acted *immediately* on receipt of mine. And she's been ill herself and isn't at all fit to do these things. Such behaviour on the part of human beings surprises me *too* much. I cannot reconcile it with what I know of Life; it is 'too good to be true'. I will send you a wire immediately I know the date of our leaving and I will make the most careful and complete arrangements possible as regards the forwarding of my letters and parcels. *Will you see I have more novels sent? Mary Hamilton's for instance?* You see I can work quite differently there and shall be so refreshed.

And please darling you will still send me papers and so on, won't you? I shall want them just the same. After I send my wire to you will you address my letters, books and papers to the new address on the card.

You see this is all arranged and managed and perfectly simple. I know I am doing the only thing, and I am sure I can make the extra money necessary.

I only hope my darling that you approve and do not still think it queer of me to find this solitary confinement insupportable. But the past is past; I look forward to the future with oh,—such joy!

Goodbye my precious. *Be happy.*

Your own devoted
Wig

Do you think you could just wire me if this plan satisfies you?

Wednesday,
L'Hermitage, Mentone,
(January 21, 1920)

. . . I have escaped. Do you know what that means? There has been a postal strike in Italy. No letters, no wires. Nothing comes through. A strike of the railways, and now from today a strike of automobiles. We just got through by taking a roundabout route and escaping the police. . . .

I have got away from that hell of isolation, from the awful singing at night, from the loneliness and fright. To tell you the truth, I think I have been *mad,* but really, medically mad. A great awful cloud has been on me. . . . It's nearly killed me. Yes. When J. took me in her arms today she cried as well as I. I felt as though I'd been through some awful deathly strain, and just survived—been rescued from drowning or something like that. You can't understand, it's not possible you should, what that isolation was when you left again and I again was ill. . . .

If I don't get well here, I'll never get well. Here—after the journey— was this room waiting for me—exquisite, large, with four windows, overlooking great gardens and mountains, wonderful flowers—tea with *toast* and honey and butter—a charming maid—and these two dear sweet women to welcome me with papers, books, etc. This is really a superb place in every way. Two doctors live here. . . . The cleanliness is almost supernatural. One feels like a butterfly. One only wants to fan one's wings, on the couch, the chairs. I have a big writing table with a cut-glass inkstand, a waste-paper basket, a great bowl of violets and *your* own anemones and wall-flowers in it. The directress is a very nice Frenchwoman only too anxious to look after me and see that there is no change in anything. . . . There is also a sort of Swiss nurse in white who has just been in and says she answers the bell at night. She is so good to look at that I shall have to ring.

I've got away from under that ghastly cloud. All is absolutely changed. I'm here with people, with care. I feel a different creature *really*—different eyes, different hair. The garden is gorgeous. There is a big shelter, chaufféd. What do you think of that?

8.30 a.m.,

(January 22, 1920)

. . . I have had such a gorgeous night in this huge room, with stars coming through the west and south windows and little airs. At eight arrived the breakfast. I really hope this place is showing off a little and this present behaviour is abnormal. If it isn't, pray see that our new house has folding doors, wide staircases. Nothing else will contain me. Oh, blankets and sheets of such rare quality—blankets that feel like lambs—sheets *glacés*. Electric lamp by the bedside under a small gold shade—great pot of hot water muffled in a real soft thick bath-towel. All these things are acting with such effect upon the infant mind of your girl, and a west view of mountains covered with little pines and a south view of distant sea and olive groves (as seen from 2 marble balconies) that she feels almost intoxicated.

Getting away yesterday was really pretty awful. Ma'am Littardi arrived asking 50 lire for the *hire* of the stove; the youth who has been sleeping arrived asking for 5 lire a night (8 nights) and the laundry arrived with a bill for 57 lire. . . . The taxi fare was £6, and he demanded 25 *francs* for having seen us through the police at Vintimille. I don't care. I'm still alive and I'm away. But the *comble* was that the day before yesterday when I was gone upstairs to fetch the revolver two beggars came and rang. The door was open. So I came down as quick as I could. But they'd gone and were at the foot of the steps—an old man and an old woman *with a bundle*. I saw them get into a small mule cart and drive away. At 11 p.m. that night I asked L.M. to fetch my overcoat as I wanted to sew on a button. It was gone—with the green scarf—the woolly. What do you think of that? Italy, my Italy!

Dearest,

I thought when I had sent my letter yesterday that you really don't know where we stand. The last letter I had from you was on a Wednesday and you contemplated spending the following weekend with the Waterlows to see The Lacket. Did you go? What happened? I know nothing after that until I received your letter about Wells yesterday. And what was the last you received from me, I wonder? It is all terribly confusing. Do you know how we stand? Oh, a hundred curses on the Italian post. It is too distracting. . . . Reviews of course— *Chinese Poetry, Sir Limpidus, Coggin*—all have been sent, and four parcels of books. These I imagine arrived before the strike. If they did, will you please let me have the money? I need every single penny I can get. You see in addition to my room I have *wine* and *medicine* and laundry and odd expenses and L.M. to not only keep but to give pocket money to and provide for. I don't care two figs. I feel perfectly reckless. Until Kay says the Bank will summons me I'll just *go on*. It's worth it. One day here makes me feel better, and only to have escaped that TRAP is such a triumph.

Connie came yesterday to see me, carrying a baby Pekinese. Have you ever seen a really *baby* one about the size of a fur glove, covered with pale gold down, with paws like minute seal flappers, very large impudent eyes and ears like fried potatoes? Good God! What creatures they are. This one is a perfect complement to Wing. We MUST have one. They are not in the least fussy or pampered or spoilt. They are like fairy animals. This one sat on my lap, cleaned both my hands really very carefully, polished the nails, then bit off carefully each finger and thumb, and then exhausted and blown with 8 fingers and two thumbs inside him, gave a great sigh and crossed his front paws and listened to the conversation. He lives on beef-steaks and loaf-sugar. His partner in life, when he is at home, is a pale blue satin bedroom slipper. Please let us have one at The Heron.

I had a long talk with Connie yesterday. She and Jinnie are really— no joking—superb women. It's a queer queer relationship. C. obviously adores J. and refers everything to her, but she is not in the least a parasite or overshadowed. She is a complete creature who yet *leans* on J. as a woman may do on a man. One feels her happiness to an extraordinary degree. That is what is so restful about these two women.

They are deeply *secure,* and they are well bred,—they are *English ladies*
—which means a great deal.

I went down yesterday for lunch and dinner. Dear love, I am here
on false pretences. I am the only healthy creature here. When I entered
the *salle à manger* I felt that all the heads were raised and all the noses
sniffed a frampold rampant lion entering. It's not that these people are
ill. They look exactly as though they were risen from the dead, stepped
out of coffins and eating again *pour la première fois.* Their hair is thin
and weak and poor; their eyes are cold and startled, their hands are still
waxen—and THIN! They are walking-sticks. All the little arts and allure-
ments they have shed and not yet picked up again. They are still sex-
less, and blow their noses in a neuter fashion—neither male nor female
blows. At the tables there are the signs and tokens of their illnesses—
bottles, boxes. *One* woman gave me a nasty knock. She had a réchaud
beside her—a lamp and a stand—and she re-heated everything, even
the plates. There, but for the grace of God, went Wig. The waitresses
of course thrive in this atmosphere. They are two pretty full-bosomed
girls, with spider-web stockings, shoes laced up their legs, little
delicate wispy aprons, powdered necks, red lips, scent—and they
move like ballet-dancers, sliding and gliding in the fullness of their
youth and strength over the polished floors. All this amuses me very
much.

Later. The masseuse has just been and ironed me from top to toe. I
am all tingling as though I had been a 10 mile walk, Boge [the word is
adorned with flourishes]. See how *very* silly I am getting. You just wait
until we meet again and you find a bran new girl.

But never never shall I cut myself off from Life again. I haven't any
illusions, darling. I know all about it and am not really a baby saying 'a-
gooh-a-gah!' but, in spite of everything, I know *il y a quelque chose . . .*
that I feed on, exult in, and adore. One must be, if one is a Wig, con-
tinually giving and receiving and shedding and renewing and examining
and trying to place. According to you, I suppose, my thinking is an
infant affair with bead frames and coloured blocks—well, it's not
important. What is important is that I adore you and I shall go up in
flame if I do not show you these cornflowers and jonquils. [There is a
little drawing of a pot of them.]

The day is cloudy, but it doesn't matter. Landscape is lovely in this
light; it's not like the sea. The mimosa—great puffs of mimosa and
great trees of red roses and oranges bright and flashing. Some boys are

460

being drilled outside. The sergeant-major keeps on saying: 'T'ois cinquante, n'est-ce pas?' and there is a most for*lorn* bugle.

Here is a story my little *femme de chambre* told me. Please read it.

'Do you know, Madame, *que les fleurs sont trop fortes* to be left dans la chambre pendant la nuit et surtout les joncs. If I put them sur le balcon —n'est-ce pas?—and bring them in early in the morning? Vous savez quand ma petite mère était très jeune, elle était la maîtresse d'une petite école pour les tout petits enfants. Et sur son jour de fête les bébés lui ont apporté un bouquet énorme, grand comme un chou, rond comme ça, Madame—de ces joncs. Elle les a mis dans sa chambre à coucher. C'était un vendredi. Le soir elle s'est endormie—et puis, tout le samedi, le dimanche, jusqu'au lundi matin, elle dort pro*fond*ement. Quand les petits élèves sont arrivés le lundi, la porte était fermée. Ils ont frappé. Pas de réponse. Enfin, mon père, qui n'était pas mon père à ce temps-là, alors est venu du village et il a forcé la porte—et voilà ma mère, qui n'était pas ma mère ni même mariée à ce temps-là;—toujours dans un sommeil *profond,* et l'air était chargé de la parfum de ces joncs qu'elle a mis sur une petite table près du lit. . . .'

Don't you like that story? Do you see the infants looking in with their fingers in their mouths, and the young man finding her blanche comme une bougie, and the room and the flowers? It's a bit sentimental, p'raps, but I love it. I see such funny little worms with satchels and socks and large tam o' shanters.

Post has been. Your Tuesday letter is arrived and here is only Friday. Isn't it a COMFORT to be out of that awful silence? But here you talk of farmhouses. Does that mean The Lacket is off? Oh, shall I ever catch up?

Why did not Sydney tell you—or why didn't you inquire at the post office about Italy? Sydney MUST have known at the F.O.

Yesterday though, I saw a copy of the *D.T.* which said the strike was over on the 20th. What a lie! It is really only beginning. San Remo you know was guarded by the military. I feel this place is so near, so *easy* to get at. It's like being out in the garden with you in the house. It really is. And it's so beautiful, darling—what I see of it, at least— superb. The one brick is the expense. I wrote to Rutter yesterday. If *he* pays me it will make a difference. Did you see the story. Did you like it? What did you think?

I must get up and open the windows.

Goodbye my precious. Give my love to the pussies and to Violet and keep it all down to the last crumb for yourself. Did Richard get a long letter from me? And a lovely inkpot posted in a diplomatic cardboard box? I shall be so thankful when you have heard from me. Perhaps you'll get a letter tomorrow or p'raps you'll be in Sussex. . . . Goodbye my own. Do write as long a letter as you can and tell me ALL.

Your own wife

Wig

Monday,

(January 26, 1920)

Darling Heart,

Letters are beginning to roll up from Italy. I am now up to date to the 18th. Only there is not a *word* about the Lacket. Did you see it? Or did you just give it up? The cheques have arrived; they are *more* than grateful. As you can perhaps imagine I am terribly hard up, and need every single sou. I meant to send Tchehov on Friday night, but in the afternoon I was stricken with a nervous headache—absolutely dished with it all that Friday—Saturday couldn't *move*—Sunday the same. I think it was the reaction after the strain; also I haven't slept since I left that cursed place. The brilliant doctors here prescribed me a forte dose of veronal (qui est si bon!) I refused to take it. They are mad. But today I can lift my head and walk. Feel a bit faible but that is all. I feel certain that the earliest of my reviews must have reached you for this week—the others will roll along and I'll send this week Tchehov. But that finishes my books. Don't novels ever turn up? Susie? OR Mary Hamilton? Or anybody? I can't *make* them up. When you said we must have novels in the paper—was that really quite reasonable? Who in God almighty's name doesn't agree? Could *I* stop the strike?

Oh, you do make me want to *stamp* so hard sometimes. Wing ought to beat you with his tail. The weather here is simply gorgeous today— the room flooded with sun. L.M. is going to try to get a job here, to help with her keep. You see she costs at least 20 *francs* a day. Then they order me wine and frictions and goûter which I *must* have. Oh—that reminds me. The *Lit. Sup.* has come. What a very nice advertisement![1] But look here, have you time to send a book of mine to Grant Richards? *Do,* darling! Look here, you old boy, I must have it sent—a book of short stories. I'll send a list of 'em, and if you approve, do for God's sake let him have it at once. I don't know what terms he will make, but let me see a copy of your letter to him. I'd sell outright for £20, of

---

[1] Of *Je ne parle pas.*

course, but I want money *now*. Later on. I can make it. But can you do this?[1]

I've just written four pages and torn them up. A wave of bitterness came over me. I *must* never let it be known.

C. and J. are coming today with their precious dog. I regret to say I burn to let them know you are an Old Boiled Egg,[2] and have already told Pa same—and intend writing Chaddie and sending V. a card. What a woman—aren't I? I must stop writing. For some horrible reason a Casetta mood is on me. It will pass in two T's. Tell me if you see that story, will you?

Always your own
Wig

For Grant Richards.

> Je ne Parle pas Français
> Bliss
> Psychology
> A Man of No Temperament
> Sun and Moon
> 'Pictures'
> Mr. Reginald Peacock's Day
> The Black Cap

I can't remember the others. There were 10 at any rate, and now my new story will be 11. I'd like them called *Short Stories*. Will you discuss this with me?

PLEASE READ THIS ALL THROUGH   Saturday,

My dear Bogey,   (January 31, 1920)

I wrote to you on Thursday last when I had heard from you of the arrival of my letters from here, but I did not post the letter. I held it over, hoping with each courier that the need to send it would be over. But now (Saturday) I can wait no longer.

I have received your letters about the house-hunting, and your Italian letters are coming in, in any order. I fully appreciate the fact that you are working extremely hard and that all your superfluous energy

---

[1] Naturally I was adamant against Katherine's plan of selling her volume of stories outright for £20, and immediately got into touch with Mr. Michael Sadleir of Constables.
[2] O.B.E.

is directed towards finding a house. At the same time, my dear Bogey, you have hurt me *dreadfully*. If you reflect for one moment, you will perhaps realize how your 'How's money?' struck me. Did I not tell you the expenses I had coming here—the bills to settle, the hire of the motor, the theft of my overcoat, the more expensive room, the extras such as *goûters* and *frictions,* and Lesley to board and keep. Yes, I have told you all these things. Now let me tell you what I 'imagined' you would do on receipt of my first letter from Menton. I imagined you would immediately wire me £10. I 'imagined' you would have written: 'It's gorgeous to know you are there and getting better. Don't worry. Of course, I shall contribute £10 a month towards your expenses.' In addition, I *counted* on your loving sympathy and under-standing, and the fact that you failed me in this is the hardest of all to bear. I don't think you read my letters. I *cannot* think you simply dis-missed them like that. This week I have been simply waiting for the letter that has not come and can't come now. It's made it impossible to work. Now I must just re-adjust things and go on and I shall try and send you more for your paper.

I have changed my room here for a smaller one, but on Wednesday last, for instance, my lungs were radiographed. It cost me 200 francs and the cocher charged me 15 francs pour aller et retour. This morning the doctor lectured me about working (I put it down to 'mon travail') and ordered me an hour's drive by the sea every day pour calmer les nerfs. *I* can't afford it.

Therefore I ask you to contribute £10 a month towards my expenses here. If you cannot do so, please *wire me at once,* for I must make immediate other arrangements. *I cannot wait a day longer.*

It is so bitter to have to ask you this—terribly bitter. Nevertheless, I am determined to get well. I will *not* be overcome by anything—not even by the letter you sent me in Italy telling me to remember AS I grew more lonely so you were loving me more. If you had read that in a book what would you have thought? Well, I thank God I read it here and not at the Casetta.

I've nothing to say to you, Bogey. I am too hurt. I shall not write again.

    Your
       Wife

You will not put me off with just a sentence or two? Consider, Bogey, what you do!

My dear Bogey,

I have just received your Thursday and Friday evening letters. Thank you from my heart for doing that for Gertie.[1] It was a beautiful little act on your part and I am so proud that you should have done it.

About the Grant Richards book (did I tell you he was coming South this month?) I think *The Black Cap* had better not be included. But I will send you another story—*A Second Helping* it is called—to go in its place. I shall try and get it typed here. My copy of *Je ne parle pas*—or your copy, isn't it?—arrived yesterday. It *looks* lovely but I am not at all satisfied with the story.

About the house. Dear Bogey, why do you TORMENT yourself, as you say? Or is that only your way of saying it? I am sure it is the wrong attitude and it will only tire and exhaust you so that you will be 'sick of the whole subject' very soon.

It's no good my writing every day. I can't; I simply don't feel you read the letters. I try and do my own work instead. There's a much better chance that you'll read that some day—though why you should I don't know.

Yes, this is a very suitable place to be in. It is safe and very healthy.

Goodbye dearest,

    Wig

Is there really a tearing hurry about the house? I fully appreciate the fact that you do not want to stay at Portland Villas. At the same time it would not matter if we were there until the middle of the summer. And when I come home L.M. can help with the househunting. I mean she could always go for a preliminary inspection in the middle of the week and so save you useless journeys. This is well worth considering. She knows just what we want.

By the way, about that story Rutter has[2]—I am awfully sorry to bother you, but I must see the proofs MYSELF before it is printed. If it's typed, 10 to 1 there will be mistakes, and at any rate I can't expect anyone to go through it as I must go through. Every word matters. This is *not* conceit—but it must be so. Will you promise to send the proofs to me if he prints the story? I'll send them back express the same day. If

[1] I had only sent her to our doctor at our expense.
[2] *The Man Without a Temperament.*

you did not live at such racing speed I would beg you to go through the typed copy with the MS and see that the *spaces* were correct—that where I intend a space, there is a space. It's sure to be wrong. But I CAN'T afford mistakes. Another word won't do. I chose every single word.

Will you please answer this when you write?

This is written before your II card and telegram. I have opened this and replied on pages III and IV

Wednesday,

Dear Bogey, (? February 4, 1920)

A slip was enclosed in a letter card but I have received no letter which explains itself. However I will tell you the situation between myself and G.R.

I wrote asking him if he would consider an MS.

He replied Delighted.

I replied saying I would send him one.

He replied the sooner the better.

Money has not been mentioned, but I think most certainly he ought to have the first look. If he wants it I must ask for an advance, and if he refuses the advance the affair is off. Please send me the note you refer to, will you?

As regards the advance money, I would rather wait and receive it for my book than that you should lend it me. I MUST have it for my overcoat, fare home etc., and I certainly do not want to borrow it from you. Perhaps I did not make clear that I ASKED you for the £10 a month—I mean, not as a loan. I am afraid from this note you may advance it for me and then take the book money. But I am afraid that will not do.

Will you please tell me *why* money is tight? I cannot understand. If it is necessary to say [these] things why do you buy a mirror? I feel, as I felt when you referred before to your heavy debts, that you are keeping something from me all the time. You have expenses, you *must* have, that I don't know of. Oh, if only you would be frank about this: it would make things so different. Can't you confide in me? Are you helping somebody? I know you are saving up for the house but you . . . don't put the house FIRST, do you, Bogey? Yet you find it necessary to again write *money is tight*. I don't want—God forbid!—to know your private affairs, but if you can tell me a little it would be a great relief.

Wig

Bogey dear,

Your telegram came this afternoon and your second card enclosing the cheque but STILL not enclosing the letter came this evening. First, about the £20. You will doubtless adhere to your intention in the letter card that it shall be an advance on my book—but you will see why I do not want that. If you can agree to allowing me £10 a month for my expenses while I am here, I shall look upon this cheque as the first 2 months instalment. I would perfectly understand your *money is tight* had I NOT consumption, a weak heart and chronic neuritis in my lower limbs.

About the overcoat, you will doubtless explain how you want it paid for. So I can't write about these things, neither will I touch the cheque till I hear from you.

My darling, I can't write every day. I love you but something has gone dead in me—rather—no, I can't explain it. Explanations are so futile—you never listen to them, you know. I shrink from trying any more. Give me *time,* will you? I'll get over this. I get over everything, but it takes time. But darling, darling, that doesn't make me love you less. I LOVE you—that's the whole infernal trouble!

Bogey, I cannot have the *German Pension* republished under any circumstances. It is far too *immature* and I don't even acknowledge it today. I mean I don't 'hold' by it. I can't go foisting that kind of stuff on the public—*it's not good enough.* But if you'll send me the note that refers to it I will reply and offer a new book by May 1st. But I could not for a moment entertain republishing the *Pension.* It's positively juvenile, and besides that it's not what I mean: it's a lie. Oh no, never! But please give me the chance of replying to whoever wants to do so and offering another book.

Wig

Thursday in bed,

Forgive me for saying this. (February 5, 1920)

Will you remember when you write that I don't go out or walk or see anybody to talk to—that you are my ALL. I lie in a chair all day. I am not strong enough yet to walk at all—and so when you say things like—that about insuring your life and breaking your neck, you have me at your complete mercy. Can you understand?[1] Try to imagine it!!

[1] I *had* insured my life and I had, unfortunately, made a feeble joke about it.

467

It is terrific torture—terrific. Don't you care about ME at all? If I must bear it, I *must*, but I'm nearly at the end of my tether when you say such things.

Bogey darling,
   I have just received your Monday letter written on the back of the Constable note[1] and hasten to reply. In the first place, *your throat*—how is it? I cannot know. I must just wait then. And that remark flung at me about insuring your life—I beg of you not to say these things. They are just like the most terrible frightful earthquake—much worse. My day breaks up into terrified pieces. You know that—you know it *quite well*. Oh, how CAN you? I don't understand. But one must be very careful and say nothing one would regret. I have no right to reproach you and I don't want to appeal to your pity—but, my Bogey, you make it very hard when you say such things—that's all. (Everything I thought at the Casetta got 'a long way from reality'.)

   Now about Constable. If they will give £40 in advance and Richards won't, it must be Constable, of course. I have explained my relations with Richards. A book including *Prelude, Je ne parle pas* and so on would be interesting. But I must make very sure of what they collect from *Rhythm*. The story *The Wind Blows* from *The Signature* is in the collection. It's the only one worth re-printing. The book had certainly better include *Prelude*: it makes a longer book. I am afraid this is adding to your great press of work. Sadler says even if an arrangement is come to nothing can be published for several months. In that case the final decision as to *which* stories could perhaps be left for my return in the first week of May.

   But this is all rubbish beside your sore throat and your remark about breaking your neck househunting. I must wire you and somehow *stamp down* my anxiety until I have your reply.
                                                            Yours
                                                            Wig

[1] From Michael Sadleir offering to take the book on fair terms.

In reply to your Tuesday letter   (? February 7, 1920)
My dear Bogey,

I have your Tuesday evening letter. That you took my letter as being primarily concerned with money is horrible. However, I'll answer that first. I send you back the cheque for £20. As you have paid £20 into my bank, I shall use that at the rate of £10 a month and by the time it is finished, that is at the end of March, I hope that my book will be paid for and I shan't have to ask you for any more money. You ask me if we haven't known each other long enough for me to wire for £20. But, Bogey, haven't we known each other long enough for you to have said to me: '*I realize* you must need money. But I'm cleaned out this month. I'll send some next'? If only you'd thought for me, or imagined for me: it was *that* that hurt.

You say I ought to have guessed you misunderstood. Curse money! It's not really a question of money. It was the question of sympathy, of understanding, of being in the least *interested,* of asking me JUST ONCE how I was—what I thought about and felt—what I did—if I was 'all right'? I can't get over the fact that it never occurred to you and it makes me feel you don't want my love—not my living love—you only want an 'idea'. When that strike was on—fool that I was!—my first thoughts always were: 'What I feel doesn't matter so much. Jack must be in such agony. When he doesn't hear he'll try to wire and the P.O. will tell him no wires are delivered and he knows I'm ill.' But your letter came 'drunk with the magnificence of the Downs'—'a day's sheer joy'—'the note of hysteria would go out of my work'—'very fit'. And when you *did* hear—good—your anxiety was over and you never referred to me again. So I *must* face the fact that you have put *me* away for the time—you are withdrawn—self-contained—and you don't want in the deepest widest sense of the word to be disturbed. As long as I'm on a suitable shelf—and ∴ YOU'RE not worried—ça va! Of course, I still love you. I love you as much as ever. But to know this is torture until I get it in hand.

'A love that might break through *if she would let it* the ghastly terror of her loneliness.' Does not that show it up? Who could write such unspeakably cruel words if he loved at the moment? You suggest that my suffering was self-imposed, in so far as it was really a failure to love enough. If I had loved you enough I need not have suffered as I did. Bogey, you must believe me, that is a DEADLY false view. A living,

469

loving, warm being could not believe that or say it. It's a vile intellectual idea and it simply appals me. I can't wire the word 'Love' because of it. (Of course I can, of course I will. You do *love* me; it's only you don't love me just now.) To make out my agony was my failure to love—that is really too much.

I want to mention something else. Lawrence sent me a letter today. He spat in my face and threw filth at me and said: 'I loathe you. You revolt me stewing in your consumption. . . . The Italians were quite right to have nothing to do with you' and a great deal more. Now I do beseech you, if you are my man, to stop defending him after that and never to crack him up in the paper. *Be proud!* In the same letter he said his final opinion of you was that you were 'a dirty little worm'. Well, *be proud*. Don't forgive him for that please.

Goodbye, I am bitterly disappointed with the answer to my letter but I *must* bear it. You say you are not ashamed. I don't want you to be ashamed. And then you say you sent the £20 the moment you had it. 'February 1 came too late.' Damn the £20. I suppose from that you look upon yourself as a man who is being bled: *you* did all in your power, but FATE and your wife would not wait. It's UTTERLY false. I wanted love and sympathy and understanding. Were you cleaned out of those until February 1st? It's a nightmare that you won't understand.

Your own
Wig

Of course you love me, of course you do. It's only since I've been away you have withdrawn yourself from me and ever since I broke down at the Casetta and appealed to you things have never been the same. It's only that you don't love me NOW. Oh, darling, do do break through. DO care. It's so hard. Wait till I'm strong before you run away for a bit. It's so awful. Bogey, you must love me. Fancy writing so coolly to me and asking me to wire if I think you do. Would I be *here* if I thought you didn't—somewhere—deep down love me?

Dear Darling, (February 8, 1920)
I received a letter from you yesterday saying (1) you had bought me an overcoat. I wish you hadn't. It is obvious that you *raced* to buy it and that you bought it with your little brains and nerves. You are the man

in the Daudet story you know—The Man with the Golden Brain. But there. When it comes I'll see. I'll cherish it. (2) You have paid £10 into my Bank. Now I'm going to ask you if you can put in another £10 in March. After that I shall need no more of your money. (3) You've sold my book. With the £40 I shall spend £10 for living expenses in the mois d'Avril and the £30 for fares and travelling home. Do you mind asking them to send the cheque to me? Pure childishness—but I want to see it with my own eyes and send it with my own hand to Kay. I feel the Bank will *close*. It is fearfully good of you to have done this for me, and I feel it has been *no* end of a nuisance.

Re the matter of the book—I suppose I have final say. I couldn't have *The Woman at the Store* reprinted *par exemple*. Anne's drawings don't matter. I do want the story called *Second Helping* that I'm at now to be included. Enough. Richards is coming here you know to see me. That will be orkid.

Another change in the near future. I have not mentioned it, but this place is *intolerably* noisy. I am so sensitive to noise, oh, so sensitive. It *hurts* me, really. They bang my door, other doors, shout, shriek, crash. I can't endure it and really can't work *or* sleep. The doctor suggested *une forte dose de véronal*. Merci. But really it's *bad*. I just mentioned this to Jinnie. She came one day when I was feeling it a bit badly. Today she arrived with a carriage and fur rugs and silk cushions. Took me to their villa. It is really superb, *exquisite* outside and in. They had a *chaise longue* in the garden—a tiny tray with black coffee out of a silver pot, Grand Marnier, cigarettes, little bunch of violets, all ready. Then we went in to tea. Their villa is really—Boge—it's a dream. I mean even the furnishing is *perfect*—Spanish silk bed coverlets, Italian china, the tea appointments perfect, stillness, maids in tiny muslin aprons flitting over *carpets* . . . and so on. Then they showed me into a room, grey and silver, facing south, with a balcony—the only touch of colour a little rose brocade couch with gilt legs—and J. said, 'Now, my dear, we want you to come here, and live here. It's *dead* quiet. You can be alone all day if you like. There is the garden. We are here. First, I must arrange that you see Dr. Rendall for him to sign that you are no longer infectious. If he does this, we want you here until May. You're going to get well. You can't afford to fight or see ugly people or have ugly trays.' And then she laughed and said, 'The Lord has delivered you into our hands, and please God we'll cure you.' What do you think of that? They want me to stay there till May and then travel home together

471

Bogey, this is really very important; it's one of the most important things that ever happened to me. These women are *right*; they are what we mean to be in our life. They are wise and at rest and deeply happy—and they are very exquisite. It all depends on Rendall. Subject to Rendall's signing I shall go, but I don't know when. Not for a week at least: I will let you know. And I shall pay what I pay here—but of course no extras. I go as a patient—and Jinnie couldn't afford to leave the room empty. Also it's right I should do that. But no money on earth can ever repay what I shall get there. You see, I'll have that *Life* to share too—the meals and the room with great wood fires and the darling baby peke and the garden and the gardener—the orange trees, the lemons, their maid to look after my clothes—you know what I mean? And my WORK always arranged for and thought of. A table in the garden and a bath chair with rug and cushions that I can lie in and write.

Why should they do that? *Why* should Jinnie say, 'Then I'll be at rest about you, darling. I shall know you're safe'? It's as though my *Mother* were here again. I miss her so. I often long to lean against Mother and know she understands things . . . that can't be told . . . that would fade at a breath . . . *delicate needs* . . . a feeling of great fineness and gentleness. But what Mother hadn't is an understanding of WORK.

The Villa is in style like Garsington. I mean that is the tone. It is very large—a huge hall lighted from above—a great double salon. It has delicate balconies and a tower. I want you to see it. I can't make you see it. I want you to see the garden and the potting-shed where I can walk and look at the little plants. Huge springing palms—great branches of orange against the sky. [A drawing of one.] No, I can't draw them. As soon as I've seen Rendall I shall know when I go.

Have you read so far? That's all, dearest, but that explains why I can't work here as I thought I could: the infernal noise, especially in the morning. You remember when I managed to ask you not to go on scraping your porridge saucer? It was so hard to say and I tried to say it nicely, but I see now how you pushed the plate away and rumpled your hair and wouldn't eat or look at me—just *went blind*. It wasn't fair, you know, Bogey, really it wasn't. You know how hard it was for me to say. Why did you take offence? You know I think and think of those things sometimes and I *can't* account for them! It's hereditary, but I wish you didn't—*pay me out* for having to say: 'I say, old boy, I'm

472

so sorry—but my nerves are so awful in the morning—DO you mind—I hate having to say it?' And, oh, he shows her how he does mind! Do you 'understand that in a novel'? I suppose you do: I wish I did. No, darling, at times you are very dark to me.

Your devoted
Wife

Urgent   Monday,
My Bogey,   (February 9, 1920)

I cannot stand it any longer. You must tell me the truth. Here is your Thursday letter: 'Well, Wig, don't give me up entirely.' If you really contemplate the possibility of it then you no longer love me or believe in our marriage. You are simply killing me again and again with every letter. Your last ASKING me to wire IF I loved you! Now tell me at once, by wire, whether all is over or not. God, to have been driven by you to write such words.

You cruel cruel—oh I am crying.

Of course when I said I would not write again I only meant until I had your answer.

No you are *too* cruel. To throw away SUCH love—throw it away. Oh how you must have lied to me! I thought we could not live without each other. But now put me out of my pain. I *can't* bear it. I am in utter despair. I must know.

Your Wife

This your Thursday letter makes mine about the Villa Flora just a silly dream. Again I *am* not. I just steel myself somehow not to weep before people—that's all.

Love,   (February 10, 1920)

Note this coincidence. I wrote to Lawrence: 'I detest you for having dragged this disgusting reptile across all that has been.' When I got his letter I *saw* a reptile, *felt* a reptile—and the desire to hit him was so dreadful that I knew if ever I met him I must go away *at once*. I could not be in the same room or house, he is somehow filthy. I never had such a feeling about a human being. Oh, when I read your reply do you know I *kissed* it. I was lying on my face—dressed in nothing but a lace cap. Mlle Burger had gone off in the middle of doing my back and I was alone for a minute. *As* I read it, *as* I kissed it, I had the queer, the *queer* feeling as though somehow one was caught in some wave of

473

tradition that passes round and round the earth—as though hundreds
and hundreds of years ago, a woman lying like I was, being massaged
by some one, had been handed a letter from her lover who swore to
smite his enemy and she kissed it and laid it against her cheek. That's
NOT nonsense. But you must hit him when you see him. There's
nothing else to do.

My Life,

This letter of yours—it's Friday evening's letter—is almost like one
of the old ones. I had a *nuit blanche*—fever—I couldn't help it. Yesterday
nearly finished me and it was so strange. I was thinking at night as I
smoked to stop crying, I love you *more*. Even though you denied me
and everything and refused to understand what I was getting at—even
though that which *could* not happen, happened—you questioned
OUR love, broke the chain that couldn't be broken—still I love you
more. You know I never dreamed of doubting your love—must I
dream of it? I simply felt you'd gone away—had enough for the time
being—and *that* was unendurable. The other—your idea—oh, you
don't love as I do—you can't have the capacity. God! at the breath of
such a possibility I am in anguish. But we are evidently very very
different. I haven't 'illusions', really not, though you think I have, but
I love. And loving I simply cannot face desolation—the desert *persists*
in blossoming—the flower *persists* in turning to the light. When you
said at the Casetta you not only believed differently but you did not
want to change—you remember—when we talked, or rather when I
said you seemed somehow to deny fertility—the living unborn child—
when you said that so deliberately, I felt there was an essential difference.
And STILL I don't believe it. I STILL think it is not you.

You see the war—the tragedy of the war was that ever since I knew
you you had been trembling towards it. (This is a secret.) The war was
no surprise to you: it was a supreme justification of all you had trembled
towards (like a compass) all your life. That's what nobody else can ever
know. It wasn't the war that broke a bright, radiant, ardent, loving,
rich spirit as all your friends and admirers think. You *never* wrote in
pictures or other than in that austere fashion, and you were talking to
Gordon about weariness of the spirit, ultimate obscenity, vultures, 'our
wounds' years and years before. But I always felt that behind all that
talk—'I am very tired' *à quoi bonisme*—there hid what I can't help
calling a bright burning angel—loving, turned to the light. Oh, my

474

child! but like some daisy—innocent as others are not—*wise* as others are not—dreaming, fulfilled, serene, a poet, the father of my children. Oh, my pride to think that!

But the war came, your dark self pulled over, and finally at the Casetta you said you did not even *want* the angel to triumph—and I knew we would never have children—we'd never be Adam and Eve lying under a tree looking up through the branches with our own little flowery branch lying between us.

My own, you are always so terrified that I want to intrude—to have you other than you are. You are always thinking there is a need of escaping from my IDEA of you. You are wrong. I adore you as you are—your deepest self, but yes, it is the 'angel' I adore and believe in for ever.

> Wig

[At top of letter a drawing]
Anemones on my table.

I'll send you a wire about the overcoat, my darling, the moment it walks into this room. I am longing for it; my cape is no good for warmth. Jinnie muffles me up in rugs when she takes me out, but then I have to be a mummy, just a head showing out, and one does or *I* do like to wave MY arms and legs sometimes [a drawing of her doing so], unlike a boy I used to know.

> Wednesday—no—Yes,

My Precious,   (February 11, 1920)

Your Saturday evening letter has come with the 'explanation'. Don't say another word about it. Let's after this put it quite away. Yes, I felt in Ospedaletti that you refused to understand and I have felt since I have been abroad this time that you have turned away from me—withdrawn yourself utterly from me. I have felt like a person in an open boat, tossing about in frightful waves calling and crying to be saved and you have seen me from your ship and refused to see me or to rescue me because you were not made of whipcord and steel. Yes, Boge, it has been a suffering such as I don't feel you ever could know. But it's over and it has taught me a lesson and I don't regret it. I could turn to it now and kiss it. I can't enter into what it has taught me, but the difference is there. It had to be. If I'm *dead* sincere, I must say that I believe in the mystery: *out of evil good shall come.* But now, put it all away, my own. And you really must give up the word *desperate* with regard to our relations. Don't let it exist. Don't make an effort to love me—my silly darling—or to fly after enamel spoons.[1] Just remember: *That From Now I am not ill.* Because that is the truth. So lean on me, give me your things to hold, confide in me, worry me, treat me as your wife. Just *rest* on the thought of me. You are absurd when you say you are no good as a lover. That is just nonsense, and it's not fair to me. I don't want a slave and an admirer, my love. You would be a perfectly rotten slave and admirer. As a lover, you are—well, simply you—just all my life and my joy and my *pride*. Call me your 'worm'—that is enough for me. But let's get over all this. What has been, has been. But, remember, *no desperate* efforts are allowed. Not being an intellectual, I always seem to have to learn things at the risk of my life—but I do learn. Let's be wise, true, real lovers from now on. Let's enter the Heron from today— from this very minute, and I shall rejoice in you and if it's not too great an effort, dear love, try and rejoice in me.

I go to the Villa Flora on Sunday. All is arranged.

Heard from Mary Cannan this morning: she is at Capri and had heard from L. that I was a 'very sick woman' and you a 'great swell'. I thereupon wrote her an intimate letter and just put her right about us and just told her what you really were like and what your loyalty to L. had been and so on. I just felt I must do this. Heard from Grant Richards who's at Cap Martin—$\frac{1}{2}$ an hour away—*very snuffy,* but still wants to see me. He suggests bringing over a car and motoring me there. Well, I'd better see him. No, he doesn't suggest a car—just that I shall go—so I don't know.

It's lunch time. I'm in bed, I must fly up. My nib will not write. It must write that I love you and you only world without end amen.

Yours

Wigchik

Tell Wing to keep both eyes on you and when you disappear again he and Athy must just hunt you out and beat you—but not hard.

Are the snowdrops out?

The cuckoo has been heard at Hurstmonceux, Sussex.

Chaddie has a wide 'border of yellow crocuses'. It sounds like an Alice Prosser,[2] doesn't it?

[1] A reference to a story by Anatole France.

[2] I seem to remember that Charles and Alice Prosser were characters of Katherine's New Zealand days—a somewhat excessively refined clergyman and his wife who had come out from England.

C. and J. have given me the most exquisite fine woollen stuff for a dress and a dressmaker to go with it.

Your Mother wrote me such a nice letter today and I replied.

(1) Tell Richard about my change of Address after Saturday. Please *be sure to do this* and give the old boy a loving hug from me.

(2) Mark the linen.

(3) Whistle on the stairs.

(4) Walk out of the steps and down the front on your hands please to show all's well.

(5) Ask Violet when she's going to be married and tell her it's worth it. But do none of these things desperately.

Thursday,

Monday evening letters (1) and (2) received   (February 12, 1920)

(1) Very well, Isabel about the *Pension*. But I must write an introduction saying it is early, early work, or just that it was written between certain years, because you know, Betsy love, it's nothing to be proud of. If you didn't advise me, I'd drop it overboard. But of course I'll do the other thing and certainly it airs one's name. But why isn't it better? It makes me simply hang my head. I'll have to forge ahead and get another decent one written, that's all.

(2) I'll repay you for the overcoat when Constable pay me. Thank you enormously for the figgers. They frighten me. You never mentioned your new suit. I don't know what colour it is or shape or anything—or whether there is any fringe on the trousers. I always rejoice when you buy clothes. When I am rich, you will have such lovely clothes—all real lace and silk velvet. You will have crimson satin sleeves, slashed with Indian green silk and embroidered gloves with sachets sewn in them. Just wait.

(3) I had your wire last night about my story. Oh dear, I hope you do find a moment just to say a little more against OR for. I burned for you to like it.

(4) You are a perfect darling to have bothered to say all this about the money. No, there's not much to play with indeed. We're both rather short of pocket money. If God would only give us a sheer 1d. a week dropped from Heaven every Saturday morning—just for us to go off and *spend*.

I've told the people here I'm leaving. It was *awful*. How I hate having to do this, especially as they have been so immoderately kind. They make such a dreadful fuss of me—everybody, down to the servants. Even the masseuse says: 'It was so wonderful just to come into the room, and then we all say we know Mrs. Murry's room by the good smell outside the door—cigarettes and flowers.' As to Armand, —oh, its been *dreadful*. These people are so queer. Just because the room is arranged as we arrange a room, and gay, and I wear my little coats and caps in bed, it seems to them amazing. It's not in the least.

Jinnie drives me round to the Villa Flora on Sunday. It will be a very famous day. Darling, there's an American woman living with them— she's a bit of a millionairess and I *can't* stop her presents. If only I could post them on. I don't *want* them. Four boxes of marquise chocolate at one time—bouquets of violets and lilies—cigarettes by the hundred. I think it's the first time I have come across unlimited money. She is terribly unhappy and I know she feels I can help her. I can. She's tremendous food for me—-I mean literary. But I wish I could send you the gifts. I'll try and post the marquise chocolat today, at any rate some of it. I don't care for such things.

It's such a delicate day—little birds are flying through it. I—love— you. I am very very well. Tell me about that house. Have you any idears? I must jump up. The overcoat isn't here yet. But I'll send what I think the Constable book ought to contain and will you discuss it with me?

     Yours for ever
       Wig

                             Friday,

My own,   (February 13, 1920)

Your 2 Tuesday letters are here but they are too late—aren't they? I mean—happily too late. We[1] do understand everything and all is over —but really beautifully over—isn't it? I'm out of the open boat and you have stopped sailing away and away....

Precious love, you know the Italian china? The 2nd kind we liked even better than the first? Its shop is here—*packed*: plates, cups, letter racks, china trays. I am going to buy a whole pile of it with my *Art and Letters* money, if you agree. Do you? And have it packed in a crate. It's such a *perfectly thrilling shop,* one of our own shops, you know.

[1] The 'W' has a blot and beautiful antennae and a line leading to "Please show it to Wingchik".

It's cold, deadly cold today. I am writing my review of *Peter Jackson* and *The Dark River*. But I feel a rag: I've got fever. Temperature 100. I shan't stir a step. It's the chauffage qui ne marche pas. But it won't matter after Sunday. Jinnie came yesterday to see me: it was her birthday: she is 64. I thought she was about 47. We are the same age when we're together—that's what's so queer. But she is a saint—a real saint—a *holy woman.* It's a great privilege to have known her.

Boge, I see Gaby Deslys is dead of pleurisy. I am so sorry. She had just given up the stage because of her lungs. She couldn't sing any more, and she was going to be married to *the man,* and now, poor little soul, she and all her hats are dead. God rest her soul!

Grant Richards is coming to the Villa Flora on Tuesday with a closed car, taking me to Cap Martin and driving me home—guaranteed *no steps.* But he says: May I hope to persuade you to let me have the first refusal of your next novel? Well, I suppose there is no harm done: I'll ask for £60 in advance, and then he'll be sorry.

Woman next door to me—inferior Belgian in bed—with fever—being SICK all day and then sighing in between and making SUCH noises—2nd class ladies' cabin noise entre Harwich and Antwerp. It's very fierce not to have this place properly heated, though.

Addio, my own darling precious ONE.

Your Wig

Pray read this from the fayr Alice: it's *comic* somehow! I bet I ask her to spend the day with us at the country and bring little Hugh. I FEEL myself asking her.

Villa Flora, Mentone,
(February, 1920)

[A drawing of Villa Flora (I think) at the top of the letter] No, it's not like that.

Love,

Will you put this letter from R. and the drawing in the file? Both are so characteristic of him and so delightful they ought to be kept. And would you please post this letter to Anne? *No* post for me today—not a letter or a paper: I am so disappointed. I had none yesterday either. I am sure they have not gone to the Hermitage; they must be *en route.* And my overcoat, Bogey, was it registered? When can I expect it? Can you know? I am worried about it; it's not that I want it so much just at this moment (though I do) but I am so afraid it may have gone astray, and yet that is surely very unlikely with a parcel in the *sac diplomatique*. But was it insured?

It's a vile day—a real mistral. One is protected from it here, though. But Rendall says I can go for walks and that makes one impatient. I want to go for gallops to the china shop. Bogey, if ever you have neuralgia or rheumatism or any pains of that kind take *Irénine*. It is in the form of cachets and it's absolutely *in*-fallible. Don't forget, darling. Any French chemist would sell it to you, I expect.

This isn't a letter today. J'attends.

Your own
Wigchik

Sunday,
(February 22, 1920)

My very own Bogey,

It is raining here, but such lovely rain! The drops hang on the rose bushes and on every tip of the palm fronds. Little birds sing; the sea sounds solemn and full and silver gulls fly over. I can smell the earth and I can feel how the violets are growing and all the small things down there under my window. It is exquisite.

Talking about flowers, you know Gentlemen's Buttonholes? (A double daisy, small.) Child, they grow here in every conceivable colour, and massed together they really are a superb sight. I am sure Sutton would have them. We *must* remember to grow them so in our garden, in a round bed. *Country Life,* of course, makes it almost impossible to wait for a garden. When one reads the collection of flowery shrubs, *par exemple*—mock orange (you remember that? It was at Mylor), four kinds of flowering quinces, Mexican fuchsia. . . . Oh *dear* me! And then the annuals that, sown in January and February, are flowering in Avrilo—there are at least 24 kinds and if you are clever you can grow them so that one kind marches up with banners after the other until the chrysanthemum is there. I think I shall become a very violent gardener. I shall have shelves of tomes and walk about the house whispering the names of flowers. We must have a tiny potting shed, too, just big enough for you and me. I see as I write little small forked sticks with labels on them. Daphne grows in England: Eden Phillpotts has a great bush. I shall write for a cutting. I read in *Country Life* of a most excellent apple called 'Tom Putts'—silly name, but it seems to be a very fine fruit and the trees bear in their second year. *Country Life* intoxicates me—the advertisements and the pictures and the way they *harp* on hardy annuals. We must have a boy for heavy work, but I want to do a fearful lot myself—large gloves again (mine this time) and very short corduroy velveteen skirt—Buff Orpington colour. Now I must lay down my trowel.

I've just remembered your bankruptcy discharge. If it could be done it would be an excellent thing, but I detest the idea that Smith or any of your creditors should get another sou. You can't borrow (?) on me for I'm not a good enough life—but could the house be bought in my name? Could any use be made of me? It's very confusing. Bogey, what is the amount? And what would you be called upon to pay? I do wish you had never gone bankrupt, but it seemed the only thing to do at the time. I think it was not, though; I think you had evil advisers. The whole affair never ought to have come about. Will you tell me more, as much as you can, and just what you think best to do?

God! what a comfort we are married—and no one can possibly start a divorce. We are *sound* as far as that is concerned.

I have given L.M. the £10. Thank you again my Darling for arranging all that affair.

Bogey, I find this Italian inlaid work is really dirt cheap. I wonder if you know what it is I mean. For instance, J. has a tray here for coffee cups. It is a kind of sea green inlaid with very delicate ivory coloured trees and kids and little loves playing among them and blowing on trumpets. It cost 35 francs!!! There is in fact a whole shop of it and a man who does the work here. Oh, I wish you were in Menton with me for a little. We should have the most ravishing prowls, but perhaps better not. I told you about the finger bowls—clear glass with faint gold and green or gold and pink stripes—the green is prettiest. I'll never rest happy until we have a house fit to be visited by—by . . . ourselves. And I want very much these two French servants. They long to come: and they love cats and chickens and country. I think it would be a kind of final cachet, don't you? The one is Marie-Louise and the other Josephine and they both dress alike. Post has just come. I'll start another page.

I have your Thursday afternoon letter and the *A.* and the *T.L.S.* First, the letter. I am afraid the house was not what it sounded because you would have wired. Your childhood horrifies me. You came upon

481

things so late, and then they were so few. But how nice Way House, Minster *sounds* doesn't it?

Now darling this is final about the coat. We must give it a bit longer. (It really can't have been lost if it did go in the sac diplomatique, it must have been stolen in London, I fancy). But if it is hopeless, just wire *No go*. I mean if I may definitely NOT expect it. For then I'll get one made on the spot at a shop here called New England. They have excellent materials—wool of the purest and thickest—and will make one for me in five days. L.M. has got *her* eye on a grey Burberry—very chic. She fancies herself in it. Burberry has a shop here. So just let me know and I'll go ahead and with my £10 windfall get a coat.

I note about stamps *re* reviews. And may I have more books. Poor Mrs. Leonard Merrick's *Mary Girl* can't stand more than a short notice. It's just dreadfully bad and she's dead. Rest her! I can't say anything against her. I'll just send a synopsis. The books are rather difficult to do: they are SO BAD!

Grant Richards said at his hotel at Cap Martin a man saw him reading the *Athenaeum* and said 'That's the paper K.M. writes in. She's very brilliant, I know her well, have known her for years . . .' and so on. It was Belfort Bax whom I *hardly* knew really and haven't seen since the old original *New Age* days. What great cheek! He thought himself such a gun then, and now he boasts about poor little K.M. But don't imagine that *I* think myself brilliant will you, my precious? Very very far from it.

May has brought me a big branch of orange blossom all wet with rain. I must get up. If it clears after lunch we're going to take a car and go up into the mountains to see if we can find wild tulips for tea. Did I tell you I am having a lovely dress made—materials and dressmaker chosen by Connie. It's very fine supple black cloth with a puritan ivory crepe collar and cuffs. Do you like that? I like you to know about my clothes. I do feel one must have very distinguished clothes—Middleton Murry clothes. The little American millionaire who is still here has a set of green and gold enamel dressing-table pots and trays. But I am going to bring you back a pile of presents. Unpacking will be a real adventure. No one must be forgotten! There's your mother and Richard, too. But the house—the house!!

[Drawing.] There is a piece of orange blossom for you—buds and leaves—but oh, I can't draw the scent.

Goodbye, my precious. Ever, for ever, your Wig

Monday,
(February 23, 1920)

Re the New Forest, I was talking about it to Cousin Connie last night, and she says it's so difficult to get anything on gravel—and that *gravel* is the *most* important thing. She thought as well dig a grave as live on clay.

Darling,

I have just read your Canterbury letter about Minster. I felt that Minster was not going to be much good. You didn't see Heaven when you were a little boy. Alas! they put you off with market gardens.[1] I have a feeling that you won't find anything till I get back (which is in about 9 weeks, as I suppose you realize. Wing knows). I shall be able to tell what is possible and what is not. People lead you a dance, love. For instance, I was positive Battle was no go: the man seemed so—almost reluctant. But, dear love, these last few days I keep on wondering whether the New Forest is any good? I've a passion for it 'as an idea' and you could keep a horse and we might run to a pony for me as well. You see Woodhay, which isn't our affair—but still *is* a highly desirable residence with garden, orchard, all improvements p. w.c. h & c and all kinds of pretty little kickshaws like awnings and summer blinds only cost £2000. . . . And I am sure the forest is *superb*. And Father found it in one go. He just walked out and happened on it. . . . What do you think? I feel a forest is a wonderful place to live near and it certainly can't be enervating. What do you think, darling?

By the way, about my coming home. DON'T come to Paris. Meet me in London with a car. There's no point in coming to Paris and as it is we shall be such a party. You wouldn't like it at all. You'd try and be a *mari* and May would laugh at you. These two have 14 trunks of their own, I have 3, L.M. 2. No, my child, don't come near Paris. Meet me at the station. Sit on a bench with a poetry book and clap it to when the steam comes waving under the roof and then find me very quickly. That will be far better.

Yesterday—it being mid-summer—Mrs.——drove me in a kerridge and pair to Monte Carlo. I take back my words about the Riviera *not* being what it is made out to be. It *is* and more. It was the most marvellous afternoon. We drove towards the sun up hill down

[1] I had been very optimistic about the house at Minster, a place of which I had a romantic childish memory.

dale, mountain roads, through lemon and orange groves—little children throwing bouquets of violets and hyacinths into the carriage—past the sea, under huge mountains—and the FLOWERS. Of course, it is all quite artificial: there's no imagination in it anywhere. *Monte is real Hell.* To begin with it's the cleanest, most polished place I've ever seen. The villas are huge and they have strange malignant towers. Immense poppies sprout out of the walls and roses and geraniums hang down like carpets. All the shops are magasins de luxe, lingerie, perfumes, fat unguents and pawnbrokers and patisserie. The Rooms are the devil's headquarters. The blinds are down, there's a whitish glare from the electric light inside—carpet on the outside steps—up and down which pass a continual procession of *whores,* pimps, governesses in thread gloves—Jews—old, old hags, ancient men stiff and greyish, panting as they climb, rich great fat capitalists, little girls tricked out to look like babies—and below the Room a huge outside café—the famous Café de Paris with *real* devils with tails under their aprons cursing each other as they hand the drinks. There at those tables sit the damned. The gardens, darling,—if you could see them—the gardens in Hell. Light, bright delicate grass grown in half a night, trembling little pansies grown in tiny beds that are nourished on the flesh of babies—little fountains that spray up into the air all diamonds—Oh, I could write about it *for ever.* We came back through pine forests, past Cap Martin and then at the edge of the brimming sea. I've never heard of Monte before—never dreamed there was such a place. Now I want to go to the Rooms and see it all. It's *dreadful,* but it's *fascinating* to me. We stopped the carriage outside the café and waited for about five minutes. I thought of the Heron and *our* life—and I thought how strange it was that at the Heron I should no doubt write a story about that woman over there, that ancient long-nosed whore with a bag made of ostrich feathers. . . . I wonder if you'd like to see such a thing, would you? I don't in the least know. Cruelty is there—and vultures hover—and the devil-waiters wear queer peaked caps to hide their horns.

It's another dead calm gorgeous summer—June—day as I write. Perfect weather! I wish you shared *that* at any rate. Take care of yourself, my own—and don't forget for a moment how perfect our house is going to be. It will be far better than we imagined in the past because all is different now. No, I can never forget anything of what has happened because it has changed everything; but I don't regret it. It *had* to be.

Your own Wig

I can get a lovely coat here I find. So don't forget to wire me if I must not expect the other. But parcels do take 3 weeks from Paris.

Tuesday,
(February 24, 1920)

We had baby lamb with infantile potatoes and nouveau né green peas today.

There is a book which we must positively not be another week without. It is Forster's *Life of Dickens.* How is it that people refer to this and have many a time and oft talked of it to me and yet—as though 'it was of course a very good Life, a very good Life indeed, about as good as you could get and immensely well worth reading'. But so dispassionately—so as a matter of course. Merciful Heavens! It's one of the most absolutely fascinating books I have ever set eyes on. I found today Vol. III in the book shelves. Whether the other two are here or not I don't know, but I do most solemnly assure you it is so great that it were worth while building a house in the country and putting in fireplaces, chairs and a table, curtains, hot wine and you and me and Richard and whoever else we 'fancy' exprès for reading this. Bogey, it's *ravishing.* What will you do when you come to the description of how his little boy aged four plays the part of hero in a helmet and sword at their theatricals and having previously made the dragon drunk on sherry stabs him dead, which he does in such a manner that Thackeray falls off his chair, laughing, and rolls on the floor. No, that's nothing. Read of his landlord *M. Beaucourt,* read of his home in Boulogne.—

Now I am exaggerating. Since I wrote all that I finished the book. It's not GREAT, of course, it's not; it's fascinating and it's a bit terrible as a lesson. I never knew what killed Dickens. It was money. He couldn't, as he grew older, resist money; he became a miser and disguised it under a laughing exterior. Money and applause—he died for both. How fearful that is! But still, my own precious, we must have the book. We must have his complete works.

I had your Saturday (home again) letter today. Fancy winter back again and here we go from sun to sun. I'll tell L.M. to write to Harlow Downs and I'll write to Belle in case she hears from any of her friends of anything. But don't get agitated or desperate for a minute. When we're back we'll get what we want. I have no possible doubt. You do realize, darling, there's a chance I may have to return here next winter

485

—a big chance? It's for the *sun,* and I can't risk taking 10 years getting well when I might take 2. If I do come, of course it will be with Connie and Jinnie and I'll leave L.M. in charge of the house and you. I'd come from November till May. Rendall saw me yesterday. He says my lung is better even in a week, but my old rheumatism which has located itself at present quite definitely in the right hip-joint is 'very trouble-some'. It could be cured by baths but then my lungs won't stand baths. So I'll have to get them going before I can cure it. It doesn't prevent me from living my life however.

Yesterday I had a wonderful afternoon. Mrs. D. took a carriage and we (she) shopped. I bought for the house, Oh dear! the most ravishing perfect—surprises you ever did see. You'll *never* recover from them. She bought some too and a dress for me, a girl's dress, blue chiffon with a pinky fringe—summer dress. No, I can't draw it. But I really think what I bought for the house will bouleverse you. I paid 77 francs of the £10 gave me (*sic*), and mean as I say to get more. This is a *frightful* town for shopping—glass, china, inlaid work, bits of brocade, trays. We had champagne for dinner, and J. seeing my softened mood gave me her Missal to read. But that's no good, darling, Who made God? (I don't mean I did.)

Wig

Wednesday,

REPLY URGENT. (February 25, 1920)

Marie-Louise—domestique de 30 ans, venant du Nord—peut faire la cuisine—travaille admirablement—désire venir avec nous comme cuisinière-femme de menage. Mais elle a avec elle sa nièce, jeune fille de 17 ans, *admirable* comme parlour-maid et sewing-maid qui veut venir aussi. Si je m'attache tous les deux? Please reply! Ce sont deux femmes superbes!!! Mais pas un mot d'Anglais. Je suis *très* anxious to bring them.

Wig

Thursday,

THE IMPORTANT LETTER. (February 26, 1920)

Darling Precious little Husband,

I want you to read this slowly and remember that I am loving you with my whole heart and putting you first in my thoughts, always. I

486

know how terribly anxious you are to leave P.V., but what are you going to do if I go abroad for the winter? Rendall said today it would be madness for me to spend the next 2 winters in England because, whatever the luxury I live in, the air is almost perpetually damp and there IS very little sun. It is not as though I were a simple consumptive who can walk, lie about and so on. I am handicapped very severely by my rheumatism which cannot be cured until my lungs are cured. It is that which prevents me from leading the normal life in a cold climate which another consumptive can do. He says that for the next two years I ought to be here from November till May. I must take this opinion into account; it is shared by these 2 women, and I dare not face a prolongation of my illness.

Now, if I do come abroad, L.M. must be with me. She would not let me come alone and she says she dare not. I think she is right. . . . You remember I was once cruel enough to suggest that we put off establishing our house: *I still suggest it.* Yes, I still think it would be 1000 times better to wait for 2 years. Please don't get angry. Please read on. You could surely get a week-end place for yourself every week-end. I would spend May till October in P.V. I suggest offering Violet and Roger the basement floor and her bedroom—with a door at the top of the kitchen stairs for them so that they live there. I would get the whole house and the feeding arrangements and so on into *perfect order* before I left and arrange that you were never left without a servant even when she was out. In the meantime you take your time, you look; if you do see the perfect thing and it's cheap, you make it your week-end cottage, and for us when I'm there until I am well enough to live there.

You'll say you can't stand P.V. any longer. Not as it is now, of course, you can't. The house wants attention, care, organisation, the life of it wants changing; you must live like a gentleman and be served like one. But all that can be done when L.M. and I get back. I'll make it my job to see you are really comfortably and exquisitely housed. There's no reason why Sydney should not stay either. I KNOW you hate London, but, darling heart, you MUST be in London, any way for a time and you certainly could get every week-end off and *when* the house is found perhaps you could spend every week-end there. P.V. when I've seen to it won't be in the least what it is now. And, Bogey, you must realize that I want to give you your heart's desire *this moment* but I must consider well what is easiest and best for us. Life in the country without your wife would not do. It would make immense demands on your energy. It can't be done without L.M. and me there all the time—and I really think I *dare* not face this rheumatism for two years.

You see what it amounts to is this: I come back, thoroughly set you up—get all *really* exquisite—you find a country place or a pied à terre and go slow just for the present. Light a cigarette. Think it well, well over. I wish you were here so that I might talk it out with you. I do so feel it's the right thing to do. Let Sydney know: ask him. Tell him how snug I mean to make P.V. and well kept in every way. And if you do agree, please read this letter to Violet and give it her immediately and, darling, please please wire me either *agree* or *don't agree*. I shall wait for that wire. I'll go into all the details once I'm home—and I promise you great comfort—no domestic worries and L.M. shall establish your country comfort.

That's all. Your devoted

Wife Wig

Fin de la grève (?)   Tuesday,

My own Bogey,   (March 2, 1920)

A perfect pile of letters came today—one telling me about Dollie Radford. Also there came the paper. I think it is vastly improved with the contents across p. 1. It looks a very good number. I have not had time to read any but your most *admirable* article yet. There'll be no me this week, I am afraid. Letters have simply not been going to England. I suppose you don't realize *là-bas* how serious this strike has been here. I have seen the *D.N.* (Jinnie takes it) and it seems to be just dismissed, but the French papers are *full* of it and full of its *esprit révolutionnaire*. Were it not for the post, I'd snap my fingers at it. What does it matter here—when Jinnie takes up a piece of omelette and says: 'Come on *hedge-sparrow*, peck away'? That's her name for me!

I want to write about a million things, but I am held up because I do not know what you are feeling about my letter about the house. I feel your keen disappointment and I'd give my eyes to be able to retract it. But I *can't*. It's no good imagining that I can live in an English winter yet. I just dare not: it might cripple me for life. And we can't have a half life. You are the very last man on this earth to have to do with an 'invalid wife'. I know that so well. I know that the springs of our life together will be poisoned if I am not well. Italy taught me that and now this rheumatism which Rendall assures me is most obstinate and which I know for agony convinces me that nothing but sun from

November till May will do. But *do* remember that I *realize* what that is to you when I say: Put it off.

L.M.'s letter came, and she was here, so she let me read it. Bogey, she can't sell her shares—not even for us and not even when it is such a sound proposition. She can't: she's *bound* not to, first by the solemn promise to her sister, and I feel as well she *cannot* for another reason which is too obscure and difficult for me to write about. It's a *compound* feeling. If you'd like me to analyze it for you, I will.

Have my letters arrived? I have written every day and I have sent a review of *Pilgrims of Circumstance* and *Jewish Children*. This week I'm awfully badly off for books. Couldn't I have Rebecca West's novel *The judge* and *The Woman called Smith* by . . . (Heinemann) and . . . some others? It's fearfully difficult to review things which ought not to have long reviews.

About the Constable excisions in *Je ne p. p.* it depends what they ask, doesn't it? I want to cut a small bit out of *Prelude,* but that I can do in proof. Bogey, are you going to review my story[1] in the Athenæum? Every week . . . I look . . . and don't see it. Your book was reviewed so I suppose it's not a question of the staff—at any rate it wouldn't be, for I don't sign. But if you'd rather let it alone, all right, darling.

Your Blunden man. . . . Oh, what a curse! he doesn't really thrill me yet. I can't 'get away with it'. It seems to me the first poem is over-weighted—over-heavy. But I KNOW I'm not fair and I understand what he must be to you, and all success to him! If any one sent a poem from N.Z., from my school, that had even *one* happy line. . . . But that is not your first interest in him, of course. Boge, do remember to be sober in your praise—temperate. You remember how little fired us when we were young, and to be over-generous is dangerous. You, of course, would shower love on anyone whom you thought was walking the right path, and I love you for it—and yet. . . . I know one *must* hold back a bit. If I'm dead down sincere I'll confess that the fact he wrote you, approached you, through *Clare* influenced me, for I have a perfect horror of Clare. The fact that he fell down in the mud at Byron's funeral and ruined his only clothes fills me with woe. So there's a female for you!

Oh, Love, my pen moves stiffly till I hear from you; it won't run or leap, and I want the strike to be over. It's *torture* not to be in the paper. E.M.F. fills me with jealousy even tho' he is such a *kleine Seele*.

[1] *Je ne parle pas français,* reviewed by J. W. N. Sullivan on April 2.

489

Bogey, I don't think you ought to talk or bother about silly people. Be quiet if you want to. Just be yourself. It's all that matters. Don't even try to be anything else. I feel it is of the highest importance you should not make an effort which you feel in your soul to be a wrong effort. I've exposed you to that sometimes—but *never never* again.

The weather day after day here is hot brilliant summer. We lie out, drive, bask. Its hot enough for cold lamb salad, champagne, and fruit and cream—*really* hot. Menton is an exquisite little town. Every time I drive into it I think it more lovely. My lungs and heart are a million times better, but my rheumatism is not. It's very bad—bad as bad can be just now. I love these women more every day, I think. But I long to be HOME and making HOME for you—as perfect as I have learned how. Goodbye, for now, my own—my darling precious Bogey. Ever your devoted

Wigchik

Thursday,
Dearest of all, (March 4, 1920)

Your telegram saying you absolutely agreed seemed to me the most wonderful gesture you had ever made. I felt your arms opened and I ran in and was folded up and *we* absolutely agreed. But all the same, dearest and most precious, I know what it meant to you—I know the cost. I deeply deeply know it and feel it. Whatever we do it will be the Best. Whatever we decide you know that my whole heart is in it *for you*. For I am yours, body and soul, my beloved—your own wife, and every single day that passes here I feel as though I am dedicate anew to OUR FUTURE. This Spring is going to be our Spring—it's going to be the crowning of our love. I wish I could explain that: I can't. But I feel I've never before been really ready for Life—able to cope with it—strong enough to give and to rejoice. Now I am. And you are my all—my very one.

Your letter about the house has come with the *quaint quaint* 1750 Bogey-eyed drawings. It sounds exquisite and I want to know what you decide. My only brick about it is—not the size, but the cheapness. After a very big scrutiny of *Land and Water* I can't see why it's not £3,800. What is the reason? There must be one. It can't be *distance*, for a house that size would mean that the people would keep a car. . . . Otherwise, it sounds marvellous. If only we could take it and play with

490

it for the 2 years until it's ours for ever and we are really planted there! But you will tell me in your next letter.

Queer you should feel that about Tchekhov. I feel it simply profoundly— a kind of 'There you are' towards him with a smile which really means 'but no one understands him *truly* and delicately as Bogey and I do'.

Please tell Wingley how very much better his grandma is—how *everybody* remarks on it and says she looks a different creature. If only her rheumatism would go, I think she'd be almost well, but it does not go at present. . . . All the same, really my lungs are marvellously better and I hardly *ever* cough!

It's the most divine spring-summer weather—*very* hot. This is the kind of thing that happens at 1-30. A big car arrives. We go in from our coffee and liqueurs on the balcony. May is waiting to dress me—I wear 'somebody's' coat—'anybody's'—we get in, there are rugs, cushions, hassocks, and yesterday the tea basket, and away we go. Yesterday we went to La Turbie (I can't spell it and am ashamed to ask). It's up, up, high, high on the tops of the mountains. It's a tiny, ancient Roman town, incredibly ancient! with old bits with pillars and capitals—Oh, dear—it is so lovely. The road winds and winds to get there round and round the mountains. I could hardly bear it yesterday. I was so much in love with you. I kept seeing it all, for you—wishing for you—longing for you. The rosemary is in flower (our plant it is). The almond trees, pink and white; there are wild cherry trees and the prickly pear white among the olives. Apple trees are just in their first rose and white —wild hyacinths and violets are tumbled out of Flora's wicker ark and are *everywhere*. And over everything, like a light are the lemon and orange trees glowing. If I saw one house which was *ours,* I saw twenty. I know we never shall live in such houses, but still they are ours—little houses with terraces and a verandah—with bean fields in bloom with a bright scatter of anemones all over the gardens. When we reached the mountain tops we got out and lay on the grass, looking down, down—into the valleys and over Monaco which is—if anything in this world is, Cinnamon's capital. The palace, seen from so high—with its tufts of plumy trees—the harbour basin with his yacht and a sail boat and a minute pinnace. Angelica's chemises were hanging out to dry in a royal courtyard. I saw them through the glasses.

The hedge sparrow had cushions and rugs for her—the American whose name is D. lay flat on her back smoking—Jinnie, never still for a moment, roamed about and one heard her singing. She couldn't keep still and Connie (of course) unpacked the tea basket and fed us all and poured cream down us and then gave away the cakes to two funny little mountain children who watched us from behind a rock. We stayed there about 2 hours and then dropped down by another road to Monte—the light and the shadow were divided on the hills, but the sun was still in the air, all the time—the sea very rosy with a pale big moon over by Bordighera. We got home by 6.30 and there was my fire, the bed turned down—hot milk—May waiting to take off all my things. '*Did* you enjoy it, Madam?' Can you imagine such a coming back to Life? It's simply incredible! But I was simply filled with thoughts of *you* all the time—every moment I lay back in the car and talked to you. . . . How can one repay them for all this? It's not money, it's not because they are *rich,*—it is the spirit of it all, the way they do it, —their voices and looks and tones. It is living by love. How I do scorn all that horrible old twisted existence. I mean really the week-ends at ——, the paralysis of everybody, the vanity and ugliness of so much. No wonder you can't speak. It's not for us, such a life—but *this* is, plus of course our work and our youth and our deep, deep love. It's *living,* Bogey. I feel even the sun is part of it in some way—and shines differently.

(March, 1920)

I heard from Violet today and will reply via you tomorrow

Dear Bogey,

Your Monday note has just come (written at 200 miles an hour, I should think). I haven't received the *A.* yet. My proof came last night a thousand thanks for correcting it so minutely. What a printer they have! I'm posting it back today together with a review.

Dearest, please do not accept any invitations for me, will you? I am coming HOME because *I want to be with you* and in my room, and not to spend part of the summer in Mrs. Locke Ellis's house, tho' it's very kind of her. I'd rather stay where I am than do that. And please don't ask anybody to dinner the day I come home or for the week following —not Brett—or anybody except of course my dear little 'brudder' whom I'm going to ask to meet me at the station. I have not the remotest desire to see anybody but you and Richard and my cats and the house and Sorapure and the willows and the shepherdess and Violet and Gertie. I am afraid you don't know how home-loving I am and how it thrills me to think—oh, bliss untold!—of opening the grey door and being in the hall! My 'perfect times' here are only *pastimes*. So don't bother to cry 'hurrah'—funny one.

At the moment (and yesterday) I'm in bed with rather a severe chill and fever, but everybody is looking after me, so 'hurrah' I suppose again.

      Yours for ever
         Wig

                                   Villa Flora,
My darling Bogey,   (March 7, 1920)

After two days and nights of misery trying to make bricks out of straw I was forced to give up. I can't write on novels unless I have some novels to write on. You see I have no intellectual stimulus here and my nerves are still so overstrained that they just fail me.

I am also exceedingly worried about you.

Except for that hurried note in reply to my important letter, you have not referred to it: you have not talked it out at all. I tried my very best darling to make you realize how deeply I felt it for you but I am afraid I did not succeed at all. But try not to forget that we are *all in all* to each other and that you, when you 'confess you are selfish' and talk of 'no compensations in London,' you are saying things which I not only know just as deeply, just as finely, as you—we have talked of them all in the deepest intimacy—but you hurt my love in speaking as though I were a stranger. Must you? Try not to! It is like your other letter saying: 'My days are very laborious and I am none too pleased with life.' Can't you feel how those words strike another? Oh, so strangely and sadly, dearest.

As soon as I get back (in 7 weeks) I shall arrange everything for you. I think the cottage idea is the right one, and we shall have a whole month. There is the summer. L.M. and I will make it perfect, I do not ask you to spend one penny on P.V. I never have. All that we buy will be for the Heron and P.V. is our storehouse. Remember this, Bogey dear. I have already spent 200 francs on most lovely things for us here— cups, saucers, trays, boxes, exquisite oddments. I bought them with such deep joy but your letter makes me feel perhaps my joy was a little premature and you will not care so greatly. It's a great effort to love just now, isn't it? Ah, Bogey—

Darling, do not drink more wine than you need. It does you great harm. Won't you get Sorapure to give you some injections as you are over-tired? May I write and ask him to come and see you?

And you will tell me in your very next letter whether you want Waterlow to stay on. As regards his money, I will pay the £13 a month. If you want him, we must fit him in somehow. It is for you to say but please tell me, won't you?

I feel your fatigue is dreadful. Take care of yourself, my precious boy and remember that in seven weeks please God you will be able to hand over many of your worries to your own devoted for ever, your very own

Wig

Do confide in me if you possibly can, won't you?

Wednesday,
My dearest Bogey,   (March 10, 1920)
Please reply to all this in detail for I shall be home now in six weeks and I must know certain things.

(a) I have just received a letter from you about your country expedition with Brett. I am in complete agreement about the cottage. As long as you can find one L.M. and I will do the rest. But I am certainly not well enough to spend the 6 months (and not 4 as you ever so airily suggest, darling!) in a cottage. As I have already told you I return to England on the 30th of April and do not leave before November. I must ∴ have Portland Villas and I beseech you to realize that QUITE DEFINITELY. I long to spend a country holiday with you but I intend when I return to see Doctor Sorapure, to go very slow and certainly it were impossible for me to pass those 6 months in the country. We shall have to make a financial scheme by which this will be 'easy'; I am sure we can. (Does 2 months make so little difference to you? Darling, what a queer lover I have!)

(b) P.V. is too small to contain Waterlow during the months that I am there in my opinion, and I would very very much prefer to have our own home for those months. I long to be alone and home with you more than ever I did. But the question of space and our own intimacy makes it I think impossible. If you agree will you please tell him immediately to leave P.V. in the last week in April so that there will be time to re-arrange the rooms and so that Violet can clean them.

(c) About Violet. You 'ignored' my plan. Did you give her my letter?

How shall I write to her if I don't know? And I must write at once and make arrangements for my coming home. Did you discuss my plan with her? I know you received it for it was in the letter which you in part answered.

I cannot tell you, my darling Bogey, how distracting it is not to know these things. You write to me as though I had been away 8 years.

(d) We shall do all that is necessary to the house and don't buy anything till I return, will you dearest?

(e) Please ask Sullivan to review my story if it is not too late. Well, darling, I am sorry to worry you, but I am so very very anxious to know these things. I felt when you talked of my 8 months away as though you hardly cared if I ever came home again. It *did* hurt.

Yours for ever

Wig

Just got your telegram about Sydney. God bless you my darling. I don't know what to say. It was FEARFULLY IMPORTANT.

'House' letter

My precious dear,   (March 14, 1920)

I hasten to answer your letter (Thursday night) about the house. Look here, we can decide practically nothing while I am away, but the main lines Bogey must be arranged. . . .

I don't see how we *can* have Waterlow. Where is he to sleep? I must have the South bedroom, Ida, the small room, and you *must* have your dressing room with a little bed in it in case I have to sleep alone. But quite apart from that, oh Bogey the idea is *detestable* to me. Surely he'd understand that he can't be there in the summer. It seems to me so sensible. The house is *much* too small and the bathroom, lavatory and so on aren't a bit suitable. But the chief question is I cannot put to you too strongly my desire to be HOME and he is NOT part of my home. I want to dine 'en famille'—to be alone with you—to have all the rooms. I'll leave the winter scheme and Violet and Roger en l'air till I return. I can see you would rather I did. It's a poor look-out to let the house furnished as I want it to be so lovely, but that must be as you wish. At any rate I cannot consider for one moment a furnished house in the country for the summer! Oh, you don't understand me a tiny bit. I'm in furnished houses all winter. P.V. is HOME. I want to be THERE with OUR things—our cats—our own little bits. I CAN'T GO ANYWHERE

ELSE. Let's go to your cottage and we'll make that cottage perfect and have a month in it, but I must have my own house. I can't be without it. You must decide what you like in the winter. If you would prefer rather dingy rooms and your cats—(who will look after *them*?) and who will look after you? No, we really had better not discuss all this till I return.

I'll write to Violet leaving all plans 'pending'. I rely on you to get rid of Waterlow and to let us be alone for those six months. If you would rather not, let me. I'll write at once. But it must be done at once. *Please wire me* if you would rather I wrote, or not—will you? But let us at least have our life together unspoiled by strangers for the little time we have together. Does that sound too 'queer' to you? Please at any rate leave it all till April 30th and DON'T unsettle Violet. I don't think you know how we depend on her. No, dearest love, the only thing is to wait, but to get Waterlow out if you can or if not, let me explain to him AT ONCE.

Your own
Wife

[a drawing] a *heart* flying to greet you and panting after the water-brooks.

I'll have to add this. Marie has just brought your Telegram about Waterlow. I am so happy I have turned a Katherine wheel and feel inclined to cheer. *Just wait till I get home* that's all the best. And we shall be alone and all the house ours and a perfect table and the new cups and saucers with their flowers and fluting. And the windows shall be open—you'll be in old clothes, I'll be in fair ones. Wing and Athy there—fruit in our Italian dish—HAPPINESS, happiness. We'll be really truly alone. I'll be able to pick up your hand—look at it—kiss it—give it back to you. I'll say Bogey, my own; you'll say Yes, Wiggiechik. We'll look at each other and laugh. Wing will wink at Athy and pretend to play the fiddle. Oh I love you. Je t'aime.

Wig

I am glad that Waterlow has been so decent Boge and I fully accept all you say. At the same time....

Dearest Bogey,   (March 17, 1920)

I have just received your Sunday letter answering my questions. Thank you darling. Now we'll cry PAX till I do come home. It's so soon now. At the same time I had a letter from——. I hesitated before

496

opening it. I felt it was not going to be pleasant . . . and it wasn't. She told me all about the 'orgies' and the 'drink' and the parties etc. I had known more or less before, but I do wish she had left me with my 'less'. I could never be part of such a world, dear Bogey, however desperate I felt. A great gulf separates me from it for ever. And then that precious Richard writes that HE thinks the sun has risen over the Heron and will never set. Well, I hope it won't, for him. I shall do my very best to make him feel it is there and bright and warm when I come home. Don't ever let him see the 'orgies' or wine parties, will you, Boge?

Poor ——! she asks me to forgive her. Of course, I forgive her—but she ought to take herself in hand. She can't afford to drift. I do feel so very deeply the need for dignity in this present life. It's the only protest one can make—to be dignified and sincere and to—somehow keep *love* of human beings in one's heart. Really, it's no wonder people are so unhappy.

Well, I cannot afford to judge any man. And, after all, I have lived another, remote and different, life. My eight months are like eight years. The 'girl you left behind you' really did die after all in that Casetta and is buried there for ever.

My dearest little mate, we shall have a month together in the summer all alone—and peaceful beyond words. We shall lie on the grass and look up at the clouds and play soldiers and you shall wear a daisy in your buttonhole and we'll blow some o'clocks and tell lady-birds to fly away home. That is MY kind of gaierty, Bogey darling.

Take care of yourself and don't forget that I love you 'absolutely' and that I am

Your own
Wig

[Drawing of a heart crossed by two arrows].

You see that combines a kiss ordinary and a heart with an arrow. It is a ∴ very powerful magick.

Darling Bogey, (March 19, 1920)

I have just received your Monday letter. I am so sorry a faint chill sounded from mine about Mrs. Locke Ellis. I did not mean it to be there. And my feeling about P.V. isn't really as unnatural as you think. I *fully* enter into yours; but you see it's OUR home to me until we have another —and ∴ the centre of my affections. I am sure when you have your cottage and when L.M., Miss James, Singer and Co and Wig have spring clung P.V. you'll feel it is rather nice and bearable until we have our permanent home. But you see until we do it is my home and I have lived many months away from it—away from the cats and the—no, I'll spare you. How thrilling about the table! But I see what you mean about chairs. I *said* don't buy any because I was sure you didn't want to. If you *see* any, of course they'd be a joy. Those red ones are too hard for anybody to sit on. What are Heal's like? Do they 'go' with the table. I'll write to Violet about the spring cleaning. If only luggage were not such a great bore here. We are not allowed more than 100 lbs. More than that is rejected or one has to take an extra full ticket for it. Isn't that *maddening*? I'm having the china sent by rail post: it's the only way. It will be a long time coming, but that can't be helped. The cups are really very very lovely—big, fluted and covered with little small flowers. But I want to buy other things here and just can't because of getting them away. I'll have to wait and bring them back next year.

I have been rather lucky about clothes here and I have some very nice hats. Perhaps you may think me a rather pretty girl when I put them on, but you needn't say so. They are all presents, of course.

About our holiday, what about the New Forest? And picnics in it? I mean it really is a perfect place. Would you like it? I could ask Marie to find us rooms. I can't go to awfully poky little cottages, Boge, you know what I mean is—oh, Blow! You know what I mean. I thought we might go to an inn—what do you think? Of course, BEST of all would be a cottage but how does one find them? And we can't do for ourselves, my darling. It's no fun. We want to be free and not to have to worry about anything. What is your idea? Perhaps the Locke Ellises know a good place. From here I feel rather helpless you see. It's high time I did without a personal maid for a month. Yesterday I was going out driving with Bunny and I really could not dress myself. Couldn't find my hat or veil or anything. I had to ask her to lend me her nigger servant as May was out. But we must find a very simple place where we can come in with leaves in our hair. . . .

And what month will it be? A hot one so that we can brown nicely. I am very brown now: the sun burns today again and after the rain there is a special sparkle on everything. I wrote a review last night of 4 books of short stories—2 columns. It's the only way to treat them— I mean, to do them by the bunch. How you have had to work! Bogey, you *must* have your holiday. Would it be too expensive and unpractical to go to Ireland? Get Beatty to find us a place? I feel it would be such a thorough change for you, but on the other hand it is a waste so far as cottage-getting is concerned and—you're English and I want to see the English summer country. But you must have a *complete* rest and I'd like you to have bathing or boating.

I am very anxious for you to send me a copy of *Prelude* if you can. Will you? And, darling, if you can send back B.C.'s Christmas card I can get a *perfect* frame for it here—in any colour. I wish you would. Is that possible? Just slip it into the pages of *Prelude*: that would be all the best. Mrs. ——'s husband arrives today. A powerful fellow—a very bad man, I imagine. We (J., C. and I) smell a cloven hoof already. But that doesn't interest Bogey. Are the tulips above ground? How is our raskal? Do you love him as much as ever? And Athy? The Chaucer is exquisite. I know the poem. I read Alexander Smith's essay on Chaucer yesterday: it's very good. He's a very pleasant fellow. Goodbye for now my blessed one.

Your very own little
Wig

Darling,   (March 22, 1920)

Sullivan's a wicked liar. I never said more than 2 years.[1] Kill him and pay no attention to his dead groans. Oh, you are working too hard, much too hard, far too hard and it's still five weeks before I am home. I am so impatient now. I want to be *there* with you. It's High Time you were looked after and not by substitutes but by your own Heronia. Can you keep going till April 29th? Then you must throw everything at me. Once you get your cottage it will be better.

> Come up here, O dusty feet,
> Here is faery bread to eat,
> Here in this enchanted room
> Children, you may dine
> On the — ◡ — of broom,
> And the smell of pine.

I forget it and it's not good but it rings in my ears—faëry bread—I feel you ought to be nourished on it, and you ought to push under your plate all the horrid old city winter crusts. Precious love, at a wave a week my slow boat has five waves to get over.

[1] 'Sullivan told me he had had a letter from you in which you said that you had to go away for the winter for years i.e. more than 2 years more.'

I am waiting for Ida to come for my reviews and a telegram for you. I'm furious about Marie D. For Heaven's sake tell her you are too busy. She's attached fast to the horrid ——'s. She'll never be allowed to sink. Why should you have to worry about her? I am so angry with C—— that I feel inclined to throw my inkpot from here to Wooden Hay.

Ida has been and gone with the reviews and telegram. The cannons are being fired for the royal wedding at Monaco. Monaco IS very romantic! Last night it and Monte were illuminated and there were Bengal lights and a torchlight procession and serenades under the Palace windows and a great ball in the gardens. I always wish in a way we were Prince Bogey of Heronia and the Princess Wig. You would have made a good Prince . . . but I wouldn't have been up to much.

B.D. is revealed as a B.H. of the worst kind. She is frightfully jealous of me and has been telling disgusting lies behind my back and altogether behaving so odiously that I can't even *look* at her. Happily, she returns to the Ritz and Claridge's in a day or two and she don't signify. But society women when they do turn and are not well bred take a good deal of beating, Boge. I've got her presents for good and all and I don't really care.

Oh, it's such a day—the sea purrs. It's so hot and fine and golden. You would bathe and brown and you'd eat oranges with me in a green shade. I love and love and love you for ever. Goodbye for now, my own *precious* darling. Don't forget I'm coming and that I am for ever your very own little mate

Wig

Villa Flora, Menton,
(abt. March 24, 1920)

[A drawing] You and Richard and me on a mule expediting.

Old Sir John to hell has gone.
Burn, devils, burn him!
When one side well is fried
Turn, devils, turn him!

I thought you might quote that one day. It's quite genuine: in a churchyard in the Isle of W.

My blessed one,

It's winter again—pouring rain, ghashly cold, pipes burst, oranges burst,—big fires, booties, Marsala, frenzied palms. I DO love Bogey so.

Why?

Just because he IS Bogey and he is mine and I am his. I dreamed last night I got home, arranged all my presents on a tray, brought them to you and the ONLY one you picked out was *the Russian spoon*. 'Tig, what a charming spoon! Why didn't you buy ½ a dozen?' And there was the tray with all the lovely things, and I had to say: 'Don't you remember you sent it me for my birthday?' Wasn't that fearful? It really was.

Country Life has come. It has some flower pictures in it. Do you know, Bogey (this is literally true) flower pictures affect me so much that I feel an instant tremendous excitement and delight. I mean as strong as if a great band played suddenly. I read a description of a certain pink magnolia which grows in Africa 150 feet high—the blooms are shell pink on silver stems and there are no leaves so that it has the appearance of a great flock of flamingoes. This was illustrated. Bogey, I *really* nearly fainted. I had to lie down.

But when I come home and show you what I've bought you you nearly must faint too. We'd better have Richard there with buckets of water. I love Richard, Bogey. He writes me such darling letters with small pictures in them and I love to think of him—so honest and true and good—and a Boy. I think he wants the kind of spoiling he could get *chez nous*—not a mother's spoiling, but a sister's (quite a different thing). When I have money he shall be my heir. We must also bring him with us here one year, and you and he must go climbing up in the mountains. I can go too on a mule. [A drawing] See us? The mule looks rather a silly.

Knock at my door. Jinnie: 'Is our little girl comfy?' 'Yes, very.' 'Are you warm enough, darling?' Now she has gone and the baby peke has dashed off with my pink mule. It's so wonderful to think that I come back here *with* them in November—to this same room, even. Bogey, you would love these women—and there is *no* effort—no need to talk or to be other than your own self—absolutely. They make old age a joke. Connie is nearly 70 and she's a *girl*! Bless them, but above all bless my little mate.

My precious Bogey,   (about March 24, 1920)

I had 2 such lovely letters from you yesterday one written on Wednesday and the other on Thursday. They were quite *old-fashioned* letters, telling me things, and they brought us so near together. I read and re-read them. Thank you, my very own.

About the novels, I'd rather do them until I come home. Then we can talk it over. But you've sent me enough now to go on with and I DO hope to work more this week. It's all I can say. I feel very refreshed today and my chill has quite gone. Rendall (the doctor man) had a talk with me on Friday evening. He says I do absolutely right to go back to England now and to return here in November, and this time next year I *ought* to be as well as I ever shall be i.e. as well as Mother was. She and I seem to be exactly the same: my heart trouble, I mean, is exactly like hers. I don't mean my temporary Casetta heart trouble, for that's gone, but my permanent kind, love, which will never go. You see, part of my *left* lung *n'existe plus*—so my heart has to do a two men's job to pump the blood through quickly enough—to oxygenate the system. It can do it of course but it won't bear strain, I mean it won't bear violent exercise ever, so if a bear runs after me you *must* run after the bear and not climb your juniper tree. But I can walk and even ride when my arthritis is better and can do all normal things *at my own pace,* that's all. I have written Father about this because I must have my £300 a year for life certain. And I must work no end. But I am very very happy—and if all is well between us, my own, we shall have a wonderful life: it will be far more wonderful than we imagined. Oh, how I long for it!

Here, I could not be more exquisitely cared for and loved and spoilt. They are more than sweetness and goodness to me in every way and the maids are the same—and the Doctor is a treasure of kindness. BUT I want to be alone with you, quite alone with my own Bogey for ever so long—away from *everybody*. I'd like a tiny baby house where just a little boy brought the milk an butter and an old man came selling cream and raspbugs and we sat at the door in the evening and read poetry. . . . That's *my* heaven: to have you to myself. Nothing less would do. Let's have a month of it. Oh, *do* let us! Nobody else, though. I felt in these 2 letters that perhaps you hadn't forgotten after all what we used to be to each other, darling, and that made me long to have you near. . . . Goodbye for now. Tickets are taken for April 27th. After that there are no more seats till the end of May. I'll be back by the 29th. 9 p.m. Victoria.

Your own

Wig

Booked tickets for April 27th. There happened to be 2 first class returned for that date (*wagon lits*). After that there are no seats till the end of May. Rendall says I must not stay here for the month of May: it's too enervating. So we shall be home about *April* 29th. Victoria 9 p.m. So will you see that Waterlow knows in time for the rooms to be put right again? The more I think of it, Boge, the more I realize he mustn't be there. The house is much too small, and besides—I can't help it—I feel he is my enemy. The luggage complication is awful. We can only take 100 lbs. each and I've bought all these things which *must* come. I wanted to buy 2 trays—large—one blue inlaid with cream and one silver grey with black and white inlay—VERY exquisite, 40 francs each but perfectly *exquisite*.

My darling Broomy,   (end of March, 1920)

Is the cottage to be ours?[1] I do long for a telegram saying that you have secured it. It sounds a perfect little GEM, and so cheap. If the worst comes to the worst we can always live there on nothing and 1d a year, darling and eat the 2 acre fields. But I long to know more. Can we make a bathroom? What is the water-supply? How is it heated? Can the dairy be made an extra room? I feel we ought to attach to it a government hut, for six rooms won't go far with 3 people and a maid. We can't live there *without* a maid. It sounds just what you are looking for and the position is ideal. Is there a shelter for a trap? But as we shall only be there week-ends and our summer holiday, we won't want a trap. A bicycle for you will do.

I loved your letters today, darling.

I am longing to be home. It is a great strain to live away from one's own tribe, with people who, however dear they are, are not ARTISTS. These people's minds are about 1894—not a day later. They still talk of such-a-pretty-book and whether one can or can't (*Oh ye Gods!*) have a platonic friendship with a man and (Oh ye Gods!) agree that you can't while the male is male and the female female!!!! I 'shock' them, but if they knew how they shock me. ——talks as I've never heard a prostitute talk—or a woman in a brothel. Her mind is a *sink*. She's sex mad. They make me inclined to roll up my sleeves, pin back my hair, lock the door and take myself and my knife off to the dissecting room— where all such idlers are shut out for ever.

[1] A cottage on Chailey Common, called Broomies, which we actually bought with borrowed money, but never lived in.

Oh, how pure artists are—how clean and faithful. Think of Tchekhov and even Johnny's talk and Anne's laughing, generous way—so remote from all this corruption. Dearest love, let us remain chaste and youthful with our work and our life and our poetry. One can't afford to MIX with people. One must keep clear of all the worldly world. And we can do it. I feel our happiness will simply be without end when we are together again.

But now that I am turned towards home, I am impatient to be there. I want to make 2 P.V. perfect in its way, and I'll strip out of it what we want for Broomies. But Broomies will be exquisite, too. No doubt about that.

I'm deaf today, with booming noises in my head. Almost idiotic with it. It must be a slight chill. So please forgive a silly letter in answer to your two darling ones. Won't Wing love the new house? He shall go down in a bastick.

Goodbye for now, dearest own. I'll try and bring the trays. I want us to have them. One thing I have got here is a present of a dressing-table set of pots and so on which is the loveliest thing of its kind I have ever seen. Do you like your pen-tray? I have bought 2 more for writing tables. PLEASE SAY.

Du reste je t'aime de tout mon cœur—je suis pour toujours—toujours—mon bien-aimé

          Your
            Broomy I

Broomy Regina ✴

My dearest Bogey,   (about March 25, 1920)

I was reading your letter so happily this morning until suddenly I came across your remarks about B.H.[1] Darling, your memory is very short-lived. Yes, it is true, I *did* love B.H. but have you utterly forgotten what I told you of her behaviour in Paris—of the last time I saw her and how, because I refused to stay the night with her, she bawled at me and called me a *femme publique* in front of those filthy Frenchmen? She is

[1] 'Today came a letter signed B.H. "Can you give me any work on your paper?" Not addressed to me by name. "Editor. . . . Dear Sir." What am I to do? She's no friend of mine, it's true; but you, I know, have memories of feelings towards her. She must, I suppose, be hard up to apply to me even in the most formal way. I'd be willing to give her something; but, you see, I never thought anything of her work—and the paper isn't a charitable organisation. I wait for your suggestion.'

loathsome and corrupt and I remember very very well telling you I had done with her, explaining why and recounting to you how she had insulted and abused me.[1] I should have thought you could not have forgotten these things. Indeed, I shall never forget your enemies— never forgive them—never forget if you tell me you have been insulted. London is a veritable sink of corruption if such mists gather and mislead your fine and pure understanding.

But darling, even though, as you say, you cannot cope with the world, don't for God's sake for that reason go to meet the world in any way. Withdraw. Be morose. Be silent. But, oh Bogey, do be proud. What is our love if it hasn't taught us *pride,* if we don't defend each other and keep the shield bright for each other. Your honour is my honour; I'll not betray you. I'll defend you: I'll keep very very straight and good because I am a Heron. I will NOT be caught on their lime twigs even for one moment.

Love, you are too lenient. Is it much to ask you to be yourself and to condemn what you don't approve of? Those horrible parties of Ottoline when you were gloomy with wine. Oh, how hot and ashamed I am that those sniggering fools could so egg you on! Wouldn't you rather it were said of us: 'Try as Lady A. did she could not persuade Middleton Murry to attend her parties, or if he did his despair was manifest' than 'he came and was perhaps a trifle more gloomy than was natural'. Oh, I am so deeply truly anxious that we shall be an example and in our small way hand on a torch. I could *never*—or I swear I never will—attend such functions unless I am my most sincere self. I'll keep away and make enemies by silence rather than by the words I wish I hadn't said. It is really a fault in your nature that you are not proud enough. Will you one day forget and forgive Lawrence—smile—give him your hand? Oh, that I should dare to write that. Forgive me. But, my own, do, I beseech you, keep clear of bad people till I return. Be fastidious. HURT bad people rather than be hurt by them. Remember that B.H. is bad, has insulted us, insults us worse by thinking she has only to write to you for you to wag your tail.

I think I am too changed. Perhaps you will think I am too exacting altogether and that it can't be done. Well, if it can't, if we can't remain pure, let us not try and be artists. That's all. I have such a profound respect and reverence for our work and for *the universe*—for all that is being discovered, for all who really seek the truth, that I want to belong

[1] See letter of March 22, 1915.

505

to them *alone*. But will you, my gentle knight, please defend me against my enemies—and I shall defend you and keep our name unspotted.

Let us be GREAT—FAMOUS Broomies through and through.

I solemnly warn you that if you stir B.H. you will discover such a nest of serpents that you will repent it. Don't forget OUR PRIDE. Not that she's so important in herself; it's what she stands for. Don't you see?

  Broomy II

[A drawing of a pot of flowers]

My little King of Broomy Castle,   (March 26, 1920)

Ever since I sent that long wire[1] I've been ashamed of it: it wasn't the wire to send *you*. Forgive me, please. This afternoon a wave of rage against myself seized me so I put on my ta-ta and went off to the poste and sent another. I couldn't *bear* to think you had that odious one for the week-end. It was so wicked of me not to have considered that your intentions were perfect and that you are too busy, my precious one, to remember everything. Forgive me again and please kiss and be friends. I'm a wicked Wig who flies off at tangents. I'll try not to....

Being out and full of love, desperately in love in fact, I went and bought a tray—about the length of this page, about ¾ the breadth, a divine shade of blue with little ivory birds in ivory boughs singing all over it—a tray for letters to be handed on and cards—to be kept on the hall table. Perfeck. This made me feel slightly better. I ordered a large one for tea and then bought another, small and square, just for handing a cup or a glass of milk—*very lovely*—silver grey with a centre design— 7.50!! I then went and bought Connie a bouquet for her birthday tomorrow, stocks and *bleuets*. They tied it with gold string, which was very kind of them for it only came to 2.75. Then I bought a large packet of lined envelopes for 1 franc (about 5d.) hailed a very sparkling little voiture and came home by the sea. Came in. Had tea, cherry jam and cream cake—threw up my hat several times and caught it—remembered we start for home tomorrow a month—looked at your photo said 'Boge' to it and . . . well, here I am. Can't get calm. Have fallen in love with a dark-haired young man with beautiful hazel eyes.

I had a letter from Brett today and answered same. She was terribly sad and kept asking me to put her into the dust-bin (like a Dickens character). Poor dear! I hope I have cheered her up a little bit. It's the tag-end or fag-end of that ghastly winter, I expect.

Oh, child, we'll have such a July—a holiday *complet* as you say. What about—phonetically-speaking—'Bewley' in the New Forest? There's an inn there and water. One can sail in a walnut shell with a match-end for a mast and an ivy leaf for a sail. I must wait and see what Marie says. We shall certainly find something. And I want you to hire a horse and go for a ride every day, leaving me under a tree. That's my idea. We shall take a camera and photograph each other, too, and we'll go off in the morning with our lunch and our poetry-book and pic-nic and make a fire (*on est permis* to make fires in the forest) and drink tea out of a muslin bag.

Do you know, Bogey, I love you. Yes, you know very well, Isabel. In the New Forest I expect they will think we are Newly married and give us the best of everything. Won't it be perfect? Think of summer evenings—when we've put on our slippers and had supper and I'm lying down and you're sitting up and we read and then go over to the window and look at the stars. I love you much more than I used to— because I'm different. But that doesn't matter. I don't expect you will notice.

I hope Wing and Athy are practising their Chorus of Welcome. I long to pick up little Wing and see his dear eyes again.

Well, I must finish my review for tomorrow morning's post. Goodbye, my true love. Do please try and rest a little and DON'T make any preparations for me except a car to be at the station. If Violet wants to know things just say: 'Look here, Violet, I'm awfully tired. Be a brick and just manage best way you can.' And she will. Tell Richard it's time he wrote to me. How is he?

My own little mate I am yours for ever with all my heart and soul.

Your
Wig-wife
[A drawing of a pot of flowers]

[Drawing] Primula and leaf

My precious little mate,   (March 30, 1920.

I've had three letters from you today—one before the pen-tray, one after, and one about Broomies. I want you to tell me C.Y.H.S.D.[1] if

[1] Cross Your Heart Straight Dinkum.

you thought the pen-tray at all 'special'. Because then I shall know what to buy. I think its simply exquis but perhaps I have gone a trifle mad-dog after so long 'on my own'. I shan't refer to B.H. again. It's explained, isn't it, love? And now shake off Marie D. Thank Heaven, she'll never be with us. Oh, please tell Tommy to take his 'sprightly stone axe' for me and bang Miss W. on the head with it. Really, her *Balzac*!!!! It is the last word in utter drivel.

Your 'Miss Cavell' is *superb*. You're doing just what I hoped you'd do in the *Nation*—putting big things into the scales. It's VERY good. Now don't forget to tell *Who's Who?* all about yourself. And your recreations are—what? Oh, I wish I looked over your shoulder! But be sure to do it. I shall be always *idly* turning over the pages and re-reading what you say. *Don't forget: do it in time.*

Could you send me a copy of *Prelude* please? And thank you for my bouquet in the *A.* for March 26th. It was a very nice one.

I am all for Broomies. I, too, have this idea we may retire there and live on love when we are old. I love the little place. It's the right size and it's remote and very simple. William and Dorothy might have lived there or any of our *own kind*. If we do have money we can always make it better and better but I am greatly desirous of our owning it (bad English). I think it's *us*. We can leave it to Richard. It seems to me nicer than anything else. I see it under the stars—so quiet—it's thorn hedges spangled with moonlight—our pony cropping—my dear love at the window, telling me how fine the night is. Please let us decide on it if you agree. I want it with all my heart.

I have (practically) taken a flat here. Connie and Jinnie have also taken one. They don't want to risk this huge place next year. We're in the same building, on the same landing—just our 2 doors next to each other. The house is exquisite—really most delightful in very fine style. It faces due South, so do all the rooms except the kitchen and the bonne's, which is best. It looks towards the frontier. There are balconies at all the big windows. Lovely rooms, a superb bathroom and geyser, and the kitchen part is shut off from the salons and chambres à coucher by big doors. There is a gas stove, 3 best bedrooms, salon, salle à manger, bonne's room, kitchen, w.c. bathroom, and housemaid's pantry. Theirs is identical across the way, so I am in hopes you may come out for a month next year or at least for a peaceful and early Xmas. What do you think?

To revert to Broomies for a minute. If the *A.* gives up at the end of its two years you drop £1000 a year. Well, we want to be in a position where this doesn't matter two shakes of Wing's tail, and we should if we had a cottage like Broomy. You'd just turn into a poet and vegetable grower if you wanted to. At any rate, there'd be nothing BIG to keep up or to be a drag, and, you being what you are, my dearest, it's always best to remember we *can* live on the cheap.

Here's supper. It's a roaring night, so we are drinking champagne to put it out of mind. Connie bought me *another* hat today—that makes *six*. She must stop. She 'dresses' me just as though she were my Grandma and I have more clothes than ever before. 'Now, that would suit you, darling. You're such a little slight thing, you'll only need 2½ metres, and I'll have it made with just a touch of . . .' and she holds it up against my cheek. Oh, it does remind me of Grandma so! It's awfully sweet.

Goodnight, dearest dear. I love you for ever and ever amen. In fack I ADORE you.

Your Wig-wife

Tell me how you love me in your next letter. . . . You see I love you so terrifically and Thursday is the 1st and then it's only 27 days. 27 bregchiks, three 'laundries', 3 Sundays—think of it. 3 Sundays and I shall be HOME. I feel quite *shy* with bliss. You'll whistle when you come in, won't you? and I'll look over the stair. Then you must gallop up or I'll let down a little ladder. We'll have very good dinners (all new food) and coffee and liqueurs. Oh, oh, oh, I could go on for ever. What will you wear at the station? What hat? When I see your precious darling face and hand lifted and feet running, I may fly into 1000 pieces. We'll walk arm in arm—forgetting our luggage. Will you be as happy as I will? Oh Boge!!

[Two drawings of children see p. 517] I can't draw our little girl till I've got a fine pen; but he's not bad, is he?

Darling Bogey,   (end of March, 1920)

I do wish I could draw. I am always wanting to put little small drawings on the tops of your letters and I had such a thrill when I made that little boy. We'll have to take our sketch books away this year.

You know—*re* the South of France—I have grown to like it far more than ever I did. The mechanical *appearance* goes and there's something

509

about the rocks and stones which reminds me of New Zealand—volcanic—and the sea is really a wonderful colour. Yes, I've grown to love it. The air in the mountains is wonderful and then the trees—the pepper trees and the lemons. If only you shared my winters and we had a minute Broomchen here where we grew jonquils, early peas and lettuces and anemones. . . . You would be unhappy, I know. I would not go to Bandol again because it's not far enough South. Between here and Nice there are lovely little unspoilt corners in the mountains. But we can wait and come in 30 years' time. That will do.

Thursday,

My precious little mate,   (April 1, 1920)

April Fool's Day and only 27 days before I start for home—I think you and Wing might begin taking one bead off the counting frame each day now. Did you learn to count on a frame? [a drawing of one] And so on? I did. I remember how blue the blue beads were now.

Your Monday letter came last night. It will not be at all difficult to supplement the well-supply with a good colonial tank, and a great tub for rainwater—barrel, I mean. The more I think of it the more I am in favour of a small place that we can live EASILY in, with our eggs and chicks and fruit and veg. and nothing to worry us about money. We oughtn't to take a place like the Canterbury one because I can't help feeling it's a burden for people like us. It's all right *for a time* but we are in harness. And I'd rather live exquisitely, dress for supper, have every possession fine as fine at Broomies. We are not really and truly earth children. I want to be very comfortable (have to be) and never to do house-work or horrid cooking or anything like that. I'm sure I couldn't light a fire even if I tried. But I don't want us to find out we're spending heaven knows what a week and have to *pull together* and manage somehow. No, let's live at Broomies when we can enlarge it a bit—keep it for our own faery house until then and keep our good old poor old despised by you loved by me P.V. for the present.

My flat idea is all in the air again. For Jinnie now wants to buy this small château and to give me rooms in it to be my very exclusive own for next year and the year after. I am torn in two for it's true the exquisite *protection* of being here no money could buy and if I had my own den it would be different. Well, I'll manage all this as I think best. Don't give it a thought. It is after all my own look out and nothing to do with you. (I mean that 'nicely and kindly', love.) Jinnie wants me so much I expect I shall be here and not at Garavan. She said: 'One of my aims in life is to make you well and you mustn't deny me that.' I've nothing to say when she puts it like that.

An awful thing happened here yesterday. Just a week ago a young woman was seen wandering about under the trees at Cap Martin and crying—all day. *Nobody spoke to her.* At dusk a little boy heard her crying for help. She was in the sea about fifteen feet from land. By the time he had told somebody it was dark and she had disappeared. Her purse and jacket were on the beach. She had a *return* ticket to Nice— five francs and a handkerchief in it—that was all. Yesterday the sea washed her up just opposite the Villa. She came rolling, rolling in with each wave and they waited till she was tumbled on the beach. All her clothes were gone except her corset. Her arms and feet were gone and her hair was bound round and round her head and face—dark brown hair. She doesn't belong to a soul. No one claims her. I expect they'll shovel her under today. Poor soul—

Wig

Vendredi Saint,

My darling love, (April 2, 1920)

Your letter on the gnu typewriter came yesterday. What a pearl it must be! I've never seen one I liked better. It is so distinguished that it's quite possible to write personal letters on it without feeling you've shouted them into the common ear—as you do with the old-fashioned kind. Two compliments flew from your letter.

I am very thankful you liked the reviews. The Beresford book was *awful*—dead as a tack. These people have no life at all. They never seem to renew themselves or to GROW. . . . The species is now adult and undergoes no other change, until its head-feathers turn white and fall out. . . . Awful!! Even if one does not acquire any 'fresh meat'—one's vision of what one possesses is constantly changing into something rich and strange, isn't it? I feel mine is. 47 Fitzherbert Terrace, p.e., is colouring beautifully with the years and I polish it and examine it and only now is it ready to come out of the store room and into the uncommon light of day.

Oh my stars! How I love to think of us as *workers*, writers—two creatures given over to Art. Not that I place Art higher than Love or Life. I cannot see them as things separate—they minister unto each other. And how I long for us to be *established* in our home with just a few precious friends with whom we can talk and be gay and rejoice. . . . *Ecce quam bonum et quam jucundum habitare fratres in unum! Sicut unguentum in capite, quod descendit in barbam, barbam Aaron.* (Now that surprised you, didn't it?) I'm a cultivated little thing, really.

It's a cold and windy day and makes me cough. I still cough, still walk with a stick, still have to rest nearly all the time. They still talk about me as tho' I were the size of a thimble. So you mustn't expect a very fierce girl and you mustn't be disappointed if I have to go slow.

Ignore it. Take it all as part of the present me. It's nothing to worry about—and I'm going to be 1000 times better as soon as I have seen Sorapure. Now goodbye for now, my own blessed *darling* little mate. You must be very sure not to make any preparations for me or to add one single worry to all your worries.

Ever your own devoted

Wig-wife

I see the *D.N.* quoted your *Nation* article. I feel there's a smile in the remark etc. 'It doesn't even make him laugh.' You seem very famous nowadays. I bought a lovely early morning T-tray shaped ⬯

Easter Sunday,

Dearest Own, (April 4, 1920)

Easter Sunday—pouring rain, 'parky' beyond words—pools in the garden, rows of goloshes in the bathroom, umbrellas in the marbil basins.

I got lovely presents. A silk egg full of chocs, a silk jersey trimmed with silver, a cigarette holder, two boxes for my dressing table, a pot of white cyclamen. The eggs were in the table napkins which were cunningly contrived birds' nests. The *Athenæum* came at lunch, but was seized and taken by Jinnie. I haven't seen it yet. I long to. Course I couldn't go and see old Schiff in this weather. I was *very* glad I couldn't. Your Thursday letter came today, darling.

I think it would be a famous idea to have sketches and stories.[1] I wrote one on the spot, called *Daphne*—about a plant. I'll try and bring a whole lot home, and you could stick them in under noms de plume—if you wanted to.

Yes, it's true about Catholics: their world is not our world—my *duty* is to *mankind*—theirs is a personal deity—a really-living KING with

In the *Athenæum*.

a flashing face who gives you rewards. I read a panegyric by a Jesuit
t'other day which did astonish me.

'God shall be our most passionate love. He shall kiss us with the kisses
of his mouth' and so on. It disgusted me. They horribly confuse
sexuality and the state of beatitude. I know really a good deal about
Catholics now. Of course there's no doubt J. is a saint. But she has
given herself up to the whole thing. She works like mad for the glory
of God—lives for his glory—refers everything to God or his saints, and
in fact it is to her what Art is to us. But it has *warped* her—even her. I
try to pretend she can see our point of view, but then she says of *Je ne
parle pas,* 'How *could* you say her big belly? I feel Our Lady would have
disliked it so much.' *Well*—what are you to say to that?

Oh, most exciting. Cousin Mac (the surgeon Laurie Macgavin) lives
a few miles from Broomies. Knows it. has been over to see it, wanted it
for Cousin Lou and Len (the deaf and dumb one, Connie's sister and
brother, great uncle Horatio Beauchamp's children). Mac says it was
too isolated for them but it's a great bargain, excellently built, could
be made up-to-date at a very small expense and is just the very climate
for me. He wrote 'Katherine could not have a better spot.' He has a
place called Dewbridge where he lives, there: I believe it's lovely. And
we are not far from the Leslies' encampment—old Kate Leslie and her
crew. They knew Broomies too. But don't be frightened, dearest love.
I won't let them disturb you. Laurie Macgavin is a fearfully nice chap
tho'—a Scottish surgeon. You'd like him and I'd value his opinion.
We *must* have that house. If we did want to sell it any time we could
always do so to one of their ramifications. But I *don't* want to sell it.

Boge, could you buy an ordinary folding canvas chair for me—
small—one that L.M. could carry on to the Heath for me and put under
a tree, so that I can work there? I've got the out of doors habit now and
like all people with lungs I feel *stifled* indoors. I mean to be the Mysterious Lady of Hampstead Heath this year. Wing can be trained to
carry me visitors' cards, can't he? Addio, precious darling love.

Ever your very own

Wig

Tuesday,

(April 6, 1920)

My own precious Bogey,

We are motoring to Nice this afternoon. Early lunch in hats and then
down come the maids with cushions and rugs for the car—the baby dog

is captured: 'Coming for nice tatas with Missie,' and he growls with joy. 'Has little Murry got her fur?' 'Where's Connie?' You know that kind of *upheaval*. It reminds me of my early days. May is going to look after me. The others want to shop, and I can't rush even if I would, so May, carrying the baby dog, trips along. 'Oh, *Ma*-dam! Isn't the little pot ever so sweet—and on a *blue* tray, Madam, with just a *little* cloth, not too big and a Mappin and Webb tea-service!' I can hear her already. She's such a little gem, carries the parcels and looks after one beautifully, and the Peke sits on her arm. 'Now, Chinnie, be a good girl, my ducksie-pet!'

Does that all sound very strange to you? I love it. I *bathe* in it. And it's all gay, and there are flowers and music and sparkling sea, and we go and have tea in a queer place and eat ice-cream, and little Murry has no choice but must drink chocolate.

'L'auto est là, Madame.'

Later: I'm in bed and have just had supper with brandy for a drink. The drive to Nice is really wonderful, Boge, through Roquebrune, Monte, Eze, Villefranche, Beaulieu—but Nice is *vile*. At least the shops are. I do hate great glaring glittering glass and gold shops where one walks miles to the ascenseur and where the employées look as though they lived on 10 francs a month. Mountains of jumpers, haystacks of *crêpe de chine* chemises—ugh! I retired and sat in the car and read the paper. On the way back we were stopped by the Deschanel cortège. Very gay—the streets marvellously decorated and a bataille de fleurs for the gentleman. It was rather fun. We cut in after the presidential car and before *La Presse* and *L'Eclaireur,* flying their flag, and were part of the procession—received the salutes and flowers and Vive Madame Deschanel. We bowed very nicely. At Roquebrune we stopped for a presentation, and the people crowded round, gaping. Connie (the Beauchamp in her) enjoyed it very much. I wish you could have seen Monaco with the minute soldiers guarding the palace and the little pepper-tree-fringed roads that lead up to it. Monaco is certainly *your* town.

But oh! I do hate the middle-class. Nice is the *paradis des bourgeois*. All the same, Boge, the Riviera isn't over-rated. It's superb. More than that one gets fearfully fond of it. It does in bits remind one so much of home, of N.Z.—the rocks and sea and the flowers. I am afraid I do want a Broomies here as well—two tiny houses: one in Sussex, one not far from Menton. Would you hate that, my darling?

My darling Boge, (April 6, 1920)

I've just got your note about *Je ne parle pas*. No, I certainly won't agree to those excisions if there were 500,000,000 copies in existence. They can keep their old £40 and be hanged to them. Shall I pick the eyes out of a story for £40. I'm furious. No, I'll never agree. I'll supply another story but that is all. The *outline* would be all blurred. It must have those sharp lines. *The Times* didn't object. As to *The Wind Blows*, I put that in because so many people had admired it (Yes, it's *Autumn II*, but a little different). Virginia, Lytton and queer people like Mary Hamilton and Bertie all spoke so strongly about it I felt I must put it in. But this had better be held over till I get back. I'll never consent. I'll take the book away first. Don't worry about it. Just tell —— he's a fool. As to *The German Governess* it *was* on my list and I asked you to include it!! (Caught out!) But don't you worry. It will have to wait. Of course I won't consent!

Wig

Wednesday,

My darling again, (April 7, 1920)

It's Wednesday. I'm off to lunch at Roquebrune with the Sydney Schiffs and to see their Gauguins and their Picassos. Your Sunday letter has come. Would you rather Richard didn't come to the station? Tell me and tell him.

Bogey, I feel I was too undisciplined about my story and Constable. I leave it to you. You're my cricket. If you agree to what they say— why then, all's well (and I DO want the money). Je t'aime.

Our queer correspondences again. I have been steeped in Shakespeare these last days with a note book—looking up every word, finding what are inkles and caddises—and I have felt that we must read more—you and I—read together. I nearly know the sheep shearing scene from *A Winter's Tale* by heart. It's the more *bewitching* scene—but that's one of my favourite plays. If I am strictly truthful I know nearly all of it *almost* by heart. And I began reading the songs in *Twelfth Night* in bed this morning early—

> Mark it Cesario, it is old and plain;
> The spinsters and the knitters in the sun
> And the free maids that weave their thread with bones
> Do use to chant it: it is silly sooth,

515

And dallies with the innocence of love,
Like the old age. . . .

Clo: Are you ready, sir?
Duke: Ay, prithee, sing.   (*Music*)
Clo: Come away, come away, death, etc.

Oh, how that does all ravish me. I think I could listen to that for a
small eternity. My dear love, we must read together—read aloud to
each other. Do you know, by the way, Alexander Smith's essay on
Chaucer?

Goodbye for now, dearest dear. What a miracle that we should love
each other and love the same other loves.

Your own

Wig-wife

(April 8, 1920)

Would you give enclosed letters to my manager, J.M.M. and ask him
to get his menials to post the necessary books to the gent? I think he
ought to have a copy of *Je ne parle pas* and be told about the Constable
book, but that's as my manager pleases. As to Biographical Note!

Née 14 Octobre à Nouvelle Zélande

Premier voyage âge de six mois

Première histoire publiée âge de neuf ans

Le reste de ma vie est passé en voyageant et en écrivant des short
'stories'. Written for Australian and English papers and reviews.

Wife of the brilliant poète et critique J.M.M. who is the famous
editor of the newly brought to life and prominent Athenæum.

Two cats.

K.M.

Your proposed amendments of Je ne parle pas are read, admired and
heartily approved by

    Your affectionate Client
        Katherine Mansfield Murry
           (Prize Scholar,
              English Composition,*   *Subject: 'A Sea Voyage'.
             Public School,
                Karori)

I cant draw no better fine herbefore find pen. but he's not bad is she?

Darling Bogey

I do wish I could draw. I'm always wanting to put little small drawings on the tops of your letters. & I had such a thrill when I made that little boy. & I'll have to take our Umbrella blows away this year. You know re the South of France I too have grown to like it far more than ever I did. The mechanical appearance goes & there usually shine the rocks & stones which remind me of New Zealand. Volcanic. & the sea is really a wonderful colour. Yes. The ground is lovely it. The air in the mountains is wonderful & then the trees. the pepper trees & the lemons. If only you shared my winters. & we had a minute Brooinchen here there re few prospects. early peas & lettuces & anemones... You would be happy I know. I'm in no fit to Bandol of air because its not fine enough I mth. Between here & Nice there are long silted unspoilt corners in the mountains. But we can build & in 30 years time. That will do.

517

Friday. Winter. Wind and raging sea. Cold. Big Fire.

My very very own, (April 9, 1920)

Do not overpraise me. When I read what you had written about the drawings I flew two pink flags. But if you like them a little I'll do you some more—better—and put them in a frame for you when they're good enough. I entirely agree with your suggestions *re Je ne p. p.* Please invest yourself with Full Powers, darling, and forgive me for giving you so much trouble. This month will end it. This letter (Tuesday) is the most astonishingly sweet letter. It's one of those letters which make me feel quite faint for joy. I feel I *must* see you—*must* hold you—*be held* —must say: 'You know . . . Bogey . . . my darling.' 'My darling'— that's what you are. Darling—darling—and my heart is full of love. I feel deeply your obligation to make the *A.* a success. It must be done. You can do it—it's your duty towards your neighbours. Yes, you're a poet but you're too true a poet not to be a poet OF your time. When I heard old Schiff the other day praising the paper (praising it so rightly) and saying what you were doing for English literature, I felt you *could* not let all these people down—you must carry the torch. They do look to you. When Schiff said the other day: 'I feel confident that in a few years it will make or break a man—the criticism passed on him by the *Athenæum*'. It's pretty terrific—or rather—you are.

L.M. is blowing off to the poste this afternoon with a wire *re* Constable. Act on it, darling, won't you? and if you *can* so fix things that they send me the money *as soon as possible* you will greatly oblige me. You see I am practically determined to take either a flat or small villa next year. I want to ∴ pay for it while the exchange is high. Not pay all—that I couldn't do—but pay part of my Constable money immediately. *This is very important* to me, old boy. As it works out, I think the advantages are greater in being my own mistress. Of course, you can't advise me, Mr. Absurdity. You're my *literary* adviser, that's all, I want it to be in Menton if possible because I simply love this little place— LOVE IT. If it weren't for you England wouldn't see me again for a very long day. I'd live at La Turbie in the summer and here in the winter. But YOU are in London and so my whole heart is there until we are free enough to live between Broomies and the S. of France. Even then I don't want to live far from Menton—because I can't live all the year round away from *music,* and opera especially. One can get both here and at Monte. You need never go. But I'll often take a slave and descend to either town to hear a symphony.

But, above all, I long for the time when we shall be together 'all the year round'. It's not yet, but it will come and now we know how to receive it. Life—strange life—teaches. Or, no—one *learns*. I wouldn't be without these months for anything in the world. Do you feel that? Without them we were going all wrong, getting into an entirely false position. This separation has been and will be for ever the great fact of my life—my secret—when, you know, 'something happened'. No one knew what—but after that 'all was changed'.

I had a lovely letter from the old boy today and one from Brett— pathetic.

L.M. arrived to take letter. Goodbye darling

Own Wig

To Bogey of Broomies   Sunday,
My very own,   (April 11, 1920)

All yesterday, off and on, I had waves of delight at the thought of Broomies. I could not have imagined that the fact of us being real little landowners could have made such an extraordinary difference. The feeling of *security*—have you got it, too? The enormous pleasure of putting up a wall if we choose or putting in a fireplace. I'll never be able to say what Broomies means, and you found it—my own explorer. It's our island. I feel the anxiety about money in the future is lessened, too, don't you? All our geese will lay golden eggs before they become swans. . . . But more than anything I keep writing short prefaces and putting in the left hand bottom-of-page corner 'Broomies, 1922'. Also, 'We shall be at Broomies until the fin d'Octobre, when we leave for Genêt Fleuri—our small villa in the South'. Oh, Destiny, be kind. Let this be. Let these two children live happy ever after.

By the way, what with these two names, we shall be calling our small son Richard Plantagenet Murry if he doesn't hurry up. I see SUCH books. Golden bees fly out of them—young dandelions sprout between the pages—the critic discovers the first small aconite on p. 54, and by the end of the book he is even slightly freckled. I'm very silly. Forgive me.

L.M. spends all next week hunting for a villa or a flat for next year. I am decided not to be with these people, and the flat I saw—perfect though it was—had more stairs than I like to remember. She'll find something and I'll take it, however. The weather was awful yesterday, il pleut averse today. But a bird sings and it is very warm. I do hope May will be warm.

Yes, my precious, we'll divide our time between Sussex which is you, and the South of France, which is me, mystically speaking. We shall never saddle ourselves with any big responsibility or large house—but we'll live beautifully. It makes another great joy in my coming back here this winter to know I'll have the Schiffs at Roquebrune. Do I take violent fancies, Boge? I must say at present I love Violet Schiff. I think you would, too. You would certainly find her very beautiful, as I do. I want you to see her and to talk to her. She is extremely sympathetic.

Jinnie has just come in with your Thursday letter. What a shower of pearls and diamonds tumbles out of your letters! Heavens, how I do love you! Yes, you are perfectly right about the book. Let it be as you wish. I am only too willing to abide by your decision. I am so sorry to have given you so much trouble, dearest love.

Hardy thrills me.[1] It's an anniversary, I expect—but whose? Oh, it's *very* thrilling. And that he should have chosen you. I confess I'd dearly love to go down and see him with you one week-end—very quietly. *I* wouldn't talk, but I like to see him and see you together. It's very good about the American publisher. Richard, of course, rushed to tell me.

How sweet you are! You are so wonderful. I wonder people don't see the gold ring round your hair. *I* think you're perfeck.

I fearfully want to see your review of James's letters. Boge, the paper wants a touch of Lytton and Forster—it looks a trifle depressing, too. There's so much small type. But that's just *en passant*. Goodbye for now, my blessed one.

Wig of Broomies

Would you *lend* me your copy of *Prelude,* if you have one?

Monday,
(April 12, 1920)

Dearest of All,

Time seems to be flying this month and I have only 2 more Mondays here after this one. If only the wedder is fine and fayre in May! I don't think it would be possible to have fogs now, do you? This gorgeous air and almost certain sunshine give one quite a horror of such things. Today for instance—it's 9 a.m.; it's hot. The sun is pure gold and a great swag of crimson roses outside my window fills the room with a sweet smell. Oh, how I have come to *love* this S. of France—and to dislike the

Thomas Hardy had written offering a poem to the *Athenæum*.

Katherine Mansfield   April 1920

French. The French here don't count; they are just *cultivateurs au bord de la mer,* but it's the voice of la France *officielle* which I loathe so. You should have read *L'Eclaireur* on this last crise; it was a very pretty little eye-opener.

But, Bogey, I do so long for you to know this country in the Spring. It's like the Middle Ages, somehow. I feel it's Elizabethan spring— earlier—far—oh, I don't know *when.* But driving up those valleys and seeing the great shower of flowers and seeing the dark silver olives and the people working in the beanfields—one feels as though one were part of the *tradition* of spring.

Outside my window are two lizards. Sometimes they come in and look at me and their throats pant in a funny way. I wish I could bring them home.

Oh, my dearest, I love the sun. I made a fuss about it at San Remo, but that was because I was ill—but I love it. To WORK and to play in our garden—in woods and fields and on mountains and pebbly shores —with you. And to sometimes draw on thin suède gloves and go into cities and look at pictures and hear music and sit at a café with a long drink watching the passing show (you with a large parcel of books on the chair by you). That's the life for me—to live like artists, always free and *warm-hearted* and always *learning.*

I can say great long pieces of poetry for you now—heavenly bits . . . and you must tell me things.

Yours, yours for ever,

Wig of Broomies

Precious Bogey *darling,* (April 14, 1920)

The Schiffs have just been. They are giving a luncheon party for me tomorrow—and they came in to beg me not to bother to talk. 'Let *them* do the running'. Also Schiff wanted to tell me he'll send a car for me and send me back in it. He has had my disease and rather exaggerates the care one ought to take. But it's all in *more* than kindness. Well, if I do take fancies to people, love, it's nothing to the fancies they take to your Wig-wife. It makes me feel so horribly unworthy and it excites me so. I long to be worthy of the sweet things they tell me. I'm not: it's all nonsense. But they find something strange in me like people do in you. We're Broomies and they know it. But Mrs. Schiff says suddenly. 'You're such a lovely little thing, I want to cry.' (I only tell you that in dead privacy: she feels like Anne feels.) It's not *false*. There are certain people who do make me feel *loving,* warm-hearted, tender, and—like children feel. Anne is one. Violet Schiff is another. Did I tell you that (it's confidential) Schiff wrote *Richard Kurt*?

Oh, to be among people with whom one can discuss *prose*—and its possibilities. Not very seriously, or well, but at any rate to discuss it and be understood. But you must meet Violet Schiff. She's one of the most attractive *women* that we have known, physically *and* mentally. You'd admire her—you'd like her and her mind. I am frightfully fatigued with talking to people who care for THE CHURCH or (D——and Co.) dress—envy, hate and all uncharitableness.

God mend all! I've had no letters today, my darling. As the time passes, I get awfully impatient for letters. Today fortnight we shall be in Paris. Oh, my plans for the future! Oh, Bogey, will you really want to be *alone* with me as I shall with you? Will you really say: 'Darling, I must have you to myself' and mean it beyond words? To be in a room with you, hearing you, watching you—my heart—to look after you again and see that you have lovely lovely food and that all is in exquisite order. Oh, will it matter to you—having a wife? Will you ask people to dine with us and will you ask me sometimes to lunch or come to tea with me? Oh—to love as I love you!!

Know that Jaeger woolly you bought me? I got a skirt of the same stuff today—all woolly and furry. It looks the *spit* of Broomies with a very funny hat which might have been made of chopped bracken. It's the best country ensemble I've ever seen because it's very amusing but at the same time it is distinguished.

Wig of Broomies

[Drawing of a sea-urchin]   Thursday,
My own Bogey,   (April 15, 1920)

Your Saturday afternoon letter is here about *King John*. It's such a dull old play, too. How horrid that you must do it! I simply long to read your article on James. What I saw in *The Times* horrified me—arrogant, monstrous pomposity—even from early youth. I thought the article was a bit of fearful pretentiousness, too, and not worth a brass farden. James makes me ashamed for *real* artists. He's a pompazoon. I am thankful we never received any favours. They can keep him. And then holding up his shocked hands at Thomas Hardy! How *great*

Hardy is beside the other. Oh, I DO hope you will speak your mind and put all right for those who are frightened to say.

Yesterday I went to the Oceanographical Museum and Aquarium at Monaco. It was one of those experiences which make me stamp with fury because you are not sharing it. I wanted to telegraph you to promise that one day we'd spend a whole week in Monaco together and live in this place. My dearest—one is richer for life by such a museum. The AQUARIUM finished me and I had to lean over a tank of slumbering tortoises and weep because of the fishes I had seen and the worm-high worm-built forests. I've got the guide for you. I'll show it you one Sunday afternoon.

The little town of Monaco is the cleanest on earth, I should think. You must see the palace courtyard with its cannons and cannon-balls (all toy), pepper-trees, limes and platanes, ancients in green with red facings, gold lace shoulders and hats [a drawing] like that. 'Tis a sweet place. There are benches where one can sit and look at it all in tumpany with nurses in black velvet bodices, white chemisettes and lace caps, tossing up month-old patriots. But all these things *without you*—that's the rub, Bogey. There was a little cream house with powder-blue persiennes and a carpet of rose geraniums hung over its pink wall. I wanted to live there with you—another life. You know I love you beyond repair—and I'll be home in a fortnight today. Oh dear! *And we are propriétaires!!!!!* My love.

Wig of Broomies

Thursday,
My darling,   (April 15, 1920)

I envy you 'madly' going to see *Cymbeline*. If you knew how full my mind is of Shakespeare! It's a perfect world—his pastoral world. I roam through the Forest of Arden and sit on the spiced Indian sands laughing with Titania. When we *do* get a small quiet moment—*what* talks! But you are going to Stratford-on-Avon. Lucky, lucky boy! And you won't remember for a moment that was the first English country your wife saw, and she used to walk about there with her hair down her back, wearing a pinky-grey hat and even in those days carrying one of those small green Shakespeares (but of course, it was Amleto, then.)

Talk about excitement, inward excitement. I wish I could keep it down. The fire—the beacon, you know—the Bon Feu of bonfires is blazing away already with a kind of soft silent roaring most difficult to bear. We meet—Heaven defend us!—this day fortnight at 9 of the clock.

Yesterday afternoon Ida and I went driving up to Castellar—it's more lovely than Gorbio even. You must come here in the spring. L.M. is hunting hard for a flat or villa. I'll have to pay about £60 for the season i.e. £10 a month. It can't be done for less in comfort—and it must be in Garavan: that's the other bay, the one towards Italy with the superb old town and old ancient port built to one side of it. L.M. has gone there today bathing.

I love your comment on *The Fair Maid of the West*. *My* day book contains a regular gallimaufry of things—from 'curtains for studio windows and landing windows must be lined' to hints for lunches and dinners taken from Annette here, to notes and drawings of flowers, and their leaves, buds and seed-pods minutely described, to observations on a peke burying a non-existent bone, to—Shakespeare again. Thus the whirligig. . . .

It's grey; it's rather cold. It's going to rain. I shan't be able to go to my party. *Oh Weh, oh Weh!*

Fair young King of Broomies thy dear Love and Queen salutes thee.

Wig Regina

Sunday,

My own,   (April 18, 1920)

This letter was never posted[1] and here's Sunday déjà. I did go to my lunch after all. It was very enjoyable. A man called Tinayre sang—and the Schiffs' house is made for singing.

Yesterday, Saturday, horrible things happened. I had my review all ready to send and Ida never came. It was not a day to go out in and I was dead tired. I finally did go out, feeling certain to meet her carriage, didn't meet it and had to rush, and couldn't get a carriage and reached the poste 5 minutes late and got a carriage and tore up to the station where nobody would help me or tell me anything. I posted it in a box there, then wired you, then got back into the carriage and you see me, don't you darling? weeping away *furiously* in face of all Menton. I got out at Rumpelmeyer's and drank boiling black coffee and ice water, came home a very pore girl and lay down with a brandy for tumpany. Schiff came in later and sat with me. His rage against the world because

1 This refers to the second letter dated April 15, 1920.

524

I had had such a bad time didn't make it better—and even now I can't get over it or quite forgive Ida until I know it has arrived. If you only knew what agony it is to fail you—what an effort to work (8 interruptions yesterday) in stranger's houses! I don't want to make a moan tho'.

I have taken my flat, paid the deposit and asked Mrs. Harrison to find me a cook for next season. The flat is *ideal*. Three bedrooms, maid's room, salon, salle à manger, bath with geyser, kitchen with gas, housemaid's pantry, cabinet de toilette for your dressing-room. It's exquisite —furnished by an Italian contessa—all dark wood in my bedroom, grey velvet curtains and hangings, lined with blue brocade and a blue silk édredon. Quite *lovely*. Big soft carpets everywhere—fine glass— with plenty of small silver teapots and so on—and at least 1 dozen copper saucepans in the tiled kitchen.

I shall be able to give little parties next year to my friends here—for the Schiffs will be here, the Tinayres, Lytton's married sister and so on. I've paid the deposit and shall leave part of the rent to be paid at the present exchange. Then I want you to come for Xmas if you can, and I thought Brett might care for a month here (12 guineas, I'd ask her: couldn't do it for less). It has the most superb view and a concierge on the premises. It looks very like Sir John and Lady Middleton Murry, which pleases me.

Darling, I love the thought of North Devon. You'd better write *soon* to that hotel. Of course I don't mind it being far from the railway. Why ever should I? But do you mind very much if I take a maid with me? It's such a bore dressing and undressing and packing and getting things, and she'd be a comfort travelling. It's such a waste of time and energy for you to do all these things, and I can't do them, and we want a *holiday*. I don't see very well how we can do without a maid for a month. All our buttons will come off and we'll have no clean hankies. I thought perhaps Violet's or Gertie's sister might come—or I'll get someone from an agency for the month.

Well, my own precious Boge—of course, I understand about the £10. But I'd like to help you, but I can't. You see, I've had to pay for 2 wagon-lits and 1st floor room in Paris, and then there is all the tipping etc. here. I'll be très hard up by the time I get back. Be sure to order a Hampstead car, won't you, that will take the luggage, and make certain of it, darling? Oh dear, I can't believe it, not even now. I just *go on*.

Your own
Wife

Tuesday,

My precious darling,   (April 20, 1920)

All being well I shall be at the Palais Lyon on Wednesday until Thursday. Do you think L'Hôte would come and see me on Wednesday afternoon—or Valéry? If they'd leave a *bleu* letting me know when to expect them, I'd be delighted. I want to see them for the firm—to have a chat, don't you know, and hear what is happening. It's the most divine day.

I am staying in bed until lunch as I had a heavy day yesterday buying small presents to bring back and so on. Exhausting work because one gets so frightfully excited as well. Connie went with me in the morning and bought *me* an antique brooch, very lovely; three stones set in silver. Then she bought me a pastel blue muslin frock with frills like panniers at the side. Ida, who was by, said she thought Connie had a very bad influence on me because she spoiled me so. And the poor old dear got pink just like Granma used to and said, 'Well, the child has had no fun, no life, no chance to wear pretty things for two years. I'm *sure* Jack would want to do what I'm doing. . . .' You remember in Italy how I longed to return to Life with all kinds of lovely possessions. Funny it should have all come true. I also bought the most exquisite fruit plates with small white grapes and gold leaves on them pour la famille Murry, and a dish, high, to match, to take the breath. I've no money. I think I must be a little bit mad. Oh, could I bring the flowers, the *air,* the whole heavenly climate as well: this darling little town, these mountains—It is simply a small jewel—Menton . . . and its *band* in the jardins publiques with the ruffled pansy beds—the white donkeys standing meek, tied to a pole, the donkey women in black pleated dresses with flat funny hats. All, all is so terribly attractive. I'd live years here with you. I'm immensely attached to it all and in the summer we'd go up to the Alpes Maritimes and live in the small spotless inns with milk hot from the cow and eggwegs from the hen—we'd live in those steep villages of pink and white houses with the pine forests round them—where your host serves your dinner wearing a clean white blouse and sabots. Yes, dearest darling, I'm in love with the Alpes Maritimes. I don't want to go any further. I'd like to live my life between Broomies and them.

Your Sunday and Saturday letter has come. You are a darling to have made the garden so fair and had the grass cut. I've been thinking about that grass. You are having a worrying time about Richard, dear love. Couldn't the decision be left till I talk it over with you? But, after all, there is nothing to talk over with me that you haven't mentioned. If Richard is going to be a *real artist* he must have his chance and if I have the good fortune to make money, you know I'll always help. As matters stand I spend every penny I have, because, you see, I *can't* live except in a rather luxurious way, and I can only get better by resting— taking carriages—living as though I had £800 a year of my own instead of £400. This journey home for L.M. and me, for instance, has cost—I really can't say what—telegraphing to Paris, to the boat, to the other side, with *wagon lits* and so on. But I can't do it except like that. I've written Rutter 3 times for the money for my story and I've not had a penny nor have I had a cheque from the paper this month. But all the same we shall be all right, I know, and we shall take Richard, and when he's here with me, he'll not cost you a sou.

I read your article on Negro Sculpture last night. It was *excellent*. I thought Fry most feeble in the *Athenæum*. As usual he was afraid to say what he felt. He wanted—a small fry—to be in the cultured swim. Will you take me to see some pictures when I get home?

I'm lunching with the Schiffs tomorrow. It will be our last meeting until they come back to London. Schiff—well, you'll see what he's like. I was at a big lunch the other day (about 10 people) at their house and you should have heard the talk against *The Nation* and FOR the *A*. Massingham, according to some really rather intelligent men there, gets his facts hopelessly wrong about French affairs. But I learnt a great deal of interesting facts about the French—not to their credit. I'll tell you in about 3 years' time when the other things have been told.

Darling, don't make my home-coming an effort—don't curse the upset of it all. I will try not to show how glad I am and so frighten my darling little mate. Don't feel you have to meet me even. It is very dreadful to know that even Love is an effort to you at times and I don't want you to make that effort. Feel—oh, well, she'll make things easy and L.M. will be on the spot, and I shan't have to think of puddings. Years ago, I wanted to change things in you—I wanted you to be less 'vague', less silent, more—almost—practical. But you must always remember that was years ago. Now I don't want you to be *anybody* but your natural self—free to wander away or to keep quiet just as it pleases you. I want you to feel that with me you can be absolutely FREE in spirit. If I find your hat's too awful I shall buy you other hats—or if.

your hair is too dreadful I shall seize the moment and brush it straight—
but you must not *exert* yourself or pretend that you have to look after
me. I'm very independent please altho' I am

Your own little

Wig

Please tell the old boy

Dearest Bogey,   (April 20, 1920)

This is about Richard. Of course I am entirely in favour of the
scheme. It is splendid to think we shall have a painter in the family and
I rejoice greatly.

As regards money—he can, as you say, always have Broomies at his
back—a sure haven. And then I'd like him to know that I am certain
to have money one of these days—certain—I mean money that will be
left me. This, as long as our children are provided for, Richard can
always count on. At any rate, however big our family (no fear of that)
I shall always $\begin{cases} \text{give} \\ \text{leave} \end{cases}$ Richard enough to live on without working. I
am determined, within the next few years, to have a house in the South
here. He can always come and paint and be free of all money worries.

I love and admire Richard and it's simply the greatest good fortune
to have a chance of making him happy. Here we are. He can take from
us without ever dreaming of paying back: he can just be our brother-
in-art as well as in Life—and all success to him and a proud sister's
blessing.

We *must* see him through.

Goodbye for now my darling

For ever and amen your

Wig

Thursday,

My dearest,   (April 22, 1920)

Your letter with the piece about Raquel Meller has just come. I hope
you have good weather at Stratford. Kay writes it's awful and that I'll
never stay over there. I *wish* it would be finer: it's quite frightening to
think of the English climate—or of Paris even. As to London with its
sights and sounds I was only saying to L.M. last night it needs a very
great gasp to swallow it. But you and home and the kittens—all are in

Hampstead, so Hampstead is the tall rock rearing its awful form with the sunshine nestling on its head. But pray *pour le beau temps!*

About your *Cinnamon and Angelica,* I am frightfully anxious to see reviews. Richard and C-S have done it beautifully. Yesterday Connie began reading part of it aloud—Angelica and Mrs. Carraway (oughtn't she to have been Mistress?) I wish to God it will be a success. It's only a question of time but I know what it means to be recognized *immediately.* There is nothing so wonderful or that has so renewing an effect upon an author. My love, I wish it for you with all my heart.

Just let me look at your list of friends again. No, we can't really include Virginia. I don't know Tomlinson at all personally. I can't call him or T. Eliot or group (3) my friends except in so far as they are people who I feel certain *are* right people. Tommy and Eliot because of their books the other (3) because you know and like them. Brett is a dear creature but again—yes, she's a friend, but much more a friend of yours than mine. Violet Schiff I'd include and Schiff without the smallest hesitation or doubt. I like him as much as I do his wife, but in of course an entirely different way. He attracts me *tremendously* and his great kindness—sensitiveness—almost childishness endear him to me. In fact, I'd head my list with those 2, but that's because I look at people from a different angle to what you do. Then I'd include Anne Rice—*definitely.* I love her as a 'being', as Kot would say.

What a silly I am! Now I see you only call your list 'nice people'. Then I subscribe to it, of course. I'm sure they are nice—but that's not enough, is it?

I am glad the singer is wonderful. I shall go to hear her as soon as I can. Let me be frank. Your article on her bears the impress of great fatigue. It saddens me that you should be so painfully overworked—painfully unable to respond 'without an effort'. 'We shall learn it chiefly from the assiduous frequentation of our own great heritage.' There—that's what I mean. You must not feel too strongly your duty to bear the age we live in upon your back. At any rate, faced with a fellow artist—I'd greet her *as* an artist and let them understand what they may. That's our privilege. We can explain later—obliquely. Do I talk nonsense?

Wig

Will you ask Eliot to supper on Sunday? I want to see him very much and have messages for him. But if you're not inclined, it's no matter, dearest.

My own dearest,

A dinner party here: 18. I'm wearing my purpil dress. I thought I shouldn't be able to get into it—but *pas de chance*. I'm also wearing *real* small pearl earrings—a farewell present. They are very lovely—being real, they have such a different feeling. I rather dread the dinner. Oh I'd so much rather go to my Schiffs. Mr. Schiff is a kind of literary fairy godfather to one. He looks after one so perfectly and so gently, and Violet Schiff seemed to me the last time far more beautiful and more fascinating than before. She will *fascinate* you—the movement of her lips, her eyes, her colour,—all her beauty. And their house is always for me the house where *lovers* dwell. He loves her perfectly. And her quick 'Darling!' and hand outstretched. I mustn't talk of these people for I should talk too much. They are so real and dear and beautiful to me, and they understand one's work. Our farewell has been postponed until tomorrow. We are going to Eze by car: it's a tiny Saracen village on the Grand Corniche road.

Stratford sounds *awful*, my darling, hopelessly awful—and no pyjamas to crown all! If we'd been there together we should have fought for good dry beds, but even then we couldn't fight for good dry skies. I think I'll learn plays by heart and give representations like Mrs. Hannibal Williams used to.

I sent you today four assiettes très anciennes and a fruit dish. They are *perfect*. There were no more to be had. And they cost me—*Oh, dear*. Now I am quite broke, really broke—it's awful!

About Devonshire—is it too remote? Are the sanitary arrangements perfect? Can one drive? Your wife can't be planted on a cliff yet, alas, and I'm a little bit frightened of your hotel. I feel I ought to be nearer civilization. But let's decide that when I return. I have an *idear*.

Sunday. Brilliant fine. Oranges for breakfast and a huge bouquet of sweet peas—AND a letter from you. That Festa, my own boy, must have been a most disgusting affair.

Oh, how I agree about Shylock! I think *The Taming of the Shrew* is so *deadly* too. I am certain Bill never wrote it: he bolstered up certain speeches, but that is all. It's a hateful, silly play, so badly constructed and arranged. I'd never go to see it. I think we shall have a Shakespeare festival one year at Broomies—get actors there to study their parts—act out of doors—a small festa—a real one. I'll be stage director. *I am dead serious about this.*

Really, it's grilling hot today! I feel inclined to make a noise like a cicada.

Just now Miss Helen Fullerton shouted from the garden: 'Come on to the balcony and be took!' She had her camera. She'd just returned from early Communion. Jinnie has just come in from Mass.

Oh, this climate, this weather, this place. Ill never leave here another year before the end of May. It's too perfect. Even June is exquisite, I am sure. Adorable South of France. How I have loved it!

Well, I won't write again. Goodbye, my precious little mate. Go slow and be a good boy—not a tired one. Be sure you have a car *engaged*, won't you? Now begins a new chapter—much newer—quite different (so I imagine) to what you think.

Your own wife
Wig

It is difficult to define so subtle an impression, but, having read these letters in their sequence many times, the feeling abides with me that, taken as a whole, the letters which Katherine wrote while she was at the Villa Flora, Menton, are less spontaneous and more 'artificial'—if the word be permissible—than any others. As I remember, that was my impression at the time of receiving them; it has become confirmed with the years. Perhaps the cause of it is to be found in some sense that Katherine had that she was in a false position. Not merely was she living a life of luxury compared to anything she had experienced before—and there was always a struggle in her soul between a desire for luxury and a desire for simplicity, in which the desire for simplicity finally triumphed; but this life of luxury had been conferred upon her for a purpose, with an arrière pensée, in order that she might be converted to Roman Catholicism. Katherine was aware of this, and resisted the pressure; but at that time she had the strength neither of body or of mind to sacrifice the comfort for the freedom of spirit, which in more normal circumstances she would have chosen.

She returned to 2 Portland Villas at the end of April. The apparent improvement in her health was not sustained. In August she arranged to rent the villa Isola Bella at Menton, and arrived there on September 13. *The first of the following letters was a note written to me while we were both at Hampstead.*

Dear Darling,   (June, 1920)

Forgive me. I believe I always do 'start it'. It's become a half-unconscious habit with me to exaggerate my opinions whenever I speak to you just to *provoke* your attention—to stir you—rouse you. It is simply horrid. I never talk in that extreme dogmatic way to others you know. I hear myself even *lying* to you to bring you out of your cave. Of course, I am not as anti-Sorley as 'all that'. What I have said to you isn't my opinion at all.

It all narrows down to the old evil. No time to talk anything *out* or to think or to be gently poised. No time for that long breath. So we are both unjust to each other very often, and sometimes I *know* I am unjust in my criticism.

It's so difficult to explain: we have to take things on trust. A whole book wouldn't explain it fully. But let's try and get free and write—live and write. Anything else isn't worth living. You see we are both abnormal: I have too much vitality—and you not enough.

Your
Wig

Villa Isola Bella, Menton-Garavan,
Tuesday,

Darling Bogey,   (September 14, 1920)

What shall I tell you first? I have thought of you often and wondered if the beau temps is chez vous aussi, now that I've gone away.

We had a good journey but a slight contretemps in Paris. Ida disappeared with the porter to find a taxi, and she forgot the door she'd gone out—rushed off to another and lost me. After about half an hour I appealed to the police but they were helpless. The poor creature had lost her head and when we did meet finally it was only because I saw her in the distance and simply *shouted*. This tired me and made my nose bleed and I had a very bad night and had to do my review in bed next day, being fanned and bathed with eau de cologne. It's of no importance *to me* but I felt *all the time* I was betraying you and the paper. Forgive me once again.

We arrived here yesterday at 4-50 after a day of terrific heat. Menton felt like home. It was really bliss to sit in the voiture and drive through those familiar streets and then up a queer little leafy 'way' and then another at right angles, to a gate all hidden by green where la bonne Annette stood waving her apron and the peke leapt at her heels. This villa is—so far—perfect. It has been prepared inside and out to such an extent that I don't think it will ever need a hand's turn again. The path from the gate to the two doors has a big silver mimosa showering across it. The garden is twice as big as I imagined. One can live in it all day. The hall is black and white marble. The salon is on your right as you enter—a real little salon with velvet-covered furniture and an immense dead clock and a gilt mirror and two *very* handsome crimson vases which remind me of fountains filled with blood. It has 2 windows one looks over the garden gate, the others open on to the terrace and look over the sea. I mustn't forget to mention the carpet with a design of small beetles which covers the whole floor. The dining room is equally charming in its way—and has French windows, too. It abounds in cupboards full of wessels and has a vrai buffet with silver teapot, coffee and milk jug which catch the flashing eye. All is delightful. There are even very lovely blue glass finger bowls. . . . On the other side of the passage is the garde-linge big enough for all our boxes as well. The linen is overwhelming. It is all in dozens—even to maids' aprons. . . . The kitchen premises are quite shut off with a heavy pair of doors. The kitchen gleams with copper. It's a charming room and there's a big larder and a scullery big enough for a workshop and outside there's a garden and three large caves and the lapinière. Upstairs are four bedrooms—the maid's on the entresol. The others have balconies and again are carpeted all over and sumptuous in a doll's house way.

Annette had prepared everything possible. The copper kettle boiled. Tea was laid. In the larder were eggs in a bowl and a cut of cheese on a leaf and butter swimming and milk, and on the table coffee, a long bread, jam, and so on. On the buffet a dish heaped with grapes and figs lying in the lap of fig leaves. She had thought of everything and moreover everything had a kind of chic—and she in her blue check dress and white apron sitting down telling the news was a most delightful spectacle.

The heat is almost as great as when we arrived last year. One can wear nothing but a wisp of silk, two bows of pink ribbon and a robe de mousseline. Moustiques and moucherons are in full blast; we are both bitten to death already. They are frightful. But so far I can accept them without a reproach, the compensations are so great.

I must tell you a very big date palm grows outside my bedroom balcony window. At the end of the garden wall—(a yellow crumbling wall) there is a vast magnolia full of rich buds. There is a tap in the garden. In the vegetable garden the French artichokes are ready to eat and minute yellow and green marrows. A tangerine tree is covered in green balls.

I hope all this description doesn't bore you, darling. But I content myself with thinking you are going to see it yourself one day, and so my description is only 'in advance'.

The view is *surpassingly* beautiful. Late last night on the balcony I stood listening to the tiny cicadas and to the frogs and to someone playing a little chain of notes on a flute.

I do not know *what* it is about this place. But it is enough just to be here for everything to change. I think already of the poetry you would write if you lived such a life. I wish you were not tied. I have always at the bottom of my deep cup of happiness that dark spot, which is that you are not living as you would wish to live.

Here is Annette with a big dish of fresh lemons, broken off with the leaves remaining. And it's lunch-time. The heat!

Goodbye darling. Take care of yourself. I hope you have good tennis and that all goes well.

Yours ever

Wig

My darling Bogey,   (September 15, 1920)

Your letter and card this morning were so perfect that (only you will understand this) I felt you'd brought up a little kitten by Wingley and put it on our bed and we were looking at it together. But it was a very kitten of very kittens . . . with wings. I must answer it this once and risk breaking the agreement *not* to write. But my letter to you was so inferior to yours to me.

Yes, that suddenness of parting—that last moment—But this last time I had a deep, strange *confidence,* a feeling so different to that other desperate parting when I went to France. We are both so much stronger and we *do* see our way and we do know what the future is to be. That doesn't make me miss you less, though. . . .

Don't ask my parding humbly. Open any letter you like. You know you can; I only pretend to mind. I like you to open them, for some queer reason. I'll reply to Methuen tomorrow. I've got the two novels for this week, thank you. I'll write to old Sorapure about that vaccine. You were right. It was a case of moral cowardice.

I'm in bed—not very O.K. The moustiques have bitten me and I've had pains and fever and dysentery. Poisoned, I suppose. It was almost bound to happen. But don't worry. Annette is in the kitchen and her soups and rice climb up the stairs.

I think I've got a maid, too, Mme. Reveilly, 5bis. Rue des Poilus. She's a police inspector's *sister* and she looks indeed as though she had sprung out of a nest of comic policemen. Fat, dark, sitting on the sofa edge, grasping, *strangling* indeed a small black bead bag. 'Si, vous cherchez *une personne de confiance* Madame et *pas une imbécile* . . .' she began. I felt that was a poor compliment to my appearance. Did I look like a person who wantonly cherched imbeciles to do the house work? But of course all the time she recounted her virtues I saw the most charming imbecile with woolly shoes like rabbits and a great broad beaming smile . . . which I couldn't help dismissing rather regretfully.

The villa is even lovelier than it was. Once I am up again and out again, I feel it will be almost *too* fair. I do miss you, tho'. I have (I've told you a thousand times) always such a longing to share all that is good with you and you alone. *Remember that.* Events move so awfully strangely. We live and talk and tear our *Daily News* up together and all the while there is a growth going on—gorgeous deep glories like bougainvilleas twine from your window to mine. . . .

Tell me all you can but don't worry to tell me. I only want just what comes into your head. After today I shall begin sending a card a day (for 40 cents pay).[1] Yes, you'll have a photograph when the moustiques are less like mousquetaires.

I've begun my journal book. I want to offer it to Methuen—to be ready this Xmas. Do you think that's too long to wait? It ought to be rather special. *Dead* true—and by dead true I mean like one takes a sounding—(yet gay withal). Oh, it's hard to describe. What do you advise? The novels, dear love, won't bear re-hashing—not *really*. I can imagine what a difficulty your Harris is. The idea of it excites me awfully—your exquisite writing!

Yours for ever

Wig

One of Katherine's particular songs: 'I worked all day for forty cents pay. . . .'

re F. The letter is of course for you to read.

Darling Bogey,   (September 16, 1920)

It is imbecile and odious that you should be so troubled. What F. refers to as the Chelsea period and good received beats me. But *it is true* that he does possess letters written during my acquaintance with him which I would give any money to recover. And it is true that especially if he is married he will never cease threatening. What I propose is this. I talked it over with Ida. She agreed to give me £40. I want you to go with F. to a solicitor, receive the letters, get his sworn statement and hand him my cheque for the amount. It's *not* a waste of £40. I couldn't ask or get it from Ida on another pretext but I don't hesitate now. Will you wire me if you agree? And that ends *all communication with him*. As to the letters, needless to say they are yours. I'd like them destroyed as they are, but that's for you to say, darling.

I'm better today, fever gone, but weak as a blutterfly and *thin* as a match. All well except I can't bear you should be troubled with all this.

                                                                                  Tig

The clock goes perfectly but it has a surprised   Thursday,
look and an interrogatory tick.   (September 16, 1920)

Hullo, darling. These are going to be my cards.[1] They are more private. Do you see the good advice written on the sides? What else would you do with it? But you know the kind of people who use these cards in France . . . people who have one pen a generation.

Let's see. What's the news? (1) Where is my *Daily News*? I haven't seen one since Saturday. This is *V.* great treachery on your part, darling Boge. I shall miss all that Eastbourne case—which ʀeally *was* interesting.

N.P. The heat is terrific. It beats Italy and the insetti are beyond imagination. Does the moustique roar *before* or *after*: this question beats the lion one. But I've a note on the moustique in my journal. (Let me hold your ears very softly, my dog, and kiss your lovely eyes.)

N.P. I've got a maid. There's matter for song in it. Not the black one. A grey one about 55, a real expert servant who does everything and is installed today because Vendredi is a mauvais jour. Her name is Marie. I believe she has real gaieté de cœur. I pay her 160 par mois. But I don't grudge it. Those old wages were *shameless*.

Letter-cards. We had covenanted to write letters only on Sundays and postcards the other days. As usual, the arrangement was abandoned.

N.P. I'm still in bed, precious, in awful spasmodic pain. Tomorrow I'll call in another doctor to consult with me. I *wish* it would go away and let me begin mending.

N.P. A bouquet of plumbago—no there's only room for LOVE

Tig

No newspapers!!

Dear Darling,   (September 18, 1920)

Thank G. for Milne. Hold fast to him. He's so nice and she's not a bit nice. She's like an unripe banana.

I'm longing to see your 'Wilde-Harris'. I am sure O.W. was negligible but he *is* an astonishing figure. His letters, his mockeries and thefts —he's a Judas who betrays himself.

. . . Which is the more tragic figure—the master without a disciple or the disciple without a master? . . . That's by the way. Can I have the *Times Lit. Sup.*? I freeze, I burn for the printed word.

You touch me so with what you say about my bouquets. I put them there expressly for you. I said to them: 'Please last as long as you can for him'—and you understood.

Do kiss the cats' noses for me. I thought I heard Wing crying the first night I was here. Which reminds me—there's a little kid tethered below and it 'kyes and kyes so drefful'.

Saturday. I sent my review last night. I do hope it arrives in time. Dearest, I'm better. Temperature normal—pain gone—up and lying in the salon. I am eating again too and now really *will* mend. But I have *never* been so thin—not even in Paris. I simply melted like a candle with that fever. I rock when I stand. But Hurrah! it's over. These cards are no good today. I will send a cleaner one tomorrow.

Your own
Wig

Sunday afternoon,

My darling little Follower,   (September 19, 1920)

It is true—isn't it—that we are going to walk out together every single Sunday? All through the week we are hard at work—you, in that horrible black town that I hate, me, on my beautiful island; but when Sunday comes (it was my first thought this morning) we adorn ourselves, and soon after midi I hear that longed for but rather peculiar, rather funny whistle. I run to the window, and there below is a lovely vision in a faded very much washed creamy linen shirt, linen trousers, a scarlet belly-band, a wide silver-grey hat just a little on one side. I kiss my hand, spin down the stairs, and away we go. But for this week at least we'll not go far—only out of sight of the world—that's far enough. For your Wig is still so weak that she can't walk straight—sometimes I fling myself at the doors or take a great high step in the air. But I *am* really on the mend, and as to my cough—fancy, I've been here five days and I cough hardly at all. This morning in fact I didn't cough *at all* and can't remember if I have until now, 6 p.m. I only have to get my strength back after this 'attack'. That is all about me.

(There is so much to tell you. I tell you in my mind and then the effort of writing is too much. Forgive for this week an infernally dull girl.)

Later.

My feeling for this little house is that somehow it ought to be ours. It is, I think, a perfect house in its way and just our size. The position— up a side road *off* a side road standing high—all alone—the chief rooms facing South and West—the garden, the terrace all South—is ideal. You could do all the garden. There's a small vegetable plot outside the kitchen and scullery—there is a largish place in the front—*full* of plants and trees—with a garden tap and at the side another bed—a walk—a stone terrace overlooking the sea—a great magnolia tree—a palm that looks as though the dates must ripen. You shall have photographs of all this. And then it's so solid inside and so, somehow, spacious. And all on two floors and as well all the kitchen premises away, shut away and again perfectly equipped. I shall, of course, keep the strictest accounts and see exactly what it would cost us to live here.

Marie, the maid, is an excellent cook—as good as Annette was. She does all the marketing, and as far as I can discover she's a very good manager. A *marvel* really. Of course she cooks with butter but then one doesn't eat butter with one's meals so it comes to the same thing. The food is far better than any possible house we go to in England. I don't know to whose to compare it—and all her simple dishes like vegetables or salads are so good. It's a great pleasure to go into the kitchen for my morning milk and see this blithe soul back from market in the spotless kitchen with a bunch of lemon leaves drying for tisane and a bunch of camomile hanging for the same.

All is in exquisite order. There are pots on the stove, cooking away—

mysterious pots—the vegetables are in a great crock—in bundles—and she tells me of her marvellous bargains as I sip the milk. She is the kind of cook Anatole France might have.

As to the weather it is really heavenly weather. It is too hot for any exertion, but a breeze lifts at night, and I can't tell you what scents it brings, the smell of a full summer sea and the bay tree in the garden and the smell of lemons. After lunch today we had a sudden tremendous thunderstorm, the drops of rain were as big as marguerite daisies—the whole sky was violet. I went out the very moment it was over—the sky was all glittering with broken light—the sun a huge splash of silver. The drops were like silver *fishes* hanging from the trees. I drank the rain from the peach leaves and then pulled a shower bath over my head. Every violet leaf was full. I thought of you—these are the things I want you to have. Already one is conscious of the whole sky again and the light on the water. Already one listens for the grasshopper's fiddle, one looks for the tiny frogs on the path—one watches the lizards. . . . I feel so strangely as though I were the one who is home and you are away. I long for you here.

Tuesday, September 21. I dropped this letter and only today I pick it up again. Your cards came and your treasure of a letter, *my own boy*, and I long to answer—I keep on answering as it were. There's so much to tell you and apart from that there's the paper—your Stendhal—so *first chop*—the books you've sent me. And I still haven't told you about this house or the life or the view or what your room is like. It all waits. Will you, my wise comprehending boy, just take me and it for granted for about a week? In a week I'll be a giant refreshed—but I've simply got to get back my strength after the last blow.

But you know how soon I come to the surface. It did pull me down. It's only a few days. It's over. I'm on the *up grade,* but there you are—just for the moment. Each day the house finds its order more fixed and just (that's not English). Marie does every single thing. I am having an awning made so that I can lie out all day. The weather is absolute exquisite radiance, day after day, just variegated by these vivid storms. It's *very* hot and the insects are a trouble, but it's perfect weather for you and me here. I am doing all wise things.

Dear darling, I'll just have to ask you to take a wave of a lily white hand to mean *all* for the moment. Yes, I am sending a review this week. I note the novels are coming across quickly. I'm going to do three together. Can you bring Wing at Xmas? If not, Ida says she will go across and fetch them both when you give up the house. They'd be happy here.

I *wish* I were stronger. I'm so *much* better. My cough is nearly gone. It's nothing but de la faiblesse and I know it will pass. But not to be able to give you all this when I want to—that's hard to bear. The papers come, thank you, dearest.

Your own loving
Wig

Wednesday,

My precious Bogey,   (September 22, 1920)

I must answer your Sunday letter. Now DON'T bother to answer this. But it sends waves and waves of love beating through me—even tho' the storm that raises them is you as a landlord or the Cuticura unguent. I had, too, my best night here, and the day is surpassingly lovely. It rained all night. You know that freshness of early morning in the South. The palm sings, rocks, the sky is in great broad bands of white and deep blue; there's a sound of someone sawing wood and a sound of hens cackling.

FIRST: About your poem. Devil take it—I am plagued in exactly the same way. I can't begin a thing yet. I've put it down to my fatigue, and then I'm so *troubled,* just as if, beneath all my other feelings, someone stirred the pool with a stick and all is muddy. The someone is L.M. I'll get over it, but my weakness has given her a chance she hasn't failed to take advantage of. I'll get over this—and perhaps it's not that at all.

Truth to tell, too, I miss you more than I'd imagined. Together, we seem to make something: we seem to be *building* something, and I don't like to think of anything stopping those building operations. Time is too short. I wonder if you know what I mean? Do you? It's hard to explain. But even while we lie in bed and the eiderdown slips to the floor it's going on. And now, it's not going on. The bricks and mortar and heavy planks are all tumbled on the long grass. Well, it can't be helped. I am going to astonish you at Xmas if I can—by then I'll have broken through.

It DELIGHTS me that Milne has ousted M. What infernal cheek! Oh, I DO rejoice. I'm so glad you were firm. I shiver to think of her in possession—with her earrings tinkling triumphantly: 'We've got the Murry's house for the winter!' My Vord, what an escape!

Re book-box. I burn for it. No, there is nothing more to come, love, in it. What I miss here terribly is odd things, *ornaments,* scraps of stuff for little table cloths, all nice things for the table, but, especially, little personal 'bits'. But those you can't provide. WHEN we live here we'll have them.

I must get up. Marie has gone to market. She bought a superb carpet sweeper yesterday acting on my orders. It cost 50 francs (£1!).

The invisible worm has got into my Founting Pen, alas!

Yours truly and faithfully

Wig

Wish I'd seen that football match.

Thursday,

(September 23, 1920)

Yesterday a man came up and measured for an awning—a top and three sides—a kind of tent to be fixed in a corner of the terrace, where one can sit the whole day. And I also bought a chaise longue and a green chair which is (privately) yours.

Dearest Dear,

DON'T worry about me; I beg you not to. I am certainly on the mend all that remains is for me to get back my strength. And I SHALL in no time now. I haven't worried an atom bit about F—— except in so far as it worried you and affects US. I won't have that Pole outside our door. Burn all he gives you—won't you. A bon fire. . . .

I'm sending my reviews tomorrow. Wish I was a trump. It's most frightfully nice to be called one. Tommy (I'll send you his letter on Sunday. It was a masterpiece) sent me Arnold Bennett's new book to do for *The Nation.* I must do it and at once. It's a chance for me. But I wish you could melt me down some iron nails, or better, make some iron tea in a jug in our backyard where we played when we were tinies,—first. WANTED: Old or New Iron. Good Price Given.

I thought on the spot *Roger* when you mentioned Violet.[1] My literary watchdog bayed at that marriage and always called it a tragedy. I hope it's not.

The newspapers arrive every day. But look here!! What a trick to play on your little pal. There was I reading away about Miners' Ulti-

---

[1] The maid at Portland Villas.

matums and Darker Prospecks per usual, and suddenly *plop* I went through the bed? just my toes waving Au secours! 'Mr. J.M.M. editor of the Athenæum writes....' Can you imagine it????? You, with your absurd little coal shovel talking about Blood Money and International Coal Scuttles. I see you with your hands behind your back at the Miner's Congress singing: 'My pay was 40 cents a day, Twing!' Oh, my preposterous Darling——

Wig

Friday,
(September 24, 1920)

I am 'getting on', darling—there's no doubt about that—but it's a stiff climb pour le moment.

My own Bogey,

A clap of thunder and the long arm of Jove thrust through the shutters with your precious telegram upon a silver fork of lightning. That is what happened last night. You are *too* thoughtful; it bouleverses me. There the matter ends I hope about F. I'll keep the letters till you come at Xmas. Your card with the cutting *re* tuberculosis came today. What a splendid letter it was! 'Advanced stage' and now 'splendid health'. What that means to read!

I want very much to know about your dinner with Kay. My theory is *drink*. Did I tell you I had another letter from B.H.? A hateful, sniggering letter—a hiccup of a thing. People are rather dreadful, Boge....

Bogey, love, Wingley is on my heart, awfully. I keep seeing him and remembering how he sat—a teapot cat—so serene in my room and how he touched my hand at meals with his gentil paw. You must love him tenderly—as you alone know how—and whisper him our secrets. No one else understands him. He's very like us, really.

I'm writing my reviews today. It has been raining—torrents of warm heavy rain—and now it is marvellously fine and warm again and one can hear the buds uncurling. WHEN you come—I am making preparations even now, not to hurry, my dearest dear, but—

Your own
Wig

Photographs included. I'll try to send some every Sunday. They are not good but—you'll see.

PLEASE { Tell me your small worries and big worries.
Tell me what annoys you and what you'd like changed and what plagues you.

My own precious Bogey,

I am beginning my Sunday letter. I can't resist the hour. It's 6-30, just on sunset—the sea a deep hyacinth blue, silver clouds floating by like sails and the air smells of the pine and the bay and of charcoal fires. Divine evening! Heavenly fair place! The great RAIN has brought a thousand green spears up in every corner of the garden. Oh, you'll be met by such Flowers on Parade at Christmas time. There's a winey smell at the corner of the terrace where a huge fig tree drops its great purple fruits. At the other the magnolia flashes leaves; it has great buds brushed over with pink. Marie has just brought in my chaise longue and the green chair which is yours to escape l'humidité du soir. . . . Do these details bore you, my darling in London? Oh, I could go on for ever. But I do think this place, villa, climate, maid, are all as perfect as can be. Marie's cooking infuriates me. Why don't I help you to her escaloppe aux tomates—with *real* purée de p. de terre—deux feuilles de salade and des œufs en neige. And her Black Coffee!!

Sharing her return from market tho' is my delight. I go into the kitchen and am given my glass of milk and then she suddenly rushes into the scullery, comes back with the *laden* basket and (privately exulting over her purchases). 'Ah cet-te vie, cet-te vie! Comme tout ça est chère, Madame! Avant la guerre notre jolie France, c'était un jardin de Paradis et maintenant c'est que le Président même n'a pas la tête sur les épaules. Allez! allez! Douze sous pour les haricots! C'est vrai qu'ils sont frais—qu'ils sont jolis, qu'ils sont enfin—enfin—des haricots pour un petit Prince—mais douze sous, douze sous . . .' etc., etc. This at a great pace of course. Does it come over? Does it seem to you the way a cook ought to talk? There's a mouse in the cupboard. When she brought my bregchik this morning . . . 'le p'tit Monsieur nous a visité pendant la nuit, Madame. Il a mangé presque toute une serviette. Mais pensez-vous—quel dents. Allez-allez! c'est un *maître*!!' I don't know. I won't bore you with any more of her—but it seems to me that this is the way people like her *ought* to talk.

I heard from Methuen today. They now say they'd like 2 books for next spring. I think there must have been some trunk work, some back stair work in this on your part. But I'll see what I can do without promising in my fatal way what I can't perform. I wish I could begin real creative work. I haven't yet. It's the atmosphere, the . . . tone which is hard to get. And without it nothing is worth doing. I have such a horror of *triviality* . . . a great part of my Constable book[1] is *trivial*. It's not good enough. You see it's too late to beat about the bush any longer. They are cutting down the cherry trees; the orchard is sold—that is really the atmosphere I want. Yes, the dancing and the dawn and the Englishman in the train who said 'jump!'—all these, with the background. I feel—this is jet sincere—that you and I are the only 2 persons who realize this really. That's our likeness and that's what makes us, too, the creatures of our time.

Speaking of something else, which is nevertheless connected—it is an awful temptation, in face of all these novels to cry 'Woe—woe!' I cannot conceive how writers who have lived through our times can *drop* these last ten years and revert to why Edward didn't understand, Vi's reluctance to be seduced or (see Bennett) why a dinner of twelve covers needs remodelling. If I did not review novels I'd never read them. The writers (practically all of them) seem to have no idea of what one means by continuity. It is a difficult thing to explain. Take the old Tartar waiter in *Anna* who serves Levin and Stepan—Now, Tolstoy only has to touch him and he gives out a note and this note is somehow important, persists, is a part of the whole book. But all these other men —they introduce their cooks, aunts, strange gentlemen, and so on, and once the pen is off them they are *gone*—dropped down a hole. Can one explain this by what you might call—a *covering* atmosphere—Isn't that a bit too vague? Come down O Youth from yonder Mountain height and give your Worm a staff of reason to assist her. What it *boils down to* is . . . 'either the man can make his people live and keep 'em alive or he can't.' But criticks better that. (Don't bother to answer if it bores you, darling.)

Reams come from ——. She ruffled my feathers. She is keeping you at tennis because of the good it does you. Your Mind can think of

Nothing Except the Flying Ball. You are not to be allowed to work too hard but she means to be wily and in the future you and I and she and Gertler are all going to live in some untidy chateau with Richard 'for a tornado' upsetting my exquisite ways and eating all the jam. This made me—all the heathen in me—rage so furiously together.

Sunday afternoon.

Really today is the Best Day. It's hot, yet there's a breeze. I'm much better. I went into Jinnie's garden and lay all the morning under the pine trees. To have all that overgrown half-run-wild garden has simply *intoxicated* me. I found it this morning. It was like a better Karori. There's not a soul there. The great shuttered villa so white in the sun-light—so serene. And she went voyages of discovery. At the end of an avenue of bamboos there was a small round bamboo parlour. Is it really there? For another time? I doubt very much. But I want and I want my playmate. Please don't mind me saying that. It leaves you as free as Ariel, love. You can go up half a hundred Amazons tomorrow or live in a tower on wheels. I don't want my cry to follow you over as a plaintive cry or a pleading cry. But just suppose there's a small gold cloud and a bird hidden behind it—it's note is a kind of hoch celestial 'Bogey'. No more than that.

I kiss you. I am proud of you. I love you for ever. I am at your side. Darling, please take care of yourself.

Wig

Monday,

Dearest Bogey, (September 27, 1920)

I want to go through the paper with you and a card won't do. Before I begin, I am thrilled about Shaw of course. All is forgiven. In fancy I slipped down to the town and sent him a straw basket of tangerines—with an inscription which rolled and rolled and rolled to small golden perfection like the ripest and fairest in the bastick. Aren't we a pair if people smile on us? But I'll be silent. I'll not exist. *You* are the one who climbs the stairs and sitting in a delightful room with some quite peculiarly delicious tea you and cette belle barbe have it out. Oh, I *do* envy you.

And what are you going to reply to Methuen?

'Dear Sir A.

Ah—there you have me, I'm afraid.'

To business.

Your Wilde, Bogey, was extremely good. You put him in his place without for a moment pronouncing a judgment that was not strictly *critical*. What I mean is: it's so very difficult with a man like Wilde to get him and keep him inside that strange sort of ring through which one gazes at one's 'specimens' at the moment of writing. Know what I mean? It's a kind of expanding and contracting ring. You can pull your specimen up very near—so near that you can count the hairs of his spiritual eyebrows—or you can send him far, far—a speck on the horizon. Wilde—the immense temptation is to take your eye away and see him *there* without its aid. You haven't. I note tho', darling, the last sentence and it makes me smile a little . . . instead of 'a great biography'. You can't resist poor old Frankie's dreadfully battered hat and his: 'I knew you as a boy, Sir!' I understand. . . .

May Sinclair's finished—good. It's a flabby dabby babby. But it will go down, no doubt. Oh, it *is* bad, isn't it?

I thought Dobrée too missish. It read like the essay one handed in on Monday and got back on Wednesday. No style, no attack, no *reason* for it. God forbid he writes the same number of lines on Shakespeare, or Hamlet—Mad or Sane?

Blunden is in danger of writing stunt prose. His Sussex (it is he?) is good, but he bangs the drum too hard himself.

I thought Aldous v. good on Thomas, didn't you?

And old Sullivan was excellent. He has got a good firm touch with him—nowadays.

D.L.M. is excellent.

410–411 look very dull, don't they? But it can't be helped, I realize.

I think our Library Table is—no, it's not dull. At the same time it's not interesting, is it? I feel the paper *lacks* something, *lacks* a column—on the lines we suggested for De la Mare. Do you feel it a bit scrappy? I don't bite *in* to it.

About the leaders—there again. I think they ought to be more pronouncedly the work of one hand. They ought to be just a touch *caustic* or (appalling word) *bright*. They can't *compel* in such a little space ∴ they ought to attract. If that can't be done I think real good pars. would be better. Talk it over with me, will you?

I wish and I wish and I wish—Why aren't you here? Even though I'm as poor as a mouse don't publish *Sun and Moon*. I'll send you a story this week. *Do* publish it if you can. Of course, don't if you're full up—

but alas! for my £25 a month—it's gone. This, however, is sheer wailing and nothing to do with my blessed little editore.

Yours EVER
K.M.

Just a line more.

The lizards here *abound*. There is one big fellow, a perfect miniature crocodile, who lurks under the leaves that climb over a corner of the terrace. I watched him come forth today—*very* slithy—and eat an ant. You should have seen the little jaws, the flick flick of the tongue, the great rippling pulse just below the shoulder. His eyes, too. He listened with them—and when he couldn't find another ant, he stamped his front paw—and then, seeing that I was watching, *deliberately* winked, and slithered away.

There is also a wasps' nest in the garden. Two infant wasps came out this morning and each caught hold of a side of a *leaf* and began to tug. It was a brown leaf about the size of three tea leaves. They became furious. They whimpered, whiney-pined—snatched at each other—wouldn't give way and finally one *rolled* over and could'nt roll back again—just lay there kicking. I never saw such a thing. His twin then couldn't move the leaf at all. I pointed out the hideous moral to my invisible playmate.

Fabretta[1]

Wednesday,
Darling, (September 29, 1920)
Your letter came today. I had looked forward to it so tremendously.
—and it told me what I wanted to know. It brought you close to me for a little moment.

I am rather upset. I have never got over that first illness, and I keep having fever. That's the truth. Fever and headache and nightmare pursue me. I should not have walked in that garden; it was too much and it has laid me low again. I must just keep dead quiet and pin my flag—a small and trembling banner—on to some less high mountain top for the present.

I *tell* you, because it's all of me for the moment. Disappointment—to be so weak and so queer. It will pass. I will be glad when Jinnie and Connie come. I feel I'd like barricades. One feels so alone when one is

---

[1] Probably a feminine diminutive of Fabre, i.e. Little Naturalist.

cast down again. Isn't it the irony of fate that just when it would be (so it seems) so much easier to get well if one were with one's darling— it's denied. Well, one must just *bear* it—that's all! But the awful sense of insecurity. . . . One puts out one's hand and there's nothing there. (Are these three years a dream?)

Now I've taken your hankyberchief and cried on your shoulder and you've kissed me—we'll wave it away. We'll get up and go on. Can you *bear* me to do that? Ah, dearest, *ought* I to? Not to make *you* sad— never that—just to hear from you: 'I know, Worm.' I too am nearer you than ever before in *spirit*—more your

Wig

(October 1, 1920)

Friday. v. warm, overclouded, with a vague dark wind.

Dearest Bogey,

I repent of having sent you that depressed card. I ought not to have, I suppose. Really, it's rather a nice point of conduct. I can't decide it for myself. Knowing you—should I refrain? But the falsity—oh, blow! Yes, of course I ought not to: I mean it's terrifically against my interests ever to gronder. I risk your loving me less nearly, less warmly: I risk you—even taking the receiver off altogether so as not to be bothered with that cursed bell. No, it's TOO difficult.

How is the house going, darling? Does it go smoothly? Are you left untroubled? Please let me know this. And do take great care of getting hot at tennis and then not putting on a thick enough coat after. Do be careful of your colds.

You've so precious little money (2d less than £1!) that I don't dare suggest the dentist—yet you ought to go. You ought to keep as fit as you can in every way to withstand the winter cold. Don't save. Spend it on keeping healthy. What in Heaven's name is there to equal HEALTH? There's no future if you're not well, no solid substantial Xmas with £50 in the pudding. There is only TODAY. That reminds me of your buying the Hardy. How fantastic it seemed when I was just holding on to the hour and the minute in Ospedaletti! But this feeling (which is making me simply reckless at present) would be very difficult to imagine if one had not been ill. Really, if one is healthy one can live on next to nothing still—of course one can. OR once one is well, one can make money—easy as winking. Why not? But if one's

548

ill—well, there one is with a grey gown and a rattle, coughing in the wake of the chariots.

Dear little Wing would make a sweet acolyte at ½d a week. I see him. He is a precious little cat. Whisper my name in his ear. I'm afraid tho' he won't smile. He'll more likely sneeze.

Oh, Bogey, that packet of letters never fetched up, nor did the signed declaration. Were they sent? The letters have been 9 days on the way, so they *must* be lost.

I shall be more than thankful for my books. It was v. silly not to have brought Shakespeare.

Suppose you didn't glance at a novel by a man called Prowse, *A Gift of the Dusk*. A simply terrible book—awful—ghastly! and about as good as it could be. It's just a kind of . . . journal the man kept while he was at a sanatorium in Switzerland. It *is* the goods if you like! But he must be a wonderful man. I wish I knew if he is dead. Will you PLEASE ask Beresford if you see him (Collins is the publisher)? I wish very much I could hear of him—One's heart goes out to anyone who has *faced* an experience as he has done. 'One must tell everything—everything.' That is more and more real to me each day. It is, after all, the only treasure, heirloom we have to leave—our own little grain of truth.

As I write I am deeply loving you. Do you feel that? Sitting opposite to you—and talking—very quietly. You *are* there? You *do* reply?

Tell me about yourself, my darling, whenever you can.

Your own
Wig

My darling Bogey,   (October 4, 1920)

It's Monday and the sun has come back—it's fine and warm. I had 2 cards from you today but you didn't tell me how your cold was. Does that mean it is better? Yesterday the paper came. I thought it was a very good number. You felt rather 'faint' about it, didn't you? and Miss Brett found it 'dull'. But I thought it was full of meat, somehow. I read it, and I thought of you and of what an amount of work it means and of how you labour at it—and I sent you that wire. *Whatever* my feelings are, I am *not* justified in giving way to them before you or in letting you see even the shadow of the border of that shadowy country that we exiles from health inhabit. It is not fair. So I'm resolute that you shan't be plagued again, my dearest darling, and determined to keep my resolution. Help me to.

I'm sending you and Milne a dozen kāhki (I don't know how to spell it: that's phonetic) to eat for your breakfasts. They are very good and very healthy. I send them unripe. You must wait until they are soft, then cut off the top, squeeze a *lot* of lemon-juice inside and eat with a teaspoon. Perhaps they won't be a treat, after all. I always long to *send* you things. Please give my love to Milne. He sounds so nice in the house. I wonder what Wing thinks of the clarinet.

Walpole's novel which I mean to do for next week (1 col) ought to be a very good prop to hang those very ideas on that I tried to communicate to you. I want to take it seriously and really say why it fails—for, of course, it does fail. But his 'intention' was serious. I hope I'll be able to say what I do mean. I am *no* critic of the homely kind. 'If you would only explain quietly in simple language,' as L.M. said to me yesterday. Good Heavens, that *is* out of my power.

The garden menagerie includes snakes—a big chap as thick as my wrist, as long as my arm, slithered along the path this morning and melted into the bushes. It wasn't horrid or fearful, however. As to the mice—Marie's piège seems to snap in the most revolting way. A fat one was offered to a marauding cat at the back door yesterday, but it *refused* it. 'Polisson! Tu veux un morceau de sucre avec?' I heard Marie scold. She is very down on the cats here; she says they are malgracieux. Yes, she is a most *remarkable* type. Yesterday afternoon, it was terribly gloomy and triste outside and she came in for the coffee tray, and said how she *hated* Menton. She had lived here 8 years with her pauvre mari and then they'd lived 2 years in Nice where he died and was buried. She said she could *bear* Nice because 'il se repose là-bas mais ici—Madame—il se promenait avec moi—partout partout—'and then she beat her little black crêpe bodice and cried 'Trop de souvenirs, Madame, trop de souvenirs'. Oh, how I love people who feel deeply. How restful it *is* to live with them even in their 'excitement'. I think for writers, for people like you and me, it *is* right to be with them—but the feeling must be true—not a hair's breadth assumed—or I hate it as much as I love the other. As I write that I don't believe it any more. I could live with you and not care 2 pins if people 'felt' anything at all—in fact, I could draw away and be very aloof if they did—*I* don't know. It's too difficult....

More reams from ——. Tennis and Gertler's threatened tuberculosis are the themes. How he mustn't be told and will crumple up if he *is* told and Dr. Sorapure says . . . and she dreams tennis. But I wish you would keep her pen off tuberculosis—she doesn't know what she is writing about and it's desperately tactless to 'tee-hee' at the idea of it. Heavens, what irony! I have no doubt Gertler's friends will subscribe £1000 and send him to Egypt for the winter. Oh, she does make me loathe London. She seems to sweep a gutterful of it into an envelope and then she *goads* me—on purpose. *She's* not ill, *she* can run, *she* can play tennis with Murry. No, I can't write to her. 'You must get better and you and I and Murry will go streaming away.' OH, BOGEY!! But people with spots on their lungs are not subjects for merriment.

I feel this letter is cold and poor; the fruit is not good to eat. It's rather like that withered fig tree. Do you know there is a kind of fig tree which is supposed to be of the family of that unfortunate one—it is dark stemmed and its leaves are black, they flap on the blackened boughs, they are like leaves that a flame has passed over. *Terrible.* I saw one once in a valley, a beautiful valley with a river flowing through it. There was linen drying on the banks and the women were beating the water and calling to one another—gaily—and there was this *sad* tree. L.M. who was with me said 'Of course the *explanation* is that one must never cease from giving'. The fig tree had no figs—so Christ cursed it. *Did you ever!* There's such a story buried under the whole thing—isn't there—if only one could dig it out.

Well, darling, I'm going back to my chaise longue. I spend all day either lying on the terrace or in this salon with both windows open and I go to bed at 8 p.m. and get up at 10 a.m. Each day is the same.

How are you? Your poem? You—the very you? Do you feel we are near each other? I love you. I think of you at the yellow table.[1] I miss you at night and in the early morning, and when I am awake at night I think of you, lying asleep. I wonder what suit you are wearing. I see you in your jersey. 'Don't be afraid'—I do not ask you, my darling own, to come under my umbellella.

But I have a deep, *pure* love for you in my heart.

Your Wig

Dear darling, (October 5, 1920)

I've just got your further notes about the *A.* I agree absolutely. (Oh, Bogey if you knew what a *bridge* such a piece of paper is to me. You

---

[1] I occupied Katherine's room at 2 Portland Villas: her writing table was painted yellow.

fling it across and it holds and I seem to somehow emerge and cross over to your bank for a minute. It's *miraculous*.) However, revenons. I'm for pars instead of leaders. They are a grind and I don't think the grind worth it. Yes, A.L.H. this last week struck me so much that I sent him a p.c. He's enormously improved. YOU mustn't do a stroke more. I agree with Shaw. You write too well to be a really good editor. You can't take your ease at the job: you can't write without your nerves being in the job. Neither in my worm-high way can I.

I turn to see a chunk of your poem. I am not in the least settled down to anything yet. The Journal—I have absolutely given up. I dare not keep a journal. I should always be trying to tell the truth. As a matter of fact I dare not tell the truth. I feel I *must* not. The only way to exist is to go on and try and lose oneself—to get as far as possible away from *this* moment. Once I can do that all will be well. So it's stories or nothing. I expect I shall kick off soon—perhaps today. Who knows? In the meantime I peg away too, darling, in my fashion.

Stick things into envelopes and send them over when you can, will you? Any old thing becomes a treasure on the way. Remember that, old boy. I must get up and take my first *cure d'air*. It's a fine day, very fine—very blue.

I've still *never* had that packet of letters—never had the document. I heard from Cook's to-day that the box has left. What an excitement it will be—unpacking it! Don't forget what *news* means—a magazine—the *L.M.*—anything that keeps me in touch. Kiss our sweet cats for me.

Fare well my precious Boge and be happy.

Wig

Your Saturday night letter   Wednesday,
Darling,   (October 6, 1920)

Forgive me my unworthiness and my failure these last days.

Your letter—surely the most wonderful letter a man ever wrote a woman—or a Boge ever wrote a Wig—almost made me cry out: 'Forgive me, forgive me.'

It is what my suffering has given me—this letter—the reward of it. I seem to have just a glimpse of something I've never known before as I sit here thinking of you and me and of our love. . . . It's as though, looking across the plains, what I had thought was cloud dissolves, lifts and behind it there are mountains. Always a new silence, a new mystery.

My precious love.

You HAVE come here. I mean—the ache of separation is over. I'm not alone. Of course, I long for you here, sharing my daily life, but I do not say 'Come!' It's not only on account of the money, Bogey. If I believed at this moment I was going to die, of course I would say 'Come!' because it would be unbearable not—to have you to see me off on the journey where you know the train drops into a great black hole.

(No, I believe even then I couldn't say 'Come!')

But what is it? I feel our 'salvation'—our 'future'—depends on our doing nothing desperate, but on holding on, keeping calm (this from *me*!) and leaving nothing in disorder, nothing undone. The 'paper' isn't really the 'paper', I suppose. It's the kind of battle that the knight has to wage, and the knight in you and me—he's our spirit. Also, my darling, I have got the queer feeling that 'holding on', we declare our faith in the future—our power to win through. *This* year is the important year for us. You ought, for your future freedom, to be where you are. You ought for THE FUTURE to keep the paper going one more year.

And there's this, too. But here I am speaking to myself. If I am to be what I wish to be I must not be rescued. That's *dead true*. Bogey and I have chosen each other for lovers in this world, and I believe absolutely in our choice. But I believe the reason beyond all other reasons why we chose each other is because we feel FREE together. I know that, at the last, I do not put the slightest chain on him, nor he on me. I feel, if he were here now—if I gave up and said 'Come!', there might be a danger—in fact the very cry is a denial of what I really believe.

But it's all mysterious: it all seems to belong to another country. This speech will not explain it. There are signs, silences, a kind of flowing from light to shadow. I can only say: My love, we shall stay as we are.

I live for you. I will prepare myself for our life. Look into my heart. Believe in me. *Would I sooner have Bogey here now?* NO (what a funny looking no—a little bit Gothic!) Oh dear, oh dear. Put your arms round me. Come at Christmas with candles in your hair. I want to hold you very tightly—I feel we are deathless when you write to me so. You HAVE come, Bogey; I say it again. You are here. And now I'm going to get up and work.

Let me not fail again. It is my dream to be here alone until Christmas and to do my work—to have a book ready by then. I shall begin my book today. It's just as though the ship has sailed into harbour. . . . Now, get off, my pilot, until next Christmas. I can manage rocks and shoals and storms—anything. (But even now your letter is unanswered. It is a GIFT. Time will show how I will use it). My darling love—you are happy? You understand?

I am your
Wig

Thursday,
My beloved darling, (October 7, 1920)

Your Sunday and Monday letters are come. With them I feel more convinced than ever that we do right to keep our promises: you know how I love you. Truly, I can't get over having troubled you like this: it seems impossible and yet now that I know you *do* understand, I can't regret it. I called upon you in my time of trouble and you heard me— that is enough. My dearest own, don't feel that you must keep on hold- ing me or that you must keep listening for another cry. . . . I have a perfect horror of demanding help, of asking you to . . . hold my hand. You're as free as can be again. You've wonderfully responded—the miracle that I couldn't have believed could happen HAS happened. If I could love you more absolutely (it seems I always can) I do. But—do you understand? I want to put my arms round you—hold you—let you hear my inmost heart, say Thank you, thank you, my Boge, and then *let you go*. Be undisturbed; be free of me now. Think of me as here and working and getting better so that all we intend to do we shall do. I feel immensely glad we have Broomies. It's somehow so important that it should be there. I feel we shall return one day, not too far off and *it* will be our home. I feel nearer than ever. There is *you* and *work*.

Don't write me any more letters now except on Sundays. Oh, my own precious little mate, do you see Wig imploring you to smile and be calm and wear a bow tie and sit at my yellow table with our teapot cat and save pennies and talk to your friends and keep warm.

As for me I am in the open day and night. I never am in a room with the windows shut. By great good fortune I've got Marie who every day looks after me better. And she is so sympathetic that all she cooks tastes especially good. She looks after me and anxiously asks if 'la viande était assez saignante'—but *sanely*—in the way one not only can stand, but one loves, and when I go into the kitchen and say, 'Marie, je tremble de faim' her 'tant mieux' as she butters you a tartine is just absolutely right. So you see I *do* count my blessings; this house, this climate, and this good soul.

It will be perfeck if you can come for Xmas, but there again you must feel free. Don't think of me as too disappointed if you can't. Just feel free. If you do come, L.M. is going to England to spend the three weeks with her sister so we'd be quite alone in the little house. . . .

It happened just as I thought it would. I began on my own work yesterday and did a big chunk. I think its alright. But today I'm reviewing Walpole as I feel you may want an extra novel or two in the paper just now as it's 'the season'. Walpole is a *real case*.

T's letter was a most pathetic document, Boge. Poor little chap! He would sweep the very office. I have an idea that B. leads him the devil of a life. What *was* her operation? I feel she had—no, it sounds indelicate. I'll not write it. But she's just the kind of woman who would have that operation and then trade on poor old T's sympathies for ever after. By the way, Maggie, Walpole's heroine, had the Kosmos behind her, too.

It's blowing guns today—a choppy sea—my favourite sea, brilliant blue with the white lifting—lifting as far as one can see, rather big unbroken waves near the shore. Butterflies love a day like this. They love to fling themselves up in the air and then be caught by the wind and rocked and flung and lightly *fluttered*. They pretend to be frightened. They cling as long as they can to a leaf and then—take a butterfly long breath—up they go—away they sail, quivering with joy, and delight. It must be a kind of surf bathing for them—flinging themselves down the wind.

You know how when one woman carries the new born baby the other woman approaches and lifts the handkerchief from the tiny face and bends over and says 'Bless it'. But I am always wanting to lift the handkerchief off lizards' faces and pansies' faces and the house by moonlight. I'm always waiting to *put a blessing* on what I see. It's a queer feeling.

Am I near you? I feel we are so near each other. I feel that our love has changed: it seems to have grown in grace.

Here are three little photographs, darling. Do you like them? L.M. always seems to take the same, and then she has (can't you see it?) *washbasins* full of prints—dozens of *one kind*.

Goodbye for now, my darling.

Wig

I think it was too sweet of the cats to have gone to the bathroom. Pathetic! Wonderful cat psychology, really. You ought to have a minute one installé with a mouse's tail for a plug.

My darling Bogey,

It's Sunday and after awful storms fine again. My darling, I can't understand why my letters don't arrive. I know they are safely posted; I am sure they are stolen your end. My mind says S. egged on by M. But it is simply more than maddening to know the letters don't come. It makes me feel so helpless. And I know the feeling too well when they don't arrive.

Is Gertler really ill? Do tell me. I always remember him swaggering up to me when I was just back from the South: 'Well, Katherine, I hear you've got it. Do you spit blood and so on? Do all the things in the books? Do they think you'll get over it?' And then he laughed out. It's like all —— 's friends having *spotty lungs*. I am very sorry, but I can't forgive these things. They may be ignorance and so on, but I not only can't forgive, I *do* condemn them. There's a kind of agitation in —— 's atmosphere that repels me.

Oh, if you knew what a joy your Shakespeare was. I straightway dipped in *The Tempest* and discovered Ariel riding on *curlèd clouds*. Isn't that adjective perfect? I'd missed it before. I do think *The Tempest* is the most radiant, delicate, exquisite play. The atmosphere is exactly the atmosphere of an island after a storm—an island re-born out of the sea with Caliban tossed up for sea wrack and Ariel blowing in a shell. Oh, my divine Shakespeare!! Oh, most blessed genius. Again I read of the love of Ferdinand and Miranda, how they met and *recognised* each other and their hearts spake. Everything—everything is new born and golden. God knows there are desert islands enough to go round—the difficulty is to sail *away* from them—but dream islands . . . they are rare, rare.

Yet, if I had not loved you I should never have understood Shakespeare as I do. His 'magic' is the same magic as our love. 'Where the bee sucks, there lurk I: In a cowslip's bell I lie.' I believe this all sounds quite quite different to us than to all the rest of the world. I feel, if I lived with you where the climate was delicate, the air most sweet, fertile the isle, we should end by talking in a kind of blank verse. (I'm smiling as I write this, my true love, and yet I mean it.) Looking back at our time in the Villa Pauline when the almond tree was in flower, remembering how I saw you come out of the *cave* in your soft leather boots, carrying logs of wood . . . it is *all* a dream.

Oh, Bogey, I don't like the world. It's a horrid place. When I think of the ——'s Sunday lunch—I feel there is no place for us except Beyond the Blue Mountains. I want to wander through valleys with you, drink out of leaves for cups, sit on warm hillsides and listen to bees in the heather. I want a house as small as possible and there to live and watch the clouds and mark the seasons—with you. There to work and *live*—no servants. Friends sometimes to see us, but all *jet simple*. . . .

(I came to the back door then with a bowl of crumbs for some migratory birds that had come to rest on our hill-top after a storm and were still too weak to fly. They were quite tame—hopping about—rather large slender grey birds with silver breasts. You came walking from the field with a pail of milk. Our lovely little fawn cow was just wandering away. The pail glittered, you *strolled* along. I looked at the cow and the birds and thought: All are enchanted. . . .)

Yes, I do understand how you must hate the idea of *dinners*. Carry me in your pocket. No, that won't do any good. I'd give my eyes to watch you dress. You'll look so lovely in your evening clothes and I've never seen you in them. But your *best dress* is that Jaeger jersey. That's the very Bogification of you. . . .

I'm hoping for the paper tomorrow. The *D.N.* for October 1ST came today (Oct. 10th). Could I have the *Mercury,* please?

Now, I want if I can to finish a story today for you. I'll write it out here. I've got a HUGE umbrella lashed to the terrace in place of that *tente* which was too expensive, of course. The umbrella does just as well. Oh, that you were here, just at this moment, sharing this sky and this gentle breeze.

Your own
Wig

Just as I folded that, I had *callers.* A M. and Madame showed on to the terrace—very gracious, but *Oh, dear!* what a ghastly idea it is! What can one say? I can't play 'ladies' unless I know the children I am playing with.

Now there's an asp come out of a hole—a slender creature, red, about 12 inches long. It lies moving its quick head. It is very evil looking, but how much nicer than a caller! I was warned yesterday against attempting to kill them. (Do you see me trying to kill them, Boge?) But they *spring* at you, if you do. However, darling, I'll catch this one for you at the risk of my life and put it in your Shakespeare for a marker at the scene where the old man carries in the basket of figs. You will have to hold your Shakespeare *very firmly* to prevent it from wriggling, Anthony darling.

Lovingly yours,
Egypt

Darling Bogey,   (October 11, 1920)

I send the story.[1] As usual I am in a foolish panic about it. But I know I can trust you. You know how I *choose* my words; they can't be changed. And if you don't like it or think it is wrong *just as it is* I'd rather you didn't print it. I'll try and do another.

Will you tell me—if you've time—what you think of it? Again (as usual) I burn to know and you see there's NO ONE here.

It was one of my queer hallucinations; I wrote it straight off. And I've no copy.

Wig

I hope you like my little boy. His name is HENNIE.
May I use that address?

My darling own Bogey,   (October 12, 1920)

It is such a Heavenly Day that I hardly know how to celebrate it—or rather I keep on celebrating it—having a kind of glorified Mass with full Choir. (But à bas the Roman Catholics!) It's just blue and gold. In the valley two workmen are singing—their voices come *pressing* up, *expanding,* scattering in the light—you know those Italian voices! I think from the sound they are building a house: I am sure the walls will hold this singing for ever, and on every fine day, put your hand there on that curve or that arch, and there'll be a warmth, a faint vibration. . . . The sun woke me at 7 o'clock—sitting sur mes pieds comme un chat d'or mais c'était moi qui a fait ron-ron. And at 7–15 Marie brought déjeuner—petits pains with miel des Alpes and hot coffee on a fringèd tray. Her old bones were fairly singing, too. I said, 'Vous allez au marché, Marie?' She said, rather aggrieved—'Mais comme vous voyez,

The Young Girl.

Madame, je suis en train d'y aller'—and then I noticed she was 'dressed' for the occasion, i.e., she had flung on her shoulders a most minute black shawl with a tiny bobble fringe. This she always holds over her mouth to guard against le frais du matin when she scuttles off with her panier and filet. She really *is* a superb type.

Good God! There are two lizards rushing up the palm tree! A Boge and a Wig. Lizards *glister*, Heaven bless them. In the trunk of the palm high up some tiny sweet peas are growing and some frail dandelions. I love to see them. As I wrote that, *one* lizard fell—simply fell with a *crash* (about 5,000 feet) on to the terrace—and the other *looked* over one of those palm chunks—really it did. I've never seen such an affair. It was Wig that fell—of course. Now she's picked herself up and is flying back. She seems as good as new—but it's a mad thing to do.

I have a hundred things—oh, a million things I want to talk about, but the sun seems to draw them away from my breast into a heaven where they are little clouds with seraphim on them singing of her love of Bogey.

The papers have come, dearest love—likewise books. I'm going to do 4 females this week. You were *excellent* on Delamare. Since I was here those two lines: 'But beauty vanishes, beauty passes, However rare, rare it be' have sounded so often in my mind. . . . I love Delamare, love the man who came to tea—with his wife sitting there by the fire and dark, young, lovely Florence. The memory of that afternoon is so precious. For one thing I felt that Delamare *recognised you*—I mean a certain 'you'—I almost mean 'us'—but that he couldn't have known. . . . And that brings with it always a sense of Peace that endures.

Ida has come for this letter and can't wait. I will write again.

You feel my love?

I am your

Wig

Last day of *my* old year.

Dearest love,   (October 13, 1920)

I want to make something clear. When I say and have said in my letters I shall not say 'Come' you must understand very very deeply that I only mean—not on my account—not because of my illness. What I mean is: I could give up the world, the sea and all the tiddimies in a blink of the eye, if you *felt* it was the thing to do. I'm not in the very slightest frightened of being poor. I am sure we shall sell our *real*

559

work. I'm confident of that, tho' it may take time. So if you arrange it to be for next Easter,[1] my darling, o BLISS is my signature to the agreement. We'll talk it out at Christmas—shall we? As a matter of fact now speaking dead true I think it's a waste of time for me to do journalism. I think I'd *make more* with stories only. Truth is I *detest novels* and think they're simply rubbish, on the whole. But in saying that, I don't mean, I couldn't mean that I want to give up my work for the *A. I could not live here without it*. But I just tell you that see? darling. Because it *is* la vraie vérité.

I think at Easter L.M. had better go off to London, meet you there, and take over the affair of settling up. Then you'll come here or hereabouts and we'll live on—love and work.

You're not to speak of yourself as a silent Boge, an irritating Boge. It makes me hang my head.

This is the last letter I shall ever write to you at 31—the very last. An End and a Beginning. Oh God, how deeply and truly I love you. I am so divinely happy, somewhere, in some still place.

Henry[2] has your note and is replying to the Yinkum people today. I just took it into him. He was sitting on his window-sill, smoking. He intends going off to Annunciata for the day.

I DESPISE and shrink from that vulgar Bennett. C-B too, with his Wordsworth complex! The queer half-hinting, half-suggesting . . . and yet what he *does* say doesn't help one in the very slightest to understand Wordsworth better.

I am amazed at the sudden 'mushroom growth' of cheap psychoanalysis everywhere. *Five* novels one after the other are based on it: it's in everything. And I want to prove it won't do—it's turning Life into a *case*. And yet, of course, I do believe one ought to be able to—not ought—one's novel if it's a good one will be capable of being *proved* scientifically to be correct. Here—the thing that's happening now is— *the impulse to write is a different impulse*. With an artist—one has to allow —Oh tremendously—for the sub-conscious element in his work. He writes he knows not what—he's *possessed*. I don't mean, of course, always, but when he's *inspired*—as a sort of divine flower to all his terrific hard gardening there comes this subconscious . . . wisdom. Now these people who are nuts on analysis seem to me to have *no* subconscious at all. They write to *prove*—not to tell the truth. Oh, I am

I had decided to resign *The Athenæum* early in 1921.
The surname of a banker in Mentone.

so dull aren't I? I'll stop. I wish they'd stop, tho'! It's such gross impertinence.

Later. I've just been to the——Louise, stolen three whopping lemons and had a talk to their jardinier who comes here le vendredi to plant flowers autour du palmier. This man drew a design of the flower bed on the gravel and then, after telling me the names of the flowers, he described them. You know, it was *terrific* to hear him. In trying to describe the scent. . . . 'C'est—un—parr-fum—' and then he threw back his head, put his thumb and forefinger to his nose—took a long breath and suddenly exploded it in a kind of AAAhhh! almost staggering backwards—overcome, almost fainting; and then in telling me of des paquerettes, 'ce sont de tout petites fleurs qui se regardent comme s'ils disent: c'est moi qui est plus jolie que toi!' Now, Bogey—Oh dear me—I wonder if it *is* so wonderful. I sat down on a bench and felt as though waves of health went flowing through me. To think the man *cares* like that—*responds*—laughs like he does and snips off a rosebud for you while he talks. Then I think of poor busmen and tube men and the ugliness of wet, dark London. It's wrong. People who are at all sensitive ought not to live there. I'll tell you (as it's my birthday tomorrow) a tale about this man. He came to see me. I had to engage him. First he passed me in the garden and went to Marie to ask for Madame Murry. Marie said—'But you've seen her already—' He said: 'No—there's only une petite personne—une fillette *de* quinze ans—enfin—sur la terrasse.' Marie thought this a very great joke. Bit steep—wasn't it? I expect I'll be about five by Xmas time—just old enough for a Christmas tree . . . [a drawing of one instead of the word.]

Doctor Mee—who was Mother's doctor, too—can't get over my improvement in the last fortnight. He's *staggered*. But he says he does wish you would go to Gamage and buy a pair of *shoulder straps*—you know the things, I mean. They're to keep me from stooping. I stoop mainly from habit. I feel so much better that I almost have to tie myself to my chaise longue. But I know now is the moment to go slow. Alas, I'm so infernally wise in these things. Oh Heavenly day. I wish you'd shared my boisson—that fresh lemon with a lump of sugar and Saint-Galmier.

Every morning I have a sea-water bath in a saucer and today after it, still wet, I stood in the full sun to dry—both windows wide open. One can't help walking about naked in the mornings—one almost *wades* in the air. As for my old feet, I've never felt them since the first

561

days I was here—never dream of wearing that awful strapping or
anything. I'm writing, facing Italy—great mountains, grey-gold with
tufts of dark green against a sheer blue sky. Yes, I confess it's very hard
work to wait for you. Can we hope for more than—how many?—
springs and summers. I don't want to miss one.

Such a strange feeling. I seem to *be* you—not two persons but one
person. You must feel my love. Do you? Precious Bogey . . . dearest
dear.

I am your true love

Wig

Thanking you for the answer to my telegram, love.

My own darling,   (Friday, October 15, 1920)

I confess it *was* a bit of a jar yesterday to have no birthday. You know
how silly I am about them. Of course, I didn't expect to hear from anybody but you this year as the children are in N.Z. But I waited and
waited for the post in my room and then when he did come and the
envelope was rather fat it was a terrific relief. I thought you'd sent me a
handkerchief or perhaps a han' made poem. Oh—it was only enclosures,
after all. I was very glad to get them, of course, but all the same——It
was a misty old day and nobody said 'Many happy returns', but when
the telegraph man came I was so relieved that I gave him 50 centimes.
Then I found you really had forgotten. First time since we've been
together—and I *did* give you a nice one, didn't I, with that almond
paste and all? I felt so désolée that I sent a wire after that myself.

How perfectly awful about your income-tax. It sounds incredible.
£198! I think one would have *more* money if one had less. I love your
little notes. They are much nicer than cards.

This AWFUL photograph L.M. took on the orchard path the day
I went lemon-stealing. She does seem to be bad at cameras. Does she
make me look like that?

I am going to see Bouchage today—just to know how much I can
do. One can't tell. One is so immensely better—then one has a fit of
coughing which—isn't better at all. One hears out of the depths of it
the old wolf howling as loud as ever when one thought he'd be driven
off and never could have to attack again. But one couldn't be as hungry
as I am and not be getting better.

I am sending my review today. It's done and ready to go. Now I am going to make another effort to write four during the week and catch up. This time I must because I'm so much older.

Ida has gone for a voiture. I must put on my chapeau.

Goodbye, my precious Boge. Tell Wing that he didn't remember either.

      Your
         Wig

(October 16, 1920)

URGENT.

☛ May I have the money for the novels I left at home and for those I've sent over? I really badly want it. Had I better send the novels direct? If so, please send me the address. I don't want to complain of my partner but my expenses are very heavy and every little counts no end. It would mean ever so much to me to have it—and it's MINE—isn't it? It is a bit cool of you to just pocket it. The female in me rebels. You wouldn't dare to do it if I could fight you.

Darling,

I've just got back from Bouchage. I expect you'd like to know what he's like. He seems to me a very decent, intelligent soul—quite as good as any other doctor. He approved absolutely of my life and conditions of life here and is going to keep an eye on me. The result of his examination was the eternal same. Of course, one can see that the disease is of long standing but there is no reason why—provided—subject to—if —and so on and so on. Not in the least depressing. Yet the foolish creature always does expect the doctor to put down his stethoscope to turn to her and say—with quiet confidence: 'I can cure you Mrs. Murry.'

He has the same disease himself. I *recognised* his smile—just the least shade too bright and his strange joyousness as he came to meet one— just the least too pronounced—his air of being a touch more vividly alive than other people—the gleam—the faint glitter on the plant that the frost has laid a finger on. . . . He is only about 33, and I felt that his experience at the war had changed him. In fact, he seemed to me awfully like what a young Duhamel might be. I'm to go on just as I'm going until he sees me again, i.e., $\frac{1}{2}$ an hour's walk—the rest of the time in my chaise longue. There's really nothing to tell. He had such a charming little old-fashioned photograph in a round frame on his mantelpiece—faded—but so delightful—a girl with her curls pinned back and a velvet ribbon round her throat. . . . His mother, I suppose. This seemed to me more important than all else.

Your Wig

Sunday,

Darling Bogey,   (October 17, 1920)

It's 3-30, Sunday afternoon. Marie is out and L.M. has gone off to tea with some cronies and a French poodle. So I have the house to myself. It's a cloudy, windless day. There is such a great stretch of sky to be seen from my terrasse that one's always conscious of the clouds. One forgets that clouds *are* in London and here they are—how shall I put it —they are a changing background to the *silence*. Extraordinary how many planes one can see—one cloud and behind it another and then a lake and on the far side of the lake a mountain. I wonder if you would feed on this visible world as I do. I was looking at some leaves only yesterday—idly looking—and suddenly I became conscious of them— of the amazing 'freedom' with which they were 'drawn'—of the life in each curve—but not as something *outside oneself*, but as part of one— as though like a magician I could put forth my hand and shake a green branch into my fingers from . . . ? And I felt as though one received— accepted—absorbed the beauty of the leaves even into one's physical being. Do you feel like that about things?

Ah, but you would have loved the golden moth that flew in here last night. It had a head like a tiny owl, a body covered with down— wings divided into minute feathers and powdered with gold. I felt it belonged to a poem of yours.

The paper has come. I think the paragraphs are an extraordinary improvement. They 'catch hold' of the reader, they draw him in. The frigidity which was a danger in the leader is gone. There's somehow a welcome touch in them as old Moult would say. Seriously, I am sure they are right. I always *miss* a long review by you. I hunt down your initials first.

Tomlinson's story was *very* good.[1] It just missed it, though, at the end. I mean judging from the Tchekhov standpoint. The thing I prize, admire, and respect in his stories is his knowledge. They are true. I trust him. This is becoming most awfully important to me—a writer *must* have knowledge—he must make one feel the ground is firm beneath

In a Coffee Shop.

his feet. The vapourings I read, the gush, wind,—give me a perfect Sehnsucht for something hard to bite on.

Darling, you know I'm bouleversé by the papers nowadays. I mean the *Times Lit. Sup.* Their reviewing is a filthy scandal. There's no other word. I mean they gave for instance Mrs. D. S. a long review and talked of her 'wisdom'—took her seriously—didn't say a word about her real *disgustingness* and absurdity; and then again to find a firm like Duckworth publishing ——. It's a book for the rubber-shop (*mes excuses!*). It's a book about what she calls 'bedroom talk'. It's not downright lewd, of course—not decent bawdy, but it's a defence of female promiscuity by an hysterical underbred creature.

I don't know whether it's I that have 'fallen behind' in this procession but truly the books I read nowadays astound me. Female writers discovering a freedom, a frankness, a licence, to speak their hearts, reveal themselves as . . . sex maniacs. There's not a relationship between a man and woman that isn't the one sexual relationship—at its lowest. Intimacy is the sexual act. I am terribly ashamed to tell the truth; it's a very horrible exposure.

I'll do Prowse, *Adam of Dublin,* the Cobden-Sanderson novel (an exception) and another this week and take these seriously—good ones after last week's bad ones.

How is the paper doing? How is our circulation? It ought to be high. Heavens! it's a top-notcher, isn't it? compared to any other.

Bogey, I loved Susannah Burns's letter. I am glad you gave the children the racquets; Chummie would have liked them to have them too. I always connect them with him.[1] I like to think little children play with them.

Connie and Jinnie and entourage have arrived. It's pleasant to feel all the life there—to let one's thoughts play with the party sometimes. It's a large open book, near enough but not too near—stimulating. The maids and old Hill, the gardener, arrived at 11.30 last night. I heard the voiture clattering up the dark lane and then presently Jinnie's *whistle* to them. She must have come on to a balcony. There was a shrill piping . . . and I saw her in my mind—grey-haired in her camel dressing-grown. For a woman of 64—NOT BAD!!

I'm working a great deal. I'll send another story this week. I ought to write a story a day. I would, I believe, if you were here and L.M. wasn't. But she is my curse, my cross that for some reason I just *have* to bear.

We used to play Badminton in the garden of 5 Acacia Road.

Now that she has nothing on earth to do, she does—absolutely nothing but make *French knots* in her bedroom and ask questions like: 'Can you tell me a book that will explain what makes the sea that funny yellow colour so far out? What is the *authority*?'

Goodbye, my darling boy,
Your
Wig

(October 18, 1920)

My darling Bogue (Yes, that is right. It's your other name you know.)

I return de la Mare's letter. I long to hear of your time with him. It's very queer; he haunts me here—not a persistent or substantial ghost but as one who shares $\left\{ \begin{matrix} \text{our} \\ \text{my} \end{matrix} \right.$ joy in the silent world—joy is not the word, I only used it because it conveys a stillness, a remoteness, because there is a far-away sound in it.

You know, I have felt very often lately as though the silence had some meaning beyond these signs, these intimations. Isn't it possible that if one yielded there is a whole world into which one is received? It is so near and yet I am conscious that I hold back from giving myself up to it. What is this something mysterious that waits—that beckons?[1]

And then suffering, bodily suffering such as I've known for three years. It has changed for ever everything—even the *appearance* of the world is not the same—there is something added. *Everything has its shadow.* Is it right to resist such suffering? Do you know I feel it has been an immense privilege. Yes, in spite of all. How blind we little creatures are! Darling, it's only the fairy tales we *really* live by. If we set out upon a journey, the more wonderful the treasure, the greater the temptations and perils to be overcome. And if someone rebels and says, Life isn't good enough on those terms, one can only say: 'It *is*!' Don't misunderstand me. I don't mean a 'thorn in the flesh, my dear'— it's a million times more mysterious. It has taken me three years to understand this—to come to see this. We resist, we are terribly frightened. The little boat enters the dark fearful gulf and our only cry is to escape—'put me on land again'. But it's useless. Nobody listens. The shadowy figure rows on. One ought to sit still and un- cover one's eyes.

See the end of *A Married Man's Story*.

I believe the greatest failing of all is *to be frightened*. Perfect Love casteth out Fear. When I look back on my life all my mistakes have been because I was afraid. . . . Was that why I had to look on death? Would nothing less cure me? You know, one can't help wondering, sometimes. . . . No, not a personal God or any such nonsense. Much more likely—the soul's desperate choice. . . .

Am I right in thinking that you too have been ridden by Fear (of quite a different kind). And now it's gone from you and you are whole. I feel that only now you have *all* your strength—a kind of *release*.

We are as different as can be, but I do believe we have the same devils as well as the same gods.

Here are your letters back again, love. They interested me deeply. Your Stendhal article . . . seemed to fetch the French ducks off the water . . . didn't it? I'm sorry about Knopf and the Yazpegs[1]—but can't be helped.

Take care of yourself, my beloved child, with all the wild men about throwing stones and striking. Make yourself small—fold yourself up. I'm (privately—it doesn't do to tell you these things) terrified that in your lunch hour you'll take your bisticks into the street and get caught in a crowd and march away. *Eat*—don't catch cold whatever you do. I want to put my hands on you—to touch you—anxiously and longingly. I *miss* you. Do you miss me? I miss your voice and your presence and all your darling ways.

Your

Wig

P.S.—Can you bring Ribni at Xmas? There is a shop at Nice which cures Poupées cassées. When I read of it I almost telegraphed for Ribni. I want him to be made good as new again. He haunts me—Ah, I can see a story in this idea. . . .

(October 21, 1920)

Did the fruit ever arrive? *Later*. Yes, I've just heard it did. Please Nota Bene my Nota Beenies.

Darling Heart,

I have your Sunday letter about finances. I am properly horrified at the whacks—the huge whacks that tout le monde takes out of your

---

Aspects of Literature which Knopf had declined.

£1000. Poor little boy with the pudding! Everybody seems to have a spoon except the child with the plate.

There is no doubt in my mind that you would fare better with £300 abroad. . . . There is also the chance that by next Avrilo we shan't want any money at all; we shall be living in caves and minding what flocks and what herds are left a leg to stand on. Even so, if you can, come to me then, my darling. Life is so terribly short. I know that, on my death bed, I shall regret the time we didn't have together.

As regards my own situation—I feel I ought to and could make a fair amount of money by my writing. It's not really health that keeps me back but the peculiarity of my relation with L.M. But don't misunderstand me: I can and am determined to stick it until April. The 'trouble' is that while it endures don't expect a terrific flowering de la part de ta femme. No, that's not quite what I mean. It suggests that I'm not making every effort to adjust the relationship and escape into my own kingdom and *write*. I am. But it's not an easy task.

Jinnie and Connie have been in several times. They are very tamed OR they are offended with me for not giving in about the Church. It's in their eyes every time they look at me. Very uncomfortable. Every pause in the conversation I hear Jinnie silently saying: 'Don't you think, dearest, you would like to see Father X?' And I have in consequence a kind of No Popery manner. What a bother!

To be free—to be free! That's all I ask. There's nine o'clock striking gently, beautifully from a steeple in the old town. The sound floats across the water. I wish you were here and we were alone. . . . Did I tell you I have a little bookcase made by a carpenter *wot* lives on the hill? He made it most rarely: dovetailed the corners—isn't that right— and cut a little ornament on the top shelves and then painted it pale yellow. 24 francs. His wife sent it with a bouquet of zinnias, the like of which I've never seen. These people with their only child, a lovely little boy of about five, live in their *own* house with their *own* garden. He seems to work for his own pleasure. Where do they get the money? The little boy who's like an infant St. John wears little white overalls, pink socks and sandals. 'Dis bon jour à Madame! Où est ton chapeau! Vite! Ote-le!' and this hissed in a *terrible* voice with rolling eyes by the father. The little boy slowly looks up at his father and gives a very slow ravishing smile.

It's really queer about these people. Marie was saying the mimosa tree *leans*—it's got a list on it—and, of course prophesying that ('espérons toujours que *non*, Madame, *mais* . . .') it will fall and crush us all. When she described how the tree leant she took the posture—she became a mimosa tree—little black dress trimmed with crepe, white apron, grey hair—changed into a tree. And this was so *intensely* beautiful that it made me almost weep. It was Art, you know. I *must* get up. The day is still unbroken. One can hear a soft roaring from the sea and that's all.

Goodbye for now, my darling heart

Wig

I think that Love is glorified childhood. Except ye become as little children, ye cannot enter. . . .

N.B. I've just got the milk book to pay. It's a minute pink *carnet de* . . . *appartenant à* . . . *commencé le* . . . you know the kind, with *broad* lines inside, and on the back the Table de Multiplication—but only up to 6 fois 1 font 6. Doesn't that make you see its *real* owner?

Later

Your Monday letter has just come. My own, forget that you forgot. I give you my pure wool guaranteed warmest Blessing. So wrap yourself up in it and don't even let your (gentlemen's size) nose show. Suffice it to say that she adores him.

About the Delamares—it's mutual. I feel just the same about that afternoon. I love them, too. It's really cold today—a winter day, but lovely all the same—charged with beauty and radiance.

Your own

Souris

Dear Love, (October 22, 1920)

I had your letter with the enclosures: all interesting indeed to me. I feel Knopf is Knopf very friendly, tho', don't you? I'd like to send him the sheets of a book that he *did* consider an absolute korker.

It's very cold here. I have a fire and a rug and a screen. But, of course, the cold is not London cold—it's pure and it's somehow *exciting*. In fact the cold here is *intoxicating*: it's as marvellous as the heat. The leaves shake in the garden—the rose buds are very tight shut—there's a kind of whiteness in the sky over the sea. I loved such days when I was a child. I love them here. In fact, I think Menton must be awfully like N.Z.—but ever so much better. The little milk-girl comes in at a run, letting the gate swing; she has a red stocking tied round her neck.

Marie predicts a strike, snow, no food, no fuel and only la volonté de Dieu will save us. But while she drees her weird she begins to laugh and then forgets. A *poor* little cat, terrified with pink eyes, looked in and begged—and then slunk away. To my joy I hear it dashed into the dining room, seized a poisson on the console and made off with it. Hooray!

What silly little things to tell you—but they make a kind of Life— they are part of a Life that, Bogey, I LOVE. If you were here you'd know what I mean. It's a kind of freedom—a sense of *living*—not enduring—not existing—but being alive. I feel I could have children here for about a farthing each, and dress them in little bits cut off one's own clothes. It wouldn't *matter* as long as they had feathers in their hats. It's all so EASY.

Would we really be so happy, so blissfully happy as I imagine? Could you delight in a little town? In this country? In burning the dry rose-mary? In tying up the very headstrong and dashing periwinkle? I could spend at least 2 years at it. Working and reading and living like this. But there must be you. You are always part of it. . . .

Dunning's was a *very* nice letter. Dent's was typical and delightful. The par. from *The Weekly Dispatch* amused me. Did you get the full flavour of the Title: *Double Harness*? Oh, darling, fancy that in cold print about Bogue and Souris. (Do you like my new name? *It's very important* to know.)

Well I must finish my reviews. Be careful of stones and bottils flying in the air. Don't shout 'Hooray!' whatever happens. I *long* for you here. But April isn't far, and I am better—and Bouchage begins to remind me of Tchekhov. But you'd like this room so. You'd love this villa so. I actually, in bed this morning, saw that there were 2 cans of hot water for your bath when you arrive. . . . You *had* a bath, put on a jersey. Supper was ready. We sat down. Marie brought the potage. Oh, *dear*!

Yours for ever.

Darling Bogue, (October 23, 1920)

You should see the colour of the sea today. Royal blue with (as Pa would say) *crests* on every wave! I've got your lunch-with-O. letter. Roquebrune isn't really near. It's near Menton but then Garavan is another bay and my villa is about five minutes from the pont which carries you over to Italy. It's at the extreme end and hard to find.

However, I bet she won't come. I don't care one way or another. She's such une feuille morte to me. I am very interested in what you say about Gertler. I wish you'd tell me more if you can. Is Sorapure his doctor? *What is his state?* It's not really morbidity that makes me ask.

Precious, please don't get pangs at my notes. I can't send them if you do. And if a thing is important I *have* to put ☞ a hand pointing to it because I know how sleepy you are in the morning and I *imagine* these devilish devices wake you or terrify you (*pleasantly*). Yes, really the papers are disgusting. —— gave —— a whole column with *Sorel* and *Syndicalism* and any-fresh-fish-to-gut-on-the-problem-of-marriage-is-to-be-welcomed, etc. She makes me feel a very old-fashioned creature. I feel if I met her I should have to say: 'And you are one of these *New Women?*'

Did you see that Connie Ediss has had the thyroid gland treatment (she's 50) and is now become 18 and climbs trees. I should just think *she did* climb trees. That seemed to me terribly significant. I remember her singing: 'It seemed a bit of all right' years ago. Poor old —— will become a *great climber,* I expect!

Well, dearest love, I seem a bit silly today. It's the wind. I feel inclined to sing,

> 'When I was young and had no sense
> I bought a Fiddle for eighteen pence.'

Perhaps it was Marie's lunch. A good cook is an amazing thing. And we have *never* had one. Heavens! it is a relief to me to do the housekeeping (I don't: Marie does)—but not to have L.M. doing it. All that awful invalid cookery[1] and then her anxiety. Here things just appear—though at a price. *Faux filet*—a piece for 3 is 11 francs!

I'm interrupted by the electrician who comes to mend a wire. He is a boy of certainly not more than 14 in a blue overall. Just a child standing on the table and fixing wires and turning over tools (rattling them!) in a box. I don't know—The world is changing. He's a *very* nice little boy. He asked Marie pour une échelle. We haven't one. 'Donnez-moi une chaise.' She brought one, 'C'est trop bas. Vous avez une table *solide*' (as tho' none of your fandangles here). But *she* scorns him and made him stand on a newspaper—nearly tied a bib round him.

Also spricht Doctor Mee: If your functions trouble you *don't* take drugs. Take an ounce of paraffin in a *glass of soda* water at night. Get 2

The word actually is 'rookery'. Perhaps K.M. meant it.

siphons from the chemist. This is really good for you—it is you see a lubricant which is what you need in cold weather. If you want anything more drastic take ONLY Cascara evacuant (Parke Davis preparation) for that is a bowel tonic. It improves the action and doesn't weaken it. How is your general health and condition? Will post reply in plain sealed envelope.

(Mee
M.D.)

Your own
Souris

le dimanche,
(October 24, 1920)

Darling, The writing in this letter goes off. But I do awfully want you to read it if you've time. Wig.

My darling Bogūe,

The paper has come. Your Baudelaire is *excellent*. I could not help comparing Eliot and you as I read. Your patient never dies under the operation. His are always dead before he makes an incision. To be serious, I thought it really remarkable because of the way in which you conveyed the *quality* of Baudelaire, as it were. That's where Matt Arnold failed so lamentably. One never feels that Shelley or Keats or whoever it was sat on his bosom's throne and though I don't mean that your subject should occupy that position when you write about him, he's got to have been there.

I am exceedingly glad you joined hands with the Oxford Professori. *The Daily Mail* FOAMED today on the subject. It almost went so far as to say the library at Liège and such acts of burning were by Professors only. It—but let it pass! In the *Times* I noted a book by a Doctor Schinz—not a good book, but the *Times* noticed it as though Schinz were kneeling on Podsnap's doormat. Faugh!

How long *can* it go on! You know whenever I go away I realise that it has happened. The change has *come*. Nothing *is* the same. I positively feel one has no right to run a paper without preaching a gospel. (I know you do, but I mean with all the force of one's soul.) I get an evangelist feeling, when I read Fashion News in the *D.N.* and then Strike News and Irish News and so many thousands out of work. But above and beyond that when I realise the 'spiritual temper' of the world, I feel as though the step *has* been taken—we *are* over the edge. Is it fantastic? Who is going to *pull us up?* I certainly had no end of an admiration for L.G. but then he's capable of that speech on reprisals—which really was a vile speech from a 'statesman'. It was perfectly obvious he had no intention of saying what he did when he got up to speak—he was carried away. It *is* all over really. That's why I shall be so thankful when you pack your rucksack and come over here. The only sort of paper for the time is an out and out *personal, dead true, dead sincere* paper in which we spoke our HEARTS and MINDS.

I want to say I was wrong about your book *The Intellectual.*[1] I was right about the spirit (or so I think.) I was wrong about the aim.

You know there are moments when I want to make an appeal to all our generation who do believe that the war has changed everything to come forward and let's start a crusade. But I know, darling, I am not a crusader and it's my job to dwell apart and write my best for those that come after.

It *is* Sunday. Don't turn away if I talk. I have no one to speak to here. And I don't only want you to listen Bogue. I want you to reply.

Does your *soul* trouble you? Mine does. I feel that only now (October 1920) do I really desire to be saved. I realise what salvation means and I long for it. Of course, I am not speaking as a Christian or about a personal God, but the feeling is. . . . I believe (and VERY MUCH); help thou mine unbelief. But it's to myself I cry—to the spirit, the essence of me—that which lives in Beauty. Oh, these *words*. And yet I should be able to explain. But I'm impatient with you. I always 'know you understand and take it for granted'. But just very lately I seem to have seen my whole past—to have gone through it—to have emerged, very weak and very new. The soil (which wasn't at all fragrant) has at last produced something which isn't a weed but which I do believe (after Heaven knows how many false alarms) is from the seed which was sown. But Bogue it's taken 32 years in the dark. . . . Without our love it would never have come through at all.

And I *long* for goodness—to live by what is permanent in the soul.

It all sounds vague. You may wonder what induces me to write this. But as I walked up and down outside the house this evening the clouds heaped on the horizon—noble, shining clouds, the deep blue waves—they set me thinking again.

The Evolution of an Intellectual.

I never felt the longing for you as I do this time—but for such other reasons.

Take care of yourself, my Beloved Boy,

Ever your
Wig

Monday,
(October 25, 1920)

My silly little Trot,

You are a nuisance to me. I can't mention money without your putting your hand in your sailor pocket, bringing out your handkerchief with a knot in it—and oh! wringing my heart by untying the knot and showing me the penny. I don't even want to borrow it from you. Take back your old cheque. I am very hard up but not to that extent. But the sooner you leave there the better. If it isn't rates, it's taxes. And now you can't chew—on your left or your right side. This put me in a panic and ∴ I sent a wire. Chew you *must* at whatever cost or you'll ruin your health and strength. And NO dentist if you're in pain should keep you waiting. You can't bear six days toothache. It's terribly bad for you. I would tie a handkerchief in two rabbits' ears on top of your head and march you off there in two winks.

Darling Precious Noble little Bogūe.

I can't scold you without kissing you. You are wicked and awfully sweet. But I DO WISH Avrilo would hurry.

By the way, would you like to give up the house at Xmas? Would it be possible? L.M. is going over for 3 weeks. She *could* stay longer —as long as necessary, I mean, if Roger and Violet don't mind. I don't know their plans—or if Mrs. K. would like them to stay on (she wouldn't).[1] If you'd like to go into rooms instead. *No, it's an absolutely mad idea.* Pay no heed to it. As long as you are there you'll do no cheaper than you do now and without any comfort. It would be a ghastly uprooting. I can't think what made me even consider it. Think of the worry and upset for 3 months. Lordy! who took hold of my pen?

No, it's April I must live for. But Xmas is near even. The station at Garavan will be open by then. This villa is only a minute away. You'll arrive 5.15 p.m. As I write, I see a fussy little engine bustling along, I see Bogue sitting in a small kerridge. I see Wig trying not to let *every-*

Our house was to be taken over by Mrs. E. V. Knox.

body see and Marie on the terrace here crying. Our 'séparation' always moves her terribly. Our bedrooms are side by side; they communicate and have a mutual balcony as well. Yours has a live writing table and a pink velvet sofa, mine a rich saignant stickleback in plush. But they are lovely rooms. *Now as you read these words* you must feel how I love you. Put your arms round me and I will hold you.

You're everything, my dear blessing—

Wig

As far as I can see from a month's full accounts we can live here EASILY as I live now on £300 each. That is saving £100 a year as we must do—I mean saving £50 each. But that's real luxurious living. I mean such living as we've never had before. The best of everything. It could be done cheaper. Of course I have L.M. to pay for now, but she won't be here when you come.

(October 28, 1920)

I'm sending 2 lots of reviews this week.

Dear Love,

The letters I have had—three from you! I expect the railway has delayed them: I mean the shortage of traigins. (That's a queer word of ours, isn't it?) I am glad to hear your tooth is better and very sorry to hear you are going to be patched by a tooth-tinker and more than sorry about my old yinkum-tags. I ought to pay that moi-même. How much is it exactly? Let me have the forms will you, darling? Never a word more came about H. King's poem. Yes, you're right to come in April—it's too marvellous to miss. I mean *Life* is and one is alive here. The weather is simply enchantment. I am taking a sun-bath cure on Doctor Bouchage's advice and at 8 o'clock the sun streams on my bed and nearly burns me. It's a very wonderful treatment. I believe in it. I'm also having those confounded iodine injections which make me an appallingly tired girl. But I believe in them, too, so I must put up with the feeling. Doctor Bouchage is of the same school as Doctor Sorapure. I have great confidence in him. He helps me greatly—so far. But I am having the iodine every other day for a fortnight. By that time I shall have to hang like a bat when I'm not walking. Like the poor Lord, who had no place to rest his head, I've no place to rest my derrière. Hugh Walpole's letter was very nice, I thought. People *are* a bit surprising, aren't they, Bogey?

575

I was very interested in what you said about ——. Queer chap! I should think he was in a way uneasy with you. Has he any children? I wish I'd seen him and Rosy. And I would have enjoyed Goodyear pa-man. I remember giving F.G. my photo and he telling me his father had said it was a *fine head*. I remember how he laughed and so did I—and I said 'I shall have to grow a pair of horns and have it stuffed to hang on Murry's door'. When I recall Goodyear I can't believe he is—nowhere—just as when I recall Chummie he comes before me, *warm,* laughing, saying 'Oh abso*lu*tely'. What a darling boy he was! You were always so beautifully generous in your thoughts of him. One—just one, my precious, of the things I love in you is the way you speak of him sometimes. Because, after all, you saw him so little.

I love this place more and more. One is conscious of it as I used to be conscious of New Zealand. I mean if I went for a walk there and lay down under a pine tree and looked up at the wispy clouds through the branches I came home plus the pine tree—don't you know? Here it's just the same. I go for a walk and I watch the butterflies in the heliotrope and the young bees and some old bumble ones and all these things are added unto me. Why I don't feel like this in England Heaven knows. But my light goes out in England, or it's a very small and miserable shiner.

This isn't a letter, darling. It's just a note. Yes, I shall provide small pink carnets for our accounts at Xmas. Slates, too, with holes burnt in them for the sponge string. Did you ever burn a hole in the frame? Thrilling deed. It was Barry Waters'[1] speciality, with his initials burnt, too—and a trimming. I can see it now.

Dearest most precious one

Wig

New Block. Bought today 7.50   Saturday,

My own Love,   (October 30, 1920)

Yesterday was so busy I didn't send you a personal letter. Only the reviews went off.

Your Tuesday letter came, telling me you intended to visit Achner (wise boy!) and that you were reading Mrs. Asquith. I read certain parts of her book and felt—just that—there *was* something decent. At the same time the whole book seems to me *in*-decent. Perhaps I feel

<hr>

The original of Pip in *Prelude*.

more than anything that she's one of those people who have no past and no future. She's capable of her girlish pranks and follies today—in fact, she's at the mercy of herself now and for ever as she was then. *And that's bad.* We only live by somehow absorbing the past—changing it. I mean really examining it and dividing what is important from what is not (for there IS waste) and transforming it so that it becomes part of the life of the spirit and we are *free of it.* It's no longer our personal past, it's just in the highest possible sense, our servant. I mean that it is no longer our master. That is the wrong image. I used to think this process was fairly unconscious. Now I feel just the contrary. With Mrs. A. this process (by which the artist and the 'living being' lives) never takes place. She is for ever driven. She is of the school of H.L., isn't she?

'I am the Cup that thirsteth for the Wine'—

These half people are very queer—very tragic, really. They are neither simple—nor are they artists. They are between the two and yet they have the desires (no, appetites) of both. I believe their *secret whisper* is: 'If only I had found THE MAN I might have been anything. . . . ' But the man isn't born and so they turn to life and parade and preen and confess and dare—and lavish themselves on what they call *Life.* 'Come woo me—woo me.' How often I've *seen* that in H.L. as her restless and distracted glance swept the whole green country-side. . . .

Oh, God! God! as I write, I want to write. I see our work. Oh! to be a writer!! What is there like it!

(By the way, Heart dearest, I do love Sir Toby's saying to Viola, 'Come *taste your legs,* Sir. Put them in motion,' when he wanted her to leap and fly. I wish I had a little tiny boy to say that to.)

Today's letter says you have been to Achner and you do think he's good. Yes, isn't he? He is a change after poor old Lucas hooking his saliva carrier on to the arum lily jar.

There's a violent N.W. wind today—a howling one—I had to go into town. The great immense waves were sweeping right up to the road and over. I wish you'd seen them. Three brigs are in—the sailors' pants hanging on lines and dancing hornpipes. Leaves are falling; it's like autumn. But the shops are full of flowers and everywhere little girls, wrapped up to the eyes, go by at a run carrying a bouquet of chrysanthemums in a paper—For tomorrow is Le Toussaint.

When I got home I found my BOX had arrived. The thrill was terrific. I wondered and wondered what little oddments you had found —whether I'd find. . . . Well, it didn't matter. I found in addition to

577

the books the 2 Indian figures and the small tan cushion. Was that all? Will you tell me in case anything was stolen. I really had a laugh over it. And the book-case made to hold the books (one shelf half full!). It was my fault. I am NOT for a minute blaming you, my precious love.

Don't forget, Mignonette, to tell me the date of your probable arrival at Xmas time.

Goodbye for now, dearest love.

Yours for ever amen
Wig

Sunday,
(October 31, 1920)

My dear Love,

Your Thursday letter and Hardy's letter have arrived. I shall keep Hardy's letter for you—unless you'd rather have it back. I'll put it in my Spenser.

In reply to your letter: I don't doubt for one instant that your feelings and mine have been alike: that we have been haunted again by our strange correspondences. Your letter might *be* my letter—if you know what I mean. You say just what I had meant to convey in my letter and I, too, feel that I don't *want* a God to appeal to—that I only appeal to the spirit that is within me.

You say you would 'dearly love to know exactly what I feel'—I thought I had told you. But my writing is so bad, my expression so vague that I expect I didn't make myself clear. I'll try to.

	'Between the acting of a dreadful thing
What a	And the first motion, all the interim is
book is	Like a phantasma or a dreadful dream;
hidden	The genius and the mortal instruments
here!	Are then in council; and the state of man
	Like to a little Kingdom suffers then
	The nature of an insurrection.'

The 'thing' was not always 'dreadful' neither was the 'dream', and you must substitute 'spirit' for genius—otherwise there you have my life as I see it up till now—complete with all the alarms, enthusiasms, terrors, excitements—in fact the nature of an insurrection.

I've been dimly aware of it many times—I've had moments when it has seemed to me that this wasn't what my little Kingdom ought to be like—yes, and longings and regrets. But only since I came away this time have I *fully realised* it—confronted myself as it were, looked squarely at the extraordinary 'conditions' of my existence.

. . . It wasn't flattering or pleasant or easy. I expect your sins are of the subconscious; they are easier to forgive than mine. You are, I *know*, a far nobler and stronger nature. I've *acted* my sins, and then excused them or put them away with 'it doesn't do to think about these things' or (more often) 'it was all experience'. But it hasn't ALL been experience. There IS waste—destruction, too. So, Bogey,—and my inspiration was our love: I never should have done it otherwise—I confronted myself. As I write I falsify slightly. I can't help it; it's all so difficult. The whole thing was so much *deeper* and more *difficult* than I've described it—*subtler*—less conscious and more conscious if you know what I mean. I didn't walk up and down the room and groan, you know. As I am talking to you I'll dare say it all took place on another plane, because then we can smile at the description and yet mean something by it.

But as I say my inspiration was Love. It was the final realization that Life for me was intimacy with you. Other things attend this. But this *is* my life on this earth. I see the Fairy Tale as our history really. It's a tremendous symbol. The Prince and Princess do wed in the end and do live happy ever after as King and Queen in their own kingdom. That's about as profound a truth as any. But I want to talk to you rather than write to you. I feel—only *now* can we talk.

And I don't want to imply that the Battle is over and here I am victorious. I've escaped from my enemies—emerged—that is as far as I've got. But it is a different state of being to any I've known before and if I were to 'sin' now—it would be mortal.

There. Forgive this rambling involved statement. But, my treasure, my life is ours. You know it.

A thousand thanks for managing the Constable affair. I am, of course, more than satisfied.

The papers have come. I've not read the *A.* yet. The *D.N.* astounds me. I believe they are making a dead set against us. But really my quotations proved the idiocy of Mrs. S.—surely. Really, I CAN'T understand this world. Then did you see their caricature of Prowse's novel? I'll send it you. It's almost *word for word*. But Prowse wrote as seriously as Duhamel. AND the *D.N.* reviewed his novel—gave it a 'good' review a week or two ago. It's like each time one picks up a dish the crack seems more evident. Each time I read the paper I get the same sharp little shock. But it will be funny to see how they will *rend* me.

It's a very cold sea-shell of a day. But I am content. That is what this climate makes me feel.

I will write about the *Athenæum* tomorrow.

Goodbye, my own love

Wig

Monday,
(November 1, 1920)

Monday: Midi: Waiting for lunch. 'En tirant la langue comme un chien' as they say here.

My own Precious,

It's simply heavenly here today—warm, still, with wisps of cloud just here and there and le ciel deep blue. Everything is expanding and growing after the rain; the buds on the tea roses are so exquisite that one feels quite faint regarding them. A pink rose —'chinesy pink' in my mind—is out—there are multitudes of flowers and buds. And the freezias are up and the tangerines are turning. A painter whose ladder I see against the house across the valley has been singing ancient church music—awfully complicated stuff. But what a choice! How much more suited to the day and the hour than—and now, I'm dished. For every song I wanted to find ridiculous seems somehow charming and appropriate and quite equally lovable.

> I put more whitewash on the old woman's face
> Than I did on the gar-den wall!

—for instance. That seems to me a thoroughly good song. You know the first two lines are:

> Up an' down, up an' down, in an' out the window,
> I did no good at all.

Sam Mayo used to sing it. Things weren't so bad in those days. I really believe everything was better. The tide of barbarism wasn't flowing in.

Oh, Bogey, I wanted to ask you: Did you care about the Mayor of Cork? It was a most terrible shock to me. I'd been reading about his appalling suffering in the *Eclaireur* and you know I never thought he *could* die. I thought he simply couldn't. It was a ghastly tragedy. Again, I feel the people ought to have rushed out of the prison and made Lloyd George or whoever it was free him. My plan (this sounds heartless; yes, but I would have done it; I'm not laughing at the Lord Mayor —God forbid!) was to kidnap Megan Lloyd George and inform the père that so long as the Lord Mayor was imprisoned she went unfed. Why don't the Sinn Feiners do things like this? Murder Carson, for instance, instead of hunger strike.

After lunch. I've read your Baudelaire. I think it's extremely fine— really *masterly*. It made me thirst after a book of such critical portraits. You've made a most extraordinary leap forward in your *power of interpreting*. One used to feel with you a certainty that the knowledge was there but a kind of difficulty prevented you from sharing it. There was in spite of your desire to express yourself *almost an involuntary* withholding of something. That's very difficult to explain. I felt it until recently—quite recently. And now that it's gone not only have I the reader's deep 'relief' but I seem (am I fantastic?) almost to rejoice in your consciousness of your liberation as well.

Goodbye dearest love. No letters today—as yet. *Next* month we meet! Oh, *Bogey*.

Your Wig

I was all wrong about the house painter!! He's just come back from lunch—in a grey flannel suit—put on his overall and started singing in English! Elizabethan airs. He must be some sensible fellow who's taken the little house and is doing the job himself. He makes me think of you —but his singing is different—more difficult, darling.

'What is milk a metre now?' L.M.

Dream I.

I was living at home again in the room with the fire escape. It was night: Father and Mother in bed. Vile people came into my room. They were drunk. B.H. led them. 'You don't take me in, old dear' said she. 'You've played the lady once too often, Miss —— coming it over me.' And she shouted, screamed *Femme marquée* and banged the table. I rushed away. I was going away next morning so I decided to spend the night in the dark streets and went to a theatre in Piccadilly Circus. The play, a costume play of the Restoration, had just begun. The theatre was small and packed. Suddenly the people began to speak too slowly, to mumble: they looked at each other stupidly. One by one they *drifted* off the stage and very slowly a black iron curtain was lowered. The people in the audience *looked* at one another. Very slowly, silently, they got up and moved towards the doors—stole away.

An enormous crowd filled the Circus: it was black with people. They were not speaking—a low murmur came from it—that was all. They were still. A white-faced man looked over his shoulder and *trying to smile* he said: 'The Heavens are changed already; there are six moons!'

Then I realised that *our* earth had come to an end. I looked up. The sky was ashy-green; six livid quarters swam in it. A very fine soft ash began to fall. The crowd parted. A cart drawn by two small black horses appeared. Inside there were Salvation Army women doling tracts out of huge marked boxes. They gave me one! 'Are you corrupted?'

It got very dark and quiet and the ash fell faster. Nobody moved.

Dream II.

In a café Gertler met me. 'Katherine, you must come to my table. I've got Oscar Wilde there. He's the most marvellous man I ever met. He's splendid!' Gertler was flushed. When he spoke of Wilde he began to cry—tears hung on his lashes, but he smiled.

Oscar Wilde was very shabby. He wore a green overcoat. He kept tossing and tossing back his long greasy hair with the whitest hand. When he met me he said: 'Oh *Katherine!*'—very affected.

But I did find him a fascinating talker. So much so that I asked him to come to my home. He said would 12.30 to-night do? When I arrived home it seemed madness to have asked him. Father and Mother were in bed. What if Father came down and found that chap Wilde in one of the chintz armchairs? Too late now. I waited by the door. He came with Lady ——. I saw he was disgustingly pleased to have brought her. 'Dear Lady ——!' and M. in a red hat on her rust hair houynhyming along. He said, 'Katherine's hand—the same gentle hand!' as he took mine. But again when we sat down—I couldn't help it. He *was* attractive—as a curiosity. He was fatuous *and* brilliant!

'You know, Katherine, when I was *in that dreadful place* I was haunted by the memory of a *cake*. It used to float in the air before me—a little delicate thing *stuffed* with cream and with the cream there was something *scarlet*. It was made of pastry and I used to call it my little Arabian Nights cake. But I couldn't remember the name. Oh, Katherine, it was *torture*. It used to *hang* in the air and *smile* at me. And every time I

resolved that next time *they let someone* come and see me I would ask
them to tell me what it was but every time, Katherine, I was *ashamed*.
Even now. . . .'

I said, 'Mille feuilles à la crême?'

At that he turned round in the armchair and began to sob, and M.
who carried a parsol, opened it and put it over him. . . .

My precious Bogey,   (November 2, 1920)

Your Saturday and Sunday letter have come—and I've read them
twice. I'll expect you then on the 20th of next month—on or about—
that's it, isn't it? Be sure to have your passport ready in time. I feel we
have such a tremendous lot to settle. We shall be talking nearly all the
time. But I expect it won't seem ½ so much once you are here. Things
will go easy. Yes, my calculation included rent. I think it's more or less
just.

About this little house—I don't *think* I shall be allowed to keep it
after May. At any rate we ought not to stay the summer through here.
I should like to have this little house by the sea. It's extraordinarily
satisfactory. In fact it's almost ideal—quite ideal in its way. So small
and yet not cramped—the position perfect—the garden perfect. I love
the little place *deeply*. It will be a great wrench to get away. But I've
got my eye on another quite near. At any rate, we shall not have great
difficulty, I don't think. I should like to keep Marie if possible wherever
we are in France. She saves enormously in time, worry, energy, everything and looks after all one's interests. But indeed Marie is such a
jewel that I expect to lose her any day. She's much too good to be true.
She's what one has always sought after.

We'd better keep all our plans *dead secret* until we have discussed
them, hadn't we?

I'm not up to much today. Yesterday was dark and stormy; today is
too. And in spite of my feelings the weather affects me physically. I
fly so high that when I go down—it's a drop, Boge. Nothing serious;
just a touch of cold, but with it to 'bear it company' a black mood.
Don't pay any attention to it. I expect it will have lifted utterly by the
time this reaches you. And it's really caused by a queer kind of *pressure*
—which is work to be done. *I am writing*—do you know the feeling?
and until this story is finished I am engulfed. It's not a tragic story
either—but there you are. It seizes me—swallows me completely. I am
Jonah in the whale and only you could charm that old whale to dis-

583

gorge me. Your letters did for a minute but now I'm in again and we're thrashing through deep water. I fully realise it. It's the price we have to pay—we writers. I'm lost—gone—possessed and everybody who comes near is my enemy.

The very queer thing is tho' that I feel if you were here this wouldn't happen. Work wouldn't then be the *abnormal* but the normal. Just the knowledge that you knew would be enough. Here's egoism!! But it's to excuse a very faded old letter.

It's so *unfair* with these letters of yours. But you understand, don't you, love? Tomorrow I expect I shall be up in the clouds again with the story finished.

And my deep love—my new love—no breath could ever touch it. It abides. I am *your*

Wig

F——'s letters came—thank you, darling—and a cheque for the books—5/- too much. Take it off the next ones.

Wednesday, 8.35 p.m.,
(November 3, 1920)

Here it is under my hand—finished—another story about as long as *The Man Without a Temperament*—p'raps longer. It's called *The Stranger*, a 'New Zealand' story. My depression has gone, Boge; so it was just this. And now it's here, thank God—and the fire burns and it's warm and tho' the wind is howling—it can howl. What a QUEER business writing is! I don't know. I don't believe other people are ever as foolishly excited as I am while I'm working. How could they be? Writers would have to live in trees. I've *been* this man, *been* this woman. I've stood for hours on the Auckland Wharf. I've been out in the stream waiting to be berthed—I've been a seagull hovering at the stern and a hotel porter whistling through his teeth. It isn't as though one sits and watches the spectacle. That would be thrilling enough, God knows. But one IS the spectacle for the time. If one remained oneself all the time like some writers can it would be a bit less exhausting. It's a lightning change affair, tho'. But what does it matter! I'll keep this story for you to read at Xmas. I only want to give it to you now. Accept my new story. Give it your blessing. It's the best I can do and therefore it is yours. If it pleases you nobody else counts—not one.

Your own Wig

Thursday,
(November 4, 1920)

Thursday: I had about 1 inch of mouse's tail from you today, but it was the gay and wavy end so it didn't matter. 'Twas writ on Monday. Good morning, my darling! There's a debonair wind blowing today and a very pale, faint jonquil sun. I send you Hugh Walpole's letter. He seems to me most awfully nice; and it is in reply to one which I sent him telling him what I really *did* think of his book—I mean as man to man—I said 'Just for once I'll be *dead frank*' and you know what that means. But I felt nobody else ever *would* and it was an opportunity. Besides his letter somehow called for one's deep sincerity. And instead of sending mine back with 'This is outrageous'—he replies—so gently. Won't you see him? I feel (what a volte face!) he's almost a friend of ours.

—— wrote yesterday too—touched one's heart. His wife has been very ill, she's had an operation and so on, and poor —— is shattered. His letter has actually 'by the Grace of God' and 'D.V.' in it. What old Death can shake out of us! But it's very touching to know how frail is one's hold on Picture Galleries and Editions de Luxe.

If the Last Trump ever *did* sound—would it frighten US? I don't think it would in the least. If God didn't take us both into Heaven I'd rather be in Hell and out of sight of anyone so stupid.

(I told poor old L.M. yesterday that after I died to PROVE there was no immortality I would send her a coffin worm in a match box. She was gravely puzzled.)

I must write my review. Goodbye my precious. The sun has gone in again—he'll have to do better than this at Christmas.

Wig

Friday,
My precious darling,   (November 5, 1920)

You've NOT done it again. I'll never mention a single thing again. I meant to be rather funny about the box with all the cardboard—the famous box—like our *grands meubles* at Paris which ended in two of the smallest tables in the world with the tiniest jugs and basins on them. *Send no more Basil,* please, love.[1] *Re* books, I'll not have any more just now. Don't worry.

[1] I *think* this is a reference to the telegram in *The Singing Lesson:* 'Pay no attention to letter must have been mad bought hat stand today Basil.'

I am glad you are going to see Elizabeth.[1] I confess I've a great *tendre* for her really, more than I'd tell anybody. Perhaps it is just sentimentality—but I feel that in her 'innermost she', . . . oh, p'raps that's too much. I'd better wait and here what you dishcover. The Flat-iron party (a VERY good joke) amused me awfully. I like Mrs. Wells, too. But no, we were never bright and young like people are.

Oh, by the way, I had my photo taken yesterday—for a surprise for you. I'll only get des épreuves on Monday tho'. I should think it ought to be extraordinary. The photographer took off my head and then balanced it on my shoulders again at all kinds of angles as tho' it were what Violet would call an art pot. 'Ne bougez PAS en souriant leggerreMENT—Bouche CLOSE.' A kind of drill. Those funny studios fascinate me. I must put a story in one one day. They are the most *temporary shelters* on earth. Why is there always a dead bicycle behind a velvet curtain? Why does one always sit on a faded piano stool? And then, the plaster pillar, the basket of paper flowers, the storm background—and the smell. I love such endroits.

Wig

[Drawing of Villa Isola Bella, see p. 593]

Re your journey   Friday,

My own Love,   (November 5, 1920)

While I think of it: Would it worry you very much to bring your big suet case (registered) with clothes in it? Things to wear. The point is this. No, I DON'T want you to dress up, or to worry, but it would be most awfully nice if you brought a clean suit for here and a pair of grey trousers to wear with your jaeger jersey—or a grey suit—I can't remember what you've got. But I fearfully want you to look a little bit pretty—for Marie, for the doctor, for Jinnie, for. . . . At the same time I know you may be a little fed up with me for suggesting it. But the journey isn't very grubby nowadays, so if you do bring your not oldest overcoat it won't get spoilt. And a Hat. I don't want to make you feel I ask you to spend D's.

Bring as much as you like: I can guard it for you here, and keep my book money in future (if you agree to the scheme) to pay for the registration. I know you thought of coming in a rucksack and spegchiks: that's why I write. It's 2 cold at Xmas for white duck trousers.

---

[1] Katherine's cousin, Elizabeth of the German Garden.

Now, just absolutely straight dinkum would a cheque for £5 help with clothes? *Please answer.* P'raps it would be more convenient for you to send the big suit-case on—in front of you? But I don't think so. It means a tagseye across Paris, but that's worth it. The Metro's *inferno* at present.

What are your idears?

Wig

My precious darling,   (November 6, 1920)

Your Friday letter has come and the new Tchehov. I'll do the column as quickly as I can. You wonder I am sure that I don't send more work; that I take so long. It's not my fault. As a matter of fact I ought not to do even what I do just now. I have had the subject out several times with Bouchage. For some reason I'm in such a queer state mentally—work excites me MADLY and fatigues me, too. I can't take it calmly. It sounds perfectly absurd, but it's an immense effort to begin and when I do begin I begin to get into a fever. And I am suffering with pains in my head-box. Awful ones. Of course with our imagination I think it can only mean my brain's going up like a rocket one day soon or I've got something pressing on it or a vine curling round it or a fox eating it up. You know our pleasant fancies. But in fair moments I think it's only the result of my long illness and coughing and nerves. But they were so severe (are) this evening that I thought I'd write and tell you about them. Not to apologise, or to frighten you but just to let you know because I think you ought to.

Another reason may be that in my cough mixture that I've been taking for 2 years there has been a certain amount of opium. I'm trying to knock it off now but it has had a certain effect and I think accounts for my sensitiveness now—nervous sensitiveness. I simply have to tell you this tonight. Not because anything might *happen,* but I know you are my own and will understand why I tell you. I'm a bit frightened (as we are) about these head pains and sensations of violent raging excitement.

Love, don't let this make you sad or worry you or *anything* like that. Just put it aside for future reference (I hope you'll never need it) and never forget that living alone is the devil for me; it starts all my terrors to life. You know that from experience. Just as I am more sensitive than other people *to* other people so am I, I suppose, to myself. I always notice that when I am *with* people these frights and premonitions die away and I forget 'whether I am going mad' or not (!) I suspect most writers of my kind share my nervousness, but in my case it's immensely accentuated by illness.

What a perfectly horrid letter—and written on the divinest evening. I've just seen all the anemones are up, too. That's much nicer than talking about my old head.

I wish Fergie would give us some little models. I always feel artists ought to give away their books more than they do—for some reason. I'll post you my photos on Wednesday—one is looking *bang* at you like you asked for and one half-bang.

You will understand this letter as I mean, won't you, darling? If I feel you do, it *relieves* me to have told *someone*: to have broken the silence about it. My head feels better already. What a wife!

Wig

Darling little Fellow,   (November 7, 1920)

Your long descriptive letter has come. Don't observe too much. I felt at the end you were GASPING. I don't want you to see more than it's easy to see. Yes, I do admire your observations, of course, and I am ashamed to say a wave of pure disgusting female relief came over me at your description of ——. I was lying on my bed, dressed in a peach-coloured handkerchief having my bang de soleil and I kicked up my toes at their dinner. Oh, how it does *bore* me—the —— type and that kind of conversation. If I were there and you were there we should do something desperate. You'd make yourself a ladder and I'd climb on to to your head and turn there on one toe. (Perhaps.)

All that you said about G.G. is extremely interesting. And the queer thing is that she only wants a *male appearance*. There's her essential falsity. Forgive my frankness: she has no use for a physical lover. I mean to go to bed with. Anything but that. That she can't stand—she'd be frightened of. Her very life, her very being, her gift, her vitality, all that makes her depends upon her *not surrendering*. I sometimes wonder whether the act of surrender is not the greatest of all—the highest. It is one of the [most] difficult of all. Can it be accomplished or even apprehended except by the aristocrats of this world? You see it's so immensely complicated. It 'needs' real humility and at the same time an absolute belief in one's own essential freedom. It is an act of faith. At the last moments like all great acts it is *pure risk*. This is true for me as a human being and as a writer. Dear Heaven! how hard it is to let go—to step into the blue. And yet one's creative life depends on it and one *desires* to do nothing else.

I should not have begun on this in the corner of a letter, darling. It's not the place.

Forgive Wig

Darling Bogey,

Kissing is a queer thing. I was standing under a tree just now—a tree that is shedding exquisite golden yellow leaves all over my garden path. And suddenly one leaf made the most ethereal advances to me and in another moment we were kissing each other. Through the silvery branches one can see the deep blue sky . . . lapis lazuli.

I think the time has come, it really has come for us to do a little courting. Have we ever had time to stand under trees and tell our love? Or to sit down by the sea and make fragrant zones for each other? Do you know the peculiar exquisite scent of a tea-rose? Do you know how the bud opens—so unlike other roses and how deep red the thorns are and almost purple the leaves?

I think it must be the orange flower which Marie has brought home from market. I have been arranging branches of it in jars and little slips of it in shallow glass bowls. And the house has a perfume as though the Sultan were expecting the première visite of his youngest bride. Marie, standing over me, chanted the while—almost chanted a hymn to the cyclamen sauvage qu'on trouve dans les montagnes and the little violettes de mon pays which grow so thick that one trempe ses pieds dedans.

If I live much longer, I shall become a bush of daphne, or you'll find no one to welcome you but a jasmine. Perhaps, too, it's the effect of receiving the sun every morning—très intime—the lady clad only in a black paper fan. But you must come here; you must live here in the South and forget greyness. It is divine here—no less

Wig

(November 8, 1920)

Always examine *both sides*. In my house both sides are buttered.

Darling,

Re your Mrs. A.[1] I thought it was *very good* but . . . your feeling was really contained in your words: 'The type it reveals is not very in-

[1] *The Autobiography of Margot Asquith.*

triguing.' She isn't your game. When all is said and done I feel that *you* haven't time for her and you don't care a Farthing Taster whether she made her horse walk upstairs or downstairs or in my lady's chamber. She would *weary* you. What is there really to get hold of? There's— nothing—in the sense you mean. The direct method (no, I can't for the life of me 'see' the other) of examining the specimen isn't really much good except in so far as one can . . . make certain deductions—discover certain main weaknesses and falsities. But it's a bit like trying to operate on a diseased *mind* by cutting open a brain. The devil is—Oh the very devil is that you may remove every trace of anything that shouldn't be there and make no end of a job of it and then in her case, in the case of all such women—the light comes back into the patient's eyes and with it the vaguest of vague elusive *maddening* smiles. . . . Do you know what I mean? Here's I think the root of the matter. What Is Insensitiveness? We know or we could find out by examination what it is NOT but it seems to me the quality hasn't been discovered yet. I mean it's x — it's a subject for research. It most certainly isn't only the *lack* of certain qualities: it's a kind of *positive unknown*. Does all this sound most awful nonsense to you? My vocabulary is awful, but I mean well and I faint, I thirst to talk. My landscape is terribly exciting at present. I never knew it contained such features or such fauna (they are animals various, aren't they?). But I do want a gentleman prepared to pay his own exes, to join me in my expedition. Oh, won't YOU come? No one else will do. But when you do it's a bit sickening—all my wild beasts get a bit funny-looking—they don't look such serious monsters any more. Instead of lions and tigers it's apt to turn into an affair of:

> 'The Turkey ran pas' with a flag in his mas'
> An' cried out: "What's the mattah?" '

Not that I think for one minute that you don't treat me au GRAND sérieux or would dare to question my intelligence, of course not. All the same—there you are—Alone, I'm no end of a fillaseafer but once you join me in the middle of my seriousness—my deadly seriousness— I see the piece of pink wool I have put on your hair (and that you don't know is there).

Queer, isn't it? Now explain that for me. Do I intrigue you? I wonder. But don't misunderstand me and think I think you can afford to laugh at me because of your great mind and my little one. The laugh is a mutual affair really.

'Oh, Wig, these subtleties are too much for me.' I am sorry, sweet-heart: I am just going. Let thy garments be always white and thy hair never lack ointment.

Your own

Wig

It came over me sudden.

In having your passport renewed, wouldn't it be worth it to remember your O.B.E.

These things are sometimes useful in foreign parts. If we wish to smuggle, steal, flay alive. If we have no money and only our poor faces for our fortunes, your O.B.E. would go miles further than my nose—say.

An O.B.E. may move a 'blighter' to some kind of respeck.

Don't scorn

Wig

My precious Bogey,   (November 10, 1920)

I am awfully excited today. It's for this reason. I have made an offer to J. for this villa for one year from May 1st next and tho' the offer has not been accepted it has also not been refused. Chances are even. *Oh dear, what torture!* Perhaps you don't know that my feelings towards this villa are so fearfully intense that I think I shall have to be evicted if she doesn't give it to me. It's the first real home of my own I have ever loved. Pauline—yes, it wasn't home tho', neither was Runcton,[1] not even Hampstead. Not really, not with this thrill. This little place is and always will be for me—the one and only place, I feel. My heart beats for it like it beats for Karori. Isn't it awful? And for us it is made in every single particular. True there's no salle de bain. But there's a huge saucer bath and a spung as big as me. So what matters! The divine incomparable situation is the trick, I suppose. Heaven from dawn to dawn. Walking on the terrace by starlight looking up through my vieux palmier I could weep for joy—running into the garden to see how many more buds are out in the morning is to run straight at—into—a blessing. The fires all burn—but not frightfully—the doors shut—the kitchen is big and the larder is down 10 steps that send a chill to one's knees. The garde-linge is immense, all fitted with cupboards and shelves. The luggage is kept there and the umbrellas and the flags

---

[1] See *Between Two Worlds*, pp. 226 sq.

that flew at my gate on the 11th. One get's ones parasol from the garde-linge. Your feltie would be there, too. There's enough garden for you to bien gratter in. At the back we could grow veg. In fack, it is the dearest, most ideal little corner. And private—just the next thing to an island.

If Jinnie accepts, I thought we'd stay on here until le grand chaleur. Then take the funicular to Annunciata for those weeks and leave Marie here. She could come up and take away our laundry and bring it back and generally keep our things in order while we were there. I mean she'd come by the day. It *only* takes 40 minutes to the hotel. We'd be back here in September and plant a *terrific* garden. Do you like the plan? You see we'd know just where we were for that first year. No worry. No moving. You'd REST. No responsibility. You'd just, I pray, get rested and happy and loaf about and garden and play with me and whistle on the stairs. There are 3 bedrooms not counting Marie's room, so you could have a guest if you liked.

Bogey, hold thumbs for me. Truly this is a great turning point. I'm trying to be calm, but it's not easy with such bliss in the balance—I had to offer an immense sum—6000 francs. That means your share of the rent is 3000 for the year and the franc is at present at 57.

Am I a little bit mad? You will find ISOLA BELLA in poker work on my heart. The baths are only 10 minutes away from you in the summer, sea baths with splash boards—no, spring boards—for you to plop off. I wait outside with a bun for you with big currant eyes (the bun I mean!).

Je t'aime. But do wish it will come true

Wig

Do you love me as I love you? It's getting frightfully urgent. I mean a kind of sweet blissful longing excitement and joy—always JOY.

Isola Bella *until* May 1922

My darling Bogey,   (November 12, 1920)

Did I tell you yesterday that Jinnie has accepted my offer for this villa? So it's mine until *May 1922*. I hope when you have seen it you will be happy to think that it's our pied à terre. I can't expect you to feel about it as I do. For me it's for some reason the place to work in. Found at last. It's the writing table. But I only want to sit and write here until May 1922. I've a horror of people or distractions—the time is more

Wed. Nov. 11. 1920

Re your journey:

Why am I so . . .

. . . while I think of it: send it with your very much thing

you big shirt case (registered) with clothes in it? Things to wear.

than ripe. And here at long last Life seems to have adjusted itself so that work is possible. Even if our finances went down and down we could live here more cheaply than anywhere else. I want you to plant veg. if you will at Christmas. Très important. Even if we had no maid we could live here (tho' God forbid)—we should just eat bread and lettuce on the Terrace and dust once a fortnight. I really feel it may not be notwendig even to go up into the Mountains. We'll have the whole garden of the Louise for ourselves after May (when Jinnie and Connie go) and, as Jinnie points out, the fruit and veg. That's bonzer cherries, oranges, tomates, pimentos, figs, grapes. The garden is simply divine with grass in it and trees. It's romantic, too, and very big, with lemon groves. Their villa and ours always seem to me to be an island. You see, we've no neighbours—only, out of sight, up the hill, a château which belongs to some Spaniards—and that garden we can wander in, too, for they never come and la gardienne is a friend of Marie's. It takes the ultimate biscuit.

But Isola Bella's the thing. Now, if you ever want to send anything over, dearest, like a bit of cretonne or—no, I'll get Ida to bring what I want after Christmas. For, of course, the furniture isn't pretty. Still, it somehow, even as it *is*, looks . . . to my doting eye.

You'll have a whole year here. Last night I walked about and saw the new moon with the old moon in her arms and the lights in the water and the hollow pools full of stars—and lamented there was no God. But I came in and wrote *Miss Brill* instead; which is my insect Magnificat now and always.

Goodbye, my precious, for now. BE HAPPY. Your last letters have been so fearfully woeful. Such a fool I was to have told you about my head. I was *confiding*. And the worst of it is I felt so infinitely better till I got your sad, desolate, crushed reply: 'Not long now,' as tho' we were waiting for *le dernier soupir*. Oh, Boge, Boge, Boge—Do let's try and not fall over! Or if we do—let's explain to each other (as I tried to) that we are falling.

Do please come back to me. I feel you've gone away and are queerly *angry*—with life—*not* as you were.

Your true love

Wig

Darling Bogey,   (November 13, 1920)

Will you have this[1] typed for me AT MY EXPENSE? Two copies.
And what do you advise me to do with it? I mean—ought I to try and
sell it?

If you can just give me your opinion. . . . I'm not registering it so
I'm asking you just to wire me if it comes for I HAVEN'T ANOTHER
COPY.

I am for ever your own

Wig

You know my state of mind
(a) He'll not like it
(b) It will be lost

*The unfortunate incident which is the theme of the following letters needs
explanation. Messrs. Constable had passed on to me a request from Mr.
Clement Shorter for a photograph of Katherine to accompany a preliminary
announcement of 'Bliss' in 'The Sphere'. It was required immediately. I, in
all innocence, gave them a photograph of Katherine which I particularly
treasured. I thought, and still think, it a beautiful photograph of her as she was
in 1913.* (It is reproduced on the following page.) *I had no suspicion
that she disliked it, and was dumbfounded to receive on November 14 the
following telegram: 'Entreat you let no one have hideous old photograph published in 'Sphere' burn it Tig.' Her statement in her letter 'I know you know
how I detest it' was untrue, and the implication that I had deliberately hurt her
hard to bear.*

*Even now I find the violence of Katherine's reaction almost incomprehensible
except as a psychological effect of her pthisis. For a time the alternation of her
moods was completely bewildering to me.*

                                                        Sunday,
Dearest Bogey,   (November 14, 1920)

I wired today about my photograph in *The Sphere*. I can't think who
gave it to the papers. My vanity is awfully wounded. What a dog's life
it is! Really, I haven't got such beastly eyes and long poodle hair and a
streaky fringe. That's one for —— and —— and all the rest of them. I
feel quite ill with outraged vanity. I've written to Sadler and sent him a
postcard. I'll take the front page of *The Daily Mirror* for two pins and
denige this other. I know you know how I *detest* it. It's not me. It's a

---

[1] *Poison*, I think.

HORROR. If it's given to any one please get it back. Fool I was not to have burnt it.

Tig.

My darling,   (November 15, 1920)

Your letter saying I could knock off (no need thanks) came today and you sound better. You told me too about the Part Eyes. If I were you, I'd never go—never. Why should you? They must be simply *too* awful. I don't believe I could go. I'd change into something frozen. Leave them alone. —— and his wife can go. He's queerly insensitive and proud of being invited to such affairs, mais ils ne sont pas pour nous. Tchehov hated them just as we do. At any rate it's not worth while to sit up till 1.20 for S.—ever. I hate —— for that. If I could see him now here, I'd say 'No'. I feel I don't ever want to speak to him again. Such disgusting indifference. He is a *clumsy* creature. I think I'm terribly intolerant of *clumsiness*.

Fine shades—fine shades—I'm all for them. Life is made up of nuances. One must be sensitive—sensitive to the very last nerve—or *I* must.

If I didn't live with you I'd live solitary. I'd go further and further away. I love to watch my people, to know them, but I like to keep very very free—what I suppose you accused me of—aloof. In fact, I confess that except with you I DO feel aloof and remote and rather fastidious. I'll only be familiar with *you*. Du reste j'ai mon travail. But just shaking those parties at me makes me—feel like Mother. Oh, people are careless, clumsy. The days when I could stand them are over. Don't ever ask —— here, will you? Your own

Wig

(November 17, 1920)

Thank you for the flower. Yes, it *did* touch me.

No, darling. If I let this letter go I shall repent it. For it is not all.

It's true I am hurt as I've never been. Perhaps it is your carelessness. But then carelessness in love is so dreadful. And yet what else can it be? Even after getting my present which I tried to make perfect for you in a case which I chose awfully carefully *and you never even gave one word to,* you didn't mention this other photograph. And to talk about too much fragility and so on—I hang my head. I feel timid and faint. I am not an ox. I *am* weak; I feel my hold on life is fainting-weak. But that is ME—the real real me. I can't help it. Didn't you know? And

596

then when you toss off my letter about 'passports, kisses, O.B.E.'—oh, I am so ashamed. Was that what I wrote about? Let me creep away and fold my wings. They quiver—you hurt me.

I must tell you; no one else will. I am not that other woman. I am not this great girl. Whether you did tell Sadler it was precious or not, I don't know. I scarcely hear you saying that to him.

But I must tell you something else. I have been ill for nearly four years—and I'm changed, changed—not the same. You gave twice to your work (which I couldn't see) what you gave my story. I don't want dismissing as a masterpiece. Who is going to mention 'the first snow'?[1] I haven't anything like as long to live as you have. *I've scarcely any time, I feel.* Richard will draw posters 100 years. Praise him when I'm dead. Talk to ME. I'm lonely. I haven't ONE single soul.

Dear Bogey,   (November 18, 1920)

For this one occasion I have the use of the Corona. It's an opportunity to write you a legible business letter. Will you regard it as such, as just the letter of one writer to another? That's to say —don't, I beg, think it is just my little joke. I am in dead earnest.

I have your letter saying you gave that picture to the press. Now I must ask you to see that it is destroyed at once. And in future please do not act on my behalf without sending me a wire. Nothing is so urgent that it cannot wait twenty-four hours. No earthly publicity is worth such a price.

I am more or less helpless over here, as you know. But that has got to be changed. I beg you not to publish one single solitary thing that I may have left in England.

And I want to put my work and publicity into the hands of an agent with whom I shall communicate direct. Is Pinker the best man? I shall be doing a great deal of work from now on, and I want to free myself from journalism, which I hate, at the first possible moment. At the same time I must have money.

If you do not understand my feelings about that photograph—could you do this? Could you ACT as if you did?

I am so bitterly ashamed of this affair that I'd pay for bookmarkers with a new photograph.

You do not understand. I cannot make you. But at least you did

[1] *The Stranger.* 'But her words, so light, so soft, so chill, seemed to hover in the air, to rain into his breast, like snow.'

know—tho' you may have forgotten—that I hated this thing. And you did possess other photographs of mine that you knew I did not mind.

I can't write to you personally, tonight. The other face gets in the way! Is that the person you've been writing to for the last four years?

I am terribly sorry about it all. But please for my sake—I'll even stoop and mention my health—put me out of my anxiety and let me feel that you will always send a wire—at my expense—before you act for me.

    Don't misunderstand your
       Wig

Until I do get an agent—you will act for me? I'm sending another story tonight. And I'd be immensely grateful if you'd suggest what I ought to do with it.

  Wig

Dearest Bogey,   (November 21, 1920)

Thank you very much for all my little drawings. The nicest you ever made was the hobgoblin with the fork dashing off to eat that sole.

'Be sprightly—thou'rt among friends,' he seemed to be saying.

I am very glad you liked *Miss Brill*. I liked her, too. One writes (*one* reason why is) because one does care so passionately that one *must* show it—one must declare one's love.

But oh, there are so many stories to write and they are all so different.

The paper came this morning and 2 *Newses* and *The Literary Supplement*. The *News* is sordid; there's no other word for it—and such sordid news. Dreadful people behaving in such an odious way. One feels—not frightened, but that never never will one return to such a city.

The paper . . . wasn't a very good number, was it? In fact I think you must have driven your cold into it and there it *rages*. Poor *Athenæum*!

Let me be frank. The tone isn't quite certain, either. 'A trumpet to the soul of the nation.' That doesn't ring: it's common property: it has been blown by so many writers that it's gone dull. Perhaps I'm out of sympathy. I suppose those leading pars must be topical—now I'm referring to the later ones.

Beresford's story was just so bad that I could hardly credit it!

I had been waiting for the review of the Grenfell brothers. This book must have been an *astonishing* document; but no one has discovered it.

The quotations in the *A.* are enough to make one glimpse what a feast was there. But C.F.! Ye—Gods—in the name of Psychology what balderdash is this! I think it's far the worst review that has been in the paper.

E.B. had Masefield delivered into his hands. It's queer how an author always gives away finally his *secret weakness*. Here is *anatomy of description instead of creative power:* it comes of course from a weakness of creative power. One thinks the effect can be produced by an *infinite piling on.* But there's a whole fascinating argument dropped there. E.B. evidently wishes to keep in with J.M. (or perhaps that's unkind of me).

The review of Ruskin, too. Fancy talking of Ruskin's 'marvellous confidence in himself'. Fancy being taken in to that extent. If the reverse was ever true of a man it was of R. His efforts are pitifully obvious to overcome this.

Sullivan tries to be a little knowing about Russia, but it's rather 'Talks to our Readers'. D.L.M. is always good, but Dent is disappointing—isn't he?

Poor old Aldous almost waves the flag off the stick! He's very exhausted on his book diet. He seems only to turn *from* books *to* books.

I hope you won't be offended by my saying all this, Boge. It's just how it struck me. The truth is I am not in a mood for papers and perhaps not sympathetic. Oh, what a trial it must be! Do you enjoy it at all?

We shall talk about all this when you come over. You're not going to tell a soul about your giving up the paper, till then, are you?

M.'s novel is here. Je tremble dans mes souliers de fourrure. The worst of it is I shall tell the truth. I shan't know M. while I read it. I shan't be able to help myself. I posted you 4 novels today. I don't want any money for them. Keep the money—you can call it *telegraph money.*

It's so cold here today—glacial. I wish I could draw you my fire— my golden stag. Or the blue glass bowl of orange blossom

Yours
Tig

Are you doing any of your *own* work?

(November 24, 1920)

Here's a photograph of the girl you are NOT in love with—sitting on the steps of her vegetable garden. It is one of her hiding places.

Answering your Sunday letter

Dearest Bogey,

I do wish you'd send me your article *Art and Morality* as soon as you can. I'd immensely like to see it. All my ideas on this subject are VERY lively just now but I simply haven't the time to write them. They will have to *filter through*. But all I know I have learnt by studying divine Shakespeare. I feel that only now do I begin to understand how mighty he is ... but one feels that every six months at least ... 'Chief nourisher at Life's feast'.

However, let me commend to your notice perhaps the most perfect written phrase in all literature: '*Reverence—that angel of the world.*' I am going to ask it to go before my new book. It says all I would say. Merciful Powers! what a man is this!

Will you send me, too, my copy of *Cinnamon and Angelica*? I am very anxious to re-read it.

I'm a little bit sorry you are writing on Art and Morality just now, because 'a clear logical statement' is nothing like enough! The breath of life is in the subject—and it must blow easy, easy, filling the sail. Perhaps that's only an uneasy fear on my part of which I ought to be ashamed.

But *do* send me the article. The subject is of FIRST importance.

It's still cold—ice cold here. Snow on the mountains. The thermometer dropped 10 degrees in 24 hours. I fear for the anemones: they are just about 5 inches high—très frisé—lovely; and the ranoncules are smaller still. They want sun. I tried to comfort them yesterday, but they referred me to my own nose! Which was in very truth all but bitten off.

I am making my Isola Bella very nice. It is shabby beyond words inside, with old faded papers and ceilings that are sicklied o'er with pale casts of dear knows what. But who cares? The windows of the salon have dear little cotton corduroy velveteen trousers to keep them warm at 10.50 the mètre. You'll see at Christmas.

Your loving
Wig

Dearest Bogey,   (November 27, 1920)

Don't let's speak of it again. These things are simply part of life. Why? One's question whispers out and out into the darkness: there *is* no answer.

And you have got a terrific case against me which is: I am OVER-sensitive, *impossible*—Life being what it is. Also, it is not within the bounds of possibility that we should be in quite the same worlds. I have hiding places—so have you. They are very different ones. We do though emerge from them strange to each other, and it's only when the strangeness wears off that we are together. This must ever be so. We share *something*—not *all*. I think by recognising that fully we shall cease hurting each other ever. What we share we prize enough to wish to share it: the rest is our own.

And forgive me if I hurt you—*ever*. Oh, I can't *bear* to hurt people! least of all my dear Bogey.

I'll write to Pinker. I have a long story here—very long—which I want to get published serially. It's supremely suitable for such a purpose. And it would bring me in money. Its form is the form of *The Prelude* BUT written today, not then.[1] *The Prelude* is a child's story. But I shall not sell it unless I am offered a good deal of money. Yes, please send *The Stranger* to *The Mercury* as soon as possible, will you?

I didn't think for one infinitesimal moment that you deliberately gave that photograph to anybody. How *could* I think such a vile thing? I thought you didn't think at all.

Just a breath of something else. Anthony Asquith has sent me a letter which makes me feel that there are young people for whom one writes! He must be a darling boy. I wrote to him explaining how you'd sent his letter to me *privately* and he says of course he couldn't be angry! Oh, but it's such a real *boy's* letter—my kind of boy, at any rate. And those quick words which are scratched out—how they express the lovely impatience of youth which knows what it wants to say and chafes at the rein!

If you see him, please give him my love. All is well, darling?

Wig

Darling little Fellow,   (November 28, 1920)

Il fait beau, aujourd'hui. I am sitting in my long chair on the terrace. The wind of the last days has scattered almost the last of the fig leaves and now through those candle-shaped boughs I love so much there is a

[1] This *may* refer to *The Daughters of the Late Colonel*.

beautiful glimpse of the old town. Some fowls are making no end of a noise. I've just been for a walk on my small boulevard and looking down below at the houses all bright in the sun and housewives washing their linen in great tubs of glittering water and flinging it over the orange trees to dry. Perhaps all human activity is beautiful in the sunlight. Certainly these women lifting their arms, turning to the sun to shake out the wet clothes were supremely beautiful. I couldn't help feeling—and after they have lived they will die and it won't matter. It will be all right; they won't regret it.

A small, slender bird is pecking the blue bayberries. Birds are much milder here, much quicker, properly on the qui vive, you know. Bogey dear, do you mind? I've *done* with England. I don't even want to see England again. Is that awful? I feel it is rather. I know you will always want to go back. I am collecting possessions at an awful rate. All my pennies go on them. Don't expect your Wig to have 2 pairs of flannel trousers; she only buys 2 pairs of curtains or a pair of coffee pots. But they are all movables. They can all be carried up the mountains. Wander with me 10 years—will you, darling? Ten years in the sun. It's not long—only 10 springs. If I manage to live for 10 years I don't think I'd mind dying at 42 and then you'd be about the age of Johnny Fergusson—very beautiful and brown and free and easy in your ways. But as to starting a theatre for ——s to come to—Lord, Lord—not I.

You are coming quite soon now—aren't you, Boge? I shan't come to meet you at the station. This station is an absolute *death-trap*. Trains are always late; you have to wait in the open and horrid men wave you away from the barriers even. Perhaps our own station will be open by then. That would be perfect for it's only one minute off. But otherwise I shall send my special cocher for you, wearing some outstanding mark for you to find him by—a red rose—and I'll be here at the gate. You can't arrive at the gate, for no horse can mount the tiny *sentier*. But that doesn't matter. I only hope you'll like my little Isola Bella like I do. I don't suppose it's perfect or anything like perfect—but—well, it *suits me*. Tchehov would be happy here. Of that I'm *certain*.

There is a train now which arrives in the early afternoon. It's a very fast train. Had you better ask about it? It leaves Paris (I believe) some time after 8 and arrives here shortly after 2. Be sure you take some FORMAMINT to suck in the train in case people have colds. Frenchies are so careless. It's a pity you can't come in a box, darling. But you know about keeping warm and eating plenty—they are the essentials of right conduct on a journey. *Don't buy biscuits.* Eat dejeuners and diners whatever they cost.

My darling Bogey,   (end of November, 1920)
   I have so much to say that I don't know what to start with. Yes, I do
First, foremost, most important, nearest is

Je t'aime
[a drawing of a heart]
'cœur petit'

If only I could make that warm—or make a beam fly out of it into your heart. Your letters make me long to hold you tight and tell you that the golden thread never COULD be broken between us. Oh, don't you know that? The golden thread is always there. Bogey, you must believe that my little drawing of a heart IS a sign, a symbol. You know whom it comes from—don't you, darling? You are my Boge, my 'veen' (whoever he is, he's *very* important) you are also Basil-love and Jag-Boge. If you were here, you would believe me. When you come, you will! You *are* coming at Xmas? I am preparing for you every single day. 'I should like it done before Xmas' is my date when I give orders.

Darling, your letter enclosing the cover of *Bliss* came today. That's all right. Thank you for sending it to me. You must not be my dog any more tho'. Pinker must. He sounds a perfectly *horrid* dog, doesn't he: one that runs sideways. Do you know the kind?

I want to tell you I have had a chill. It's over now or rather it's turned the corner. Never was serious. But it took it out of me and I have been a farthing candle for light and warmth. I wouldn't bother to mention it except that I feel my novel review suffered so dreadfully in consequence. It took me 11 hours!! and the result was only that!! Is it too bad to print? I simply could not squeeze a review out of my head. But I'll make up for it this week and try and send you two bonzers.

About the punctuation in *The Stranger*. Thank you, Bogey. No, my dash isn't quite a feminine dash. (Certainly when I was young it was). But it was intentional in that story. I was trying to do away with the

603

three dots. They have been so abused by female and male writers that I fight shy of them—*much* tho' I need them. The truth is—punctuation is infernally difficult. If I had time I'd like to write an open letter to the *A.* on the subject. Its boundaries need to be enlarged. But I won't go into it now. I'll try, however, to remember *commas.* It's a fascinating subject, ça, one that I'd like to talk over with you. If only there was time I'd write all one wants to write. There seems less and less time. And more and more books arrive. That's not a complaint. But it *is* rather cursed that we should have to worry about —— —— when we might be writing our own books—isn't it?

Oh, darling—here's a Perfectly Dreadful Discovery of mine. Poor little M.'s book is the continuation of Opal Whiteley's Diary. He is in fact (this is for your ear alone) Opal Whiteley. Even the cat is called William Shakespeare and there are bits about roses in her cheeks and babies coming and horses having some tired feelings. In fact, if I didn't know poor M. I should have said so in print.

And about *Poison.* I could write about that for pages. But I'll try and condense what I've got to say. The story is told by (evidently) a worldly, rather cynical (not wholly cynical) man *against* himself (but not altogether) when he was so absurdly young. You know how young by his idea of what woman is. She has been up to now, only the *vision,* only she who passes. You realise that? And here he has put *all* his passion into this Beatrice. It's *promiscuous love,* not understood as such by him; perfectly understood as such by her. But you realise the vie de luxe they are living—the very table—sweets, liqueurs, lilies, pearls. And you realise? she expects a letter from someone calling her away? *Fully* expects it? That accounts for her farewell AND her declaration. And when it doesn't come even her *commonness* peeps out—the newspaper touch of such a woman. She can't disguise her chagrin. She gives herself away. . . . He, of course, laughs at it now, and laughs at her. Take what he says about her 'sense of order' and the crocodile. But he also regrets the self who dead privately would have been young enough to have actually wanted to *marry* such a woman. But I meant it to be light —tossed off—and yet through it—oh, subtly—the lament for youthful belief. These are the rapid confessions one receives sometimes from a glove or a cigarette or a hat.

I suppose I haven't brought it off in *Poison.* It wanted a light, light hand—and then with that newspaper a sudden . . . let me see, *lowering* of it all—just what happens in promiscuous love after passion. A glimpse

of staleness. And the story is told by the man who gives himself away
and hides his traces at the same moment.

I realise it's quite a different kind to *Miss Brill* or *The Young Girl*.
(She's not 'little', Bogey; in fact, I saw her big, slender, like a colt.)

Will you tell me if you see my point at all? or do you still feel it's
no go?

Here is an inside and an outside photograph of me in and out of my
Isola Bella. Would you like some more? I have more here if you'd like
them. And shall I tell you the conversation which just went on between
Marie and the carpet woman? Oh, no, it's not interesting really without
the voices. Even old Marie *attend Monsieur* now. 'J'ai l'idée, Madame,
d'acheter une belle tranche de veau—*alors* de faire une poch-e dedans et
de la farcir avec un peu de jambon—*un* œuf—' and so on and on and
on—the song becoming more and more triumphant and ending 'mais
peut-être il vaudrait mieux que nous attendions l'arrivée de Monsieur
pour ça. En effet un bon plat de nouilles est toujours un bon plat,' and
then she puts her head on one side and says,' Monsieur aime le veau?'

Pleased to tell you mice have made a nest in my old letters to L.M.
Would that I could always be certain of such behaviour. The mice in
this house are upstarts.

Goodbye for now, darling

I am your Tig

[Drawing of Xmas Tree and Boat]

Dearest Bogey,   (End of November, 1920)

Your new book arrived today.[1] Let me congratulate you on its
appearance, darling. Ah, you know! I wish it Every success. I greatly
look forward to reading it carefully before you come and discussing it
with you. Collins has certainly done you proud. It is a pleasant and
entirely dignified volume. I am very fond of a longish-shaped book
with a narrow page; it is especially suited to criticism, somehow.

Yesterday, I had your letter about the finances of the *A*. Really,
there is nothing to be said. B. has sat on the poor egg to some purpose.
The picture of you was life-like. Your very legs were under the table.
I would have known them among a million pairs. But, child! you have
a terrible pen for these small drawings. Dear! Dear! they are so
pathetical. When Mother came back from Switzerland 1894 she
brought me a tie-pin made like a violet, and one shut one's eye and

[1] *Aspects of Literature.*

looked through it at the Lion of Lucerne!! *Your* tie-pins, darling, all are made of a diamond that's really a tear-drop. I shut one eye and look through at my own little Lion—and my heart *faints* to see his sweet mane all in knots over his sums.

However, Liony dear, I am very happy to hear of your costume de flannelle and I think rich brown gravy shoes would look awfully nice with it. What about a *Daily Mail* hat? They look, in pictures, really top-hole. Orpen I saw in one and thought immediately of you. They are, I imagine, the result of leaving a bowler hat and a felt hat between the hatter's sheets. Will you try and get one? They haven't got *Daily Mail* written on 'em.

Yes, I'll send a Christmas story before the end of the 2nd week in December. And when you know when you are coming you'll let *me* know, won't you, dearest?

It's still freezing cold. Oh, I do feel the cold most cruelly. I *cannot* keep warm. Blankets over my knees, two pairs of everything that one has two of, a fire, soup—nothing saves me. I frissone and fade and curl up. And as soon as the sun so much as shakes his fiery head, I feel better. Bogey, when I leave here it will be to go further south.

My good Marie is ill with rhumatisme dans les reins and a fierce cold. Jinnie is laid low; Connie too. As to L.M. we have just had a fearful fight on the subject of MEN and I think she must be frozen. She always talks of 'a man is a man'—'that's a man all over'—'clearing up after men'. This is so extremely offensive to me—so *repellent* that I could bear it no longer. Why are people so coarse? It's unthinkable. I mean— and I always mean—by 'coarse': Why do they *so offend against human dignity?* Also, I expect it's Nature speaks in her tho', too. It's not all her fault. Nature is starved and she's provided with no substitute for what would have been for her the real thing.

I confess since I've been away this time my need or my wish for people has absolutely fled. I don't know what it is to be *lonely* and I love to be *solitary*.

Bogey, if my book is to be reviewed in the paper, who is to do it? May I have a say? Of course you can't and I don't want —— to, because I don't like her work at all at all at all. It wasn't for nothing that she got so excited by a mark on the wall, my Jo! that was a revelation. I'd prefer to have it done by someone who'll—oh, I don't know —Santayana, I prefer. Now I'm not being serious. I mean of course,

my darling, that's only my wicked preference. But his idea of friendship and mine are alike—that is beaucoup, isn't it?

Your very cold but loving Wig

Did you read in *The Times* that Shelley left on his table a bit of paper
with a blot on it and a flung down quill? Mary S. *had a glass case* put
over same and carried it all the way to London *on her knees*. Did you
ever *hear* such rubbish!! That's her final give-away for me. Did she
keep it on her knees while she ate her sangwiches? Did everybody
know? Oh, *didn't* they just? I've done with her.

I was fearfully shocked by ——'s stupidity about Juliet. That *was*
a blow. He has never had the faintest idea about the whole play,
evidently. What a *foolish* article! But it was worse than that. It was very
ignorant and stupid.

(End of November, 1920)

Here's a card for them—and I'll enclose the cheque for you to make
out. DO be careful of the cheque, Boge, won't you? No, I'm frightened
to enclose a blank cheque. I'll send it filled as soon as I hear.

Dear Bogey,

No {
You know that blue-green curtain that used to be on the sofa
in the studio—an Indian thing—a djellim, I think? You know the
one I mean? It's on the top shelf of the linen cupboard. Could
you send it here to me if it's worth it? I have a dark red velvet
sofa which is too dreadfully gory. I cannot afford to buy a cover for
it here and I don't want a loose cover made, for that's just waste.

If you think it would be better to send a new one (to 'go with'
old gold curtains) would you call at Liberty's, buy one, give
them this address and I'll send you + a cheque by return.[1]

♡
S
D

Yes {
Yes, that's all the best. I don't want that dirty old one again, and
they can post it and pack it and send it for tea.[2] But the colours
must be not extreme you know—not violent—just what you
would put with OLD GOLD. And if this is too much trouble—
well, just don't do it for

Wig

[1] Cross my Heart Straight Dinkum.   [2] Cp. 'Nick it and pick it and cross it with T.'

Wednesday,

My darling,

(December 1, 1920)

Two letters today from you. You are generous not to have resented what I said about *Art and Morality*.[1] It's a queer thing. You always manage to surprise me whatever I think (and you know how highly I do esteem) of your powers as a critic. I don't agree with all of your book, rather I feel you yourself would *enlarge* and *expand* much now. But your book is ASTONISHING as a whole. There's a note in it, not always loud, but clear and challenging and absolutely new, my boy. It rings through the forest of literature, my child—it is so finely purposeful. What do I mean by that? I mean you are not thinking for thinking's sake, or reading for reading's sake. One has the feeling that you are out to discover, to explore literature in the name of Life. I am only saying general things now—for I've only read through your book—but trust me, Bogey. Trust my 'flair', if you like. I still think your Sorley's a mistake, for example. You've made him up. But your Hardy—your remarks on Coleridge, and above all—much above all—your first essay. BRAVO! It is very, very thrilling when the one you believe in calmly goes one better. So, just to go on with, accept my admiration, please. (Here a salute of guns is heard.)

I have written to Squire. I was polite. His letter though was a bouleversement. He'd never even begun to see what I was getting at. Of course, I can't change the sentence. I *want* the *L.M.* to publish my serial in the spring. I am so glad you feel like that about Anne. Them's my sentiments exactly. And nothing really suits my feelings except to hug her.

I had a letter from —— today, telling me *Miss Brill* was *quite* good, quite *nice* and full of *feeling* and happy phrase—But didn't I think that it was a mistake to rate the Russians above de Maupassant? And that Proust is not only the greatest living writer but perhaps (I like the perhaps) the greatest novelist that ever has been!!!!! And what a dastardly shame to have dismissed L.'s novel (one of the 'freshest' voices of our day) in a short notice. And—but that's enough. And to spare. I will reply I would give every single word de Maupassant and Tumpany ever wrote for one short story by Anton Tchekhov. As to Proust with his Morceaux de Salon (who cares if the salon is 'literary') let him tinkle away. He must be beaten simply.

[1] See letter of November 24, 1920.

608

In very truth, Bogey, Koteliansky's saying: 'This man must be beaten plainly' is profound.

Oh, by the way, Sullivan's a silly about Santayana—and his 'scornful stare'! Rubbish! That's romancing. It's far too obvious and it's not even true. Sullivan isn't finely subtle enough for Santayana—scientific carefulness won't do. You can't dissect him with an instrument; he's not the kind. And I do wish S. could eat his dinner for once without a bottle of G.K.C. on the table. Even if he doesn't dash his viands with it he always points to the bottle. . . . His shoes will always carry a trace of Fleet Street, and he's too proud of the trace to have 'em cleaned.

Oh dear what a bother!

I am fainting with hunger. It's choux farcis for dinner with purée of pommes de terre, salade de rave and Roquefort cheese and fresh oranges—un jour demi-maigre, as Marie says. My last preparation for you is a yellow tin of Berlingots de Carpentras. Well, my dear darling, try and be a good boy and don't forget to now and then think of

Tig

[a drawing of a growing flower]

Darling Bogey,   (December 2, 1920)

Just a line in reply to your letter all about A. and H. I *should* resent the getting there as I'm sure you won't get Godber to take you. But I expect you'll enjoy the rest. H. understood food very well and an atmosphere of admiration is never wholly unpleasant at 31, is it, Monsieur? I don't quite believe in your cry against fine ladies. At least I take a big grain of salt out of my salt-cellar while you're telling me and *say*: 'I think your hair wants parting a little more to the left.'

H. too, is no end artful with those she wants to please.

I was walking about in the garden last night. It was wonderfully starry. Not a breath stirring. And pleasant it is to walk in and out of one's windows as one does in France. I'd much rather look at the stars than at the bubbles in my glass in *any* company.

But I'm very sorry you're so pressé, darling. For *heaven's sake* don't bother to tell me all about it!

Your
Wig the eremite

My darling Bogey,   (December 3, 1920)

I am so very sorry you had all that extry hard labour. And I hope
your boat's out of the storm now, at any rate, and that it will sail in
smoother waters until you've had a holiday. I 'note' you'll get here
about the 22nd; you're very sensible to travel 1st class. It's madness to
risk 2nd class anything, anywhere, for the next 50 years at least. I'll go
through the paper today with a pencil and give you *my* views. Also
your *Art and Morality* is come. I'll read that today, too. I sent off my
reviews last night. Tomorrow I'm going to *wade* into my story. Oh,
dear—curse this question of time! It's terrible here. I want to work all
day—I shall never have the whole afternoon to spend looking at things
or talking, darling, if you do come in Avrilo. I'm simply *rushing*
to catch up and shall be for evermore—whatever evermore may
mean.

You see, I was right about the dinner—after all. It was very nice of
A. to give you a lift home. Don't be suspicious about women. Are you
really? Or is that *your way*? You're very attractive to women, as you
know, but as long as they don't interfere—surely you like knowing
them. And you always can escape, darling, for though you are so
tender-hearted, you're ruthless, too. I mean if it was a question of a
woman or your work, there wouldn't *be* a question, would there?
Otherwise, I think you ought to enjoy them. There is even a strong
dash of the lady-killer in you! And think of the way you look in a glass
if a glass is in the room—you return and return and return to it; it's like
a woman to you—I have often noticed that. Don't forget you're only
31, Boge, and get all you can out of life!! You see, Bogey, your position
is difficult. I'm a writer first and a woman after ∴ I can't give you *all*
you want—above all, a kind of easy relaxation which is essential to you,
and which the glass (I don't mean that in the least scornfully) provides.
A man with your kind of mind can't go on being strenuous and ex-
erting himself the *whole* time, for your mental activity is as it were
separate from your life. Mine is all one—so it's no effort to me. The
story isn't always at a crisis, don't you know, but it is all part of the
story. This is an essential difference. I was blind not to have understood
it in the B. affair—but no—that *was* 'wrong', as we say. However, *do
feel free*. I mean that.

It's a lovely day, but by the time you come all the leaves will be gone.
The last are falling. I don't know about mes roses; at present the whole

610

garden is roses—where it's not violets. The different smells of different roses, I've only this year realized. There are 6 in my garden. I go from one to the other until I feel like a bee.

Well, darling, I must go out and sit in my tent with the *A*. and a pencil.

Take care of yourself

Tig

Darling Bogey,   (December 4, 1920)

I hasten to return this story which I haven't read and wouldn't read for £5. Oh, *no! no! no!* I'm sorry, sir, but I'm MUCH too busy—and I'm not a bit, not a morsel, interested. That is the harsh truth. And please, darling, don't tell me about A. Forgive me for saying this. But . . . the love-story in the motor-car and so on . . . oh, DON'T tell me! For I can't just listen and keep quiet, and if I do reply I shall only offend you. So I am sitting here with about 5 bearing-reins . . . and one bull's eye to keep me quiet.

Thank you most awfully for all you say about *Poison*. I agree.

If Delamare would do my book, I'd rather him than anybody. Otherwise, if you'll do it unsigned, love. If not, E. M. Forster. I mean yes, E.M.F.

And I'd love a striped silk piece for my sofa—any colour you like.

Oh, Bogey, I caught your glimpse of Clovelly[1] so plainly. I often turn and turn those days over—hold them up to the light—almost wear them again.

What *I* thought I drew was a dove with a laurel wreath, Sir Peckham. You aren't much of a finder out. The little picture of you in the D.M. hat is simply ravishing. Have you a revolver in one hand, too? *Boge*—off to see his Fine Ladyes is my name for it and it makes me laugh.

It's a pure silver day. I have a blue and white glass of tiny hyacinths on my table. The day and the flowers say—Greece, to me, and if I were a poet, they would have a poem. It's cold though. I must knock off now. Tomorrow I'll write re *Art and Morality* and paper.

Yours for ever

Tig

---

[1] The flat in Gray's Inn Road where we lived in 1912.

611

Business

D. Bogey,   (December 5, 1920)

   re The Athenæum.

I think the list suggested by you cannot be improved on. It's a pity the Exhibitions of the Week has to go because it's awfully readable at present. I don't know how sound Drey is but he certainly seems to have improved greatly. Pity he can't do something on the paper.

I think poetry ought not to be cut down and it's hard to get a story shorter than between 2½ and 3 cols.

Novels ought to be 2 only and I think you ought to aim at getting more 1 col. reviews—I mean for books generally.

Have you got your number for Nov. 19? Turn it up if you have. As regards make-up it's awfully good. The reviews are fairly short, and yet the paper has not a scrappy appearance. I think it's rather a no. to aim at.

Correspondence ought to be 2 cols. only—don't you think? And D.L.M. ought not to be more than 2.

The whole paper needs a stricter form—or could do with one, I feel, a more stringent form that is scrupulously adhered to. But I realize the difficulty of this with writers like K.M. and Co. who never can learn the length of a page. Still they ought to be hauled over the coals. A big nasty cut now and again would larn 'em.

The front pars. are—not very interesting, are they? They want more diversity—the *par.* one subject. If they run on they might as well be a short article. I think the Science article is valuable. It's a pity it can't be more varied. Where's your medical man—the man who wrote about the fatigued frog? *Orton* ought to be sent a book or two for 1 col. reviews, too.

Marginalia is utterly feeble. It had a moment, a little spurt, a few weeks ago, but ever since then it has been dead as a nib. '100 years ago' is the dust-bin, tho', Boge.

If the paper is shorter, it wants to be more *defined, braced up, tighter.*

In my reckless way I would suggest all reviews were signed and all were put into the first person. I think that would give the whole paper an amazing lift-up. A paper that length must be *definite, personal,* or die. It can't afford the 'we'—'in our opinion'. To sign reviews, to put them in the 1st person stimulates curiosity, *makes for correspondence,* gives it (to be 19-eleventyish) GUTS. You see it's a case of leaning out of the

612

window with a board and a nail, *or* a bouquet, *or* a flag—administering whichever it is and retiring *sharp*. This seems to me essential. Signed reviews are tonic: the time has gone by for any others. I do wish you could work this. I am sure it would attract the public. And there's rather a 'trop de livres, trop de livres' faint cry in it. I read the first par. of about 4 reviews and I begin to whimper faintly.

You're all right, but the others are not. A letter ought to be drafted to your regular contributors asking them, now that the reviews are to be signed (supposing that to happen)—asking them to pull themselves together and make their *attack* stronger. Do you know what I mean? I feel inclined to say to them, as if I were taking their photographs: '*Look Fearless*'. They are huddled up.

I think the shorter paper might be all to the good. But it *must* be swifter, too. If all those cobwebs are gone, we must show the bare boards.

I do wish you were here to talk it over. Writing is the very devil—specially as my pen won't go. It's not out of order—it's merely wicked—sitting on its hind legs and scratching its ear. As I write this I burn with enthusiasm for the paper—yes, it's as undiminished as ever. And this new form seems to me a great clearing of the ground, and easier for you to manage.

Only wish I had more to say, darling. Is this any good?

Ever your

K.M.

(December 6, 1920)

I've just finished a story called *The Lady's Maid* which I'm sending for the paper. I do hope you will care to print it. It's what I meant when I said a Xmas story. Dear knows, Xmas doesn't come in it after all and you may think I'm a fraud. But I think, all the same, people might like to read it at Xmas time. The number of letters I've had about *Miss Brill*! I think I am very fortunate to have people like my stories—don't you? But I must say it does surprise me. *This* one I'd like you and Delamare to like—other people don't matter.

Curtis Brown's letter and your reply came today. I am deeply grateful to you. Yes, I feel I may make enough money in America to free myself to make money.

It's *hell* to know one could do so much and be bound to journalism for bread. If I was a proper journalist I'd give the day to reviewing and

613

so on—but no! Reviewing is on my chest—AND a sense of GUILT the whole week! However it can't be helped. I'll win out and then I don't want to read another novel for——

But isn't it grim to be reviewing Benson when one might be writing one's own stories which one will never have time to write, on the best showing!

I've not written to Pinker yet for the reason that I have not any reserve stock to offer him. I hope after Xmas to have at least 3 stories ready. But it only confuses things to get into touch with him and not have the goods. He's bound not to have any interest. So Brown had better go ahead with *The Stranger* and I'll write promising him my 3 stories which will be ready at the end of this month. It was a nice letter.

Personally I want to make money by my stories *now*—I can't live poor—can't worry about butter and cabs and woollen dresses and the chemist's bill and work too. I don't want to *live rich*—God forbid— but I must be free—and ça coûte cher aujourd'hui. It's most awfully kind of you, darling, to have written to Brown.

Just while I'm on the subject I suppose you will think I am an egocentric to mind the way Constable has advertised my book and the paragraph that is on the paper cover. I'd like to say that I mind so terribly that there are no words for me. No—I'm DUMB!! I think it so insulting and disgusting and undignified that—well—there you are! It's no good suffering all over again. But the bit about 'Women will learn by heart and not repeat'. Gods! why didn't they have a photograph of me looking through a garter. But I was helpless here—too late to stop it—so now I *must* prove—no, convince people ce n'est pas moi. At least, if I'd known they were going to say that, no power on earth would have made me cut a word. I wish I hadn't. I was wrong—very wrong.

The story will go to you Wednesday morning. A typist has been found at 7 francs a 1000. *I* think she is mad as well. But I can't afford not to send corrected copies.

What a horrible note this is. And there's the evening star, like an emerald hanging over the palm. Forgive me, evening star. Bogey, forgive me. These are only sparks on my coat—they are not my real fur. But the ancien couteau burns faintly in my left lung tonight—and that makes me wicked. Wicked, but loving—loving

Tig

I have sent back the books today.

My dear Bogey, (December 8, 1920)

It is with the most extreme reluctance that I am writing to tell you K.M. can't go on.

The fact is she ought to have given up months ago but money was so urgent that she dared not. I know you suggested a month's holiday—but a month's holiday doesn't fit the case. She won't be well in a month. The strain will begin all over again and I think she has told you fairly often *what* a strain it is.

She would not, however, have taken this step if Doctor Bouchage had not made her realize it was *absolutely necessary*. He has. It is not that her health is worse than it was in London. But it's no better. She has good days she didn't have then; but she has BAD ones she didn't either. And she is not improving, as they say.

In two words—and plain ones: it's a question of shortening her life—to keep on. And that she can't do.

But you must realize how deeply she 'appreciates' the awkwardness of this for you. She knows it all: feels it all.

One thing must be perfectly clear. She wants NO money from you and no sacrifice. She hates even discussing money affairs with you. She knows you have paid debts of hers; she hopes they will be the last you'll ever pay. *This is final.* You may smile at this and say: 'I haven't any money to give her.' Right-o. But she just had to tell you.

And now I'll be personal, darling. Look here, you ought to have sent me that Corona! You really ought to have. Can't you possibly imagine what all this writing out has meant to a person as weak as I *damnably* am? You can't, or a stone would have sent it. You knew what a help it was to me in London.

But oh dear I don't mean to accuse you, because I can't bear, as you know, to make you feel unhappy. But what you would have saved me —I can't say! Isn't it awful that I haven't dared to *add to your burdens* by reminding you before? That's Mother in me. And you rather count on it, darling.

But don't feel sad—or knocked over—or don't take any of this too seriously. Easy to say, isn't it? Yes. All the same it's not RIGHT to LIVE among mountains of gloom—or to sweat blood as one climbs them. One must just run on top and be careless. I don't mean that in putting you in this hole I'm laughing at the hole. But think of the hole I might so easily trip into!! It's far bigger—far blacker—but I won't moan.

This is a very mixed letter. You ought just to love me—that's all the best—and you *must* understand.

Your own

Tig

Darling,

I open this letter to say I've just got yours of the 5th. *The Morning Post* is very whiskery, isn't it? But oh, I wish I didn't have to send my letter! Your letter makes it so hard.

My chill is a bit better today but always there. 'C'est pas grand' chose mais enfin' . . . is the feeling.

I've had a letter from Squire saying my story is at the printer's and asking for another as soon as and whenever I have one. I'll give you one to take back.

Now about things you ought to bring. Do you mean—for me? I have no commissions for you. Bring warm clothes for yourself. It's v. cold here and the last leaves are gone. We are very exposed—all our lovely trees are bare. I fear you will not think it is very pretty at all. The lemons shine on bare boughs and the freckled tangerines have two little leaves left to fly with.

I feel so queer—so *abnormal* shorn of my job that I can scarcely write to you until I have heard. And it pains me to think I shan't be in the paper. I'm shut out. But it can't be helped. No complaining.

Farewell my darling

Wig

[A drawing of Boge and Wig sailing in a boat towards the sun]

Darling little Fellow, (December, 1920)

I've just had the wire about the £30. Now this is just what I wanted to avoid. I presume it is my *A*. cheque augmenté to that sum by you.

Will you believe me or I shall be cross. I am in no need of money. I'll pay you back every cent—il y a de plus. I'm as rich as Crœsus (who *was* Crœsus?) My kine are fat; my sheep are all jaeger. Stop now! Calmez-vous! What do you mean by jumping up, you Jack-in-the-Box? What can I do with you?

Doctor B. has just gone. We talked over the affair again. He was quite definite. I shall now tell you exactly so that you know where you are.

I *have* injured my heart for the moment by over-work—but not permanently. If I had persisted I should have endangered my life. It is difficult to explain to any one as wise as you the gigantic strain of one weekly article—to a person as 'weakly' (as Pa would say) as I am. It sounds fantastic. It hung over me like a cloud. But (1) money and (2) my feeling for the paper and you made me cling. However it was (1) which kept me at it too long, I fear. At present too both my lungs are enflammés as the result of a chill. It's not serious or urgent, but if I tried to exert myself it would be. My heart is, however, the trouble at the moment. It needs rest. So I have to lie low and rest the little *fiend*. It will then get better.

However, I am not forlorn. Je suis si bien ici. J'ai ma petite villa—ma bonne—un feu d'enfer flambe dans la chéminée and lying here I can do my work when I'm not too tired. I can take it up and put it down à mon aise.

There. I only tell you all this because you're such a bad wicked Boge to worry. Stop! I'll tell you when to worry. I solemnly assure you I am afraid of NOTHING. I mean that. I do not want to die because I have done nothing to justify having lived. I mean to jolly well keep alive with the flag flying until there is a modest shelf of books with K.M. backs. Which reminds me I do think Constable might have sent me a copy of *Bliss*—don't you? But only vanity makes me want to see i. *Confession:* I want to leave it about for Marie to see and exclaim over.

Goodbye, darling. Help me to keep all fair—all serene and fine. Why should it be otherwise? No, you are not a Teddy Bear. You are a Boge and I am a

Wig

About your Book

My dear Bogey,   (December, 1920)

I have now read your book, and though we can't really discuss it until you come, I should feel ungracious were I not to write you quelques mots.

Well, Bogey, I'm your admirer. Accept my admiration. It's from my heart and head! There is real achievement in that book. While I read you on Tchekhov, Butler, the first essay, Shakespeare criticism, I liked to pretend you were a stranger. I imagined what I'd feel like if this book had fallen out of the sky—and that really gave me your measure. (There's a female standard!) At your best no one can touch you. You simply are first chop. For the first time *je me trouve* under-lining your sentences—putting marks in the margin—as one so *very* seldom does, Boge. You re-create—no less—Tchekhov, for instance. I want to make you feel what a great little fellow you are for this book! And how it makes me believe in you—stand by you in my thoughts and respect you. There! Shake hands with me. And of course I want 'to criticise'—to tell you all I feel. But not before you realize how firm and unyielding are the foundations of my praise. Here goes.

Your Hardy doesn't quite come off to my thinking. You seem to be hinting at a special understanding between yourself and the author. That's not fair: it puts me off. You (in the name of your age, true, but not quite, not wholly) intrude your age, your experience of suffering. . . . This destroys the balance.

Your Keats is performance, right enough, but it's more promise. Makes me feel you ought to write a book on Keats. It's deeply interest-ing. The last paragraph is a pity—when you praise Sir Sidney.[1] Here again I seem to catch a faint breath of *pride*.

I think Edward Thomas is seen out of proportion. It's not in his poems; he's not *all that*. Your emotions are too apparent. I feel one ought to replace Thomas with another and say it all about *him*. There was the beginning of all that in Thomas but you've filled it out your-self—to suit what you wanted him to be. It's not wholly sincere, either, for that reason.

Let me make my meaning clearer. Take your Tchekhov. Now you make Tchekhov greater than one sees him but NOT greater than he was. This is an *important dangerous* distinction. A critic must see a man as great as his potentialities but NOT greater. Falsity creeps in immediately then.

You ought to guard against this. Its another 'aspect' of your special pleading danger—as in your essay on Hardy. In your tremendously just desire to prove him a major poet, you mustn't make yourself Counsel for the Prisoner! I mean that in all its implications.

You might have borne this trick of yours in mind when you are so down on S.T.C. for his idolatry. Remember how Shakespeare *was*

[1] Sir Sidney Colvin.

618

regarded at that time—the extraordinary ignorance, stupidity and meanness of the point of view. I don't think you take that into account enough. It's too easy to talk of laudanum and soft brainedness. The reason for his *überfluss* is more psychological. (I don't defend S.T.C. but I think he and you are both wrong in 'considering' far too specially a 'special' audience). On the other hand you are splendidly just to his amazing *Venus and Adonis* criticism. (I must say that chapter on *V. and A.* is a gem of the first water).

Ronsard is interesting because you have conveyed the chap's quality so well, tho' I deeply disagree with one of the 'charming' quotations— the complexion one is perfect.

Now, I'll be franker still. There are still traces of what I call your sham personality in this book and they mar it—the personality that expressed itself in the opening paragraphs of your Santayana review in *The Nation*. Can't you see what a *farce* it makes of you preaching the good life? The good life indeed,—rowing about in your little boat with the worm-eaten ship and chaos! Look here! How *can* you! How can you lay up your sweat in a phial for future generations! I don't ask for false courage from anyone but I do think that even if you are shivering it is your duty as an artist and a man *not* to shiver. The devil and the angel in you both fight in that review. I must speak out plainly because your friends flatter you. They are not really taken in by your 'sham personality', but they are too uncertain of themselves not to pretend that they are, and you are deceived by their pretence because you want to be. It is this which mars you and it is for this reason you will not be popular. It's the BAD in you people can't stomach—not the good. But tho' they don't understand it, they sense it as treachery—as something that *is not done*. Don't be proud of your unpopularity, Bogey. It is right you should be unpopular for this.

Now let me point to your remark in the preface that you can 'do no less than afford your readers . . . a similar enjoyment in your case'. My dear Bogey! How could a person say such a thing. It's so naive as to be silly, or so arrogant as to be fantastique. Suppose I wrote: 'I have dated my stories as I venture to hope my readers may enjoy tracing my development—the ripening of my powers. . . .' What *would* you think! You'd faint! It is indecent, no less, to say such things. And one doesn't think them!

It always seems to me you let yourself go in *The Nation* especially; you count on Massingham's weakness. The worst of it is that whenever one is less than true to oneself in work, even what is true becomes tainted. I feel whenever I *am* true my good angel wipes out one bad mark—doesn't give me a good one—but, at any rate, next time, there is one bad mark the less to get over. Now you only get half-marks, and they are no marks at all, because you cannot resist this awful insidious temptation to show your wounds. Until you do, you are a great writer marred. Lynd called it 'highbrowism'. It's much more subtle.

There you are. If you were to send me back my 1/9 wedding ring for this letter, I should send the letter just the same and keep the ring in a match-box and be very sorry.

I must risk being wrong. In my efforts to be clear I am crude. I must risk that. For as long as I live I never will be other than dead honest and dead sincere with you, as I would have you with me. Do not think I imagine I know all about you. Ah, my darling, I never shall. Forgive me if I hurt you—please forgive me!

But I love you and believe in you.

That's all.

Wig

(December 1920)

I made these notes. Read them, will you?

The Lost Girl

It's important. It ought not to be allowed to pass.

The Times gave no inkling of what it was—never even hinted at its dark secret.

Lawrence denies his humanity. He denies the powers of the Imagination. He denies Life—I mean *human* life. His hero and heroine are non-human. They are animals on the prowl. They do not feel: they scarcely speak. There is not one memorable *word*. They submit to the physical response and for the rest go veiled—blind—*faceless*—*mindless*. This is the doctrine of mindlessness.

He says his heroine is extraordinary, and rails against the ordinary. Isn't that significant? But look at her. Take her youth—her thriving on the horse-play with the doctors. They might be beasts butting each other—no more. Take the scene where the hero throws her in the kitchen, possesses her, and she returns singing to the washing-up. It's a *disgrace*. Take the rotten rubbishy scene of the woman in labour asking the Italian into her bedroom. All false. All a pack of lies!

Take the nature-study at the end. It's no more than the grazing-place for Alvina and her sire. What was the 'green hellebore' to her? Of course, there is a great deal of racy, bright, competent writing in the early part—the 'shop' part. But it doesn't take a writer to tell all that.

The whole is false—*ashes*. The preposterous Indian troupe of four young men is—a fake. But how on earth he can keep it up is the problem. No, it's not. He has 'given way'. Why stop then? Oh, don't forget where Alvina feels '*a trill in her bowels*' and discovers herself with child. A TRILL—what does that mean? And why is it so peculiarly offensive from a man? Because it is *not on this plane* that the emotions of others are conveyed to our imagination. It's a kind of sinning against art.

Earth closets, too. Do they exist *quâ* earth closets? No. I might describe the queer noises coming from one when old Grandpa X was there—very strange cries and moans—and how the women who were washing stopped and shook their heads and pitied him and even the children didn't laugh. Yes, I can imagine that. But that's not the same as to build an earth-closet because the former one was so exposed. No.

Am I prejudiced? Be careful. I feel privately as though Lawrence had possessed an animal and fallen under a curse. But I can't say that. All I know is, This is bad and ought not be allowed. I feel a horror of it— a shrinking. But that's not criticism. But here is life where one has blasphemed against the spirit of reverence.

(December 12, 1920)

This is much harsher than I feel, but you compel me to speak out. It isn't even *as* I feel; it's so crude. But I simply CAN'T . . . bear your lack of a sense of proportion. It will be the ruin of us both.

Bogey,

A letter has come from you in which you say you are 'annihilated' and tell me of A. because you think your . . . what shall I call it? . . . meeting her may have had something to do with my illness. Well, Bogey—please let me speak.

I told you to be free because I meant it. What happens in your personal life does NOT affect me. I have of you what I want—a relationship which is unique but it is not what the world understands by *marriage*. That is to say I do not in any way *depend* on you, neither can you shake me.

Nobody can. I do not know how it is, but I live *withdrawn* from my personal life. (This is hard to say.) I am a writer first. In the past, it is

621

true, when I worked less, my writing self was merged in my personal self. I felt conscious of you to the exclusion of almost everything, at times. (All this is just outline).

But now I do not. You are dearer than anyone in the world to me—but more than anything else—more even than talking or laughing or being happy I want to write. This sounds so ugly. I wish I didn't have to say it. But your letter makes me feel you would be relieved if it were said.

Can't we stop this *horrible drama!* I hate explaining myself: it's so unnatural to me. It makes me feel indecent.

Let us quit ourselves like men.

Tig

On December 15th I received a telegram 'Pay no heed to my letters illness exasperated me. Are you arriving Tuesday? If so, won't write again. Fondest love, Tig'. I set out for Mentone as soon as I could. I found Katherine very seriously ill indeed. Possibly my own stupidity had contributed; but there was no doubt that the root of the trouble, apart from the phthisis itself, was over-work. In the three months since October, in addition to her weekly article for 'The Athenæum,' she had written 'The Stranger,' 'The Daughters of the Late Colonel,' 'The Lady's Maid,' 'Miss Brill,' 'The Young Girl,' 'Poison,' and I think 'The Singing Lesson' and 'The Life of Ma Parker'. I stayed with Katherine three weeks during which it was decided that I should resign 'The Athenæum' immediately and return to London only for the purpose of winding up my connection with it and getting rid of our Hampstead house. I left Mentone for this purpose on January 11, 1921.

Katherine's health seemed to improve while we were together at Christmas; but immediately I left there was a relapse. As soon as I heard of it I went to Mentone again on January 19. I returned to London early in February, finished winding up my affairs, and returned to Mentone by the middle of the month.

Tuesday,

My precious darling,
(January 11, 1921)

I shall never forget your beautiful gesture in handing me that letter. I read it and I drove home with you and you are still here. You have been in every moment of the day; it is as though you had gone up to the mountains for a long afternoon. I have never loved you so. No, my precious, until now I did not know what it was to love *like this*. This peace and this wonderful certainty are quite new.

Take care of yourself. Depend on me. Tell me anything—and feel that I am with you. My one drop of 'sorrow' is that I am not helping you. But you *know* how I am with you. Oh, my Veen, how happy you have made me! I sit here on the striped couch and Rib does sentry-go up and down it with the feather for a gun and I am still possessed by memories of my darling. On the red box there is the snail shell. It said to me this evening: 'Am I not one of your treasures, too?' Darling little snail shell—found by Boge—perfect little blue flowers brought by him. Oh, my heart, how can I ever thank you for everything!

Wig

This exquisite paper has just arrived. I must send a note to the Villa Louise—to impress them. . . . Bogey, our photographs are very important.

Wednesday,

My precious Boge,   (January 12, 1921)

It has been a perfect day. I was out on the terrasse from ten o'clock on: Marie even brought me my déjeûner there sur une petite table. I wished you had been there to share it.

I sent you a wire this afternoon, for it will be so long before my letters arrive, and I don't want you to be without a sign.

Yes, I *miss* you, my darling. But *tout va bien* and I am working and that marvellous serenity is unchanged.

Marie has got her bitter oranges. A small pot of the confiture is to be sent to Monsieur. Now that she knows 'us', I think she will turn into our nurse.

When I emerge from my work, it is to follow my darling's journey. I see him take out his pocket-book, put it up, read, (but I never can think of him asleep—ça me serre le cœur). And now you go up the gangway and now you are on deck. Oh, my beloved Veen!

Goodbye.
Your
Wig

Thursday,

Dear Bogey,   (January 13, 1921)

Thank you for your little letter 'en route'. Dear Bandol! I should like to see it again. Do you really imagine those days . . . incorrigible optimist!

All is as usual here. My cough is a great deal worse pour le moment. It has never ceased—so it seems—since yesterday morning. But perhaps it will be quieter today. It's devastating.

The more I think of it, the more I hope *The Athenæum* shuts down. But I *feel* it won't. B. is now going to prove what he is capable of . . . I mustn't let my fancy run on.

Lebe wohl!

Wig

Dear Bogey,
Wednesday,
(January 19, 1921)

No post today, Wednesday. Ida brought me a copy of the horrid *Daily Mail* which says the weather is appalling in London. Do try and see that you don't catch cold. The London climate is *infinitely* dangerous. By the way, I chanced to read a doctor's letter which said that tuberculosis transferred from a wife to a husband or vice versa was so rare as to be absolutely left out of account. It is perhaps the rarest form of contagion. This may reassure you in a mauvais moment.

No news. No change. I hear the walking world go up and down the petit sentier outside. But they don't realize their good, their heavenly fortune.

Lebe wohl

Wig

Dear Bogey,
Thursday,
(February 3, 1921)

This letter has come for you. That's all the post there was. As soon as you know your plans you might send me a wire, will you? Then I shall know when to stop writing. I have an idea you will be away a good deal longer than you arranged for. Please tell me straight out if this is so, and don't bother de faire des explications. . . . Find I can't get a room in Bordighera for weeks. . . .

I hope things are going well with you and that Bonwick et Cie are not putting too much pressure on you.

All serene here. I am still in bed, of course.

Yours

Wig

Dear Bogey,   (February 7, 1921)

I haven't a postcard but this will serve. All goes well here. I mean there is no change at all.

Try not to rush things. Don't hurry back. If you want to stay longer I'll arrange to go away as soon as I am 'up and about again,' as they say. I hope your journey was not too horrid.

Yours ever
Wig

Katherine was seriously ill during February and March 1921. A gland in her throat became tubercular and very painful and had to be drained. The Spahlinger treatment for tuberculosis was much talked about at this time, and Katherine decided to go to Switzerland to make contact with those who practised it. We arranged to leave Mentone early in May, when I had to go to Oxford to deliver some lectures. She went to Baugy, near Montreux.

Nevertheless, in spite of Katherine's poor health, the rest of this year was a happy time, or so it seems to have been in memory. The immense strain of continual separation and the burden of The Athenæum were gone. In comparison with what had gone before our separation in May was a trivial affair.

Katherine left Baugy for Sierre where I rejoined her at the beginning of June. At the end of the month, after some hesitation because of the weakness of her heart, we went up to Montana, where I hoped she would stay for at least two or three years. It was a bitter disappointment to me when, towards the end of the year, Katherine began to set her mind on going to Paris to take the Manoukhin treatment.

Saturday,
Baugy, Switzerland,

My darling Bogey,   (May 7, 1921)

I have been walking round and round this letter, treading on my toes and waving my tail and wondering where to settle. There's *too* much to say! Also, the least postcard or letter penned within view of these mountains is like presenting one's true account to one's Maker. Perhaps their effect will wear off. But at present, Boge . . . one keeps murmuring that about cats looking at Kings, but one feels a very small cat, sneezing, licking one's paw, making a dab or two at one's tail in the eye of Solemn Immensities. However, the peasants don't mind, so why should I? They are cutting the long brilliant grass; they are wading waist high through the field with silver stars—their scythes, winking bright in the sun—over their shoulders. A cart drawn by a *cow* (I'm sure it is a cow) drags over a little bridge, and the boy driver, lying like a drunken bee on his fresh green bed, doesn't even *try* to drive. It's a perfect, windless day. I'm, as you have gathered, sitting on the balcony outside my room. The sun is wonderfully warm, but the air is just a little too clean not to be chill. The cleanliness of Switzerland! Darling, it is frightening. The chastity of my lily-white bed! The waxy fine floors! The huge bouquet of white lilac, fresh, crisp from the laundry, in my little salon! Every daisy in the grass below has a starched frill—the very bird-droppings are dazzling.

Boge: 'But, Wig, this is all jolly fine, but why don't you tell me things? Get down to it!'

I'm sorry, my precious; I'll have another try. You got my telegram? The journey was excellent. The *lits salons* were horrid—when they unfolded they were covered thickly with buttons so that one felt like a very sensitive bun having its currants put in. But it was soon morning, and my mountains appeared as of yore with snow, like silver light, on their tops, and beautiful clouds above, rolling solid white masses. We passed little watery villages clinging to the banks of rivers, it was raining, the trees dripped, and everybody carried a gleaming umbrella. Even the fishers fished under umbrellas, their line looked like the huge feeler of a large water beetle. And then the rain stopped, the cows began to fatten, the houses had broad eaves, the women at the book-stalls got broader and broader, and it was Switzerland.

I sat on a neat green velvet chair in Geneva for three hours. L.M. brought tea on a tray. Do you see her, coming from afar, holding the tray high, her head bent, a kind of reverent beam on her face, and the smoke of the teapot rising like the smoke of sacrifices?

Then we mounted an omnibus train and *bümmelt*ed round the Lake. The carriage was full of Germans; I was imbedded in huge ones. When they saw a lilac bush, Vater und die Mamma and even little Hänse all cried: 'Schön!' It was very old-world. Also they each and all read aloud the notice in the carriage that a cabinet was provided for the convenience of passengers! (What other earthly reason would it have been there for?) We reached Clarens at 7. The station clock was chiming. It was a cuckoo clock. Touching—don't you think, darling? I was *very*

626

touched. But I didn't cry. And then a motor car, like a coffee-mill, flew round and round the fields to Baugy. The manager, who is very like a goldfish, flashed through the glass doors and our journey was over. . . .

This hotel is admirable. The food is prodigious. At breakfast one eats little white rolls with butter and fresh plum jam and cream. At lunch one eats—but no, I can't describe it. It could not be better though. I suppose in the fullness of time, I shall take soup at midday, too. But at present I can only watch and listen. . . . My rooms are like a small appartement. They are quite cut off and my balcony is as big as another room. The sun rises in the morning vers les sept heures, and it sets, or it begins to set (for it takes its setting immensely seriously here) at seven in the evening. It has no connection whatever with the South of France sun. This is le soleil père—and she's a wanton daughter whose name is never mentioned here.

The air, darling, is all they say. I am posing here as a lady with a weak heart and lungs of Spanish leather-o. And so far, I confess I hardly cough except in the morning. One mustn't be too enthusiastic though. Perhaps it is the hypnotic effect of *knowing* one is so high up. But the air is amazing!

It's all very German. Early German. Fat little birds, tame as can be— they look as though their heads unscrewed and revealed marzipan tummies—fat little children, peasants, and—I regret to say—ugly women. In fact, everybody seems to me awfully ugly. Young men with red noses and stuffy check suits and feathers in their hats ogling young females in mackintoshes with hats tied with ribbons under the chin! Oh weh! Oh weh! And if they try to be 'chic'—to be French— it's worse still. Legs—but legs of mutton, Boge, in silk stockings and powder which one feels sure is die Mamma's icing sugar.

Of course, I quite see the difficulty of being chic in this landscape. I can't quite see . . . yet. Perhaps a white woollen dress, a Saint Bernard, a woollen Viking helmet with snowy wings. And for your. . . . ? More wool, with your knees bare, dearest, and boots with fringèd tongues. . . . But I don't know—I don't know. . . .

I am sure you will like Switzerland. I want to tell you nicer things. What shall I tell you? I should like to dangle some very fascinating and compelling young carrots before your eminent nose. . . . The furniture of my salon is green velvet inlaid with flesh pink satin, and the picture on the wall is *Jugendidylle*. There is also an immense copper jug with lovely hearts of imitation verdigris. . . .

Goodbye, my darling. I love you v. much and I'm fond of you and I long to hear from you.

Wig

Monday,
(May 9, 1921)

Dearest Bogey,

It was a great pleasure to hear from you today and get your post cards of Bandol and Arles. *This* time I am numbering and keeping your letters. . . . You took me back to Graviers—especially those big pebbles. They are so plain in my memory, big, round, smooth. I see them. I am glad you saw the Allègres, even tho' it was sad. The post cards are very impressive. So was your desire to see a bull-fight. I rolled my eyes. *()*

After my hymn in praise of the weather it changed on Saturday night, to heavy rolling mists and thick soft rain. The mountains disappeared very beautifully, one by one. The lake became grave and one felt the silence. This, instead of being depressing as it is in the South, had a sober charm. I don't know how it is with you; but I feel the South is not made pour le grand travail. There is *too much light*. Does that sound heresy? But to work one needs a place (or so I find) where one can spiritually dig oneself in. . . . And I defy anybody to do that on the Riviera. Now this morning the mist is rolling up, wave on wave, and the pines and firs, exquisitely clear, green and violet-blue, show on the mountain sides. This grass, too, in the foreground, waving high, with one o'clocks like bubbles and flowering fruit trees like branches of red and white coral. One looks and one becomes absorbed. . . . Do you know what I mean? This outer man retires and the other takes the pen. In the South it is one long fête for the outer man. But perhaps, after your tour in Provence, you won't be inclined to agree (I mean about it's not being ideal for working.)

I feel, at present, I should like to have a small chalêt, high up somewhere, and live there for a round year, working as one wants to work. The *London Mercury* came on Saturday with my story.[1] Tell me if anybody says they like it, will you? That is not vanity. Reading it again, I felt it might fall dead flat. It's so plain and unadorned. Tommy and Delamare are the people I'd *like* to please. But don't bother to reply to this request, dearest. It's just a queer feeling—after one has dropped a pebble in. Will there be a ripple or not? . . . You know how much I shall want to hear about your lectures. Tell me what you want to. No

The Daughters of the Late Colonel.

628

more. I expect you'll be busy and not inclined for letters. All the same I shall expect letters.

What do you feel about Broomies now? This weather, so soft, so quiet, makes me realise what early autumn there might be. It's weather to go and find apples—to stand in the grass and hear them drop. It's Spring and Autumn with their arms round each other—like your two little girls in Garavan.

The packet arrived safely, thank you. Your remark about Tiz reminded me that in a paper here I read a little letter by Gaby Deslys saying that Reudel's Bath Saltrates made her feet 'feel so nice'. A little laughing picture and a bright string of bébé French. I felt, if I went on reading there'd come a phrase, 'Quand on est mort, tu sais. . . .'

Goodbye for now, dear darling Bogey.

Thursday

Dearest Bogey,   (May 12, 1921)

The inventory came from Pope's last night. I am keeping it in the file. We don't pay this bill, do we? (*Re* money: L.M. destroyed that cheque you gave her. I don't know why.) The list of our furniture would make any *homme de cœur* weep.

> 1 Tin Box Doll's Tea Service.
> 1 China Figure of Sailor.
> 2 Liqueur decanters.
> 1 Liqueur glass.
> 3 Light Dresden Girandole.
> 1 Glass Bowl.
> 9 Paper Knives.

Doesn't it sound a heavenly dustbin? Did you know there was a Fluted Comport? and a Parian Flower Jar?

Since my first letter the mountains have been mobled kings. They have un-mobled themselves today, tho'. I have not had one word sent on from the office, not a paper. This is *queer*, isn't it? I am glad it was 'rather beastly' to feel absolutely cut off. Thank you for this flourë smale. Goodbye, dear love. Is it to be postcards, postcards *all* the way?

Tig

I am in the middle of one of my *Giant Coups*. Yesterday evening I decided to look no longer for doctors in Montreux. In fact I felt the hour had come for something quite extraordinary. So I phoned Montana—asked Dr. Stephani to descend by funiculaire to Sierre and meet me here at the Château Bellevue at 3 o'clock today—then engaged a car and started off this morning shortly after 9 o'clock. It is years since I have done such things. It is like a dream.

Sweethert myn,

I got back from Sierre at about 7.30 last night. I rather wish I hadn't sent you that little note from there. It was so confuged. Tear it up, love. . . . While I write a man is playing the zither so sweetly and gaily that one's heart dances to hear. It's a very warm, still day.

Will you please look at this picture of the lake at Sierre? Do you like it? It's lovely—really it is. If we spend a year here in Switzerland I don't think you will regret it. Yesterday gave me such a wonderful idea of it all. I feel I have been through and through Switzerland. And up there, at Sierre, and in the tiny mountain towns on the way to Sierre it is absolutely unspoilt. I mean it's so unlike—so remote from—the Riviera in that sense. There are *no* tourists to be seen. It is a whole complete life. The only person I could think of meeting was Lawrence before the war. The only thing which is modern (and this makes me feel the Lord is on our side) is the postal service: it is excellent everywhere in Switzerland, even in the villages. There are two posts a day everywhere. As to telegrams, they simply fly—and your letter posted 8.30 P.M. on May 12th arrived here 9.30 A.M. May 14th. All these remarks are, again, of the carrot family. I heard there are any number of small chalêts to be had in Sierre and in Montana. We should take one—don't you think, darling? and have a Swiss bonne. As to cream-cows, they abound. And the whole country side is full of fruit and of vines. It's famous for its small grapes, and for a wine which the peasants make. The father brews for his sons, and the sons for their sons. It's drunk when it's about 20 years old, and I believe it is superb.

Queer thing is that all the country near Sierre is like the Middle Ages.

There are ancient tiny castles on small round wooded knolls, and the towns are solid, built round a square. Yesterday as we came to one part of the valley—it was a road with a *solid* avenue of poplars, a green wall on either side—little wooden carts came spanking towards us. The man sat on the shafts. The woman, in black, with a flat black hat, earrings and a white kerchief, sat in front with the children. Nearly all the women carried huge bunches of crimson peonies, flashing bright. A stream of these little carts passed, and then we came to a town and there was a huge fair going on in the market square. In the middle people were dancing, round the sides they were buying pigs and lemonade, in the cafés under the white and pink flowering chestnut trees there were more people, and at the windows of the houses there were set pots of white narcissi and girls looked out. They had orange and cherry handkerchiefs on their heads. It was beyond words gay and delightful. Then further on we came to a village where some fête was being arranged. The square was hung with garlands and there were cherry-coloured masts with flags flying from them and each mast had a motto framed in leaves—AMITIE—TRAVAIL—HONNEUR—DEVOIR. All the men of the village in white shirts and breeches were stringing more flags across and a very old man sat on a heap of logs plaiting green branches. He had a huge pipe with *brass fittings*.

Oh dear! in some parts of the Rhone valley there are deep, deep meadows. Little herd boys lie on their backs or their bellies and their tiny white goats spring about on the mountain slopes. These mountains have little lawns set with trees, little glades and miniature woods and torrents on the lower slopes, and all kinds of different trees are there in their beauty. Then come the pines and the firs, then the undergrowth, then the rock and the snow. You meet tiny girls all alone with flocks of *black* sheep or herds of huge yellow cows. Perhaps they are sitting on the bank of a stream with their feet in the water, or stripping a wand. And houses are so few, so remote. I don't know what it is, but I think you would feel as I did, *deeply pleased* at all this. I like to imagine (am I right?) that you will muse as you read: Yes, I could do with a year there. . . . And you must know that *from* Sierre we can go far and wide—in no time. I believe the flowers are in their perfection in June and July, and again the *Alpine flora* in September and October.

I see a small chalet with a garden near the pine forests. I see it all very simple, with big white china stoves and a very pleasant woman with a tanned face and sun-bleached hair bringing in the coffee. I see winter—

snow and a load of wood arriving at our door. I see us going off in a little sleigh—with huge fur gloves on, and having a picnic in the forest and eating ham and fur sandwiches. Then there is a lamp—*très important* —there are our books. It's very still. The frost is on the pane. You are in your room writing. I in mine. Outside the Stars are shining and the pine trees are dark like velvet.

Farewell, Bogey. I love you dearly, dearly.

Wig

Thank you for Mrs. Hardy's nice letter. I long to hear of your time there. I was not surprised at ——. He's so *uncertain* at present, I mean in his own being, that it will come natural to him to pose. I don't know how far you realise that you *make* him what he is with you—or how different he is with others. Also at present he has no real self-respect and that makes him *boast*. Like all of us he wants to feel important and that's a *right* feeling—we *ought* to feel important—but while he remains undisciplined and dans le vague he *can't be* important. So he has to boast. I mustn't go on. You are calling me a schoolmistress. . . .

Please give Mother and Richard my love.

Tuesday, 4.30 p.m.,

My darling Bogey, (May 17, 1921)

About the Journal.[1] I wish it were ever so many times as long again. You can imagine how I read it: a kind of special façon de lire. Really, there is nothing more fascinating than this vision of the other's mind— independent, personal, detached as it can't be in letters, and yet intimate as it can't be in another form of writing.

Bandol is *beautiful*—there's no other word. There's such 'leisure'— a dreaming quality . . . it's like a boat swinging idle on a still sea. I feel you were at the place at Arles, for instance, for months. That your room there *was* your room—you did without a carafe *the whole time*. I have now an idea of all that country and of the kind of life which I did not even glimpse before. The farmer class—the asparagus—the grossness—the lovely tiles—the talk. Good Heavens! Are there really only a few pages of it? The procession seen from the window might be the middle of the book.

As to Paris. I never read anything about a child more exquisite than your little girl's remark 'Il pleut' when someone put a sunshade up.

[1] I kept a journal of my journey through France for Katherine's benefit.

It's the most profound thing about a very young baby's vision of the world I've ever struck. *It's what babies in prams think.* It's what you say long before you can *talk*. She's altogether a ravishing person—no, so much more than that. She is a tiny vision there in those gardens for ever. Your tenderness is perfect—it's so *true*.

I liked Valéry and his household. It seemed somehow 'extremely right', as Kot would say, that his mother should be there and that she should be so small. I expect she thought you were a boy. I should like to have been there.

I am writing in the thick of a thunder-storm. They are regular items now in the late afternoon. It gets misty, the birds sound loud, it smells of irises and then it thunders. I love such summer storms. I love hearing the maids run in the passages to shut the windows and draw up the blinds, and then you see on the road between the vineyards people hurrying to take shelter. Besides, I've such a great part of the sky to see that I can watch the beginning, the middle and the end.

Darling, I can't thank you properly for the blue book. I'll take care of it for you.

Let's see. What is the news of the outside world? A letter from Sorapure. *Awfully nice.* A letter from Bouchage and his bill (2000 francs). Awfully nasty. A letter from —— appealing to the past when he first knew us and quoting your old letters to him. Yes, it *did* touch me. A bundle of press-cuttings—stray shoots that ought to have been cut off long ago—and Jeanne in Montreal and Jinnie just off to Rome— and so on, love. It's so hot that one pulls up one's sleeves to write— above the elbow, you know—and thinks in terms of fans. I decided last night that we should have our first dinner up here in the little salon. It was the first—in fact it was the airy fairy *foundation stone* of the dream which is called *Arrival of Bogey*.

Tig

Veen dear,   (May 19, 1921)

Read this criticism. It takes the bisquito. The gent is evidently playing Paris to Miss W.'s Helen. But why a half-brick at me? They do hate me, those young men. The *Sat. Review* said of my story[1] 'a dismal transcript of inefficiency'. What a bother! I suppose that, living alone as I do, I get all out of touch and what seems to me even *lively* is ghostly glee....

---

[1] *The Daughters of the Late Colonel.*

Sorry you forgot your braces and your toothbrush. I can't imagine either you or me without toospeg brushes. I feel they'd come flying after.

I am very glad you lunched with ——. Don't they get a funny crew together? But they are a kind pair.

O my dear sweet-hert, I like these two torn pages written at such a terrific lick—funny long y's and g's tearing along like fishes in a river when you are wading.

One word more. I was not honest about not 'facing all facts'. Yes, I *do* believe one ought to face facts. If you don't, they get behind you and they become terrors, nightmares, giants, horrors. As long as one faces them one is top-dog. The trouble is not to *steel oneself*—to face them calmly, easily—to have the habit of facing them. I say this because I think nearly all my falsity has come from *not* facing facts as I should have done, and it's only now that I am beginning to learn to face them.

Thursday,

Darling,   (May 19, 1921)

I can't tell you how Tigs love to be told they are missed and that their Bogies think of them—especially when they are in 'some strange hotel'.[1] I shall be very glad when you can come back. I hope you will not have to go away too soon again. . . .

S. has 'gone' for the time being, hasn't he? I confess I do not want to see him here—not now—nor B. In fact, I *cannot* see B. or other people just now. I wish they would understand that. If they suggest coming across, will you tell them the plain truth which is I am too busy this year? Leave it to them to understand or not, darling. There it *is*.

I wish you weren't such a modest little fellow. I'd love an outside opinion of your lectures. *Are you happy about them?* No, you can't answer that—you're feeling your way yourself. There is just the one point. What about leaving out the quotation from K.M. and replacing it by someone else? I don't think it's in quite good taste. At any rate, I have a feeling about it. What do you think?[2]

Of course, I remember old Grundy.[3] It was Goodyear's laugh I heard when I read his name—a kind of snorting laugh, ending in a chuckle and then a sudden terrific *frown* and he got very red. Do you

From a music-hall song.
A quotation from *Prelude* (*The Problem of Style*, p. 103).
Dr. G. B. Grundy, a famous Oxford figure who died in December 1948.

remember? And you remember the stick he brought from Bombay? He was very pleased with that stick. Your mention of Grundy gave me Goodyear again—living, young, a bit careless and *worried*, but enjoying the worry, in the years before the war, when a pale moon shone above Piccadilly Circus and we three stood at the corner and didn't want to separate or to go home....[1]

I went out yesterday in a Swiss kerridge to see Mercanton, who is Stephani's man here. The Swiss kerridge was a rare old bumper, and the driver who weighed about eighteen stone leaped into the air and then crashed back on to the seat. It was raining. A massive hood was down. I could just put forth a quivering horn from beneath it. Montreux is *very ugly* and quite empty. But in the shops the people are awfully nice. They are simple, frank, honest beyond words and kind in the German way. The thing about Switzerland is that there is absolutely no *de luxe*. That makes an enormous difference. It's simply not understood. And one is not expected to be rich. One isn't expected to spend. This is very pleasant indeed. I suppose there is a sort of surface scum of what the *Daily Mail* calls the 'Jazzing World,' but it doesn't touch the place. To put it into a gnut shell, love, there simply is no *fever*—no fret. The children are really beautiful. I saw a baby boy yesterday who took my heart away. He was a little grub in a blue tunic with a fistful of flowers—but his *eyes*! his *colour*! his *health*! You want to lie in the grass here and have picnics. Monte Carlo is not in the same world. It's on another planet almost. But you'll feel what I mean.

Tig

Saturday evening,

My precious Bogey,   (May 21, 1921)

I am rather conscious that my letters have fallen off just these last days. Especially so since this evening I have read yours written at Oxford on Thursday. You know how it is when just the letter you get is the letter you would love to get. That was my experience with this one of yours, my darling. I dipped into that remote Oxford and discovered you there. Heard that click of the cricket ball and I saw the trees and the grass. I was with you, standing by you, not saying anything, but happy.

I love you with my whole heart, Bogey.

The reason why I haven't written is that I am fighting a kind of

---

[1] For Frederick Goodyear see the *Journal*, p. 58.

Swiss chill. It will go off. Don't please give it another thought. I've a tremendous equipment of weapons.

All day, in the sun, the men have been working in the vineyards. They have been hoeing between the vines, and then an old man has been dusting certain rows with powder out of a Giant Pepper-pot. The heat has been terrific. The men have worn nothing but cotton trousers. Their bodies are tanned almost red brown—a very beautiful colour. And every now and then they stop work, lean on their pick, breathe deeply, look round. I feel I have been watching them for hundreds of years. Now the day is over; the shadows are long on the grass. The new trees hold the light and wisps of white cloud move dreamily over the dreaming mountains. It is all very lovely. . . .

How hot is it in England? Here it is really—as C. would say—almost tropical. The nights are hot too. One lies with both windows wide open, and my toes as usual, get thirsty. . . .

Yes, what you say about your exercises. . . . You know, the vision of you 'with naked foot stalking within my chamber' is somehow most awfully *important* in the story of my love for you. And seeing you in the mirror and seeing you on the floor . . . all so marvellously jewel clear! And you—a radiant—very free being—revealed in some way—in no need of the least 'protection' or 'covering'. I wonder if you see what I am getting at. It seems to me that my *false* idea of your helplessness was put absolutely, beautifully *right* by the sight of your nakedness. But here I 'spec' you're smiling at Wig for making such a big bone about it. Nevertheless, I mean something 'very profound,' love.

Thank you for Tchehov. Came tonight. I am simply captivated by Chaucer just now. I have had to throw a bow window into my cœur petit to include him with Shakespeare. Oh, dear! His *Troilus and Cressid*!! And my joy at finding your remarks and your pencil-notes.

I read today *The Tale of Chaunticleer and Madame Perlicote*: it's the Pardouner's tale. Perfect in its way. But the *personality*—the *reality* of the man. How his impatience, his pleasure, the very tone rings through. It's deep delight to read. Chaucer and Marlowe are my two at present. I don't mean there's any comparison between them. But I read *Hero and Leander* last night. That's incredibly lovely. But how extremely amusing Chapman's *finish* is! Taking up that magical poem and putting it into a body and skirt. It's *v.* funny.

As I write there's a subdued roar from the salle à manger where Lunn's Lions are being fed. Fourteen arrived today for A Week by the

Pearl of Lac Leman. It's nice to think I have this salon and don't need to go among them except when so dispoged.

I do hope you will be happy with Hardy. I feel it ought to be most awfully nice. I feel they are simple. There'll be no need to explain things. The kind of people who understand making jam, even—and would love to hear of others making it. I liked so what she said about their way of living. It was almost egg-weggs for tea.

I *look forward* to June. Be happy, dearest mine,

Tig

Monday night,
Dearest Bogey darling, (May 23, 1921)

I have been trying to write out a long explanation of the reasons why I have felt out of touch with you. But I don't think such explanations are of the smallest good. If you were here I could tell you what I felt in a minute, but at a distance it's different. I don't think it's good.

Do you know, darling, what I think Love is? It is drawing out all that is noblest and finest in the soul of the other. Perhaps the other isn't conscious this is what is happening and yet he feels at peace—and that is why. That is, I think, the *relationship* between lovers, and it is in this way that, because they give each other their freedom (for evil is slavery) they 'ought' (not in the moral sense) to *serve* each other. By service I mean what Chaucer means when he makes his true knights wonder what they can do that will give joy to their love. (But the lady must, of course, serve equally.) And, of course I do not mean anything in the least 'superficial'. Indeed, I mean just what there was between us in the last months at the Isola Bella—that—and more perfect.

You ask me how I am, darling. I am much the same. This chill has been the worst I have ever had since I was ill, and so I feel weak and rather shadowy—physically. My heart is the trouble. But otherwise I feel . . . well, Bogey, it's difficult to say. No, one can't believe in *God*. But I must believe in something more *nearly* than I do. As I was lying here today I suddenly remembered that: 'O ye of little faith!' Not faith in a God. No, that's impossible. But do I live as though I believed in *anything*? Don't I live *in glimpses* only? There is something wrong, there is something small in such a life. One must live more fully and one must have more *power* of loving and feeling. One must be true to one's vision of life—in every single particular—and I am not. The only

637

thing to do is to try again from tonight to be stronger and better—to be *whole*.

That's *how I am,* dear love. Goodnight.

Tig

I heard today that Spahlinger costs 14 horses to begin with!!!!

Tuesday,

My dear love,   (May 24, 1921)

Last evening came your perfect letter written on Friday. I mean the one in which you wonder whether you 'ought' to have said more about Stephani's report.[1] Love, as I *read* it, I understood your saying you loved me was the answer and especially your speaking of our future. I wanted nothing else. It was just as though, after I'd said something important to you, you crossed the room and for some heavenly reason —kissed me. You see, my precious? It was a perfect reply.

The fact is, Veen, that we have decided (those mysterious two have) not to speak about my illness any more than is 'necessary'. They just don't. There is no need to, any more. It's for the same reason that when they are together it may happen that they don't talk to each other at all and even look out of different windows. It seems to me it all began going one day to Castellar. No, I could trace it back deeper still. But n'importe. It isn't possible to love any one more than I love you. I wish I were a better girl in all ways. I mean to write a *work* one day which will be my kind of a love poem. Oh, heavens! to think you're coming over here and we shall gather fruit together this autumn. Did I tell you Sierre is renommé for its golden grape? I told you about the wines. But in September, so they say, the whole little town goes into the vine-yards. Shall you be there? Shall I? Bogey and Wig with brown hands and leaves in their hair. Sitting at the foot of a tiny green mountain that has small leaping white goats on it. It makes an awfully nice piggleture.

Know that goldfinch I have *tamed*. He comes right into my bedroom now and eats breakfast crumbs beside the bed. He is a ravishing little bird. If only he were carpet-trained. But I'm afraid you can't train birds. He seems just as surprised as I am. The sparrows, now that he has come in, grow bold and come as far as the parquet, too. But I won't have them. I aspire to having taught this goldfinch to present arms with my founting pen by the time you come—to do you honour.

The report of the Swiss exponent of the Spahlinger Treatment on her condition.

I also dream of its singing an address of welcome—holding the address, you know, in one claw.

During the past two nights I have read *The Dynasts*. Isn't it queer how a book eludes one, and then suddenly opens for you? I have looked into this book before now. But the night before last when I opened it I suddenly understood what the poet meant, and how he meant it should be read! *The point of view* which is like a light streaming from the imagination and over the imagination—over one's head as it were—the chorus and the aerial music. I am talking carelessly, because I am talking to you, and I am relying on you to more than understand me. But it did seem to me that if the *poetic drama* is still a possible 'form,' it will be in the future like *The Dynasts*—*As if* for the stage and yet not to be played. That will give it its freedom. Now when one reads *The Dynasts* it's *always* as though it were on the stage. . . . But the stage is a different one—it is within us. This is all *très vague*. Yet on my life I saw a play by you . . . which was the outcome of this form. In fact, I *long* to talk about this.

Squire has written asking for another story and also begging me to write a novel. Mrs. Belloc Lowndes says Won't you telephone her if you have time? Every single afternoon there is a thunderstorm.

Here I stopped. The doctor came. It's really funny. I must tell you. My chill is slightly better, but I have symptoms of whooping cough! *Il n'a manqué que ça.*

Oh, Boge,
I am your
Wig

Wednesday,
(May 25, 1921)

Darling Bogey,

In a small letter from you last night you seem to suggest that my letters weren't arriving. When I heard that all my peaceful thoughts flew out of the tower—wheeled—circled—wouldn't come back. Not getting my letters? Not hearing from me? Is there a letter-eater at the office? Someone steals them? I can't bear to think they disappear. Dear love, I write so often.

I understand exactly what you feel about Oxford. I expect you will be glad to go to London for some days. Tell me what you do. Just the facts, and I'll embroider them. I'd like to ponder over them . . . to see you and Raleigh at dinner.

It seems to me—the more I read the papers and now from what you say, too—that you and I are in some way *really different* from other writers of our time. I mean it seems to us so natural and so easy to link up with Flaubert or another. It's part of our *job* and the people whom we read as we read Shakespeare are part of our *daily lives*. I mean it doesn't seem to me QUEER to be thinking about Othello at bregchick or to be wondering about the Phœnix and the Turtle in my bath. It's all part of a whole. Just as that vineyard below me is the vineyard in the Song of Solomon, and that beautiful sound as the men hoe between the vines is almost part of my body, goes on in me. I shall never be the same as I was *before* I heard it, just as I'll never be the same as I was before I read the death of Cleopatra. One has willingly *given* oneself to all these things—one is the result of them all. Are you now saying 'intellectual detachment'? But I've *allowed* for that.

Other people—I mean people today—seem to look on in a way I don't understand. I don't want to boast. I don't feel at all arrogant, but I do feel they have not perhaps lived as fully as we have. . . . However. . . . Did you know that Turgenev's brain *pesait deux mille grammes?* Horrible idea! I couldn't help seeing it *au beurre noir* when I read that. I shall never forget that brain at Isola Bella. It was still *warm from thinking*. Ugh!

Oh, Bogey, I shall be very, very glad to see you, darling. I have a mass of things to talk about. 'The great artist is he who exalts difficulty' —do you believe that? And that it's only the slave (using slave in our mystical sense) who pines for freedom. The free man, the artist, seeks to bind himself. No, these notes aren't any good. But I have been finding out more and more how true it is that it's only the difficult thing that is worth doing; it's the difficult thing that one deliberately chooses to do. I don't think Tchehov was as aware of that as he should have been. Some of the stories in *The Horse-Stealers* are—rather a shock.

Tell me, (I've changed my pen and my *sujet*) how is this? There is no Saint Galmier here, only Eau de Montreux, which according to the bottil, is saturated with carbonic acid gas. But my physiology book said that carbonic acid gas was a deadly poison: we only breathed it out, but never, except at the last desperate moment, took it in. And here are Doctors Schnepsli, Rittchen and Knechloo saying it's a sovereign cure for gravel, and makes the urine sparkle like champagne.

It is all so very difficult, as Constantia would say.

Be a good Boge. And don't walk on both sides of the street at once. It distracts people and makes it difficult for them to continue the conversation.

As for me, I simply love you.

Tig

At first Katherine was very happy at the Chalet des Sapins. She was once more 'in some perfectly blissful way, at peace'—the mood in which she could return to the vein of 'Prelude'. She wrote 'At the Bay,' its companion piece, and besides this 'The Voyage,' 'The Garden Party,' 'The Doll's House'. 'Life of Ma Parker,' as well as a number of minor stories to fulfil a contract with 'The Sphere'. The months from July to December 1921 must therefore be reckoned the most fruitful period of Katherine's writing life. No less than five of the dozen stories she wrote during it belong to the very finest of her work. It is not surprising that she was exhausted by it. Had she been content to lie fallow afterwards and await the spring, the story might have been different. For, at this time, Katherine came nearer to following a regime than ever before or after, and there is no doubt that the condition of her lungs was greatly improved. Until the end of the year, she seemed reconciled to a long stay. Her much loved cat, Wingley was brought out to her.

'It's awful the love one can lavish on an animal. In his memoirs, which he dictates to me, Murry's name is always Masteranman—one word—my name is Grandma Jaeger—the Mountain is always called Fostermonger and for some reason our servant he refers to as the Swede. He has rather a contempt for her.'

Before the snow had fallen, the wild flowers in the forest, and when the snow had fallen the migrant birds held an incessant fascination for her. As her Journal for this period shows, she was very severe with herself for idleness, which was unreasonable. What she called idleness was really lassitude after much exhausting creative work. In retrospect, it seems to me that she set her ideal of spiritual perfection too high. She demanded of herself the impossible, by refusing to accept the limitations which her condition of health imposed upon her; and when she failed to achieve it, turned too precipitately to two alternative and in essence contradictory notions: one, that there was a physical or medical technique which would abolish her disease, and annihilate her limitations; the other that there was a psychological or spiritual technique which would enable her to ignore them. Whereas I, on the other hand, believed and still believe that she was most deeply at peace, and doing her finest work, in

x 641 K.M.

the months when she came nearest to accepting her limitations and using her own spiritual powers, which were simple and great, to make contact with the source of all strength.

When Katherine first mooted her desire to try the Manoukhin treatment, at the beginning of December 1921, I was not greatly disturbed, because we were both under the impression that the treatment could be carried on by her doctor at Montana, where I fervently desired that she should stay. I had not much faith in the treatment, as such, any more than I had had in the Spahlinger treatment which had excited Katherine's hopes a year before. As that had been forgotten, so (I hoped) the Manoukhin treatment would be. What I dreaded above all else was that Katherine should begin her journeying again, for an instinct warned me that that would be fatal.

I have regretted nothing more bitterly than that, when Katherine discovered that the Manoukhin treatment required a consultation with the inventor in Paris, I did not resolutely oppose her going. As the subsequent letters show, it was the slippery slope which led to Katherine's confinement in Paris, her abandonment of the Swiss mountains, and a disillusion the more shattering because her hopes had been set so high. And it had for me the peculiarly dismal consequence that it set a barrier between Katherine and myself. I was required 'to have faith' in the Manoukhin treatment. I had little.

It was, I am sure, no mere coincidence that, at the same time that her thoughts were turning towards the 'miracle' of Doctor Manoukhin, in which I could not believe, Katherine became deeply attracted to the doctrines expounded in 'Cosmic Anatomy,' a book of occult doctrines, which had been sent me in Switzerland at the instance of A. R. Orage. My prejudice against occultism was great; and it is as deep-rooted now as it was then. There is no doubt that this book set Katherine's mind on the train of thought which took her, when she was disillusioned by the results of the Manoukhin treatment, to the Gurdjieff Institute at Fontainebleu. I was as much opposed to the one as to the other. Both seemed to me to be off the line of truth. I felt that there was something equally wrong about the expectation of a complete physical cure, and the expectation of acquiring spiritual 'powers' such that the condition of her body could be ignored. I obscurely felt that Katherine was driving herself towards a terrible dilemma: demanding that her disease should be physically or mentally annihilated, as it were presenting Life or God with an ultimatum. It was inordinate, and I feared the consequences.

In her complete physical cure I could not believe. Too many doctors had been explicit to me about her condition. The utmost it admitted was that the active disease should become quiescent, and the process of destruction halted. In

642

Montana for the first time some definite progress had been made in that direction. The consequences of her alternative—a concentration on the acquisition of spiritual powers which would enable her to ignore her bodily disease—were fearful to contemplate. It was impossible for me to believe in that.

What I did believe was that if Katherine could have reconciled herself to living in the Swiss mountains where we were, her life could have been considerably prolonged.

I think now that I ought to have strained every nerve to persuade her to my modest faith and to dissuade her from her own determination at all costs to be 'well'. We might have been spared the pain of drifting apart. As things were, the burden of my unfaith became to Katherine too grievous to be borne. That was natural enough. I understood and accepted her feeling. But I could not change my nature to meet her demand, however much I desired it. I had been driven down to bedrock. I could not believe the things I was required to believe. I could not then; I cannot now.

Thus it was that for the first time since we first loved each other, we knew ourselves to be travelling different paths. The ways, at last, really had parted. Hitherto, in spite of separations and misunderstandings, or indeed because of them, we had always grown closer together. With all its trials, 1921 had been the most equably happy year of our life together. The peace of the Chalet des Sapins was the peace of the Villa Pauline in a new dimension. I may be wrong; but it is my surmise that the very quality of our happiness in the Chalet des Sapins set in motion in Katherine the overwhelming desire to be 'well', in order that we should be completer friends, companions and lovers than we were. She felt that I was sacrificing something, whereas in truth, I was sacrificing nothing at all. Her longing to be 'no longer an invalid' took entire possession of her.

By the beginning of December her hopes were centred on the Manoukhin treatment. To her first letters to Dr. Manoukhin she received no reply. She wrote to Brett on December 19.

'As to Doctor Manoukhin, I got the Mountain to 'phone Paris yesterday and found he was absent and only there from time to time, très rarement. So that doesn't sound very hopeful. I am disappointed. I had made him my 'miracle'. One must have a miracle. Now I'm without one and looking round for another. . . . Have you any suggestions?'

That reveals how conscious Katherine was of her own desire to deceive herself. She did not herself really believe in the miracle; but she demanded of me *that I should have faith in it so great that it would convince herself. I could not satisfy the demand. I felt distinctly bitter about those who encouraged her to believe in miracles, whether physical or spiritual.*

In January Katherine got into touch with Dr. Manoukhin and, in spite of the fact that she was only just recovering from a congestion that had confined her to bed for six weeks, insisted on going to see him in Paris. It was agreed that she would return immediately, but, if she were found to be a suitable subject for the treatment, she would begin it in May. She left for Paris with L.M. on January 30, 1922.

What I feared would happen, happened. No sooner had she seen Dr. Manoukhin than she wanted to commence the treatment immediately. Very reluctantly, I agreed. There seemed to me nothing else to do. Her heart was now set on it. Having agreed by telegram, I at first intended to remain at the Chalet des Sapins, chiefly because I shrank from giving it up. I wanted Katherine to return there; it was to me the symbol of salvation and sanity. The idea that it should be abandoned drove me almost to despair. But Katherine took it for granted that in agreeing to her remaining in Paris I was abandoning the Chalet, and writing Finis to the chapter. Her disappointment that I clung to it was so obvious that I gave it up and joined her in Paris on February 11.

> Victoria Palace Hotel,
> 6 rue Blaise Desgoffe,
> Paris
> Tuesday morning,
> (February 1, 1922)

My precious dear,

Although I have not seen Manoukhin yet and am in fact waiting for bregchik I must write you a little note to be posted in all haste. To tell you what you call news. Bogey, Montana is a *wonderful* place. Since I left I have not once had shortness of breath or a second's trouble with my heart. I am exactly like an ordinary common garden person in that respect. I had to walk at the Gare de Lyon quite a long way and except that my pegs were tired—I have been scoring on paper for so long now (oh, it dies hard, my dearest, notre jeu)[1]—I felt as I used to 5 years ago.

Perfect journey. The hotel is extremely quiet. There is a huge salle de bains. I have a bedroom, hall with private door, and this—well, it's a dressing-room bath-room—for 20 francs a day. I wallowed in a bath

---

[1] Cribbage, which we played regularly at the Chalet des Sapins.

on arrival, put on clean clothes and am lying down. It's like a dream not to be out of breath and to be alone with one's own sponge again.

Of course, numbers and numbers of marvellous things happened on the journey. I am keeping a journal instead of putting them in letters. It's less boring for anyone to read them unashamedly put forth like that. But I suppose my love of you is at the root of everything. Meine Wurzeln sind tauig begiessen with that und mit frischen Bühlen erfüllt. Dear Eckermann and dear Goethe! I slept last night in the little hollow of the bed between the two of them.

Wasn't that review —— *sickening*? Didn't it make —— a sorry worm? There was nothing in the paper (*D.N.*) but a white satin tea-cosy hand-painted with flags of the Empire for Princess Mary.

Ida's boots have made a *profound* impression here. I feel she ought to carry a little whip to keep them in order.

But all this is nothing except love. The essence of it is Love for you. I'll tell you all tomorrow—if I see M. today. Do let me know about you. I embrace you, my dear love, and if this sounds hurried and unimportant, forgive it. It's written between 2 stools as it were.

Your own
Tig

Tuesday,

Dearest, (February 1, 1922)

I went to see M. tonight. I found him a tall formal rather dry man (not in the least an 'enthusiast') who speaks scarcely any French and has a lame Russian girl for his interpreter.

He read Bouchage's report and I brought him up to date. He then very thoroughly examined me and reported as follows:

I can promise to cure you—to make you as though you had never had this disease.

You have T.B. in the second degree—the right apex very lightly engaged. All the left is full of rales (as usual).

It will take 15 séances—then a period of repose preferably in the mountains for 2–3–4 months just as you like. Then 10 more.

After the 15 you will feel perfectly well. The last 10 are to prevent any chance of recurrence. Fees as he stated.

I then explained our 'situation', exactly—what we wished to do, what would be more convenient in every sense, financially and otherwise. He said as follows:

It would be very much better for you to start now. Your condition is favourable. To begin now, to leave Paris in the 2nd week in May, to return in—even September if you liked for the last séances.

I do not insist on your beginning now. I do not say you will be greatly harmed by waiting.

I do say it is much better not to wait and especially, as you have taken a journey, not to take another, or to have the re-effort of the altitude, again. Nothing is worse than travelling. He insisted on that and the great advantage in beginning now. At the same time he said of course he cannot really say anything if we prefer to wait until April. He asked me to write all this to you and to give the answer as soon as possible. His secretary told me that he had treated 8000 cases in Moscow —that here in Paris patients in the 3rd and 4th degree—far, far worse than I—were now as well as possible. She also said of course do not wait. And especially they kept on speaking of the double journey again. I then left.

What do you think? Will you give me your opinion? The truth is it was a mistake that we did not see him together. It would have been far better. All my inclinations are to come back, not to 'upset' our life. All my wishes are for that. At the same time I must first put it all to you impartially. I said: Suppose I go for February and come back at the end of March. He said: You must be in Paris in June and July which is *not* good. It is very puzzling. The best thing of course would be for you to see him. But that's no good. Supposing you think I ought to take the treatment now I can of course send Ida back for as long as necessary. It is possible we might be able to sub-let.

My desire is not to stay. Why? Because of our life. I feel I cannot break it again. I fear for it. If it were possible for you to come 3rd perhaps and just stay a couple of days. Is that a foolish idea? Consider well. Please darling think of this calmly. There is no hurry. I never felt less excited in my life. What do you think, my little King of Hearts? Shall I come *bang* back at the end of my fortnight? That is what I want to do. If I am leaving you to decide something hard, then just give me your 'advice'. But don't forget that above all I love you

Tig

Next day early.

I am going to send Ida out with this at once. I feel this morning perhaps we forget what a difference it's bound to make to us if I was well. It would make our lives very wonderful. And to wait for that

646

longer than we have waited is perhaps foolish. Two things remain. His opinion that I would do far better to start the treatment now—his remark that he did not insist on my starting before April.

Of course, were I alone, I should begin at once. But I am not alone and my life with you is nearly the whole of life. It is so precious that to endanger it by making you unhappy is, I find, equal to endangering my own life. Remember Ida can do all that is necessary at Montana. And should you decide to come just tell Ernestine simply and leave stamped addressed envelopes with her for the post and some money for her food.

I have learnt, my dear love, that if we act calmly and do not forget our *aim* . . . it's not so hard. That's why I don't wire, or feel even excited. I refuse to. We must be superior to these things.

Forgive me if I am worrying you my heart's dearest.

My precious,

Wednesday,
(February 2, 1922)

I rested all day, but after sending your letter I wrote one to Manoukhine, saying that before I decided anything I would like to know all there was to know about this treatment, whether one ran risks, what its effects were on the heart, and so on. I told him that I was very much in the dark, that I could not afford an experiment; and in a word that I would be obliged if he would let me see his French partner and talk it all over. His reply was to ask me to see them both at 5 o'clock at their cabinet médicale. So we took a taxi and I went.

The general impression was good—all in the highest degree simple, scientific, professional, unlike anything I have seen before. Manoukhin came and took me into Donat. He (D) is an elderly man, rather like Anatole France in style, wearing a white coat and skull cap. Quite unaffected, and *very* clever, I should imagine. I told them my difficulties. It was a little bit awkward, especially as Donat has evidently a great regard and admiration for M. But there you were. This matter is serious and past pretending. And they were awfully kind. Donat delivered an absolute lecture; they drew diagrams, described the process, told me of its effects and so on. There is no *risk*. It is, as you know, the application of X-rays to the spleen. It produces a change of blood. It is a kind of immensely concentrated sun action. What the sun does vaguely and in a dissipated way this gently forces. He discovered it while working at typhus and cholera and applied it to tuberculosis. Donat spoke of it always as my' colleague's discovery'. 'Dr. M. has taught us . . .' 'Doctor M. then experimented on so many animals and so on and found such and such results.' The whole thing is *new*. That I realized keenly. It is the latest thing in science. That was what one felt. At the same time there was a very good responsible atmosphere at this place. One felt in the presence of real *scientists*—not doctors. And Donat never says a fantastic word. He is dead straight: one does feel that. It's what I always imagined a Pasteur institute to be. Donat agreed I could be cured. He has healed an Englishman in the 3rd degree, who after 12 applications has no more bacillus at all in his sputum. . . . He asked me about Montana. He and Manoukhine said that if I had been anywhere really healthy and led a quiet life free from worries I would have had the same amount of benefit. But in their united opinion Montana was too high for my heart in its present state. If I stayed absolutely still in bed there—*bien*—but to make a continual effort of that kind is not and cannot be good. One is living on *l'energie nerveuse*. He ended by saying: 'It is easy to see you are not a little ill. You have been ill for a long time. One has not an endless supply of force. You ought to get well. L'air de Paris et les rayons de Docteur Manoukhine will make you well. Of that I am confident.' I then came away.

I am glad I saw this man as well as the other. But isn't it strange now all this is held out to me—now all is at last *hope,* real *hope,* there is not a throb of gladness in my heart. I can think of nothing but how it will affect 'us'.

Dear love, don't worry about me though. The food in this hotel is excellent. I have such a nice airy room with a comfortable chair. It could not be better in all those ways, and I rest, I take my evening meal in bed.

In all things, though, you are my first thought—you know it. Remember Ida asks for nothing but to manage everything for us—and at all times.

Your own
Wig

Friday,
(February 4, 1922)

My precious Bogey,

Your telegram came yesterday as a complete surprise—a very marvellous one—a kind of miracle. I shall never forget it. I read it, scrunched it up, then carefully unscrunched it and put it away 'for keeps'. It was a very wonderful thing to receive. I agree absolutely it is best that I start now and I telephoned the same moment to M. whose reply was: 'Deux heures'. (But before I speak of my time there I want to say your two letters, my dear one, are simply such perfect letters that one *feeds* on them. I don't know. You have become such a wonderful person—well, you always were—but the beams are so awfully plain now, *on se chauffe* at every word you write. And there is a kind of calmness which I feel too. Indeed, I feel we are so changed since the days before Montana—different people. I do feel that I belong to you, that we live in our own world. This world simply passes by—it says nothing. I do not like it, but that's no matter. It is not for long. Do you realize that if the miracle happens we May Go to England This Summer Together? That's just an idear of what the future holds. May it make you a hundredth part as happy as it makes me!)

I went to the clinique today and there the French doctor with Manoukhine went over the battlefield. Really, it was the first time I have ever been 'examined'. They agreed absolutely after a very prolonged examination that I had *no* cavities. *Absolument pas de cavernes.* They tested and tested my lungs and always said the same. This means I am absolutely curable. My heart, rheumatism, everything was gone into and finally I passed into another room and had a séance.

I want to ask you something. Do you really believe all this? There is something that pulls me back the whole time and which won't let me believe. I hear, I see. I feel a great confidence in Manoukhine—very great, and yet. . . . I am absolutely divided. You know how, to do anything well, even to make a little jump, one must gather oneself together. Well, I am not gathered together. A dark secret unbelief holds me back. I see myself, after 15 goes, apologizing to them for not being cured, so to speak. This is very bad. You realize I am in the mood now when I confess to you because I want to tell you my bad self. But it may be it's not me. For what is bad in me (i.e. to doubt) is not bad in you. It's your nature. If you do feel it, please tell me—please try and change. Try and believe. I know Manoukhine believes. I was sitting in the waiting-room reading Eckermann, when he came in, quickly, simply, and took my hand and said: 'Vous avez décidé de commencer. C'est très bien. Bonne santé!' But this was said beautifully, gently.

(Oh, Boge, I do love *gentleness*!). . . . Now I have told you this I will get over it.

It has been a marvellous day here, very soft, sunny and windy, with women selling les violettes de Parme in the streets. But I could not live in a city ever again. That's done, that's finished with. I read Shakespeare (I am with you as I read) and I am half way through a new story. I long for your letter which follows mine. Oh, those precious birds at the coconut. How I see and hear them! And it's fig pudding. You write the word 'fig' in such a nice way that all your precious darling self walks in the word. Goodbye for now, my blessed one. I feel a bit mysterious, full of blue rays, like a deep sea fishchik.

YOUR

Wig

Ref. No. Letter X.   Saturday,

My darling Bogey,   (February 5, 1922)

Your letter came as a surprise to me, but I absolutely agree with every word of it! It's far and away the best plan. I understand perfectly your feeling about your work and here is an opportunity. I, too, shall put in a great deal of work. I feel this year must float our ships if we are going to bring any cargo home. Goethe has filled me with renewed longing to be a *better writer*. No, I have no other idea to offer at all. Except—wouldn't it be far less unsettling if instead of your coming down for that week, I got Brett over while Ida went up there? She'd come like a shot. In fact, she begged me to let her come for a weekend. You know what energy a journey takes. We have nothing to talk over, darling, that can't be done by letters. And then when you come in May all will be so different. I think we'd better leave the Oiseau Bleu[1] in the air—in flight—until we are certain we shall want to go there. But I hope you will agree with the Brett suggestion. Nothing is gained by your coming here for a week and you would lose a great deal by the geographical change. I don't think anyone can realize how different a city is until they come right into it. It makes a most extraordinary impression. I have a definite aim and hope in being here, so I can ignore the effect—but for you at present in the middle of your novel it would be bad.

It seems to me there is no more to say about it all. You see when Ida comes back she can settle everything, and then when you come

A chalet in the next village to Montana which we had planned to take.

650

down in May she can go up again (it's like a see-saw isn't it?) and finish up the Chalet des Sapins. By the way coconut II is *under* the house. Ida saw it fall, near the bathroom. I am so glad E. is improved. I thought she would be all right on her own. She's an honest creature and Wingley makes it proper, there being 2 gentlemen in the house instead of one.

What wretched *posts* are arriving. I am glad about Pinker and Massingham. I must get Alice Jones to find me an English typist. She sent me *The Lancet* today with Manoukhine's article in it. Shall I send it to you?

The only thing I don't quite understand in your letter is your 'breaking the back of your year's work' and so on. It's all right—isn't it? You're not working in secret at something I know nothing about? It sounds so very appalling.

Well, I shall end this letter here for I want Ida to send it at once. It's Saturday night. I am afraid it may not reach you until Tuesday. Please reply at once about the Brett idea. And thanks most awfully for sending the letters. Will you go on sending them? I long to see the Tchekhov books, too, when you have finished with them.

Your loving
Wig

Monday,

Darling Bogey,   (February 7, 1922)

I have just received your Friday-Saturday letter—full of snow. The whole of Switzerland according to the papers is snowing. It must be horrid! I hope it is over. No, it's not been really bad weather here, and April-mild until yesterday when it froze. But today the sun is in-and-out again.

Will you send me the *Lit. Sup.* And *The Dial*? I'd be very glad of both if it's not too much bother.

Ida is arranging to return on Friday, leaves here Friday night, that is. Don't feel any doubt about *not* coming here. I'd far rather you didn't come. There's no point in it and it would unsettle us both. Hotels are odious places for two. If one is alone, one can work and forget, but that's not so easy *à deux*. No, let the red peg and the white peg meet in May—not before. . . .

Have you read that Goethe-Eckermann? I shall give it to Ida to return to you. But I mean to order a whole one for myself. That taste has given me *such* an appetite. It's a mystery to me that so fascinating a book should be so little talked of. In fact it's one of those books which, once discovered, abides for ever. It's such a whole (even in part, as I have it). These two men live and one is carried with them. The slight absurdity and the sentimental bias of Eckermann I wouldn't have not there! Delightfully human—one smiles but one can't help smiling always tenderly. And then outside sounds come in—the bells of Weimar ringing in the evening—the whisper of the wheat as the friends walk together, the neighbours' little children calling like birds. But all this human interest (Ah! how it draws one) apart, there is Goethe talking, and he did say marvellous things. He was great enough to be simple enough to say what we all feel and don't say. And his attitude to Art was noble. It does me good to go to Church in the breasts of great men. Shakespeare is my Cathedral, but I'm glad to have discovered this other. In fact, isn't it a joy—there is hardly a greater one—to find a *new book,* a living book, and to know that it will remain with you while life lasts?

How is your novel? Does it go steadily? I write slowly here because it takes time to abstract oneself. I feel I have a terrible amount to do, though. I hardly dare look out of this story because of all the others. They are in rows in the waiting-room. But one would not have it otherwise.

I've read *Antony and Cleopatra* again last week, and upon my word it is appalling to find how much one misses each time in Shakespeare—how much is still new. Wonderful play! But, Bogey, you remember "Tis one of those odd tricks which sorrow shoots out of the mind.' That is familiar enough, but it still leaves me gasping. There is something over and above the words—the meaning—all that I can see. It is that other language we have spoken of before. I feel that, as I am, I am not great enough to bear it. The image that for some reason comes into my mind is of an old woman in a cathedral, who bows down, folds herself up in her shawl, mournfully closes herself against the sudden stirring of the organ. You know when the organ begins and it seems to ruminate, to wander about the arches and the dark altars as though seeking some place where it may abide. . . .

I must get up. I hope you have my letters, and that Wingley is a good little pussy-wee.

Your loving

Wig

My darling Bogey,   (February 8, 1922)

I have had no news from you today yet (3 p.m.). I expect it is the snow. Arctic conditions prevail in Switzerland, so the papers say. I hope that you manage to keep warm and that Wingley's tail is not frozen.

Advise me—will you? I am looking for a tiny flat—very small— a mouse's hole just big enough to nibble a pen in. If I find anything suitable I shall take it until the end of May and L.M. will look after it to save money on servants and so on. But (this is where I want your advice) to whom can I apply for a reference? They are sure to ask me for at least two. Can you think of anybody? I wish you could answer this as soon as possible, Bogey. A card will suffice, as they say. It's rather urgent. Flats are so scarce here and I want to be settled as soon as possible once something is found. Of course, it may all be a wild goose's chase. L.M. has gone off to an agent this afternoon. But there it is!

I have started a new Shakespeare note book. I hope you will let me see yours one day. I expect they will be legion by that time. And, reading with the point of view of taking notes, I begin to see those marvellous short stories asleep in an image as it were. For instance,

> . . . 'Like to a vagabond flag upon the stream,
>   Goes to and back, lackeying the varying tide,
>   To rot itself with motion.'

That is terrible, and it contains such a terribly deep psychological truth. That *rots* itself' . . . and the idea of 'it' returning and returning, never swept out to sea finally. You may think you have done with it for ever, but comes a change of tide and there is that dark streak reappeared, more sickeningly rotten still. I understand that better than I care to. I mean—alas!—I have proof of it in my own being.

There are awful good oranges to be had in Paris. But there's nothing else good that I know—nothing *fresh, sound,* or *sweet.* But mine's a partial view, of course. I have done with cities for ever. I want flowers, rather sandy soil, green fields, and a river not too deep to paddle in, also a large number of ancient books and a small but *very* pretty cow. In fact, I should like the cow to be strikingly pretty. I shall put it in the advertisement. 'No plain cows may apply.' No, I can't do that. It's too cruel. But it's an airy-fairy herd for a long time, I'm afraid. How is your work going? If I am very dull for five weeks, you must remember

653

that for 5 weeks this treatment makes one rather worse. After that you will have to snatch my letters (like snapdragons) all blaging out of the postman's bag.

Your loving
Wig

In reply to your telegram.   Wednesday,

My darling Bogey,   (February 9, 1922)

I do not 'understand' why you have sent this telegram, so my reply is rather in the dark. Still, I must send it. Please do not come here to me. That is what I wish to say and I say it deliberately. It is not *easy* to write so to you. I will try and explain my reasons.

I want you to have your freedom as an artist. You asked for it at Menton. I thought it was a mistake—that you did not mean it and only wrote under influence. But then after I left Montana you asked for it again. You were willing to join me *if I wanted* you—you were pre-pared, like a shot, *to be of help to me*. (But that is exactly like saying to a person: If you want to borrow money, borrow from me—or Father's telling me I could count on him up to £50 if the necessity arose. It is not the gesture of people who deeply understand each other.) On the other hand your own personal feeling was not that at this most critical of all the moments in her life I could not leave Wig. Golly—no! It was my work—May would be too late—my novel—and so on. Reverse the positions, darling. *Hear* me saying that to you!

It is no good. I now know that I must grow a shell away from you. I want, I 'ask' for my independence. At any moment in the future you may suddenly leave me in the lurch if it pleases you. It is a part of your nature. I thought that it was almost the condition of your working that we were together. Not a bit of it! Well, darling Boge, for various reasons I can't accept this. And now that I am making a bid for health —my *final bid*—I want to grow strong in another way, too. Ida is leaving here on Saturday. She will be with you on Sunday. Tell her what you want her to do, if you intend leaving Switzerland. And write to me about everything.

But my very soul rebels against when it's fine you prefer your work and your work is more urgent than this affair in Paris has been. When it snows you might as well be playing cribbage with me! And also that remark: 'Moreover, the rent is paid here!'

No, darling, *please*. Let me be alone here. This queer grain in you does not for some extraordinary reason in the very least atom lessen my love for you. I'd rather not discuss it. Let it be! And I must work now until May. These 'affairs' are 1000 times more disturbing than 1000 train journeys. Pax, darling. You will see Ida on Sunday. But for the last time I ask you not to join me. I cannot see you until May.

Your loving
Wig

Please just accept this. It's awfully hard having 'it' to fight as well as my other *not* dear Bogies.

Later.

Dearest Bogey,

I have just opened my letter to say your Sunday and Monday ones have come—about the snow, about Elizabeth, about your staying there. If the weather is fine by now I daresay your doubts will have taken wings, too. But for my part I would rather stay here alone. I have seen the worst of it by myself i.e. going alone to Manoukhin, having no one to talk it over, and so on. I want now intensely to be alone until May. Then IF I am better, we can talk things over, and if I am not I shall make some other arrangement. There's no need to look ahead. But that is my very *calm collected* feeling. So if you do want to leave the chalet before May—let us still be independent of each other till then, shall we?

I hope that horrible weather is over. Don't we get dreadfully few letters! I am going to see a little flat tomorrow which I hope will be suitable. Here—I can't stay longer than necessary.

Your loving
Wig

P.S. We haven't read *The Schoolmaster*, have we? Are you certing? Don't send *The Daily News* about E.B.

We settled down, as far as was possible in a Paris hotel, to the routine of the Chalet. Chess took the place of the more homely and cheerful cribbage, which we were accustomed to play. 'We live here like two hermits in our caves at the end of a long dark passage. We work, play chess, read. M. goes out and does the shopping; we make tea and drink it out of dove-blue bowls', Katherine wrote, early in March, to Lady Ottoline Morrell. 'For some reason, it's all

*very nice'. At first, Katherine was able to work a little and wrote 'The Fly'.
But in a little while the 'forte réaction' produced by the irradiation of the spleen
made her feel very ill, and the attempt to work had to be abandoned.*

*We lived in the hotel for four months, while the treatment continued. The
miracle did not happen. Katherine gained some weight; but probably that
would have happened anyhow with the diet imposed upon her. Whether the
condition of her lungs was improved it is impossible to say. But Katherine
was deeply disappointed with the result. I felt that the modest promise of
Montana had been sacrificed in vain.*

*On June 4, 1922 we left Paris and returned to Switzerland—to a hotel 750
feet lower down the slope at Randogne-sur-Sierre. But the spell, or the rhythm,
of existence in the mountains had now been finally broken. A deep restlessness
had now taken hold of Katherine. She found it very difficult indeed to work.
Her mind was now moving fast towards the expectation of the other miracle—
the attainment of such psychic control as would enable her to ignore her bodily
condition. Into this realm I could not enter at all.*

*Disagreement on a matter so fundamental created a situation that was painful
for us both. It was at this point that we agreed to separate for the time being.
I acknowledged my inability to give her the kind of faith that she sought. It
was completely beyond my power now even to pretend that I saw any hope in
'occultism'. Since I had no faith of my own to offer, and I felt that I had no
right to criticize her search for one, it was decided that I should stay at
Randogne while Katherine descended to Sierre. We agreed that we now had
a depressing effect upon one another, and that we ought not to live together
until one or other of us had found a faith to live by.*

*Katherine went to Sierre at the beginning of July. I went to stay with her
at the week-ends. We telephoned one another daily; and the following notes
passed between us.*

Wednesday,

Dearest,(July 5, 1922)

With one eye on the future—if you can possibly manage to write a
short note to my Da it would, I think, be a good idea. He has seen a
doctor who finds him 'in fairly decent shape'—so you'd only have to
say you were glad to hear that the Doctor reported favourably and
hoped he'd be well in England. . . . This is extremely boring. My pen
won't write any more of it. If I didn't wish for a chimley stack, I'd
not suggest it.

Was yesterday nice, I wonder? Brett is very chastening. God has sent her to me as a trial. I shall fail. It serves him right.

There are the most darling swallows here—little forked tails and wings like gold fins. And some one calls drowsily from a window 'Fraülein *Wir*-kel?' Then the soft sound of the gardener raking the paths . . . Summer.

A bientôt

Tig

Many thanks for the papers. I hate the *N. & A.* worse than ever. I despige it. The *Lit. Sup.* was bad, too. There seems to be a positive blight on English writing. Really, really nothing to say. Their review of Garnett made me realise again how first-chop your criticism is.

D.B.   (July, 1922)

We could not phone you last thing, when this letter came, because of the Festa. Will you decide what you would like to do and phone Ida here? She will then get through to Zürich.

I am glad it's nice where you are. We had a quite wonderful time here in the garden before the rain fell. (Huge great drops like $\frac{1}{2}$d. buns). But the garden was lighted by lanterns and a faraway band played and there were Bengal lights, golden rain, rockets. Marvellous! There was a special dinner, too, with a whole great salmon lying on a bed of roses with little crayfish adoring.

I am v. glad the ladies are nice. Isn't it pleasant to sit in friendly tumpany again?

Yes, Somerset Maugham lays it on too thick. It's too downright good a story—don't you think?[1] Too oily! And there's not enough rain in it. The rain keeps stopping. The whole story ought to have been soaked through and through—or steamed with the after the rain feeling. And it isn't and doesn't.

What about *Northanger Abbey*? Is it possible? And the *New Statesman*?

I like you awfully

Wig

Monday

D.B.   (July 31, 1922)

I was quite wrong about Arco. L.M. had 'made a little muddle about the a.m.s and p.m.s. The truth is you start from here at about

---

[1] *Rain.*

657

11 o'clock one morning and you are in Arco the next evening at about 8-30. That is, if you spend the night in Milano. If you don't you change at midnight and so on and so on. If you would like still to go I will find out everything very exact. I sent your toospeg cream after you today. What an awful man on this p.c.! Why s [a blot]. After that I say no more, Betsy.

Early Edition. (August, 1922)

I think *Amos Barton* is awful and there is nothing to say for it.

In the first place poor George Eliot's *Hymn to the Cream Jug* makes me feel quite queasy (no wonder she harps on biliousness and begins her description of a feast: 'Should one *not* be bilious there is no pleasanter sight,' etc.). In the second place, the idea of lovely, gentle, fastidious, Madonna-like Mrs. Barton having 8 children in 9 years by that pock-marked poor 'mongrel' (her own words) with the blackened stumps for teeth is simply disgusting! If I thought the poor little pamphlet was designed to put in a word in favour of Birth Control I could bear it. But far from it. Each chubby chubby with a red little fist and TEN *black nails* (how is that for charm?) rouses a kind of female cannibalism in G. E. She gloats over the fat of babies.

I have always heard *Amos Barton* was one of her best stories. You know, it's very very bad that we haven't sincerer critics. Having spread my peacock tail to that extent I had better depart. *Not* before saying what a truly frightful need England hath of thee.

Later edition.

I have just got your Lawrence review and note. You didn't send the Pope, love. . . . But I'll get L.M. to ask for the two receipts and will print the address in a faire white linen hand. About your review. I think you are absolutely right in every word of it—every word. I think you occasionally use more *words* of praise than are necessary; it sounds too effusive and will raise suspicion. Shall I tone it down a bit on my typewriter, or send it as it is? I'll phone you and ask. Gerhardi comes off with a nice little pat. But can't be helped. Oh, I *long* for a paper this morning!! I have been 'making up' a paper since I read your review. I *shall* start one, too, jolly soon. For three years only. But what years!

Don't you think it might be a good idea if this week you came on Sunday instead of Saturday? Give us a longer week. That is if you are at all pressé or inclined to the notion. Otherwise you won't mind, will you, dear, if I do a bit of work on Saturday while you are in the garden?

H'm yes. After my Spartan suggestion has been written, I *take it back*. I say instead what I have said about working . . . and *hope* I'll be able to look out of window and see your summer feltie below. Yes, indeed, come Saturday unless you don't want to, or think that the female will is determined to drag you here. It's not, my dear darling.

Once *The Dove's Nest* is finished I shall leave here. But it will take a fortnight, not a week. It's too expensive. I *must* draw in my horns for the next six months, somehow. Blow!

My watch is still a li'll golden angel. And what a big brown angel that chest is![1] With two little windows at the sides and a chimney at the top we could almost live in it—open the lid softly for the milkman and the wild strawberry man.

Ever your

Wig

Katherine's original plan had been to return to Paris on August 20 to continue the Manoukhin treatment; but shortly before she decided suddenly to go to London. Ostensibly, the purpose was to consult Dr. Sorapure about the condition of her heart, which had been troubling her. In fact, Katherine's heart was relatively sound, though she always believed it was her weak spot. But she must have been visited at this moment by a strong premonition of approaching death, for on August 14 she made her will. She arrived in London on August 17. I went with her.

I say that 'ostensibly' the purpose of her visit was to get Dr. Sorapure's opinion about her heart, because I believe her real purpose, though it was probably not admitted to consciousness, was to get into touch with A. R. Orage who had been instrumental in sending 'Cosmic Anatomy' to us in Switzerland. At any rate I was surprised by the swiftness with which she joined the circle formed about M. Ouspensky, to which Orage and J. D. Beresford belonged. Katherine was staying in Dorothy Brett's house at 6 Pond Street, Hampstead, while I had a room in Boris Anrep's house next door.

We sometimes talked of the matter which most deeply concerned us, but now our love spoke across a vast; and my memory of these days is one of despair and anguish. It was as evident to me as it was to Katherine that rebirth was the only remedy. But how to be born again? It was impossible for me to follow her into the Ouspensky circle; or at least it seemed impossible

---

[1] Two presents from me to Katherine.

without violating my own integrity. Thus I had no part in what had now come to be Katherine's absorbing interest. I had to acknowledge that I was now utterly useless to her—even worse, a positive hindrance to her effort towards liberation.

Dr. Sorapure's verdict on her heart was reassuring, and he also found the disease of her lungs quiescent. Katherine arranged to have the Manoukhin treatment continued by a London radiologist. But by this time that had become a secondary matter. When finally, having declared the London radiologist unsatisfactory, she left London for Paris on October 2, for the avowed purpose of resuming the treatment under Dr. Manoukhin himself, I was pretty certain that her real purpose was to try to enter the Gurdjieff Institute. Probably the reason why she did not openly acknowledge it to me was that she was fully aware of my opposition to such a step.

Meanwhile I had arranged to live at Vivian Locke Ellis's house at Selsfield. On September 1 Katherine and I went there together for a week-end. When she returned to London I stayed on, but visited her at the week-ends.

Tuesday,

Dearest Bogey,   (September 5, 1922)

I am still so sorry about your neck. Is it better? I told Sorapure this morning, who said no tonic will do you as much good as a régime of *milk* and *oranges*. Not alone. Not together. But in this order.

Every morning drink a large glass of milk and $\frac{1}{2}$ an hour after eat an orange.

Every afternoon—do the same.

The lime salts are what you need, and they are helped to disperse by the citric acid. $\frac{1}{2}$ an hour after you have drunk that milk it reposes, a solid curd, in your stomach. Along comes the orange juice and a most important meeting with very valuable consequences takes place. . . . Will you do this? It's about 200 per cent stronger than Sanatogen.

The weather is absolutely grey here, every day not a spot of blue sky. In fact the sky is like a big enamel pail. People don't seem to mind, though. I don't think they even notice.

Did I tell you I'm having my first treatment tomorrow? I hope I shall get off with 8.

Ask for anything you want done, or sent. And tell me about your health, won't you? Did you see the perfectly lovely sketch of Johnnie Keats in Sunday's *Observer*?

Ever, darling, Wig

Dearest Bogey,   (September, 1922)

I'm so glad to hear from you. Our goodbye reminded *me* of the goodbye of a brother and sister who aren't each other's favourites. . . . But it didn't matter a little bit.

L. M. has been to Pope's. I'll tell her about Turner's Hill in case she cares to telephone.

I don't think I can come to Selsfield until my treatment here is over. I regret, very much missing autumn that I love so. But at the same time I am happy in London just now. Not because of people, but because of 'ideas'. At last I begin to understand the meaning of 'Seek, and ye shall find.' It sounds simple enough, but one seems to do anything *but* seek. . . . However, that sounds a little too airnest for a letter.

Darling, I'm too shy to write proposing myself to Will Rothenstein.[1] If you care to send him a card saying I'm agreeable, I'd be pleased to be in a book. But wouldn't that be the best way to do it? Richard came yesterday and did a drawing. It was extremely well done. He's been to the Aeolian Hall and chosen rolls for the pianola. So this little house sighs like a shell with Beethoven.

Ah, Bogey, I had such a sad letter today from Roma Webster. Goodbye Arco! She is afraid there will be no Arco for her. And goodbye Paris and the Manoukhin treatment! It cannot be for her. 'Every day I am getting worse.' Brave, noble little soul shining behind those dark, lighted eyes! She has wanted so much, she has had so little! She wants so terribly just to be allowed to warm herself—to have a place at the fire. But she's not allowed. She's shut out. She must drive on into the dark. Why? Why can't I go to Rome? I should like to start for Rome today, just to kiss her hands and lay my head on her pillow.

It is so terrible to be alone.

Outside my window there are leaves falling. Here, in two days, it is autumn. Not late autumn, but bright gold everywhere. Are the sunflowers out at the bottom of the vegetable garden? There are quantities of small Japanese sunflowers, too, aren't there? It's a mystery Bogey, why the earth is so lovely.

God bless you!

Wig

Later. Richard has just been in again to finish his drawing. Then we

[1] Will Rothenstein had suggested to me that Katherine should sit for a drawing.

went downstairs and he played. But what am I telling you? Nothing! Yet much, much happened. Don't you think it's queer how we have to talk 'little language' to make one word clothe, feed and start in life one small thought?

My dear Bogey,

Wednesday,
(September 20, 1922)

There seems to me little doubt that the wave of mysticism prophesied by Dunning is upon us. Don't read these words other than calmly! But after yesterday to read that little leader in *The Times* this morning was quite a shock. We had a most interesting after-lunch talk at Beresford's. Orage gave a short exposition of his ideas and we asked him questions and made objections. It seemed strange to be talking of those dark matters (with passionate interest) in a big sunny room with trees waving and London 1922 outside the windows. Ask Sullivan about it when you see him in the country. He liked Orage and he found a very great similarity between his ideas and Dunning's. In fact, the more we talked, the more apparent the resemblance. This pleased me for I felt that you would accept what Dunning believed and like that you and I would find ourselves interested equally in these things.

I came back and found Richard here. He had tea and we had a most *terrific* talk. Nice is not the word for your little brother. Richard does believe it is possible to 'imagine' an artist a much more complete being than he has been up till now—not that exactly—but more *conscious of his purpose*. But if I try to reproduce his youthful conversation I shall antagonise you. For I can't put in all the asides and all the implications. Sullivan came back for supper and he and I talked of all these ideas afterwards. It was, as he said, a 'simply stunning evening'. I do hope you see Sullivan for a longish time and that you see Dunning, too. Is this interference? It's hard not to interfere to the extent of wishing you found life as wonderful as it seems to me. Even the least idea—the fringe of the idea—of 'waking up' discovers a new world. And the mystery is that 'all' of us, in our unlikeness and individual ways, do seem to me to be moving towards the very same goal. Dear, dear Bogey, I hope I don't sound like Mrs. Jellaby.

Give my dear love to Selsfield—to the stairs especially and the chimney room and, oh dear! the late light coming in at the small window by the fireplace—and *all* the garden. I love Selsfield.

I had a card from Lawrence today—just the one word 'Ricordi'. How like him! I was glad to get it though.

Do you want anything sent—anything bought? Command me; I'll command Ida. It's a warm still day with a huge spider looking in at my windy pane. Spider weather.

Greet Locke-Ellis for me. Accept my love

Yours

Wig

Dearest Bogey, (September 27, 1922)

I have changed my plans and am going to Paris on Monday for the treatment i.e. for 8–10 weeks. I am not a little bit satisfied with the purely experimental manner of it here. And as I realise more than ever these last foggy days how dreadful it would be to go back and not to go forward, I would endure any hotel, any Paris surroundings, for the sake of Manoukhin himself. I'm sure you'll understand. You see Webster is simply a radiologist. He doesn't examine one, or weigh one, or watch the case as they did at the clinic. Everything was different. It's quite natural—he knows nothing. He is experimenting. And I don't feel I'm in the mood for experiments.

If I leave on Monday I'll get another treatment next Wednesday at 3 Rue Lyautey.

I shall leave my rooms here just as they are. If Brett cares to let them furnished, she may. I shall be only too pleased. But no harm will come to them. And in the spring when I am at Selsfield it will be nice to have them. (That's not sincere. Ugh! how I hate London and all its works! Perhaps I shan't then, though.) But there it is. It couldn't be helped. I suppose I was too quick. At any rate no harm has been done yet. I shall have to count on making money in Paris. I have over £80 in the bank. Money does not worry me. I'll go to the Victoria-Palace for the first week or so, and Ida has a famous list of hotels. She will find another and a better one I hope, then—somewhere more *cosy*. It's a little pity you can't take these rooms and let your flat. They are so fearfully nice and self-contained, with hot baths, attendance, food, telephone and so on. Brett is a very good creature, too. This won't alter anything, will it? It only means that instead of being in London I shall be in Paris. I really have a very great belief in Manoukhin. So have you, I know. Do you care to come up for Sunday night—say?

There is no need to. Phone me if you don't, dear Bogey, and write me anything you would like done before I go. I'm seeing Orage Saturday or Sunday evening, but otherwise I am free. I don't expect you to come and don't even recommend the suggestion. It's so unsettling just as you are I hope beginning to settle down. I think I'd better say—it's fairer—that I am engaged on Saturday from 8 to 10-30 and on Sunday from 8 to 10-30, even though the engagement is only provisional. All the rest of the time I am free.

Ever

Wig

Select Hotel,

Place de la Sorbonne, Paris

Tuesday, 11-30 a.m.,

Dearest Bogey, (October 3, 1922)

After great grief and pain we have at last found a hotel. Ida has gone off for the bagage registré and I'm in one of those gaps, looking before and after, in a room that's not ready, with luggage half unpacked. . . . You know? It's not bad, though—rather nice, in fact. My room is so pleasant after all the rooms I saw yesterday night! I even went back to the Victor-Pal and had a glimpse of the 'uncles', still there, and the Mlle at the Bureau—toujours la même camisole. Happily, it too was full. It was a glorious, soft, brilliant night—very warm. Only man was vile. . . . This hotel is the one I stayed at during the war. My room is on the 6ième, rather small and low but very possible. Shabby, but it gets the sun. Outside the window there's the Sorbonne roofs with tall grave signors in marble peignoirs holding up a finger. Also a coy, rather silly-looking eagle poised over a plaque called Géologie.

I think you'd find a change in Paris even since we were here. The lower orders are much more disagreeable—downright horrid, in fact. One has to fight with them for everything, even the right of sitting in their taxis. There's a queer feeling that the war has come back. Even waiting in the Victoria-Palace last night I noticed an immense advance in de-civilization in the faces. I don't think it's just fancy.

Yesterday at Calais reminded me so of our first voyage to France together.[1] It was so hot and the train didn't go. Outside the windows old women held up baskets of pears. The sun was positively fiery.

[1] In May, 1912.

Oh, I meant to suggest to you to ask for Yeats's Memoirs to review. I think they are coming out this autumn. I believe you would find them very interesting. He's not a 'sympathetic' person, as far as I know, but he's one of those men who reflect their time. Such men have a fascination for me. Haven't they for you?

I wish we lived nearer to each other. I should like to talk more to you. But there is time. When this jungle of circumstances is cleared a little we shall be freer to enjoy each other. It is not the moment now. Tell me what you can about yourself. Not even you could wish for your happiness more than I do. Don't forget that dragons are only guardians of treasures and one fights them for what they keep—not for themselves.

Goodbye, darling Bogey. I hope to see Manoukhin tomorrow. I'll tell you what he says.

Ever yours lovingly
Wig

Wednesday,

Dearest Bogey, (October 4, 1922)

I don't *feel* influenced by Ouspensky or Dunning. I merely feel I've heard ideas like my ideas, but bigger ones, far more definite ones. And that there really is Hope—real Hope, not half-Hope. . . . As for Tchehov being damned—why should he be? Can't you rope Tchehov in? I can. He's much nearer to me than he used to be.

It's nice to hear of Richard sawing off table-legs and being moved by the greengrocer. Why is it greengrocers have such a passion for bedding people out? . . . In my high little room for 10 francs a day with flowers in a glass and a quilted sateen bed-cover, I don't feel far from Richard either. Oh, it's awfully nice to have passed private suites and marble-tops and private bathrooms by! Gone! Gone for ever! I found a little restaurant last night where one dines ever so sumptuous for 6-7 francs, and the grapes are tied with red satin bows, and someone gives the cat a stewed prune and someone else cries: 'Le chat a mangé une compôte de pruneaux!'

True, one is no longer *of* people. But was one ever? This looking on, understanding what one can, is better.

I've just come from the clinic. Manoukhin is far and away nicer. Donat's beard is cut in a very chic way. Poor Madame who opened the door has had a terrible *grippe* and still her fringe is not curled. She said she thought she was *filée de mauvais coton*. But Manoukhin is an old friend, you know. Language doesn't matter. One talks, as Natasha in *War and Peace* says, 'just so', and it's quite enough. He and Donat promise me complete and absolute health by Christmas. My heart is much better. Everything is better. The sparks, the dark room, the clock, the cigarettes, Donat's halting steps—all were so familiar one didn't know how to greet them with enough love! Dear, what wonderful people there are in this world. There's no denying *that*, Bogey!

Is it really warm in England? Here one wears thin stockings again, and my window is wide open day and night. Today is especially lovely —the air just moves on fanning wings—the sky is like a pigeon's breast.

I'm sending you some copies of Manoukhin's and Donat's pamphlets. Do you feel inclined to send them to—Sorapure, say, and Massingham, and any one you know? I told him you would do this for him.

Goodbye, dearest. I hope you see Elizabeth and she's nice. (Haunted by the word 'nice'.)

Wig

Hippius and Dmitri and the Bunins live in a HUGE château—all together. Dmitri rides out on a dragon while Hippius watches from a tower. She puts pins in Bunin's bread, but he doesn't notice *yet*. Manoukhin has moved into a *pension de famille*. 'Il le faut'. He seems much happier. Donat's mysterious daughter whizzed her *père* away *dans un auto* for the summer. I think they went *over* the Mediterranean as well as by it.

I wish I could send you some of our brown bread. You know the kind. It's better than ever. I have a little food cupboard with 'snacks' in it. You'd like it. Green and black figs are 1d. a 100 or thereabouts.

<table>
<tr><td></td><td align="right">Friday,</td></tr>
<tr><td>Dearest Bogey,</td><td align="right">(October 6, 1922)</td></tr>
</table>

How very strange about your soldier! I wish I had seen him. Petone! The Gear Company! And fancy your remembering about those rugs. The way you told me the story reminded me of Lawrence somehow. It was quite different. I saw the soldier so plainly, heard his voice, saw the deserted street on early closing day, saw his clothes, the sack. 'Old boy . . .' It was strangely complete.

By the way, I wonder why things that happen in the rain seem always more wonderful? Do you feel that? There's such a freshness about them, something so unexpected and vivid. I could go on thinking of that for hours.

I heard from Jeanne this morning. She is marrying her young man on October 10th (before he sails) and wondered if you'd go to the wedding. Just in case you should have the faintest feeling I'd like you to go (you know these queer feelings) this is to say I haven't.

It's the most lovely morning. There's just a light sailing breeze and the sun is really hot. Thinking of London is like thinking of living in a chimney. Are there really masses and masses of books? I hope you don't forget to send me that Tchekhov. I look forward to it *very* much. Can one get hold of Tolstoy's diaries? Is there a cheap English edition that is not too cut and trimmed? I wish you'd let me know....

I enclose a letter from Gerhardi. He is passing through rather an awkward age, it seems,—cutting his teeth, poor young man, to the accompaniment of many a coral rattle. But if he's any good, he'll come through.

I'm so glad your neck is better and that your lecture is finished. Have you ever been to Newcastle? It's on Tyne, isn't it? Sounds so mysterious.

I was wondering if next time you went to the Dunnings' you took a bottle of barley-sugar to those young heroes. I feel things like barley-sugar are apt to be a little scarce in that household, and, however wonderful your Da may be, to have a pull, take it out and look at it and put it back again—does mean something. I am sure Michael especially would agree. And then you'll be for ever after the barley-sugar man—which is a nice name.

Your

Wig

Sunday,

(October 8, 1922)

My darling Boge,

Do not bother to write to me when you are not in the mood. I quite understand and don't expect too many letters.

Yes, this is where I stayed *pendant la guerre*. It's the quietest hotel I ever was in. I don't think tourists come at all. There are funny rules about not doing one's washing or fetching in one's cuisine from *dehors* which suggest a not rich an' grand clientèle. What is nice too is one can get a tray in the evening if one doesn't want to go out. Fearfully good what I imagine is provincial cooking—all in big bowls, piping hot, brought up by the garçon who is a v. nice fellow in a red veskit and white apron and a little grey cloth *cap*! I think some English traveller left it in a cupboard about 1879. The salt and pepper stand, by the way, is a little glass motor car. Salt is driver and Pepper Esquire is master in the back seat—the dark fiery one of the two, so different to plain old Salt. . . . What a good fellow he is, though!

Yesterday the wind was nor' north by north by east by due east by due east-north-east. If you know a colder one, it was there, too. I had to thaw a one-franc piece to get the change out of it. (That is a joke for your Sunday paper only!)

I've just read you on Bozzy. You awe me very much by your familiarity with simply all those people. You've always such a vast choice of sticks in the hall-stand for when you want to go walking and even a vaster choice of umbrellas—while I go all unprotected and exposed with only a fearful sense of the heavens lowering.

Lawrence has reached Mexico and feels ever so lively. Father has reached Port Said. He quoted a whole poem by Enid Bagnold to say so. 'I am a sailor sailing on summer seas.' All the same a marvellous wash of the blue crept up the page as I read his letter, which had nothing to do with E.B.

By the way, do you read letters at Selsfield? Do you ever read letters? You never do. You only skate over them. 'Here's a letter!' And down you sit, clamp on your skates, do a dreamy kind of twirl over the pages, and that's all. Or is that libelling you?

Mary! There's a most beautiful magpie on *my* roof. Are magpies still wild? Ah me, how little one knows!

I must go out to lunch. Goodbye, my darling. I hope to send you some MSS to type this next week. Give my love to L.-E. Tell him of this hôtel in case he comes to Paris. I think he'll like it. My room is on the 6ème. Didn't I tell you? I felt sure I did.

I know that water music. It is lovely—so very watery—reminds me too in bits of Spenser's Swans.

Ever
Wig

Dearest Bogey,

I have a letter and a card of yours to answer. How horrid your Father is—really horrid! I am so sorry for your Mother. Do you think your policy of keeping silent for her sake is really a good one? I quite see quarrelling would be no use but I do feel a few *chosen words,* so that he can't preen himself on 'having had the best of it', would be worth while. Give him something to think over.

J.M.M. (quite quietly): 'You know, Dad, you're a horrid bully. Nobody loves you.'

I'm afraid he'll live for ever, too. Why should he die? All his life is there, coiled up, unused, in a horrid way *saved.* He is a very odd character. I feel you left your Mother thinking of her with real tender love, seeing her at Selsfield even, helping her out of the car. Or am I wrong?

That lecture must have been a queer little aside—wasn't it? A sort of short loop line.

It has got very cold here. I feel it. I am adjusting myself to it and it makes me feel rather dull—*distrait,* you know. I have had to leave my dear little *grenier au 6ème* for something less lofty, more expensive, but warmer. However, it's a very nice room. 'Et vous avez un beau pendule,' as the garçon said. *He* thoroughly approves of the change. All the same, you say 'Tell me about yourself.' I'll have a try. Here goes.

A new way of being is not an easy thing to *live.* Thinking about it, preparing to meet the difficulties and so on, is one thing, meeting those difficulties another. I have to die to so much; I have to make such *big* changes. I feel the only thing to do is to get the dying over—to court it, almost. (Fearfully hard, that.) And then all hands to the business of being reborn again. What do I mean exactly? Let me give you an instance. Looking back, my boat is almost swamped sometimes by seas of sentiment. 'Ah, what I have missed! How sweet it was, how dear, how warm, how simple, how precious!' And I think of the garden at the Isola Bella and the furry bees and the house-wall so warm. But then I remember what we really felt there—the blanks, the silences, the anguish of continual misunderstanding. Were we positive, eager, real, alive? No, we were not. We were a nothingness shot with gleams of what might be. But no more. Well, I have to face everything as far as I can and see where I stand—what *remains.*

669

For with all my soul I do long for a real life, for truth, and for real strength. It's simply incredible, watching K.M., to see how little causes a panic. She's a perfect corker at toppling over.

I envy you Selsfield. How I should like to be there now, this morning! How beautiful it is! How gracious! I am so glad you are there, my darling Bogey. I feel it *is* the house of your dreams. Do you have flowers on your writing table? Or only pipes in pots, and feathers? You won't forget the Tchekhov, will you? I'd like the *Lit. Sup.* with your review if it isn't too much of a bore to send it.

Ever your
Wig

Friday,
(October 13, 1922)

Don't mind if I don't talk about health, will you?. . . It's a *useless* subject.

My dearest Bogey dear,

That was a massive 1st instalment from Newcassel. What an observer you are become! But I don't think the North is at all simpatico—do you? Those big bones make one feel like a small Jonah in a very large cold whale.

It's a divinely beautiful day—so was yesterday. I hope you are having the same weather at Selsfield. The sky is as blue as the sky can be. I shall go to the Luxembourg Gardens this afternoon and count dahlia and baby heads. The Paris gardens are simply a glorious sight with flowers—masses of beloved Japonica—enough Japonica at last. I *shall* have a garden one day and work in it, too. Plant, weed, tie up, throw over the wall. And the peony border really will be staggering. Oh, how I love flowers! I think of them with such longing. I go through them —one after another—remembering them from their first moments with love—oh, with rapture, as if they were babies! No, it's what other women feel for babies, perhaps. Oh Earth! Lovely, unforgettable Earth! Yesterday I saw the leaves falling, so gently, so softly, raining down from little slender trees golden against the blue. Perhaps Autumn is loveliest. Lo! it is Autumn. What is the magic of that? It is magic to me.

At that very minute in came your letter with the rose, and the aspen tree, the two little birds, the ring from the anvil, and the far away rooster. You never gave me such a perfect birthday present before. A divine one. I love you for it. Beautiful Selsfield sounds. I hope you *do* care for de la Mare—warmly. I feel that he is different to the others, but he too is hidden. We are all hidden, looking out at each other; I mean even those of us who want not to hide. But I understand perfectly what you say of friendship. With you it is love or nothing, and that you are in love with Elizabeth when she loves you. A relationship which isn't what you call a *warm* one is nothing to me, either. Feel I must. But then, darling, oughtn't you to express your feeling and risk losing those people who think you 'ridiculous' or who don't understand it? That's hard to decide. For instance, *I* feel you and Locke Ellis only touch the fringe of what your relationship might be if you both were 'free' with each other. But perhaps I'm quite wrong. Yes, I care for Lawrence. I have thought of writing to him and trying to arrange a meeting after I leave Paris—suggesting that I join them until the spring. Richard, too, I think of with love. That reminds me. Won't you ask Milne down for a week-end? But he is so shy, perhaps he would refuse. Do you know what I think he is? A Dreamer. A real one. He chooses to dream.

I am going to Fontainebleau next week to see Gurdjieff. I will tell you about it. Why am I going? From all I hear he is the only man who understands there is no division between body and spirit, who believes how they are related. You remember how I have always said doctors only treat *half*. And you have replied: 'It's up to you to do the rest.' It is. That's true. But first I must learn how. I believe Gurdjieff can teach me. What other people say doesn't matter—other people matter not at all.

But you matter to me—more and more. I'd like to say I believe as never before in the possibility of real living relationship between us— a true one.

  Ever
   Wig
Again, my love, I thank you for the rose.

         Saturday,
My darling Bogey,   (October 14, 1922)
Your sweet telegram and letter are here. Thank you, my angel. I do think Selsfield sounds perfect, but it's no good my coming there while I am a creeping worm. When I can fly, I will come if you will

have me—so very deeply gladly. I am more than happy to know you are there. Most blessed house! How it lives in my memory. Fancy the blackberries ripe. There are some, aren't there? along the fence on the way to the hen houses, I seem to remember. Michaelmas daisies remind me of a solitary bush in Acacia Road. Do you remember? I like them. They have such delicate arrowy petals.

I send back Elizabeth's letter. If that is grist, you have a very superior mill indeed. Why do you mind punching holes in me? If you punch holes in her?[1] I do think *she* writes the most fascinating letters. If I were a man I should fall in love every time I had one. What qualities she has—and tenderness—real tenderness—hasn't she? I feel it—or perhaps I want to feel it.

About doing operations on yourself. I know just what you mean. It is as though one were the sport of circumstance—one *is,* indeed. Now happy, now unhappy, now fearful, now confident,—just as the pendulum swings. You see one can control nothing if one isn't conscious of a purpose—it's like a journey without a goal. There is nothing that makes you ignore some things, accept others, order others, submit to others. For there is no reason why A. should be more important than B. So there one is—involved beyond words—feeling the next minute I may be bowled over or struck all of a heap. I *know* nothing.

This is to me a very terrible state of affairs. Because it's the cause of all the unhappiness (the secret profound unhappiness) in my life. But I mean to escape and to try to live differently. It isn't easy. But is the other state easy? And I do believe with all my being that if one *can* break through the circle one finds 'my burden is light'.

I have met two awfully nice men here. One is Mr. Pinder—did I tell you about him? The other is a Doctor Young. He came up from Fontainebleau today to meet Orage who arrives tonight. And on his way to the station he spent a couple of hours with me, talking about Gurdjieff and the Institute. If I were to write it all to you, it sounds fabulous and other-worldly. I shall wait until I've *seen* it. I still hope to go on Monday and I'll take a toothbrush and *peigne* and come back on Wednesday morning, only.

I've had such a queer birthday. Ida brought me a *brin* of mimosa. And I had my poem and the telegrams. Wasn't it awfully nice of L.-E. and de la Mare to send one? It's been sunny, too. But all the same I'd rather not think about my birthday.

I had a letter file which required this operation.

Oh, the little Tchekhov book has come. Do you think I might have the *Lit. Sup.* with your article in it? I see no papers here at all. That's not a complaint, though. For Paris flaps with papers as you know. I haven't seen a single newspaper since leaving London. There! Does that shock you?

My *darling* Bogey,

I am your

Wig

Sunday,

(October 15, 1922)

I have opened my letter, darling, to add something. It's this. Darling Bogey, in your spare time, however little that is, get nearer the growing earth than that wheelbarrow and spade. *Grow things.* Plant. Dig up. Garden. I feel with all the force of my being that 'happiness' is in these things. If it's only cabbages, let it be cabbages rather than chess. Sweep leaves. Make fires. Do anything to work with your hands in contact with the earth.

You see chess only feeds your already over-developed intellectual centre. And that regular spade-and-barrow becomes a habit too soon, and is likely only to feed your moving centre—to exercise your machine. Does that sound awful rot to you?

Why don't you get some animals? I'm not joking. Two hours a day would be enough for them. Birds—rabbits—a goat—anything, and live through it or them! I know you will say you haven't the time. But you'll find your work is 100 times easier if you come to it re-freshed, renewed, rich, happy. Does this sound like preaching? Don't let it. I am trying to tell you what I feel deep down is your way of escape. It is to really throw yourself into life—not desperately, but with the love you even don't feel yet. People won't do. We know too well that unless one has a background of reality in oneself, people can't endure in us. When we have a table spread we can afford to open our door to guests, but not before. But enough of this. I am afraid of boring you.

Did you ask L.E. about tulips? Has he got anemones in the garden? *You* ought to see to them; they are your flowers. Why don't you write to Sutton's and ask their advice?

Oh, if you knew how I believe in Life being the only cure for Life.

Ever your own Wig

About being like Tchekhov and his letters. Don't forget he died at 43. That he spent—how much? of his life chasing about in a desperate search after health. And if one reads 'intuitively' the last letters, they are terrible. What is left of him? 'The braid on German women's dresses . . . bad taste'—and all the rest is misery. Read the last! All hope is over for him. Letters are deceptive, at any rate. It's true he had occasional happy moments. But for the last 8 years he knew no *security* at all. We know he felt his stories were not half what they might be. It doesn't take much imagination to picture him on his deathbed thinking 'I have never had a real chance. Something has been all wrong.'

Monday

Dearest Bogey, (October 16, 1922),

Here is a note from Jeanne that you may care to read. I received at the same time a card from Marie to you telling you where to go for the wedding. It had been posted to me by mistake. So to prove *your* good faith I posted it back to her. Poor Marie! She writes that she is heart-broken to be giving up her little Jeanne.

Thank you, darling, for the *Times* article. It is extraordinarily interesting. I read it twice. The writing, apart from everything else, is so good, too—clear and not too persuasive. Do you know what I mean? I don't want any more books at present of any kind. I am sick and tired of books, and that's a dreadful fact. They are to me like sandwiches out of the Hatter's bag. I'll get back to them, of course.

A queer thing. I have cramp in my thumb and can hardly hold the pen. That accounts for this writing. Ida and I are off to Fontainebleau this morning. I am taking my toothbrush and comb. Young phoned me yesterday that there is a lovely room all ready. I'll see Gurdjieff and come back tomorrow. It's not sunny today. What a terrible difference *sun* makes! It ought not to. One ought to have a little core of inner warmth that keeps burning and is only added to by sun. One has, I believe, if one looks for it.

An extremely fat *Nation* has come with your review of ——. So Marie Lloyd is dead, is she? Poor old H.M.T. He *is* a sentimentalist, isn't he? I mean his article on M.L. begs the question so utterly. What's the good of that? What's the good of turning a blind eye to half of her? It was a painful copy of the *Nation* altogether. Massingham's Holiday Moods and his visit to the Old Vic made one hang one's head.

Did you ever see such squiggles as I am making? Forgive them, darling. But for the sake of your reine claude eyes I shall stop until my hand is a little rested.

I feel I shall have masses to tell you of my adventure today. Oh, Bogey, I am so glad W.J.D. was real. I felt he would be. If he gets that house it would be wonderful in the spring, wouldn't it? to have them all so near.

I must get up. The puffi train is, as usual, steaming up and down my room at the very idea of going away, even for half a day.

White enfin! Oh, how lovely! I don't think much of Albert[1] though. You ought to take him in hand. Why is Albert such a very queer name?

Ever, my darling Bogey,
Your
Wig

Le Prieuré,
Fontainebleau-Avon
(Seine-et-Marne)
My dear, darling Bogey, (October 18, 1922)

I have been through a little revolution since my last letter. I suddenly made up my mind (for it was sudden, at the last) to try and learn to live by what I believed in, no less, and not as in all my life up till now to live one way and think another. . . . I don't mean superficially, of course, but in the deepest sense I've always been disunited. And this, which has been my 'secret sorrow' for years, has become everything to me just now. I really can't go on pretending to be one person and being another any more, Boge. It is a living death. So I have decided to make a clean sweep of all that was 'superficial' in my past life and start again to see if I can get into that real living simple truthful *full* life I dream of. I have been through a horrible deadly time coming to this. You know the kind of time. It doesn't show much, outwardly, but one is simply chaos within!

So my first Leap into the Dark was when I came here and decided to ask Mr. Gurdjieff if he would let me stay for a time. 'Here' is a very beautiful old château in glorious grounds. It was a Carmelite monastery, then one of Madame de Maintenon's 'seats'. Now, it is modernised

The gardener at Selsfield.

675

inside—I mean, *chauffage centrale*, electric light and so on. But it's a most wonderful old place in an amazingly lovely park. About 40 people—chiefly Russians—are here working, at every possible kind of thing. I mean, outdoor work, looking after animals, gardening, indoor work, music, dancing—it seems a bit of everything. Here the philosophy of the 'system' takes second place. Practice is first. You simply *have* to wake up instead of talking about it, in fact. You *have* to learn to do all the things you say you want to do.

I don't know whether Mr. Gurdjieff will let me stay. I am 'under observation' for a fortnight first. But if he does, I'll stay here for the time I should have been abroad and get really cured—not half cured, not cured in my body only and all the rest still as ill as ever. I have a most lovely sumptuous room—a kind of glorified Garsington—for the fortnight. As for the food, it is like a Gogol feast. Cream, butter—but what nonsense to talk about the food! Still, it's very important, and I want you to know that one is terribly well looked after, in every way. There are three doctors here—real ones. But these, too, seem details. The chief thing is that this is my Selsfield for the time, the house of *my dreams*. If Mr. Gurdjieff won't let me stay, I shall go to the South, take a little villa and try and learn to live on my own, growing things and looking after rabbits and so on, getting into touch with *Life* again.

No treatment on earth is any good to me, really. It's all pretence. Manoukhine did make me heavier and a little stronger. But that was all if I really face the facts. The miracle never came near happening. It couldn't, Boge. And as for my spirit—well, as a result of that life at the Victoria Palace I stopped being a writer. I have only written long or short scraps since *The Fly*. If I had gone on with my old life I never would have written again, for I was dying of poverty of life.

I wish, when one writes about things, one didn't dramatize them so. I feel awfully happy about all this, and it's all as simple as can be. It's just the same for us, darling, as though I had stayed on in Paris, *except* that I hope I shall be well when you see me again, instead of knowing it would be a variation on the old theme.

Will you send me letters here for a fortnight? Ida will be at the Select Hotel for that time, so, if you prefer to send them there, she'll post them on. At the end of that time, I'll either stay on here or, as I say, go off to some warm place where I can turn into a worker. But I hope it will be here.

Mr. Gurdjieff is not in the least like what I expected. He's what one wants to find him, really. But I do feel *absolutely confident* he can put me on the right track in every way, bodily and t' other governor.

I haven't talked money to Mr. Gurdjieff yet. But in any case I shan't write any stories for 3 months, and I'll not have a book ready before the Spring. It doesn't matter.

When we have discussed finances I'll tell you. The fact is I've hardly talked with him at all. He's terribly busy just now and he only speaks a few words of English—all is through an interpreter. I can't say how 'good' some of the people seem to me here—it's just like another life.

I start Russian today, and my first jobs: which are, eat, walk in the garden, pick the flowers and rest *much*. That's a nice calm beginning, isn't it? But it's the eat much which is the job when it's Gurdjieff who serves the dish.

I must stop this letter, dearest. I'm awfully glad Delamare is a real person: I know just what you mean about Sullivan and Waterlow. It seems 'right', somehow, in a queer way.

I take back my words, Betsy, about your quarrying. It sounded very different when you told me about the sand.

Goodbye for now, darling heart.

Ever your own
Wig

My darling Bogey, (October 20, 1922)

I'll tell you what this life is more like than anything; it is like Gulliver's Travellers (*sic*). One has, all the time, the feeling of having been in a wreck and by the mercy of Providence got ashore . . . somewhere. Simply everything is different. Not only language, but food, ways, people, music, methods, hours—*all*. It's a real new life.

At present this is my day. I get up 7.30—light the fire, with kindling drying overnight, wash in ice-cold water (I'd quite forgotten how good water is to wash in and to drink) and go down to breakfast—which is coffee, butter, bread, gorgonzola cheese and quince jam and eggs. After breakfast, make my bed, do my room, rest, and then go into the garden till dinner, which is 11 a.m. Which is a very large meal with things like—beans mixed with raw onions, vermicelli with icing sugar and butter, veal wrapped in lettuce leaves and cooked in cream. After dinner, in the garden again till 3 o'clock, tea-time. After tea, any light job that is going until dark—when all knock off work, wash, dress and

677

make ready for dinner again at 7. After dinner most of the people gather in the salon round an enormous fire, and there is music—tambourine, drums and piano—dancing and perhaps a display of all kinds of queer dance exercises. At ten we go to bed. Doctor Young, a real friend of mine, comes up and makes me up a good fire. In 'return' I am patching the knee of his trousers today.

But it's all 'stranger' than that. For instance, I was looking for wood the other evening. All the boxes were empty. I found a door at the end of the passage, went through and down some stone steps. Presently steps came up and a woman appeared, very simply dressed, with her head bound in a white handkerchief.[1] She had her arms full of logs. I spoke in French, but she didn't understand. English—no good. But her glance was so lovely—laughing and gentle, absolutely unlike people as I have known people. Then I patted a log and she gave it to me and we went our ways. . . .

At present the entire Institute is devoted to manual work, getting this place in order, out and inside. It's not, of course, work for the sake of work. Every single thing one does has a purpose, is part of a system. Some of the English, 'arty' and theosophical people are very trying, too. But one can learn to use them, I am sure—though I'm not much good at it yet. On the other hand, some of the advanced men and women are truly wonderful. I am still on my fortnight's probation, simply spending a fortnight here. Mr. Gurdjieff hardly speaks a word to me. He must know me pretty well.

But even if he won't let me stay here, I am finished for the time being with *old circumstances*. They have just not killed me, and that's all there is to be said for them. All the people I have known don't really matter to me. Only you matter—more and more, if that is possible, for now that I am not so 'identified' with you I can see the real tie which holds us.

Ida, of course, was very tragic. She had got to the pitch of looking after me when she gave me a handkerchief without my asking for it. She *was* me.

However, I am sure Ida will recover. There is something rock-like in her under all that passion for helplessness.

Jeanne's wedding made me feel sad, Bogey. I think the fat purple fellow was McGavin, for some reason. Thank you for telling me about it. I must write to Marie in a day or two. Forgive this hasty writing.

[1] This was the Olga Ivanovna mentioned below.

Do send *Lit. Sups.* They are so good for lighting fires. I wish you were here. It's such happiness.

Ever, my darling,

Your

Wig Voyageuse

Tuesday,

My darling Bogey,   (October 24, 1922)

I was so glad to get your second letter today. Don't feel we are silently and swiftly moving away from each other! Do you *really*? And what do you mean by us meeting 'on the other side'? Where— Boge? You are much more mysterious than I!

I have managed this badly for this reason. I never let you know how much I have suffered in these five years. But that wasn't my fault. I could not. You would not receive it, either. And all all I am doing now is trying to put into practice the 'ideas' I have had for so long of another, and a *far more truthful* existence. I want to learn something that no books can teach me, and I want to try and escape from my terrible illness. That again you can't be expected to understand. You think I am like other people—I mean: *normal*. I'm not. I don't know which is the ill me or the well me. I am simply one pretence after another. Only now I recognise it.

I believe Mr. Gurdjieff is the only person who can help me. It is great happiness to be here. Some people are stranger than ever, but the strangers I am at last feeling near, and they are my own people at last. So I feel. Such beautiful understanding and sympathy I have never known in the outside world.

As for writing stories and being true to one's gift—I wouldn't write them if I were not here, even. I am at an end of my source for the time. Life has brought me no FLOW. I want to write—but differently—far more steadily. I am writing this on a corner of the table against orders, for the sun shines and I am supposed to be in the garden. I'll write again, my darling precious.

Ever your own

Wig

Darling Bogey,   (October 27, 1922)

I was so glad to hear of your Sullivan excursion. But doesn't his chess obsession bore you dreadfully? It did me. But Beethoven and the stars and the baby all sounded nice.

What are you going to do to the fruit trees? Please tell me. We have masses of quinces here. They are no joke when they fall *exprès* on your head.

I do hope you are having this glorious weather. Day after day of perfect sunshine. It's like Switzerland. An *intense* blue sky, a chill in the air, a wonderful clarity so that you see people far away, all sharp-cut and vivid.

I spend all the sunny time in the garden. Visit the carpenters, the trench diggers. (We are digging for a Turkish Bath—not to discover one, but to lay the pipes.) The soil is very nice here, like sand, with small whitey pinky pebbles in it. Then there are the sheep to inspect and the new pigs that have long golden hair—very mystical pigs. A mass of cosmic rabbits and hens—and goats are on the way, likewise horses and mules to ride and drive. The Institute is not really started yet for another fortnight. A dancing hall is being built and the house is still being organized. But it has started really. If all this were to end in smoke tomorrow I should have had the very great wonderful adventure of my life. I've learnt more in a week than in years là-bas. As to habits. My wretched sense of order, for instance, which rode me like a witch. It did not take long to cure that. Mr. Gurdjieff likes me to go into the kitchen in the late afternoon and 'watch'. I have a chair in a corner. It's a large kitchen with 6 helpers. Madame Ostrovsky, the head, walks about like a queen exactly. She is extremely beautiful. She wears an old raincoat. Nina, a big girl in a black apron—lovely, too—pounds things in mortars. The second cook chops at the table, bangs the saucepans, sings; another runs in and out with plates and pots, a man in the scullery cleans pots—the dog barks and lies on the floor, worrying a hearthbrush. A little girl comes in with a bouquet of leaves for Olga Ivanovna. Mr. Gurdjieff strides in, takes up a handful of shredded cabbage and eats it . . . there are at least 20 pots on the stove. And it's so full of life and humour and ease that one wouldn't be anywhere else. It's just the same all through—*ease* after *rigidity* expresses it more than anything I know. And yet I realize that as I write this, it's no use. An old personality is trying to get back to the outside and observe, and it's not true to the present facts at all. What I write sounds so petty.

In fact, I cannot express myself in writing just now. The old mechanism isn't mine any longer and I can't control the new. I just have to talk this baby talk.

I would like you to see the dancing here. There again you see it's not to be described. One person sees one thing; one another. I have never really cared for dancing before, but *this*—seems to be the key to the new world within me. To think that later I shall do it is great happiness. There may be a demonstration in Paris in a month or two. If so, I wish you could see it. But would it just look like dancing? I wonder. It's so hard to tell.

Oh, about money. I don't need any, thank you, Bogey. If ever I do need money I shall ask you first, but at present I don't.

I wish you'd ask Ouspensky out to dinner when you are in London. His address is 28 Warwick Gardens. He is an extraordinarily sympathetic person.

There are masses of work going on in this garden—uprooting and digging and so on. I don't see why there isn't in yours. Or perhaps you are more forward.

Won't you send Ida a card to Paris 'Select Hotel' and ask her to spend a week-end with you if she returns to England? I don't know her plans.

Still got cramp in my thumb. Oh, I wish I could write to you from this self, not the other.

Suppose you throw up every single job in England, realize your capital, and come over here to work for Gurdjieff. Burn every single boat for once! Do you like the idea? That's why I thought you might care to see Ouspensky. Do you like that old mechanical life at the mercy of everything? And just living with a little tiny corner of yourself?

You could learn the banjo here and if the worst came to the worst always make enough to keep you with playing it—or anything. But perhaps this sounds very wild talk. We are not really wild here, at all. Very serious, in fact.

My darling precious Bogey,

Yours ever

Wig

Saturday,

Darling Bogey,   (October 28, 1922)

Forgive me if I don't write often just now. I am so glad you are happy. I am happy, too. And our happiness does not depend on letters.

I feel certain we shall move towards each other. But we shall do it in our several ways. If I write at present I 'falsify' my position and I don't in any way help yours. It's absurd to give you the news here. News there is none that can be so expressed. As to the people I have known I know nothing of them and they are out of sight just now. If I am sincere, I can only say we *live* here—every moment of the day seems full of life. And yet I feel I can't enter into it as I shall be able to; I am only on the fringe. But write about it I can't.

Dunning's phrase is ½ good, I feel—no more. He always seems to me ½ way in everything. He has insight but not direction. Can he really help?

There is always this danger of deceiving oneself. I feel it, too. I only begin to get rid of it by trying and trying to relax—to give way. Here one *learns* how to do it. Life never would have taught me.

But I am sure you will understand why it is so hard to write. We don't move in our letters. We say the same things over and over.

As I tried to explain, I'm in such a state of transition. I could not if I would get back to the old life, and I can't deal with the new.

But *anxiety* I never feel. Perhaps I shall; I cannot tell. But I am so busy and so many people are here—so much is happening.

Goodbye for now, darling

Wig

Let us speak the new truth. What present relationship have we? None. We feel there is the possibility of one. That is deep-down truth, don't you feel? But no more. It doesn't mean we are moving away, though! It's a thousand times more subtle.

My own Bogey, (November 2, 1922)

Ever since my last letter to you I have been so enraged with myself. It's so like me. I am ashamed of it. But you who know me will perhaps understand. I always try to go too fast. I always think all can be changed and renewed in the twinkling of an eye. It is most fearfully hard for me, as it is for you, not to be 'intense'. And whenever I am intense (really, this is so) I am a little bit false. Take my last letter and the one before. The tone was all wrong. As to any new truth—oh, darling, I am really ashamed of myself. It's so very wrong. Now I have to go back to the beginning and start again and again tell you that I have been 'over-fanciful', and I seem to have tried to force the strangeness.

682

Do you know what I mean? Let me try now to *face facts*. Of course, it is true that life here is quite different, but violent changes to one's individuality—of course, they do not occur. I have come here for a 'cure'. I know I shall never grow strong anywhere in the world except here. This *is* the place, and here at least one is understood entirely, mentally and physically. I could never have regained my health by any other treatment. And all my friends accepted me as a frail half-creature who migrated towards sofas. Oh, my dearest Bogey, just wait and see how you and I will live one day—so happily, so splendidly. But in the meantime, love, please never take what I say for 'absolute'. I do not take what you say for 'final'. I try to see it as relative. Essentially, you and I are together. I love you and feel you are my man. It's that I want to build on and realise and live in, one of these days.

So I shall write at least twice a week and tell you any odd things that are happening. Will you tell me, too?

Last night, for instance, in the salon we learnt to make rugs from long pieces of corn. Very nice ones. Very easy to make, too. I have been in the carpenter's shop all the morning. The small forge is alight; Mr. Gurdjieff is planing, a Mr. Salzmann is making wheels. Later on I shall learn carpentry. We are going to learn as many trades as possible, also all kinds of farm work. The cows are being bought today. Gurdjieff is going to build a high couch in the stable where I can sit and inhale their breath! I know later on I shall be put in charge of those cows. Every one calls them already 'Mrs. Murry's cows'.

This letter must be posted, love. Do please forgive my two silly ones. I learn terribly slowly, my precious Veen, and I must not hurt you.

Ever your own
Wig

I am making a cure of goat's milk—4 times a day!

£5 note enclosed.

My darling Bogey,   (November 7, 1922)

I had a letter from you today saying you had bought a pruning-knife. I hope you succeed with the old trees. Here it is part of the 'work' to do a great many things, especially things which one does *not* like. I see the point of that. It's the same principle as facing people whom one shrinks from and so on. It is to develop a greater range in oneself. But what happens in practice is that no sooner do the people begin doing those

683

things they don't like than the dislike changes. One feels it no longer. It's only that first step which is so terribly hard to take.

Are you having really divine weather? It's marvellous here—like late spring today—really *warm*. The leaves are still falling. The park belonging to this château is incredibly beautiful, and with our livestock roaming about, it begins to look like a little piece of virgin creation.

I am fearfully busy. What do I do? Well, I learn Russian—which is a terrific job—have charge of the indoor carnations—no joke—and spend the day paying visits to places where people are working. Then every evening about 50 people meet in the salon and there is music and they are working at present at a tremendous ancient Assyrian group Dance. I have no words with which to describe it. To see it seems to change one's whole being for the time.

Until I came here I did not realize with what a little bit of my mind, even, I lived. I was a little European with a liking for Eastern carpets and music and for something that I vaguely called The East. But now I feel I am turned to that side far more than the other. The West seems so poor, so scattered. I cannot believe knowledge or wisdom are there. I expect this is a phase. I tell it you because I said I would tell you my reactions. . . . In three weeks here I feel I have spent years in India, Arabia, Afghanistan, Persia. That is very odd, isn't it? And oh, how one wanted to voyage like this—how bound one felt! Only now I know.

There is another thing here—Friendship. The real thing that you and I have dreamed of. Here it exists between women and women and men and women, and one feels it is unalterable, and living in a way it never can be anywhere else. I can't say I have friends yet. I am simply not fit for them. I don't know myself enough to be really trusted, and I am weak where these people are strong. But even the relationships I have are dear beyond any friendships I have known.

But I am giving the impression that we all live together in brotherly love and blissful happiness. Not at all. One suffers terribly. If you have been ill for 5 years, you can't expect to be well in five weeks. If you have been ill for 20 years (and according to Mr. Gurdjieff we all of us have our 'illness') it takes very severe measures to put one right. But the point is there is hope. One can and does believe that one will escape from living in circles and will live a CONSCIOUS life. One can, through work, escape from falsity and be true to one's own self—not to what anyone else on earth thinks one is.

I wish you could meet some of the men here. You would like them very very much, especially a Mr. Salzmann, who speaks very little. I must stop this letter. Is it a rigmarole?

I don't know what you mean, darling, by seeing me as an angel with a sword. I don't feel at all like one. There is another thing. You can't *really* be happy in my happiness. No-one ever is. The phrase is only a kind of buffer—don't you think? It's like people living through their children. Well, they may do it. But it's not life. Neither can I ever teach you how to live. How is it possible? You are you. I am I. We can only lead our own lives together. But perhaps I am treating too seriously what you said.

Goodbye for now, my darling heart,

Ever your
Wig

I enclose a £5 note. Will you pay Heal's bill and keep the rest for any odd bills I may send you later. I know there are some. If you know anyone coming to Paris do give them 2 pairs of grey milanese stockings (for size 5 shoes) to post on to me. I need them awfully. *Merci en avance.*

Darling Bogey,   (November 12, 1922)

I am so sorry for you when you speak of your life as emerging from your study and disappearing into it again. Don't you *sicken* of shutting that door and sitting down to that table? One feels like a spider in an empty house. For whom this web? Why do I strain to spin and spin? Here, I confess, after only five weeks, there are things I *long* to write! Oh, how I long to! But I shall not for a long time. Nothing is ready. I must wait until *la maison est pleine.* I must say the dancing here has given me quite a different approach to writing. I mean some of the very ancient Oriental dances. There is one which takes about 7 minutes and it contains the whole life of woman—but everything! Nothing is left out. It taught me, it gave me more of woman's life than any book or poem. There was even room for Flaubert's *Cœur Simple* in it, and for Princess Marya.... Mysterious.

By the way I have had a great talk about Shakespeare here with a man called Salzmann, who is by 'profession' a painter. He knows and understands the plays better than anyone I have met except you. He happens, too (this is by the way) to be a great friend of Olga Knipper's.[1]

Tchekhov's wife.

His wife is the chief dancer here—a very beautiful woman with a marvellous intelligence.

Dear Bogey, I'm not 'hypnotized'. But it does seem to me there are certain people here who are far beyond any I have met—of a quite different order. Some—most—of the English here don't even catch a glimpse of it. But I am sure. I remember I used to think—if there was one thing I could not bear in a community, it would be the women. But now the women are nearer and far dearer than the men. Of course, I don't speak of Mr. Gurdjieff. I couldn't say he was *near* or *dear* to me! He is the embodiment of the life here, but at a remote distance.

Since last I wrote to you I have changed my room. Now I am in another wing—another kind of existence altogether. Where all was so quiet outside the door, all is noise and bustle. My other room was very rich and sumptuous. This is small and plain and very simple. When Olga Ivanovna and I had arranged it and she had hung her yellow dancing stockings to dry before the fire we sat together on the bed and felt like two quite poor young girls . . . different beings altogether. I like being here very much. I hope Mr. Gurdjieff does not move us again too soon. But it is a favourite habit of his to set the whole house walking. Easy to see why when one saw the emotions it aroused.

About my stockings, darling. I heard from Ida today saying she goes to England tomorrow and would like to come to see you. She intends to return to France where she goes to work on some farm. Would you give the stockings to her? I'll ask her to write to you. I never think of Ida except when I get letters from her. Poor Ida! When I do, I am sorry for her.

I must finish this letter, darling. It is written on the arm of a chair, on a cushion, on my bed, as I try to escape from the heat of my fire. Oh, I have so much to do this afternoon! It's terrible how the days pass. I had a bath this morning—the first time since leaving England! There's a nice confession. But it's wonderful what can be done with a basin and a rough towel.

Have you read Elizabeth's new novel? What do you think of it? Please tell me. How is your gardening getting on? Have you learnt to drive the car?

Goodbye, my dear darling.

Ever your

Wig

Darling Bogey,

Sunday 6.30,
(November 19, 1922)

I am thankful you have your little flat, darling. Rob mine to make yours snug. Take all you can or care to, away. But do you keep warm enough? And what about food, I wonder? I have asked Ida to buy me a number of things while she is in England and to bring them over to Paris with her. Bogey, I have not got a cheque book for the moment. Would you send her a cheque for £10 0 0 on my behalf? I'll let you have it back in a week or two. But would you send it at once? As Ida is going to stay such a short while in England. Thank you ,dearest.

It is intensely cold here—quite as cold as Switzerland. But it does not matter in the same way. One has not the time to think about it. There is always something happening, and people are a support. I spent the winter afternoon yesterday scraping carrots—masses of carrots—and half way through I suddenly thought of my bed in the corner of that room at the Chalet des Sapins. . . . Oh, how is it possible there is such a difference between that loneliness and isolation (just waiting for you to come in and you knowing that I was waiting) and *this*. People were running in and out of the kitchen. Portions of the first pig we have killed were on the table and greatly admired. Coffee was roasting in the oven. Barker clattered through with his milk-pail. I must tell you, darling, my love of cows persists. We now have three. They are real beauties—immense—with short curly hair? fur? wool? between their horns. Geese, too, have been added to the establishment. They seem full of intelligence. I am becoming absorbed in animals, not to watch only, but to know how to care for them and to know *about* them. Why does one live so far away from all these things? Bees we shall have later. I am determined to know about bees.

Your idea of buying some land and building a little house *does* seem to me a bit premature, darling. You know so little. You have never tried your hand at such things. It's not quite easy to change from an intellectual life like yours to a life of hard physical work. But your remark made me wish you did care for my 'ideas'—I mean by my 'ideas' my desire to *learn to work in the right way* and to live as a conscious human being. They are not much more than that. There is certainly no other spot on this whole earth where one can be taught as one is taught here. But life is not easy. We have great 'difficulties'—painful moments—and Mr. Gurdjieff is there to do to us what we wish to do to ourselves and are afraid to do. Well, theoretically, that is very wonderful, but practically it must mean suffering, because one cannot always understand.

Ouspensky came over last week. I had a short talk with him. He is a very fine man. I wish you would just see him—out of—let's call it curiosity.

I must get dressed for dinner. I badly need a good *washing*. Remarkable how clothes fall into their proper place here. We dress in the evening, but during the day . . . the men look like brigands. Nobody cares, nobody dreams of criticising.

Oh, Bogey, how I love this place! It is like a dream—or a miracle. What do the 'silly' people matter? And there are silly people who come from London, see nothing and go away again. There *is* something marvellous here if one can only attain it.

Goodbye for now, my dearest.

Ever your own

Wig

I will write Elizabeth.

My darling Bogey,   (after Nov. 19, 1922)

I hope you and Sullivan do find a place together in the country somewhere near Dunning. I am glad you feel Selsfield is too luxurious. It is very, very lovely, but it is not living. There is too much 'Dinner is served, sir!' about it. Do you ever feel inclined to get into touch with Lawrence again, I wonder? I should like very much to know what he intends to do—how he intends to live now his *Wanderjahre* are over. He and E.M. Forster are two men who *could* understand this place if they would. But I think Lawrence's pride would keep him back. No one person here is more important than another. That may not sound much of a statement, but practically it is very much.

I shall be interested to hear of your meeting with Ida. That reminds me again of the stockings which arrived in perfect order. What an extraordinary brain-wave to hide them in *The Times*! They are very lovely stockings, too, just the shade I like in the evening. One's legs are like legs by moonlight.

It is intensely cold here—colder and colder. I have just been brought some small fat pine logs to mix with my *boulets*. Boulets are unsatisfactory; they are too passive. I simply live in my fur coat. I gird it on like my heavenly armour and wear it ever night and day. After this winter the Arctic even will have no terrors for me. Happily, the sun *does* shine as well, and we are thoroughly well nourished. But I shall be glad when the year has turned.

Darling, I must sit down to a Russian lesson. I wish you knew Russian. I have also been learning mental arithmetic beginning $2 \times 2 = 1$, $3 \times 3 = 12$, $4 \times 4 = 13$, $5 \times 5 = 28$ and so on, at great speed to the accompaniment of music. It's not as easy as it looks, especially when you start from the wrong end backwards. In fact at 34 I am beginning my education.

I can't write to E. about her book. I thought it so dreadfully tiresome and silly. It didn't seem to me like a fairy tale; I saw no fairies. In fact, I saw nobody. And jokes about husbands, double beds, God and trousers don't amuse me, I'm afraid. In fact to me a sad tinkle from an old music box.

Goodbye for now, my dearest Bogey,

Ever your own
Wig

My darling Bogey,   (November, 1922)

I understand affairs much better from your last letter. I am very glad you are going to be near Dunning. Of course, I do not feel that my way is 'the only way'. It is for me. But people have such hidden energy, such hidden strength that, once they discover it in themselves, why should they not do alone what they have to learn to do here? You were only joking, weren't you? when you said you might find Le Prieuré was your way. For one can only come here *via* Ouspensky and *it is a serious step*. However, one can always go again if one finds it intolerable. That is true, too. But the strangeness of all that happens here has a meaning; and by strangeness I don't mean obvious strangeness—there's little of it—I mean spiritual.

Are you having really perfect weather (except for the cold)? It is absolutely brilliantly sunny—a deep blue sky, dry air. Really, it's better than Switzerland. But I must get some wool-lined over-boots. My footgear is ridiculous when I am where I was yesterday—round about the pigsty. It is noteworthy that the pigs have of themselves divided their sty into two: one, the clean part, they keep clean and sleep in. This makes me look at pigs with a different eye. One must be impartial even about them, it seems. We have 2 more cows about to calve in 3 weeks' time. Very thrilling. Also our white goat is about to have a little kid. I want to see it very much. They are so charming.

You know I told you a Turkish Bath was being built. It is finished and working. It was made from a *cave* used for vegetables and of côurse all labour, including the plumbing, the lighting and so on was done by our people. Now one can have seven different kinds of baths in it, and there is a little rest room hung with carpets which looks more like Bokhara than Avon. If you have seen this evolved, it really is a miracle of ingenuity. Everything is designed by Mr. Gurdjieff. Now all hands are busy building the theatre which is to be ready in 2 weeks. I have to start making costumes next week. All the things I have avoided in life seem to find me out here. I shall have to sew for hours on end just as I have to puzzle over these problems in mathematics that we get sometimes in the evening.

But I wish I could tell you of the people I live with. There is not only my friend, Olga Ivanovna. There are the Hartmanns, husband and wife. He was—is—a musician. They live in one smallish room, awfully cramped, I suppose. But to go and sit there with them in the evening before dinner is one of my greatest pleasures. Dear precious people! She is very quick, beautiful, warm-hearted. No, it's no good. I can't describe her. He is small and quite bald, with a little pointed beard, and he generally wears a loose blouse spotted with whitewash, very full trousers, wooden boots. He is a 'common workman' all day. But it is the life between them; the feeling one has in their nearness. But so many people come forward as I write. They are all very different; but they are the people I have wanted to find—*real* people, not people I make up or invent.

Tell me about your new plans when you can, my darling, will you? Was L.M. just the same. It is a horrible thing; I have almost forgotten her. And only two months ago it seemed I could not have lived without her care. Do Dunning's children have lessons? Why don't you offer to teach them something? It's good to be in touch with children; one learns very much.

Goodbye for now, my darling Bogey. I do feel we are nearer than we were. But there is so much—so very much one cannot write. One can only feel.

Ever your own

Wig

My darling Bogey,

I seem to have snapped at that £10 like a dog with a bone, and never even said Merci in my last letter. I am most awfully grateful for it. I accept it with joy, though I *did* mean—yes, truly—to send it back to you. Did you see L.M. I wonder. Wayside Cottage reminded me of Rose Tree Cottage. The name only. They are of the same type. I hope you are snug in it. I suppose you couldn't (or wouldn't care to) snare L.M. as working housekeeper and gardener. I don't see Sullivan as a great help in such matters. But perhaps I wrong him.

About Christmas. I want to be quite frank. For many reasons I would rather we did not meet till the Spring. Hear my reasons before judging me for that, will you? For one thing the hotels at Fontaine-bleau are closed—the decent ones. You could not come to the Institute as a guest at present. It's not running smoothly enough. You would simply *hate* it. No, let me be very careful. I have not asked Mr. Gurdjieff if you could come. He might say 'Yes'. But I can't think what on earth an outsider could do here just now. It's winter. One can't be out of doors. One can't just stay in one's room. Meals are at all hours. Sometimes lunch is at 4 p.m. and dinner at 10 p.m. And so on.

But the chief *reason that matters* is this. Physically there is very little outward change in my condition so far. I am still breathless, I still cough, still walk upstairs slowly, still have to stop and so on. The difference is that here I make 'efforts' of a certain kind all day and live an entirely different life. But I have no life to *share* at present. You can't sit in the cowhouse with me at present or in the kitchen with seven or eight people. We are not ready for that yet. It would simply be a false position. Then, when I first came here, I had a most sumptuous luxurious room and so on. Now I rough it in a little, simple, but very warm room. But it's tiny. We couldn't sit in it.

Deeper still is the most sincere feeling I am capable of that I do not want to see you until I am better physically. I cannot see you until the old Wig has disappeared. Associations, recollections would be too much for me just now. I must get better alone. This will mean that we do not meet until the Spring. If this sounds selfish, it must sound selfish. I know it is not and I know it is necessary. If you do not understand it, please tell me, darling.

I don't feel the cold as much as I have in other winters. It's often sunny, too, and I have just bought for 23 francs very good *boots,* lined with felt with felt uppers.

But I'll say no more just now. I hope you will understand and not be hurt by my letter, dearest heart.

Ever your

Wig

Wednesday,

My darling Bogey, (December 6, 1922)

Your Sunday letter arrived today. Until I have your answer to mine suggesting that we do not meet until the spring, I will not refer to the subject again. . . . I think that's best.

Your little house and way of life sounds so nice. I am very, very glad that you feel Dunning is your friend. Do you have something of your Lawrence feeling for him? I imagine it is a little bit the same. And Mrs. Dunning—you like her? And do you play with the little boys? There are nine children here. They live in the children's house and have a different mother every week to look after them. But I remember now I have told you all that before. I'll tell you instead about that couch Mr. Gurdjieff has had built in the cowhouse. It's simply too lovely. There is a small steep staircase to a little railed-off gallery above the cows. On the little gallery are divans covered with Persian carpets (only two divans). But the white-washed walls and ceiling have been decorated most exquisitely in what looks like a Persian pattern of yellow, red and blue by Mr. Salzmann. Flowers, little birds, butterflies and a spreading tree with animals on the branches, even a hippopotamus. But, Bogey, all done with the most *real art*—a little masterpiece. And all so gay, so simple, reminding one of summer grasses and the kind of flowers that smell like milk. There I go every day to lie and later I am going to sleep there. It's very warm. One has the most happy feelings listening to the beasts and looking. I know that one day I shall write a long long story about it.

At about 5.30 the door opens and Mr. Ivanov comes in, lights the lantern and begins milking. I had quite forgotten the singing wiry silvery sound of milk falling into an empty pail and then heavier—plonk—plonk! 'Mr.' Ivanov is a very young man. He looks as though he had just finished his studies, rather shy, with a childlike beaming smile.

I don't know how you feel. But I still find it fearfully hard to cope

692

with people I do not like or who are not sympathetic. With the others all goes well. But living here with all kinds I am simply appalled at my helplessness when I want to get rid of someone or to extricate myself from a conversation, even. But I *have* learnt how to do it, here. I have learnt that the only way is to court it, not to avoid it, to face it. Terribly difficult for me in practice. But until I really do master this I cannot get anywhere. There always comes the moment when I am uncovered, *so zu sagen*, and the other man gets in his knock-out blow.

Oh, darling—I am always meaning to ask you this. I came away this time without a single photograph of you. This is *intolerable*. I really must have one, Bogey. Not only because I want it fearfully for myself, but people keep on asking me. And I am proud of you. I want to show them what you look like. Do please send me one for Xmas. This is very important.

Goodbye for now, my own Bogey. I am

Ever your loving
Wig

Don't forget the photograph.   Saturday,

My darling Bogey,   (December 9, 1922)

I have never had a letter from you that I so 'understood' as your last about your house and how you are living and the wages you give to John and Nicholas. I can't say what a joy it is to know you are there. It seems to me very mysterious how so many of us nowadays refuse to be cave-dwellers any longer but in our several ways are trying to learn to escape. The old London life, whatever it was, but even the life we have led recently wherever we have been, is no longer even *possible* to me. It is so far from me that it seems to exist in another world. This, of course, is a wrong feeling. For, after all there are the seeds of what we long after in everybody and if one remembers that any surroundings are possible . . . at least.

What do you read? Has Dunning any unfamiliar books? You have rather a horror of anything at all. . . . Eastern, haven't you? I read Ouspensky's *Tertium Organum* the other day. For some reason it didn't carry me away. I think it is extremely interesting but—perhaps I was not in the mood for books. I am not at present, though I know that in the future I shall want to write them more than anything else in the world. But different books. There is Mr. Hartmann here with whom I have great talks nearly every evening about *how* and *why* and *when*.

I confess present-day literature simply nauseates me, excepting always Hardy and the other few whose names I can't remember. . . . But the general trend of it seems to me quite without any value whatsoever.

Yesterday when I was in the stable Mr. Salzmann came up. He had just returned from his work—sawing logs in the far wood. And we began to talk about poverty. He was talking of the absolute need for us today to be *poor again,* but poor in the real sense. To be poor in ideas, in imagination, in impulses, in wishes—to be simple, in fact. To get rid of the immense collection with which our minds are crammed and to get back to our real needs. But I shall not try to transcribe what he said. It sounds banal; it was not. I hope you will meet this man one day. He looks a very surly, angry and even fierce workman. He is haggard, drawn, old-looking, with grey hair cut in a fringe on his forehead. He dresses like a very shabby forester and carries a large knife in his belt. I like him almost as much as I like his wife. Together they seem to me as near an ideal couple as I could imagine.

Bogey, are you having fine weather? Today is perfectly glorious. There was a heavy frost last night, but it's marvellously clear and fine. No, I don't want any money just now, thank you, darling heart. What nonsense to say those W.S. certificates are mine! Why? They are yours! And don't go building a 7-roomed house. 7 rooms for 2 people! I will write again in a day or two. Goodbye for now, dearest darling Bogey,

     Ever your own
        Wig

My darling Bogey,   (December 17, 1922)

I am so delighted to hear of your ½ motor-car. I think it is a most excellent idea. What fun you and Sullivan will have with it. It is so pleasant to think of you two together and I like to know that Sullivan will now understand you from a real standpoint—after sharing your life and working with you in the real sense. Do you teach him to cook and to sew and to knit? The fairies in the keyholes must have a quiet laugh or two of a gentle kind. As to those four little wood-gatherers, I love them.

I hope your tooth is better. Just the same thing has happened to me. My biggest and brightest stopping has come out. But I shall have to hang on until the Spring when I can get to Paris. So far all is well.

My fortunes have changed again. I have been moved back from my little bare servant's bedroom on the general corridor to my beautiful sumptuous first room overlooking the lovely park. It seems almost incredible grandeur. I suppose—I feel I have learnt the lesson that other room had to teach me. I have learnt that I can rough it in a way you and I have never done, that I can stand any amount of noise, that I can put up with untidiness, disorder, queer smells, even, without losing my head or *really* suffering more than superficially. But how did Mr. Gurdjieff know how much I needed that experience? And another mystery is that last week when it was intensely cold I felt that I had come to an end of all that room had to teach me. I was very depressed and longing beyond words for some real change and for beauty again. I almost decided to ask him to send me away until the weather got warmer. Then on Saturday afternoon when I was in the stable he came up to rest, too, and talked to me a little. First about cows and then about the monkey he has bought which is to be trained to clean the cows. Then he suddenly asked me how I was and said I looked better. 'Now', he said, 'you have two doctors you must obey. Doctor Stable and Doctor New Milk. Not to think, not to write. . . . Rest. Rest. Live in your body again.' I think he meant Get back into your body. He speaks very little English, but when one is with him one seems to understand all he suggests. The next thing I heard was that I was to come into here for the rest of the winter. Sometimes I wonder if we 'make up' Mr. Gurdjieff's wonderful understanding. But one is always getting a fresh example of it. And he always acts at precisely the moment one needs it. That is what is so strange. . . .

Dear Bogey darling, I shall not have any Xmas present for you. But you know that £5 I sent you. How much did you spend? Would you buy a book each for Chaddie and Jeanne for me and keep the rest for yourself? Jeanne would like Delamare's new poems, *Down-a-Down-Derry*, I am sure (it's 7/6 isn't it?) and Chaddie—h'm—that is difficult! Some book that looks pretty and tastes sweet—some love poems. Is that too vague? And may I ask you to execute these commissions for me? I hope there will be something left over for you, darling. Buy it with my love. I'll tell you what I want for a present. Your photograph. The proof of the drawing, of course, I should simply treasure, but why should you send me that? Keep it. Of course, if you could have it copied. . . .

There is a man here who is going to take a photograph of me one day. I have changed. I have no longer a fringe—very odd.

We had a fire here the other night. A real one. Two beautiful rooms burnt out, and a real fear the whole place would go. Cries of 'Vode! Vode!' (Water!), people rushing past all black and snatching at jugs and basins. Mr. Gurdjieff with a hammer, knocking down the wall. The real thing, in fact.

What is the weather like with you? It's so soft and spring-like here that actually primroses are out. So are the Christmas roses under the espalier pear-trees. I *love* Christmas; I shall always feel it is a holy time. I wonder if dear old Hardy will write a poem this year.

God bless you, my darling precious!

Ever your
Wig

Saturday,
Darling Bogey,   (December 23, 1922)

Just a note to wish you a Happy Xmas. I am afraid it will not arrive in time for today is Saturday *not* Friday as I imagined. But there! Put the blame on the poor Xmas postman. No, even to think of such a thing won't do at all. . . . A Happy Xmas, my dearest Bogey. I wonder very much how you who always say you hate Xmas so will spend it this year. Perhaps the Dunning children will make it seem real at last. Do tell me about them.

Here we are to have great doings. The Russian Christmas is not due for another fortnight. So Mr. Gurdjieff has decided the English shall have a real old-fashioned English Xmas on their own. There are so few of them, but that makes no difference to his ideas of hospitality. We are to invite all the Russians as our guests. And he has given us a sheep, a pig, two turkeys, a goose, two barrels of wine, whiskey, gin, cognac etc., dessert of all kinds, an immense tree and carte blanche with which to decorate it. Tomorrow night we have our tree followed by the feast. We shall sit down to it about 60. Whoever gets the coin in the pudding is to be presented with our new-born calf—a perfect angel. Would that it were mine!

I do love to hear about your Dunnings. What a queer thing you should have found them just at this time. Not really queer, for it does seem to be a truth than when one is in real need one finds someone to help. Are you and 'Bill' friends? I mean more friends than you and Frieda were, for instance, for you had no separate relationship with her really, did you? I would like to know them both.

Darling precious Bogey, this is not a letter this time—only this note written on a table piled with paper chains, flowers, little bon-bon cases, gold wire, gilded fir cones—you know the kind of thing.

I attended the obsequies of the pig this morning. I thought I had better go through with it for once and see for myself. One felt horribly sad.... And yesterday I watched Madame Ouspensky pluck, singe and draw our birds. In fact, these have been gory days, balanced by the fairy-like tree. There is so much life here that one feels no more than one little cell in a beefsteak, say. It is a good feeling.

God bless you darling.

Ever your
Wig

Boxing Day: Tuesday
(December 26, 1922)

My darling Bogey,

I think the drawing of you is quite extraordinarily good—and in a very subtle way. I had no idea Rothenstein was that kind of artist. People will say it makes you look old. That is true. But you have that look. I am sure *c'est juste*. I am more than glad to have it and I shall keep it v. carefully. Thank you, my dearest. The photograph I don't like so well for some reason. But photographs always pale before good drawings. It's not fair on them.

How is the old Adam revived in you, I wonder? What aspects has he? There is nothing to be done when he rages except to remember that it's bound to be—it's the swing of the pendulum—and the only hope is when the bout is exhausted to get back to what you think you really care for, aim for, wish to live by, as soon as possible. It's the intervals of exhaustion that seem to waste so much energy. You see, my love, the question is always: '*Who am I?*' and until that is answered I don't see how one can really direct anything in oneself. '*Is there a Me?*' one must be certain of that before one has a real unshakeable leg to stand on. And I don't believe for one moment these questions can be settled by the head alone.

It is this life of the *head,* this formative intellectual life at the expense of all the rest of us which has got us into this state. How can it get us out of it? I see no hope of escape except by learning to live in our emotional and instinctive being as well and to balance all three.

You see, Bogey, if I were allowed one single cry to God, that cry

697

would be: *I want to be REAL*. Until I am that I don't see why I shouldn't be at the mercy of old Eve in her various manifestations for ever.

But this place has taught me so far how unreal I am. It has taken from me one thing after another (the things never were mine) until at this present moment all I know really, really is that I am not annihilated and that I hope—more than hope—believe. It is hard to explain and I am always a bit afraid of boring you in letters.

I heard from Brett yesterday. She gave a very horrid picture of the present Sullivan and his views on life and women. I don't know how much of it is even vaguely true, but it corresponds to Sullivan the Exhibitionist. The pity of it is life is so short and we waste about $\frac{9}{10}$ of it—simply throw it away. I always feel Sullivan refuses to face the fact of his wastefulness. And sometimes one feels he never will. All will pass like a dream, with mock comforts, mock consolations.

Our cowshed has become enriched with 2 goats and two love-birds. The goats are very lovely as they lie in the straw or so delicately dance towards each other, butting gently with their heads. When I was there yesterday, Mr. Gurdjieff came in and showed Lola and Nina who were milking the cows the way to milk a goat. He sat down on a stool, seized the goat and swung its hind legs across his knees. So there the goat was on its two front legs, helpless. This is the way Arabs milk. He looked very like one. I had been talking before to a man here whose passion is astrology and he had just written the signs of the Zodiac on the whitewashed stable door. Then we went up to the little gallery and drank koumiss.

Goodbye for now, my darling. I feel this letter is flat and dull. Forgive it.

I am ever your own loving
Wig

Sunday,
My darling Bogey,   (December 31, 1922)

My fountain pen is mislaid, so as I am in a hurry to write please forgive this pencil.

Would you care to come here on January 8 or 9 to stay until 14–15? Mr. Gurdjieff approves of my plan and says will you come as his guest? On the 13th our new theatre is to be opened. It will be a wonderful experience. But I won't say too much about it. Only on the chance that you do come I'll tell you what clothes to bring.

698

One sports suit with heavy shoes and stockings and a mackintosh and a hat that doesn't matter. One 'neat' suit with your soft collar or whatever collar you wear and tie (you see you are my husband and I can't help wanting you to look—what shall I say?) slippers and so on. That's all. If you have a cardigan of course bring it and a pair of flannel trousers in case you get soaking wet and want a change.

I am writing to ask Brett to go to Lewis' and get me a pair of shoes. Will you bring them? I may ask her to get me a jacket too. But she will give you the parcel. Will you wire me your reply—just 'yes' or 'no' and the date, if 'yes', of your arrival.

There is a London train that reaches Paris at 4 something. You could then come on to Fontainebleau the same day. Otherwise it's far better to stay the night in Paris as no cabs meet the late train.

You get out of the train at *Avon* and take a cab here which costs 8 francs *with* tip. Ring the bell at the porter's lodge and I'll open the gate.

I hope you will decide to come, my dearest. Let me know as soon as you can, won't you? I hope Tchekhov's wife will be here. I have gone back to my big lovely room, too, so we should have plenty of space to ourselves. We can also sit and drink *kiftir* in the cowshed.

I can't write of other things in this letter. I hope to hear from you soon.

      Your ever loving
          Wig

I arrived at the Gurdjieff Institute early in the afternoon of January 9, 1923. Katherine was very pale, but radiant. We talked for a while in her room over-looking the garden. She told me that she had wanted me to come very much indeed, because the moment had come for which she had been waiting. She had had to disentangle herself from our love, because it had become an agony of concern for each other which threatened to strangle us. At the Institute, she had worked herself free of it, and from the fear of death, with which it was so deeply entwined. Now she could come to me as a free being, in a love that was purified of all fear.

The greatest obstacle she had to overcome in taking the plunge and making the final decision to enter the Institute had been her fear of losing me. But that fear had been the source of the falsity that had steadily grown upon her since her illness began. Only at rare and terrible moments had she dared—or been driven—to reveal to me the deadly fear that was taking possession of her soul, the blackness that engulfed her; and then I had been dismayed. When she had cried to me to help her out of the gulf, I could do nothing: I almost seemed to turn away as from something intolerable. And so our love had become a dream of happiness to be in some unattainable future. And she had had to pretend, and to go on pretending, to herself and to me that she was not the sick and frightened Katherine that she was, until her own identity was lost and she did not know which was her true self.

Suddenly, she had known that, if she was to escape this living death, she must make a clean sweep of all her fears. The Institute had offered her the opportunity. Even to enter it had been the cause of fear: she had been fascinated by, but afraid of its doctrines. She had been afraid of ignoring her illness. She had been afraid of finally alienating me. By acting in spite of her fears, she had overcome them. By risking losing me, she had found her love for me: it was entire and perfect.

And truly as I looked at her, while I listened, she seemed a being transfigured by love, absolutely secure in love. She had no desire to defend the Institute; as indeed I had none to criticise it. She spoke quite quietly of her feeling that she had perhaps now gained all that it had to give her, and that she might be leaving very soon. When she did, she would like to live with me in extreme simplicity in a small cottage in England, and she would like me to cultivate the land.

It was a great happiness to me to be with her again. She led me out first to her gallery in the cowshed, then to where the company was putting the finishing touches to the dancing hall which had been erected in the garden. Though it was built with trusses, hangar fashion, it immediately impressed me by its likeness to a huge nomad tent, though I have never seen one. She introduced me to some of her friends—to Hartmann and Salzmann and Dr. Young, to Olga Ivanovna and Adela, a young Lithuanian girl who was devoted to her. Under instruction I took a hand in painting coloured designs upon the windows of the hall. I met Orage again, for the first time for many years; and he seemed to me a changed man, much gentler and sweeter than I remembered him. Indeed there was a blend of simplicity and seriousness in most of the people I met there, and in the company as a whole, which impressed me deeply.

Many of them were very tired. They had been working against time, and often all night long, to finish the hall in time to open it on January 13. The work appears, in memory, to have gone on uninterruptedly all through that afternoon and evening. I cannot remember that there was any formal meal. But later in the evening Katherine and I went to sit in the salon. At about 10 o'clock she said she was tired, and began to go to her room. As she slowly climbed the big staircase to the first floor where her room was, she was seized by a fit of coughing. I took her arm and helped her into her room. No sooner were we inside, than the cough became a paroxysm. Suddenly a great gush of blood poured from her mouth. It seemed to be suffocating her. She gasped out 'I believe . . . I'm going to die'. I put her on the couch and rushed out of the room calling for a doctor. Two came almost immediately. Wisely, I suppose, they thrust me out of the room though her eyes were imploring me. In a few minutes she was dead.

She died at the age of 34 and was buried in the communal cemetery of Avon near Fontainebleau. On the stone was carved a sentence from Shakespeare which she particularly loved. 'But I tell you, my lord fool, out of this nettle, danger, we pluck this flower, safety.'

It is not for me to pass judgment on the Gurdjieff Institute. I cannot tell whether Katherine's life was shortened by her entry into it. But I am persuaded of this: that Katherine made of it an instrument for that process of self-annihilation which is necessary to the spiritual rebirth, whereby we enter the Kingdom of Love. I am certain that she achieved her purpose, and that the Institute lent itself to it. More I dare not, and less I must not, say.

A

PR9639.3.M258 Z556 1951   c.1
Mansfield, Katherine   100106 000
Letters to John Middleton Murr

3 9310 00079939 3
GOSHEN COLLEGE-GOOD LIBRARY